PERSPECTIVES
ON PERSONNEL/HUMAN RESOURCE
MANAGEMENT

**The Irwin Series in Management and
The Behavioral Sciences**

L. L. CUMMINGS and E. KIRBY WARREN   *Consulting Editors*
JOHN F. MEE   *Advisory Editor*

PERSPECTIVES ON PERSONNEL/HUMAN RESOURCE MANAGEMENT

Edited by

HERBERT G. HENEMAN III

DONALD P. SCHWAB

both of
The University of Wisconsin—Madison

1978

RICHARD D. IRWIN, INC. Homewood, Illinois 60430
Irwin-Dorsey Limited Georgetown, Ontario L7G 4B3

ISBN 0-256-02071-X
Library of Congress Catalog Card No. 77–088282

Printed in the United States of America

1 2 3 4 5 6 7 8 9 0 K 5 4 3 2 1 0 9 8

To our parents and our families

PREFACE: TO THE INSTRUCTOR

When we first began thinking and talking about this book, we wanted to improve on previous books of readings in the personnel/human resources area. Foremost in our minds was a feeling that the normal book of this type is more of a burden to instructors (and students as well) than a positive instructional device. We thus set as an objective the development of a book that could stand on its own, one that would not require excessive instructional time at the expense of other course activities.

Two moderately unique features are used to achieve this objective. First, through careful selection and editing, we believe we have put together a set of readings that students will find readily understandable and interesting. Second, we have written an extensive commentary at the beginning of each chapter. These commentaries are designed to offer a background for the student that many instructors would otherwise feel obligated to provide. We begin each commentary by introducing students to the basic principles, concepts, and issues in the area. In the second portion of the commentary we summarize each article, indicate major points and highlights, clarify any confusing or complex statements, and sometimes suggest debatable issues or potential limitations of a reading. The commentary is thus aimed at preparing the students for the readings and enhancing their understanding and appreciation of them.

Our own teaching, research, and consulting experiences have understandably influenced the structure and content of this book. As you will see from the table of contents, we approach personnel/human resource management primarily from a functional perspective. The emphasis is on the various personnel activities conducted in organizations and how they can contribute to enhancing both employee effectiveness and employee participation (their willingness to join and remain with the organization). Incorporated into these readings and commentaries is explicit recognition that the functional activities are conducted in an increasingly complex legal environment.

The last three chapters deal with three relatively recent, innovative issues that transcend any specific functional activity: hours of work, design of jobs, and equal employment opportunity. As we indicate in our commentaries, virtually all of the personnel functions are affected by these three issues. As a consequence, we deal with them at the end of the book, on the assumption that students will find them more understandable having first been exposed to the specific functional activities. Also, these chapters truly illustrate the integrative aspects of personnel/human resource management.

The order of the chapters reflects our preferences about the organization of material and our view of the personnel/human resource management field. It is possible, however, to use the chapters in virtually any order if you choose to accommodate them to a textbook. In this latter regard, we have prepared a cross-reference grid which matches each chapter in this book to the most appropriate chapter(s) in several standard textbooks. This grid is shown following the table of contents.

Regardless of your ordering preferences, however, we strongly recommend that you have students read Chapter 1 first. In it we outline our view of the personnel/human resource management field, and set the tone for the remainder of the book. The readings in the introductory chapter present an overview of the personnel/human resource function in the organization by describing its excitement, complexity, and ever-increasing importance.

Overall we chose articles not only for their coverage of important topics, but also for the interest they might hold for students. In this context we included a paper showing a "real-world" application of the functional activities in most chapters. We hope your students will find all of the readings and the commentaries to be stimulating and helpful in their learning efforts.

Acknowledgments

Many instructors, colleagues, and students have contributed to our thinking about the field of personnel/human resource management. Much of that contribution is reflected in this book. We thank them for their contributions. Special thanks go to Larry Cummings, Lee Dyer, Dave Robertson, and Tom Stone for their numerous helpful suggestions and comments. Anna Berg and Nancy Pearson provided excellent secretarial assistance to the first author while he was on leave at the University of Washington. Equally fine assistance was provided by Betty Lane and Janice Zawacki at the University of Wisconsin—Madison.

February 1978 **Herbert G. Heneman III**
Donald P. Schwab

CONTENTS

part III
PERSONNEL/HUMAN RESOURCE ACTIVITIES

part IV
INNOVATIONS IN WORK

CROSS-REFERENCE GRID
Relationship between Chapters in This Book and Chapters in Other Personnel/Human Resource Textbooks

Heneman and Schwab	Anthony and Nichol	Beach	Burack and Smith	Chruden and Sherman	Crane	French	Glueck	Mathis and Jackson	Megginson	Miner and Miner	Robbins	Pigors and Myers	Sayles and Strauss	Yaney
Overview	1, 2, 11	1, 2, 3, 4, 7, 30	1, 2	1, 3, 4, 24	1, 3, 20	1, 2, 3, 4, 7	1, 3, 20	1, 2, 15, 19	1, 2, 3, 4, 5, 6, 25	1, 2, 3, 22	1, 2, 15	1, 2, 4, 7, 23	1, 2, 20	1, 12, 14, 15
Employee attitudes and behaviors	—	17	3, 4	2, 11, 15, 23	2	6, 8	2, 20	3, 18	15	8, 21	8	6, 11, 12	3	3, 13
Performance and its evaluation	7	12	12	10	7	15	9, 11	10	14	8, 9	9	16	13	10
Forecasting, planning, and recruitment	5, 6	9	5, 7, 15	5	4	11	4, 5	5, 6	7, 8	6	3, 4	3, 15	7, 8	2, 9
External staffing	6	9, 10	7	6, 7	5, 6	12, 13	6, 11	5, 7	9, 10, 11	10, 11, 12, 13	5	15	8	2, 5
Internal staffing	8	13	16	15	11	14	8, 9	—	11, 14	18	5	12, 17	7	—
Learning and training	7, 8	14, 15, 16	8, 16, 17	8, 9	9, 10, 11	16, 17, 18, 26	7, 10, 12	11, 12, 13	12, 13	14, 15	6, 7	3, 16	9, 12, 14	11
Compensation	4, 9, 10	25, 26, 27, 29	10, 11	19, 20, 21, 22	12, 13, 14, 15	8, 19, 20, 21	13, 14, 15	8, 9	16, 17, 18, 19	5, 16, 20	11, 12	20, 21	15, 16, 17, 18	7
Labor-management relations	10	5, 6, 24	13	16, 17, 18	17, 18, 19	8, 22, 23, 24, 25	18	16, 17	21, 22	5, 19	14	8, 13, 18	4, 6	8
Safety and health	—	28	14	12	16	10	16	14	24	5, 17	13	11, 22	19	12
Hours of work	—	29	14	2	15	10	3	13	—	7	10	19	11, 16	—
Design of jobs	4	8	9	2	2, 13	9	4	4	5	7	10	19	—	11
Equal employment opportunity	6, 10, 11	9, 10, 11	4, 6, 7	5, 6, 7, 14	4, 5	11, 12, 13, 16	4, 5, 6, 11, 17	5, 6, 7, 8	4, 6, 7, 8, 10, 17	5, 10, 11, 15	4, 5, 6	4, 15	10, 11	5, 6, 12

part I

INTRODUCTION

1

OVERVIEW OF THE PERSONNEL/HUMAN RESOURCE FUNCTION

This book is about how organizations deal with their employees and prospective employees. To be more specific, it is concerned with personnel or human resource activities that are carried out in organizations. It focuses on how organizations can obtain and retain a workforce and on how a workforce can be developed and treated so that it performs its functions effectively.

PERSONNEL/HUMAN RESOURCE OBJECTIVES

Organizations typically have two major objectives for personnel/human resources. One of these we refer to as the *participation* objective. This objective or goal involves obtaining and retaining a workforce. Obtaining a workforce requires making the organization visible to prospective employees and encouraging them to join the organization. Once in the organization, retention is desirable so that a stable and experienced workforce can be maintained.

The second major objective pertains to the *effectiveness* of the workforce—how successfully it performs the work to be accomplished in the organization. Effectiveness depends on the motivation of the workforce combined with its abilities.

The two objectives are clearly and closely intertwined. Organizations seek out prospective employees who are likely to perform their jobs effectively. Thus the effectiveness objective is a paramount consideration in obtaining a workforce. Retention of a workforce is also of concern largely because of its implications for effectiveness. Employees typically benefit from their experience and the training received after joining an organization. Experienced employees are thus more likely to be effective performers. Effectiveness may also aid the participation objective. People are often more likely to stay on those jobs on which they believe they are performing successfully.

All in all, the two major personnel/human resource objectives tend to complement each other. Organizations that are successful in meeting the participation objective are more likely to be successful in meeting the efficiency objective, and vice versa. At the same time, however, one must recognize that the factors or activities influencing people to participate in organizations frequently are different from the factors influencing their effectiveness. Consequently, organizations must devote substantial effort to the successful accomplishment of each objective.

The above objectives are common to all organizations that employ a workforce. They are as important to public and nonprofit organizations as they are to profit-seeking firms. Hospitals, voluntary organizations, and local governments have these objectives as surely as manufacturing firms. Therefore, the subject matter of this book is appropriate for any organization that hires people to engage in work.

Moreover, organizations have these objectives even though they may not have a personnel/human resource department as such. Indeed, most organizations employing less than 100 employees do not have a formal personnel/human resource department. Such organizations must still achieve the participation and effectiveness objectives, and they still must conduct the activities that such a department would perform.

IMPORTANCE OF PERSONNEL/HUMAN RESOURCES

The importance of personnel/human resource objectives to the organization should be obvious from the discussion so far. The quality of the organization's workforce is critical to the organization's overall success. This observation is especially appropriate in several expanding areas of our economy such as the service sector. The success of governmental organizations, for example, is almost exclusively dependent on their ability to have effective employees. However, personnel/human resource activities are also critical in capital intensive industries such as automobile manufacturing or petroleum production.

It would be a mistake to believe that the personnel/human resource objectives are of interest only to the organization. Society as a whole is also very concerned with both participation and effectiveness. Effectiveness in the aggregate is influential in determining our national wealth. It strongly influences such things as our ability to accomplish collective environmental objectives, compete in international affairs, and support those members of our society who cannot provide for themselves. Participation is also of concern at a societal level. Most personal income is obtained through wages and salaries so that participation is the major determinant of income in our society. The quality of participation is also important. A reasonably stable workforce performing psychologically acceptable jobs makes a necessary contribution to a stable and cohesive society.

Ultimately, however, personnel/human resources probably is most important to individual employees or prospective employees. The activities engaged in by organizations to achieve participation and efficiency objectives have their greatest impact on individuals. The type of organization one is attracted to, the type of job one performs, the working and interpersonal conditions associated with the job, and the financial rewards connected with performing the job all result from personnel/human resource activities. When you recognize that these activities are affecting most males between the ages of 20 and 65 and a majority of females in this age group, you can see the tremendous impact of personnel/ human resource objectives and activities on people.

PERSONNEL/HUMAN RESOURCE ACTIVITIES

To this point we have spelled out major personnel/human resource objectives and tried to point out their importance to various groups. We turn now to a discussion of major personnel/human resource *activities* that are designed to help the organization achieve these objectives.

To a large extent personnel/human resource activities are aimed at creating a close correspondence or match between the individual and the job the individual does. This matching takes place in two different ways. First, any job has certain skill and ability requirements for successful performance, and the organization must match individuals' skills and abilities that they have, or can acquire, with these job requirements. A second match has to do with the needs and expectations that the individual brings to the job and what the job offers in terms of the satisfaction of those needs and expectations. The latter include such things as the financial rewards attached to the job, relationships with fellow employees and supervisors, and the satisfaction associated with doing the work itself. Clearly, the organization's success in matching people and jobs in both ways will influence its ability to achieve its effectiveness and participation objectives.

Personnel Planning and Staffing. The process of creating a match between the individual and the job begins before the individual even joins the organization. One important set of personnel/human resource activities has to do with identifying (*forecasting*) its expected future personnel needs. Included in these activities is an assessment of the jobs that will need to be performed. Based on these job assessments, organizations develop plans about how many employees of various skills they will require in future time periods. These plans, in turn, are followed by *recruiting* activities which are aimed at attracting persons to seek employment in the organization.

An attempt is usually made to attract more applicants to the organization than it expects to hire so that the organization can choose those applicants that are likely to perform best, and remain, on the jobs to be filled. Often applicants are required to take tests, provide biographical and work history information, and be interviewed. While these activities are far from perfect, they can often aid in obtaining a better workforce than would have been obtained had they not been used.

The need to identify the right person for a particular job does not apply just to persons seeking work with an organization for the first time (usually called *external staffing*). Equally important is the movement of current employees to different jobs in the organization through transfer and promotion. Such *internal staffing* occurs for many reasons. Some jobs require experiences that only can be obtained on other jobs within the organization. Jobs often change, and new people may be needed to meet the new skill and ability requirements. And employees themselves change in both abilities and needs, so that movement to a different job may lead to a better match than the current one.

Personnel Training. Staffing is aimed at identifying people with abilities and needs that correspond to the ability requirements of, and reward systems associated with, the job. As noted, however, this can be achieved only imperfectly. Moreover, even when an initial match between person and job is highly congruent, changes in the person and/or the job over time are likely.

Organizations engage in *training* because staffing can only be partially successful in meeting personnel/human resource objectives. Training efforts are aimed at both participation and effectiveness objectives. For example, new employees are often given orientation training. These programs are designed to familiarize individuals with their job and work environment so that they will feel comfortable and remain with the organization. The effectiveness objective is paramount in training programs aimed at increasing skill on current jobs or preparing employees for new job assignments in the future.

Compensation. Employee *compensation* is a personnel/human resource activity of great importance to the organization. Compensation is by far the most expensive personnel/human resource activity. Taking all cost factors into consideration, oftentimes compensation may be the greatest single organizational expense.

It should not be surprising, therefore, that compensation is usually aimed at both personnel/human resource objectives. Organizations make attempts to see that their compensation is comparable to other organizations as a way of encouraging persons to both join and remain on the job. In addition, organizations usually try to have compensation aid in achieving effective work performance. They do this primarily by attempting to reward employees according to how effectively they perform their jobs.

Safety and Health. Employee *safety and health* is still another area that is typically the responsibility of personnel/human resources. Naturally there are substantial differences in the importance of safety and health activities depending on the type of work performed. Examples of highly dangerous occupations include miners, construction, and lumber workers. On the other hand, insurance salespersons, college professors, and clerical personnel all have relatively safe jobs. Even in relatively safe occupations, however, safety is important because of the extremely undesirable physical and economic consequences of accidents.

An area of related concern is the employment of persons who have already experienced an accident or have some other health-related difficulty. Such persons can often perform certain tasks as well as nonhandicapped persons. The role of personnel/human resources in these situations is to match individuals to jobs that they are capable of performing effectively.

Labor-Management Relations. Employees frequently feel that the employer is unacceptably powerful in establishing personnel/human resource policies. Dissatisfactions like this may cause employees to organize into *unions* to promote their employment interests through collective action. These unions and union-like organizations *negotiate* with employers about terms and conditions of employment. Historically these negotiations dealt mainly with compensation issues. Over the years, however, the issues that unions and managements negotiate over have broadened considerably. For example, most unions seek to have management take employee seniority (length of time on the job) into account when making promotion, transfer, and layoff decisions.

The result of the negotiation process is a *contract* signed by the union and employer. This contract specifies and spells out just what employment terms the organization has agreed to. The organization retains responsibility for administration of the terms of the contract. The union, however, ordinarily reserves the right to challenge that administration through a *grievance process*. Thus, whether one is positively or negatively inclined toward unions, it is obvious that the organization needs personnel/human resource specialists to help negotiate and administer labor management contracts.

EVALUATING PERSONNEL/HUMAN RESOURCES

A very important activity for personnel/human resources is the *evaluation* of the function's effectiveness. Evaluation involves comparing actual achievement against established objectives. This comparison, in turn, requires the ability to measure achievement.

The effectiveness objective requires that employee performance contributions be measured. Physical measures of productivity are possible for a few jobs where there is measurable output and employee control over work pace. Frequently, however, performance measures must be obtained by having one person (usually the supervisor) observe and evaluate the performance of another. This procedure is called *performance appraisal*.

Measures of effectiveness, whether they be physical productivity or performance appraisals, are used in a number of ways. One of the most important ways is to evaluate the effectiveness of various personnel/human resource activities, especially the staffing and training functions. They are also frequently used as a basis for making reward decisions and as an aid to motivation and self-development.

Participation indicators are also of two types. One type assesses directly and in quantitative terms various forms of participation: examples include measures of *turnover* (persons leaving the organization during some time period) and *absenteeism* (persons not reporting for work although still with the organization). The second type attempts to assess the quality of participation from the employees' perspective. These measures are usually aimed at obtaining *employee attitudes* about their work, rewards, and the organization. *Job satisfaction surveys* are usually conducted to obtain this attitude information.

Measures of participation, both quantitative and attitudinal, are also used as a basis for evaluating various personnel/human resource activities. For example, an organization may assess both turnover and employee attitudes before and after a substantial change in compensation practices to see what impact the change had on employee turnover. Without such an assessment, it would be impossible to determine if changes in personnel/human resource activities were beneficial or harmful.

REGULATION OF PERSONNEL/HUMAN RESOURCES

One cannot understand personnel/human resources and the problems encountered in its development without mentioning the role of public regulation.

Two time periods in particular have provided regulation of nearly every facet of the personnel/human resource function. This regulation, for better or worse, has had a tremendous impact on the development and growth of the personnel/human resources function.

Before the 1930s there was relatively little public regulation of organizations or how they carried out their personnel/human resource activities. The prevailing attitude was that organizations and individuals could work out any contractual arrangement that was acceptable to both parties. Thus, while there was little formal regulation, state and federal courts took a fairly dim view of unions which were typically seen as an artificial constraint on the competitive process. Laws pertaining to the economic security of employees on or off the job were also viewed as essentially unnecessary. The one major exception to this philosophy had to do with *workmen's compensation* laws passed by many states prior to the Great Depression. These laws established that loss of income and medical expenses, due to work-related injuries and illnesses, should be a public responsibility borne through employer-financed insurance programs.

The depression of the 1930s led to a substantial change in public thinking about individual responsibility for economic misfortune. With nearly 25 percent of the workforce unemployed during much of this decade, people came to view the need for much greater participation in, and responsibility for, the welfare of workers or those who wished to work. Thus, during the 1930s laws were passed regulating (a) minimum wages employees could receive, (b) hours employees could work before the employer is required to pay overtime, (c) benefits to persons experiencing temporary unemployment, and (d) benefits to persons of retirement age, to name but a few. In most cases these benefits were financed at least partially through taxes on employers.

The 1930s also saw a remarkable change in public attitude toward unions. Before this decade unions were regulated primarily through *common law* (that is, judicial precedent). Often unions were viewed as illegal or nearly illegal institutions. In 1935, however, the *Wagner Act* was passed which encouraged the development of unions. Employees were given the right to organize into unions without employer interference. Moreover, where a majority of workers desired a union, the employer was legally obligated to bargain with the union in good faith over wages and working conditions. While subsequently modified by several amendments that have attempted to shift some power back to employers and individuals who are not interested in unionism, the Wagner Act provided a major impetus for the strength that unions enjoy today.

The laws of the 1930s were aimed primarily at economic security issues and at the legitimacy of unions. Over the years, however, it became apparent that certain groups of workers were not benefiting from these laws as much as certain other groups. Minorities, females, and older workers and job seekers, in particular, continued to experience employment difficulties not experienced by other workers and job seekers.

The 1960s and early 1970s saw much legislation and other federal regulation aimed at providing additional employment opportunities and protections for these "special" workforce groups. Major laws or amendments to existing laws included the *Equal Pay Act* passed in 1963 and designed to insure that females received pay equal to males when they performed similar work. The major legislation passed during the decade was *Title VII* of the *Civil Rights Act* of 1964. It prohibited discrimination in employment based on race, sex, color, religion, or national origin. This is a highly significant act affecting virtually every aspect of personnel/human resources. Another important piece of legislation was the *Age Discrimination Act* of 1967 which extended the protection of Title VII to workers and job seekers aged 40 to 65. In 1970 the *Occupational Safety and Health Act* was passed. Title VII of the Civil Rights Act was amended in a number of important ways by the *Equal Employment Opportunity Act* of 1972. The most recent major piece of legislation was the *Pension Reform Law* of 1974.

Some of the most significant regulation occurred, not as a function of legislation, but from presidential orders. During the Kennedy and Johnson administrations, a number of *executive orders* were issued that apply to nearly all private and public organizations doing business with the federal government. These orders frequently require organizations to establish *affirmative action* programs aimed at increasing the employment representation of minorities and females.

All told, these regulations have had an extremely important impact on the development of personnel/human resources. Indeed, without such regulation it is likely that personnel/human resources as practiced in organizations would be entirely different today. Almost certainly, the function would not be as important as it has become in many organizations. The utilization of skilled specialists in labor relations is substantially the result of the Wagner Act and its amendments. Minimum wage laws, occasional maximum wage laws, pension laws, and the social security law have all had a profound effect on the complexity of the administration of compensation. Laws and executive orders designed to protect minorities and females have impacted on all personnel/human resource activities, but they have been especially important in the area of staffing. Recruiting and selection decisions are closely regulated for their potential adverse impact on the employment opportunities of minorities and females.

OUTLINE OF THIS BOOK

Personnel/Human Resource Outcomes. Part II of this book examines major issues regarding personnel/human resource outcomes. *Outcomes* are the operational indicators (measures) of the participation and efficiency objectives. Logically they are considered first because they serve as the basis for evaluating the success of all other personnel/human resource activities.

Since personnel/human resource activities are aimed at impacting on people, we begin Chapter 2 with a discussion of (a) characteristics of people that influence both their motivation to perform and hence their effectiveness and (b) attitudes that bear on participation. Chapter 3 is devoted entirely to the assessment of effectiveness. A chapter is given over to effectiveness because of its importance and complexity.

Personnel/Human Resource Activities. Part III of this book is devoted to considering the traditional activities of personnel/human resources. Chapters 4 and 5 deal with the activities associated with obtaining employees. Chapter 4 is concerned with forecasting, planning, and recruiting employees. Chapter 5 focuses on the external staffing processes and techniques used to choose from among the applicants.

Chapters 6 and 7 deal with creating a congruence between the skills and abilities of existing employees and the skill/ability requirements of the available jobs. One of these chapters deals with internal staffing, the allocation of employees among existing jobs. The other deals with changing employee skills and abilities through training.

Chapters 8, 9, and 10 deal with three critical personnel activities. Chapter 8 focuses on decisions organizations make regarding employee pay and how the results of these decisions may influence employee effectiveness participation. Chapter 9 is aimed at providing an understanding of the processes organizations and unions go through in negotiating and administrating a contract specifying employment conditions. Chapter 10 deals with issues involved in providing a safe and healthy work environment.

Innovations in Work. Part IV deals with a number of issues that have received much recent attention and have significant implications for the conduct of personnel/human resource activities. Chapter 11 has to do with workhours. It focuses on the problems and promises of greater flexibility in the scheduling of worktime. Chapter 12 has to do with the structure of work itself—job design or redesign. Clearly, changes in the design of jobs has direct and serious implications for all personnel/human resource activities. Chapter 13 is concerned with the many important facets of equal employment opportunity regulation. Again, this regulation has profound consequences for all aspects of personnel/human resource activities.

INTRODUCTION TO READINGS

The personnel/human resource function has tended to be viewed in two quite different ways by organizations. One view, unfortunately in the minority, has perceived personnel/human resources as a function that can make a positive contribution to the overall effectiveness and survival objectives of the organization. Personnel/human resource officials in such organizations are typically well trained, well rewarded, and make substantial inputs into important decisions of all types. In the majority of organizations, however, personnel/human resources has not historically enjoyed such prestige. It has frequently been perceived as a function that must carry out necessary clerical and record-keeping activities (often required by law), but not activities that contribute to the efficiency objectives of the organization.

The two readings in this chapter reflect the organizational ambivalence toward personnel/human resources. The first and decidedly more upbeat of the two is by Herbert E. Meyer, who sees personnel/human resources as expanding in both importance to the organization and as an increasingly attractive career path for upwardly mobile managers. His observations are undoubtedly true, but still they occur in only a small number of organizations.

The second article by Fred K. Foulkes and Henry M. Morgan develops two ideas aimed at making the personnel/human resource function of greater consequence to the organization. The first focuses on the types of issues that personnel/human resources needs to be concerned with. The second centers on how the personnel/human resources department should be organized. Much can be learned about the personnel/human resources function by reading this article.

Foulkes and Morgan are especially concerned about the appropriate role of personnel/human resources vis-à-vis the rest of the organization. They argue, for example, that the contribution of the personnel/human resource function will be suboptimal if it is allowed to become the servant of line management. Their concern about the appropriate role is also reflected in their recommendations regarding the staffing of the personnel/human resources function. They suggest that line managers be rotated through the personnel/human resources department. Such a strategy would bring persons with broad organizational knowledge to the personnel/human resources department.

We agree that active line management participation in the personnel/human resources function can have positive benefits. There are, however, potential dangers. The main danger is line management's lack of understanding of the specialized skills necessary to personnel/human resources. These skills have resulted from technologies developed in fields such as industrial psychology, labor economics, and industrial engineering, as well as personnel management. We believe that a major reason why the personnel/human resources function is frequently not accorded much power or prestige in the rest of the organization results because persons in personnel/human resources do not have the appropriate professional skills. We are hopeful that this book will encourage the development of those skills in the next generation of individuals that participate in the personnel/human resource function.

1. PERSONNEL DIRECTORS ARE THE NEW CORPORATE HEROES

HERBERT E. MEYER

The personnel department has been represented on many a corporate organization chart as an orphaned box—one that came from nowhere and didn't seem to fit anywhere. To many businessmen, including many chief executives, the people who worked in "personnel" appeared to be a bunch of drones whose apparent missions in life were to create paperwork, recruit secretaries who couldn't type, and send around memos whose impertinence was exceeded only by their irrelevance. As a result of this perception, personnel directors, whatever their individual competence, suffered the *sui generis* image of being good-

Source: Reprinted by permission from *Fortune* Magazine; © 1976 Time Inc.

 r 'd-Joe types—harmless chaps who spent their careers worshiping files, arranging company picnics, and generally accomplishing nothing whatsoever of any fundamental importance.

In some cases, this depressing image was accurate. Companies *have* been known to use their personnel departments as a sort of dumping ground for executive misfits, or for burned-out vice presidents who needed just a little while longer on the payroll to be eligible for their pensions. But there have always been some personnel directors who found the job a springboard to higher corporate office, and in some companies the executive in charge of personnel management has traditionally been regarded, not as an outcast, but as an heir apparent.

The current chairman and chief executive of Delta Airlines, W. T. Beebe, was once Delta's senior vice president for personnel. Both Richard D. Wood, the chairman of Eli Lilly and Company, and one of his predecessors as chief executive served as corporate personnel directors on their way to the top—and a former president had followed the same route. Right now, the top Lilly executive responsible for personnel, Harold M. Wisely, holds the rank of executive vice president and has a seat on the company's board of directors.

A Step Toward the Top

In the last few years, many companies have joined Delta and Lilly in putting their personnel departments in the hands of powerful senior executives. That old chestnut about a transfer to personnel being a one-way ticket to oblivion is no longer true. Absolutely no one at First National City Bank viewed it as a setback for Lawrence M. Small when he was transferred from the commercial-banking division to head the personnel division in August 1974. Indeed, it was universally regarded as one very impressive step up the ladder: the job carries the title of senior vice president, and Small was only 32 years old at the time. And at IBM, to cite just one other example, the former director of personnel resources, David E. McKinney, is now president of the Information Records Division, an important marketing and manufacturing unit.

Those good-old-Joes of yesteryear would be stunned by the amount of power and prestige today's personnel directors can claim within their companies. At Dow Chemical Company, for example, the man in charge of personnel, Herbert Lyon, reports directly to President Ben Branch, the chief executive. Lyon is a member of Dow's board of directors and is responsible for, among other things, global product planning and corporate administration. At Warnaco, Inc., most of the executives promoted to jobs in top management during the last three years were singled out for advancement by John Limpitlaw, the company's vice president for personnel.

The executives who are being put in charge of personnel departments today are hard-driving business managers who speak what they call "bottom-line language"; they are as interested in profits as any other executives. George A. Rieder, senior vice president for personnel at Indiana National Bank in Indianapolis, provides an almost textbook example of how today's personnel executives perceive their role. "I'm not a personnel manager," Rieder says, in a tone of voice conveying scorn for that traditional title. "I'm a business manager with responsibilities for personnel."

Rieder quickly adds that this difference is much more than merely semantic.

It's a difference of style, scope, and approach. I view myself as a businessman first, whose job has as much of an impact on the bottom line around here as anybody else's. To be effective I have got to understand every aspect of my company's business, and I have got to participate actively in major management decisions before they're made.

As a senior vice president, Rieder reports to John R. Benbow, the bank's president, and participates actively in day-to-day management of the business.

"Good Ones Are Worth a Lot"

Salary scales provide a measure of the growing importance of personnel. When the average salaries of executives in different specialties are compared—manufacturing, finance, and so on—personnel directors come out as the lowest paid. But they've begun catching up, bcause they are getting bigger raises than other executives. According to the American Management Association, the average compensation for personnel directors of industrial companies with sales of $500 million to $1 billion was $61,-400 in 1975. Executives in charge of manufacturing for those companies got an average of $83,400, chief financial officers got $103,400, and chief executives $225,700. But since 1970, the average compensation of personnel directors has increased by 20 percent, compared with just 13.5 percent for chief financial officers, 15 percent for manufacturing executives, and 18 percent for chief executives.

It's likely that personnel directors will continue to receive larger raises than other kinds of executives, according to Pearl Meyer, a compensation expert who is executive vice president of Handy Associates. "These poor guys in personnel won't be at the bottom of the scale for too much longer," Mrs. Meyer predicts. "Companies are recognizing that good ones are worth a lot." Last year, when Chase Manhattan Bank went looking for an executive to head its human-resources division (modern corporations don't have personnel departments anymore), the bank put out word that for the right man, it would pay up to $120,000. Chase was obviously not in the market for a mere picnic planner. (The right man turned out to be Alan Lafley, from General Electric.)

Clearly, things are not at all what they used to be in the once dull world of personnel or, if you please, human-resource management. And just as clearly, much of the pressure for change came from the economic environment in which corporations have been operating. As Warnaco's John Limpitlaw points out, "The business climate out there today is a whole lot different from what it was ten years ago." In the economy of the 1970s, just about everybody has found the going tough and profits hard to come by. The cost of labor—union contracts, executive salaries, pension plans, and so on —keeps moving up.

Furthermore, many companies that had expanded geometrically during the 1960s discovered that their acquisition programs had left them a tangle of incompatible compensation plans, and with scores of highly paid executives who now seemed to be in the wrong jobs or, worse, were superfluous. And with the stock market remaining in the doldrums, stock-option plans that had looked like money machines during the 1960s suddenly seemed most unsatisfactory; new compensation plans had to be devised to keep key executives contented. The job of personnel director took on new dimensions—especially as chief executives began scrambling to minimize the adverse effects of the recession.

Companies eager to increase their workers' productivity—and which were not?— discovered that an alert personnel director was in a unique position to contribute to the company's welfare. For example, George Sherman, the vice president of industrial relations at Cleveland's Midland-Ross Corporation, got to wondering just why productivity rates in Japanese factories were so high. He flew to Japan, visited some factories, and concluded that part of the answer lay in the use of committees, made up of both workers and supervisors, that met regularly to hear suggestions for meeting production goals. On his return to the U.S., Sherman got clearance to form Japanese-style committees of workers and supervisors at the company's electrical-equipment plant in Athens, Tennessee. One modification of the Japanese plan involved the offer of a cash bonus to both workers and managers if productivity really did increase beyond the goal set by Midland-Ross. One year and 400 suggestions later, productivity at the Athens plant was up by 15 percent. The company was able to cancel plans to invest $250,000 in added manufacturing capacity, because output increased without it. Now Sherman expects to set up similar committees at other plants.

Time Off When It Counts

An idea developed by IBM's vice president for personnel, Walton Burdick, further illustrates how a personnel executive can help his company, and its workers, through a difficult economic period. Burdick developed a policy allowing IBM's employees to defer vacation time for as long as they wanted. Postponement was actively urged during years of booming business activity, thus keeping a lid on the number of employees. The payoff for both IBM and its employees came during the past year, when the recession took a bite out of IBM's production. Workers who had saved up weeks or even months of vacation time were encouraged (rather firmly, one gathers) to use it.

IBM Chairman Frank Cary credits the policy of deferred time off for helping the company get through a rough period without any layoffs.

You can't put a dollar sign on this sort of thing. Cary says: The real benefit is in terms of morale. Our people know our policies are designed to keep them on the payroll. It makes them a lot more willing to go along with organizational changes we propose from time to time.

Pressure on American corporations from their not-so-silent partner, Uncle Sam, has done a great deal to add luster to the job of personnel director. In the last 20 years, there have been more than 100 individual pieces of federal legislation directly affecting the relationship between corporations and their employees—for example the Work Hours Act of 1962, the Occupational Safety and Health Act of 1970, and the Employees Retirement Income Security Act of 1974. There has been a whole basket of laws and regulations to outlaw discrimination, including the Civil Rights Act of 1960, the Equal Pay Act of 1963, and the Age Discrimination in Employment Act of 1967.

Suits That Concentrate the Mind

Personnel directors complain that the federal rules and regulations are poorly conceived, sloppily written, and almost impossible to comply with because they change so rapidly. But many of those same personnel directors concede that the federal government's anti-discrimination activities have done wonders for their own prestige and power. To paraphrase Samuel Johnson,

there is something about being sued for a lot of money that concentrates a chief executive's mind wonderfully. While some antidiscrimination suits involve just one aggrieved person and not much money, there have also been some class-action suits whose costs to corporations have been considerable. American Telephone and Telegraph Company has settled two antidiscrimination suits—one for $38 million and another for $25 million—and nine steel companies settled one for a total of $31 million. The threat of class-action suits by aggrieved employees or disgruntled job applicants has made chief executives very much interested in having their personnel directors come up with ways to avoid even the appearance of discrimination. "Boy, do they listen to us now," says one personnel expert rather cheerfully.

In addition to setting affirmative-action goals, such as for the number of women and blacks to be hired during the coming year, and the number to be promoted into various levels of management, personnel directors develop procedures to make sure the goals are reached. That may involve new hiring systems or special training programs for those already hired and marked for fast promotion. Personnel directors must spend a lot of time these days with supervisors at all levels, helping them to meet their targets.

At Chemetron Corporation, Melvin Shulman, corporate director of human resources, works directly with Chief Executive John P. Gallagher to set the affirmative-action goals and develop the procedures for reaching them. Then he works with Chemetron's line executives to make sure they understand what those goals are, and also that they understand how serious could be the consequences of failing to reach them. Says Shulman:

I tell them of the possible damage to the company, but in a sense I'm making sure they realize that their own careers here are involved. When they understand how directly the chief executive is involved, and that in effect I'm representing him, they're more than willing to get cracking.

Personnel directors probably would have come in from the cold even without the help of a topsy-turvy economy or a flood of legislation. It would have happened because attitudes within the American corporation itself have been changing steadily for at least a generation—the attitude of chief executives toward their subordinates as well as the attitude of employees at all levels toward the companies for which they work.

It is so commonplace now for chief executives to deliver speeches extolling "people" as their companies' most important resource that one tends to dismiss the phrase as cant. For some chief executives, of course, it may be. But a growing number of them really do realize that the quality and morale of their employees can make the difference between success and failure for their companies. One chief executive who is especially articulate on the importance of a company's human resources is Delta Airlines' Tom Beebe. He says emphatically:

The name of the game in business today is personnel. You can't hope to show a good financial or operating report unless your personnel relations are in order, and I don't care what kind of a company you're running. A chief executive is nothing without his people. You've got to have the right ones in the right jobs for them, and you've got to be sure employees at every level are being paid fairly and being given opportunities for promotion. You can't fool them, and any chief executive who tries is going to hurt himself and his company.

Since Beebe is a former personnel man, there is some temptation to pooh-pooh his views as those of a man loyal to his old specialty. But one cannot argue with success. Delta hasn't had a strike in 20 years, and as airlines go, it is uncommonly profitable.

Courses for the Comers

Every chief executive has to be especially concerned about bringing along capable successors. One company that is justifiably famous for the breadth and quality of its management-training programs is IBM. Frank Cary works closely with Walton Burdick, the vice president for personnel, to develop those programs and to assign the executive "graduates" to appropriate jobs within IBM. "It's the chief executive's responsibility to make sure the company has personnel policies and practices that can select the best people, then train them for management positions," says Cary.

Dresser Industries' senior vice president for industrial relations, Thomas Raleigh, spends a lot of time with President John V. James developing and administering the company's executive-training programs. At the recently established Dresser Leadership Center, a campus-like training center near the company's Dallas headquarters, executives enroll for courses lasting one to four weeks. They take courses in business management and also study aspects of Dresser's energy-related business that may be unconnected to their immediate assignments. And Raleigh gets a chance to size up Dresser officials who work far from Dallas.

Few personnel managers work only with executives, of course, and the changed attitudes of employees toward their companies present a constant flow of new challenges. Today's blue- and white-collar workers want more from their jobs than just a paycheck; they want satisfaction, and they want to be treated fairly. Specifically, they want a salary that's fair in relation to their co-workers' salaries, and they want a fair chance for promotion that's based on an objective evaluation of their performances rather than the subjective whims of their immediate supervisors, or on their sex or skin color.

When Harold Johnson joined Philadelphia's INA Corporation as vice president for personnel a few months ago—he was formerly with American Medicorp Inc.—the insurance company did not have a fully developed system for setting the salaries of new employees. Nor were there clear ground rules for awarding raises, or for evaluating employee performance. "Things worked pretty much according to the whims of individual supervisors," says Johnson:

There were no company-wide standards at all. The employees were unhappy because they felt their salaries were sometimes unfair, and because they felt top management wasn't aware of the quality work they were doing. And top management needed a tool to help identify the high performers so they could be promoted, or selected for advanced training.

INA Chairman Ralph Saul has ordered Johnson to develop a system to identify the company's most promising executives and to establish corporate salary scales so that employees in similar jobs will be paid within an established range. Johnson is also devising an evaluation system to assure that raises will be awarded in a consistent way, based on individual performance. Once the system is in effect, Johnson will be responsible for getting supervisors to use it. Saul has told Johnson that the latter's own job performance will be measured in part by how quickly he can get the new pay and evaluation system working.

Power for the Team

In many companies the personnel director's responsibilities have become so complex that they can only be shouldered by topflight business managers who have the backing of the chief executive. The people who do the job like to say that in the years to come, a tour of duty in the personnel department (more likely the division of human resources) will be mandatory for any executive who aims to be chairman. Though that may prove to be an exaggeration, it is true that more companies are transferring up-and-coming executives into personnel for a while, en route to greater things. Dow Chemical's Herbert Lyon says it's a good thing for personnel departments to have a mix of professional experts, who have worked exclusively in personnel, and generalists who are brought in for a tour of duty from other parts of the company. IBM's Walton Burdick agrees and adds that in his view the professional personnel types—of whom he is one—benefit even more than the generalists from having a mix. "It gives the specialists a better sense of what's really going on out there," he explains.

Citibank's Larry Small reflects a perspective common to executives who have moved into personnel but who do not expect to remain in it forever. "I'm not a personnel guy," he says carefully, displaying the annoyance of a man who has explained this to others before and who knows he'll have to explain it again to somebody else. "I'm a businessman—a manager. I just happen to be handling personnel at the moment, because it's a very important part of managing a business today."

As more and more personnel departments become populated with managers like Small, what were once enclaves will increasingly be seen as key corporate divisions. And the executives who run them, whether they are called personnel directors or executive vice presidents for human resources, will finally be recognized for what they now are and what in retrospect they always should have been—power-wielding members of their companies' management teams.

2. ORGANIZING AND STAFFING THE PERSONNEL FUNCTION

FRED K. FOULKES and HENRY M. MORGAN

We recently had the opportunity to study and evaluate the effectiveness of the personnel departments of several large organizations. During the study, line managers clearly indicated a desire to make the personnel function more effective. Typical of their many comments are the following:

We need better coordination into a corporate viewpoint on personnel practices—there are still too many instances of personnel practices and programs developed and pursued without recognition of the total corporate implication.

We need better methods of identifying and developing management talent. We also need help in finding ways to move out older managers with long service, short of terminating them and ending up with an age discrimination charge.

Reclassifications take months and they are tacky. There is confusion at the first level of personnel management. They are not about to get out of a reactive mode. They are just not able to say no to requests.

The image of personnel is zero, though some of the gripes are unjustified. Personnel is reluctant to get rid of its obvious nonperformers. The image of personnel in the community is poor.

Personnel should have more contact with line managers to exchange ideas before policies are frozen. They need a better knowledge of the profit impact of the suggested actions.

Personnel tends to be a tower unto itself. If personnel does not perceive a problem as important, it is not handled. It is too interested in new gimmicks, and ignores day-to-day needs.

Such comments raise questions, to say the least, about the performance of personnel departments in different companies. Why

do other parts of the organization view personnel departments as so apparently ineffective? Why do line managers often view the personnel department with contempt?

In this article, we will focus on the critical issues of organizing and staffing the personnel department for greater usefulness. We warn at the outset that personnel programs of every sort, other than those involving routine service matters, often fail. Properly or improperly, personnel usually gets the blame for such failures, while line managers generally take credit for any successful personnel program. In reality, personnel programs succeed because line managers make them succeed.

The Jewel Companies, for example, have been very successful in attracting and retaining outstanding MBA students. It is significant that at Jewel either the president or the chairman interviews every MBA who is being seriously considered for a job. Jewel's innovative personnel program also features for each MBA a mentor or sponsor relationship with a senior executive.

We could argue that if an organization has both a top management that is involved in personnel matters and a reward system that gives weight to success in personnel activities by means of performance appraisals, merit raises, and bonus determination, then neither the organization nor the staffing of the personnel department really matters. Our experience, however, suggests that appropriate organization and staffing of the personnel department can enhance the effectiveness of the personnel function.

ORGANIZATIONAL ISSUES

The long-accepted approach to understanding the organizational role of the personnel department is through a discussion of line-staff relationships. On examining these relationships, we find little consideration of the complexity and geographical dispersion of large modern organizations. Is traditional line-staff language appropriate for discussing the multidivision, multilocation organization? Where do line and staff come into contact? Is the staff function performed only in central headquarters, or is there a line-staff relationship at each location? If so, are there differences in the roles and issues at headquarters and local offices?

We found that the tasks of the personnel department at corporate headquarters differ from those at operating offices. We also think that the old line-staff concepts are no longer completely adequate. An issue today is as much staff-staff relations (corporate staff versus division staff versus plant staff) as it is line-staff relations. Such geographically dispersed and functionally diversified corporations as Du Pont, General Motors, and Tenneco obviously require different personnel functions for different locations.

Consider a relatively modest-sized company such as Polaroid. With about 10,000 employees, 95 percent of whom work in laboratories, factories, and offices within 50 miles of its Cambridge, Massachusetts headquarters, it is less complex than Du Pont or General Motors, but more so than a single-plant corporation.

In fact, most organizations that are large and complex enough to need a well-defined personnel department probably resemble Polaroid. Does Polaroid's personnel department need to provide the same service to its highly automated film division in Waltham that it does to the research laboratories in Cambridge—or to the camera assembly factory in Norwood, the patent department, or the international division? Is there one personnel manager's job? Or are there many similiarities with some differences based on the client served? Does the location of the personnel department in any way determine the function?

From our studies we have developed a way of looking at the total personnel function and breaking out aspects that are best handled at different places by different people. Thus we can identify four distinct aspects of the personnel function:

1. Formulation of personnel policy—a top management responsibility.
2. Implementation of policies by the line managers—the service function.
3. Audit and control—the establishment of standards and procedures to see that organization policies are maintained.
4. Innovation—research and development of new practices, procedures, and programs.

We find that many personnel departments are not organized to get the whole job done. In fact, service and audit activities bog some of them down so that they can give only scant attention to policy formulation and innovation—the most important functions in the view of a number of line managers, including chief executive officers, whom we interviewed.

Most managers recognize the longer-range critical policy problems. Many of them, however, demand administrative or maintenance type of help at the expense of policy problem solving. The urgent always gets in the way of the important, and, consequently, the personnel function should be organized to get both jobs done.

Policy Formulation

Undoubtedly, a most critical issue for any organization is the formulation of personnel policy. In an evaluation of the personnel department of a large organization, we asked a high-level administrator how personnel policy was formulated. His answer was, "I don't know. I don't have a good picture of it." When the personnel director of the same organization was asked the same question, his answer was, "Each policy has a different process." When pressed, he said that policies were developed on an "as needed" basis in response to some new problem or crisis.

Confusion arises because people mean different things by "personnel policy." At the extremes, policies range from simple administrative procedures such as schedules for coffee breaks to crucial institutional issues relating to growth strategy, location of plants, and attitudes toward unions.

While much input from various people and in different ways is essential, we believe that top management should formulate the critical policy decisions relating to personnel. Such decisions should not be allowed to develop in response to crises, and they should be integrated with basic corporate strategies.

In general, the formulation of personnel policy is simply too important to be left to the personnel department alone. Personnel policies need to take into account the law, ethics, and the developmental needs of people and costs. Above all, they should reflect accurately the goals and values of the organization.

Edwin H. Land, chief executive officer of the Polaroid Corporation, describes the strategies of his company:

We have two basic aims. One is to make products that are genuinely new and useful to the public, products of the highest quality and at reasonable cost. In this way we assure the financial success of the company and each of us has the satisfaction of helping to make a creative contribution to the society.

The other is to give everyone working for the company a personal opportunity within the company for full exercise of his talents—to express his opinions, to share in the progress of the company as far as his capacities permit, and to earn enough money so that the need for earning more will not always be the first thing on his mind. The opportunity, in short, to make his work here a fully rewarding and important part of his life.

All personnel strategies at Polaroid flow from the second basic aim. The personnel policy committee consists of top corporate officers and is chaired by a senior vice president, with members of the personnel department serving as staff to the committee.

In addition, all levels of the organization, through a "yellow draft" system, extensively review proposed policy changes before their formal adoption.

Needless to say, personnel policies have to be well administered, for the essence of policy is administration. In personnel, as in everything else, good policies poorly administered mean little.

There is no question about the role of personnel in the implementation of policy, but what should its role be in the formulation of policy? A good personnel department can provide feedback into policy from two directions. First, it knows the concerns of employees and traditionally has represented their views. Second, in response to a world of increasing complexity, it has an outward perspective on social changes and their resulting legislative and regulatory impact on policy.

Policy formulation has two aspects: the process and the content. In the personnel area, where effective implementation counts for so much, the process can be as important as the content of the policies themselves. Thus we would recommend that personnel join with others in top management as a partner in the balancing of values that is the heart of the process.

In one large company, a recent personnel policy change upset so many people that it had to be modified considerably. The company had long had a job-posting system, but the change called for selecting the most senior qualified applicant as opposed to the prior policy of selecting the "best qualified." This change raised so much havoc that the company went back to the old policy for all exempt jobs. The new policy continues, amidst much disagreement, for nonexempt employees.

Regardless of the equity of the approach, the issue would have fared differently, we feel, if it had been discussed by a method similar to that used by Polaroid's personnel policy committee of line managers.

In another case, Honeywell recently formed an executive employee relations committee composed of five operating group vice presidents and five staff vice presidents. This committee serves as a senior policy board in respect to employee relations. Commenting on this, Charles Brown, Honeywell's vice president for employee relations, said:

We go to the committee with one or more proposals for changing something at every meeting, and we have had practically 100 percent acceptance. Once an idea is endorsed by the committee, its implementation becomes relatively easy.

The executive employee relations committee at Honeywell is also responsible for evaluating the top 200 management positions in the company.

At Honeywell, proposals approved during 1976 included a significantly upgraded employee communications program, improvements in the company's merit pay plan, and increased emphasis on recruiting talented minorities and women.

Does any set of personnel policies universally fit all situations? We think not. If they did, management could simply find and adopt them. The best personnel policies are like the best organizational strategies—they are contingent upon the particular situation, and they depend on the strategy of the company.

Within a company, with respect to both setting and administering personnel policy, one must ask where and when uniformity is essential and when it is unnecessary. Given the different missions and diversity of some organizations, some local autonomy and flexibility is frequently desirable. While discretion can result in inconsistency, a certain amount of inconsistency can be lived with, at least in some organizations. And the price of a detailed set of uniform rules and regulations may be very much higher than the price of discretion.

We admit, however, that inconsistent policies at times bring difficulties in equitable administration and in compliance with government regulations. Good sense suggests that sometimes people are being treated fairly when they are not being handled in a uniform manner. Yet, unfortunately, the law sometimes makes it hard these days to justify such action.

The best personnel policies for Polaroid, Xerox, or IBM arise from different contexts from those for U.S. Steel, Kennecott Copper, and the Ford Motor Company. Good personnel policies must be judged by how well they serve the particular management and employees. Do they work? Are they easy to understand and implement? Do they contribute to the attainment of corporate goals?

Good personnel policies cannot stand apart from the basic strategies for the organization as a whole. The two aims of Polaroid, for example, each form an essential part of one inclusive corporate strategy, neither part separable from the other.

Policy Implementation

The "bread and butter" of the personnel job is service to line management. Personnel assists in the hiring, training, evaluating, rewarding, counseling, promoting, and firing of employees at all levels. Personnel administers the various benefits programs such as educational reimbursement, health and accident programs, retirement, vacation, and sick leave. The department also has a role with respect to grievances.

Personnel must, however, guard against becoming a servant to, as opposed to a service to, the line organization. As one personnel vice president put it, "if you get into that servant role, you're asked to arrange the Christmas party and the retirement parties and that's about it."

While most good managers recognize that dealing with personnel matters is an integral part of their own jobs and that they generally must retain the responsibility for final selection of job applicants and other crucial decisions, the personnel representative can provide valuable support such as the initial screening and all necessary signing-in processes after the final decision.

Although personnel departments have had to develop specialized expertise to maintain their usefulness and justify their existence, it is often this special expertise that brings about dissatisfaction with personnel departments. For example, dealing with people is a critical part of any manager's job, and most managers believe they are competent at the practical level. They may seek help when they are overextended, but they do not want the personnel department to do things for them that they feel competent to do.

Thus the personnel representative who provides service to line managers must understand their needs and provide the help asked for—help that may require little special expertise. The personnel representative at the decentralized level, working as part of the management team, must be more of a generalist. (We will discuss the role and place of the personnel specialist in a later section of this article.)

The personnel department must also be accessible. We observed that wherever there is a physical decentralization of operations, the personnel function should be similarly decentralized. Those performing the personnel function should be where the people and the problems are. There should be a strong sense of mutual "ownership" of the personnel department by both management and employees at the local level. Correspondingly, personnel needs to identify with the organization and feel a part of it.

Consider the recent experience of a large and highly decentralized company. One of its plants produces five major product lines. Within the past two years, product management teams have been established for each line consisting of two technical or operations people and one marketing person. Each team has the authority to draw on all resources available for the profitable production and sales of its set of products.

The company noted that because of the technical nature of the manufacturing and sales involved, these teams found a definite need for personnel planning within the or-

ganization. In fact, this need became so strong that, in three of the five teams, personnel people have been physically moved to the team location and are directly participating in the work of the team. The personnel people, moreover, have the same evaluation of their work as do the line managers under the company's management by objectives program.

In smaller organizations that are physically decentralized but without the resources to employ local personnel representatives, the personnel function can be performed on a part-time basis by someone other than a member of the personnel department. We believe it better to perform the service function locally, even if it is not assigned to a specialist in personnel, than to insist that a central personnel group try to serve where its people are not seen as members of that organization. One organization has made the administrative assistant to a department manager the official provider of personnel service to that department.

In a bank we studied, a line officer, who is responsible for a large clerical operation, said:

I wish personnel would realize that this part of the bank is a factory with three shifts. What we need are blue-collar types rather than traditional bank types. If only the personnel people would visit us sometime, they might better understand what it is we do.

While this comment says something about the staffing of the personnel department, it is also relevant to our organizational point. It would probably be better to designate someone in the department as a personnel coordinator.

However, management can go too far with a decentralized approach. Decentralization in the personnel area has both costs and benefits. Ways need to be found to lower the costs. For example, at one large company, a former senior personnel administrator, who was promoted from personnel to a line job, said:

I think our decentralized approach to personnel is one of our strengths and also one of our weaknesses. By aligning the personnel function with the line organization, it becomes much closer to the action, really learns to understand what pressures line people are under, and becomes actively involved in working with line managers to meet their goals.

However, from a corporate standpoint, this results in a somewhat fragmented personnel function. The separate groups tend to function independently and, as a result, much effort is spent in reinventing the wheel. It is very difficult to coordinate with this type of organization.

Therefore, as personnel service is provided locally and as implementation is decentralized, there is a corresponding need to strengthen, but not necessarily enlarge, the centralized personnel function to help maintain organizational consistency and integrity. There should be strong and centralized auditing to ensure proper and consistent policy implementation by the generalists at the local level.

Audit and Control

Of the four organizational issues we are dealing with here, a most critical one today is that of audit and control. The coherence and integrity of the entire personnel service function depends on good personnel policies that, in turn, require follow-up to ensure that they are indeed being properly practiced. This follow-up requires a strong and centralized audit of actual practice.

One organization we studied has recently implemented a job-audit program. Under this program, a central personnel member checks what employees actually do on their jobs against the job descriptions to ascertain whether there are any serious discrepancies. This company adopted its approach after some women employees filed an equal-pay suit.

Management, doing what it thought proper under its affirmative-action plan, had consciously given these women additional responsibilities for development purposes. The women, however, claimed they were doing more than the men were and that they were not being paid accordingly. A job audit revealed that this was indeed the case and thus the women were given back pay. Afterward management adopted a job-audit program to avoid future legal challenges.

The various requirements of state and federal regulations (for example, the Occupational Safety and Health Act, the Equal Employment Opportunity Commission, wage and hour acts, Employee Retirement Income Security Act) make increasing demands on both profit and nonprofit organizations. In 1940 the U.S. Department of Labor was responsible for enforcing 16 statutes and executive orders. By 1960 the number had grown to 40. Today it is more than 130.

While the reader could argue intelligently that the regulatory list is too long to permit proper enforcement, in the meantime compliance is necessary. Responses and reports to these regulators can be made only from a central group supplied with accurate information. In addition, this centralized group must be made up of specialists—well trained in legal requirements and in accounting and reporting techniques, and well reinforced by the full power and authority of top management.

Unfortunately, too many organizations suffer from inadequate and incompetent staff in their central audit and control group. This function should be in the hands of personnel specialists. Compliance with the laws relating to OSHA, EEOC, and ERISA demands expertise. Expertise is also needed in the content of, installation of, and administration of wage and salary plans; in the increasingly complex field of employee benefits; and in surveying what is happening in the outside world. Labor relations and grievance procedures also require the knowledge of an expert. And crucial to the entire audit and control function is the need for a superior employee information system.

Separation of the service function from the auditing function can relieve a large part of the anxiety and ambiguity of the service-control conflict. This will make the personnel function more effective and better accepted as part of the management team.

There should be more innovative ways to perform the audit and control function. Line managers need to develop further their personnel knowledge and skill. Two companies use impressive approaches to accomplish these objectives: one for labor relations and one for health and safety.

One company has added a Step 3½ to its grievance procedure (Step 4 is arbitration). At this step, managers from nearby plants hear grievances. This procedure encourages a plant manager to get involved in day-to-day labor relations in order not to be embarrassed in front of his fellow plant managers.

Another company requires that all of its plant managers devote two weeks a year to safety and health inspections at two plants other than their own. One week is spent at each plant. The inspection team, with the help of a company safety specialist, conducts a complete safety audit. This exercise not only educates the plant managers about safety and health and their importance but also motivates them to keep their own houses in order, since the manager knows that sometime during the year a team will be inspecting his plant and making a report to top management.

Innovation Role

The final important function of the personnel department is to provide up-to-date information on current trends and new methods of solving problems. We call this the innovation role. Personnel departments can escape their errand-boy guise and gain the respect of other members of management by providing credible information on trends concerning human resources and related policy proposals. Such a role will permit top management to plan its course of action rather than operating on an emergency basis. A personnel department able to provide timely advice to management on how to shape and use its human resources will have no trouble making its voice heard in executive councils.

Naturally, the innovative role must be in tune with the times and the set of issues confronting a particular company. In periods of rising inflation and escalating wage and salary demands, the emphasis may be on compensation issues. In times of retrenchment and falling profits, creative work sharing and layoff plans may be needed.

Currently, there is a great deal of interest in improving the quality of work life to fight boredom and decreased productivity in both blue-collar and white-collar jobs. More and more promising executives in their 40s are deciding to get away from high-pressure, treadmill jobs and are abandoning careers they have pursued for years, thus leaving gaping holes in the ranks of the up-and-coming. Employees are demanding changes in the ways in which work is organized. There is an increasing concern and growing legislation about privacy. There are proposals to encourage employee stock ownership.

All these issues require the attention of personnel. And, since the issues change with the times, personnel must be responsible, adaptive, anticipatory, and, especially, innovative. Because of the changing nature of demands, the personnel function must be characterized as pragmatic rather than doctrinaire.

Let us look at some of the specific issues and consider how and where innovation can best take place according to our concepts of central versus dispersed operations.

Attitude Surveys. The purpose of this activity is to assess and evaluate employees' attitudes. Who needs this information? The central office of corporate headquarters? The plant or office manager? Or both?

It seems to us that attitude surveys trigger action at the local level. The local manager certainly needs to have the survey information as a measure of the local pulse. Does a central office need the same data? Is a local situation purely local, or is it often part of a large system trend? We believe that attitude surveys should be made locally and sent to central office for audit, since action and service belong at the local level with auditing and control at the central level.

Work Hours and Work Life. Can management allow flexible working hours at one location and not at another? Should local personnel managers be allowed, or encouraged, to engage in research and experimentation, or should this research be done only at a central point to maintain equity and uniformity?

Depending on the status of union contracts or the potential for union organization, local experimentation and research can be desirable or disastrous. Basic changes in working conditions and hours of work are critical issues of policy and should be carefully controlled corporation wide. This does not mean that variations cannot be allowed or encouraged in response to local conditions, but they should be administered in the light of overall policy.

Job Design. It can be argued that job design is an integral part of a compensation system and must be developed and audited centrally. But the knowledge about the job and persons holding jobs obviously resides at the local level. Compliance with corporation-wide standards can be too rigid, so that managers have little or no incentive to try something new in job design.

Perhaps central specialists should assemble the basic tools of job design, with the information gathered and the implementation carried out at the local level. When job redesign involves new classifications and hence changes in compensation systems, some central authorization and monitoring is necessary; but, without local initiative and participation, it is unlikely that much will ever change.

Pay and Benefits. Because of the critical factor of equity, pay and benefits must be established and controlled centrally. The requirements of various governmental regulatory bodies, on top of the continuing need to ensure conformity with corporate strategy, have forced greater uniformity and less arbitrariness in compensation.

Government regulations form part of a societal trend that is sounding the death knell for many types of merit pay plans. Too many of these plans have been administered in such a way that the recipients cannot comprehend them. As a result, most wage and salary plans have become minor variations of a straight seniority system.

This subject is too complex for detailed discussion in this article. For our purposes here, however, we should simply remark that compensation requires centralized standardization.

Our analysis and prescriptions for the placement of different activities could be called a contingency approach to organization. Basic to this approach is task, since we find that certain tasks are better performed in different places.

Another element of concern in the contingency approach is the environmental forces. Many of the pressures on the personnel department today arise externally, as we have discussed. It is exactly these external changes that an innovative personnel department must sense and track to anticipate the need for internal response ahead of situational crisis.

PERSONNEL AS "CHANGE AGENT"

One danger requires a strong warning. That is the self-appointment by personnel to the role of "change agent." Any personnel director who appoints himself his company's change agent is presumptuous. Anybody in a business who sets out without invitation to reform his senior colleagues is headed for trouble. In addition, simply as a practical matter, the role of internal change agent is difficult, especially on a part-time basis, added to the administrative responsibilities of an entire department.

On the other hand, if the personnel director is indeed to be a part of the executive team, can he also be a satellite of the organization? Are these two functions, personnel manager and change agent, compatible? Many organizations, struggling for stability in a stormy sea of external change, will not look kindly on the change agent in their midst.

In our experience, most of the people who try to fill this role do not see themselves as trying to institute the change, but sincerely consider that they are helping the organization respond, adapt, and survive. But their colleagues in management see them as the proverbial messenger bringing bad news, creating change, and creating trouble. And, like the messenger, they often suffer a disastrous fate.

As a consequence, the personnel manager often works himself into the position of feeling excluded from major management decisions and then, donning the robe of missionary and reformer, the position of defender of the downtrodden with whom he identifies. This role will further alienate him from management, because he will be seen as working against things as they are, and against established policy. He will be seen as leading the charge against the ramparts of status quo. At this point, the only direction for the personnel manager to charge is out the door.

One personnel manager we knew felt it was his responsibility to educate his top management. He developed training programs to identify and deal with social change issues. Although the effort was well intended, it required that a cultural change take place within that company. The company's operative style was one of reaction to crisis, and these training programs required an anticipatory or proactive response. These programs required more than the support of top management; in fact, top management had to institute and lead them. The personnel manager as change agent, as a satellite, cannot even produce an adaptive mode, let alone produce change itself. As one company chairman put it:

One weakness of personnel people is that they think they are God's favorite children. Too many simply want to rock the boat rather than solve the problem. They need to take responsibility. It is easy to come up with ideas. But there is a need to think things through. Things can't be done that quickly, especially when they involve sales and production people. Personnel people don't seem to understand that things can't be implemented tomorrow.

With respect to change, the personnel manager plays a role similar to the one he plays with respect to personnel policy. He should be the agent to look at change rather than the change agent. Personnel can be the expert staff that identifies areas of concern, researches choices, and provides certain skills in training and implementation. But personnel alone does not decide what changes are needed, nor does it deliver the solutions. Change strategy, like policy information, must be "owned by" the appropriate leaders in the organization. There must be an institutionalized process for developing policy and for change.

In our view, it is important to recognize, however, that while it is difficult and frequently inappropriate for the personnel officer to assume a Janus role, the chief personnel officer should be sufficiently tuned to the needs of employees via his personnel network to make certain that the employees' viewpoint is given appropriate consideration on critical matters. Sometimes it is legitimate for a personnel director to play a change agent role. As one personnel vice president put it:

The ideal situation is when the personnel guy is a consultant. But in the real world there are a number of people in responsible positions who have no interest at all in the growth and development of their people. Personnel may be the only one an employee can turn to in a nonunion company. Sometimes I have to be a bad guy with the manager. I have to be a change agent or a catalyst.

What makes this personnel vice president's behavior appropriate is the fact that he has the backing of his company's president and chairman. Personally recruited for his job by the president, this man has a value system congruent with the value system of the president and chairman of this family-controlled company.

In summary, self appointment to a change agent role can be suicidal for the individual and dysfunctional for the organization. For the change agent role to be effective, not only does the personnel officer need to be part of top management, but other members of top management need to be committed to the appropriateness of one of their members in a change agent role.

Earlier we referred to two aspects of policy formulation, process and content. In regard to change, we see the personnel manager as the custodian and protector of the process of change. In this role, he keeps channels of communication open—channels up and down and sideways, channels that flow in and out of the company.

Line management, particularly at and near the top, must be responsible for the content of change. In assuming process as a fundamental part of his job, the personnel manager gains strength and avoids the risk we have warned against.

STAFFING CONSIDERATIONS

While the personnel function must be organized properly to be effective, competent staffing is equally important. Though we have already said a little about staffing, we wish to deal more explicitly with this subject. How large should the staff be? What is a competent personnel department member? How has he or she been trained? How can competence be recognized and rewarded?

Too often, personnel members have been called incompetent. Too often, other departments have used personnel as a dumping ground for their failures. Some personnel departments are staffed by people recruited from outside. They do not know the business, and sometimes they show no interest in learning it. Some company personnel departments are staffed by people who have been somewhat less than successful in the line organization. Weak people who do not engender respect and who cannot hold their own at staff meetings do not add to a department's credibility. Too often, people seek personnel work because they "like working with people."

Effectiveness in much of personnel work has little to do with liking or disliking people; rather, it requires a willingness to take the time to understand the individual needs of employees in order to identify with their problems. This is true in a direct counseling session, in labor negotiations, or in dealing with another member of senior management or the chief executive officer.

While many companies have faced up to the need to get properly trained, talented, and motivated people into the personnel function, the old image is sometimes still there. Personnel people, to be effective, ought to have a working knowledge of what goes on in a plant or office.

Specialists and Generalists

We recognize the need for a wide variety of talents. We see the need for the specialist, particularly in the areas of audit and innovation. However, we also see a strong need for the generalist in the areas of service and policy.

As we have described it, the auditing function requires detailed knowledge of the legal and regulatory aspects of personnel. It requires the development and understanding of systems and the collection, storage, and use of large quantities of information. Personnel must have the ability to understand the needs both of the line organization and of the various branches of state and federal government.

In many respects, all elements needed cannot be found in any one person. Rather, we suggest that a team be developed. This team would include specialists trained in personnel compensation and benefits, in the uses of computers and data systems, and in law, either in the department itself or on call.

However, because a team of personnel specialists will lack the ability to understand the needs of the line client, both manager and nonmanager, we suggest that people trained in other ways should supplement the auditing and control part of the department.

Line Managers and Supervisors

One source of talent will come from line managers and supervisors who have needed personnel information themselves to help them be good managers. In effect, these are the consumers of personnel services. They will bring to personnel the knowledge, language, and requirements of the line. Such managers will improve immeasurably the communication links within the company, and line managers will get help from someone who talks their language.

After a stay of perhaps two to five years, when the temporary member of personnel returns to the line, he or she will serve as a valuable ally of, and interface with, the personnel department. Half of IBM's corporate personnel staff consists of line managers who remain in that function for no more than two or three years.

The increasing demand for personnel to be better integrated with the rest of the organization appears in nearly every situation we have met. A woman personnel officer at a trade association talked about the changes she had noted in the caliber of people going into personnel work in an industry that increasingly draws union interest. Commenting on this, she said:

Top management has finally realized that the people costs are as important as other costs. Lately I've noted more forceful people in the personnel and labor relations field. They now have more of a voice in top management. You can't just talk it; you have to do it. The person entering the field today isn't the "has been" who used to hang around in this field.

Current and Future Superstars

Management now pays greater attention to who heads the function. Where seniority and grandfather clauses used to prevail, many organizations today ask their current and future superstars to lead the personnel department. In one company, after a long conversation about personnel's role and other topics, the vice president of personnel casually stated, "When the president is away, I run the company." Attracting and holding a person of this caliber, one who can and does take over the reins when necessary, is becoming increasingly common.

One of the immediate effects of asking a superstar from the line organization to head the personnel function is to increase the salary of the position, for good people do not move for less money. Thus it is important not only to rotate managerial talent into and out of personnel but also to alter the reward system to show that the organization values such service.

In addition to having credibility with top management, the line executive who becomes the personnel vice president has to, in turn, rely on the staff people because they possess the specialized knowledge that he is lacking. Staff people thus have greater influence.

It is also more natural, perhaps, to put the personnel vice president with line experience on the executive committee and on the bonus committee, positions that indicate influence to other line managers. Such status and influence have been and will continue to be obtained by the well-prepared and trained personnel specialist who becomes a personnel generalist through his training and experience.

But does this mean that there is no great future for the well-trained specialist in the personnel department? No, but the well-trained specialist must learn the language of the rest of the organization and go beyond his own special language, jargon, and concepts. Some who have done so have become very effective personnel vice presidents.

Just as we have suggested that line managers and supervisors take a turn through personnel, so should the personnel specialist take a rotation through a line job in order to increase the ability to understand and deal with the organization as a whole.

It may be, however, that some personnel staff jobs have become so specialized that such people cannot handle a line job. If this is so (though we suspect these cases are rarer than is commonly thought), then such people should, in addition to teaching or taking courses in psychology, law, human relations, and personnel, take courses in marketing, finance, and general management. They also need to find ways to spend more time in offices and plants so that they become more familiar with what actually happens on a day-to-day basis.

Interested Employees

Many nonunion companies have still another source of personnel talent. These companies generally have highly developed communication networks for a two-way flow of information. Employees must know what management is thinking, and managers must also know what employees are thinking.

In such companies, interested and articulate members of the nonsalaried, non-exempt ranks can become important resources for personnel. In fact, the best potential new members for personnel have often been the harshest critics. Far from bringing such employees into personnel to co-opt or silence them, the company should give them an opportunity to make improvements in the very things they found to criticize.

In one company, several key division personnel managers had been at one time hourly employees. The training in personnel, coupled with their previous hourly work experience, had made them effective with both management and workers.

While such a transition may be more difficult in unionized companies, those companies ought to have people in personnel who have seen a side of the company other than that learned through the route of college,

MBA, and several years of management experience. It is just as important for personnel people to understand the language, goals, and values of top management, we should add.

Thus we see many sources of talent for a well-rounded, effective personnel department: the college-trained specialist, the line manager taking a rotation through personnel, the line manager with a career commitment to the function after years in the line, and the hourly employee who is upwardly mobile. Above all, look for talent, not among those who "like working with people," but among those who want to be effective and who like to be part of the total organization.

Naturally, besides selecting people for personnel, management must think about their development. To provide the focus, attention, and coordination this activity requires, IBM has a director of personnel development who reports to the personnel vice president. His sole responsibility is the development of personnel people in IBM on a worldwide basis.

GUIDELINES FOR EVALUATION

We are left with one final question: How does management evaluate the effectiveness of the personnel department? This question obviously needs to be thought through in the context of the particular organization and its specific goals. What is effective for Texas Instruments may not be for Polaroid, or vice versa. But there are some common questions and guidelines.

While people like to think that their organization is unique, the personnel job in reality does not differ greatly, whether it takes place at Macy's, INA, Citibank, or IBM. Organizations do face common problems. In the area of personnel, the similarities may in fact be greater than the dissimilarities. Every organization has to handle people and define personnel's role, particularly how it relates to top management, and to develop the appropriate policies.

From our study of personnel departments and interviews with line managers, we can define three important measures for evaluating the effectiveness of the personnel functions.

1. Operating measures: Budget for the function as a percentage of company or division sales. Size of personnel staff to size of employee group serviced.
2. Quantity measures: Number of nurse visits and of industrial accidents per month. Cost per professional employee hired. Number of days to process insurance claims.
3 Quality measures: Analysis of grievances and of the issues personnel is involved in plus the nature and the level of its involvement. Employee feedback on specific corporate issues. Effectiveness and professionalism of personnel staff (that is, group as well as individual performance).

Undoubtedly, other criteria could be added to this list. But the point, it seems to us, is that personnel, like all staff work, has to be evaluated with rigor, and not only as to its results, but also as to how efficiently those results are achieved. To do so, the organization should develop measures and criteria in accord with its objectives. Any such evaluation should include periodic checks with line managers, the clients of the personnel department.

part II

PERSONNEL/HUMAN
RESOURCE OUTCOMES

2

EMPLOYEE ATTITUDES AND BEHAVIORS

Chapter 1 indicated that the personnel/human resource function is concerned with two major objectives. The *effectiveness* objective has to do with insuring that employees perform their jobs adequately. The *participation* objective is aimed at attracting persons to the organization and retaining their services once hired.

Since both objectives concern the behaviors of people, it is appropriate to examine and ultimately judge the success of the personnel/human resource function in terms of its impact on people. Such a perspective points to the need for an understanding of how people become and remain effective performers, and how they make decisions about joining and remaining with an organization. The present chapter is concerned with this understanding of people.

EFFECTIVE PERFORMER MODEL

Whether or not an employee is an effective performer depends on a number of factors that occur outside of the employee. The way the work is organized, the technology available, and the nature of supervision are examples of environmental characteristics that typically have an impact on whether or not employees perform their job successfully. Ultimately, however, performance depends on how employees behave. Thus, environmental factors such as those already identified influence performance *through* their impact on the individual.

There are two characteristics of people that are essential for effective performance; one of these factors is the *ability* to perform, and the other is the *motivation* to perform. Ability can be thought of as reflecting the employee's capacity to be an effective performer. It indicates the specific knowledges, skills, and experiences that the employee has gained or is capable of gaining. Motivation refers to an employee's willingness to perform the job. It is a fairly complex topic, and it will be discussed in more detail in Reading 3 by Donald Schwab.

It is important to note here that personnel/human resource activities and other mechanisms of organizational control influence performance only insofar as they influence the individual's ability and/or motivation. This influence process is shown in Figure 1.

FIGURE 1
Organizational Influences on Employee Performance

While probably all of the personnel/human resource activities that are performed in organizations have some implications for both ability and motivation, some are more directly aimed at one than the other. For example, employee selection is aimed primarily at assessing and obtaining persons with the appropriate abilities for the jobs they will be expected to perform. Compensation policies and practices, alternatively, are typically aimed more at increasing motivation to perform. Training is an activity that is often aimed at influencing both employee ability to perform and motivation to perform.

EMPLOYEE PARTICIPATION MODELS

Participation behaviors differ from effectiveness behaviors and are partially influenced by different factors. Moreover, as we noted in Chapter 1, there are several different types of participation behaviors. Three of these are (1) job seeking, (2) attendance and length of service, and (3) job satisfaction.

Job Seeking. Decisions to join an organization depend initially on the organization's ability to attract the job seeker's attention. Having been attracted to the organization, a decision to join is influenced primarily by the type of work offered and the job seeker's perception of the organization's rewards such as the compensation associated with the job. When there are several job offers, job seekers will tend to choose that organization which is relatively most attractive in the rewards associated with each job. The role of compensation in this choice process is discussed in Chapter 8.

Attendance and Length of Service. Once in the organization, two critical employee behaviors are *regularity of attendance* and *length of service*. Their opposites, absenteeism and turnover, are often serious and expensive problems for the organization.

A distinction needs to be made between absenteeism or turnover which is initiated by the employee versus that which is not. The former is called *voluntary* and is the type that organizations typically seek to reduce. An example of voluntary absenteeism would be an employee choosing to stay home, even though he or she was not actually ill. Voluntary turnover is illustrated by an employee leaving one employer for a more attractive job with another employer.

Job Satisfaction. To some extent, attendance and length of service can be viewed as behaviors to be motivated, much as performance. Certain rewards can be connected with both attendance and length of service in order to motivate employees to behave in desired ways. For example, some organizations have designed cash bonus systems for employees who have perfect attendance in some time period. These programs have often been successful in reducing absenteeism.

There is, however, another useful way of approaching the attendance and particularly the length of service problem. This latter approach focuses on the favorability of the attitudes employees hold about their work and the work environment. In Chapter 1 we referred to these attitudes as reflecting the quality of participation. This is often called *job satisfaction*. Job satisfaction refers to an emotional reaction to the job and its surrounding conditions. It can be thought of as resulting from an evaluation by employees of the rewards they perceive the job actually provides compared to their expectations of the rewards the job should provide.

When the job and conditions associated with it meet the expectations of the employee, satisfaction results. The higher the employee's satisfaction, the less likely the employee is to be absent or to leave the organization for voluntary reasons. Satisfaction is especially likely to influence absenteeism and turnover when the employee can make such choices without being penalized by the organization. For example, the relationship between attendance and satisfaction will likely be very high among managers who would not be penalized for occasional absences.

Investigations suggest that employees often experience satisfaction/dissatisfaction over several aspects of the work. One important component for many people involves the nature of the job itself. The job is often referred to as a source of *intrinsic* satisfaction/dissatisfaction. Oftentimes employees appear to prefer work which is challenging and provides them with a sense of accomplishment when the job is performed adequately. Other sources of satisfaction/dissatisfaction include the people one works with—both superiors and peers. Personnel policies and practices pertaining to rewards and opportunities such as pay and promotion also are important sources of satisfaction/dissatisfaction.

It is very important to note that satisfaction/dissatisfaction results from an evaluation of what one perceives the job to be providing against one's expectations of what the job should provide. Thus, even though people may have identical jobs and experience identical personnel practices, they probably will not be equally satisfied with their work. This occurs because they bring different expectations to their work. Personnel/human resource activities that do not account for these differences between people are likely to fail.

ATTITUDE SURVEYS

Organizations need to assess how well they are accomplishing their effectiveness and participation goals. This clearly involves the need to measure employee effectiveness and participation such as attendance and length of service. The measurement of effectiveness is so important and complex that Chapter 3 is devoted entirely to its examination.

If an organization wants to more effectively meet its personnel/human resource objectives, steps must be taken to find out about the factors that influence those objectives. These wide-ranging steps include many of the issues discussed throughout this book. Some of the steps, however, involve finding out about how employees feel about their work and organization. This activity is usually referred to as a *survey of employee attitudes.*

Ordinarily attitude surveys should be done formally. A formal survey involves several components. One component involves the use of a standardized questionnaire or interview format. Standardization permits comparisons of responses between different employees at the same time or across time. Second, the employees asked to respond to the questionnaire or interview (the sample) must be chosen carefully. For example, conditions may vary substantially in various parts of the organization or across different types of jobs. Thus, it is important to capture feelings representative of the entire organization. It is also highly desirable to conduct the survey on a periodic basis. Such a procedure permits the organization to identify any changes going on in employee feelings which would indicate the desirability of changing personnel/human resource policies or other organizational characteristics.

INTRODUCTION TO READINGS

Motivation in Organizations

In the past 15 years, thinking about motivation in the personnel/human resource area has become much more sophisticated. The first reading by Donald P. Schwab attempts to explain a number of these developments. Schwab makes one very important distinction between motivational *contents* and *process.* Contents refer to the needs or rewards that are attractive to people, while motivational process, on the other hand, refers to the factors that influence how people will go about trying to obtain the rewards.

The process aspect of motivation is particularly important to successful management. The organization typically has many potentially powerful rewards such as pay, opportunities for upward advancement, supervisory praise and recognition, and interesting and challenging work assignments. The critical process issue is how to use these rewards in such a way that they will influence such things as attendance and performance.

Schwab describes a very useful process model called *expectancy theory.* You will see that there are two critical links in this model. The first link is the connection, as employees see it, between their efforts and behaviors such as good job performance. This link is called *expectancy.* The second link is called *instrumentality* and refers to the connection employees see between their behavior and the likelihood that the behavior will lead to obtaining a desired reward. Using these concepts, expectancy theory says that employees will be motivated to perform well:

1. If they feel working harder will lead to higher performance.
2. If they feel higher performance will lead to higher rewards.

3. If the rewards they can obtain are rewards they desire.

Employee Satisfaction Survey

The second article by Karlene H. Roberts and Frederick Savage focuses on issues to be considered in conducting a survey of employee satisfaction. One of the most important observations they make has to do with whether or not a survey should be conducted. They argue that a survey is appropriate only if management is willing to make changes that are suggested by the results. This is a very important point worth reemphasizing. Surveys of opinion will almost certainly raise employee expectations; and unless the organization is willing to act on the results, it may find satisfaction lower after a survey than before.

Developing a questionnaire is a difficult, time-consuming activtiy. Fortunately, in the case of satisfaction this effort has already been done by others who have developed a variety of standardized questionnaires. Roberts and Savage identify and describe the characteristics of a number of these.

Much of what Roberts and Savage have to say about satisfaction surveys would also be applicable to surveys of other types of employee attitudes. For example, a survey of motivation needs to be followed by explicit managerial actions that are suggested by the results. The latter type of survey would, however, according to the earlier selection by Schwab, need to include questions about desirable rewards or outcomes, as well as questions about employee instrumentality and expectancy perceptions.

Job Satisfaction and Turnover

The last paper in this chapter reports the results of an excellent study that was conducted by Charles L. Hulin to reduce turnover. You will see that two satisfaction surveys were conducted on a group of clerical workers who were experiencing very high turnover rates relative to employees doing similar work in nearby organizations. In the first survey[1] a strong relationship was found between satisfaction and length of service. In addition, the workers in the organization studied were found to be relatively dissatisfied with all dimensions of work measured.

As a result of these findings, the organization made an effort to change policies regarding pay and promotions. In the study you will read, the results of these changes are reported. Turnover rates declined appreciably to rates that were similar to other organizations employing the same types of employees. Between the two surveys there was some increase in satisfaction with several aspects of the job. The major increases, however, occurred with the pay and promotion systems, as expected. All told, Hulin makes a persuasive case that the changes implemented by the organization resulted in increased satisfaction and that the increases in satisfaction resulted in a reduction in voluntary turnover. This paper is a very good illustration of how the intelligent use of attitude surveys combined with appropriate organizational changes can lead to desirable participation effects.

---

[1] Charles L. Hulin, "Job Satisfaction and Turnover in a Female Clerical Population," *Journal of Applied Psychology* 50 (1966): 280–85.

3. MOTIVATION IN ORGANIZATIONS

DONALD P. SCHWAB

Motivation is a term that has been used frequently and in many contexts. Thus, a precise unitary definition would not only be arbitrary, but probably also dysfunctional. Generally speaking, however, persons who have thought and written about motivation have considered two distinct but interrelated sets of ideas.

1. One of these focuses on the environmental or personal characteristics that serve to energize, activate, or "motivate" the individual. These approaches have been referred to as *content* theories of motivation (Campbell, Dunnette, Lawler and Weick 1970: 341) since they aim at identifying classes of variables that serve to stimulate the individual.

2. A second approach has been concerned with explaining how the individual chooses to engage in a particular behavior. Campbell et al. (1970: 341), refer to these orientations as *process* approaches since they focus on the mechanisms linking content variables to specific actions that the individual may perform.

A bit of reflection will suggest that knowledge of both motivational contents and processes is important if we are to understand and ultimately influence motivation. In an organizational context, for example, we must have information on the needs persons experience or the outcomes they seek (contents) in order to provide the types of rewards persons will find attractive. At the same time, however, these rewards must be administered so that persons will be encouraged to engage in the behaviors required by the organization. This requires knowledge of motivational process.

This entry is concerned with motivation as it applies to organizational contexts. It is thus aimed at furthering understanding about motivational contents and processes as they apply to work-related behaviors such as job choice, job maintenance, and, particularly, job performance.

MOTIVATIONAL CONTENTS

Content Theories. Motivational content can be viewed from two complementary perspectives (Cummings and Schwab 1973: 22–23). One is to view contents in terms of the deficiencies, deprivations, imbalances, or needs that activate the individual to behave. This is the traditional way of considering contents; it views them as internal to the individual. In this entry it will be referred to as the *needs* approach. A second, more recent, approach focuses on rewards or outcomes that serve to satisfy needs. Thus this approach considers contents in terms of consequences of the individual's behavior and will be referred to as the *outcome* approach.

Need Approaches. A number of theories have emphasized taxonomies that propose to identify needs possessed by individuals. By far the best known of such theories to persons interested in organizational behavior is Maslow's (1970) *need hierarchy* theory. According to this theory, individuals may experience five classes of needs: (1) *physiological* (hunger and thirst); (2) *safety* (primarily bodily); (3) *social* (friendship and affiliation); (4) *esteem* (both self and the esteem of others); and (5) *self-actualization* (growth, realization of potential). These needs are hypothesized to be arranged in a hierarchy such that each lower level of need must be predominantly satisfied before the individual experiences higher level needs.

Source: Donald P. Schwab from *Encyclopedia of Professional Management* edited by Lester R. Bittel. Copyright © 1978 by McGraw-Hill, Inc. Used with permission of McGraw-Hill Book Co.

Moreover, Maslow hypothesized that as physiological-through-esteem needs are satisfied, they cease to motivate. Self-actualization needs, alternatively, are hypothesized to become more active as they are satisfied.

Outcome Approaches. Although explicitly aimed at identifying sources of satisfaction rather than motivation, Herzberg's *two-factor* taxonomy is the best known attempt to identify motivating work outcomes (Herzberg, Mausner and Snyderman 1959). According to this approach, there are two types of work outcomes: (1) *intrinsic* factors which have to do with promotion, recognition of one's work, and with the work itself; and (2) *extrinsic* factors which have to do with the work environment including formal rewards other than promotion such as salary, relations with co-workers, supervision and organizational administration, and working conditions. In subsequent writings regarding this taxonomy, Herzberg (for example, 1966) has hypothesized that only the attainment of the intrinsic outcomes can initiate sustained motivation toward organizational goals. . . .

Implications. The typical organizational environment has four characteristics that may serve as sources of motivational outcomes:

1. First is the *work itself* that can provide intrinsic or task mediated outcomes.
2. *Personnel policies and practices* pertaining to rewards and discipline constitute a second source of outcomes.
3. Interpersonal relations with one's *supervisor*, the extent to which the supervisor provides recognition and allows for participation is a third outcome source.
4. Finally, one's *co-workers* are typically a source of socially oriented outcomes.

Content theories and their interpretations have too often emphasized one of these sources of outcomes to the exclusion of others.

A more appropriate interpretation of employee outcome preferences would take into consideration the following observations. *First*, substantial differences exist between individuals in their preferences for outcomes. *Second*, organizations probably have little influence on the types of outcomes employees find motivating (Lawler 1973: 38). *Finally*, employee preferences for outcomes, whatever the specific patterns, are likely to be fairly stable through time (Dawis, England, and Weiss 1968).

Organizations interested in providing motivating outcomes for a majority of employees would do well to heed the implications of these observations. In some respects, they put organizations in a passive role. Rather than attempting to change outcome preferences through communication or development programs, for example, these observations suggest the importance of identifying preexisting preferences. Attempts to change outcome preferences of employees probably have to come over time through selection procedures aimed at changing the labor force of the organization.

Most importantly, these observations suggest that organizations maintain a balanced approach to the administration of work outcomes. For example, while job enrichment may be appropriate for certain tasks and employees, it cannot by itself "solve" organizational motivation problems. Attention must also be paid to the other sources of outcomes.

MOTIVATIONAL PROCESSES

Practical considerations of motivation inevitably lead managers to the question of how needs or outcomes can be harnessed or linked to behaviors the organization wishes to encourage. That is, how can needs or outcomes serve to motivate certain types of behavior? This is the basic question about the *process* of motivation.

Over the years many process theories

have been proposed in several different branches of psychology. Interestingly, however, it was not until fairly recently that industrial psychologists and others interested in human behavior in organizations began to seriously consider and investigate theories that are essentially aimed at understanding motivational process. While a number have been proposed, Vroom's (1964) formulation of expectancy theory clearly has become dominant in recent years.

Expectancy Theory. Expectancy theory has been used to explain choices between different actions such as decisions about what job to accept. It has also been used to explain levels of intensity regarding a single activity—such as whether or not an employee will attempt to be a high, average, or low performer (Campbell and Pritchard 1976: 74). The theory is thus obviously aimed at explaining behaviors of interest to organizations.

The theory is frequently referred to as a *cognitive* one in that it emphasizes the importance of the ability to think in determining voluntary activity. All told, one must consider three concepts that people pre-

occur in the work environment. Unlike the content theories discussed earlier, however, expectancy theory makes no a *priori* statements about what outcomes individuals will find valent or nonvalent.

Instrumentality Perceptions. A second concept has to do with individual's beliefs about the connection or linkage between some activity and an outcome. These perceptions can be thought of as subjective probabilities and are referred to as *instrumentality* perceptions. In a work environment, for example, individuals would be expected to have instrumentality perceptions regarding the link between performance and potential outcomes such as salary increases. Note that there is a potentially unique instrumentality perception for each outcome.

Expectancy Perceptions. A third concept pertains to the individuals' beliefs about the connection (or linkage) between one's effort to engage in an activity and the likelihood that the activity will be accomplished. These are called *expectancy* perceptions and may also be thought of as subjective probabilities. For example, an individual's

FIGURE 1
Motivational Components in Expectancy Theory

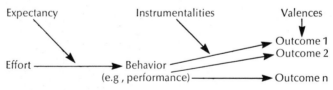

sumably think about to understand the process of motivation according to this theory.[1]

Valence of Outcomes. One concept has to do with the attractiveness (or *valence*) of outcomes that may be associated with an activity. We have already discussed types of intrinsic and extrinsic outcomes that may

---

[1] Readers interested in the nuances of the theory are encouraged to read Vroom (1964: 14–28) and Campbell and Pritchard (1976: 74–84).

expectancy perception regarding work performance might be thought of as his/her response to the question: What is the likelihood of performing this task successfully if you exert a reasonable amount of effort?

Expectancy theory states that: *Motivation to engage in an activity will be high when an individual's expectancy perception regarding that activity is high and when instrumentality perceptions linking the activity to positively valent outcomes are high.* Thus, we would expect an employee to be motivated to be a high work performer if that employee believed:

1. High performance was attainable through effort (high effort-performance expectancy).
2. High performance would lead to outcomes (high performance-outcome instrumentalities).
3. The outcomes were generally attractive (positively valent outcomes).

The major elements of the theory are diagrammed in Figure 1. Note that the motivational components of the theory speak only to the effort an individual may be expected to expend toward the accomplishment of some activity. Actual accomplishment depends not only on motivation, but also on ability (Vroom 1964: 196–204). *Thus, the complete theory states that behavior (for example, performance) = Motivation × Ability.*

Evaluation. Since its formulation by Vroom in 1964, many studies have been conducted testing various aspects of the theory. For the most part, these studies have been conducted in actual public and private organizations. A wide variety of occupational groups have been investigated including managers, professionals, and white- and blue-collar workers. Most of the research has been aimed at testing whether the theory can predict measures of employee performance or effort to perform. A few have used the theory in attempts to predict job choice.

By and large, findings from these studies have been favorable.[2] That is, it is frequently found that beliefs concerning valences of outcomes, and particularly concerning instrumentalities and expectancies, are associated with measures of effort and performance. Higher performers, or those exerting greater effort to perform, tend to have higher expectancies and higher instrumentalities that performance will lead to positively valent outcomes. While it is important to recognize that support for the theory has not been universal, nor always strong, it has been quite consistent.

Implications for Practice. Expectancy theory is very rich in implications for administrative action. Motivation can be enhanced to the extent that the organization is able to appropriately influence valence, expectancy, or instrumentality perceptions of employees. Since we have already indicated that organizations have little influence over the types of outcomes employees find important (valent), the discussion which follows will focus on the latter two perceptions.

It should be noted at the outset that employees' perceptions are ultimately influenced most importantly by the objective state of affairs. Thus, administrative policies will be unsuccessful if they communicate expectancy or instrumentality linkages that are not consistent with the actual implementation of those policies.

At the same time, however, individuals taken singularly or as group members bring to the work environment a set of partially unique historical experiences. These may tend to shade their feelings and beliefs regarding the important motivational components. Thus, majority relative to minority, rural relative to urban, female relative to male, advantaged relative to disadvantaged employees may hold somewhat different motivational perceptions regardless of organizational characteristics. Organizations must, therefore, show special sensitivity in establishing and implementing policy whenever persons of diverse backgrounds are employed.

Influencing Instrumentality Perceptions. There is little doubt that an organization can have the most immediate impact on motivation through its influence on instrumentality perceptions (beliefs regarding the links between behavior and outcomes). Instrumentality perceptions can be strength-

---

[2] A critical review of early research on expectancy theory has been performed by Heneman and Schwab (1972) and on the more recent research by Campbell and Pritchard (1976: 84–95).

ened by making rewards contingent or dependent on desired behavior. Thus, if the organization wishes to encourage motivation to perform among its employees, it must reward the high performers with positively valent rewards. In addition, low performers must not be rewarded.[3] The key to establishing appropriate instrumentality perceptions is both in *differentially* rewarding and in not rewarding. Rewarding indiscriminately will not have positive motivational impacts.

Given the cognitive nature of expectancy theory, it follows that instrumentality linkages should be communicated. Employees need to be informed that behaving in desired ways will be rewarded. The more specific the organization is about the exact behavior desired and the exact rewards to be expected, the better. While contingent administration of rewards may influence behavior in any event, the impact can be more effective in a shorter time if it is explicitly communicated (for example, Bandura 1974).

There is substantial literature from reinforcement theory that has dealt with methods for linking rewards to desired behavior. This literature is frequently interpreted as suggesting that partial reinforcement schedules (that is, where not every desirable behavior is rewarded) are most effective for motivation (for example, Hamner 1974: 491–94). The evidence for this type of conclusion, however, has not been established on adults working in organizational settings. Field studies in the latter context suggest that continuous reinforcement (where every desirable behavior is rewarded) is at least as effective as partial reinforcement (Cummings 1976). This latter observation is consistent with expectancy theory which would hypothesize that instrumentality perceptions would be maximized when every desirable behavior was rewarded.

In summary, organizations can have positive impacts on their employees' instrumentalities by:

1. Communicating in specific terms the linkage between the behaviors and the rewards.
2. Implementing the communicated linkages, including withholding rewards from persons who do not engage in the desired behavior.
3. Where possible, offering the rewards for every or nearly every desired behavior.[4]

While the organization probably has the greatest impact on instrumentality perceptions through the processes described above, keep in mind that individuals also differ in how they respond to these processes.

Influencing Expectancy Perceptions. Expectancy perceptions (beliefs regarding the links between effort and behavior) can also be influenced by the organization. Since they pertain to an individual's feelings about his/her capabilities to perform some activity, they will depend mostly on the individual's perception of his/her ability *relative* to the ability requirements of the activity.[5] That is, expectancy perceptions depend jointly on the individual and the task to be done.

Such a formulation suggests that a number of organizational activities may have impacts on expectancy perceptions.

1. *Training and development programs* are an obvious method for attempting to change individuals. By sending employees through training programs, organizations typically attempt to increase their job skills. These changes, in turn, can frequently be expected to enhance expectancy perceptions.
2. *Selection* provides another method for changing, not individuals, *per se*, but characteristics of the workforce in the aggre-

---

[3] This is not to suggest that low performers should be punished. Punishment does not generally influence behavior in a direction opposite of positive rewards and hence should not be thought of as falling on the opposite end of a continuum from positive rewards (for example, Campbell and Pritchard 1976: 71).

[4] This latter recommendation is the most tentative of the three because of the paucity of evidence from studies of humans in work organizations.

[5] The ideas expressed in this section have been substantially influenced by the theory of work adjustment (Dawis, England and Weiss, 1968).

gate. By changing employment standards, organizations can influence the ability levels of those hired and consequently influence expectancy perceptions.

3. *Job simplification or enlargement* may manipulate work content favorably, also. Simplification has been recommended as a mechanism for increasing productivity through an emphasis on employees' ability to perform. Recently, many persons have advocated enlarging or enriching jobs (i.e., making them more demanding and difficult). Emphasis has been placed on employees' *motivation* to perform. Here it is sufficient to indicate that manipulation of the job will likely influence the ability requirements of the job and hence employees' expectancy perceptions.

4. *The employee-job "mix"* may be changed by reallocation of persons within the organization. Transfers and promotions are frequently used examples of this method for changing employees' relative ability to perform and hence their expectancy perceptions.

Viewing expectancy as proposed here suggests that it is a very dynamic construct. Employees change through time, jobs change, and hence expectancy perceptions change. It can frequently be expected that expectancy perceptions will be fairly low for employees starting on a job. With experience and/or training, these perceptions will likely increase. Changes in jobs, either through transfer/promotion or technological change, may dramatically alter expectancy perceptions of experienced employees, however. Thus, the organization must be continually alert to the implications of the congruence of worker abilities with job ability requirements for expectancy perceptions.

As with instrumentality perceptions, we can also expect individual differences in expectancy perceptions, primarily as a function of one's previous experience. Those who have a history of coping successfully with their environment in the past will probably have more positive expectancy percep-

tions than those who have been less successful. . . .

REFERENCES

Bandura, A. "Behavior Theory and the Models of Man," *American Psychologist* 29 (1974): 859–69.

Campbell, J. P., Dunnette, M. D., Lawler, E. E., III, and Weick, K. E., Jr. *Managerial Behavior, Performance, and Effectiveness.* New York: McGraw-Hill, 1970.

Campbell, J. P., and Pritchard, R. D. "Motivation Theory in Industrial and Organizatonal Psychology." In M. D. Dunnette, ed,. *Handbook of Industrial and Organizational Psychology. Chicago:* Rand McNally, 1976, 63–130.

Cummings, L. L. "Reinforcement in Management: Principles and Cases." Unpublished Paper, Graduate School of Business, University of Wisconsin-Madison, 1976.

Cummings, L. L., and Schwab, D. P. *Performance in Organizations: Determinants and Appraisal.* Glenview, Ill.: Scott, Foresman, 1973.

Dawis, R. V., England, G. E., and Weiss, D. J. *A Theory of Work Adjustment: A Revision.* Bulletin 47. Minneapolis: Minnesota Studies in Vocational Rehabilitation, 1968.

Hamner, W. C. "Reinforcement Theory and Contingency Management in Organizational Settings." In H. L. Tosi and W. C. Hamner, eds., *Organizational Behavior and Management: A Contingency Approach.* Chicago: St. Clair Press, 1974, pp. 86–112.

Heneman, H. G., III, and Schwab, D. P. "Evaluation of Research On Expectancy Theory Predictions of Employee Performance." *Psychological Bulletin* 78 (1972): 1–9.

Herzberg, F. *Work and the Nature of Man.* New York: World, 1966.

Herzberg, F., Mausner, B., and Snyderman, B. B. *The Motivation to Work.* 2d ed. New York: Wiley, 1959.

Lawler, E. E., III. *Motivation in Work Organizations.* Monterey, Calif.: Brooks/Cole, 1973.

Maslow, A. H. *Motivation and Personality.* 2d ed. New York: Harper, 1970.

Vroom, V. H. *Work and Motivation.* New York: Wiley, 1964.

4. TWENTY QUESTIONS: UTILIZING JOB SATISFACTION MEASURES

KARLENE H. ROBERTS and FREDERICK SAVAGE

During the last decade the issue of employee job satisfaction has received considerable attention. There are several obvious reasons for measuring satisfaction.

There is a growing concern with the human as well as the physical assets of organizations. Among these human assets are the values employees hold about their employers and their jobs.

Some researchers and some managers believe that satisfaction contributes to job performance; that the dissatisfied employee will perform poorly.

There is ample evidence that satisfaction is negatively related to absenteeism and turnover, both of which are costly to organizations. Managers can better allocate their personnel resources if they understand the attitudes of their various groups of employees.

It is always a good idea for managers to know how their employees feel about their jobs. Our research shows that different kinds of employees in the same organization respond to their jobs with different attitudes and values.

Unfortunately, having information about employee satisfaction is futile unless the firm is willing to take positive steps where there is low morale. However, even where there is a commitment to action and a desire to collect reliable information about employee attitudes, there are at least two further problems. How does a manager know whether he should conduct a job satisfaction survey? And, if he does conduct one, how should he measure satisfaction?

To date, no one has attempted to present managers with an effective strategy for determining whether their companies should conduct attitude surveys, and there is no groundwork for selecting appropriate job satisfaction measures. To remedy this situation, we offer the following strategy, based primarily on our own research.

The "Twenty Question" Strategy

At one time or another most of us have seen the television program "What's My Line?" As in the game, "Twenty Questions," the "What's My Line?" panel attempts to guess the occupation of a guest by asking a series of questions which can be answered "yes" or "no." After watching the program, most of us are amazed at how quickly the panel usually guesses the guest's occupation. On closer examination, we note that a skillful panel member first asks questions of a very general nature. As these are answered, he narrows his scope of interest, ignoring certain options and concentrating on increasingly specific questions to elicit the appropriate information. Arlene Francis' famous question, "Is it bigger than a breadbox?" illustrates the skillful use of partition question to zero in on an individual's occupation.

This "Twenty Questions" strategy can be equally useful in deciding the cost-benefit trade-offs of conducting a job satisfaction survey. The more general questions force an examination of an individual's managerial goals and the goals of his company and force him to ask *if* conducting a job satisfaction survey will benefit the firm. If such a survey is recommended, the narrower questions will help determine how it might benefit the firm and how one should go about measuring job satisfaction. The eco-

Source: © 1973 by the Regents of the University of California. Reprinted from *California Management Review*, vol. 15, no. 3, pp. 21–28, by permission of the Regents.

nomical questioning strategy helps conserve time and money.

To illustrate this strategy consider the following situation: The president of Barrow Company, a manufacturing firm with 1,000 employees, notices that the female clerical personnel are not doing their jobs well. This group is characterized by high absenteeism and turnover rates. To correct this situation he decides to restructure the clerical job so that each girl has more opportunity for growth and responsibility. After the jobs are restructured, however, job performance drops more, absenteeism and turnover increase another 15 percent per year.

Question No. 1: Should the Manager Conduct a Job Satisfaction Survey?

Yes, if he is prepared to make some changes in those job facets which are particularly dissatisfying to his employees. Employees may think that in providing the manager, or an outsider who conducts the survey, with information about their job related feelings, they can expect some attempt to change those job facets related to attitudes.

In our example, the workers may value pay more than they value responsibility. A job satisfaction survey would probably have revealed this. A company's deteriorating organizational climate may well be a result of failing to consider this kind of need in restructuring jobs. If a job satisfaction survey had been conducted before the jobs were restructured, the situation of increased absenteeism and turnover might have been avoided. Our research, as well as that of many other authors, shows that different employee groups want different things from their jobs. Even if a survey indicated that girls wanted greater job responsibility, their participation in job restructuring might have been crucial to the effectiveness of such a change. By not directly participating in the change, employees can feel left out of decision processes directly affecting them, and they may sabotage efforts at change.

In situations similar to that in our example, job satisfaction surveys may help in two ways: first, they provide a means for employees to communicate their feelings to higher management and thus participate indirectly in job restructuring; second, questions concerned with the desirability of employee participation in decision-making can be a part of the survey—employees may or may not indicate a need for direct participation in such matters and management can act accordingly.

But what if the situation has gone as far as it has in our example? The jobs have already been changed. A job satisfaction survey still could be profitable. First, it will provide information on employee attitudes about the restructured jobs and can include questions about attitudes the employees had before the changes took place. Such information can furnish insight as to whether the restructured jobs caused the company's deteriorating organizational climate. (For the most convincing case to be made, however, job satisfaction information should have been collected both before and after the job restructuring.) Second, open-ended questions about future job changes considered by the company can be included in the survey. Finally, a job satisfaction survey will allow employees to participate in proposed changes by encouraging them to evaluate such changes. Again, none of this will benefit a company in which management is unwilling to act on the results of the survey. Thus, management philosophy may ultimately determine whether or not to conduct a job satisfaction survey.

Question No. 2: Could Information About Employee Attitudes Really Be Useful in Improving a Firm's Organizational Climate?

Yes. As evidenced from our example and the foregoing discussion, a job satisfaction survey might help managers make decisions related to improving organizational climate. Research has shown a positive relationship between job dissatisfaction and such components of organizational climate as accidents, grievance rate, absenteeism, and turnover.[1] By ascertaining those job factors associated with dissatisfaction and working with employees to correct them, grievance rate, absenteeism, and turnover can be decreased. Because hiring and training personnel are expensive, reducing turnover rate alone might more than repay the cost of conducting a job satisfaction survey.

Job performance is also a facet of organizational climate. However, the relationship between satisfaction and performance is less clear than are the relationships we have just discussed. In the past it was thought that high satisfaction produces good performance. Research, however, has questioned this notion of causality.[2] It may be that high performance causes satisfaction, or that the two are unrelated. Obviously, it is fallacious to conduct a job satisfaction survey based on the single assumption that from knowing the degree to which an employee is satisfied, you can predict his performance. Other factors, such as employee expectations concerning their rewards and the value of these rewards to them, may contribute to both satisfaction and performance.[3] Your satisfaction survey might include a measure of how employees view their rewards. With this additional information you can look at both satisfaction and performance in relation to these rewards.

[1] V. H. Vroom, *Work and Motivation* (New York: Wiley, 1964), p. 186; C. L. Hulin, "Effects of Changes in Jobs Satisfaction Levels on Employee Turnover," *Journal of Applied Psychology* 52 (1968): 122–26; C. L. Hulin, "Job Satisfaction and Turnover in a Female Clerical Population," *Journal of Applied Psychology* 50 (1966): 280–85; and I. C. Ross and A. F. Zander, "Need Satisfaction and Employee Turnover," *Personnel Psychology* 10 (1957): 327–38.

[2] V. H. Vroom, p. 186, and A. H. Brayfield and W. H. Crockett, "Employee Attitudes and Employee Performance," *Psychological Bulletin* 52 (1955): 396–424.

[3] V. H. Vroom, *op. cit.,* pp. 14–19; and L. W. Porter and E. E. Lawler, *Managerial Attitudes and Performance* (Homewood, Ill.: Irwin, 1968).

Question No. 3: If a Job Satisfaction Survey Were to Be Conducted, Should More Than One Measure of Satisfaction Be Used?

Yes. Too often managers rely on information obtained from only one estimate of job satisfaction. Yet all of our measures are imperfect. Any measure of this kind is subject to bias; but the kind of bias inherent in one instrument, say a questionnaire, is different from that inherent in another measure, perhaps another questionnaire.

Again, let's look at our example. If a job satisfaction survey had been done at any point in time and had included only questions about pay and supervision, management would have entirely missed obtaining any information about the feelings these girls associated with the amount of responsibility in their jobs. For a *complete* picture of employee attitudes, then, results obtained from two or more instruments must be looked at, each with its independent sources of error, and each tapping different aspects of employee satisfaction. One measure may be concerned with employee feelings about pay and supervision, another with general attitudes toward the job. Using multiple measures improves the probability of measuring exactly what is intended. That is, it improves the validity of the assessment.

To see how this works, let's take the concept of job satisfaction and look at it a little more systematically, as in Figure 1. Assume that any measure of the concept contains some error (either it measures something other than job satisfaction or it measures nothing at all). If each of your measures is contaminated with different errors, or bias, combining the measures should cancel out the effect of these random errors. Note the relationship, then, of the concept job satisfaction and the various paper and pencil measures of it.

The central circle represents the concept to be measured, job satisfaction, and the

other circles are imperfect measures of that concept. Some parts of a measure (maybe particular questions on a questionnaire) may fail to overlap the concept at all (measurement error), and other parts of the measure are good indicators of job satisfaction. Some of these may overlap each other. For instance, in order to measure specific facets of job satisfaction, novel questions are designed. But they happen to measure some of the same and some different aspects of job satisfaction as the standardized instrument(s) also used.

Job satisfaction measures can be direct or indirect. Direct measures are those which ask employees in a straightforward way how satisfied they are. For example, employees are asked to check on a seven-point scale the degree to which they are satisfied with their work, or with their supervision. One problem in using such measures is that they may elicit answers employees think you want to hear. Indirect measures of job satisfaction get around this problem. These are measures of feelings acquired in ways other than by asking the people involved. They are often obtainable from data your com-

pany regularly collects. A manager might, for example, find that increased thievery is an indicator of employee dissatisfaction. Only if the relationship between direct measures of job satisfaction and such indirect designators of it as thievery can be established, should the less stable indicators be accepted as reflections of morale.

Our research has attempted to establish a relationship between employee satisfaction and some inexpensive, indirect indicators of it. We have not yet met with success. We find it is better to ask employees directly how they feel about their jobs than to search futilely for such elusive indirect estimates. However, we know of one firm which noticed that employees in work units characterized by low satisfaction tended to lose work gloves more frequently than did workers in better satisfied units. By establishing a definite relationship between employee dissatisfaction with company policies (as measured in a straightforward manner) and glove loss rate, the company gained an easily accessible and inexpensive job satisfaction measure.

Finally, one cannot simply look informally at the answers to questions on the various instruments and expect to arrive at reasonable conclusions about employee job satisfaction. Nor can one look casually at some combination of direct and indirect measures for such conclusions. Instead, it is important that appropriate statistical techniques be used in the reduction and analyses of data. Both indirect and direct measures of job satisfaction are easily tallied for application of data analyses techniques which are relatively robust.

To recapitulate, to measure employee job satisfaction use more than one measure, each tapping a different aspect of satisfaction. Questionnaires are less expensive than interviews. Indirect measures, if they can be found, and only when they are shown to be related for a firm to the more stable direct measures, might offer quick cheap indicators of general employee morale. Once data are collected they should be coded and analyzed using appropriate statistical methods.

Question No. 4: Should a Manager Rely Only on His Own Tailor-Made Job Satisfaction Questionnaire?

No. Unless the firm's workforce and organizational characteristics are particularly unique, standardized job satisfaction measures should be used. In our example, these characteristics were not sufficiently unusual to warrant the use of tailor-made measures.

Even when management decides to do a job satisfaction survey, the most frequent next step is for someone to design a set of questions they think will measure satisfaction. In doing this they have no history against which to evaluate the answers to their questions, and no information about the reliability and validity of their measures. Reliability asks whether the instrument measures whatever it measures consistently. Validity is concerned with how well the instrument measures what it is intended to measure. For instance, we ask the girls in our example: "Answer on a seven-point scale (from highly dissatisfied to highly satisfied), how happy are you with the kind of supervision you have?" We obtain a mean score for the group of four on this question. Does this mean our sample is any more or less satisfied than is any other group of workers? If we measure these employees' satisfaction with their supervision the same way tomorrow, will we get the same answer? And, does this question really elicit employees' feelings about their supervision? Standardized job satisfaction measures are available which are both relatively consistent and relatively valid. They should be used wherever possible and perhaps supplemented with other questions, the answers to which can be examined in relation to results of more stable measures.

In our example, it might be useful to compare employee job satisfaction with the morale of similar work groups. We know,

for instance, that different aspects of their jobs contribute to satisfaction for males and females. The same holds true for urban and rural workers.[4] It would not be useful to compare our employees to some nondescript group. There is a great deal of information about age, sex, education, industry, and job function of the people who have responded to some instruments. In some cases there is even information about the communities in which these people work. All of these factors can be expected to influence job satisfaction. Where possible it is advisable to compare employee satisfaction to that of groups similar to them on these dimensions.

Question No. 5: In Searching for Appropriate Standardized Job Satisfaction Instruments, Should All Available Instruments Be Examined?

No. Because of the sheer number of job satisfaction instruments available, the search should be restricted to only the major ones. In selecting any instrument for your package, the following questions should be asked:

What theoretical assumptions underlie the instrument? Instruments are based on different definitions of job satisfaction. Consequently, some may measure a concept of job satisfaction not appropriate to the needs.

Have adequate reliability and validity been demonstrated for the instrument?

Under what conditions should the instrument be used?

Some of the major instruments to be considered are the Job Description Index, the Brayfield-Rothe Index, the General Motors

---

4 C. L. Hulin and M. R. Blood, "Job Enlargement, Individual Differences, and Worker Responses," *Psychological Bulletin* 69 (1968): 41–55; and P. C. Smith, L. M. Kendall, and C. L. Hulin, *The Measurement of Satisfaction in Work and Retirement* (Chicago: Rand McNally, 1969), p. 96.

Faces Scale, the Porter Instrument, and the Minnesota Satisfaction Questionnaire.

Job Description Index: A Job Facet Instrument.[5] One well-known authority describes the JDI as the most carefully constructed job satisfaction instrument in use today. The JDI taps five dimensions of job satisfaction: work itself, co-workers, supervision, pay, and opportunities for promotion. Instead of directly asking respondents to evaluate their satisfaction with each of these job facets, the JDI uses a list of adjectives from which respondents check those which describe their job situation. This format was selected so that people who are not very good readers or who are in a hurry to finish filling out the instrument can easily complete it. The JDI can be a very good instrument to use with employees like those in our example. To compare employees' scores on the five dimensions with those of other groups, an extensive amount of information available for groups characterized by different personal, community, and industrial variables can be examined.

Brayfield-Rothe Index: An Explicit Measure of Overall Job Satisfaction.[6] Designed in 1951, this index is an explicit type of overall job satisfaction measure. That is, each of the 18 items in the questionnaire attempts to describe directly the respondent's overall job environment. By summing the respondent's score on each item, an overall index of job satisfaction is obtained. Although our research suggests that some of the items are out of date, the total score on the 18 items is reliable and is highly intercorrelated with other measures of job satisfaction. Very little information exists about the characteristics of people who have responded to this instrument.

General Motors Faces Scale: A Projective Measure of Overall Job Satisfaction.[7] While

the Brayfield-Rothe Index is an example of an explicit measure of job satisfaction, the GM Faces Scale is a projective technique. According to the scale's developer, some degree of error is inherent in all questionnaires which rely on words to represent feelings. This error is greatly magnified when the questionnaire is given to people with poor verbal ability. To solve this problem, Kunin developed an overall measure of job satisfaction (as opposed to a measure of satisfaction with various job facets) which utilizes a series of 11 faces to project job satisfaction. The faces "smile or "frown" in different degrees, and the respondent checks that face which is most representative of how he feels about his job. A great deal of research, including ours, indicates that the Faces Scales is a fairly good measure of overall job satisfaction. Considerable information exists about the characteristics of the instrument respondents.

Porter Instrument: A Measure of an Employee's Need Structure.[8] This measure is based on a theory of job satisfaction which says that dissatisfaction occurs when actual rewards fail to meet what the employee perceives as equitable. To measure "perceived need deficiency" Porter developed a questionnaire based on four need categories. They are social needs, ego needs, esteem needs, and self-actualization needs. The instrument, then, emphasizes the employee's need structure rather than his satisfaction with individaul job facets or his overall satisfaction with his job.

There are two problems involved in using this measure. First, respondents must be adept at abstract thinking. People with poor reading skills have great difficulty filling out this questionnaire. It may not be useful for groups such as the girls in our example and has been primarily used with managers. Second, our research indicates that the

[5] Smith, Kendall, and Hulin, ibid.

[6] A. H. Brayfield and H. F. Rothe, "An Index of Job Satisfaction," *Journal of Applied Psychology* 35 (1951): 307–11.

[7] T. Kunin, "The Construction of a New Type of Attitude Measure," *Personnel Psychology* 8 (1955): 65–77.

[8] L. W. Porter, "Job Attitudes in Management: I. Perceived Deficiencies in Need Fulfillment as a Function of Job Level," *Journal of Applied Psychology* 46 (1962): 375–84.

questionnaire may not measure the needs indicated.[9]

Minnesota Satisfaction Questionnaire: A Measure of Work Adjustment.[10] Based on a theory of work adjustment, this job satisfaction instrument conceptually overlaps Porter's in some respects. Both instruments define job satisfaction as a function of how well an individual's work environment provides for his needs. The Minnesota Satisfaction Questionnaire comes in a long form and a short form. Each item in the long form refers to a reinforcer, some aspect of the individual's work environment which can fulfill a specific need. From these items, 20 scales were derived, based on such reinforcers as ability utilization and working conditions. The instrument has been extensively researched and is reliable. It also appears to tap those reinforcers it purports to measure. Furthermore, a great deal of information is available about the way various kinds of workers fill it out. Thus, it is possible to compare workers' responses on this instrument to those of other workers with similar or different characteristics.

Question No. 6: Are There More Specific Considerations to Be Made in Selecting One or More of the Above Instruments?

Yes. Besides thinking about using measures of overall satisfaction and job facet satisfaction, one should consider the relative merits of job satisfaction instruments which emphasize employee need structure. To determine whether or not such needs as the opportunity for growth, friendship, and self-esteem are fulfilled, the instruments to use are those other than those used to investigate employee satisfaction with pay, promotion, and co-workers. The selection of overall, job facet, or need structure instruments depends on the goals.

Let's look back at our example. Before restructuring the jobs, the manager should have had information about employee needs. However, once the restructuring occurred, it may have been more useful to examine satisfaction with job facets. An instrument package, given both before and after job restructuring, containing overall, job facet, and need structure measures would have filled the bill. This combination of instruments also meets the goals of a multi-method approach to measuring job satisfaction.

Question No. 7: Should Only Standardized Measures of Job Satisfaction Be Utilized?

No. In really thinking about the uses to which information about employee morale can be put, specific questions not contained in any of the available instruments will suggest themselves. As implied in the answer to question four, these should be added to the package, but not substituted for it, because there will be little evidence of reliability and validity for these questions.

Second, only by collecting information about respondents' personal characteristics, job functions, and so on, can job satisfaction be compared across groups and the comparisons understood. Third, in general, job satisfaction measures have been used in conjunction with interest in absenteeism, turnover, and other personnel behaviors. These data should be collected for each respondent's unit so that summaries of unit job satisfaction can be looked at in relation to summaries of unit personnel behaviors.

[9] K. H. Roberts, G. A. Walter, and R. E. Miles, "A Factor Analytic Study of Job Satisfaction Items Designed to Measure Maslow Need Categories," *Personnel Psychology* 24 (1971): 205–20.

[10] D. Weiss, R. Dawis, G. England, and L. Lofquist, *Manual for Minnesota Satisfaction Questionnaire*, Bulletin 45, (Minneapolis: University of Minnesota, Industrial Relations Center, 1967).

Question No. 8: If Standardized Job Satisfaction Measures Are Used, Will the Answers the Employees Give Be Specifically Influenced by the Firm's Workforce Characteristics and Organizational Structure?

Yes. Our research shows that such individual characteristics as education are related to the utility of various satisfaction instruments. Again, because of its conceptual complexity, the Porter Instrument cannot be answered adequately by poorly educated respondents. Other personnel variables such as employee race, and whether they work part-time or full-time may influence satisfaction. For a sample of 495 hospital employees at several job levels, we found significant differences in satisfaction level for whites and nonwhites as measured by the JDI, the Brayfield-Rothe items, and the GM Faces Scale. Not only do these racial groups differ in overall satisfaction, they respond to different aspects of their jobs. That is, their satisfaction patterns are different. The same is true for part-time versus full-time hospital employees.[11]

Organizational characteristics also contribute to job satisfaction. We found increased satisfaction associated with higher job level, increasing organizational flatness, and with whether hospitals are teaching or nonteaching facilities.[12] The job of the as-

tute manager is to try to understand the separate contributions of individual, organizational, and job function variables to employee satisfaction, and to consider the useful changes in these characteristics it is possible for him to make. He should also be aware of the fact that differences in community characteristics influence the degree to which employees are satisfied.

CONCLUSION

Although the "Twenty Questions" strategy is somewhat structured and slightly artificial, it presents one effective way to determine whether a job satisfaction survey should be conducted, what measures should be used, and what outcomes can be expected. Of course, many of our questions are best answered "maybe," and management can always expend more resources for additional information about them where it is desired. The "Twenty Questions" strategy will merely force consideration of the costs and benefits associated with job satisfaction surveys and provide the groundwork for selecting instruments.

We have discussed here the importance of asking a series of increasingly specific questions prior to advocating a job satisfaction survey. These questions are broadly concerned with managerial goals in conducting the survey, attention to corporate philosophy and structure, and the influence of employee characteristics and the external environment on job satisfaction. If a survey is to be conducted attention must be given to the selection of instruments by considering their theoretical bases, reliability and validity. Figure 2 provides a guide to the considerations involved in job satisfaction surveys.

[11] C. A. O'Reilly and K. H. Roberts, "Job Satisfaction Among Whites and Non-Whites: A Cross-Cultural Approach," *Journal of Applied Psychology* 57 (1973): 295–99, and N. Logan, C. A. O'Reilly, and K. H. Roberts, "Job Satisfaction Among Part-Time and Full-Time Employees," *Journal of Vocational Behavior* 3 (1973): 33–41.

[12] N. Imparato, S. Sedeck, H. T. Baker, R. J. Day, and K. H. Roberts, "An Exploratory Study of the Effects of Community and Organizational Characteristics on Job Satisfaction of Nursing Personnel" (in press).

FIGURE 2
Guide to Considerations Involved in Job Satisfaction Surveys

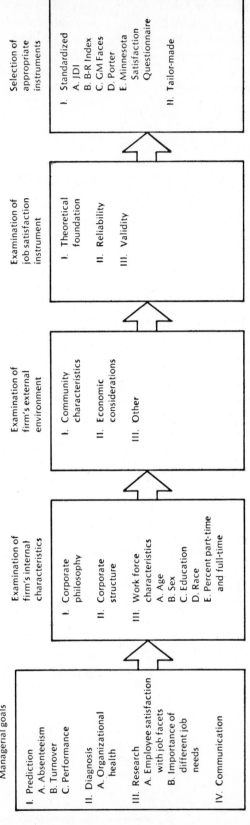

5. EFFECTS OF CHANGES IN JOB-SATISFACTION LEVELS ON EMPLOYEE TURNOVER

CHARLES L. HULIN[1]

[In a previously reported study (Hulin 1966)] I indicated the presence of an abnormally high turnover rate among the female clerical workers employed by the corporate offices of a large Canadian manufacturing firm. The turnover rate among the female employees of this company (30 percent per year) was not only high on an absolute basis but was high relative to 15 other large firms located in Montreal who had a mean annual turnover rate of only 20 percent. The company involved ranked either first or second in turnover rate during each of the last ten years among this group of companies. Many of the ecological factors which contribute to high turnover rates (general economic conditions of the area, labor market conditions, competition from other firms) and the characteristics of females in the workforce (age, marital status, previous experience, domestic responsibilities, pregnancy, marriage) were uncontrolled but were common to the other firms in the area who had much lower turnover rates. Therefore, consideration was given to the role job satisfaction and dissatisfaction played in contributing to the high turnover rate.

The relationship between job satisfaction and turnover was also investigated in this earlier study. Job-satisfaction questionnaires were administered to 345 female clerical workers employed at this company. The questionnaire measured satisfaction with six aspects of work. A year after the questionnaires were administered, 43 of the participants had quit.

The satisfaction scores of the 43 terminators were compared to the satisfaction scores of a group of nonterminators who were similar in age, years of education, and mother tongue. It was found that the terminators were much less satisfied than those who stayed.

On the basis of these results the question was raised as to whether the turnover rate for this company could be reduced by increasing the job satisfaction of the clerical workers. In order to answer this question a program was initiated by the company to attempt to increase job satisfaction in the hope of reducing turnover. It is not the purpose of this article to analyze the program *per se*. However, a brief description may be in order. The results of the scores on the Job Description Index (JDI) indicated that dissatisfaction of the clerical workers was occurring in all areas. . . . Analysis of their responses to open-ended questions substantiated this finding and also indicated that their dissatisfaction with pay was directed as much at the wage and salary *administration* as it was at wage *levels*. Examination of the workers' responses on the satisfaction with promotions scale indicated that the girls felt dissatisfaction was due to their feelings of being on "dead-end jobs" with little or no chance for promotion and not due to their feelings about the fairness of the policies.

These analyses led the company to revise their wage and salary administration policies to make them more nearly constant across departments and to institute regular salary reviews and formalize the merit-raise procedure. Also a policy was initiated of allowing and encouraging intracompany transfers so the girls could move from one department to another where they would have a better chance of being promoted. In con-

Source: *Journal of Applied Psychology,* 1968, vol. 52, no. 2, 122–26. Copyright 1968 by the American Psychological Association. Reprinted by permission.

[1] The writer would like to thank James Anderson and Susan Pfeifer for their assistance on the data-analysis stages of this research and Milton Blood who read and commented on an earlier draft of the paper.

junction with this latter procedure the girls were encouraged to make changes in their own job so that they could have a more responsible job within their present job classification. The most compelling reason for choosing these job aspects to concentrate on in the program was because they are the job characteristics which are most fully under the control of the company. The entire program was put into effect in October 1964.

The purpose of the present article is to analyze the changes which have occurred in this company since July 1964 regarding satisfaction scores, turnover rates, and the relationship between satisfaction and termination decisions.

METHOD

Research Setting

The company in which this study was carried out . . . is a large international manufacturing company which employs approximately 400 female clerical workers in the corporate offices. During the 3 years (1961, 1962, 1963) preceding the initial study, the turnover rate among the female clerical staff was 30.3 percent, 30.0 percent, and 30.0 percent. This company's rate of turnover was stable and had shown no tendencies in either direction over the past 10 years. Turnover rate was computed by obtaining the ratio of number of quits per year to average number of female employees where average number of employees was equal to the average of the number at the start of the year and the number at the end of the year.

Subjects

The entire female clerical staff was asked to participate in the job-satisfaction survey which was to be conducted by the company. The workers were informed of this by their supervisors and by a letter from the personnel department. They were told that the questionnaires were completely anonymous and that their individual responses would never be revealed to the company. . . . Of the 350 members of the clerical staff present during the week of the survey, 298 (85.1 percent) participated in the survey. (Not all of the staff was present due to sickness, vacation, travel, etc.)

Variables

The job satisfaction of these clerical workers was measured by the Job Description Index (JDI). In addition to the five satisfaction variables, measures were also obtained of each worker's age, education level, job level, socioeconomic background . . . and mother tongue. Measures of all variables were obtained during the first week of July 1966. By the first week of April 1967, [an additional 16 females had terminated].

RESULTS

The turnover rate among female clerical workers during 1966 was 12 percent. This is significantly lower than the turnover rate of 30 percent in 1964 before the changes in the company's programs and policies were initiated. The turnover rate during 1965 was 18 percent indicating that there has been a steady decrease.

As in the 1964 survey, mean satisfaction scores were computed for each of the five job areas. Table 1 shows these mean satisfaction scores as well as those obtained in 1964. t tests of the significance of the difference between the 1964 and 1966 means were computed. The results of these t tests are shown in Table 1. Of the five job areas, four—pay, promotion, supervision, and co-workers—showed a significant increase in satisfaction from 1964 to 1966. Promotion and pay satisfaction showed the biggest increases. . . .

For each of the 16 terminators who could be identified, two control subjects were drawn who were matched in terms of age,

TABLE 1
Mean 1964 and 1966 JDI Satisfaction Scores

Variable	Mean 1964 Scores (n = 345)	Mean 1966 Scores (n = 298)	t
Satisfaction with:			
Work	35.33	36.11	.85
Pay	15.01	32.83	10.27**
Promotions	10.78	24.58	10.38**
Co-workers	41.53	43.49	2.45*
Supervision	40.85	43.23	2.76**

* $p < .05$.
** $p < .01$.

years of education, job level, and mother tongue. [As in the earlier study, it was found that the terminators were much less satisfied than those who remained with the organization.]

DISCUSSION

The results of this study indicate that there was a decrease in turnover of 18 percent after the changes in the company's pay and promotion policies were instituted. In addition, there was a significant increase in satisfaction with four out of five of the job areas. Considering these results, one is tempted to conclude that the company program initiated in 1964 brought about an increase in the job satisfaction of these female clerical workers, and that this increase led to a reduction in turnover in 1966. However, since this was not a true experimental study, . . . several alternative explanations must be considered.

One explanation which could account for the decrease in turnover without attributing it to increased satisfaction is history. A change in the labor-market conditions from 1964 to 1966 may have occurred. It could have been much easier to get a job in 1964 than it was in 1966. If a girl was dissatisfied with her job, she could quit and easily find another job. However, an examination of the condition of the labor market for these two years indicates little change. One would expect that changes in the labor market

would be reflected in the turnover rates of the other companies located in Montreal. The average annual turnover rates for the other 15 large companies in Montreal were 18.4 percent, 20.2 percent, and 20.0 percent in 1961, 1962, and 1963. These turnover rates have not decreased during 1964, 1965, and 1966. The average turnover rate among these 15 companies was 24.3 percent in 1966. An explanation for the decreased levels of turnover based on changes in the labor market conditions can be rejected. . . .

Another explanation which could account for the results of this study is that there were changes in the composition of the female clerical workers employed at this company from 1964 to 1966. A certain pattern of these employee characteristics might predispose the worker to remain on the job and also to be more satisfied with her job. This pattern could be more frequently found among the 1966 clerical staff. If this explanation is correct, then one would expect to find differences between the composition of the 1964 and 1966 clerical staff. However, a comparison of the compositions of the two staffs in terms of age, job level, years of education, and mother tongue revealed no such differences.

It would also be difficult to postulate random factors which could explain the particular pattern of results obtained. To argue that one set of uncontrolled factors accounted for the large increases (t ratios of 10.27 and 10.38) in pay and promotion satisfaction, which were the two job aspects concentrated on in the program, and small increases in the three areas not stressed and that other uncontrolled factors simultaneously led to decreased turnover strains credibility. . . .

The final remaining weakness of this design would be in the use of reactive measures (Campbell and Stanley 1967; Webb, Campbell, Schwartz and Sechrest 1966). However, if the simultaneous reduction in turnover and increase in satisfaction are due purely to obtrusive measurement in combination with an otherwise ineffective program, then the millennium has indeed arrived. For if this explanation were true, then a combination of obtrusive measurement and any poorly designed, inappropriate program will solve turnover problems. This does not seem reasonable. . . .

REFERENCES

Campbell, D. T., and Stanley, J. C. *Experimental and Quasi-Experimental Designs for Research.* Chicago: Rand McNally, 1966.

Hulin, C. L. "Job Satisfaction and Turnover in a Female Clerical Population, "*Journal of Applied Psychology* 50 (1966): 280–85.

Quinn, R. P., and Kahn, R. L. "Organizational Psychology," *Annual Review of Psychology* 18 (1967): 437–66.

Vroom, V. *Work and Motivation.* New York: Wiley, 1964.

Webb, E. J., Campbell, D. T., Schwartz, R. D., and Sechrest, L. *Unobtrusive Measures.* Chicago: Rand McNally, 1966.

3

EVALUATION OF PERFORMANCE

Whether or not an organization is successful depends largely on how effectively employees perform their jobs. Indeed, most of the functional activities of personnel/human resources are aimed directly at improving the performance levels of existing employees—as in the case of training—or at improving the potential performance of job applicants—as in the case of selection. It should not be surprising, therefore, to find that the evaluation or appraisal (we will use the two terms interchangeably) of performance effectiveness is one of the most important personnel/human resource activities carried out in organizations.

OBJECTIVE AND APPROACHES

The primary objective of performance appraisal is to improve employee performance levels. Organizations attempt to accomplish this objective through two distinct approaches. The first and traditional approach has been to use the results of performance evaluations to make *judgmental decisions* about individuals, groups of employees, or prospective employees. Some of these decisions involve positive rewards such as who will be promoted or who will receive salary increases. Others are more neutral such as who would benefit from training or even punitive such as who should be disciplined or terminated. In any event, these decisions are often based on formal or informal assessments of how effectively employees perform their jobs.

The second approach to performance appraisals has to do with the direct *development* of employees so that they may perform their tasks more effectively. In this context, appraisals are viewed primarily as mechanisms for increasing employee commitment or motivation to task accomplishment. It is generally assumed that the feedback the employee receives through the appraisal process can be helpful in more effectively directing work energies toward the goals of the organization.

While the *objective* of judgmentally and developmentally oriented appraisals is similar, the *processes* through which the objective is achieved are quite dissimilar. Judgmental uses of appraisals necessarily emphasize the authority of the superior over the subordinate and tend to be oriented toward the measurement of past performance. A developmental approach to appraisals, alternatively, tends to emphasize subordinate contributions to both work planning (goal-setting) and assessment of completed work and focuses on how performance levels can be improved in the future. Not surprisingly, these two approaches to appraisal necessarily conflict to some extent. For example, the use of appraisals by superiors for judgmental decisions almost certainly inhibits the subordinate openness with, and trust in, the superior which is so necessary in using appraisals to aid development.

APPRAISAL VALIDITY

Validity is a fundamental issue whatever approach is chosen. In appraisal, validity refers to the correspondence between employees' *measured* contributions (that is, the appraisal result) and their *actual* contributions to the organization's goals. This type of validity is called *construct* validity.

Construct valid appraisals require two ingredients. First, the organization must identify how each employee should contribute to organizational goals. This requires an analysis of job objectives and can be thought of as *defining the performance domain*. The process of defining the performance domain is done as a part of a *job analysis*. Job analysis is a method for identifying (a) what must be done on a job, (b) what employee skills and abilities are necessary to perform the job acceptably, and (c) what objectives or dimensions are a part of the job. It is the latter that constitutes the performance domain insofar as performance appraisal is concerned.

The second validation requirement involves measuring each individual's performance on the dimensions identified in the previous step. Typically a superior assesses the subordinate using some instrument which specifies the dimensions of concern. On a typing job, for example, the important job dimensions may be accuracy, efficiency, neatness, and relationships with others. The appraisal instrument thus should contain some way, such as rating scales, for the superior to indicate the evaluation of each employee on each of these dimensions. Valid appraisal results are obtained if the evaluations correctly identify each employee's organizational contribution on these performance dimensions.

APPRAISAL INSTRUMENTS

There are two somewhat different methods for developing appraisal instruments. One, and the more traditional, method focuses on creating *standardized instruments* for a job or set of jobs. This method is based on the assumption that the major dimensions for a job or jobs are identical or very similar so that all persons can be evaluated against the same standards. The second method presumes that each job is sufficently unique to justify the establishment of unique objectives for every individual. In a sense this latter approach involves a unique job analysis of each individual's job. It is usually referred to as *management by objectives* (MBO).

Standard Instruments. Two general types of standardized appraisal instruments have been developed. In *comparative procedures* an employee's performance is evaluated relative to the performance of other employees. For example, a supervisor may rank subordinates from "best" to "worst." Probably the major limitation of comparative procedures, from a validity standpoint, is that they are ordinarily not based on a careful analysis of job dimensions. Thus, the evaluator is generally asked to make relative judgments only about employees' overall effectiveness. As such, comparative procedures frequently fail to capture the contributions employees make to each dimension of their job.

Appraisal instruments using *absolute standards* typically attempt to measure numerous dimensions of job performance, although the dimensions may or may not be derived from a job analysis. Each employee's performance on each dimension is assessed against written statements (absolute standards) on a rating scale, rather than against the performance of others as in comparative procedures. A typical rating scale for a dimension might look like this:

	1	2	3	4	5
Accuracy of Work	Unacceptable	Below Standards	Meets Standards	Exceeds Standards	Far Exceeds Standards

The evaluator must decide which number best describes the performance of each appraisee on the dimension.

Management by Objectives. The focus of MBO is more on a procedure than on a particular instrument. The procedure typically involves four steps. Step one consists of the setting of objectives to be completed by the performer. Often the performers participate with their supervisors in the establishment of these goals. The critical component, however, is that goals are individually set for each employee. After the employee has had time to carry out the objectives, the second step involves an evaluation of actual performance against the objectives established in the earlier step. Again, the performer often participates with the supervisor in this review process. Step three consists of whatever administrative use is made of the evaluation results. They may, for example, serve as the basis for a salary increase decision. They may also serve as a basis for increasing the employee's motivation to perform at higher levels in the future. The feedback that the supervisor provides may increase motivation by showing employees where their efforts resulted in acceptable performance and those performance dimensions on which improvement is necessary. The planning for performance improvement occurs in the fourth step, where goals for the next time period are set. Thus the MBO process continues to repeat itself.

ADMINISTRATION

There are a number of important administrative issues that must be dealt with in any appraisal program. One has to do with who should actually conduct the appraisal. From a validity standpoint, it is essential that the evaluator be knowledgeable about the appraisee's performance. This means that superiors, peers, and the appraisees themselves could potentially be evaluators. Both judgmental and developmental appraisal approaches involve managerial issues so that the supervisor must participate in any event. There are situations, however, where jobs are structured in a manner that peers can add valuable and potentially unique appraisal inputs. Peer appraisal is very common among professionals such as doctors, lawyers, and professors. Moreover, fear that peers pervert appraisals into a "buddy system" appears largely unfounded. The appraisee may also provide valuable information when appraisals are used for developmental purposes. Where appraisals are used for judgmental decisions, however, evidence understandably indicates that appraisees overevaluate their own performance.

Another administrative issue has to do with the frequency of appraisals and their timing. Organizations typically require that superiors conduct appraisals at regular fixed intervals, usually every six, eight, or twelve months. Such policies have the advantage of requiring the superiors to perform their appraisal responsibilities on a regular basis. When jobs involve nonroutine and major tasks, however, a more appropriate procedure would be to appraise when measurable units of work output are scheduled for completion. The latter schedule could be modified for new, inexperienced employees who might benefit from more frequent reviews of their work activities.

Communicating the results of the appraisal to the appraisee is another important and difficult issue. Feedback is obviously essential if the appraisal program is to have any positive impact in a developmental context. Indeed, developmental appraisal is essentially a formalized procedure to encourage superior-subordinate interaction about work performance. Feedback is also important when appraisals are used for judgmental reasons since employees have a right to know how the organization views their work. Moreover, there is evidence that feedback, when connected with personnel decisions such as merit salary increases, can have positive motivational implications. Despite its importance, it should not be surprising to observe that supervisors frequently have difficulty providing appraisal feedback. Subordinates, even though they desire to know how they stand, likewise often have difficulty accepting feedback. The problems for both are clearly most severe when the feedback must be negative in a judgment context. Supervisors frequently need (a) *assistance* in developing feedback skills and (b) encouragement to insure that they exercise those skills.

INTRODUCTION TO READINGS

Behaviorally Anchored Rating Scales

The first article in this chapter by Donald Schwab and Herbert Heneman discusses a standardized appraisal instrument called behaviorally anchored rating scales (BARS). Recall that standardized instruments are the type that are generally used on jobs where every individual does essentially similar work. BARS have been developed for jobs such as police officers, secretaries, grocery clerks, and nurses.

BARS is a relatively new and promising approach to the development of a standardized appraisal intsrument. Schwab and Heneman begin by describing the five steps necessary to develop a BARS. Note that the first three steps (obtaining critical incidents of behavior, performance dimensions, and retranslation) are aimed at defining the performance domain. The last two steps are aimed at producing an instrument that can be used to obtain valid assessments on the dimensions identified. An example of a completed scale for one performance dimension (knowledge and judgment) of a grocery clerk's job is shown in Figure 1. The illustrative descriptions of behavior on the right of the scale are the critical incidents that survived the five developmental steps.

Despite the intuitive appeal of BARS, the authors' review of research finds little evidence that the results using BARS are demonstrably superior to results using traditional rating methods. There are two important considerations to keep in mind when evaluating that evidence, however. First, as the authors note, research has not investigated the effectiveness with which BARS procedures define the performance domain. It is likely that BARS, because it uses the critical incidents method, is superior in this regard to the *ad hoc* procedures associated with the development of most appraisal instruments. It should be noted that judicial interpretations regarding equal employment opportunities now require a formal job analysis to define the performance domain. Critical incidents is a procedure that will probably satisfy these emerging legal requirements.

The second observation to keep in mind relates to the importance of the instrument *per se* in the evaluation process. No instrument, no matter how carefully developed, can guarantee valid appraisal results. The critical element in the appraisal process is the people who actually do the evaluating. Unless they are properly trained and motivated to make valid appraisals, the results will most certainly be unsatisfactory.

Management by Objectives

The article by Robert Hollmann deals with management by objectives (MBO) which represents the other major method for appraising performance. In reading this article recognize that MBO is often viewed as more than a method for individualizing the appraisal process. MBO is probably most frequently implemented as a method to increase employee effectiveness by increasing employees' motivation to perform.

In this context a heavy emphasis is often placed on the desirability of subordinate participation in the establishment of objectives and in the review process. Hollmann reviews some of the literature on this issue and concludes that participation by subordinates in the goal or objective setting process is indeed generally desirable. Be sure to note, however, that this conclusion applies primarily to subordinates who have had previous participation experience. Job experience is also necessary before participation makes much sense. It would certainly be unwise to have a new, inexperienced employee participate substantially in the objective setting process. More important than participation, in terms of whether MBO will lead to improvement, is whether or not objectives are set. The establishment of specific, moderately difficult objectives frequently leads to improved performance.

For purposes of this chapter, pay special attention to Hollmann's discussion of the review process. His remarks are specifically focused on reviews within

FIGURE 1
Behaviorally Anchored Rating Scale of Grocery Clerk's Knowledge and Judgment

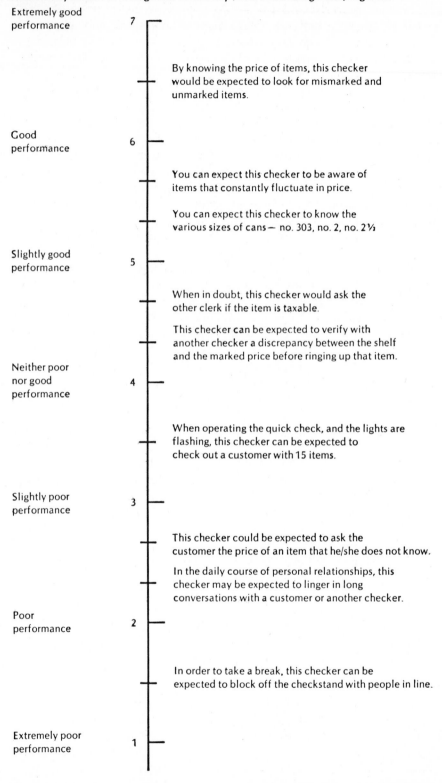

Extremely good performance — 7

By knowing the price of items, this checker would be expected to look for mismarked and unmarked items.

Good performance — 6

You can expect this checker to be aware of items that constantly fluctuate in price.

You can expect this checker to know the various sizes of cans— no. 303, no. 2, no. 2½

Slightly good performance — 5

When in doubt, this checker would ask the other clerk if the item is taxable.

This checker can be expected to verify with another checker a discrepancy between the shelf and the marked price before ringing up that item.

Neither poor nor good performance — 4

When operating the quick check, and the lights are flashing, this checker can be expected to check out a customer with 15 items.

Slightly poor performance — 3

This checker could be expected to ask the customer the price of an item that he/she does not know.

In the daily course of personal relationships, this checker may be expected to linger in long conversations with a customer or another checker.

Poor performance — 2

In order to take a break, this checker can be expected to block off the checkstand with people in line.

Extremely poor performance — 1

Source: L. Fogli, C. L. Hulin, and M. R. Blood, "Development of First-Level Behavioral Job Criteria," *Journal of Applied Psychology* 55 (1971): 3–8. Copyright © 1971 by the American Psychological Association and reproduced by permission.

an MBO process and how they can be used to increase subsequent performance. The observations he makes, however, can be applied whatever the appraisal method since performance improvement is a major objective of any appraisal system.

EMPLOYEE GROWTH THROUGH PERFORMANCE MANAGEMENT

The article by Michael Beer and Robert Ruh describes a true systems approach to performance appraisal that has been developed for Corning Glass Works. You will see that the system has three major components. MBO is used to establish work goals and to assess the degree of goal accomplishment. The emphasis in MBO is on *results* or *outcomes*.

A second component, called performance development and review, is aimed at assessing appraisee behaviors. The concern here is with the *processes* appraisees utilize to achieve results. It is reasoned that a results orientation only tells if employees have been successful and not how they might improve. The performance development and review is designed to accomplish the latter.

The results from MBO and the performance development and review feed into the third or *evaluative* (judgmental in our terminology) component of the system. Beer and Ruh provide few details on how each of the first two components contribute to the decisions made in the third. Presumably, however, the MBO results would be a major input into salary increase decisions; the performance development and review would be influential in decisions about developmental activities such as training.

There are a number of other issues worthy of note in this article. The careful construction of the questionnaire used in the performance development and review is one. Critical incidents were obtained and used much as they are in BARS to help identify an appropriate managerial performance domain. Another noteworthy feature is the attempt to separate the developmental and judgmental aspects as much as possible by the separation of the three components in time. While it would be naive to assume that appraisees would ever completely separate the developmental and judgmental aspects, the procedure used likely helps somewhat. It is also important to observe that Corning established a training program to implement the appraisal system. They correctly recognized that a personnel system, no matter how carefully developed, must be sold, and explained, to line management if it is to be used. Finally, note that an evaluation of the system was performed and that the results, while generally encouraging, nevertheless indicated some resistance by managers to participate in the appraisal system.

6. BEHAVIORALLY ANCHORED RATING SCALES

DONALD P. SCHWAB and HERBERT G. HENEMAN, III

Every personnel practitioner knows the sorrows and frustrations associated with developing, implementing and administering an effective performance appraisal system. Difficulties plague every step. Moreover, the courts and the EEOC [Equal Employment Opportunity Commission] are beginning to recognize the potential that performance appraisal has for employment discrimination (5, 8).* It is likely that many existing appraisal systems, if challenged, would fail the test of law.

In view of all these problems, it is not surprising that practitioners take an interest in any new developments in the appraisal area. One such development is behaviorally anchored rating scales (BARS). . . .

BARS are a form of appraisal ratings initially proposed by Smith and Kendall (10). They differ from other scales (e.g., typical graphic rating scales) primarily in the *process* by which they are developed and the fact that the focus is on employee *behaviors* rather than on traits, which is typically the case. We will briefly review the development process, indicate potential advantages of BARS and then summarize the evidence on the effectiveness of BARS in actual performance appraisal.

DEVELOPING BARS

Space permits only a brief summary of the five major steps involved in the development of a BARS (more detailed descriptions can be found in 6 and 10). These steps, adapted from (9), are:

1. Critical Incidents. Persons with knowledge of the job to be investigated (job holders and/or supervisors) are asked to describe specific illustrations of effective and ineffective performance behavior. These illustrations are referred to as critical incidents.

2. Performance Dimensions. Incidents are then clustered into a smaller set of performance dimensions which they define (usually five to ten).

3. Retranslation. A second group of persons familiar with the job are then instructed to retranslate the critical incidents. They are given the dimensions' definitions and critical incidents and asked to assign each incident to the dimension that it best describes. Typically, an incident is retained for further consideration if some percentage (usually 50 percent to 80 percent) of the group assigns it to the same dimension as did the group in step 2. Such incidents are said to have been retranslated.

4. Scaling Incidents. This second group is generally also asked to rate the behavior described in the incident as to how effectively or ineffectively it represents performance on the appropriate dimension. The average rating assigned the incident identifies the degree to which the incident describes effective performance on a dimension. The standard deviation of the ratings for each incident represents the amount of agreement among raters regarding the effectiveness level of performance described by the incident (the *lower* the standard deviation, the *greater* the agreement). Typically, incidents that have standard deviations of 1.50 or less (on a seven-point scale) are retained for potential inclusion in the final instrument.

5. Final Instrument. For each performance dimension, the incidents that meet both the retranslation and standard deviation criteria are retained (some may be discarded if there are too many). These incidents serve as *behavioral anchors* for the

---

Source: "Research Round-Up" *The Personnel Administrator,* January 1977, pp. 54, 56.

*Research sources are listed at the conclusion of the article. Each reference is acknowledged by using the number corresponding to the appropriate research source.

numbers on the rating scale. The incidents are located along the scale points according to their average ratings as determined in the preceding step. The final BARS instrument consists of a series of scales (one for each performance dimension) anchored by the retained incidents.

POTENTIAL ADVANTAGES OF BARS

Many specific *potential* advantages of BARS have been suggested (see, e.g., 6). Two of the most significant are (a) defining the performance domain and (b) reducing appraisal error.

Defining the Performance Domain. The development steps in BARS clearly indicate that the rating scales are developed on the basis of a thorough job analysis. As such, the dimensions and critical incidents should adequately define the domain of performance for the job (note that separate BARS are required for each job; BARS are not general forms). The scales can thus be described as content valid (or job-related). Having a content valid instrument is desirable since the focus of the appraisal is on *performance* and not on vague traits so often found on graphic rating scales. In addition, it appears that use of content valid instruments is a must for EEO purposes (5, 8).

Reducing Appraisal Error. A problem that plagues performance appraisal is the occurrence of errors such as halo, leniency, and lack of interrater reliability. BARS may help to reduce these errors because of employee participation in the development of BARS, a focus on performance (not trait) dimensions, and use of critical incidents to help define rating scale points in behavioral terms. Thus, both the process of development and the resultant scales may help the rater(s) reduce error.

RESEARCH ON BARS

To date most of the research has looked at the second potential advantage discussed above—reducing appraisal error. We reviewed the studies on this point through most of 1975 (9). On the basis of that evidence we arrived at the following conclusion:

Despite the intuitive appeal of BARS, findings from research have not been very encouraging. On the three issues that have been investigated most thoroughly (leniency, dimension independence and reliability), there is little reason to believe that BARS are superior to alternative evaluation instruments (9, p. 557).

Since our review, a number of other studies on BARS have been reported (1, 2, 3, 4, 7). In general, the results of these studies are not overly encouraging either. There is some indication, however, that the specific steps used in the development of BARS (1) and the training of raters in conjunction with BARS (2) may influence the extent to which appraisal error is reduced.

The other potential advantage of BARS, namely defining the performance domain, has not yet been investigated. This is unfortunate since it may well represent the area in which the BARS are superior to traditional rating scales.

We do not want to be overly pessimistic about BARS, nor do we want to make any hasty conclusions about their worth. More research is needed before we will know the true payoff on BARS. In this vein, it is commendable that so many organizations have sponsored and/or conducted research on BARS, and we hope that this trend will continue.

At the same time, however, it is time to recognize that the type of appraisal instrument itself is only one of many factors that influence the quality of appraisal results. Not enough attention has been paid to the rater and the context of the appraisal (such as its intended purpose). It may be, for example, that the biggest payoffs in terms of improved ratings may occur as a result of rater training; not as a result of new rating forms and instruments.

REFERENCES

1. Bernardin, H. I., LaShells, M. B., Smith, P. C., Alvares, K. M. "Behavorial Expectation Scales: Effects of Developmental Procedures and Formats." *Journal of Applied Psychology* 61 (1967): 75–79.

2. Borman, W. C. "Effects of Instructions to Avoid Halo Error on Reliability and Validity of Performance Evaluation Ratings." *Journal of Applied Psychology* 60 (1975): 556–60.

3. Borman, W. C., and Dunnette, M. D. Behavior-Based versus Trait-Oriented Performance Ratings: An Empirical Study." *Journal of Applied Psychology* 60 (1975): 561–65.

4. Friedman, B. A., and Cornelius, E. T. "Effects of Rater Participation in Scale Construction on the Psychometric Characteristics of Two Rating Scale Formats." *Journal of Applied Psychology* 61 (1976): 210–16.

5. Holley, W. H., and Field, H. S. "Performance Appraisal and the Law." *Labor Law Journal* 26 (1975): 423–30.

6. Kearney, W. J. "The Value of Behaviorally Based Performance Appraisals." *Business Horizons,* June 1976, 75–83.

7. Keaveny, I. J., and McGann, A. F. "A Comparison of Behavorial Expectation Scales and Graphic Rating Scales." *Journal of Applied Psychology* 60 (1975): 695–703.

8. Sandman, B., and Urban, F. "Employment Testing and the Law." *Labor Law Journal* 27 (1976): 38–54.

9. Schwab, D. P., Heneman, H. G. III, and DeCotiis, T. A. "Behaviorally Anchored Rating Scales: A Review of the Literature." *Personnel Psychology* 28 (1975): 549–62.

10. Smith, P. C., and Kendall, L. M. "Retranslation of Expectations: An Approach to the Construction of Unambiguous Anchors for Rating Scales." *Journal of Applied Psychology* 47 (1963): 149–55.

7. APPLYING MBO RESEARCH TO PRACTICE
ROBERT W. HOLLMANN

According to a recent survey, management by objectives (MBO) is one of the most popular management techniques used in organizations today.[1] This same survey, however, found that 15 percent of the firms using MBO were highly dissatisfied with it. Similarly, a survey of the Fortune 500 showed that 181 of the 403 responding firms were using MBO, but only 10 companies felt their programs were highly successful.[2]

While one cannot reach any definitive conclusions from only two surveys, it seems reasonable to suggest that many MBO programs have room for improvement.

Organizations can either improve their existing MBO programs or initially introduce better MBO programs by selectively and systematically incorporating the results of MBO research into their programs. In the field of management, it is unfortunate that sometimes the roads traveled by researchers and practitioners do not intersect as often as they should. The purpose of this article is not to castigate either MBO researchers or MBO practitioners for such a limitation, but to provide a research-practice "intersection." The intent is twofold: (1) to highlight some of the more salient MBO research, and (2) to discuss the pragmatic implications this

Source: Reprinted from *Human Resource Management,* vol. 15, no. 4, Winter 1976, pp. 28–36. Graduate School of Business Administration, University of Michigan, Ann Arbor MI 48109.

1 "EDP Leads the Thirteen 'Most Popular' Management Techniques," *Administrative Management* 34, 6 (June 1973): 26ff.

2 F. E. Schuster and A. F. Kindall, "Management by Objectives Where We Stand—A Survey of the Fortune 500," *Human Resource Management* 13, 1 (Spring 1974): 8–11.

research has for MBO users and potential users.

Any article of this nature must be limited in scope, and accordingly, the author has been guided by three self-imposed constraints. First, the analysis is restricted to empirically based studies of actual MBO programs or programs that are MBO in nature but called something else, such as work planning and review (WPR). This restriction is not intended to degrade the usefulness of case studies,[3] for much empirical field research is generated by perceptive case analyses, but rather to reflect a preference for the greater rigor of empirical designs. Second, the analysis concentrates on research in profit-oriented firms, not to undercut the increasing use of MBO in educational, governmental, and health care institutions, but to keep the article's scope within reasonable magnitude. And third, while there are surely many variables important to the success of MBO, the present discussion concentrates on six areas that have received a reasonable amount of attention in the MBO research and would appear to be of particular interest to MBO users: (1) introduction of MBO into the organization, (2) the manner in which objectives are set, (3) characteristics of objectives, (4) nature of the review process, (5) support for the MBO program, and (6) monitoring the program.

INTRODUCING MBO

The introductory phase of MBO is perhaps the most critical element in the program's success. Since introducing MBO represents an organizational change, a firm should take reasonable actions to minimize the resistance to change that can often occur. In addition to the usual forewarnings for careful and thorough planning of the program and the wisdom of using MBO in only those organizations or departments where managers are willing to try it, there are some other ways a firm can achieve a smoother introduction of MBO.

First, researchers at the University of Kentucky (7)[4] found that an MBO program introduced by top management had a more positive effect on satisfaction of managers' needs than a program introduced by the personnel department. Under the former approach, top managers not only used MBO in their jobs from the very beginning, but also trained their subordinates in the MBO process. A two-pronged approach (introduction and training) such as this can go a long way in establishing creditability of the program and top level support for it— much farther than top management merely describing the virtues and benefits of the "new MBO program" in a memo and turning the introductory phase over to the personnel manager, who is then faced with the difficult task of "selling" MBO to managers throughout the system. Under this second strategy, managers often view MBO as just another fad or gimmick pushed on them by an overzealous personnel manager who is trying to "make his mark" in the company; naturally, this type of managerial reaction is usually accompanied by a fairly high degree of resistance to the new MBO program.

Second, introduction of MBO should include a clear statement of the purpose(s) of the program. It is easy for managers to become confused over the intent of MBO. For example, Tosi and Carroll (12)[5] found little

---

[3] For case studies of MBO, See E. R. Frank, "Motivation by Objectives—A Case Study." *Research Management* 12, 6 (November 1969): 391–400; J. W. Humble, ed., *Management by Objectives in Action* (New York: McGraw-Hill, 1960); J. B. Lasagna, "Make Your MBO Pragmatic," *Harvard Business Review* 49, 6 (November–December 1971): 64–69; and W. S. Wikstrom, *Managing by—and with—Objectives* (New York: National Industrial Conference Board, 1968).

[4] Because of frequent references to MBO research studies throughout this article, footnotes are not used for these references. Instead, the MBO research sources are listed at the conclusion of the article and each reference to a study is acknowledged by using the number corresponding to the appropriate research source. The usual footnote method is used for references other than those listed at the end of the article.

[5] For a summary of all the MBO research conducted by Carroll and Tosi, see S. J. Carroll and H. L. Tosi, *Management by Objectives: Applications and Research* (New York: Macmillan, 1973).

agreement among managers on the purpose of the WPR program they investigated; of the nine purposes identified, only one was cited by more than 30 percent (35.4 percent) of the managers participating in the study. This is not to suggest that MBO cannot be used for multiple purposes. Indeed, if MBO is viewed as a "way of managing," it most likely would encompass a variety of purposes, such as planning, controlling, appraising, and developing. The problem occurs when managers are uncertain as to why MBO is being introduced. For instance, top management may be introducing MBO as a more viable method of appraising performance, but managers in the company, particularly those at the lower-middle and lower levels, may see MBO as just another way of forcing top level objectives down their throats.

Admittedly, subordinate managers may still feel this way if objectives are autocratically handed down to them regardless of the stated purpose(s) of the program, but under these circumstances the problem is more one of implementation than introduction. They key point at this juncture is that lack of understanding why MBO is being introduced could easily undermine managers' attitudes toward the program as well as its success. Top level clarification of the purpose(s) of MBO right at the start is one way of reducing this likelihood.

Third, care should be exercised so as not to introduce an MBO program heavily laden with forms, charts, and reports. The "paperwork problem" was an often-cited limitation of MBO in a number of studies (10, 11, 12). Managers are quite likely to resist any change that overburdens them with paperwork. A wise approach in this regard would be to develop a basic and simple form for recording objectives and performance.[6] As managers gain more experience and confidence with MBO, they will probably request constructive revisions in the forms and may even propose additional forms to aid them in the MBO process.

And fourth, it is unwise to assume that a thorough knowledge and understanding of the MBO process and its purpose(s) will "filter down" through the hierarchy. Proper introduction of MBO requires detailed orientation and training for managers at all levels.[7] This is not to suggest that MBO should be implemented simultaneously throughout the firm. A more judicious approach might involve introducing MBO to successively lower levels of management according to a predetermined, but still flexible, time schedule that allows ample time for each level to acquire reasonable facility with the process before it is introduced to the next lower level.

SETTING OBJECTIVES

Discussions on the process of setting objectives typically focus on the question of how much influence the subordinate manager should have over the final set of objectives—or, to what extent should the subordinate participate in the objective-setting process? While answers to this question vary somewhat, it appears to this writer that most MBO proponents explicitly or implicitly advocate a relatively high degree of subordinate participation. However, MBO research has found the degree of subordinate influence on objectives to vary along the entire traditional autocratic-participative continuum.

A study by Tosi and Carroll (13) showed that the percentage of managers reporting the use of four different types of goal-setting processes within the same organization varied as follows: (1) superior and subordinate independently prepare objectives and

---

6 For examples of MBO forms, see A. P. Raia, *Managing by Objectives* (Glenview, Ill.: Scott, Foresman, 1974); and W. S. Wikstrom, *op. cit.*

7 An excellent description of a thorough MBO training program is provided by J. Douglas, A. J. Grimes, J. M. Ivancevich, and S. M. Klein, "A Progression, Training Approach to Management by Objectives," *Training and Development Journal* 27, 9 (September 1973): 24–30.

reach mutual agreement after discussion—28 percent; (2) subordinate prepares list of objectives, superior edits list, discussion, and agreement based upon superior's edited list—21 percent; (3) subordinate prepares list of objectives and superior accepts list without any discussion—21 percent; and (4) subordinate is given a set of objectives as prepared by the superior—28 percent. Tosi and Carroll also found that managers' "perceived influence" over objectives varied according to the goal-setting process used, and that middle and lower managers felt they had less influence over their objectives than did top level managers. Managers participating in Raia's studies (10, 11) also reported less influence over objectives at lower hierarchical levels.

In terms of operational implications, these research findings highlight the need for periodic checking of MBO goal setting throughout the organization. The existence of highly participative goal setting in some departments of the firm is no guarantee of participative processes throughout. Similarly, the commitment to the participative form of goal setting often found at higher management levels may not be shared by lower levels—an occurrence that is perhaps partially explained by the more narrow scope of activities and limits of discretion typically found in lower level positions. While these narrower limits need not preclude the use of participative goal setting, they do make the participative form somewhat more difficult to achieve and, accordingly, create the need for greater scrutiny of the goal-setting processes at this level.

The preceding comments assume that a highly participative form of goal setting is a requisite of a successful MBO program. How valid is this assumption? As stated earlier, it seems that most proponents of MBO stress the participative form. Does the research support their position?

The effects of increased participation in the MBO goal-setting process have been examined in two research settings. First, Tosi and Carroll (15) have described the results of a systematic effort to increase subordinate participation in setting objectives in one company's MBO program. By comparing managers' "before" and "after" questionnaire responses, they found a definite increase in the number of managers reporting the use of a mutual goal-setting process. Although there were no significant changes in these managers' perceived influence over objectives or perceived superior-subordinate relationships, the results did show statistically significant improvements in managers' (a) effort to achieve objectives, (b) satisfaction with MBO, (c) belief in the applicability of MBO to their job, and (d) belief that MBO helped them perform their job.

Researchers at the General Electric Company (4, 8) have also investigated the impact of subordinate participation in goal setting. In this experimental study, managers were divided into two groups—those operating under "high" participation and those under "low" participation. Comparison of the two groups showed that those in the high participation group (a) achieved a greater percentage of their improvement goals, (b) had greater acceptance of their goals, (c) had better relationships with their boss, (d) had more favorable attitudes toward the program, and (e) felt greater self-realization on the job.

The GE researchers also learned that the effects of increased participation in goal setting were significantly moderated by a manager's "usual level of participation." Of those managers in the high participation group, the five positive effects listed in the previous paragraph were greater for managers who normally operated in a highly participative setting than for those who typically worked in a low participative setting. This finding is summarized by Meyer, Kay, and French:

In general, our experiment showed that the men who usually worked under high participation levels performed best on goals they set for themselves. Those who indicated that they usually worked under low levels performed best on goals that the managers set for them.(8)

The results of these two studies provide tentative support for those advocating a highly participative approach to MBO goal setting. On the surface, the pragmatic implication would appear to be that a firm should diligently strive to achieve a high degree of subordinate involvement in the objective setting process. Yet, one must not overlook the GE findings on the effect of a manager's usual level of participation. These results clearly suggest that *an organization should perform a thorough diagnosis of its internal climate and leadership patterns before encouraging and training managers in any particular form of MBO goal setting.*

Upon completion of the climate analysis, a company will most likely have to choose from the following alternatives. First, it can encourage a form of MBO that is consistent with the climate, based on the belief that if managers are accustomed to high levels of participation in their daily routines, they will respond more favorably to a relatively participative version of MBO goal setting, and vice versa. Second, if the climate is relatively nonparticipative and top management prefers the participative form of MBO, it may be better to try to change the climate (through management and leadership training) before introducing MBO. Or third, the firm may encourage the participative form of MBO regardless of the climate, and in cases of a relatively nonparticipative climate hope that MBO will serve as an effective means for shifting the climate in a more participative direction.

CHARACTERISTICS OF OBJECTIVES

It makes intuitive sense that managers' attitudes toward MBO and the success of the program are partly contingent upon the nature of objectives set in the MBO process. The present discussion shall not deal with the pros and cons of different types of objectives (e.g., performance, self-improvement, problem-solving, etc.) nor the controversy over performance standards vis-à-vis objectives. While these are important issues,

space requirements limit the focus of attention to the characteristics of objectives, regardless of their nature.

Research on the characteristics has been conducted by Carroll and Tosi (2). The findings of an early phase of their studies are summarized below:

1. Managers had more positive attitudes toward WPR when goals were relatively difficult and clear.
2. Managers who felt their goals were clear also felt their boss spent more time on WPR and that there was more organizational support for the program.
3. Managers felt an improved relationship with their boss when goals were clearer and when goal priorities were set.
4. When there were well-defined goal priorities, goal success was related to (1) the time the boss spends on the program, (2) organizational support for the program, (3) the extent of perceived participation in goal setting, and (4) the manager's satisfaction with his boss.

In a follow-up study, Tosi and Carroll (15) found that when managers were more involved in setting their objectives they had a better knowledge of the importance of these objectives and felt the objectives were clearer, more important, and more difficult.

The Carroll and Tosi research highlights two important characteristics of objectives —clarity and priority—that seem to be positively related to a number of end result variables. Beyond the obvious statement that objectives should be clear and prioritized, what pragmatic implications do these results have for MBO users?

First, a company's MBO training program should include a phase devoted exclusively to the formulation of objectives. Simply encouraging managers to write clear objectives is not enough. The objective-formulation phase of MBO training can be conducted in a workshop manner, which is an approach that adequately accounts for two important principles of learning: (1) providing the trainee with the opportunity to practice what he/she is supposed to learn, and (2) providing feedback to the trainee. Managers can practice setting objectives (either real objectives for themselves or hypothetical objectives for a case situation) and workshop colleagues can evaluate and comment on the clarity of each other's objectives. While an objective-setting workshop can provide an initial foundation in goal setting, it is not a panacea; only through hard work and continued practice "on the job" will a manager be able to fully develop skills in preparing clear objectives.[8]

The second action a firm can take with respect to the characteristics is to require that every manager's statement of objectives contains some type of priority for each objective. The easiest way to do this is to provide a space for each objective's priority right on the MBO form. Different methods of prioritizing can be used, with the two most common being a straight ranking method or some type of classification method in which each objective is classified in one of a number of different categories, such as "must achieve," "ought to achieve," and "should achieve." The primary advantage of prioritizing objectives is that the manager and his/her boss have a better understanding of the relative importance of each objective, which is particularly helpful during the end-of-the-period evaluation. If the manager has attained all of the "should achieve" objectives but the "must achieve" and "ought to achieve" objectives are partly or largely unattained, he/she probably needs some guidance with respect to where to direct further efforts. In other words, the priorities can aid a manager who is under pressure and who must make a decision regarding which objective should receive attention at any particular time. Obviously, it

is equally important that a manager does not spend all or most of his/her time on one objective at the neglect of other objectives or other responsibilities that are not covered in the objectives.

NATURE OF THE REVIEW PROCESS

A great deal has been written on the subject of performance appraisal over the years, and there is no need to rehash these ideas in this article. In this section attention is directed to one of the often-neglected aspects of the review phase of MBO—namely, the periodic checking of a manager's progress toward objectives. All too often managers using MBO fall into the trap of thinking that because MBO is touted as an objective method of appraising performance, the review process simply consists of a detailed end-of-the-period assessment of subordinates' performance on their objectives. While this evaluation is very important to MBO, it is only half of the review process. Periodic feedback to each manager on progress toward objectives is equally important. This feedback enhances the likelihood of a manager's performance being on target since it provides him/her with the information necessary for adjusting behavior, changing the plan of attack for achieving objectives, or even modifying the original objectives if necessary.

Research on feedback to managers using MBO has concentrated on two primary dimensions—the *frequency* of feedback and the *content* of feedback. With respect to frequency, Carroll and Tosi's (1) questionnaire study of 150 managers involved in a WPR program showed significant positive relationships between feedback frequency and managers' (1) attitudes toward WPR, (2) success in achieving objectives, (3) perceptions of goal clarity, (4) belief that superior-subordinate relationships had improved and satisfaction with their boss, (5) perceptions that their boss supported them and the WPR program, and (6) feelings that they can participate in the MBO process. Fay and Beach

---

[8] A number of writers present guidelines for preparing clear objectives. For example, see P. Mali, *Managing by Objectives* (New York: Wiley, 1972); G. L. Morrisey, *Management by Objectives and Results* (Reading, Mass.: Addison-Wesley, 1970; G. S. Odiorne, *Management by Objectives* (New York: Pitman, 1965); and A. P. Raia, op. cit.

(3) also found a greater percentage of favorable attitudes toward MBO among those managers who had more frequent progress reviews. Raia (11) reported that a complaint of managers was the lack of a sufficient quantity of periodic performance reviews, and managers responding to Tosi and Carroll's (12) questionnaire felt that the WPR program could be improved by increasing the opportunities for review and feedback. And finally, Ivancevich, Donnelly, and Lyon (7) found that most managers felt their own needs were better satisfied when they had four feedback sessions annually instead of just one end-of-the-period evaluation.

Organizations using MBO must encourage their managers to conduct regular feedback sessions with each of their subordinates. However, as Ivancevich et al. (7) point out, the optimum number of feedback sessions will vary from firm to firm. Chances are that it will even vary within the same firm. A number of factors should be considered when deciding how often feedback sessions are held. First, the subordinate's experience with MBO; those who are new to MBO may need more frequent feedback. Second, the length of time covered by the objectives; annual objectives may require more frequent feedback than quarterly or semi-annual objectives. Third, the nature of a manager's job; more complex and/or frequently changing jobs require more frequent feedback than relatively simple and stable jobs. Fourth, the subordinate's previous success in achieving objectives; those who have been less successful in goal achievement may need more frequent feedback. Fifth, the subordinate's need for independence; those with a low need may require more frequent feedback than those with a high need. And last, the subordinate's desire for feedback, which will undoubtedly be determined by the first five factors.

Content of feedback sessions is also important to the MBO process. Major findings regarding feedback content have been obtained by the GE researchers (4, 8), who learned that managers who received an above average number of criticisms in their review sessions generally showed less achievement of objectives 10 to 12 weeks later than managers receiving fewer criticisms. Furthermore, managers improved considerably less in the criticized areas than they did in the noncriticized areas. The study also showed that when specific goals were set in review sessions, managers' performance improved more than twice as much as when review sessions consisted of criticism without goal setting.

Although the GE results highlight the limitations of criticism-oriented feedback sessions, they must not be interpreted as suggesting that a superior should only lavish praise upon subordinates. While too much criticism can easily lead to enough subordinate defensiveness to render the session useless, unwarranted praise can result in a false sense of accomplishment and unjustified complacency, either of which can make the session equally useless. The superior must learn to use criticism when necessary, but must also augment this criticism with a problem-solving approach concentrating on what can be done to improve the subordinate's performance. According to Myer, et al., (8) managers reacted more positively to the WPR program when their superiors functioned in a problem-solving or "counselor" role than when they operated in a "judge" role. In other words, managers offered criticism, but used this as the basis for jointly determining solutions to problems that hampered the subordinate's job performance.

Periodic progress reviews, or feedback sessions, are a vital element of the MBO process. Managers must assume two major responsibilities with respect to these sessions. First, they must assess the numerous factors likely to determine how often they should hold progress reviews with subordinates, and they must be flexible and willing to vary the frequency of feedback according to the needs and expectations of each subordinate. Second, they should shape the content of the sessions according to an ob-

jective assessment of the nature of the feedback data itself. Both praise and criticism should be given when deserved; however, the criticism should be constructive and serve as the foundation for a problem-solving session aimed at removing barriers to subordinates' performance. The relationship between these two responsibilities is straightforward: the content of feedback sessions and the behavior of the superior during them will significantly influence how frequently subordinates wish to have such sessions.

SUPPORT FOR THE MBO PROGRAM

As is the case with most new programs introduced into a company, the success of MBO is largely contingent upon the support given to the program. Support for MBO can occur in two ways. First, from a micro point of view, behavior of individual managers using MBO can be supportive of the program. And second, in a macro sense, overall organizational practices and policies can support MBO. What specific kinds of supportive behavior and practices have been found to be effective in the MBO research?

Looking at managerial behavior first, one of the most important factors seems to be the amount of time the boss spends on MBO. Tosi and Carroll (14) found that the time the boss spends on MBO is positively and significantly related to subordinate managers' (1) satisfaction with MBO, (2) perceived success in achieving objectives, and (3) perceived improvement in boss-subordinate relationships. In a follow-up study, Tosi and Carroll (15) learned that the company's systematic effort to increase subordinate involvement in goal setting resulted in a belief among subordinates that their boss was spending considerably more time on MBO. In other words, the amount of time the boss spends on MBO is an outward reflection of his/her support for it.

Supervisory behavior that supports subordinates as they use MBO can also be helpful. For example, Tosi and Carroll (14) describe such behavior to include actions by the boss to help subordinates perform their jobs and visible superior concern for subordinates' careers as affected by achievement of objectives. In a similar vein, the positive effects of participation reported in the GE studies (4, 8) were dependent upon a background of supervisory support consisting of helping subordinates improve on their present jobs, showing appreciation of subordinates' efforts to contribute new ideas, and minimal use of threats to ensure goal attainment.

Attention should also be drawn to the fact that a number of the behaviors discussed in earlier portions of this article actually represent supportive supervisory behavior. For example, if the organization is encouraging a high degree of subordinate involvement in the goal-setting process, but particular managers are unilaterally setting objectives for their subordinates, this behavior would not seem to be supportive of the MBO program. Likewise, infrequent feedback sessions and/or a heavy use of nonconstructive criticism in these sessions would not be considered supportive of MBO.

Organizational support for MBO can occur through a variety of actions relating to the "Three Is" of MBO—introduction, implementation, and improvement. With respect to the first factor, the manner in which the program is initially introduced in a company can provide very visible support for it. As discussed earlier, an MBO program introduced by top management was more positively received than a program introduced by the personnel department (7). Similarly, a new MBO program that is characterized by a thorough and systematic orientation and training phase is likely to be viewed as having strong organizational support.

When MBO has progressed to the operational or implementation stage, various reinforcement measures can demonstrate continued organizational support for the program. To illustrate, Ivancevich (6) describes a six-month reinforcement schedule consisting of letters, group meetings, memos, and telephone discussions used in one plant of a large manufacturing firm. This study showed significant performance improvement in the plant using the reinforcement schedule as compared to two other plants not using such measures. Ivancevich cautions, however, that these particular reinforcement measures should not be viewed as the ideal form of organizational support for MBO; he suggests that the effectiveness of such measures may decrease over time and too much use of them may result in managers feeling they are being manipulated.

Perhaps the ultimate way of reinforcing MBO is to link the MBO program to the organizational reward system. A study by Mobley (9) found that 37 percent of 625 middle and top level managers in a large corporation felt that goal attainment should have some bearing in merit compensation decisions, while 54 percent believed it should have considerable bearing, and 4 percent felt it should be almost the sole determinant. Furthermore, Mobley found significant positive correlations between managers' evaluation of MBO and the extent to which goal attainment was related to their merit compensation. Tying MBO performance to the reward system is not an easy undertaking. In fact, not all MBO proponents believe it should be attempted.[9] Nonetheless, it would behoove the firm to thoroughly evaluate the possibility of such a linkage before discarding the idea as unfeasible.

Continued efforts to improve the MBO

program also represent a viable form of organizational support. For example, Carroll and Tosi (14) report that after a company had attempted to improve its program by conducting a series of much more intensive goal setting meetings throughout the hierarchy, managers felt that company interest in and support for MBO had increased significantly. Efforts to improve the MBO program should be based upon an objective evaluation of the attitudes and suggestions of those using MBO. Accordingly, a firm needs to develop a systematic method for assessing the program. By using the information collected in these assessments to constructively improve the program, an organization is clearly manifesting its continued support for MBO.

MONITORING THE MBO PROGRAM

Many of the implications described in this article relate to comprehensive training in MBO. While such training is invaluable, an excellent MBO training phase could give an organization a false sense of security. For example, Ivancevich (5) found that MBO did not result in any significant improvement in the satisfaction of managers' needs over an 18-month period and concluded that "The lack of a sustained effect upon managers' needs suggests that the training and implementation impact of MBO is short lived in the present study (5)." While this finding provides support for the use of some reinforcement measures, it also illustrates the need for continual monitoring of the MBO program.

A comprehensive monitoring of MBO would consist of three phases: (1) an attitude check, (2) a relationship check, and (3) a performance check. The attitude check would examine managers' feelings toward MBO. Specific attitudinal dimensions assessed would depend upon the purpose(s) of the program; for instance, if MBO has been introduced primarily to replace an antiquated personality trait method of performance appraisal, do managers in fact feel

---

[9] For varying opinions on this issue, see R. J. Hunady and G. H. Varney, "Salary Administration: A Reason for MBO," *Training and Development Journal* 28, 9 (September 1974): 24–28; D. L. Kirkpatrick, "MBO and Salary Administration." *Training and Development Journal* 27, 9 (September 1973): 3–6; T. H. Patten, Jr., "OD, MBO, and the R. P. System: A New Dimension in Personnel Administration," *Personnel Administration* 35, 2 (March–April 1972): 14–23; and G. Strauss, "Management by Objectives: A Critical View," *Training and Development Journal* 26, 4 (April 1972): 10–15.

that the program is helping them appraise performance in a more objective manner?

The relationship check should concentrate on relationships between superiors and their subordinates. These relationships are critical to the program's success regardless of whether MBO is conducted in the more traditional one-to-one, boss-subordinate fashion or on a team basis.[10] Efforts should be made to assess the effects of superior-subordinate relationships upon the MBO process, and conversely, the effect MBO might be having upon these relationships.

The performance check represents an attempt to measure the effect of MBO on organizational effectiveness and efficiency; as such, it is a measure of the real payoff of MBO. Studies of performance under MBO have produced mixed results. Ivancevich (6) found that performance in the production and marketing[11] departments of three plants did not improve significantly over a three-year period. On the other hand, Raia (10, 11) found that an MBO program led to increases in goal attainment, productivity, and the overall level of production goals set. While direct causal relationships between MBO and performance may not always be clearly visible, it seems reasonable to assume that if the performance check shows consistently even or decreasing levels of performance, the MBO program could use an increased emphasis on setting performance objectives that reflect an improvement over previous objectives.

SUMMARY

MBO research studies provide a rich source of information that can be quite helpful to organizations using or planning to use MBO. This article has attempted to bridge part of the gap between researchers and practitioners by describing research findings and their pragmatic implications for a number of variables that this writer believes are particularly significant for MBO users. To recapitulate, the major points are as follows:

1. Introduction of MBO can be facilitated by (a) having top management introduce the program, (b) communicating a clear statement of its purpose(s), (c) minimizing the paperwork involved in it, and (d) conducting a thorough orientation and training phase for all managers using it.

2. Subordinate participation in setting objectives will probably vary within the company; if highly participative goal setting is a desired element of MBO, regular monitoring of goal-setting processes throughout the firm is necessary.

3. Increased subordinate participation in MBO goal setting generally has positive results; however, the extent of these results is conditioned by the degree of participation managers are accustomed to. Careful examination of the organizational climate is necessary in order to minimize the likelihood of encouraging an MBO goal-setting format that is incongruent with the existing climate and leadership patterns.

4. Clarity of objectives and priorities for objectives are generally related to positive attitudes toward MBO and goal performance. Goal clarity can be improved through proper training, and priorities can be required as part of the MBO form.

5. Frequency of performance feedback is positively related to managers' attitudes toward MBO and success in achieving objectives. Superiors must learn to accurately assess and respond to the numerous factors determining how fre-

---

[10] A description of how MBO could be conducted on a team basis is provided by W. L. French and R. W. Hollmann, "Management by Objectives: The Team Approach," *California Management Review* 17, 3 (Spring 1975): 13–22.

[11] For discussions of how MBO can be applied to marketing operations, see M. J. Etzel and J. M. Ivancevich, "Management by Objectives in Marketing–Philosophy, Process, and Problems," *Journal of Marketing* 38, 4 (October 1974): 47–55.

quently feedback should be provided to each subordinate.

6. Performance feedback sessions primarily characterized by criticism do not generally lead to improved performance. Superiors should augment criticism with a problem-solving approach to improving subordinate performance.

7. Supervisory support for MBO is very important. Supportive supervisory behavior includes an increase in the time spent on MBO as well as other actions that reflect a support of subordinates as they use MBO.

8. Organizational support for MBO is equally important. Such support can be given through (a) proper introduction of the program; (b) thorough orientation and training in MBO; (c) use of various reinforcement measures, including a linkage of the MBO program and the reward system; and (d) visible efforts to improve MBO based upon a regular assessment of the program.

9. Continual, systematic monitoring of MBO would consist of an attitude check, a relationship check, and a performance check.

REFERENCES

1. Carroll, S. J., and H. L. Tosi. "The Relationship of Characteristics of the Review Process as Moderated by Personality and Situational Factors to the Success of the 'Management by Objectives' Approach." *Proceedings of the 29th Annual Meeting of the Academy of Management* (1969), pp. 139–43.

2. Carroll, S. J., and H. L. Tosi. "Goal Characteristics and Personality Factors in a Management-by-Objectives Program." *Administrative Science Quarterly* 15, 3 (September 1970): 295–305.

3. Fay, P. P., and D. N. Beach. "Management by Objectives Evaluated." *Personnel Journal* 53, 10 (October 1974): 767ff.

4. French, J. R. P., Jr., E. Kay, and H. H. Meyer. "Participation and the Appraisal System." *Human Relations* 19, 1 (February 1966): 3–19.

5. Ivancevich, J. M. "A Longitudinal Assessment of Management by Objectives." *Administrative Science Quarterly* 17, 1 (March 1972): 126–38.

6. Ivancevich, J. M. "Changes in Performance in a Management by Objectives Program." *Administrative Science Quarterly* 19, 4 (December 1974): 563–74.

7. Ivancevich J. M., J. H. Donnelly, and H. L. Lyon. "A Study of the Impact of Management by Objectives on Perceived Need Satisfaction." *Personnel Psychology* 23, 2 (Summer 1970): 139–51.

8. Meyer, H. H., E. Kay, and J. R. P. French, Jr. "Split Roles in Performance Appraisal." *Harvard Business Review* 43, 1 (January–February 1965): 123–29.

9. Mobley, W. H. "The Link Between MBO and Merit Compensation." *Personnel Journal* 53, 6 (June 1974): 423–27.

10. Raia, A. P. "Goal Setting and Self-Control." *Journal of Management Studies* 2, 1 (February 1965): 34–53.

11. Raia, A. P. "A Second Look at Management Goals and Controls." *California Management Review* 8, 4 (Summer 1966): 49–58.

12. Tosi, H. L., and S. J. Carroll. "Managerial Reaction to Management by Objectives." *Academy of Management Journal* 11, 4 (December 1968): 415–26.

13. Tosi, H. L., and S. J. Carroll. "Some Structural Factors Related to Goal Influence in the Management by Objectives Process." *MSU Business Topics* 17, 2 (Spring 1969): 45–50.

14. Tosi, H. L., and S. J. Carroll. "Some Factors Affecting the Success of 'Management by Objectives.'" *Journal of Management Studies* 7, 2 (May 1970): 209–23.

15. Tosi, H. L., and S. J. Carroll. "Improving Management by Objectives: A Diagnostic Change Program." *California Management Review* 16, 1 (Fall 1973): 57–66.

8. EMPLO[YEE GROWTH THROUGH]
PERFORM[ANCE MANAGEMENT]

"I'd like t[o be able to give you a larger] raise, Chris. [But as your supervisor, just the] other day, yo[u were still having trouble getting] Pat and John [to cooperate with each other,] and of cours[e, that's an important part of] your job. So I [wonder . . ." Meanwhile, one's] hypothetical, [well-meaning supervisor has is] all too famili[ar to many a manager. On the] one hand, he [is expected to help his sub]ordinates imp[rove their performance which] means that he [must openly talk with them] to understand [how he can help them. On] the other hand [he must use the information] he has about a [particular person in order to] make intellige[nt promotion and pay deci]sions. But too [often the manager may feel] so uneasy ta[lking with his subordinates] about their performance that he gives up trying, or he is so unaware of the difference between helping and judging that he confuses his subordinates. They might like his advice, but they see too great a risk in asking for it. After looking into the nature of such conflicts and risks, management at Corning Glass Works has adopted a system that lessens them. The authors, who helped design and implement the system, describe in this article how it works.

In recent years, management by objectives (MBO) has enjoyed a good deal of popularity. Both personnel specialists and line managers have responded enthusiastically to the emphasis that MBO places on subordinates' results and accountability rather than on their personal qualities. MBO's popularity is easy to understand.

First, many if not most managers feel quite uncomfortable judging the means by which their subordinates accomplish their

goals. There are, of course, many reasons for this discomfort. Some managers find evaluating people incompatible with the egalitarian ideals of our society. Others shy away from the job of providing feedback because they face emotionally laden interpersonal situations. Still others are simply so results-oriented that they have no time for such "personnel stuff."

Second, MBO has proved to be a useful vehicle for increasing the quantity and quality of communication between line managers and subordinates concerning responsibilities, objectives, plans, and results. In addition research has shown that the setting of specific objectives generally increases the individual's motivation to do certain tasks well.

Despite its usefulness, many managers have found that MBO also has its limitations. In fact, its major strength is its major weakness: MBO focuses the attention of the boss and the subordinate exclusively on task results. For example, a manufacturing manager reviewed the objectives of his plant manager and found that objectives for cost reduction as well as for gross margins had been exceeded. He was pleased. He was not so pleased when he learned sometime later that the MBO process had failed to uncover crucial information: the plant manager had not developed a cohesive plant staff and was not getting along well with managers in other functional areas. MBO does not, therefore, help the manager to observe and evaluate the behavior of his or her subordinates; yet, such observation and evaluation is vital to making intelligent promotion decisions and helping employees improve their performance.

Take, for example, the case of a hypothetical sales manager whose job is to improve the performance of his sales force. Suppose that this manager has two salesmen performing substantially below standard; both are achieving only 80 percent of their revenue budgets. How is the manager to help these people improve? Clearly, his first step must be to analyze why each salesman is doing so poorly. It's possible that one salesman lacks the forcefulness and agressiveness needed to overcome objections and "close" sales, while the other salesman may be alienating customers with his aggressiveness and overconfidence. Obviously, different approaches are called for to help these two people improve, even though their results are about the same.

The dilemma the vice president of sales would have in the same hypothetical organization illustrates the deficiency of MBO as far as making promotion decisions goes. Let's suppose that the VP has one sales management position to fill and that the two most logical candidates both consistently achieve 150 percent of their quotas. In order to pick the better of the two, the VP must analyze their behavior patterns.

Imagine that one salesman achieves his outstanding results through sheer strength of drive. Fiercely competitive, he is effective because he is a hard worker and persistent. Unfortunately, this salesman is not very organized. Indeed, he is rather sloppy with paperwork, and most of his colleagues find him quite difficult to work with. In contrast, imagine that the other salesman performs so well primarily because he does a good job at analyzing his territory and customers and because he plans and organizes effective selling strategies. In addition, he is particularly adept at gaining the help and cooperation he needs from others on the sales force and the marketing staff. Clearly, which of these two people would make the best sales manager cannot be determined by results alone.

For a number of years, managers at Corning Glass Works have used MBO. But because of its shortcomings, staff psychologists and personnel specialists began to look for a system that would incorporate its strengths with a better way to help managers observe, evaluate, and aid in improving the performance of subordinates. After several years of research and development, we produced what we call the performance management system. The PMS is the formal vehicle now used by Corning to manage, measure, and improve the performance and potential for advancement of approximately 3,800 managerial and professional employees.

Our purpose in this article is to describe and analyze this system. It is working at Corning, and we think it can work in other companies. But because a system is only as good as the commitment and skill of people who must use it, we shall also discuss the strategy and tactics used to introduce it as a corporate program and then its strengths and deficiencies. First, however, we would like to share the thinking behind the system with you and why we thought it would be effective.

MANAGING, JUDGING, AND HELPING

One of the most critical problems facing corporations is management development. A central thesis underlying Corning's PMS is that, while classroom learning has its place, effective managerial performance is best developed through practical challenges and experiences on the job with guidance and feedback from superiors. Analysis of current organizational life indicates that the element most frequently missing or deficient in this equation is accurate and objective performance feedback.

PMS was developed to help managers give such feedback in a helpful and constructive manner and to aid the supervisor and subordinate in creating a developmental plan. It is distinguished from other performance appraisal systems by the following characteristics: (1) its formal recognition of the manager's triple role in dealing with subordinates, (2) its emphasis on both development and evaluation, (3) its use of a profile displaying the individual's strengths and developmental needs relative to himself rather than to others, and (4) its integration

EXHIBIT 1
Managing Performance

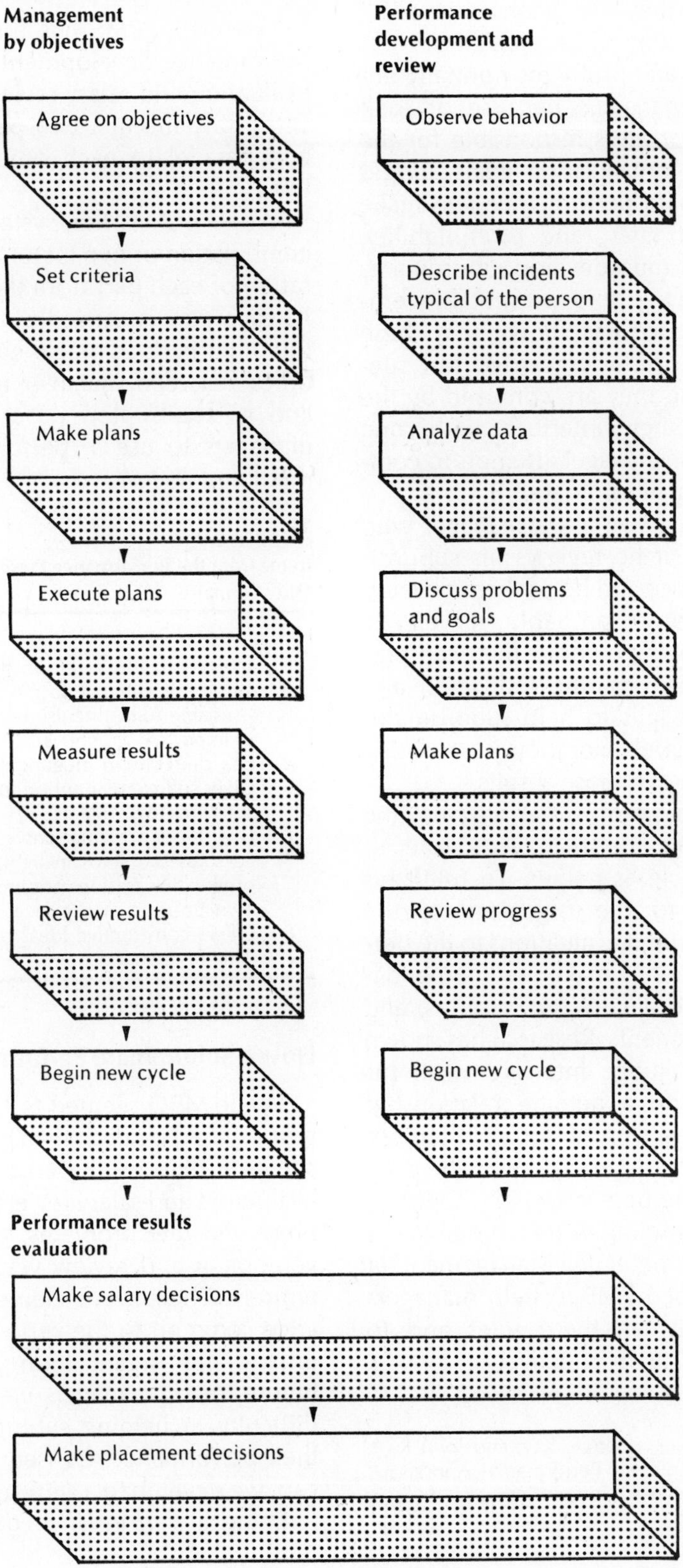

Management by objectives

Performance development and review

Agree on objectives

Observe behavior

▼

Set criteria

Describe incidents typical of the person

▼

Make plans

Analyze data

▼

Execute plans

Discuss problems and goals

▼

Measure results

Make plans

▼

Review results

Review progress

▼

Begin new cycle

Begin new cycle

▼

Performance results evaluation

Make salary decisions

▼

Make placement decisions

of the results achieved (MBO) with the means by which they have been achieved.

The development of Corning's PMS was triggered by several problems normally encountered by managers because of their triple role as *managers* responsible for the achievement of organization goals, *judges* who must evaluate performance and make decisions about salary and promotability, and *helpers* who must develop subordinates into more effective and promotable employees. Experience has shown that these functions are not always carried out successfully because they are confused by the manager and they interfere with one another when the manager attempts to communicate with a subordinate.

For example, if you ask a manager who uses only MBO if he reviews his subordinates' performance and helps them develop and improve, he will probably answer yes. Yet, while managing by objectives can play a critical part in ensuring individual and group results, it fails to help subordinates understand what behavior they must modify or adopt to improve those results.

Another typical problem arises from the conflict between the manager's role as judge and his role as helper. To fulfill his responsibilities to the organization, the manager must submit evaluations to the personnel department, make recommendations about subordinates' promotions, and make salary judgments. Research has shown that his role as judge interferes with his ability to develop a helping relationship with subordinates.[1] A subordinate often begins to feel so defensive that he or she does not hear what the boss is saying, especially when the boss is trying to be a judge and a helper at the same time. Management at Corning developed PMS to help managers differentiate between these roles and to perform each of them effectively.

---

[1] Herbert H. Meyer, Emanuel Kay, and John R. P. French, Jr., "Split Roles in Performance Appraisal," *Harvard Business Review* January–February 1965, p. 123.

DESIGNING THE SYSTEM

Essentially, PMS has three parts—MBO, performance development and review, and evaluation and salary review. Exhibit 1 indicates how the first two parts, independent and parallel to each other, feed into the third.

What makes the system unusual is a combination of two factors—a careful separation of each part from the other two (that is, each part is carried out separately from the other parts in meetings held at different times between manager and subordinate) and a step-by-step process for company managers to use in performance development and review.

EXHIBIT 2
Items from the Performance Description Questionnaire

Individual performance

1. Objects to ideas before they are explained.
2. Takes the initiative in group meetings.
3. Is unable to distinguish between important and unimportant problems.
4. Has difficulty in meeting project deadlines.
5. Gives sufficient attention to detail when seeking solutions to problems.
6. Gives poor presentations
7. Sees his problems in light of the problems of others (that is, does not limit his thinking to his own position or organizational unit).
8. Offers constructive ideas both within and outside his own job.

How a Subordinate Performs

While MBO seemed to be a process better designed by each manager to fit his own situation than by the corporation, and the evaluation and salary review process in itself presented few problems, performance development and review was another matter entirely. There were elements of performance common to the various functions and units of the organization, and, as we said before, many managers were encountering difficulty in helping subordinates improve their performance. Consequently, to fill this gap, we developed a step-by-step approach.

Using a *performance description ques-*

tionnaire, the manager first observes and describes his subordinates' behavior. Then, using a *performance profile,* he analyzes their strengths and weaknesses. Finally, through one or more *developmental interviews,* he attempts to help his subordinates see what changes in behavior are needed and plan for them. In these interviews, boss and subordinate jointly identify areas for improvement and establish plans to develop the abilities needed.

Critical Questions. The performance description questionnaire contains 76 items on which the performance of an exempt salaried person is evaluated by his immediate supervisor. Each item describes a specific type of behavior that has been identified as an important component of effective performance. Exhibit 2 lists eight items from the questionnaire. The supervisor is asked to indicate on a six-point rating scale the extent to which he agrees that his subordinate behaves in ways similar to those described in the questionnaire. Space below each item provides the superior a chance to add comments or examples that substantiate the descriptive rating—"critical incidents" he has actually observed.

Taken together, the behavioral statements represent a comprehensive picture of effective performance within Corning Glass Works. They were identified through extensive research throughout the company and thus reflect the nature of the business environment as well as the company's culture and values and the nature of the tasks to be performed. What this means, of course, is that, while some of the performance items are common to many organizations, others are of significance only to Corning. It also implies that periodic research to update the list is needed as Corning's business, strategy, culture, and tasks change.

At Corning, the first step in the research was to pool what supervisors considered the critical incidents in the job performance of their exempt employees. We asked 50 supervisors representing a cross section of levels, functions, and divisions within the

company to describe subordinates' specific actions that had led to either significant improvements or significant decrements in in their departments' performance. The supervisors identified approximately 300 critical incidents, which we then translated into 150 general behavioral descriptions.

After further research to test the validity of these general descriptions on 300 employees (selected at random), we arrived at 76 items having a statistically significant correlation with performance and management potential throughout the company.

Individualized Profiles. While a supervisor can easily evaluate each of his subordinates on all 76 items, it would be extremely time-consuming to review all 76 with each of his subordinates. So we had to invent some "shorthand" he could use to transmit to his subordinates the complex information obtained in the questionnaire.

First, we summarized the 76 items along 19 performance dimensions, 8 relating to supervision and 11 to individual performance, which are listed on the left-hand side of Exhibit 3. We will not describe here the statistical methods used to arrive at these dimensions; suffice it to say that problems were encountered.

The most troublesome problem was that the supervisors tended to rate items quite similarly for a particular subordinate depending on whether they saw him as a good performer or a poor one in the first place. This tendency of the rater to allow his initial impressions to influence all subsequent descriptions is known as the "halo error." The good performer would not receive feedback that would help him better himself for promotion, and the poor performer would feel "dumped on" and be unable to marshal his energies to work on anything.

We felt that everyone has developmental needs, even the best performers in the corporation. Thus everyone could gain from working on the few performance dimensions for which he had received the lowest ratings.

EXHIBIT 3
Performance Profile

	Subordinate A		Subordinate B		Subordinate C	
	Weakness	Strength	Weakness	Strength	Weakness	Strength
Individual performance						
Openness to influence	XX		XXXXX			XX
Constructive initiative		XX		XXX		XXXXXX
Priority setting		XX		XXX	XXXXXX	
Work accomplishment	XX		XXXXXXXXXX		XX	
Thoroughness and accuracy		XX		XX		XX
Formal communications	XX			XX	XXXXXX	
Organizational perspective		XX	XX			XXXXXX
Credibility	XX			XXXX	XX	
Cooperation		XX	XX		XX	
Decisiveness	XX			XXX	XX	
Flexibility		XX		XX		XXX
Supervisory performance						
Delegation/ participation		XX		XXX	XXXXXX	
Support for company		XX	XXXXXXXXXX		XX	
Communication and positive motivation	XX			XX		XX
Follow-up and control		XX		XX	XXXXXX	
Unit improvement	XX		XX			XXXXXX
Selection, placement, and instruction		XX		XXXX	XX	
Unit productivity	XX		XX		XX	
Conflict resolution		XX		XXX	XX	

To break the halo effect, we next developed the performance profile, a tool to help managers discriminate among a subordinate's strengths and developmental needs. For each subordinate, the supervisor receives a performance profile like the three samples shown in Exhibit 3. The center line indicates the person's own average. The dimensions extending to the left are the subordinate's weaknesses; the dimensions extending to the right are the subordinate's strengths. The number of X's indicate specific degrees of weakness or strength. Note that these three profiles should not be com-

General Areas Where Improvement Is Needed	Strategies for Improvement						
	Training Job-Related Skills or Knowledge	In the Laboratory or on the Job	Counseling Professional Consulting or Counseling	Supervision Coaching	Observing Boss's Managerial Style	Job Enrichment, Job Redesign	Job Rotation
Understanding of role				XXX		XXX	
Effort motivation, attitude				XXX	XXX	XXX	XXX
Knowledge of job or ability	XXX	XXX		XXX		XXX	XXX
Interpersonal skills ...		XXX	XXX	XXX			
Personality traits		XXX	XXX	XXX			

pared with each other, since each is structured to reflect only the individual's performance.

We have found that managers are surprised when they receive the profile because they are not used to thinking about their subordinates as having negative qualities, or perhaps at least not the particular ones listed. To us, their surprise indicates that the profile is breaking the halo effect. In fact, the profile has four distinct advantages:

1. It helps both the supervisor and the subordinate to be analytical and discriminating in their evaluation of performance.
2. It, therefore, helps ensure individuals fair recognition for their strengths and constructive criticism for their shortcomings.
3. It reduces the supervisor's defensiveness and his need to "prove" the validity of his judgments.
4. It reduces the subordinate's defensiveness and his need to enhance his superior's judgment of him in relation to his "competitors."

The Interview. A subordinate's performance profile is developed by computer after his supervisor has filled out and sent in his performance description questionnaire. After receiving the profile, the manager is urged to use it to analyze his subordinate's performance in preparation for the developmental interview. Often the supervisor will want to identify the specific behavioral ratings that have caused a dimension to come out as a developmental need. In the interview, the specific behavior that needs attention can be discussed.

Some supervisors have found that asking subordinates to fill out questionnaires on themselves encourages open and nondefensive discussion of their performance. Each dimension can be reviewed and discrepancies between superiors' and subordinates' impressions discussed.

It is not our intent here to describe the ground rules for effective developmental interviews; much has been written about this elsewhere.[2] We do wish to point out that in the PMS the developmental interview is a meeting distinct and separate from a MBO session or an evaluation session. The questionnaire and the profile are tools that help the manager differentiate development from MBO and evaluation and that reduce the anxiety associated with the developmental interview.

Finally, it is our belief that developmental plans and objectives are needed if change is actually to occur. The manager needs tools to help him form a developmental plan with his subordinates. These come in the form of (a) an interview guide, for translating explicit developmental needs into specific areas for which training programs have been identified and (b) a matrix framework as shown in Exhibit 4 for translating broad needs into general strategies for development.

How a Subordinate Is Evaluated

As we mentioned earlier, evaluation interviews of a subordinate's current performance, potential, promotability, and salary increase are distinct from MBO and appraisal sessions. It is best to make these evaluations when the subordinate is due for a salary increase. The manager rates each subordinate's overall performance and potential. The ratings, which are shared with subordinates and endorsed by the supervisor at the next level, reflect both the whats and the hows of performance.

SEEKING COMMITMENT

Since the effectiveness of any personnel system, no matter how well designed, is largely determined by the understanding, commitment, and skills of the line managers who must actually implement the program, we introduced PMS with these managers in mind.

[2] Norman R. F. Maier, *The Appraisal Interview: Gestures, Methods, & Skills* (New York: Wiley, 1958).

The best way for a staff function to engender resentment or apathy toward a program is to "cram it down the throats" of the people who must implement it, so we did not attempt to introduce the system throughout the corporation all at once. Instead, we gained the approval and support of top corporate management first and then introduced the system to one division at a time on a quasi-voluntary basis. In essence, we sold each division vice president on the program with no pressure from top corporate management. In accordance with what is known about effective change, we started with the divisions that seemed the most receptive and the most likely to succeed in using the program.

After selling the program to corporate and divisional managers on an individual basis, our primary vehicle for introducing the program within each division was a workshop training session. These sessions, which lasted either two full days or one very long day, covered the following points:

The need for and importance of effective performance appraisal.

The rationale for a program that integrates behavior with results-centered approaches to appraisal.

The research that led to performance development and review.

The MBO approach to performance appraisal and how it is implemented.

The use of the questionnaire and the profile.

The way to conduct a developmental interview in a constructive, problem-solving manner.

In addition to the traditional lecture-and-discussion format, we used a variety of instructional techniques including informal discussion groups, films, and role playing.

GAINING ACCEPTANCE AND MAKING REFINEMENTS

To investigate the extent to which PMS was being used and its effectiveness, we conducted a study in the four divisions having the most experience with the program, ranging from approximately two years to less than one year.[3] We found that 230 of the 351 supervisory personnel in seven plants and four division staff groups had participated in a performance development and review interview, either as bosses or subordinates or as both. Mobility was the primary reason that not all of the managers had participated; an employee or his supervisor very often changed jobs before they had worked together six months. Another reason appeared to be cases of little or no perceived encouragement to use the system.

Through a questionnaire we sent out, however, more than 90 percent of those who had participated in an interview provided us with detailed feedback on their impressions of the program. In addition, we checked our interpretations with the division management staffs during subsequent meetings we held with them. They confirmed and often elaborated on our interpretations.

Of course there are bound to be some complaints with any new, complex system involving a large number of people. Our data, however, indicated a generally high acceptance of PMS among those who had used it. First of all, all supervisors accepted some form of performance feedback as part of their jobs. Second, PMS in general and the questionnaire and profile in particular were seen as greatly helpful in the performance appraisal and development process.

Reduction of Anxiety

It is interesting that the person who found PMS the most helpful was the interviewer. Apparently, the active role of the supervisor placed more responsibility and pressure on him than on the subordinate.

[3] Jack E. Dawson and B. B. (Steve) McCaa, "Performance Development and Review: An Evaluation of its Utilization," a paper presented at *Performance Management System: Research, Design, Introduction and Evaluation,* a symposium of the American Psychological Association Convention, New Orleans, 1974.

For some, simply having the more formal, scientific-looking results of the questionnaire and profile rather than depending solely on their less systematized observations and conclusions helped set an easygoing tone. For most people, the profile appeared to function as an agenda that furthermore helped stimulate discussion of all aspects of a subordinate's performance. Despite these advances, the superiors we sampled still seemed to feel that they greatly needed to improve their skills in conducting developmental interviews, and a related study on the effectiveness of the PMS workshop confirmed this finding.

Important Line Relationships

One would think a highly accepted system like PMS would spread itself by word of mouth at least within a single plant. Our results do not confirm this optimistic notion. In fact, it seems that few people communicate their positive views to others in the company. The availability of a good system is not enough to spread its use; a vigorously active program is necessary.

For instance, we found a couple of chains of supervisor-subordinate relationships that had not used the PMS. These people reported that although they hadn't been told *not* to use it, they did not feel that they should until the man at the top of the chain told them to or at least had used it with his own subordinates. Other people seemed to want PMS and indicated that they were "waiting for follow-up," that is, pressure from someone in authority.

Organizational Asset

If we accept the premise that the manager's most important task is managing the performance of his subordinates and that constructive performance feedback is a key element in developing managers, then PMS is definitely an organizational asset.

In order to use PMS most effectively, significant resources are needed to follow the introductory workshop with on-the-spot consultation in planning and conducting developmental interviews. Too often, training is thought of as the final step in the introductory process. We recommend, instead, that personnel specialists help managers go through the PMS process at least once. In order to ensure that a performance management system will be used in the first place, key managers at all levels must state their commitment to it and model its use.

At Corning, many managers have found that just identifying the performance dimensions that are important to organizational effectiveness helps develop a common language for discussing performance and making decisions about people, something that is absent in most organizations. Thus a performance management system can increase the objectivity and enhance the validity of personnel decisions.

part III

PERSONNEL/HUMAN RESOURCE ACTIVITIES

4

PERSONNEL FORECASTING AND RECRUITMENT

What Is Personnel Forecasting?

Personnel forecasting is the process by which organizations develop quantitative estimates of their future personnel needs. This may be done for the total organization and for specific subunits (for example, divisions, departments, job classifications) within the organization. If forecasting is done by subunit, the subunit results can be aggregated to form the forecast for the total organization.

Personnel imbalances frequently occur over time. As technologies and products change, organizations find themselves confronted with shortages and/or surpluses of employees for various kinds of jobs. Through forecasting the organization is able to identify the probable magnitude of these imbalances and where they are most likely to occur. If the forecasts are sufficiently accurate and cover a long enough time interval, the organization will be able to use the results as a basis for *planning* how to cope with imbalances. Without forecasting, the organization is more or less placed in a situation of simply *reacting* to imbalances as they occur.

Elements of Forecasting

Personnel forecasts are usually made over one- to five-year time intervals, and there are considerable differences among organizations in the specific techniques used for making the forecasts. Regardless of time intervals and techniques, there are three major elements of forecasting. These are *labor demand, internal labor supply,* and *net personnel requirements.* These elements, and their relationships, are shown in Figure 1.

FIGURE 1
Elements and Results of Personnel Forecasting

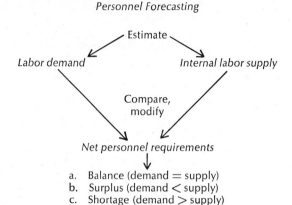

Personnel Forecasting

a. Balance (demand = supply)
b. Surplus (demand < supply)
c. Shortage (demand > supply)

Consider a personnel forecast and its results for the *total* organization. Labor demand refers to an estimate of the total size of the organization's workforce that will be necessary to achieve organization goals in some future time period. These estimates would take into account many factors such as sales, product or service demand, productivity, and technological change.

The internal labor supply element involves an estimation of the number of current employees that will still be with the organization at some point in the future. This estimate will obviously be based on anticipated turnover rates over the forecast interval. Usually consideration of past turnover rates would have a major influence on the estimated future turnover. Extrapolation from past to future can be dangerous, however, if external labor market conditions change appreciably.

The organization's *net* personnel requirements are the result of comparing the numerical demand and supply estimates (that is, demand minus internal supply). If net personnel requirements are positive, there is a projected shortage, meaning that internal labor supply will be insufficient to meet anticipated demand. In turn, the organization will have to fill this shortage by external recruitment and selection of new employees. If net requirements are negative, on the other hand, more current employees will be available than will be needed. This surplus will either have to be absorbed by the organization, or steps will have to be taken to reduce it (for example, through layoffs).

While the example in Figure 1 illustrates the basic elements of forecasting, it greatly simplifies the actual complexity of the process by focusing only on demand and internal supply estimates for the *total* organization. In practice, it is usually necessary to derive separate estimates of demand, internal supply, and net personnel requirements for *specific subunits* within the organization. The reason for this is simply that demand and internal supply, and thus net personnel requirements, can vary considerably among subunits.

Consider the case of labor demand. In some subunits demand may be estimated to increase (for example, due to a projected sales increase). In other subunits just the opposite may occur because of a projected sales decrease or the introduction of new technology that will increase labor productivity.

In the case of internal labor supply, the estimate for the total organization only reflects projected movement out of the organization. At the subunit level, however, it is also necessary to consider the movement of employees among subunits. These movements reflect the occurrence of employee promotion, transfer, and demotion. For the subunit, therefore, the estimate of internal supply requires three subestimates: (a) the number of current employees who will remain in the subunit, (b) the number of employees who will enter the subunit, and (c) the number of employees who will leave the subunit, either to move to another subunit or to leave the organization. To make these estimates, past movement patterns (promotion, transfer, demotion, and turnover) are usually examined and then extrapolated into future movement estimates. In other words, it is assumed that past movement is the best indicator of future movement. The accuracy of internal supply estimates greatly depends on the validity of this assumption.

In summary, personnel forecasting involves estimating labor demand, internal labor supply, and net personnel requirements. The latter estimate is based on the demand and supply estimates, though it may be modified. Precision of forecasting, and thus of planning on the basis of the forecasts, requires that the above estimates be made for specific subunits within the organization if at all possible. These subunit estimates may then be aggregated to yield more general estimates for the total organization.

Note that the estimation process described focuses almost exclusively on quantity of personnel required, and not on quality. Quality is, of course, very important and is considered by the organization. Usually, however, organizations attempt to control the quality of their workforce primarily through staffing and training, subjects to be considered in subsequent chapters.

Forecasting and Recruitment

One of the most immediate and direct impacts of forecasting results will be on the planning of employee recruitment efforts. This impact will be felt in both projected surplus and shortage situations. Projected surpluses serve as a signal to plan for reducing or halting recruitment efforts. In the case of shortages, current recruitment efforts will have to be maintained or expanded. The shortage figures can actually serve as recruitment goals or quotas to guide the planning of recruitment strategy. Indeed, having these figures available makes it possible to plan precise strategies by subunit.

One strategy would be to fill all projected vacancies by recruiting applicants from outside the organization. This external strategy would involve decisions about the use of recruitment sources such as employee referrals, advertisements, walk-ins, previous employees, public employment agencies, private employment agencies, educational institutions, and professional societies. An internal strategy would be to plan to fill vacancies by recruiting current employees from within the organization. This strategy assumes that the organization will have programs to publicize vacancies and identify qualified recruits.

The choice of strategy should depend on a number of considerations. The factors include the relative availability of qualified applicants outside and inside the organization, whether or not the vacancies will occur for *entry level* jobs (jobs that individuals from the external labor market are hired into), promotion from within policies, and the relative costs of external and internal recruitment. Importantly, forecasting makes it possible to have a choice of strategies and to plan implementation of the choice. Where forecasts are made on a subunit basis, it becomes possible to tailormake strategies to subunits. Thus, in some subunits "pure" external or internal strategies may be used, and in other subunits a combination of internal and external strategies may be most appropriate.

There is a major potential drawback, however, to the use of net personnel requirements as recruitment goals. Specifically, this may lead to a tendency to evaluate the subsequent effectiveness of the strategy solely on the basis of whether or not it produced the required number of applicants or new employees. If it did, the strategy is considered effective because the numerical goal was met. This may be particularly true in the case of external recruitment.

Unfortunately, this approach to recruitment effectiveness tends to overlook potentially more qualitative, long-run aspects of effectiveness. For example, consider the case of external recruitment sources. Might not the sources used have an impact on subsequent employee satisfaction, length of service, and job performance? In the first two instances, at least, there are some indications (discussed in the following section) that it might. In other words, how the organization recruits new employees may influence how they react to, and succeed in, the organization. There is thus a need to assess recruitment effectiveness on a number of different dimensions, both quantitative and qualitative.

INTRODUCTION TO READINGS

An Integrated Personnel Forecasting and Planning System

In the article by William Bright we find a description of a personnel forecasting and planning system that was developed at Union Oil for managerial and professional employees. As Bright notes, the basic motivation for developing the system was to help provide answers to many long-run human resource questions—questions that were not answerable through the company's existing personnel human resource activities. The system uses a five-year forecasting interval with annual updates. There are five major elements or programs in the system. Three of these deal with forecasting labor demand and internal labor supply, and the other two represent the strategic programs built around the forecasting results.

In terms of estimating internal labor supply, the company first developed an information system that assembled and permitted easy retrieval of necessary information about current employees. This is labeled the *Industrial Relations Information System* (IRIS). The information made available through this system serves as the basic input the *Organizational Change Model* (OCM). Though somewhat loosely stated, the model apparently does two things. First, on a subunit basis it catalogs current employees according to age, turnover rates, and replacement ratios (number of employees eligible to fill each vacancy that will occur among employees in the next highest age bracket). This information thus provides managers with a "snapshot" of the current personnel situation in their own, and other, subunits (see Bright's Exhibit 1). Second, the model is used for forecasting internal labor supply. The result is estimates of

"How many of what kinds of employees the organization will contain five years from now *if present experience, policies, and practices continue*" (emphasis added). In other words, the model is based on the assumption that past personnel movement patterns will continue into the future.

To forecast labor demand, the company developed the *Manpower Indicators Forecast* (MIF). Though the actual techniques are not described, the forecasts seem to be based on a large number of factors. Thus include output-per-employee trends (productivity), operating goals, product demand, and changes in corporate policy.

Through these demand and internal supply forecasts, the company is able to generate, five years in advance, what we previously called *net personnel requirements*. Bright indicates that these estimates serve as the primary basis for planning two major personnel human resource activities—employee recruitment, and managerial succession (promotion) and career development. The former is analogous to an external recruitment strategy and the latter to an internal recruitment and selection strategy. Bright describes the planning and operating of both programs in some detail. He also indicates some of the major problems encountered with the programs.

Recruitment Sources and Turnover

We already noted that organizations may use a number of sources of external recruits and suggested that there is a need to evaluate the effectiveness of these sources in a more qualitative, long-run sense than is often the case. Martin Gannon's study illustrates this by looking at the quit rates of employees recruited through different sources.

Gannon studied a bank in New York City that used seven sources of recruitment (referral in Gannon's terms). These were reemployed, referred by high school, referred by present employee, walk-ins, newspaper ads, major hiring agency, and other hiring agencies. For each source, the percentage of employees who quit within one year was computed; this was done over four successive years. Overall, the quit rates varied from 21.3 percent (reemployed) to 40.0 percent (major hiring agency). Further analysis showed that three of the sources consistently had significantly higher quit rates than the other four. Finally, Gannon computed a general estimate of the cost savings to the bank if they would not have used these three sources, and the savings are quite substantial.

Recognize, however, that it is difficult to explain why there were these consistent differences in quit rates among recruitment sources. In fact there is the possibility that the differences are not really due to the sources themselves, but to factors associated with their use. For example, younger applicants may have a tendency to use some sources more than others, and since younger employees typically have higher quit rates, the sources they used would naturally have higher quit rates. Likewise, certain jobs may have higher quit rates than other jobs, and it is possible that these jobs are typically filled by different recruitment sources. Again, this would make it appear as though the recruitment sources themselves were responsible for the differences in quit rates.

Regardless of the exact reasons for the differences in quit rates, Gannon's study is an excellent example of why it is desirable to evaluate the effectiveness of personnel/human resource activities. There is much to be learned, and possibly saved, by doing analyses of this sort.

Job Information and Recruitment Effectivness

Another explanation for Gannon's results (described in the previous section) is that recruitment sources may differ in the amount and/or realism of the information they provide applicants about the job and the organization. If applicants receive relatively little information, they will have little basis on which to make an informed choice of whether or not to accept a job offer. If they do accept it, the job may turn out to be not what they really "had in mind," and thus they may tend to leave the job rather quickly. Even if applicants receive a large amount of information, it may be quite unrealistic because the organization wants to present itself and the job in a favorable light. This may create unrealistic expectations which, if subsequently not fulfilled, will cause people to leave the job soon after taking it.

Some support for the realistic job information notion is provided in the article by John Wanous. Wanous first summarizes the little previous research (which found that realism reduces turnover). He also reports the results of an experimental study he conducted on how realistic job previews (RJPs) influenced newly employed telephone operators. Realism was varied by showing applicants one of two 15-minute films—the traditional film that was sometimes used by the company, and the RJP film that was specially constructed for the study. The similarities and differences between the films are described very thoroughly.

The major criterion of effectiveness was job survival—defined as still being on the job three months after hire. The survival rate for the RJP and traditional groups were 62 percent and 50 percent, respectively. Some other results were that the expectations of the RJP group were lower than the traditional group after seeing the film, and that the RJP group had higher satisfaction than the traditional group after three months on the job.

The results of the Wanous study and others he reviews lends fairly strong support to the organizational value of providing job applicants with accurate information about the jobs they will perform if hired. Interestingly, in the Wanous study, at least, it was found that realism had no impact on job acceptance rates (almost everyone in both groups accepted an offer). As Wanous notes, however, this result may be fairly unusual. Organizations may ordinarily expect that the price for the better survival rates occurring among recruits obtained with realistic job previews will be somewhat lower acceptance rates. Such a price seems small, however, compared to the alternative price of providing misleading information with resulting employee dissatisfaction and turnover.

9. HOW ONE COMPANY MANAGES ITS HUMAN RESOURCES

WILLIAM E. BRIGHT

A few years ago we were building a plant overseas. Planning its financing and construction had consumed months of executive time. Just one element was missing. No one had so much as raised the question of staffing.

When the issue finally did come up, the executive in charge seemed surprised. "We've got all the planning done," he said, "When the plant is built, we'll think about staffing."

To a human resource planner, that comment sounded disturbingly like, "When the horse has been stolen, we'll lock the barn door." By then, many of the employees best qualified for the new plant would have been assigned to other projects. To reassign and then replace them would disrupt other operations. Measurable costs would obviously be high. Solving the problem by too much hiring of new employees, for example, would increase the costs of training. The usually unmeasured costs—organizational effectiveness and the impact on employees' families, to name just two—would likely be higher still.

Fortunately, the executive in charge did reconsider his position. He decided to try to plan staffing carefully, and the benefits soon became evident. This experience helped to involve Union Oil in a deliberately inclusive approach to human resource planning. As the process matures and establishes credibility, it is joining financial and operations planning as an essential third dimension of our corporate one-, three-, five-, and ten-year planning.

For many years, we had been using some of the elements of human resource plan-

ning. We maintained replacement charts for upper echelons. Competitive pressures had led to our planning to recruit employees with professional or managerial potential. One-year staffing budgets were a well-established instrument of managerial planning and control.

There were many human resource questions, however, for which we had no answers:

Will the organization have the mix of talents, skills, maturity, and drive required to compete in the economic environment five years hence?

How many openings will occur among the top five echelons of the organization in the next few years? Will the replacements we appoint strengthen or weaken us—how do they compare with incumbents at parallel stages of their careers?

Are there places in the organization where managerial replacements are hard to find, and other places where once eager prospects are going to seed because positions above them are blocked?

When related to financial and operations planning and to outside economic events, what do our productivity trends tell about our manpower needs?

Does most of our recruiting occur in high-profit years when the level of starting-wage offers is high and the competition for good recruits is strongest?

Are our turnover costs under control, and where are they heading?

Are we keeping the employees with greatest career potential and weeding out marginal performers, or do our personnel policies, including wages and benefit plans, have greater appeal for employees who prefer security to the risks of growth and innovation?

Raising these and other related questions identified human resource planning as a frontier we needed to explore. That day began our search for concrete ways to understand and apply it.

So far, the search has led to the development of five programs:

1. Before Union Oil could mobilize its human resources effectively, we had to have ready access to our data. Hence, we first set up a comprehensive data bank that would store the information we had gathered.
2. Since both organizations and individuals change, we also needed a way to look into the future. We adopted a simulation model that would allow us to do this as well.
3. Moreover, we noted that erratic recruiting practices over the years had resulted in shortages of manpower in critical disciplines. The solution was to forecast our company-wide recruiting needs over a five-year period.
4. The next logical step was to put a succession planning system in place that would allow us to fill managerial openings up the line as they arose.
5. Finally, in order to tie all of these programs to the changing needs of the organization, we developed a method that allows us to relate output per employee to a reasonable range of operating goals.

I shall first discuss each of these five programs and then assess their impact on the Union Oil Company.

ASSEMBLING THE INFORMATION

While we had automated the organization's payroll, it did not provide ready access to the kind of information we sought. Past attempts to answer human resource questions through using payroll data had encountered long delays at the low-priority end of the systems department's request queue. If processing did occur, there were often costly programming charges, and the output seemed incomplete.

Research and visits to other companies indicated little that met the needs we had identified. We found that we needed more than the typical skills inventory. Many of the systems we surveyed had proved cumbersome and expensive to operate. Frequently their use had been discontinued. Then, as Russell Conwell described in his famous "Acres of Diamonds" address, we made the first major breakthrough in our own backyard.

One of our profit centers was successfully operating an automated inventory of employee information that met some of our requirements. When expanded and refined, it became a data base of vital organizational information. Its structure permits immediate retrieval of almost any desired item or combination of items of employee-related information. Nicknamed IRIS, for Industrial Relations Information System, the data base is quite different from many so-called skills inventories; yet, all of the information needed only amounts to two sides of one page for each employee.

IRIS can be thought of as a giant honeycomb containing over 600,000 individual items of factual, cross-referenced information about employees, information such as "John Doe has a bachelor's degree in chemical engineering," or "Fred Roe was manager of corporate accounting in 1959." IRIS also contains some information about employees' skills, career interests, and activities not related to their jobs, but the emphasis is on demonstrable fact versus what employees say about themselves.

How We Retrieve the Data

Crucial, however, to our human resource planning is the fact that each item of information has an "address" in the honeycomb where it can be located easily, an address as pragmatic as "the third floor conference room in the Honeycomb Motel, 2000 First Street, Valley Forge." IRIS retrieval programs thus use short-cut routes to specific items of information and display them in patterns useful to their seeker, whether a line manager or a staff member.

Each employee annually corrects and updates his IRIS profile, thus enabling Union Oil to fulfill one of the basic requirements of governmental "right-to-privacy" legislation, namely, that the data are correct. Operation of the data base meets other regulatory requirements as well. (Incidentally, the IRIS file is also useful for keeping management informed about other employee-relations matters, including equal employment opportunity, labor relations, employee benefit plans, employment, salary administration, and training.)

The millenium, however, is still on the horizon. We have, for example, encountered many problems in keeping the file accurate and current. We are constantly working to strengthen follow-up methods to ensure that new employees supply information on a timely basis and that old-timers correct and update their profiles on schedule. Sometimes the computer center is overloaded and retrieval searches must wait on higher priority matters. On occasion, the familiar systems gremlins go to work and produce erroneous reports. Our studies show, however, that nine-plus times in ten the file does what we want it to, accurately and on time. Without IRIS, human resource planning, as described here, would be economically impractical.

MODEL OF THE CHANGING ORGANIZATION

Thomas Wolfe wrote, "You can't go home again." You are different now and your home as you knew it no longer exists. Consider the magnitude of the problem from the point of view of an organization containing a few thousand employees, give or take a hundred, depending on the time of month and year. Today, one or two dozen will leave, and some of their replacements will be hired. Twenty-five to seventy-five will change assignments. Five hundred will learn new skills. Some segments of the organization will grow and others will inevitably decline. Next year those who remain will, of course, be one year older.

Earlier I compared the IRIS data base to a honeycomb, but under the magnifying glass an organization itself is not unlike an anthill. The workings of each are difficult to understand without a conceptual model.

In our human resource planning, we use a mathematical simulation called the organizational change model (OCM) to keep us current and help us identify potential problems. The model sorts the organizational anthill into age, function, geographical distribution, status, and skill categories, tracks newcomers and deserters, and recognizes both operational relationships and the aging process.

How the Model Works: Its Design

The model is based on the following three assumptions:

1. In a career-oriented organization, the age distribution of employees is roughly related to their years of service; thus we can categorize employees in five-year age groups.
2. The hiring rate for a given five-year age group within a particular segment of the organization is fairly constant.
3. Similarly, the attrition rate for a particular age group and segment can be assumed to be constant.

None of these assumptions is wholly true, of course. It is more accurate to say that these factors are sufficiently constant to be of value in human resource planning. For example, while attrition among pipeline engineers at Union Oil may decline by half between annual updates of the model, the proportion of this changing attrition that occurs among such engineers who are 25 through 29 years of age will remain about the same. A related assumption says that each year about one-fifth of the members in the 25–29 age group will move up into the next older age category. When they do, their attrition rate changes to a new constant for the older category. (Again, this is roughly true, and only because the model averages the attrition within each five-year category.)

Each annual update of the model is based primarily on experience in hiring and attrition during the previous year. The narrowness of this base is partially offset, however, by a formula in the model that draws together pairs of hiring and attrition rates that are abnormally divergent.

Powered by these and a host of similar assumptions about what goes on inside a career-oriented organization, the OCM is able to predict what the organization and all of its significant components will be like during the next five years. And, for several years when a new update has been compared with the old model's major trend predictions, they have fallen within a 5 percent, plus or minus, accuracy range—a figure which is adequate for planning purposes.

How It Aids the Manager: A Case Example

So much for the design of the model. What does it do for the division head who is concerned about improving his or her management of human resources?

Exhibit 1 is a report that highlights some of Union Oil's OCM findings. Companion summaries contain similar information about *trends*. Exhibit 1 presents just the *current* age distribution, turnover, and availability of degreed employees in divisions A, B, and C. As the exhibit shows, the report draws the manager's attention to anomalies within a particular division or age group. Turnover rates can be too low, indicating insufficient weeding-out, or too high, indicating excessive costs. High replacement ratios indicate blocking; low ones indicate a relative shortage of replacements. Parallel data for the whole company are shown for comparison.

Let's assume you are the president of division A. You can see that 125 of your 602 degreed employees are crowded into the 45–49 age group. Moving across the columns, you see divisions B and C, as well as the company, also have disproportionate

EXHIBIT 1
Organizational Change Model Summarized for Degreed Employees (in divisions A, B, C, and the company)

Ages	Age Distribution				Turnover Rates				Replacement Ratios*			
	A	B	C	Company Total	A	B	C	Company Total	A	B	C	Company Total
60–64	15	12	74	119	25%	27%	39%	34%	0	0	0	0
55–59	27	21	86	160	0	4	2	3	7	8	3	5
50–54	45	41	134	267	0	4	5	3	60	41	73	60
45–49	125	43	197	434	0	1	3	2	60	41	27	46
40–44	94	30	58	327	8	3	7	6	89	26	25	38
35–39	75	16	134	268	0	4	14	10	27	9	12	14
30–34	91	28	193	352	6	2	15	11	33	28	12	15
25–29	91	29	351	515	0	9	10	9	45	14	14	14
20–24	39	8	88	140	0	3	7	6	6	7	3	4
Totals ..	602	228	1,415	2,582	3	4	10	8	47	26	21	26
Percent past mid-career	42	56	39	43								

Note: The bold face figures indicate anomalies with respect to the division or the whole organization.
* To be read, "7 to 1" and "60 to 1," for example.

numbers of degreed employees who are in their early forties. Your situation, however, is worse than the others. You wonder about the morale of the 94 employees aged 40–44. Will the better ones among them be tempted to move to another company where their career paths are not blocked by so many older employees? Will others lose some of their effectiveness while waiting for promotions that are usually slow in coming? You decide to ask your staff to look into the matter and see what can be done.

Next you look at the middle section of the chart to see how your turnover rates compare with others. Your total turnover rate is the lowest of those listed, less than half that of the company as a whole. This is good from the standpoint of turnover costs, but not so good if viewed as a warning that you may not be weeding out marginal performers. Also, except for retirees, your highest turnover rate is in the 40–44 age bracket you have already decided to examine more closely. Are you losing the ones you want to lose, or are these the ones with superior career potential?

Finally, you check the replacement ratios section of the chart. The boldface figure in your column here is 89, read 89 to 1, which means that there are 89 employees aged 40–44 waiting to fill each opening that occurs among age 45–49 employees. It is the highest ratio on the whole chart. In fact, your total replacement ratio of 47 to 1 is highest among the divisions shown and almost twice that for the company as a whole.

You have seen studies that show that in career-oriented organizations, replacements are selected from employees who are in the next younger five-year age group— not always, of course, but most of them are. So your replacement ratios identify another organizational matter to investigate.

Are your employees staying so long in a particular position that their productivity falls off? Your turnover is low, so apparently waiting for promotions is not causing them to leave. Maybe reassignments are being made just when openings normally occur. You try to recall promotions made recently where openings were engineered to provide career development opportunities for employees with high career potential. The list is short. So your staff will take a closer look at this as well.

At the foot of Exhibit 1, you find some good news for a change. The percentage of your employees who are past midcareer (over 42 years of age) is in line with the company average. It is your associate who heads up division *B* who may well have a problem in this regard.

Forming the Decision: Policy Simulation

Exhibit 1 is just a sample of the kinds of information the OCM provides for the line manager. As noted earlier, other reports indicate trends, that is, whether problem situations will become better or worse during the next five years without management intervention. Still other reports show the executive how his segment of the organization compares with other segments in regard to: (1) all employees; (2) exempt employees (salaried employees not subject to regulations concerning overtime); (3) employees with critical skills (for example, chemical engineers); (4) minority employees; and (5) female employees.

For the executive who decides to act on the basis of information the OCM provides, there is a satellite model that allows him to simulate policy changes and study their outcomes. For example, if he wants to double his hiring of engineers aged 30–34, the satellite model can show him how this change will affect the total organization, as well as give him an estimate of the cost of such a change.

AVOIDING THE COSTS OF CYCLICAL RECRUITING

Our third major element in human resource planning is recruiting.

In the far Pacific there is at least one island society, that of the Melanesians, that has for centuries been a matriarchy. These Melanesians have one very busy day each year when every self-respecting uncle loads his canoe with provisions and delivers them to the often distant home of his sister's children in token of his support during the coming year. Observers say that the traffic resembles the traffic during rush hours on a California freeway.

In affluent years, a similar traffic jam occurs in the placement quarters of many American universities as the end of the school year approaches. When business profits decline, however, the number of industrial recruiters diminishes. The dollar rise in job offer levels is less than usual, and high caliber recruits are more readily available.

Establishing Policy

Some years ago, we at Union Oil decided to examine our recruiting practices. The age distribution of our professional employees contained gaps—some in critical disciplines —that suggested cyclical rather than consistent recruiting. At that time, the company's field divisions submitted requests for various kinds and numbers of recruits to the corporate manager of employment. The company's recruiting quota for the year was simply the sum of these field division requests.

Analysis confirmed that our recruiting had taken little account of replacement needs either in total or by fields of study. So we searched for some statistical series or combination of series that did at least correlate with the numbers of recruits secured in previous years. The best correlation occurred when a series combining annual earnings and capital expenditures was plotted with the number of professionals hired. We discovered that we were following a crowd of competitive recruiters to placement offices in the years when profits were high and cutting back on recruiting when they

were low. This meant, of course, that we were doing most of our recruiting in expensive years when high caliber recruits were hardest to employ.

Because the profit pinch had hit some company functions harder than others, our age distribution of educated skills was seriously out of balance. For example, Exhibit 2 shows complementary curves for the age distributions of two kinds of engineers that are both critical to Union Oil's operations. Most type B engineers were old, while type A were generally young. In the past, both types had supplied approximately equal numbers of executive replacements, but without deliberate intervention this situation seemed likely to change.

Judging from the curves, we decided to establish a five-year forecast of company-wide recruiting needs as the basis for future recruiting. We negotiate the hiring of needed recruits (as indicated by each annual update of the forecast) with the field divisions. Besides smoothing out cyclical recruiting and placing appropriate emphasis on replacement needs for critical disciplines, the forecast has had another sigficant value. It has helped persuade the field divisions to take the manpower needs of the corporate departments into account rather than simply to fill their own short-term requirements. Since most recruits are hired in the field and acquire experience there before moving up to corporate assignments, this has helped materially to maintain recruiting at a realistic level.

Correcting Practice

But our first low profit year under the forecast demonstrated once again that unlike "The Colonel's lady and Judy O'Grady," policy and practice are not always "sisters under the skin." Retrenchment in one of our most populous functions occurred, and so the field divisions reverted to previous practice; in some cases, where a 20 percent retrenchment occurred, recruiting was eliminated entirely. Naturally, it is difficult

EXHIBIT 2
Percentage Age Distributions, as of 1971, of Professional Employees

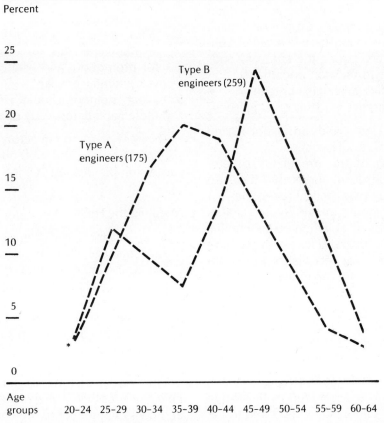

Percent

Type B engineers (259)

Type A engineers (175)

Age groups   20–24   25–29   30–34   35–39   40–44   45–49   50–54   55–59   60–64

* Age 20–24 estimated to within 75 percent accuracy.

to persuade field managers to recruit when they are having difficulty finding assignments for highly valued long-service employees.

Here the organizational change model came to our rescue. It reported a sudden rise in attrition rates among the organization's technical professionals, combined with a projected shortage in some of the most critical disciplines because of past cyclical recruiting. Appraised of this, top management took immediate action. Recruitment of employees with professional and managerial potential became an integral part of the company's one-year profit planning, in which variance from budgeted guidelines is reviewed at the fourth and seventh months by the executive committee. As a result,

our recruiting stays fairly close to forecast levels.

Forecast Recipe

Except to emphasize that it takes companywide replacement needs into account better, I have said little about the makeup of the recruiting forecast. Its preparation begins by using the organizational change model to determine the present and likely future complement of Union Oil's employees of professional and managerial potential—generally speaking, that is to say, our employees with formal education in scientific, engineering, and business disciplines. The OCM also provides estimated attrition rates. Next we mesh these data with a forecast of the company's human resource needs, still to be described, that relates output-per-employee trends to the company's long-term operating goals by major function (marketing, for example). Corporate department and other administrative needs are determinied by comparing the ratio of trends at these levels to those in operations.

There are five other elements in the recruiting forecast design. They encompass:

1. The need to avoid professional and managerial obsolescence.
2. Correction of the irregularity of employee age distributions that have resulted from past cyclical recruiting.
3. Variance in the capability (and, alas, willingness) of at different geographic locations (San Francisco seems to have more appeal for recruits than Detroit).
4. Variance in the capability (and, alas, willingness) of the field divisions to take companywide recruiting needs into account.
5. Trends in the availability of recruits from various disciplines.

Finally, the results of recruiting efforts in the past few years are added to the recipe and a kind of hunter's stew is offered to the organization. The metaphor is deliberate since the companywide recruiting forecast has proved nourishing to the organization, but not necessarily appetizing.

PLANNING FOR SUCCESSION

Without a sound succession planning process, the other elements in human resource planning would be of little avail. Even as we move toward industrial democracy in the wake of European experiments in participative management, someone probably should steer the ship. Perhaps someone should even drop anchor short of the completely democratic state. We may not yet be ready for the completely democratic industrial organization.

While traditional lines of authority at Union Oil do prevail, there are three basic questions that succession planning has to answer:

1. How many managers will we need at given points in time?
2. Who are our most promising managerial candidates, how ready are they for promotion, and what are their developmental needs?
3. What methods should we use to get these candidates ready on time?

The AIM program (an acronym for analysis, identification, and methodology) is our succession planning element.

Manning the Helm

In an organization where a majority of topside managers are (or were) engineers, it has sometimes seemed that managers communicate even more clearly in numbers than in words. It may have been because of this that we secured better attention to the importance of succession planning outside the division where it began by quantifying the dimensions of the tasks.

Our managerial needs forecast (MNF) now performs this service for each corporate and divisional officer of the company; individual units of the forecast are consolidated for officers to whom other officers report and for the organization as a whole. In all, the forecast covers about 500 positions.

We supply a two-page unit forecast annually to each unit head. Page one predicts the number of openings to occur in the next five years. It also compares 20 percent of the previous year's prediction with the number of openings that actually occurred. Page two contains a list of the members of the manager's unit, with asterisks placed after the names of those who will reach the company's average retirement age of 62 within the forecast period.

The forecasting method is actuarial. Each prediction is the sum of the likely retirees, a historically based estimate of separations for other causes, and an estimate of openings to result from the unit's supplying managers to other segments of the organization. In forecasting, of course, it pays to be lucky as well as to do your homework. In our first five years of annual updates, the number of openings predicted was 355, while 358 openings actually occurred. Accuracy has varied with population size, of course, but even for small units the predictions have been accurate enough to establish credibility.

Setting the Direction

What is important, however, is not the makeup or accuracy of the forecast, but how it is used. When the corporate or divisional officer receives his managerial needs forecast each year, he discusses it in detail with his employee relations staff head. Together they customize the forecast's findings, adding what they know of their own intent that will affect the planning. The customized forecast becomes the basis for their succession planning.

Once the number of managers needed is known, the AIM succession planning process puts planning in the hands of the people most responsible for each segment of the organization. Take marketing as an example. The AIM planning group consists of the vice president of marketing and refining; the vice president of marketing; the general manager of divisional sales; the six field division sales managers; and the manager of industrial relations for marketing and refining.

This group of ten meets for a half-day each quarter to plan succession toward the field division sales managers' position, the "apex" position toward which they have elected to plan.

They take into account their intimate knowledge of the field division sales manager's job (most having held it themselves), along with their personal knowledge of subordinates and annual employee appraisals, IRIS profiles, and quota performance information. Their purpose is to single out only those employees who have the potential to become a field division sales manager. Once identified, the succession candidates are placed in a time frame, ranging up to ten years, on the basis of their current readiness to assume the apex position. (Typically, about 15 percent–20 percent of the salaried group in question will be candidates.)

If a candidate is not "ready now," the next step is to find out what he or she needs to become ready. Whatever the candidate needs is written down on the AIM spread sheet, with deadlines for action specifically prescribed. This becomes the candidate's individual development plan. It is the responsibility of his manager to see that the development plan is carried out.

The planning spread sheet must reflect organizational circumstances that change, interim changes in the evaluation of candidates' potential, developmental actions that have taken place, and new candidates as their performance demands recognition. In a typical year, most of the entries on the spread sheet will change.

Ensuring a Straight Course

I have, of course, greatly simplified my explanation of a complex succession planning process. There are other elements that deserve mention because they characterize the effective application of that process or are hazards in its use.

First, these are a few of the criteria that were involved in success:

Apex positions toward which succession planning is done must be high enough in status to deserve executive attention and involve candidates of above average career potential; ideally, the apex position should be one with more than one incumbent, and apex positions should include key staff assignments as well as line positions.

The role of the planners in the AIM group should combine those of an interested observer, a resource person, and occasionally a referee; the present holders of the apex position should be the active planners.

The employee relations staff man must be a resource person, an asker of challenging questions, a consultant and recordkeeper who makes sure meetings are arranged on schedule and that all the required employee information is at hand (not just on marketing employees, for instance, but for others who have the necessary qualifications as well).

Except in rare instances, the vice president must be guided by the spread sheet in making his placement decisions; this applies not just in promotions to the apex position, but also to lower-echelon reassignments needed as developmental experience for succession candidates.

There are, however, a number of hazards in using an AIM approach to the planning of succession and related career development:

AIM succession planning seems to work best below the corporate officer level in the organization; at the top, succession plans must include both complex and highly personal elements.

The approach must be strongly supported by executive review with occasional intervention to prevent divisional inbreeding and to move candidates with the potential to become corporate officers from one division to another.

Since the results are officially top secret and thus fair game for the grapevine's distortions, the equity of the AIM process needs to be understood throughout the organization. Employees need to know that the system is open and flexible, that it responds to the demonstration of individual merit and potential.

Like most continuous processes, this planning must occasionally be spiced

with new evaluation techniques and other variety; devices to implement paired comparison of candidates, situational evaluation, and managerial style analysis are examples.

And, finally, the highest ranking AIM planner must be alert to generic changes in the organization or its environment that will alter the profile of an apex position in ways beyond the ken of lower-ranking members of the planning group; otherwise, they may select candidates who are qualified for an apex position that in effect will no longer exist.

By attending to these precautions, we have seen the AIM process serve the most populous segments of our organization effectively for several years. It is not uniformly applied where used, nor is it used in all parts of the organization, but its use is improving and expanding each year.

RELATING OUTPUT TO GOALS

So far, I have described four basic elements of human resource planning: (1) accumulating the necessary information, (2) using the organizational change model, (3) forecasting recruitment needs, and (4) planning managerial succession and career development.

Human resource planning, however, cannot be done in a vacuum. The organizational change model predicts how many of what kinds of employees the organization will contain five years from now if present experience, policies, and practices continue. Quite apart from this, however, does the OCM imply that the predicted size and configuration of the workforce are optimal? Since the answer is obviously no, there is another dimension that needs to be recognized: this is done through what we call a manpower indicators forecast (MIF). MIF predicts the organization's optimal future size and configuration by:

1. Relating output-per-employee trends to

operating goals in the company's major functions.

2. Using these and other trends to determine the size of the administrative group.
3. Weighing the organizational impact of significant internal statistical and external economic data, such as a distinctive turnover rate for one segment of employees or an unusual shift in consumer demand for a product.
4. Adjusting to anticipated major changes in corporate policy.
5. Providing for anticipated changes in the company's external environment (for example, increased governmental regulation).

As in the case of the organizational change model, a mathematical model is used to prepare the managerial indicators forecast. Multiple regression analysis helps to determine the mix and weighting of the statistical and economic data series employed. These vary from year to year, but the company's capital expenditures and country's gross national product are usually among them. The driving force behind the MIF model, however, is the relationship between functional output-per-employee trends and the company's operating goals.

For example, suppose marketing has five-year operating goals lower than its current volume, and no major shift in marketing policies is likely. Assume too that the output per employee in marketing is rising. Then fewer marketing employees will be needed five years from now. (Output per marketing employee is measured in barrels of sales per day adjusted for a number of factors; crude oil input to refineries and crude oil production, similarly adjusted, are other functional output measures.)

In 1972, our first MIF predicted that the number of Union Oil's marketing employees would decline about 15 percent during the next five years. This was difficult for marketing management to accept at a time when product demand seemed likely to rise forever. But the international oil crisis and related events had in fact caused our 1972 forecast to err in the direction of optimism: between 1972 and 1975, the marketing force actually declined by 25 percent. (The 1975 update of the forecast indicates a further decline of 15 percent by the end of 1979.)

It would be pleasant to claim that the manpower indicators forecast predicted and therefore led to a logical marketing retrenchment—normal attrition rather than mass layoffs. What actually happened was analogous to the fable about the dog who barked up the sun each morning. Management independently recognized the folly of expanding the sales volume of an increasingly scarce and costly commodity, and as a matter of policy began in 1972 to set more modest five-year operating goals. As subsequent events confirmed its wisdom, goals were further reduced and the MIF simply called timely attention to the need for reducing the number of marketing employees.

Among other services the forecast has performed are (1) recognizing early a need to shift domestic exploration and production employees into foreign operations and (2) calling attention to a rising ratio of administrative to operating employees that is only partly caused by the increasing amount of government regulation.

IMPACT ON CORPORATE PLANNING

Used independently, these five instruments of human resource planning supplied useful information to the management and staff of Union Oil's departments and divisions. When they saw major storm signals, it was possible to get an audience with the executive committee, one that usually resulted in appropriate remedial action. The previously mentioned tying-in of the recruiting forecast to corporate budget reviews is an example.

Human resource planning did not begin to approach its optimal impact upon the organization, however, until it came to be thought of as another dimension of corporate planning.

Our first formal step in this adoption process was to add a chapter on human resources to the written corporate strategic and tactical plans. Each year we search the sociopolitical, economic, and industrial organization literature for environmental trends, study our findings on the five elements of human resource planning, individually and as a whole, and hold discussions with the corporate and divisional industrial relations staff. Where appropriate, the treatment of an urgent issue is extended to include possible courses of action, likely outcomes, and a specific action proposal. Where approved, such action is subject to regular executive review and control procedures.

The keystone in the integration of human resource planning with overall corporate planning has just recently been put in place. The executive committee has begun to review regularly (1) the major divisions' planning of succession and career development and (2) their performance in the management of human resources. The first such formal review has set a sound and well-received pattern for others to follow.

Trouble Spots

Yet, we have identified defects. It is not surprising that there are large elements of subjectivity and intuition in human resource planning, and that therefore many of our managers have taken issue with the degree to which we have quantified our planning. The useful reaction, and fortunately its incidence increases as managers become more used to working with the program, is that human resource predictions, while helpful, need to be taken with the proverbial grain of salt. Thus a generous rounding off of the numbers arrived at has helped to secure a more appropriate reaction; various cautionary footnotes to forecasts have also seemed to help.

A related problem exists in the *techniques* we have used. Many of these techniques are relatively new and untested. Much of the quantitative data available to other kinds of corporate planning are yet to be developed and integrated into the organization's other accounting procedures. Despite numerous attempts, for example, no widely accepted way has yet been found to place a meaningful dollar value on an employee's service to the organization. Attempting to cost out the probable impact of a human resource decision can occasion more than enough "puzzlement" to tax the patience of a King of Siam. And here the scenario and Delphi methods of prediction occasionally have proved useful.

More specifically, some elements of the instruments we have used in human resource planning are measurably weaker than others:

Maintaining a reliable inventory of employee skills in the IRIS data base continues to present many problems.

The organizational change model is driven by an algorithm in which many of the assumptions need further testing and refinement.

The companywide forecast of professional and managerial recruiting needs makes only a token adjustment to evolving environmental trends.

The AIM approach to the planning of succession and career development undoubtedly errs in the direction of perpetuating the profile of the presently effective manager. Consensus evaluation of career potential may also favor the candidate whose personality corners are smoothed at the expense of the irritating genius and the entrepreneur.

The manpower indicators forecast is relatively new; it is still too early for us to be confident in separating coincidence from cause and effect or even, in all instances, in distinguishing between cause and effect.

What We See as Standout Values

Remember the overseas plant we were building a few pages ago? "We have done the financial and facilities planning," the manager said, "When the plant is built, we'll think about staffing."

Well, today that order of events would be reversed, or more accurately, the planning of human resources would be incorporated into the total planning process.

Years ago, a friend who worked for a meat-packing company was telling me some of his problems. "I wish," he said, "that I I could get my management to be as concerned about inventorying employees as they are about inventorying pickled pigs feet." Our IRIS file of employee information has taken us well past that aromatic point. We now know as much about human as other resources. Current information about human resources flows regularly throughout the line and staff organization, and increasingly it receives appropriate implementation.

Spotting potentially troublesome trends in the organization in their early stages has helped to avoid the costs of emergency action. An organization is controlled somewhat like a great supertanker. The captain signals, "Stop," the screws are reversed, and ten miles later the motion of the ship is arrested. If you drop anchor suddenly; you may lose it. Planning your human resources carefully will measurably reduce the possibility of losing that anchor.

10. SOURCES OF REFERRAL AND EMPLOYEE TURNOVER

MARTIN J. GANNON

One of the persistent theoretical and practical problems facing industrial psychologists is employee turnover. The literature on this problem stresses a variety of predictors such as age, relations with supervisors, and interest tests (Schuh 1967; Vroom 1964). One possible explanation of employee turnover may be the sources from which employees are drawn. In this regard, previous published research has primarily delineated sources of referral or recruiting patterns without relating them to employee turnover. For example, Mandell (1956) shows that companies with 500 or fewer employees tend to favor employment agencies while larger firms generally have recourse to newspaper advertisements (Mandell 1956; Malm 1954).

Source: *Journal of Applied Psychology* 1971, vol 55, no. 3, 226–28. Copyright 1971 by the American Psychological Association. Reprinted by permission.

The objective of this article is to test the hypothesis that recruiting patterns or sources of referral are predictive of employee turnover. If the hypothesis is valid, it should be possible to eliminate unstable employees even before the application of interest and psychological tests through the use of particular sources of referral.

METHOD

The personnel department of a New York bank has been studying the problem of employee referral for several years; the data presented in this article have been supplied by this bank. This department categorizes their seven sources of referral as follows: (a) The employee saw an advertisement for work in a newspaper. (b) The employee was hired by the major hiring agency under contract with the bank. (c) The employee was hired by hiring agencies other than the major one under contract with the bank. (d) The employee was referred to the bank by a present employee. (e) The employee has been reemployed after a period of time away from the job. (f) The employee was referred by his high school. and (g) The employee came to the bank through some other method, mainly by walking into the personnel office and asking for work. For each source of referral, the bank then develops a quit rate, that is, the number of employees hired through a particular source within a specific year divided into the number of employees from that source who were hired but quit within that year. Thus, the quit rates can be compared in order to discover the best and worst sources of referral.

In order to ascertain if the differences in the quit rates were significant, 2 × 2 tables were constructed, the rows of which were two sources of referral and the columns of which were the number of employees not quitting and the number who quit. Chi-square was then used to test the significance of the differences (see Table 2).

RESULTS

Four years are investigated: 1961–64. In Table 1, the quit rates for each of the seven sources of referral are presented. A total of 6,390 employees were hired during this period, and 1,934 terminated before completing their first year of service with the bank.

TABLE 1
Percentage Quit Rate by Source of Referral: 1961–1964

Source of Referral	No. Hired	No. Quit	Percent Quit
Reemployed	253	54	21.3
Referred by high school	602	131	21.8
Referred by present employees	2320	615	26.5
Others (mainly walk-ins)	1212	349	28.8
Hiring agencies except "major"	637	241	37.8
Newspaper advertising ..	512	202	39.4
Major hiring agency	854	342	40.0
Total	6390	1934	

As shown in Table 1, the quit rates range from a low of 21.3 percent for employees who were reemployed to a high of 40.0 per-

TABLE 2
Matrix of Chi-Square Values Showing the Association between the Sources of Referral

Source of Referral	Reemployed	Lower Quit Rates[a]			Higher Quit Rates[b]		
		Referred by High School	Referred by Present Employees	Others (Mainly Walk-Ins)	Hiring Agencies except "Major"	Newspaper Advertising	Major Hiring Agency
Reemployed		.04	3.40	6.14***	22.83*	25.57*	30.46*
Referred by high school			5.67***	10.23**	38.06*	41.33*	53.83*
Referred by present employees ..				2.10	31.16*	34.24*	54.32*
Others (mainly walk-ins)					15.70*	18.80*	28.49*
Hiring agencies except "major"						.31	.75
Newspaper advertising							.05
Major hiring agency ...							

[a] 21.3%–28.8%.
[b] 37.8%–40.0%.
* $p \leq .001$.
** $p \leq .01$.
*** $p \leq .05$.

cent for employees who came to the bank through the major hiring agency. Table 2 is a matrix of chi-square values showing the association between the sources of referral. Clear and significant differences between the sources of referral were discovered. Thus, four sources of referral were uniformly and significantly different from three other sources of referral ($p \leq .001$). The four sources are the reemployment of former workers of the bank, the hiring of individuals referred by their high schools, the hiring of individuals referred by present employees, and others (primarily walk-ins). These four sources of referral have low quit rates ranging from 21.3 percent to 28.8 percent and can be considered as suppliers of stable employees. Conversely, the three sources of referral which have quit rates ranging from 37.8 percent to 40.0 percent can be viewed as suppliers of unstable employees. These three sources are the employment of individuals who come to the bank through the major hiring agency, the employment of individuals who come because of newspaper advertising, and the employment of individuals who are contacted through hiring agencies other than the major one.

There are no significant within-group differences for the three poor sources of referral. However, within the group of good sources there are three significant differences. "Others, mainly walk-ins" is a poorer method for recruiting employees than reemployment ($p \leq .05$) or recommendations by high school administrators ($p \leq .01$), although it does not significantly differ from recommendations by fellow employees. Reference by present employees is a poorer source than recommendations by high school administrators ($p \leq .05$).

The final methodological point of importance concerns the stability of quit rates for each method over time. In the analysis thus far the total figures for the period 1961–64 have been presented. It is entirely possible that a particular recruiting method is characterized by a low quit rate one year but a high quite rate the next. Such inconsistencies would tend to undermine the analysis. However, as shown in Table 3, there are no inconsistencies when the quit rates are analyzed by year. In this table the quit rates for each year have been converted to ranks. In each year the three poor methods of recruitment uniformly have higher quit rates than the four good methods of recruitment. While there are some differences within groups—for example, newspapers ranked seventh in 1961 but sixth in 1962—there are no exceptions when the two groups of good and poor recruiting methods are compared.

TABLE 3
Conversion of the Quit Rates for Each Recruiting Method to Ranks for Each Year

Recruiting Method	Ranked Data			
	1961	1962	1963	1964
Newspapers	7	6	5	5
Major hiring agency	6	7	7	—[a]
Other agencies	5	5	6	—[a]
Referred by fellow employee ..	3	2	2	3
Reemployed	1	1	3	2
Referred by high school	2	4	1	1
Others (mainly walk-ins)	4	3	4	4

[a] No employees were hired through these sources in 1964.

DISCUSSION

Even before an employee approaches a firm in order to fill out the application form, it is possible to improve the selection process by utilizing some sources of referral rather than others. This study has demonstrated that four sources of referral are predictive of stable employees, namely, the reemployment of former workers of the bank, the hiring of individuals referred by their high schools, the hiring of individuals referred by present employees, and others (primarily walk-ins). However, three sources of referral are predictive of unstable employees, namely, the use of hiring agencies other than the major one, newspaper advertisements, and the major hiring agency.

The practical significance of this study is relevant for many firms. There has been some research into the cost of hiring and training new employees (see Canfield 1959; Gaudet 1958; and McManemin 1960). A conservative estimate of such costs is $1,000 per employee. The significant difference in the quit rates for the seven sources is 9.0 percent, since the two groups of sources identified as good and poor in reference to employee turnover are divided into their respective components by "others (mainly walk-ins)" (28.8 percent) and "hiring agencies other than the major one" (37.8 percent). In the four years under examination, approximately 2,000 employees left the bank without completing their first year of employment. Given a quit rate of 9 per 100 that could have been avoided if the three poor sources had not been used, the total cost to the bank is $180,000 (9 × 20 × $1,000).

This analysis assumes that enough employees could be gathered through the four good sources of referral. In a tight labor market, such an assumption may be unrealistic. However, the analysis does suggest that, even if a firm were to spend $40,000 or $50,000 in increasing the number of individuals hired through the four good sources rather than through the three poor sources, the investment would probably be a good one.

Although further research into the sources of referral is necessary so that the demographic and attitudinal characteristics of these workers can be assessed, the present analysis indicates that a substantial proportion of employee turnover can be eliminated through the judicious use of various procedures for attracting employees.

REFERENCES

Canfield, G. "How to Compute Your Labor Turnover Costs." *Personnel Journal* 37 (1959): 413–17.

Gaudet, F. "What Top Management Doesn't Know About Turnover." *Personnel* 34 (1958): 54–59.

Malm, F. "Recruiting Patterns and the Functioning of Labor Markets." *Industrial and Labor Relations Review* 7 (1954): 507–25.

Mandell, M. *Recruiting and Selecting Office Employees.* New York: American Management Association, 1956.

McManemin, J. "A Practical Method of Calculating Turnover Cost." *Personnel* 37 (1960): 73–77.

Schuh, A. "The Predictability of Employee Tenure: A Review of the Literature." *Personnel Psychology* 20 (1967): 133–52.

Vroom, V. *Work and Motivation.* New York: Wiley, 1964.

11. TELL IT LIKE IT IS AT REALISTIC JOB PREVIEWS

JOHN P. WANOUS

In analyzing the recruitment process, industrial psychologists traditionally have focused attention on how companies select new employees. More recently, however,

Source: Reprinted by permission of the publisher from *Personnel*, July–August 1975, © 1975 by AMACOM, a division of American Management Association.

organizational behaviorists have taken a hard look at how applicants choose one organization over others, and old assumptions about how new employees should be recruited are being questioned.

The traditional approach to recruitment and selection views the applicant as passive rather than active. An individual is typically selected for a job on the basis of tests, interviews, and background information. Almost completely ignored in the process is the organizational choice made by the applicant—how and why he showed up in the first place. To obtain a favorable selection ratio—that is, a large number of applications in relation to the number of job openings—companies sometimes present themselves to potential new employees in a more favorable light than the facts justify. In the end, this kind of policy can produce dysfunctional results, costly to both the organization and the employee.

Recent research suggests, however, that recruitment can be made more effective through the use of *realistic job previews* (RJPs), an atypical, untraditional approach that stresses efforts to communicate—before an applicant's acceptance of a job offer—what organizational life will actually be like on the job. A study conducted by the author at Southern New England Telephone Company and related research by others at Prudential Insurance Company, the U.S. Military Academy, and Texas Instruments utilized the RJP approach to recruitment. Major findings from these studies show:

> Newly hired employees who received realistic job previews have greater job survival than those hired by traditional recruiting methods.
>
> Employees hired after RJPs indicate higher job satisfaction.
>
> An RJP can "set" the job expectations of new employees at realistic levels.
>
> RJPs do not reduce the flow of highly capable applicants.

WHY TRADITIONAL RECRUITMENT PRACTICES NEED REEXAMINATION

Traditional recruitment practice is characterized by its emphasis on having the organization "look good" to potential employees, usually to attract a large pool of job applicants so that a cream-of-the-crop selection may be made.

In selecting employees, most organizations try to match individual and organization. This usually means selection of those who the employer predicts will be good *performers*. Selection according to who also will be a good risk on turnover or absenteeism is sometimes considered, but this factor typically plays second fiddle to selection based on job performance predictions.

This approach deserves reexamination, however, because it has hidden costs and because of laws now controlling personnel selection and recruitment.

1. Emphasis on expected job performance as the dominant—almost exclusive— criterion in selection overlooks possible turnover costs resulting from mismatches between the employee and the organization. The forces influencing performance on the job and those influencing an individual to remain on the job have important distinctions. Job performance generally is considered to be influenced by an individual's abilities and his motivation, that is, his need to achieve. On the other hand, a person's tendency to remain in the organization is seen as a result of that person's need fulfillment, for example, satisfying his need for security, and resulting job satisfaction.

2. In most organizations highest turnover occurs among newly hired employees— those in their first six months on the job. Employees new to the job and organization have a higher turnover rate than those with more experience in the organization because they may simply be "testing out" the new environment to see if it suits their particular needs. And their "test" may be necessitated by the company's practice of overselling the attractiveness of jobs during the recruitment process.

Much research, spanning 40 years or more, shows that the higher the job satisfaction, the lower the turnover. But the relationship between job satisfaction and job performance is much less clearly understood and has been the focus of controversy over the years among both researchers and theorists in the field.

Selecting new employees on the basis of performance criteria thus will not necessarily result in long-tenure employees. In fact, it is not unusual to find that the best job performers are high-turnover employees because of the thrust of their upward mobility internally or in other organizations.

Careful attention must be paid, therefore, to the results desired in organizational recruitment and selection. For example, companies risk increased turnover problems if they elect to:

Select new employees exclusively in terms of the company's interests rather than in terms of the balanced interests of both the company and the employee.

Present the organization in overly attractive terms to encourage people to apply for jobs.

Select new employees only on the basis of matching limited performance requirements to individual capabilities rather than on the basis of both performance and satisfaction requirements and capabilities.

Companies that cannot shift their personnel policies to recognize the interests of their employees may face personnel costs stemming from high turnover caused by mismatches between an individual's desires for human need satisfaction and the organization's capacity to fulfill these needs.

THE RJP: WHAT IS IT AND HOW DOES IT WORK?

A realistic job preview should be given to an applicant before the job offer has been accepted. It should try to communicate important information to the potential employee—especially information that is closely tied to employee satisfactions and dissatisfactions.

But just what is "reality," and how can it be designed into a job preview?

It must be understood than an RJP is not an indictment of a particular job nor does it exclude positive information. An RJP must be balanced to include important facets of a particular job (and the organization) that the typical employee experiences as satisfying and those that are commonly dissatisfying. The final balance between positive and negative characteristics will vary, depending on the nature of the job in question. Figure 1 illustrates RJP logic and the rationale underlying the research findings.

Impact of the Traditional Approach. The traditional job preview is not a homogeneous procedure. Organizations recruit new

FIGURE 1
Typical Consequences of Job Preview Procedures

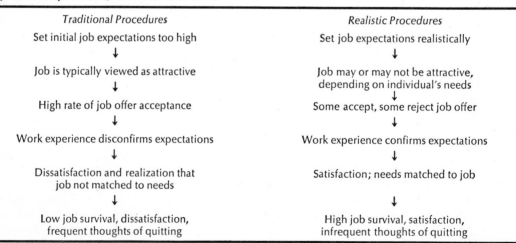

Traditional Procedures	Realistic Procedures
Set initial job expectations too high	Set job expectations realistically
↓	↓
Job is typically viewed as attractive	Job may or may not be attractive, depending on individual's needs
↓	↓
High rate of job offer acceptance	Some accept, some reject job offer
↓	↓
Work experience disconfirms expectations	Work experience confirms expectations
↓	↓
Dissatisfaction and realization that job not matched to needs	Satisfaction; needs matched to job
↓	↓
Low job survival, dissatisfaction, frequent thoughts of quitting	High job survival, satisfaction, infrequent thoughts of quitting

employees in a variety of ways, ranging from systematic attempts to "sell" the organization to the individual (via advertising techniques) to informal, unsystematic distribution of information given in the course of testing, interviewing, and selecting. Although there are wide degrees of conscious intent to sell an organization and widely varying methods for doing so, there is the common thread that an organization almost always presents itself attractively to outsiders who may become new employees.

Thus it often turns out that recruits have unrealistic initial expectations of what the job and the company are like. If these expectations, unrealistic as they may be, approach the recruit's personal preferences or desires, he is likely to conclude that the organization is an attractive place to work.

But what happens after a period of on-the-job experience? Typical reactions are disappointment and dissatisfaction because the initial expectations have not been realized. The employee probably will conclude the job is really not matched to his needs, and since this mismatch was not discovered until after work began, there is a good chance he may quit—or if the labor market is tight, he may stay on the job as a dissatisfied worker, think often about quitting, and be absent often.

Impact of a Realistic Preview. An RJP also "sets" the initial expectations of recruits, but in this case they are realistic expectations. To avoid pitfalls of the traditional preview, an RJP provides important job information—both positive and negative—completely and without bias. Thus when an individual compares his realistic expectations about the job and organization to his own desires, an appropriate organizational choice (or self-selection) can be made.

If the RJP has an impact on the individual's organizational choice, then those who actually go to work will tend to be better matched to the new environment than those recruited via the traditional procedure. This

combination of "innoculating" the individual against disappointment and the more effective organizational choices typically results in greater job survival, higher job satisfaction, and fewer thoughts of quitting.

AN EXPERIMENT: RJP VERSUS THE TRADITIONAL

The author's study of RJP versus the traditional job preview involved a sample of about 80 female telephone operators at several employment offices of Southern New England Telephone Company.

Prior to the study, which covered a period of about nine months, the overall turnover rate for operators varied between 30 and 40 percent per year. But for operators in their first six months on the job, the rate often rose to 100 percent or higher.

To compare the effects of the two contrasting job preview approaches, the previews were presented to job candidates in the form of 15-minute films shown on portable units in each employment office. Figure 2 shows the sequence of events in this experiment for each job preview approach as well as the typical sequence used prior to the experiment. Applicants were assigned at random to the preview groups.

The operator applicants also were asked to complete several questionnaires designed (1) to measure the impact of each preview on *initial expectations,* (2) to obtain a measurement of each individual's own *job preferences,* and (3) to assess *on-the-job satisfaction* and thoughts of quitting after some work experience.

The traditional preview film used in the experiment existed prior to the study. Dealing with the operator's job, it had been used in high school recruiting and in several other ways, but it never had been systematically applied as a job preview for all candidates on a regular basis.

Figure 3 shows some of the major differences between the preview films, but as a chart, it captures only part of the "flavor" of the sequences. Subjective impressions of

FIGURE 2
Selection Procedures for Operators

Preexperiment	Realistic Experiment	Traditional Experiment
Receptionist	Receptionist	Receptionist
Initial interview	Initial interview	Initial interview
	Questionnaire 1	Questionnaire 1
Testing, medical questionnaire	Testing, medical questionnaire	Testing, medical questionnaire
Application blank	Application blank	Application blank
Selection interview	Selection interview	Selection interview
	Realistic film	Traditional film
	Questionnaire 2	Questionnaire 2
Job visit	Job visit	Job visit
Training	Training	Training
Work experience	Work—1 month: Questionnaire 3	Work–1 month: Questionnaire 3
	Work—3 months: Questionnaire 4	Work–3 months: Questionnaire 4

company managers and colleagues of the author indicate that this RJP was about 60–40 negative in balance. Compared to the traditional preview film, this was quite a difference.

FIGURE 3
Job Characteristics Emphasized by Each Job Preview Film

Overlap between films

1. Customers can be quite unfriendly at times
2. Work is fast paced
3. Some operators receive satisfaction from helping out customers
4. Action sequences of operators at work:
   a. Emergency call
   b. "Wise guy" calling operator
   c. Credit card call
   d. Overseas call
   e. Directory assistance operators at work
   f. "Nasty" customer calling operator
5. Dealing with others (customers, co-workers) is a large part of the job

Nonoverlap characteristics

Realistic film

1. Lack of variety
2. Job is routine; may become boring
3. Close supervision; little freedom
4. Limited opportunity to make friends
5. Receive criticism for bad performance, but no praise when deserved
6. Challenging initially, but once learned is easy and not challenging

Traditional film

1. Everyone seems happy at work
2. Exciting work
3. Important work
4. Challenging work

WHAT THE STUDY SHOWED

In terms of "job survival" (being on the job three months after starting to work), 62 percent of the realistic group of newly hired operators survived compared to 50 percent of the traditional group. This was similar to other research studies of the RJP concept.

For example, the first study of life insurance agents found a difference of 68 percent survival for the realistic group compared to 53 percent for the traditional after a period of five months. In a second study the difference was 71 percent versus 57 percent survival over a six-month period.

The original West Point study found that 91 percent of the first-year cadets survived who received a realistic booklet before choosing to accept the appointment. Of those who received the traditional material from West Point, 86 percent survived the first year. A second West Point study analyzed the effects of an RJP booklet on voluntary resignations during the summer training period prior to the first year at West Point. Of those receiving the RJP, 94 percent survived as compared to only 88.5 percent of a control group, which had no such preview.

The study at Texas Instruments was not a job preview but an on-the-job first day indoctrination and did not report job survival data. But, in every case, to my knowledge, the RJP has increased job survival over traditional methods of recruitment.

In addition to higher job survival rates, members of the realistic group in the telephone study indicated higher job satisfaction after three months on the job and had thought much less about quitting after one month. The basis for these attitudes appears to be in the gap between expectations created by the traditional preview and the reality of being an operator.

Figure 4 charts a typical attitude pattern that emphasizes the sharp contrast between preview expectations and on-the-job reality for traditional and realistic groups.

Along with assessing the impact of an RJP on end-result variables, it was important to understand why an RJP "works." The questionnaire administered *before* job previews measured "naive initial job expectations," but the results of the post-preview questionnaire showed clearly that the expecta-

tions of those who received the traditional preview were raised, and the expectations of the RJP group were significantly lowered. For example, a sampling of the questionnaire tabulations shows that expectations particularly affected by RJPs included:

Receiving praise for doing a good job.

Having freedom to use one's own judgment.

Making use of one's abilities and using one's own methods.

Feelings of accomplishment from the job.

Whether supervisors handle employees well.

The preview films did not touch all facets of the operator's job, just some of the most important. Thus some questions showed no differences between the two groups because the films included nothing pertaining to them. But while lowering certain expectations in comparison to the traditional job preview, the effect of realism was selective because it only affected expectations included in the previews and did not spill over to others.

FIGURE 4
How Attitudes about Work Change

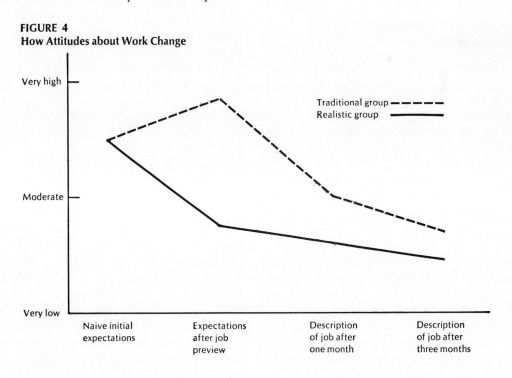

Contrary to predictions, the realistic preview made no noticeable impact on actual job decisions; the effect of an RJP on applicants' organizational choices did not materialize. Only two out of about 80 applicants refused offers, and the fact that job-offer acceptances were not influenced could be one reason why job survival rates were not even further apart.

Two explanations seem reasonable. First, the study was conducted during a period of high and sharply increasing unemployment. Second, the job previews occurred "late" in the sequence of events in the recruitment and selection process. Each applicant involved in the study had made considerable personal effort to obtain a job—making trips to the employment office, taking tests and interviews, and so forth. Research data show that the more effort individuals put forth, the more attractive the object of their effort becomes. Thus it was quite possible that the operators hired had made some type of advance psychological commitment to accept if a job offer were made.

FUTURE USE OF REALISTIC
JOB PREVIEWS

The results of the telephone operator study suggest the following guidelines for implementation of RJPs as an on-going personnel procedure.

Diagnose the Situation. Before adopting an RJP policy, thoroughly diagnose the jobs to be considered for an RJP. Check on job-survival-rate data. Are the rates high or low? What is the rate pattern? How does it vary in relation to job experience?

If a job survival problem involving new employees is indicated, make a hard, objective assessment of job characteristics and other information given to recruits to ensure the validity of the data. For example, in identifying all facets of a particular job, a variety of data sources should be tapped. When diagnosing the nature of job information given to recruits, check all potential

sources. Then compare these two assessments to determine whether any root problems can be corrected by using an RJP.

The Medium May Be the Message. An effective RJP must realistically depict the the important facets of a particular work environment. The study of telephone operators showed that the job visit portion of the recruitment and selection process did not fully communicate the job to an unfamiliar person. A short snatch of the action in an operators workroom did not accurately reflect the long-term reactions of boredom and lack of autonomy that many operators experience.

Although the job visit was intended to be a realistic preview, it probably had the effect of enhancing the attractiveness of this job. In a film format the long-run reactions to this job were portrayed by experienced telephone operators who talked about them.

In contrast to the above example where the medium (film) turned out to affect the message, there are counter examples. The studies at Prudential and West Point used booklets effectively. The Texas Instruments' first-day "realistic orientation" used a small group of peers to set initial expectations and reduce first-day anxiety.

Use Previews Early Rather Than Late. An RJP can funcion in two ways:

As a "screening device" to help job candidates decide for themselves on their organizational choices.

As an "innoculation" against disappointment with the realities of organizational life.

Early use of the RJP in the recruitment/ selection/placement process could be difficult, however, because of the costs involved in adding it to standard personnel operating procedures. Thus it may be less expensive to wait until after the first few selection hurdles have thinned the list of applicants. In some situations there even may be a tradeoff between maximum influence on the organizational choice process and the costs of administration, as in the telephone operator study. In any case, whether used early or late, the effectiveness of an RJP to innoculate new employees against disappointment seems unimpaired.

High-Unemployment Rates May Affect Outcomes. Because of the distinction between an RJP's effect on organizational choice versus its value as an innoculation, high unemployment may reduce the impact of an RJP on organizational choices. It has the same effect as that of an RJP administered too late, that is, after psychological commitment to accept a job offer has developed.

Is an RJP Limited to a Certain Type of Job? As we have seen, realistic previews have been used successfully on a variety of jobs in differing organizations. How far one can generalize from this is not completely clear. It seems reasonable, however, to assume that RJPs will be effective for a number of entry-level jobs—whether in white-collar insurance sales or as a telephone operator. But in the end, each job situation must be analyzed to assess the potential usefulness of the RJP approach.

5

EXTERNAL STAFFING

PREDICTORS AND VALIDITY

Organizations use a wide array of selection procedures for making hiring decisions about applicants from outside the organization. Tests, biographical data, and interviews represent three major categories, and there is considerable diversity of specific techniques within each category. These techniques and procedures are generally referred to as *predictors*.

Use of the term *predictor* suggests a major reason for their use by organizations. Specifically, they are designed to provide information about applicants that is predictive of the subsequent effectiveness of job seekers if hired. In other words, use of a predictor may help the organization to hire (reject) more successful (unsuccessful) people than would be the case if the predictor was not used.

Given this intention, it is necessary to ask whether use of a particular predictor will improve the organization's selection "batting average." This is the question of the *validity* of a predictor, and it is the fundamental question one must ask of any selection procedure. A predictor is valid to the extent that the information it provides about individuals is related to their success within the organization. Obviously, there is little if any reason for using predictors that are not valid, whereas use of valid predictors is highly desirable from the organization's standpoint.

Validity of predictors must be distinguished from the validity discussed as a part of performance appraisal in Chapter 3. That type is called *construct* validity and refers to the relationship between a measure and the construct to be measured. Validation of predictors, alternatively, is ordinarily done through two approaches. One of these is called *criterion-related* or empirical validation. The other is somewhat similar to construct validation and is called *content* validation. Each of these is described below.

CRITERION-RELATED VALIDITY

Criterion-related validation compares scores on a predictor with scores on a measure of success—known as the *criterion*—for a sample of individuals. Validity is thus indicated by the extent to which predictor scores are criterion-related.

To illustrate the process assume we want to validate a predictor for a job involving the assembly of miniature electronic components. We would first have to define what is success on the job and then develop a measure of success (that is, our criterion measure). Defining success requires that we do a *job analysis*. Through job analysis, perhaps we find that quality of assembly is a critical element of success. We then develop a quality measure, based on number of components rejected.

Our job analysis may also suggest that the manual dexterity of assemblers is an important factor in their quality of performance. Thus, we decide to use a test of manual dexterity as our predictor. We administer this test to a sample of assemblers (usually 30 or more) and then collect our criterion data for each assembler. We now have two scores for each assembler—a score on the test and a score on the criterion. We can compare these two sets of scores to see if, and how much, they are related.

Scatter Diagram. One way to conduct this comparison would be to plot a scatter diagram, as shown in Figure 1. Test scores are on the horizontal axis and criterion scores are on the vertical axis. Each x represents the plot of the predictor and criterion scores for a single assembler. In our example we find a very definite tendency for scores on the test to be related to scores on the criterion. Persons who score highest on the test also tend to have the highest quality ratings and vice versa. This relationship indicates that our test has criterion-related validity.

The value of these results can also be understood by considering lines A and B in Figure 1. Line A represents a possible cutoff between what the organization considers successful and unsuccessful quality of performance. Line B represents a possible cutoff score on the test that the organization might use for making selection decisions.

These two lines divide the scatter diagram into four parts or quadrants. If the test had actually been used for making selection decisions about these assemblers, there are four possible decision results and these correspond to the four quadrants. Persons in quadrants I and III represent correct selection decisions. Persons in quadrant I would be correct acceptances because they scored above the cutoff on the test and were subsequently successful. Persons in quadrant III would be correct rejections because they scored below the cutoff on the test and would have been unsuccessful on the job if they had been hired despite their test score. But there are also two types of incorrect decisions that would have occurred. These are erroneous acceptances (persons in quadrant II) and erroneous rejections (persons in quadrant IV). The former group of persons are often called *false positives* (they have positive test scores but do not perform successfully); the latter *false negatives* (they would have performed successfully if hired).

Having a valid predictor thus allows the organization to make more correct decisions than would be made without the predictor. Moreover, the higher

FIGURE 1
Hypothetical Scatter Diagram

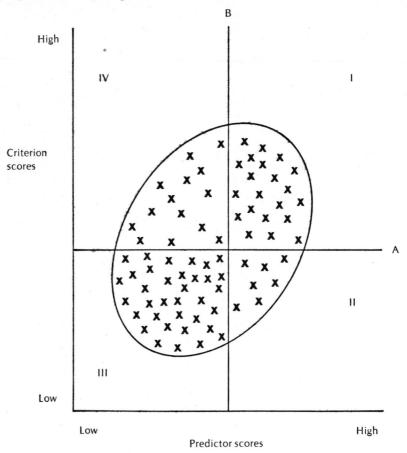

Predictor scores

the better. But no predictor will ever be perfectly valid, and consequently there will always be selection error. Since validity is never perfect, it is possible to reduce one type of error only by increasing the other type of error. To see this, simply move the cutoff test score (line *B* in Figure 1) to the right or left. Raising the score reduces the number of erroneous acceptances, but it results in an increase in erroneous rejections. Just the opposite occurs if the cutting score is lowered.

Correlation. So far, the criterion-related validity of a predictor has been illustrated visually. To complement this, the validity of a predictor can also be indicated statistically by computing the *correlation coefficient* (also called the validity coefficient in a selection context). The correlation coefficient is a simple numerical summary of the relationship between predictor and criterion scores. The symbol for the correlation is *r*. The values of *r* range from $r = -1.0$ (a perfect negative relationship) to $r = +1.0$ (a perfect positive relationship). Since, as we stated before, perfect relationships are unheard of in validation studies, in practice *r* will rarely exceed $r = \pm.60$. The scatter diagram in Figure 1 roughly corresponds to $r = +.40$. The more the scatter diagram resembles an ellipse, the greater the value of *r*; the more the resemblance to a circle, the lower the value of *r*.

CONTENT VALIDITY

Content validation involves making a judgment about the *probable* criterion-related validity of a predictor. This is done by assessing the similarity between the content of the predictor and the content of the job. The greater the similarity, the greater the content validity.

A content validation study requires that one start with a job analysis in order to define the content of the job. This knowledge can then be used to choose an existing predictor, or develop a new predictor, whose content "matches up" to the content of the job. The first part of the criterion-related validation study described earlier was actually a content validation study that involved a job analysis to define a critical element of the job of assembler, and then the choice of a test of manual dexterity as the predictor. If we had stopped at that point, we would have conducted a crude content validation.

We may thus think of content validity as a subset of criterion-related validity. The crucial difference between the two is that in content validation one never collects actual criterion scores. Consequently, in content validation it is not possible to empirically demonstrate that scores on the predictor are related to a measure of success on the job. Through erroneous judgment, what is thought to be a content valid predictor may not actually be predictive of job success.

Unfortunately content validity may be the only validity evidence possible in some situations. Content validity is necessary where there is too small a sample to do criterion-related validity (usually a sample less than 30) and/or where it is not possible to get criterion data. In these situations having content validity evidence is preferable to having no validity evidence at all.

INTRODUCTION TO READINGS

Test Validity Types and Methods

E. J. McCormick and J. Tiffin provide a nontechnical description of the major types of validity and methods for assessing it. They discuss the three types of validity—content, criterion-related, and construct—that we have identified in this chapter and Chapter 3. In addition the authors discuss methods for assessing criterion-related validity. McCormick and Tiffin refer to these procedures as methods for validating tests. It is important to recognize, however, that the methods are just as applicable and necessary for validating any kind of a selection predictor such as an interview.

They describe and discuss the merits of two procedures that can be used to examine criterion-related validity. The first, *present employee (concurrent)* method involves obtaining predictor and criterion scores from a sample of current employees. Our validation example above (involving a manual dexterity test as a predictor and rejects as the criterion) used the present employee method. In the second, called the *follow-up method,* predictor information is obtained from a sample of job applicants. The applicants are then hired regardless of their predictor scores (not all have to be hired; the crucial thing is not to hire on the basis of the predictor scores). After they have been on the job for some time, criterion scores are collected.

In either method, the results may be analyzed by plotting a scatter diagram and computing a correlation coefficient. In addition, McCormick and Tiffin suggest constructing an *expectancy table* or chart, which is very analogous to a scatter diagram. It shows the percentage of successful employees (that is, those above line *B* in Figure 1) that scored at various intervals on the predictor.

McCormick and Tiffin then discuss the advantages and disadvantages of the present employee and follow-up methods. They clearly favor the follow-up method and indicate a number of reasons for their preference. There are, however, a number of advantages of the present employee method. Those are that the study can be done quickly, it is relatively inexpensive, and results can be determined very rapidly. While these administrative advantages may not offset the disadvantages of the present employee method, it is well to recognize that neither method is inherently superior to the other.

McCormick and Tiffin conclude by briefly discussing two other criterion-related methods of validation. Neither method is considered very "conventional," and it is difficult to assess their potential usefulness. It seems likely that the present employee and follow-up methods will continue to be the major ones for determining criterion-related validity.

Validity of Aptitude Tests

There are a variety of types of potential predictors that organizations can use in the selection process. Major ones include various types of psychological tests, biographical and work history information that is typically obtained on application blanks, and information obtained in interviews. Edwin Ghiselli's article reviews criterion-related validity evidence on aptitude tests. Evidence is summarized for 20 different types of aptitude tests (Ghiselli included personality and interest tests as aptitude tests; many would disagree with this). Validity is frequently reported separately for the two different criterion measures—success in training programs and job proficiency (performance). Moreover, the evidence is presented for eight broad occupations that include 21 more specific jobs. For simplicity and space reasons, however, we have included the specific evidence for only the managerial and clerical occupations. Ghiselli's concluding statements, however, apply to the evidence for all eight occupations.

In each study reviewed, validity was expressed as the correlation between test and criterion scores. This makes it possible to summarize the validity evidence by calculating average correlation (validity) coefficients. It is these average values that Ghiselli reports and discusses. His overall summary indicates that "the average of the validity coefficients for all tests for all jobs taken together is .39 for training criteria and .22 for proficiency criteria."

These average correlation coefficients are obviously not too high. It should be observed, however, that there is considerable variability around these averages so that in some instances validity may be quite a bit above the average. Thus, there are situations where even a single test can make a substantial contribution to the organization's selection process. These results can often be improved upon by using more than one test and by using other types of predictors as well.

Validity of Biographical Data

James Asher points out in his article that biographical data, as obtained from an application blank for example, is a potentially rich source of information about job applicants. It is possible and desirable to conduct criterion-related validation studies on biographical data. This is usually done through use of a procedure known as *item analysis*. In this procedure, responses to each question (*B*-items as Asher calls them) are correlated with some criterion. For example, responses to the question "How far do you live from the organization?" might be correlated with length of service in the organization. Those items that do significantly correlate with the criterion may then be combined into a set of scoreable items, much like items on a regular test. The relationship between the total "score" on the application blank and the criterion can then be indicated by the correlation coefficient. In addition, the results can be checked out on a second sample to see if they hold true. This is technically known as *cross-validation*.

Asher reviews validity evidence from studies that used historical and verifiable *B*-items (for example, "What was your high school rank?"). These and other characteristics of *B*-items are discussed and illustrated by Asher. Overall, Asher finds that in these studies, 55 percent of the correlations were above $r = .50$, and that 97 percent of the correlations were above $r = .30$. In addition, he compares this validity evidence with the validities of various tests. In all instances he finds that *B*-items have greater validity.

All in all, the validity evidence for *B*-items is impressive. Asher gives three possible reasons for these generally strong results. The first of these deals with the factual nature of most biographical information. The other two relate to the item analysis procedures, described earlier, that are used in validation. The effect of using these procedures is that only the *B*-items that correlate with the criterion are "scored," so that only criterion-relevant items are used for predictions. This differs from the typical validation of a test in which a total score on all the items, regardless of whether or not the items are "relevant" to the criterion, is correlated with the criterion. Including nonrelevant items in the total score lowers the correlation between that score and the criterion.

Validity of the Interview

As with biographical data, it is possible and desirable to perform criterion-related validation on the employment interview when it is being used to make selection decisions. Such validation requires that an interviewer systematically evaluate a group of interviewees on one or more dimensions. For example, the interviewer might use rating scales to record his/her evaluations of the interviewee on the dimensions sociability, previous work experience, and overall suitability for the job. Each rating dimension yields scores for interviewees and thus serves as a predictor to be correlated with the criterion.

While validation of the interview is straight forward, the results are usually quite disappointing. Robert Carlson, Paul Thayer, Eugene Mayfield, and Donald Peterson note this in the beginning of their article by concluding that "It is common knowledge that selection interview probably contributes little in the way of validity to the selection decision."

Because of this dismal state of affairs, Carlson and associates undertook a program of basic research among organizations in the life insurance industry in an attempt to discover why validity was so low. The basic strategy in this research was to focus on factors that might influence interviewers' evaluations of interviewees. It was assumed that many of the factors considered by interviewers were extraneous and, hence, reduce validity. If the extraneous factors could be identified, then validity could possibly be improved by controlling and/or eliminating them. Thus, Carlson and associates conducted a number of studies that examined the impact of many different variables on interviewers' evaluations. The results of these studies, and possible implications for the interview practice, are summarized in the first part of the article.

These results then served as a basic input into the design and implementation of a complete selection process for choosing life insurance agents. The characteristics of the process, and the major principles underlying them, are described in the second half of the article. Note that in implementing the system considerable emphasis was placed on training managers in the use of the system. Ultimately, of course, there is the question of the validity of the system. Unfortunately, the evidence has not been reported.

12. VALIDITY OF TESTS
E. J. McCORMICK and J. TIFFIN

In a very broad sense, the *validity* of a test refers to the degree to which the test is capable of achieving the aims or purposes it is intended to serve. The nature of the "evidence" about the validity of a test depends very much upon the particular circumstance.

TYPES OF VALIDITY

Our current interest in tests is related primarily to their use for personnel selection and placement. However, it is helpful to be aware of the various specific *types* of test validity that are appropriate in the use of tests in various situations, such as education, vocational counseling and clinical practice, as well as in personnel work. There are basically three types of validity, which are related to the different aims or purposes of testing.[1]

1. Content Validity. Content validity is evaluated by showing how well the *content* of a test samples the subject matter or kinds of situations that the test is intended to measure. It applies particularly to achievement tests. Generally speaking, the determination of content validity needs to be made on the basis of the *judgments* of "experts" with regard to the *appropriateness* of the questions or problems (the "content" of the test) as measures of whatever the test is supposed to measure.

2. Criterion-Related Validity. This is determined by comparing test scores with one

Source: Ernest J. McCormick, Joseph Tiffin, *Industrial Psychology*, 6th edition, © 1974, pp. 101–8. Reprinted by permission of Prentice-Hall Inc., Englewood Cliffs, New Jersey.

[1] A thorough discussion of the concepts of validity and reliability of tests is included in *Standards for Educational and Psychological Tests and Manuals*, available from the American Psychological Association, 1200 Seventeenth St. N.W., Washington D.C. 20036.

or more independent criteria. In personnel selection and placement, the criterion usually is a measure of job performance of individuals, but it also may consist of "membership" in different groups, such as occupational groups. There are two kinds of criterion-related validity—concurrent validity and predictive validity.

Concurrent validity is established by relating test scores with the criterion values or categories that are available at the same time. Usually this involves the correlation of test scores with currently available criteria of job performance of the individuals in question. (The procedures used in this process are covered a bit later in the discussion of the present-employee method of test validation.)

As related to the use of personnel tests, *predictive validity* is determined by relating test scores obtained at one time (such as at the time of employment) with criterion measures (such as job performance) obtained at a later time. (The procedures used in determining predictive validity are covered later in the discussion of the follow-up method of test validation.)

3. Construct Validity. Construct validity is evaluated by determining what phychological *quality* a test measures, such as "introversion" or "intelligence." Such validity frequently is determined by correlating one test with another that previously has been found to measure the quality in question, or by using a statistical process called "factor analysis" to identify the extent to which various tests measure the same human quality.

. . . The present treatment of personnel tests in industry typically involves the concepts of criterion-related validity, which covers both predictive validity and concurrent validity.

METHODS OF TEST VALIDATION

It is of utmost importance that tests never be used for any purpose unless there is reasonable evidence that they are valid for that purpose. This means that there must be some sort of evidence that scores on the test for some sample(s) of individuals have been found to discriminate among those in the sample(s) in terms of a suitable criterion of job performance. Among the methods for obtaining such evidence in relation to personnel tests are the following (along with the type or types of validity involved):

Method	Type of Validity
Present-employee	Concurrent
Follow-up	Predictive
Job status	Usually concurrent; could be predictive
Job component	Depends on procedures used

Of these, the first two require the use of individual criterion measures (such as job performance criteria) of all of the individuals in the sample(s) used. The last two more typically involve the use of a criterion of membership in some group (e.g., working on a particular job or occupation). Of these, the present-employee and follow-up methods are the most commonly used in industry and are sometimes referred to as "testing the test."

Present Employee Method of Test Validation. This method of test validation involves the use of a sample of present employees on the job in question. The procedure is as follows:

1. Select Battery of Experimental Tests. An early step in a test validation project is the selection of a battery of tests to be tried out. These tests should be chosen in terms of the extent to which they are considered to measure attributes that are judged to be important to job success. This selection preferably should be made on the basis of information obtained from a job analysis.

2. Administer Tests to Present Employees. The tests selected are then given to employees presently on the job. When an organization plans to carry out a test validation research project that will involve the experimental testing of present employees, the organization should make such participation voluntary and should give full assurance that the tests are being given *strictly* for experimental purposes and that the results will not in any way affect the employees' relationships with the organization. It is usually desirable to distribute among the employees a sheet such as this:

The Personnel Department is conducting a series of experiments. You have our assurance that this testing is being done to "test the tests" and that the results will *not* be used, now or later, in any way that will affect your standing with the company.

3. *Select Appropriate Criteria.* At some early phase of a test validation project, it is necessary to determine what criterion of job performance to use. . . . We will only remind you that the criterion or criteria used in any test validation study should be *relevant*, meaning that it should reflect the standards by which the performance of employees should be evaluated in terms of management's objectives.

4. *Obtain Criterion Information on Present Employees.* After determining what criterion or criteria to use, it is then in order to obtain criterion information on the individual employees now on the job. Depending on the criterion in question, this may involve the accumulation of available records (such as production records, sales volume, and the like), or it may consist of obtaining ratings from supervisors on job performance of the employees, or other appropriate processes.

Depending on the manner in which the results are to be analyzed, the criterion information may be used to divide the total employee group into two groups such as "high" (or above average) and "low" (or below average), or it may be expressed in quantitative terms such as units of production or numerical ratings.

5. *Analyze Results.* After the test scores and criterion information have been obtained, the results may be analyzed in several different ways. One method consists essentially of three steps. First, the total

group of employees is divided into a "high" criterion group and a "low" criterion group, as mentioned above. Next, the employees are divided on the basis of test scores into two test score groups, those scoring in the top half on the test and those scoring in the lower half. Then the percentage of "high" criterion employees in each test score group is determined. If there is a higher percentage of high criterion employees among the employees in the top half on the test than there is among those in the lower half on the test, the difference is subjected to a statistical check to determine whether it is "significant." (This check is a common procedure in statistics and shows the probability that the obtained difference could have occurred by chance. If the analysis shows that the difference could have occurred by chance only 1 time in 100, the difference is said to be significant at the .01 confidence level. If the difference could have occurred by chance 5 times in 100, it is said to be significant at the .05 confidence level. It is standard practice in the field not to use tests when the confidence level is not at least at the .05 level.)

When a test has been found to be acceptable on this basis, employees are then split into smaller groups by test score, such as fifths—i.e., the highest fifth on the test, the second fifth, the third fifth, the fourth fifth, and the lowest fifth. The percentage of "high" criterion employees is then computed for each of these test score groups and the resulting data are then plotted in an expectancy chart such as the one shown in Figure 1.[2] The chart shows the "odds" of being a superior employee for employees in each test score bracket.

An even more effective method of determining the relationship between test results and job performance is to compute a coefficient of correlation between the test

---

[2] The procedure for constructing a five bar expectancy chart such as the one shown in Figure 1 is given in detail in C. H. Lawshe, and M. J. Balma, *Principles of Personnel Testing* (New York: McGraw-Hill, 1966).

FIGURE 1
Expectancy Chart Showing the Relation between Scores Made on the Minnesota Paper Form Board and Rated Success of Junior Draftsmen in a Steel Company

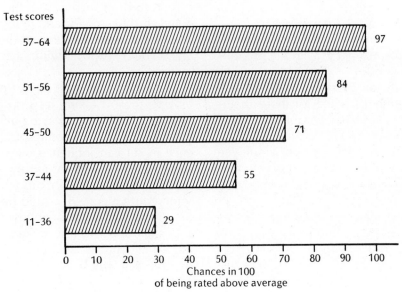

Test scores

57–64	97
51–56	84
45–50	71
37–44	55
11–36	29

0 10 20 30 40 50 60 70 80 90 100

Chances in 100
of being rated above average

scores of the employees and their criterion values. This has certain advantages over the expectancy chart method mentioned above. In the first place, it gives a more accurate indication of the *amount* of the relationship between test scores and job performance. In the second place, it enables the employment manager more effectively to take advantage of the all-important selection ratio in using the test. In the third place, it makes possible the computation of the relative importance of several tests in an employment battery so that the tests may be "weighted" according to their importance. Finally, the use of the correlational method makes it possible to offset, statistically, whatever influence such factors as experience on the job or age may have had both on the test scores and on job performance of the employees. Further mention will be made later of these possible influences.

Although the correlational approach has certain advantages over the expectancy chart method, these are largely statistical advantages. In terms of understanding by nonstatisticians, the expectancy chart method probably cannot be excelled.

Follow-Up Method of Test Validation. This method consists of administering tests to individuals at the time they are candidates for the job in question. The tests, however, are *not* used as the basis for selection. Rather, the individuals are selected just as they normally would have been selected if the test had not been administered, and the test scores are later related to whatever criterion is appropriate. The steps involved in this method are described below.

1. Select Battery of Experimental Tests. This step is essentially the same as with the present-employee method.

2. Administer Tests to Applicants. The tests are administered to applicants who are to be employed for the job in question, but the applicants should not know at the time that a decision has been made to employ them. The test results are then filed until a later date.

3. Select Appropriate Criterion. This determination is made in the same way as with the present-employee method.

4. Obtain Criterion Information on the New Employees. The criterion information on the new employees should not be obtained until after sufficient time has elapsed for them to demonstrate their actual abilities on the job. Usually this would be after completion of training, or at least after the completion of most of the training.

5. *Analyze Results.* This step is carried out in the same manner as with the present-employee method.

Comparison of Present-Employee and Follow-Up Methods. Each of these methods of test validation has certain advantages and disadvantages. In the validation of aptitude tests with the present-employee method, it is possible that a test may in part be measuring some ability that is improved significantly by experience on the job. In other words, it may be measuring achievement more than aptitude. In validating aptitude tests by this method, then, it is necessary to be sure that the tests, besides differentiating between employees in terms of a criterion of actual job performance, do *not* show a significant correlation with length of experience on the job, for an aptitude test should be one on which the employees who score high on the test do not score high simply because they have had the opportunity—on the job—to develop the ability which the test measures. If test scores *do* show some correlation with length of experience, the net relationship between test scores and job performance, after the effect of experience has been eliminated, can be determined by partial correlation. The procedure for computing partial correlations may be found in any standard textbook of statistics.

Although the influence of experience on test scores in such a situation can be eliminated by the use of partial correlations, a more straightforward manner of getting around such a problem is through the use of the follow-up method. In this case the test scores are obtained *prior* to any experience on the job and, therefore, cannot be influenced by job experience.

The present-employee method has certain other possible disadvantages. In some instances, the *present* employees on a job may represent a highly select group, inasmuch as most of those who were *not* satisfactory either were dismissed or left of their own accord. In such a case, the correlation between test scores and criterion values would *not* represent the relationship that one would expect with the follow-up method.

Further, the "mental set" of present employees toward taking tests on a voluntary "experimental" basis may be different from the "mental set" of applicants. This difference in set can influence performance on some types of tests, especially personality and interest tests. Where this influence is of some consequence, it would be preferable to validate the test by the follow-up method. If this is done, the test is then validated in the same type of situation as the one in which it will later be used.

Another disadvantage of the present-employee method is that the arrangements for testing present employees sometimes are difficult to work out, especially because it is necessary to take people away from their jobs in order to test them.

The follow-up method is clearly the preferable method for validating tests, except for the possible disadvantage of the time required. Fortunately, it is possible in some cases to use the present-employee method for developing a battery of tests for immediate use and still plan on later "follow-up" of those selected. Although the range of test scores (and of criterion values) for those so selected usually would be restricted (thus bringing about a low correlation), it sometimes is possible to adjust for this restricted range statistically. Such an adjustment makes it possible to obtain an estimate of what the follow-up validity coefficient *would* have been had the tests *not* been used for initial selection. This adjustment procedure would not be appropriate, however, if some nontest basis (e.g., membership in a minority group) has been used for excluding some applicants.

Job Status Method of Test Validation. In this method the "criterion" categories consist of those individuals who are in specific jobs or occupations. When this method is used, the test scores of employees on each of two or several jobs are compared to ascertain whether there are significant differences. In one company the Bennett Test of Mechanical Comprehension was administered to employees on each of several jobs. Following are the mean test scores for those on certain jobs:

Job	Mean Test Score
Insulators	30.9
Pipefitters	33.8
Electricians	36.4
Welders	39.7
Instrument mechanics	42.4

The use of this method is predicated on the assumption that by "natural selection" people in an organization tend to "gravitate" into the kinds of jobs that are reasonably in line with their abilities. If it can be assumed that, in general, most persons on a job are achieving a reasonable degree of success on that job, it is then possible to *compare* the employees on various jobs in order to ascertain what *differences* there are from job to job, as in the above example. It is then possible to select for initial placement, or for promotion, those individuals whose test scores most nearly correspond with the test scores of individuals now on the job.

JOB COMPONENT VALIDITY

The conventional validation methods are the present-employee and follow-up methods previously described. But in some cases —e.g., jobs with small numbers of employees—such empirical, situational validation procedures simply may not be possible, or may be too time-consuming and costly. Thus one would wish for a generalized, simplified, and yet valid method that bypasses conventional test validation procedures for ascertaining what tests to use for selection of personnel for a given job.

In this regard, one could hypothesize that those jobs that have in common the same basic kind of human behavior or job characteristic or job component would require the same human attributes. In turn, it would seem that the same test(s) should be valid for personnel selection purposes for all such jobs. Thus, if one could, by some method, identify a test that is valid for the selection of individuals for a sample of jobs with a given human behavior or job characteristic in common, it would be reasonable to expect the test to be valid for all jobs with that *same* behavior characteristic. These hypotheses give rise to the concept of job component validity. This concept generally has been referred to as "synthetic validity" ... but ... we feel that the term *job component validity* is somewhat more descriptive. ...

13. THE VALIDITY OF APTITUDE TESTS IN PERSONNEL SELECTION

EDWIN E. GHISELLI

Traditionally Munsterberg's experiment with motormen is taken to be the beginning of research in the use of tests for personnel selection. Nevertheless, anecdotal evidence

Source: *Personnel Psychology* 26 (1973): 461–77.

strongly suggests that even before 1910 other psychologists conducted similar studies with tests, studies which were small in scope and which went unpublished and unpublicized. Furthermore, under the impetus of the scientific management movement some of the so-called efficiency experts at about that time were using a few simple tests for evaluating applicants for jobs, and even reported fragmentary evidence of validity in the attempt to justify and to publicize their activities. During World War I the large-scale testing both of soldiers and industrial workers provided stimulation, methodology, and respectability to the examination of the utility of tests in the assessment of occupational aptitude. This all led to a great postwar surge of systematic research in personnel testing. So beginning about 1920 substantial amounts of data pertaining to the validity of various sorts of tests for the evaluation of workers in many different jobs began to become available.

For something over half a century, then, there has been an accumulation of experience with the use of tests as devices for assessing men and women for positions in business and industrial establishments, and an enormous amount of information has been collected. The purpose here is to summarize this information in as simple and compact form as is possible. Such a summary will at least permit an examination of general trends in the validity of tests for personnel selection.

METHOD

The description of the utility of a particular test for the selection of personnel for a given job is commonly given as the Pearsonian coefficient of correlation between test and criterion scores, the familiar validity coefficient. The findings of the different researches which have to do with the occupational validity of tests, then, have the unique quality of being expressed in the form of the same numerical index. As a consequence, they can be quite conveniently summarized by means of averages, the averages of the validity coefficients that have been reported for each type of test for each type of job. On an earlier occasion the author (1966) has summarized the literature pertaining to the occupational validity of

tests in this way. The present report brings up to date the most recent of these summaries.

The classification of tests which was used is as follows:

Tests of Intellectual Abilities

Intelligence. This category includes all tests which are termed intelligence or mental alertness tests, as for example, the Otis and Wessman tests.

Immediate Memory. These tests present material, e.g., five- to ten-place numbers, which the individual studies and after a very short period of time tries to recall.

Substitution. With these tests the individual learns and applies a code.

Arithmetic. These devices involve the computation of arithmetic problems of various kinds, which are presented in simple form or as practical problems such as making change.

Tests of Spatial and Mechanical Abilities

Spatial Relations. Spatial judgments about the size and form of figures are required by these tests. The Minnesota Paper Form Board is a good illustration.

Location. With these tests the individual must identify the location of a series of points and make judgments about the distances between them. Examples are furnished by the copying and location subtests of the MacQuarrie Mechanical Ability Tests.

Mechanical Principles. Tests of this sort, such as the Bennett Mechanical Comprehension Test, present in pictorial form problems which require knowledge of various mechanical principles to solve.

Tests of Perceptual Accuracy

Number Comparison. The stimulus material in these tests consist of a series of pairs of numbers, both members of each pair consisting of the same number of digits. The digits in some of the pairs are exactly the same and in others one digit is different.

As in the number comparison part of the Minnesota Clerical Test, the individual is required to indicate which pairs are the same and which are different.

Name Comparison. These tests are similar to the number comparison tests except that they consist of pairs of names instead of pairs of numbers. The Minnesota Clerical Test includes items of this sort.

Cancellation. A continuous series of numbers or letters in random order is presented by these tests, and the individual crosses out all numbers or letters of a specified sort.

Pursuit. This type of test presents a tangle of lines, and by eye alone the individual is required to follow each line from its beginning to its end. The pursuit subtest of the MacQuarrie Mechanical Ability Test is an example.

Perceptual Accuracy. The speed and accuracy with which similarities and differences between simple figures can be perceived is measured by these tests.

Tests of Motor Abilities

Tracing. With measuring devices of this sort, the individual is required to follow a path with a pencil, both speed and accuracy being important in the performance. The tracing subtest of the MacQuarrie Mechanical Ability Test is an illustration.

Tapping. These tests present a series of circles or squares into each of which the individual places two, or perhaps three, dots with a pencil. The tapping part of the MacQuarrie Mechanical Ability Test is representative.

Dotting. These tests are similar to the tapping tests except that by using smaller circles or squares precision of movement is stressed. For instance, in the dotting subtest of the MacQuarrie Mechanical Ability Test the individual places a single pencil dot in each of a series of quite small circles.

Finger Dexterity. This category includes all pegboard tests, together with tests which involve mating simple assemblies such as placing washers on rivets which are then inserted into holes. The O'Connor Finger Dexterity Test and the Purdue Pegboard Test are examples.

Hand Dexterity. While to some extent these tests do involve finger dexterity, their purpose is to measure grosser manual motions involving the wrist. In the Minnesota Turning Test, for example, blocks are picked up, turned over, and replaced in their original position.

Arm Dexterity. As in the Minnesota Placing Test, these tests involve the very gross movements of picking up blocks and placing them in another position.

Personality Traits

Personality. Included here are all of the sundry inventories that ask questions which presumably are indicative of one or another of the many personality characteristics. A number of different trait names are used to distinguish the various aspects of personality. In some cases different names are used to denote the same, or very nearly the same, quality, and in others the same name is used to denote quite different qualities. As a consequence it is impossible to classify the measured traits into specific categories. Furthermore, in some instances inventories are developed for a given job and are not identified by a specific trait name. Therefore, only those results were included in the present summary where the trait seemed pertinent to the job in question, or where the inventory was developed specifically for the job through item analysis, and cross-validation data were reported. An example of this category of tests is the Guilford-Zimmerman Temperament Survey.

Interest. Inventories of this sort ask questions about interests in, and preferences for, such matters as avocations, occupations, and school subjects. Interest inventories were included in this summary on the same basis as were personality inventories.

The following classification of occupations was used:

Managerial occupations
  Executives and administrators (e.g., plant managers, department heads)
  Foremen (e.g., first-line industrial supervisors)
Clerical occupations
  General clerks (e.g., coding clerks)
  Recording clerks (e.g., typist, stenographers)
  Computing clerks (e.g., bookkeepers, calculating machine operators)
Sales occupations
  Salesclerks (e.g., retail sales persons)
  Salesmen (e.g., insurance salesmen, industrial salesmen)
Protective occupations (e.g., policemen, firemen)
Service occupations (e.g., waiters, hospital attendants)
Vehicle operators (e.g., taxicab drivers, bus drivers)
Trades and crafts
  Mechanical repairmen (e.g., automobile mechanics, typewriter repairmen)
  Electrical workers (e.g., electricians, radio repairmen)
  Structural workers (e.g., carpenters)
  Processing workers (e.g., petroleum refinery workers, electric substation operators)
  Complex machine operators (e.g., printers, weaving machine operators)
  Machine workers (e.g., machinists, turret lathe operators)
Industrial occupations
  Machine tenders (e.g., punch press operators, bottle-capping machine operators)
  Bench workers (e.g., assemblers)
  Inspectors (e.g., pottery inspectors, gaugers)
  Packers and wrappers (e.g., package wrappers)
  Gross manual workers (e.g., unskilled laborers)

The literature summarized here includes reports which pertain to the occupational validity of tests that were published during the period from 1920 through 1971. To these published findings was added a great amount of unpublished material which was obtained from private sources in a number of business, industrial, and governmental organizations. In all instances validity was expressed as the coefficient of correlation between test and criterion scores. The criterion, of course, was different for different jobs. In all but a very few instances the criterion was intended to be a measure of overall success and was generally in the form of ratings, although occasionally they consisted of objective measures or combinations of different kinds of measures. The validity coefficients were differentiated in terms of whether they referred to the prediction of success in training, or to the level of proficiency attained on the actual job itself. Only those cases were included in the prediction of training where the training was preparation given the individual before he was actually placed on the job and was not refresher training.

For each of the 20 types of tests, 21 types of jobs, and 2 types of criteria, the mean of the validity coefficient was calculated. Because of the nature of the Pearsonian coefficient, the means were obtained through Fisher's z transformation, the coefficients entering into a mean being weighted in terms of the number of persons on which each of those coefficients were determined.

The circumstances in which studies of validity of occupational aptitude tests are conducted are of such a nature that in almost all instances, if not all, their findings were attenuated. As a consequence the validity coefficients that are reported for the tests almost invariably are underestimates of their true predictive power. . . .

RESULTS

Managerial Occupations

The average validity coefficients for the managerial occupations are given in Table

1. It should be noted that the studies of the prediction of trainability which were included here were only those wherein the attempt was made to provide total training for the job and not just training in some specific area such as leadership.

In Table 1 it will be observed that in general the prediction of training criteria is better for foremen than it is for executives and administrators, whereas the reverse is true for job proficiency criteria. For both types of criteria, tests of intellectual abilities, spatial and mechanical abilities, and perceptual accuracy tend to be the best and are of moderate validity for both types of managerial occupations. Tests of motor abilities have lesser, though apparently some, validity for proficiency criteria. Measures of personality and interest also are of moderate value in predicting the level of proficiency executives and administrators attain on their jobs, but they are much less useful for foremen.

Clerical Occupations

As may be seen in Table 2, while there are some differences in terms of the validity of the various sorts of tests for the three types of jobs which constitute the clerical occupations, there is, nevertheless, a considerable degree of consistency among them. Success in training for the clerical occupations is exceptionally well predicted by tests of intellectual abilities, and nearly as well by those indicative of perceptual accuracy. Oddly enough, tests of spatial and mechanical abilities also give rather good prediction of training success. More limited validity for training criteria is exhibited by measures of motor abilities. The personality and interest inventories which have been tried for this purpose have not proven to be of any great value.

Forecasts of success attained on the actual job is equally well given by tests of intellectual ability and perceptual accuracy,

TABLE 1
Validity Coefficients for Managerial Occupations

	Executives and Administrators		Foremen		All Managers	
	Trainee	Professional	Trainee	Professional	Trainee	Professional
Intellectual abilities	.27[b]	.30[e]	.33[b]	.26[e]	.30[c]	.27[f]
Intelligence	.28[b]	.30[c]	.31[b]	.28[e]	.29[b]	.29[f]
Arithmetic	.25[b]	.29[c]	.36[b]	.20[d]	.33[b]	.23[d]
Spatial and mechanical						
Abilities	.25[b]	.23[e]	.36[a]	.22[e]	.28[b]	.22[e]
Spatial relations	.25[b]	.22[e]	.36[a]	.21[d]	.28[b]	.21[d]
Mechanical principles		.42[a]		.23[e]		.23[e]
Perceptual accuracy	.18[b]	.24[c]	.26[b]	.27[b]		.25[e]
Number comparison		.14[a]		.37[b]	.23[b]	.31[b]
Name comparison	.18[b]	.23[b]	.26[a]	.14[b]	.21[b]	.21[c]
Cancellation		.32[b]				.22[b]
Pursuit			.25[a]		.25[a]	
Motor abilities	.02[b]	.13[d]	.38[a]	.15[b]	.02[b]	.14[d]
Tapping	.09[b]	.17[b]	.04[a]	.20[a]	.07[b]	.18[c]
Finger dexterity	−.02[b]	.13[b]		.23[a]	−.02[b]	.14[c]
Hand dexterity	−.02[b]	.10[b]		.02[a]	−.02[b]	.09[c]
Personality traits	.53[a]	.29[e]		.16[e]	.53[a]	.22[f]
Personality		.28[e]		.15[e]		.21[f]
Interest	.53[a]	.30[d]		.17[c]	.53[a]	.28[d]

[a] Less than 100 cases.
[b] 100 to 499 cases.
[c] 500 to 999 cases.
[d] 1,000 to 4,999 cases.
[e] 5,000 to 9,999 cases.
[f] 10,000 or more cases.

TABLE 2
Validity Coefficients for Clerical Occupations

	General Clerks		Recording Clerks		Computing Clerks		All Clerks	
	Trainee	Pro-fessional	Trainee	Pro-fessional	Trainee	Pro-fessional	Trainee	Pro-fessional
Intellectual abilities	.47[f]	.28[f]	.46[f]	.26[f]	.52[e]	.25[e]	.47[f]	.28[f]
Intelligence	.46[f]	.32[f]	.43[f]	.26[e]	.54[d]	.23[d]	.46[f]	.30[f]
Immediate memory	.21[b]	.29[d]	.32[d]	.36[b]	.46[a]	.26[c]	.32[d]	.31[d]
Substitution		.24[d]	.24[c]	.23[c]	.34[b]	.24[c]	.25[d]	.24[e]
Arithmetic	.49[f]	.25[f]	.50[f]	.27[d]	.51[d]	.29[d]	.50[f]	.26[f]
Spatial and mechanical Abilities	.35[f]	.12[e]	.30[f]	.17[d]	.52[d]	.26[d]	.34[f]	.17[f]
Spatial relations	.39[e]	.11[d]	.32[e]	.15[d]	.55[c]	.25[d]	35[f]	.16[e]
Location		.05[b]	.24[c]	.12[c]	.49[a]	.30[b]	.27[c]	.16[d]
Mechanical principles	.32[e]	.20[c]	.29[f]	.23[d]	.50[c]	.26[c]	.32[f]	.23[d]
Perceptual accuracy	.36[b]	.27[e]	.41[f]	.27[d]	.31[b]	.31[d]	.40[e]	.29[f]
Number comparison	.42[b]	.28[e]	.28[b]	.29[d]	.35[b]	.32[d]	.34[c]	.30[e]
Name comparison	.34[b]	.25[d]	.35[b]	.35[d]	.19[b]	.33[d]	.33[c]	.30[e]
Cancellation		.22[c]	.58[b]	.19[d]	.11[a]	.24[c]	.49[b]	.22[d]
Pursuit		—.17[a]	.21[b]	.12[b]		.35[b]	.15[b]	.12[b]
Perceptual speed		.40[b]	.42[e]			.46[b]	.42[e]	.45[c]
Motor abilities	.07[b]	.16[e]	.14[d]	.18[d]	.14[b]	.14[d]	.14[d]	.16[f]
Tracing		—.09[a]	.17[b]	.11[b]	.08[a]	.42[b]	.16[b]	.16[b]
Tapping	.00[b]	.20[d]	.23[b]	.25[c]	.16[b]	.15[c]	.21[c]	.20[d]
Dotting	.32[b]	.14[c]	.15[b]	.17[c]	.16[a]	.03[c]	.18[b]	.12[d]
Finger dexterity	.01[b]	.16[d]	.09[c]	.18[c]		.18[c]	.08[d]	.17[d]
Hand dexterity	.06[b]	.14[d]	.30[a]	.17[c]		.12[c]	.14[b]	.14[d]
Arm dexterity		.13[b]	.09[a]	—.09[a]		.34[a]	.09[a]	.14[b]
Personality traits	.17[d]	.30[c]		.15[c]		.19[b]	.17[d]	.22[d]
Personality		.30[c]		.18[c]		.17[b]		.24[d]
Interest	.17[d]			—.01[b]		.23[b]	.17[d]	.12[b]

[a] Less than 100 cases.
[b] 100 to 499 cases.
[c] 500 to 999 cases.
[d] 1,000 to 4,999 cases.
[e] 5,000 to 9,999 cases.
[f] 10,000 or more cases.

both of which have moderately high validity coefficients. Tests which measure spatial and mechanical abilities, and motor abilities, and inventories which are designed to measure various personality traits have much more restricted utility. . . .

THE PREDICTIVE POWER OF OCCUPATIONAL APTITUDE TESTS

Considering the considerable differences in the times when the investigations summarized here were performed, together with the large differences in the nature of the organizations in which they were conducted, and the marked variations among the samples in such factors as age, sex, education, and background, the average validity coefficients presented here can be said to

have a good deal of generality. Furthermore, since most of them are based upon a number of separate and distinct determinations, they have a substantial measure of dependability and meaningfulness.

The general run of the validity coefficients is quite respectable for training criteria, and it is somewhat less so for proficiency criteria. The grand average of the validity coefficients for all tests for all jobs taken together is .39 for training criteria and .22 for proficiency criteria. However, for every job there is at least one type of test which has at least moderate validity. If for each job, the highest average validity coefficient is observed, it will be found that for the 21 jobs these values range from .28 to .65 for training criteria, and from .24 to .46 for proficiency criteria. The averages of these maximal validity coefficients are .45 for training criteria and .35 for proficiency criteria. In view of the attenuating effects upon validity coefficients. . . . , the foregoing values clearly are conservative as descriptions of the predictive power of occupational aptitude tests. It will be recalled that single tests are being considered here, and that judiciously selected combinations of tests would have been of higher validity.

REFERENCE

Ghiselli, E. E. *The Validity of Occupational Aptitude Tests.* New York: Wiley, 1966.

14. THE BIOGRAPHICAL ITEM: CAN IT BE IMPROVED?[1,2]

JAMES J. ASHER

Biographical items may be found in measures that have names such as Application Blank, Biographical Information Blank, Individual Background Survey, and Life History Blank. Exactly what items should be classified as biographical is quite controversial (Henry 1965). For example, a biographical item may vary on any of these dimensions: verifiable-unverifiable; historical-futuristic; actual behavior-hypothetical behavior; memory-conjecture; factual-interpretive; specific-general; response-response tendency; and external event-internal event. For specific examples of biographical items representing each dimension, see Table 1.

Some have advocated that only an individual's historical experiences, events, or situations that are verifiable should be classified as biographical items (*B*-items). Using this system, most items on the usual application blank would be classified as *B*-items. For example, what was your rank in your high school graduating class? List each prior job with inclusive dates.

If only historical items that are verifiable are included as *B*-items, then questions such as this would *not* be asked, "Did you ever build a model airplane that flew?" Cureton (see Henry 1965, p. 913) commented that this single item, although it cannot be easily verified for an individual, was almost as good a predictor of success in flight training during World War II as the entire Air Force Battery.

Other researchers feel that any person-type item which describes the individual may be classified as a *B*-item. This would include such items as personality, motivation, aspiration, attitudes, and values. From this enlarged classification, any item is included that answers one of these questions:

What have I done?
Where have I been?
What do I believe?
What do I want to be?
How do I feel?
What am I apt to do?
What interests me?
What relationships have I had with others?

While the enlarged classification of *B*-items obviously expands the amount of personal information collected, a more constrained classification may reduce a ten-

Source: *Personnel Psychology* 25 (1972): 251–69.
[1] Although murder is not usually thought of as work behavior, Kahn (1965) used biographic items in an interesting attempt to predict the behavior of murderers.
[2] Appreciation is expressed to Professor Edwin E. Ghiselli for a critical reading of this paper.

TABLE 1
A Taxonomy of B-Items

Verifiable	*Unverifiable*
How many full-time jobs have you had in the past five years?	What aspect of your last full-time job did you find most interesting?
Historical	*Futuristic*
List your three best subjects in high school.	Do you intend to further your education?
Actual Behavior	*Hypothetical Behavior*
Did you ever build a model airplane that flew?	If you had the training, do you think you would enjoy building innovative model airplanes for a toy manufacturer?
Memory	*Conjecture*
Before you were 12-years old, did you ever try to perform chemistry experiments at home?	If your father had been a chemist, do you think you would have performed chemistry experiments at home before you were 12-years old?
Factual	*Interpretive*
Do you repair mechanical things around your home such as appliances?	If you had the training, how would you estimate your performance as an appliance repair man?
Specific	*General*
As a child did you collect stamps?	As a child were you an avid collector of things?
Response	*Response Tendency*
Which of the following types of cameras do you own?	In buying a new camera, would you most likely purchase one with automatic features?
External Event	*Internal Event*
Did you ever have private tutoring lessons in any school subject?	How important did you view homework when you were in high school?

dency toward fictionalization. *B*-items that are historical and verifiable may result in a narrow, yet representative, set of data about the individual, while the enlarged classification may be quite unrepresentative. For example, even when *Ss* have a set to respond honestly, items calling for conjecture, interpretation, and supposition may have enough ambiguity to enable an individual to respond with a sort of leniency rating error about himself. Illustrations of such items would be:

Have you:
a. Often been double-crossed by people
b. Sometimes been double-crossed by people
c. Been double-crossed once or twice by people
d. Never been double-crossed by people

Were your parents:
a. Always very strict with you
b. Usually very strict with you
c. Seldom very strict with you
d. Never very strict with you

Using the constrained classification that *B*-items should be historical and verifiable, the reliability and validity of these items will be reviewed for 1960 through 1970. Then, what has been done to improve the *B*-item, and what innovations could be attempted in future research.

RESULTS

The scorable application blank was used to predict work behavior that ranged from unskilled to skilled, as may be seen in the following list:

Adolescent girls (art and writing)* (Anastasi and Schaefer 1969)
Architects* (MacKinnon 1962)
College students
Credit applicants* (McGrath 1960)
Door to door salesmen
Engineers

Executives* (Laurent 1970)

Female office personnel* (Fleishman and Berniger 1960; Dunnette, Kirchner, Erickson, and Banas 1960; and Buel 1964)

Food Company salesmen

Foreign service clerical workers

Foreign service junior officers

High school students

Hospital aids

Insurance salesmen

Life insurance salesmen

Peace corp workers

Petroleum research scientists

Pharmaceutical research scientists* (Tucker, Cline, and Schmitt 1967)

Research scientists* (Cline, Tucker, and Anderson 1966)

Unskilled workers* (Scott and Johnson 1967)

Vocational rehabilitation trainees* (Ehrle 1964)

From the list, studies were selected which had these characteristics: (a) there was cross-validation data expressed in a correlation statistic; (b) biographical items were used in a combination as a predictor rather than as single items; and (c) the definition of B-items was judged to be historical and verifiable. There were 11 studies with the attributes described, and these were found in the categories marked with an asterisk. No study was selected in which B-items were used to predict grade point average for students, since this issue has been thoroughly reviewed by Freeberg (1967).

Using only cross-validated data from the 11 studies, there were 31 validity coefficients. The cross-validated correlations were distributed as follows: 35 percent were .60 or higher; 55 percent were .50 or higher; 74 percent were .40 or higher; and 97 percent were .30 or higher.

In a recent review by Schuh (1967), it was found that in 19 of 21 studies, one or more biographical items had a predictive relationship with job turnover. Schuh concluded,

". . . Some items in an applicant's personal history can be found to relate to tenure in most jobs" (p. 145).

Compared to Other Predictors.

The predictive power of biographical items may be evaluated with greater clarity when compared with other predictors. Fortunately, Ghiselli (1966) has published the proportion of validity coefficients which resulted when tests were tried for specific jobs. For example, in his book are validity coefficients for mechanical repairmen on mechanical principles tests; general clerks on intelligence tests, bench workers on finger dexterity tests, and machine tenders on spatial relations tests. The criterion was job proficiency in all cases except mechanical repairmen for whom the criterion was success in training.

In Figure 1, when the minimal cutoff for validity was .50, biographical items excelled the intelligence test 2 to 1 and spacial relations by 18 to 1.

In Figure 2, when the cutoff was arbitrarily taken as .40, B-items outperformed the intelligence test by 23 percent and the spacial relations test by 8 to 1.

In Figure 3, when .30 was the cutoff, B-items were still substantially ahead of all other predictors.

In Figures 1 through 3, B-items may be compared with another type of personal item which has a "cousin" relationship, the personality inventory. These data were taken from a paper by Ghiselli and Barthol (1953) who reviewed 113 studies from 1919 to 1953 in which the personality inventory was a predictor of work behavior. The results showed that B-items had 43 percent more validity coefficients of .50 or higher, 52 percent more validities at .40 or higher, and 55 percent more at .30 or higher.

. . . For a complex range of work behavior, biographical items seem to yield higher validity coefficients than other predictors. By contrast, the usual selection

FIGURE 1
Proportion of Validity Coefficients .50 or Higher with Job Proficiency as the Criterion

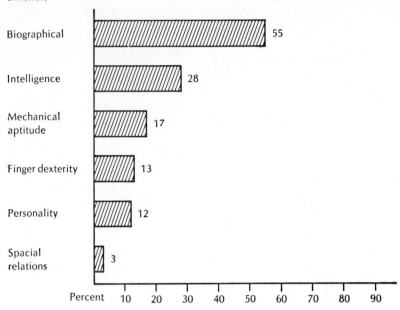

FIGURE 2
Proportion of Validity Coefficients .40 or Higher with Job Proficiency as the Criterion

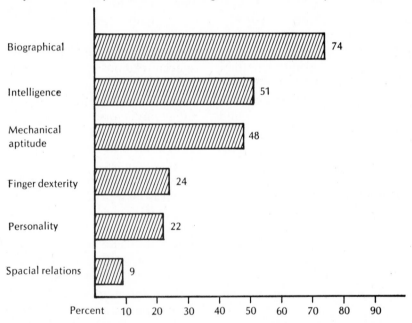

FIGURE 3
Proportion of Validity Coefficients .30 or Higher with Job Proficiency as the Criterion

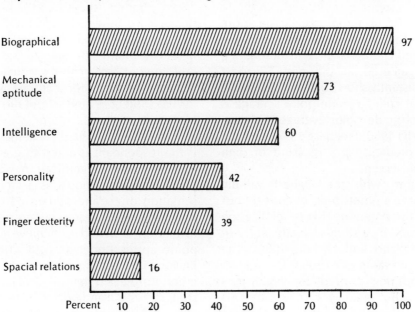

Biographical — 97
Mechanical aptitude — 73
Intelligence — 60
Personality — 42
Finger dexterity — 39
Spacial relations — 16

Percent 10 20 30 40 50 60 70 80 90 100

interview has produced such low reliability and validity in study after study that many researchers have recommended its discontinuance (Dunnette 1962; England and Paterson 1960).

Three Theoretical Explanations

The Nonfiction Theory. Why is it that *B*-items seem to have accuracy in predicting specific work behavior? One explanation is that the scorable application blank is representative of an individual's history while other predictors, especially the unstructured selection interview, may be caricatures. For instance, in the interview, the individual can present a fictionalized concept of himself, while the scorable application blank is more apt to be a systematic, comprehensive collection of factual information about the individual. *B*-items may be to the selection interview, what nonfiction is to fiction.

The Relevant Item Theory. Lykken and Rose (1963) have made the point that the validity of any test may be dampened because it is a set of "relevant" and "irrele-

vant" items. For example, all parts of the predictor space are not likely to be equally valid. The predictor space for a test is heteroscedastic since all of the test items will not be relevant for predicting a specific criterion behavior.

The scorable application blank, by contrast, has a predictor space that is homoscedastic since only "relevant" items are selected in the set used to predict the specific criterion behavior in the cross-validation.

The Point-to-Point Theory. The scorable application blank may "work" because it escapes the fallacy of attempting to make predictions by measuring general mediators. For instance, a classic strategy in testing is to assume that criterion behavior is controlled or determined by generalized mediators as traits, aptitudes, or intelligence. The problem, then, is to measure the general mediators. The more accurate the measurement, the higher the probability that criterion behavior can be estimated with precision.

The data seem to suggest, however, that

accurate prediction is a function of a point-to-point correspondence between predictor space and the criterion space. The more points they have in common, the greater the validity coefficient. As an illustration, the evidence gathered in the past 50 years rather consistently shows that the best single predictor of college grade point average is high school grade point average (Fishman and Pasanella 1960; Freeberg 1967), and the next best predictor is a measure of high school achievement.

Information with the highest validity seems to have a point-to-point correspondence with the criterion. This generalization was supported by a study of National Merit finalists (Holland and Nichols 1964). The attempt, using samples of 500 boys and 500 girls, was not only to predict college freshmen grades, but creative accomplishments in specific areas as leadership, science, drama, literature, music, and art. As might be expected, student achievement in high school was the best indicator of college achievement. The results further showed a point-to-point relationship between what the student did in high school and his behavior in college. For instance, high school grades predicted college grades, scientific activity in high school predicted similar achievement in college, and this specific one-to-one-relationship held for leadership, drama, writing, music, and art.

High school grade point average is predictive of college GPA, but if the one-to-one principle holds, then adult achievement probably *cannot* be predicted from information as college grade point average. Hoyt's review (1965) concluded that achievement in business, engineering, medicine, science, and law cannot be predicted, even with modest accuracy, from college GPA. . . .

SUMMARY

In comparison with other predictors as intelligence, aptitude, interest, and personality, biographical items had vastly superior validity. This conclusion may be limited to "hard" rather than "soft" biographical items. Hard B-items would be those classified as historical and verifiable. For instance, here is a "hard" B-item: "What was your rank in your high school graduating class?" A "soft" B-item, for contrast, could be: "What subject in high school did you enjoy most?"

It may be that "hard" B-items, especially if the respondent is asked to grant his permission for item verification with former employers and schools, is a factual representation of the individual's past behavior. Beginning with these accurate data, the information is sorted to achieve a point-to-point correspondence with criterion behavior. This sorting of items to find only criterion-relevant items is rarely the analytic strategy with standardized measures. Usually a standardized predictor is applied as a ready-made collection of items many of which may or may not be criterion-relevant.

Future research with biographical items should attempt to discover how item dimensionality is related to predictive validity. For instance, how important are item dimensions as verifiable-unverifiable, historical-futuristic, actual behavior-hypothetical behavior, etc? There is some evidence (Walther 1961; 1962) that certain "soft" B-items can have unusually high validity. A theoretical explanation is needed. It may be that item transparency and item fakability are more powerful variables than any classification of B-items as, for instance, hard or soft.

REFERENCES

Anastasi, A., and Schaefer, C. E. "Biographical Correlates of Artistic and Literary Creativity in Adolescent Girls." *Journal of Applied Psychology* 53 (1969): 267–73.

Buel, W. D. "Voluntary Female Clerical Turnover: The Concurrent and Predictive Validity of a Weighted Application Blank." *Journal of Applied Psychology* 48 (1964): 180–82.

Cline, V. B., Tucker, M. F., and Anderson, D. R. "Psychology of the Scientist: 20. Cross-Validation of Biographical Information Predictor Keys Across Diverse Samples of Scientists." *Psychological Reports* 19 (1966): 597–606.

Dunnette, M. D. "Personnel Management." *Annual Review of Psychology* 13 (1962): 285–314.

Dunnette, M. D., Kirchner, W. K., Erickson, J. R. and Banas, P. A. "Predicting Turnover of Female Office Employees." *Personnel Administration* 23 (1960): 45–50.

Ehrle, R. A. "Quantification of Biographical Data for Predicting Vocational Rehabilitation Success." *Journal of Applied Psychology* 48 (1964): 171–74.

England, G. W., and Paterson, D. G. "Selection and Placement—The Past Ten Years." In H. G. Heneman, Jr., L. C. Brown, M. K. Chandler, R. Kahn, H. S. Parnes, and G. P. Schultz, eds., *Employment Relations Research* (New York: Harper, 1960): 43–72.

Fishman, J. A., and Pasanella, A. K. "College Admission-Selection Studies." *Review of Educational Research* 33 (1960): 298–310.

Fleishman, E. A., and Berniger, J. "One Way to Reduce Office Turnover." *Personnel* 37 (1960): 63–69.

Freeberg, N. E. "The Biographical Information Blank as a Predictor of Student Achievement: A Review." *Psychological Reports* 20 (1967): 911–25.

Ghiselli, E. E., and Barthol, R. P. "The Validity of Personality Inventories in the Selection of Employees." *Journal of Applied Psychology* 37 (1953): 18–20.

Ghiselli, E. E. *The Validity of Occupational Tests.* New York: Wiley, 1966.

Henry, E. R. *Research Conference on the Use of Autobiographical Data as Psychological Predictors.* Greensboro, N. C.: The Richardson Foundation, 1965.

Holland, J. L., and Nichols, R. C. "Prediction of Academic and Extra-Curricular Achievement in College." *Journal of Educational Psychology* 55 (1964): 55–65.

Hoyt, D. P. "The Relationship Between College Grades and Adult Achievement. A Review of the Literature." *American College Testing Program Research Reports,* 1965, No. 7.

Kahn, M. W., "A Factor-Analytic Study of Personality, Intelligence, and History Characteristics of Murderers." *Proceedings of the 73rd Annual Convention of the American Psychological Association,* 1965, 227–28.

Laurent, H. "Cross-Cultural Cross-Validation of Empirically Validated Tests. *Journal of Applied Psychology* 54 (1970): 417–23.

Lykken, D. T., and Rose, R. "Psychological Prediction from Actuarial Tables." *Journal of Clinical Psychology* 19 (1963): 139–51.

McGrath, J. J. "Improving Credit Evaluation with a Weighted Application Blank." *Journal of Applied Psychology* 44 (1960): 325–28.

MacKinnon, D. W. "The Nature and Nurture of Creative Talent." *American Psychologist* 17 (1962): 484–95.

Scott, R. D., and Johnson, R. W. "Use of the Weighted Application Blank in Selecting Unskilled Employees." *Journal of Applied Psychology* 51 (1967): 393–95.

Schuh, A. J. "The Predictability of Employee Tenure: A Review of the Literature." *Personnel Psychology* 20 (1967): 133–52.

Tucker, M. F., Cline, V. B., and Schmitt, J. R. "Prediction of Creativity and Other Performance Measures from Biographical Information Among Pharmaceutical Scientists." *Journal of Applied Psychology* 51 (1967): 131–38.

Walther, R. H. "Self-Description as a Predictor of Success or Failure in Foreign Service Clerical Jobs." *Journal of Applied Psychology* 45 (1961): 16–21.

Walther, R. H. "Self-Description as a Predictor of Rate of Promotion of Junior Foreign Service Officers." *Journal of Applied Psychology* 46 (1962): 314–16.

15. IMPROVEMENTS IN THE SELECTION INTERVIEW

ROBERT E. CARLSON, PAUL W. THAYER,
EUGENE C. MAYFIELD, and DONALD A. PETERSON

The effectiveness and utility of the selection interview has again been seriously questioned as a result of several comprehensive reviews of the research literature.[1] Not one of these classic summary reviews of the interview research literature arrived at conclusions that could be classed as optimistic when viewed from an applied standpoint. Yet, none of this is new informaticn. As early as 1915, the validity of the selection interview was empirically questioned.[2] Despite the fact that it is common knowledge that the selection interview probably contributes little in the way of validity to the selection decision, it continues to be used. It is clear that no amount of additional evidence on the lack of validity will alter the role of the interview in selection. Future research should obviously be directed at understanding the mechanism of the interview and improving interview technology. As Schwab has stated:

Companies are not likely to abandon the use of the employment interview, nor is it necessarily desirable that they do so. But it is grossly premature to sit back comfortably and assume that employment interviews are satisfactory. It is even too early to dash off unsupported recommendations for their improvement. A great deal of research work remains, research which companies must be willing to sponsor before we can count the interview as a prime weapon in our selection arsenal.[3]

This was essentially the conclusion that the Life Insurance Agency Management Association reached some six years ago. In addition, the life insurance industry, through LIAMA, took action and sponsored basic research on the selection interview.

The research reported here is an attempt to improve the use of the selection interview in the life insurance industry. The role of the interview in selection presented a particularly difficult problem for the life insurance industry where each agency manager is responsible for many of the traditional personnel management functions. In addition, these agencies are scattered across the U.S. and Canada and make centralizing the selection process difficult. In order to strengthen the role of the selection interview in each manager's selection system, LIAMA has been doing basic research on the selection interview for the past six years.

The research reported here is part of a long-run research program concerned with how interviewers make employment decisions. Its purpose is to try to determine the limits of an interviewer's capability in extending his judgment into the future. This summary covers the early studies in a program of research to develop interim tools and the training necessary to make the selection interview a useful selection instrument.

The first step in the interview research program was to observe and record numerous interviews, to interview in depth the

Source: *Personnel Journal* 50 (April 1971): 268–75, 317.

[1] See, for example, R. Wagner, "The Employment Interview: A Critical Summary," *Personnel Psychology* 2 (1949): 17–46; G. W. England and D. G. Paterson, "Selection and Placement—The Past Ten Years," in H. G. Heneman, Jr., et al., eds., *Employment Relations Research: A Summary and Appraisal,* New York: Harper, 1960, pp. 43–72; E. C. Mayfield, "The Selection Interview: A Reevaluation of Published Research." *Personnel Psychology* 17 (1964): 239–60. L. Ulrich and D. Trumbo, "The Selection Interview Since 1949," *Psychological Bulletin* 63 (1965): 100–16.

[2] W. D. Scott, "The Scientific Selection of Salesmen," *Advertising and Selling* 25 (1915); 5–6, 94–96.

[3] D. P. Schwab, "Why Interview? A Critique," *Personnel Journal* 48, 2 (1969): 129.

interviewers on their decision process, to conduct group decision conferences where the interviewers discussed their perception of their decision process for a given taped interview, and to examine the published research on the selection interview. Based upon this information, a model of the selection interview was constructed that specified as many of the influences operating during the interview as could be determined. Initially, there appeared to be four main classes of influences operating to affect/limit the decision of the interviewer. They were:

The physical and psychological properties of the interviewee.

The physical and psychological properties of the interviewer.

The situation/environment in which the interviewer works.

The task or type of judgment the interviewer must make.

The research strategy has been to systematically manipulate and control the variables specified in the model, trying to eliminate variables that do not have any influence, trying to assess the magnitude of those variables that have an influence, and adding variables that other research has shown to be promising. The first section of this article will describe some of the research findings; the second section will describe some of the materials that have been developed; and the third section will describe the interviewer training that has been developed.

WHAT ARE SOME FINDINGS?

Structured versus Unstructured Interviews

One question that has often been asked is "What kind of interview is best?" What interview style—structured, where the interviewer follows a set procedure; or unstructured, where the interviewer has no set procedure and where he follows the interviewee's lead—results in more effective de-

cisions? In this study live interviews were used. Each interviewee was interviewed three times. Interviewers used the following three types of interviewing strategies: structured, where the interviewer asked questions only from an interview guide; semi-structured, where the interviewer followed an interview guide, but could ask questions about any other areas he wished; and unstructured, where the interviewer had no interview guide and could do as he wished. The basic question involved was the consistency with which people interviewing the same interviewee could agree with each other. If the interviewers' judgments were not consistent—one interviewer saying the applicant was good and the other saying he was bad—no valid prediction of job performance could be made from interview data. Agreement among interviewers is essential if one is to say that the procedure used has the potential for validity.

The results indicated that only the structured interview generated information that enabled interviewers to agree with each other. Under structured conditions, the interviewer knew what to ask and what to do with the information he received. Moreover, the interviewer applied the same frame of reference to each applicant, since he covered the same areas for each. In the less-structured interviews, the managers received additional information, but it seemed to be unorganized and made their evaluation task more difficult. Thus, a highly-structured interview has the greatest potential for valid selection.[4]

Effect of Interviewer Experience

In the past it had been assumed that one way to become an effective interviewer was through experience. In fact, it has been hypothesized that interviewers who have had the same amount of experience would

[4] R. E. Carlson, D. P. Schwab, and H. G. Heneman III. "Agreement Among Selection Interview Styles," *Journal of Industrial Psychology* 5, 1 (1970): 8–17.

evaluate a job applicant similarly.[5] To determine whether this was indeed the case, a study was done that involved managers who had conducted differing numbers of interviews over the same time period. Managers were then compared who had similar, as well as differing, concentrations of interviewing experience. It was found that when evaluating the same recruits, interviewers with similar experiences did not agree with each other to any greater degree than did interviewers with differing experiences. It was concluded that interviewers benefit very little from day-to-day interviewing experience and apparently the conditions necessary for learning are not present in the day-to-day interviewer's job situation.[6] This implied that systematic training is needed, with some feedback mechanism built into the selection procedure, to enable interviewers to learn from their experiences; the job performance predictions made by the interviewer must be compared with how the recruit actually performs on the job.

Situational Pressures

One of the situational variables studied was how pressure for results affected the evaluation of a new recruit. One large group of managers was told to assume that they were behind their recruiting quota, that it was October, and that the home office had just called. Another group was ahead of quota; for a third group, no quota situation existed. All three groups of managers evaluated descriptions of the same job applicants. It was found that being behind recruiting quota impaired the judgment of those managers. They evaluated the same recruits as actually having greater potential and said

they would hire more of them than did the other two groups of managers.[7]

One more highly significant question was raised: Are all managers, regardless of experience, equally vulnerable to this kind of pressure? Managers were asked how frequently they conducted interviews. Regardless of how long the person had been a manager, those who had had a high rate of interviewing experience—many interviews in a given period of time—were less susceptible to pressures than were those with a low interviewing rate. The interviewers with less interviewing experience relied more on subjective information and reached a decision with less information. It was concluded that one way to overcome this problem of lack of concentrated interviewing experience was through the general use of a standardized interview procedure and intensive training in its use.

Standard of Comparison

Another condition studied was the standards managers applied in evaluating recruits. It was found, for example, that if a manager evaluated a candidate who was just average after evaluating three or four very unfavorable candidates in a row, the average one would be evaluated very favorably.[8] When managers were evaluating more than one recruit at a time, they used other recruits as a standard.[9] Each recruit was compared to all other recruits. Thus, managers did not have an absolute standard —who they thought looked good was partly determined by the persons with whom they were comparing the recruit. This indicated that some system was necessary to aid a manager in evaluating a recruit. The same

[5] P. M. Rowe, "Individual Differences in Assessment Decisions," Unpublished doctoral thesis, McGill University, 1960.

[6] R. E. Carlson, "Selection Interview Decisions: The Effect of Interviewer Experience, Relative Quota Situation, and Applicant Sample on Interviewer Decisions," *Personnel Psychology* 20 (1967): 259–80.

[7] Ibid.

[8] R. E. Carlson, "Effects of Applicant Sample on Ratings of Valid Information in an Employment Setting," *Journal of Applied Psychology* 54 (1970): 217–22.

[9] Carlson, "Selection Interview Decisions," pp. 193–207.

system should be applicable to each recruit. This implied that some standardized evaluation system was necessary to reduce the large amount of information developed from an interview to a manageable number of constant dimensions.

Effect of Appearance

Some of the early studies utilized photographs to try to determine how much of an effect appearance had on the manager's decision. A favorably rated photograph was paired with a favorably rated personal history description and also with an unfavorably rated personal history. It was found that appearance had its greatest effect on the interviewer's final rating when it complemented the personal history information.[10] Even when appearance and personal history information were the same (both favorable or both unfavorable), the personal information was given twice as much weight as appearance. However, the relationship is not a simple one and only emphasized the need for a more complete system to aid the manager in selection decision-making.

Effect of Interview Information on Valid Test Results

In many selection situations, valid selection tests are used in conjunction with the interview data in arriving at a selection decision. Two recent studies have investigated how the emphasis placed on valid test results (*Aptitude Index Battery*) is altered by the more subjective interview data. Managers do place great emphasis on the AIB knowing that the score does generate a valid prediction.

However, how much weight is given to the score depends on other conditions; e.g., a low-scoring applicant is judged better if

preceded by a number of poor applicants, unfavorable information is given much greater weight if it is uncovered just prior to ending the interview, etc. This finding suggested that what is needed is some system that places the interview information and other selection information in their proper perspective.[11]

Interview Accuracy

A recent study tried to determine how accurately managers can recall what an applicant says during an interview. Prior to the interview the managers were given the interview guide, pencils, and paper and were told to perform as if *they* were conducting the interview. A 20-minute videotape of a selection interview was played for a group of 40 managers. Following the videotape presentation, the managers were given a 20-question test. All questions were straightforward and factual. Some managers missed none, while some missed as many as 15 out of 20 items. The average number was 10 wrong. In a short 20-minute interview, half the managers could not report accurately on the information produced during the interview! On the other hand, those managers who had been following the interview guide and taking notes were quite accurate on the test; note-taking in conjunction with a guide appears to be essential.

Given that interviewers differed in the accuracy with which they were able to report what they heard, the next question appeared to be "How does this affect their evaluation?" In general it was found that those interviewers who were least accurate in their recollections rated the interviewee higher and with less variability, while the more accurate interviewers rated the interviewee average or lower and with greater

[10] R. E. Carlson, "The Relative Influence of Appearance and Factual Written Information on an Interviewer's Final Rating," *Journal of Applied Psychology* 51 (1967): 461–68.

[11] R. E. Carlson, "The Effect of Interview Information in Altering Valid Impressions," *Journal of Applied Psychology* 55 (1971): 66–72.

variability. Thus, those interviewers who did not have the factual information at their disposal assumed that the interview was generally favorable and rated the interviewee more favorable in all areas. Those interviewers who were able to reproduce more of the factual information rated the interviewee lower and recognized his intra-individual differences by using more of the rating scale. This implied that the less accurate interviewers selected a "halo strategy" when evaluating the interviewee, while the more accurate interviewers used an individual differences strategy. Whether this is peculiar to the individual interviewer or due to the fact that the interviewer did or didn't have accurate information at his disposal is, of course, unanswerable from this data.

Can Interviewers Predict?

The ultimate purpose of the selection interview is to collect factual and attitudinal information that will enable the interviewer to make accurate and valid job behavior predictions for the interviewee. The interviewer does this by recording the factual information for an applicant, evaluating the meaning of the information in terms of what the interviewee will be able to do on the job in question, and extending these evaluations into the future in the form of job behavior predictions. The question is "How reliably can a group of interviewers make predictions for a given interviewee?" Without high inter-interviewer agreement, the potential for interview validity is limited to a few interviewers and cannot be found in the interview process itself.

In this study, a combination of movies and audio tapes were played simulating an interview. In addition, each of the 42 manager-interviewers was given a detailed written summary of the interview. The total interview lasted almost three hours and covered the interviewee's work history, work experience, education and military experience, life insurance holdings, attitude toward the life insurance career, family life,

financial soundness, social life and social mobility, and future goals and aspirations. After hearing and seeing the interview and after studying a 20-page written summary, each interviewer was asked to make a decision either to continue the selection process or to terminate negotiations. In addition, each interviewer was asked to make a list of all the factual information he considered while making his decision. Also, the interviewer was to rate the interviewee in 31 different areas. The ratings were descriptive of the interviewee's past accomplishments, such as his job success pattern, the quantity and quality of his education, his family situation, financial knowledge and soundness, etc. Finally, the interviewers were asked to make job behavior predictions in 28 different job specific activities such as Could he use the telephone for business purposes? Could he make cold calls? Would he keep records? Would he take direction? What about his market?

The interviewers agreed quite well with each other on which facts they reportedly considered in making their employment decision. Almost 70 percent of the factual statements were recorded by all the interviewers. The remaining 30 percent of the factual statements were specific to interviewers. This tended to confirm a hypothesis of Mayfield and Carlson where they postulate that the stereotypes held by interviewers consist of general, as well as specific, content.[12] It was concluded that interviewers do record and use similar factual information with agreement.

The interviewers agreed less well with each other on the evaluation or value placed on the facts. The median inter-interviewer correlation was .62, with a low of .07 and a high of .82. This means that the interviewers still agreed reasonably well on the evaluation—good versus bad—quality of the information they received. They would

---

[12] E. C. Mayfield and R. E. Carlson, "Selection Interview Decisions: First Results from a Long-Term Research Project," *Personnel Psychology* 19 (1966): 41-53.

make similar selection-rejection decisions.

The job behavior predictions of the interviewers, however, were not nearly as high in agreement. The median inter-interviewer correlation was .33 with a low of —.21 and a high of .67. This means that the interviewers do not agree with each other on how well the interviewee will perform the job of a life insurance agent in 28 different areas. In addition, those predictions that required the interviewer to extend his judgment further into the future had significantly greater inter-interviewer variability than did those predictions that could be verified in a shorter period of time. Thus, interviewers can agree more with each other's predictions if the job behavior is of a more immediate nature.

These findings imply that although interviewers probably use much the same information in making a decision, they will evaluate it somewhat differently. Furthermore, the interviewers are not able to agree on how well the individual will perform on the job.

Thus, it was concluded that interviewers evaluate essentially similar things in an applicant; they agree reasonably well whether an applicant's past record is good or bad, but they cannot agree on good or bad for what. Yet here, and only here, is where the clinical function of the interviewer is difficult to replace with a scoring system. In being able to make accurate and valid job behavior predictions, the interview can pay for itself in terms of planning an applicant's early job training and as a mechanism whereby a supervisor can learn early how to manage an applicant. In order for the interviewer to be able to make accurate and valid job behavior predictions, it follows that he must have a feedback system whereby he can learn from his past experiences. Only through accurate feedback in language similar to the behavior predictions can the interviewer learn to make job behavior predictions. The results further imply that the interviewer must be equipped with a complete selection system that coordinates all the selection steps and provides the interviewer with as relevant and complete information as possible when he makes job behavior predictions.

Conclusions

These early studies in LIAMA's interview research program provided little in the way of optimism for the traditional approach to the selection interview. However, this research did indicate specific areas where improvements in selection and interview technology could be made. It did indicate where interim improvements could be tried and evaluated while the long-term research on the interview continued.

Two major applied implications may be derived from the interview research to date. First, the selection interview should be made an integral part of an over-all selection procedure, and to accomplish this, new and additional materials are needed. The new materials should include a broad-gauge, comprehensive, structured interview guide; standardized evaluation and prediction forms that aid the interviewer in summarizing information from all steps in the selection process; and an evaluation system that provides feedback to the interviewer in language similar to the preemployment job behavior predictions he must make. The second major applied implication is that an intensive training program for interviewers is necessary if interviewers are to initially learn enough in common to increase the probability of obtaining general validity from the selection interview. Thus, the early studies have provided specific information that has been used to change the way selection is carried out in the insurance industry.

Implementation: Development of a Selection Process

As a result of and based upon the early interview research, LIAMA constructed the *Agent Selection Kit*. This is a complete agent selection procedure to be used by agency branch managers and general agents in the field. Selection begins when the agency head secures the name of a prospective recruit and ends when the new agent has been selling for six months or when negotiations or employment is terminated. Because research demonstrated the necessity of formally taking into consideration each step in the selection process, each step in the procedure is carefully placed to maximize the potential of succeeding and following steps. The *Agent Selection Kit* introduced the following new ideas to the insurance industry:

1. *Selection Should More Properly Be Viewed as Manpower Development.* The *Agent Selection Kit* is a completely integrated process, more properly described as manpower development; it goes beyond just selection. The assumption is that if industry is really going to have an appreciable effect on the manpower problem, it will have to think of recruiting, selection, training, and supervision as parts of a total manpower development process and not as entities by themselves. Quantity and quality of recruiting have an impact on selection—selection affects training—training capabilities, in turn, should affect selection. Unless viewed as a continuous, dependent process, maximum use cannot be made of the information the tools provide. If viewed as a complete process, the information gained from each step is carried forward to make future steps and the final decision more powerful.

2. *Organizational Differences Must Be Taken into Consideration in Selection.* Because the *Agent Selection Kit* is a complete selection process, it can be modified to meet company and agency differences. By clearly spelling out the philosophy and principles behind the steps in the *Agent Selection Kit*, the company and the agency head are able to evaluate what is being gained or lost by altering the steps in selection. Further, because the agency head is forced to make job behavior predictions, he can begin to consider each recruit in terms of his particular agency needs, style, and strengths. Agency differences, as well as individual differences, enter into the employment decision in a systematic manner.

3. *A Career with Any Company Should Be Entered into Based on Realistic Job Expectations.*[13] The company should know what the job recruit expects from his association with the company. Under such a condition, the manager can make a manpower development decision that properly considers selection, early training, motivation, and supervision practices of the applicant in question. The job recruit should know what the company expects of him, how the company is going to help him accomplish these goals, and the difficulties and benefits he may encounter in undertaking the job. With such knowledge, the recruit can make more than a job decision. He can make a career decision. The creation of realistic expectations further implies that the employment decision be one of "mutual consent." Professional management of the future will not be able to rely on a slanted job presentation to attract recruits to a career in hopes that one or two applicants will succeed. Manpower development decisions will replace selection decisions. The *Agent Selection Kit* is built around the concept of "mutual consent" with respect to a career decision. There are already indications that the recruit of the future will respond to a "mutual exploration" theme, where together he and the manager will examine the individual's future in an industry. The *Agent Selection Kit* provides a systematic fact-finding procedure that appeals to the recruit.

4. *The Selection Interview Should Proceed According to a Highly Structured Format.* The *Agent Selection Kit* contains two self-contained structured interview guides. The first interview guide is to be used with applicants who have had extensive prior work history and concentrates on this work experience. The alternate interview guide is

---

[13] Life Insurance Agency Management Association, "Realistic" Job Expectations and Survival, Research Report 1964–2 (File 432).

to be used with applicants just completing their education or military experiences and without any work experience. In addition, both interview guides cover the recruit's education, military experience, attitude toward insurance and toward the insurance agent's job, family commitments, finances, social mobility, social life, and future goals and aspirations. The interview guides present the initial series of questions and several alternative probes. Experience and pretesting have indicated that recruits are receptive to a structured approach and that interviewers can learn to use the guides after brief, but intensive, training.

5. *Employment Decisions Should Be Based on Predictions of Future Job Behavior.* The *Agent Selection Kit* considers decision-making from the point of view of a prediction of future behavior, rather than from vague, over-all impressions of potential or character. The manager manages the agent's activity, use of the telephone, recordkeeping, prospecting, etc. The *Agent Selection Kit* enables the manager to make predictions about such job behaviors.

6. *The Manager Should Be Able to Learn From and Correct His Selection System.* The *Agent Selection Kit* procedure contains a built-in "feedback system" that enables the manager to learn from and correct his selection process. LIAMA interview research has shown that managers do not learn from the traditional approach to selection interviewing. To correct this, the *Agent Selection Kit* includes an Agent Performance Rating Form that the manager uses to compare to his final decision ratings. Discrepancies between his prediction and results point to areas in his selection and early training process that need extra effort.

Implementation: Training in Selection and Interviewing

To ensure at least uniform initial introduction to the material, LIAMA designed a three-day skill-building workshop. Three general training objectives and 16 specific behavioral objectives served as guides in setting up the training program. The first general goal was to develop in each trainee *knowledge* of selection and interview techniques; the second goal was to create favorable *attitudes* in the managers toward selection and self-confidence in their ability to conduct a technically good selection interview; and third, to develop *skill* in actually using the selection and interview materials. As a result of participating in the training, the agency heads are to actually be better at selection and interviewing than they were prior to training, to know they are better, and to be able to immediately use the new material with some skill. Thus, the goals of the training are to change attitudes as well as to develop knowledge and skill. These specifications dictated that the workshops be built around small-sized classes, class participation, and practice with standardized case material and controlled feedback.

To accomplish the goals of the training program, the first step in the workshop is to help the agency manager to understand and accept the principles behind the steps in the selection process. This helps to make the trainees receptive to discarding their current approach to selection and to accepting the new approach. Once the agency head accepts the logic of the principles on which the *Agent Selection Kit* is based, the next step is to get the trainee to recognize and question how he is currently conducting his selection process. This is accomplished through the use of edited tapes that demonstrate some of the effects of violating the selection principles. At the end of this first phase of the training, the agency heads are receptive to a new procedure and are aware of what a good procedure should contain.

The skill training that follows is designed to make the agency head more proficient in the use of the interview and evaluation procedures. The interview technique training includes taped examples, practice, and critique. The final evaluation practice sessions are extremely important to agency heads. Here the manager is asked to combine information from all the selection methods he has utilized—the interview, reference checks, credit reports, interview with the wife, precontract training, etc. The manager practices making job behavior predictions in areas such as use of the telephone, night work, markets, prospecting activities, etc. For the first time, managers recognize that they will not be managing the recruit's character or how impressive he looks, but rather they recognize that they must manage his work activities. Managers begin to recognize that selection should try to predict the recruit's performance in these activities.

During the workshops, the participants' attitudes swing from skepticism to receptivity, from impatience with the training detail to complete acceptance. These swings in attitude are built into the schedule, since early experimental workshops showed that they were necessary to modify and solidify managers' attitudes.

The managers leave their workshop with greater knowledge, with a skill that is well along in development, and with much greater self-confidence in their selection and early training procedure that they can put into practice immediately.

The Future

The *Agent Selection Kit* was introduced to LIAMA's 300-plus member companies in 1969. By mid-1970, 40 major life insurance companies had introduced it to their general agents and managers. Obviously, at this time it is much too early to evaluate its effectiveness. However, it is currently being evaluated as part of LIAMA's research program on the selection interview. In addition, it also provides a natural field setting for further pure research on the selection interview. Thus, LIAMA's research on the interview is an example of pure research generating an improved product, which, in turn, furthers the pure research effort.

6

INTERNAL STAFFING

RELATIONSHIP TO FORECASTING

We previously suggested that the purpose of personnel forecasting was to identify probable imbalances (shortages or surpluses) in the organization's workforce for future time periods. It is then possible to plan how to deal with these imbalances. Both shortage and surplus conditions will have an impact on external recruitment and staffing strategies, particularly for entry level jobs. Yet, both conditions will also influence internal staffing strategies and programs.

To illustrate the internal staffing implications of anticipated imbalances, consider first the problem of projected surpluses in certain subunits of the organization. How is this to be dealt with? The most immediate reaction is usually to assume that layoffs will have to occur. A layoff strategy, however, is only one of many strategies that can be considered in the planning process. An alternative to layoffs would be to transfer and/or promote employees out of surplus subunits into shortage subunits. Transfers, and particularly promotions, will probably also require the design of training programs to qualify the employees for these jobs. Demotion of employees into subunits where shortages are anticipated is another possibility. Yet, another possibility would be to establish provisions for early retirement, perhaps coupled with a onetime cash bonus as an added inducement.

In the case of projected shortages, numerous facets of internal staffing will likewise be affected, particularly if the shortages will be occurring in nonentry-level jobs. The most immediate requirement will be to identify the employees who are qualified now, or will be qualified, for transfer and promotion. The necessary qualifications themselves may be reviewed and revised, especially if a substantial amount of internal job changing is anticipated. Again training programs may have to be considered as a method of upgrading the skills of current employees, particularly if transfer and promotion rates will be increasing.

In short, all facets of internal staffing, and even training, are potentially affected by forecasted shortages and surpluses. The crucial point is that if the imbalances can be identified far enough in advance, the organization will have the opportunity to consider a wide variety of options for dealing with them.

VALIDITY OF INTERNAL STAFFING DECISIONS

When making internal staffing decisions the organization may use a number of predictors to assist in the decisions. Some of the predictors may be very similar to the types used in external staffing, such as paper and pencil tests. In addition, however, the organization may use predictors unlikely to be found in the external staffing process. For example, both formal and informal assessments of on-the-job performance for each individual within the organization may serve as bases for decision-making. In addition, length of service or seniority, types of previous jobs, and types of training received may also be considered.

Recently, many organizations have developed what are known as *assessment centers* as a basis for evaluating promotability. In addition to the types of predictors mentioned above, the participants will be required to perform in job-related simulation exercises such as the *in-basket, leaderless group discussions,* and *business games.*

Despite these differences between internal and external staffing in the types of predictors used, there is little difference between them in the underlying processes and objectives. In both internal and external staffing, the organization must make inferences or predictions about individuals' probabilities of success on the job for which they are being considered. Therefore, the question of the validity of predictors used in external staffing is equally applicable to the predictors used in internal staffing. Moreover, as in external staffing, both criterion-related and content validation approaches would be appropriate for investigating validity. With the exception of the assessment center, however, there has been surprisingly little research on the validity of internal staffing decisions.

SENIORITY AND INTERNAL STAFFING DECISIONS

Under most circumstances employee seniority will receive some consideration in internal staffing decisions. This may occur in any number of ways. When considering a group of candidates for say promotion, the decision-makers may implicitly assume that the more senior employees deserve greater attention and consideration. On a more formal basis, the organization may have definite lines of job progression established. Associated with these will often be minimum seniority requirements specified for upward movement. An illustration of this is the promotion systems in civil service jurisdictions.

In situations involving employees covered by a labor contract, there will usually be very precise contract provisions about seniority and internal staffing. These will deal with such issues as the seniority unit (department, occupation, plant, and so on) in which employees accrue seniority, how seniority is to be computed and when it is broken, the specific decisions that will be influenced by seniority, and the relative weight that seniority (as opposed to other factors such as merit or ability) will carry in such decisions. Such provisions may also be stated in the personnel policies of an organization in nonunion situations.

The relative weight that seniority (versus merit or ability) should carry in internal staffing decisions has long been an issue of debate and controversy. In part, the controversy involves issues of reliability and validity of measurement. Proponents of seniority argue that seniority is a more objective and reliable measure than assessments of merit and ability, simply because everyone can agree on how much seniority an individual has accumulated. On this basis alone, seniority is to be preferred. In addition, however, seniority proponents argue that seniority has some validity due to its natural reflection of job experience, which in turn is presumed to be related to success on new jobs into which individuals might progress.

The arguments for seniority, however, go beyond issues of reliability and validity. For example, some proponents of seniority note that as employees grow older, their needs for job security and additional income increase. Since age and seniority are usually related, seniority is a logical mechanism for fulfilling older workers' needs. In addition, the use of seniority permits employees to know where they "stand" in terms of probability of job movement or layoff. Thus, employee anxiety is reduced by creating a degree of predictability to the internal staffing process.

INTRODUCTION TO READINGS

Career Management and Development

If the organization is likely to be faced with continual shortages of critical personnel, a powerful stimulus will be created for the organization to develop long-range plans for enhancing the utilization of its personnel. The result will often be a complex set of programs that fall under the general heading of career management or development. At the present time career management has its greatest application for managerial, professional, and technical employees. The selection by William Glueck discusses career management within this context.

As Glueck notes, career management is not simply short-term training and development for the purpose of preparing individuals for their next transfer or promotion. Rather, career management is based on the premise that individuals will spend their entire working career within the organization. Because of this, career management is best thought of as a whole series of planned experiences for the individual. As such, it incorporates elements of on- and off-the-job training, performance appraisal and feedback, job rotation, and well-defined job transfer and progression paths. In one sense, therefore, career management is nothing really unique, at least in terms of its elements. In another sense, it is unique due to the planning and integrating of its elements with a long-term time perspective.

Glueck then reviews the potential advantages of career management. In essence, he ends up concluding that both the organization and the individual stand to benefit from it. Unfortunately, he neglects to consider possible disadvantages of career management. These would include such things as excessive inbreeding and the disarray that could occur if the organizational structure changes.

Descriptions of two career management models are then given. One model involves a hypothetical plan for a company with numerous geographic locations, and the other model is a general career plan for U.S. Air Force officers. Note that both models represent plans from time of entry into the organization all the way to the anticipated time of retirement from the organization.

The Assessment Center

The assessment center involves a complex set of procedures used to assess current employees primarily for the purposes of making internal placement and promotion decisions. Ann Howard describes the characteristics of a typical assessment center in the first part of her article. Participants are assessed off the job through the use of numerous techniques (or components, as Howard refers to them). As we previously noted, these include various ability and personality tests, biographical questionnaires, and situational tests such as the in-basket exercise. The information about participants derived from these techniques is then evaluated by groups of *assessors*. Typically, these evaluations require that assessors rate each participant on specific behavioral dimensions (for example, decision-making, communication, organization ability) and also make a rating of the participant's overall potential, taking into account all the information about the participant. The rating scores, plus scores on the techniques themselves, all may be viewed as predictors.

Howard then reviews the evidence on assessment centers in terms of *interrater reliability* (the amount of agreement between two or more assessors' ratings of participants) and validity. High interrater reliability is important because unless assessors can agree with each other, there is little possibility that their ratings will be valid. Fortunately, the evidence indicates that interrater reliability is acceptable (see her Table 1).

Validation of the assessment center involves correlating participants' assessment ratings and scores with criteria of success obtained at some point after the assessment center. These criteria are usually actual numbers of promotions received or ratings of promotability. During validation it is important that the assessment center evaluations not be used in the actual promotion decisions or promotability ratings. If they are used, then what Howard calls *criterion contamination* occurs. In turn, this may inflate the correlations between the predictors and criteria. Unfortunately, Howard indicates that criterion contamination may be a problem in many of the validation studies.

In most of the validation studies, the assessors' ratings of the participants' overall potential were correlated with the types of criteria just discussed. Based on the results she presents in Tables 2 and 3, Howard concludes that "overall ratings of potential or performance from assessment center procedures generally have shown impressive predictive validity, especially for managerial jobs."

How does this compare with the validities of the separate components (for example, test scores and assessors' ratings of participants on the specific dimensions)? Though the results vary from study to study, Howard concludes that the validities of the components are generally less than the validity of the overall ratings.

Finally, Howard discusses a number of additional advantages ("aesthetics") and potential problems ("blemishes") associated with assessment centers. She notes the need for more research on all of these issues.

Seniority Provisions in Labor Contracts

The Bureau of National Affairs (BNA) maintains a file of 5,000 labor contracts on a continual, updated basis. This file serves as a basic input into the development of written summaries of basic patterns and provisions in labor contracts. The BNA selection, dealing with general seniority provisions, is based on a sample of 400 of the 5,000 contracts.

Specific seniority provisions dealt with in this selection are too numerous to summarize. However, we would like to make a few general observations about these provisions. First, the data show that provisions vary considerably from industry to industry. This is best seen in the last table in the article, which summarizes provisions by manufacturing and nonmanufacturing, and by specific industries within each of these two categories.

The data also indicate that the role of seniority in layoffs, promotions, and transfers is quite complex. For example, seniority is much more likely to be a factor in layoffs than in promotions and transfers. And when it is a factor, its weight, relative to other factors such as ability and merit, varies considerably. This is shown by classifying contracts according to whether seniority is to be the sole factor, the determining factor, a factor given equal consideration with other factors, or a secondary factor. Thus, the seniority versus ability and merit controversy previously discussed is reflected very precisely in labor contracts.

Finally, we should point out that this selection only deals with the more general types of seniority considerations and provisions. In practice, seniority provisions in contracts are usually more complex and apply to many specific internal staffing problems.

16. CAREER MANAGEMENT OF MANAGERIAL, PROFESSIONAL, AND TECHNICAL PERSONNEL
WILLIAM F. GLUECK

This article will define career management and its relation to manpower planning, and will also discuss the usefulness of

Source: "Career Management of Managerial, Professional, and Technical Personnel" by William F. Glueck which appeared in *Manpower Planning and Programming* by Elmer H. Burack and James W. Walker, © 1972 by Allyn and Bacon, Inc.

career management to organizations and to individual employees, as well as the consequences of ineffective career management. A model of career management, along with some examples of career planning, is given, and the importance of the geographic transfer aspect of career management is discussed. Finally, there are some hints on how to plan and program careers.

CAREERS, CAREER MANAGEMENT AND MANPOWER PLANNING

Career management is the part of manpower planning that is designed to develop programs or paths by which employees progress in the organization, that helps them develop themselves to their fullest capacity, and that makes the best use of their talents from the organization's point of view. Optimally developed with the encouragement of, and after consultation with, the employee involved, the career plan includes a combination of securing information and developing attitudes and skills in technical, administrative, and strategic or cognitive domains. These are acquired by training on and off the job, by counseling and coaching with superiors, and by planned rotation in positions of varying functions and in different locations. Career management is not simply "management development" as this term is normally used in the literature. For "management development" frequently connotes individual or group studies or off-the-job programs designed to improve the managerial abilities of the subjects, but little else. Career management's purpose is to design programs to "grow" effective managers (or professionally or technically competent individuals) for the improved goal achievement of the organization and increased satisfaction of the employee.

To understand adequately the implications and the uses of career management, the term *career* must first be defined. *Career* has long been an important concept to sociology and to vocational guidance counselors. It has been defined in various ways. Gusfield defines the terms as: . . a long time commitment to an occupation and/or work place in which an individual places his economic life chances in a particular occupation or organization.[1] Thompson says: A career is any sequential set of relationships to or participation in a social institution.[2] And Simon defines it as: . . . an honorable occupation which one normally takes up in youth with the expectation of advancement and pursues it until retirement.[3]

There are two emphases in careers: those pursued (1) primarily within an organization, and (2) primarily within an occupation. Some may build careers by moving among organizations to achieve the best professional position; others are tied to an organization and shift positions and job orientations within it.[4] Our focus will be on the management of careers with organizations.

FUNCTIONS OF CAREER MANAGEMENT

An individual can perceive his work position as one of two extremes: as a job or as a career. Some individuals view their work only as a "job," a means to an end. "I must go to work to pay the bills," this type of employee might say. As the employee moves through his work life, his job may be changed but his attitude may not. The employee could, however, look upon his work time with the organization as a career —a meaningful series of positions that contribute to the organization and to his or her own development. Whether he perceives work as a "job" or "career" depends on the attitudes and personality he brings to the workplace and the work environment created for the employees by the organization.

Maslow, in his theory of motivation, would contend that the "job" oriented employee would have only his physiological and security needs satisfied and possibly his

---

[1] Joseph Gusfield, "Occupational Roles and Forms of Enterprise," *American Journal of Sociology* 66, 4 (February 1960): 571–88.

[2] James Thompson and Donald Van Houten, *The Behavioral Sciences: An Interpretation* (Reading, Mass.: Addison-Wesley 1970), p. 92.

[3] Herbert Simon et al., *Public Administration* (New York: Knopf, 1950), Chapter 6.

[4] The sociologist Alvin Gouldner referred to these orientations as cosmopolitans (occupationally oriented careers) and locals (organizationally based careers). See his "Cosmopolitans and Locals: Towards an Analysis of Latent Social Roles," *Administrative Science Quarterly*, Part 1. 2, 4 (December 1957): 281–306; Part II. 3, 1 (March 1958): 444–80.

social needs. He could still actuate his higher level needs for "recognition" and "self-actualization" with potential improvement in satisfaction and productivity.[5] McClelland and Atkinson might point out that an organization which did not develop careers for these employees would fail to bring out the achievement motive in these talented employees.[6] Schoonmaker contends that the desire for control of one's own career is a basic human need for those employees and has important implications for employee satisfaction and organizational productivity.[7] Hughes, Gross, and Becker and Strauss argue that an individual's view of his work and/or career is crucial to his satisfaction as a human being and development of his personality. It provides dignity and meaning to his work life.[8]

Implicit in these arguments is that most professional, managerial, and technical employees would prefer to feel that their talents are well used in the workplace, and that the employing organization is impressed with the employee's dignity and talents enough to plan or help him plan how his life is spent for a significant part of his life. It is assumed that, other things being equal, the employee would prefer to join or continue to work in an organization that evidenced these career interests.

The complement of this argument is that the organization benefits when it develops and manages careers for professional, technical, and managerial positions. As Slocum says:

> The need for proficient and loyal officials and workers has induced corporations, universities, government agencies, and other formal work organizations to establish occupational career lines with graded steps. . . . It may be hypothesized that occupational career lines will be established if management considers it necessary to do so in order to attract and retain employees with highly prized occupational knowledge and skills. Career lines may also be established to reward and help to retain loyal and competent workers with lesser skills.[9]

Grusky contends that more rewarding careers will lead to greater commitment to the organization,[10] and Pearson believes that career management will lead to more productive employees.[11]

If there are positive results for the employee and his organization that develops and manages careers, those organizations that do not do so should have negative results. Whyte says that employees feel like "checkers" under these circumstances.

> No one likes to be played checkers with and the man that the organization needs most is precisely the man most sensitive on this point. To control one's destiny, to know which way the path will fork, to have some index of achievement, is an independence he will never have in full measure, but he must forever seek it.[12]

And Ferguson says that organizations which do not plan careers experience excessive turnover and serious underutilization of employees' talents.[13]

[5] Abraham Maslow, *Motivation and Personality* (New York: Harper & Row, 1954), especially chapters 4 and 5.

[6] See, for example, David McClelland, *The Achieving Society* (New York: Free Press, 1967); J. W. Atkinson, *An Introduction to Motivation* (New York: American Book Company, 1964); and Norman Feather, *A Theory of Achievement Motivation* (New York: Wiley, 1966).

[7] Alan N. Schoonmaker, "Individualism in Management," *California Management Review* 11, 2 (Winter 1968): 9–22.

[8] Everett C. Hughes, *Men and Their Work* (Glencoe: Free Press, 1958), especially chapters 3, 7; Edward Gross, *Work and Society* (New York: Thomas Crowell, 1958), especially chapters 1, 5; and Howard E. Becker and Anselm L. Strauss, "Careers, Personality, and Adult Socialization," *American Journal of Sociology* 62, 3 (November 1956): 253–63.

[9] Walter Slocum, "Occupational Careers in Organizations," *Personnel and Guidance Journal* 43, 9 (May 1965): 858–59.

[10] Oscar Grusky, "Career Mobility and Organizational Commitment," *Administrative Science Quarterly* 10, 4 (March 1966): 488–503.

[11] Andrall E. Pearson, "Sales Power Through Planned Careers," *Harvard Business Review* 44, 1 (January-February 1966): 105–16.

[12] William Whyte, Jr., *The Organization Man* (New York: Simon & Schuster, 1956), p. 167.

[13] Lawrence L. Ferguson, "Better Management of Managers' Careers," *Harvard Business Review* 44, 2 (March–April 1966): 139–52.

Some consequences of the lack of career management include:

1. Hoarding of good people by managers to the detriment of the total organization.
2. Promotion from among acquaintances alone without considering others in the organization.
3. Overdependence on present supervision for future positions.
4. Lack of development when individuals are not promoted but the reasons are not explained.[14]

In spite of these persuasive arguments that organizations should help plan careers for their employees, most students of career management contend that most organizations do not do so.[15] Recently, the U.S. Army in a study of 12 large corporations—American Telephone and Telegraph, Chrysler, Du Pont, Ford, General Electric, General Motors, Gulf Oil, IBM, Mobil Oil, Montgomery Ward (division Marcor), Standard Oil of Indiana; and Standard Oil of New Jersey)—had this to say about career programs in industry:

The paths which employees follow in progressing upward in companies are universally understood but seldom recorded. Only one company (in this sample) has identified and recorded normal lines of progress in the managerial hierarchy. The purpose of this effort is to provide managers with a guide for developing and promoting high potential employees into proper channels where their abilities will be utilized to the fullest.[16]

Schoonmaker argues that, in most organizations today, the supervisors and organization are indifferent to the career development of these individual employees. He en-

courages the employee to develop his own career, for without a career attitude, the employee will not be satisfied with his life.[17] This orientation toward individual responsibility (by default or otherwise) is also evident when Ivey and Morrill define a career as: . . . a continuing process through which a person engages in a sequence of developmental tasks necessary for personal growth in occupational life.[18]

If it is true that few organizations manage the careers of their most important employees, this is ironic. For these same organizations frequently do not neglect the management of materials, machines, and funds. Yet, the most complex resource, the one most likely to lose its creativity or usefulness without company or self-management—the human resource—is often neglected. And if little or no attention is given to career management by the organization, it may also be difficult or impossible for the individual employee to plan his own career or to help advance himself, since few cues are given by the firm on what kinds of individuals the firm wishes developed.

CAREER MANAGEMENT: A MODEL

A career plan includes a mix of positional experience and on- and off-the-job-training. After an individual is hired, he or she will experience assignments that develop the individual and use his talents. While in these positions, he or she will serve as an understudy, being counseled and coached by his superior. He also will be assigned to a series of different positions that develop him, in different locations, if this is significant. He or she also will receive appropriate additional training or information to improve technical knowledge (for example, operations research), managerial skills, attitudes (for example, sensitivity training, human relations courses), and conceptual skills (ad-

---

14 Theodore M. Alfred, "Checkers or Choice in Manpower Management," *Harvard Business Review* 45, 1 (January–February 1967): 157–69.

15 See Ferguson, "Better Management"; also David Monent, "Career Development," *Personnel Administration* 30, 4 (July–August 1967): 6–11.

16 *Special Study of Career Programs in Industry* (Washington: Department of the Army, Deputy Chief of Staff for Personnel, May–June 1968).

17 Schoonmaker, "Individualism in Management."

18 Allen Ivey and Weston Morrill, "Career Process: A New Concept for Vocational Behavior," *Personnel and Guidance Journal* 46, 7 (March 1968): 645.

vanced management courses, management gaming, etc.).

A career plan for a young man that could lead to a position of top manager for a company such as Southwestern Bell Telephone Company might look something like the model given in Figure 1. (This is not Bell's plan; rather it is a plan that they might use.) As soon as he is hired, the new "Southwestern Bell employee" becomes exposed to the company by participating in the training program of one year, in a series of understudy roles in which he is closely observed, coached, and counseled by experienced managers. Perhaps he is hired in St. Louis. After the training year, he is given a first line job, for example, in operations. If he is successful, he might be transferred to Topeka, Kansas, where he performs similar duties but with a slightly enlarged scope. Assuming continued progress, he is rotated at Topeka into a position in the commercial department a year or so later. Bell has the employee participate in its financial management training program and transfers him to Houston, Texas. There he works successively in finance, operations, and personnel departments. At this point he is sent to the University of Houston's business school for additional course work and then transferred to New York for positions with the parent company's long lines department. Here he works in several functional jobs and is transferred to California; he receives additional "Bell" training programs and then is returned to "Southwestern Bell" after 16 years to its Dallas office. After several new positions, he is sent to the University of Texas' Top Management Program. After this, he is transferred (at 20-year point) to Arkansas to head up these operations for about five years, then to similar positions for Texas. Next he might attend Harvard's Advanced Management Program. Then, after 27 years, he is transferred to the home office in St. Louis to complete his career as a top manager for Southwestern Bell. Again, this is a hypothetical career plan for a manager. Career plans vary a great deal. Some,

for specialists and staffs for example, are much flatter, or peak early. Form and Miller have pointed this out, as have Thompson and Van Houten.[19] Comparing the young manager's career with that of a personnel career, which may have only three levels of positions, is an example.

Early in the employee's history the career plan is likely to be rather standardized, since there are many rather similar positions to be filled. Later the plan becomes more differentiated or individualized as the employee progresses along the career path and develops somewhat different competencies.

One large organization that has tried to develop and manage careers perhaps even more than others have is the United States Air Force. The Air Force employs approximately 135,000 officers, 350,000 civilian employees, and 750,000 enlisted men. It has a very sophisticated manpower planning system (determination of needs) and personnel planning (determining assignments) system. Its classification system is elaborate (for officers alone there are approximately 400 major classifications). Each month a compute printout of officer manning analysis by command, speciality, and grade level is made at Randolph Air Force Base, Texas. These data are used to plan training, development, and procurement programs. They are also used for sophisticated computer simulation of possible utilization of personnel (such as benefits systems).

The Air Force has developed a complex career development plan for its officer force. The purpose of career development (as stated by the Air Force) is to assure that enough highly qualified officers are available and promoted to responsible positions (it takes years to stimulate intellectual and professional growth and to commit

[19] William Form and Delbert Miller, "Occupational Career Pattern as a Sociological Instrument," *American Journal of Sociology* 53, 4 (February 1947); 317–29. See also Thompson and Van Houten, *Behavioral Sciences*, pp. 106–12; and Victor Vroom and Kenneth MacCrimmon, "Toward a Stochastic Model of Managerial Careers," *Administrative Science Quarterly* 13, 2 (June 1968): 26–46.

FIGURE 1
Career Plan for General Manager: Utility Company

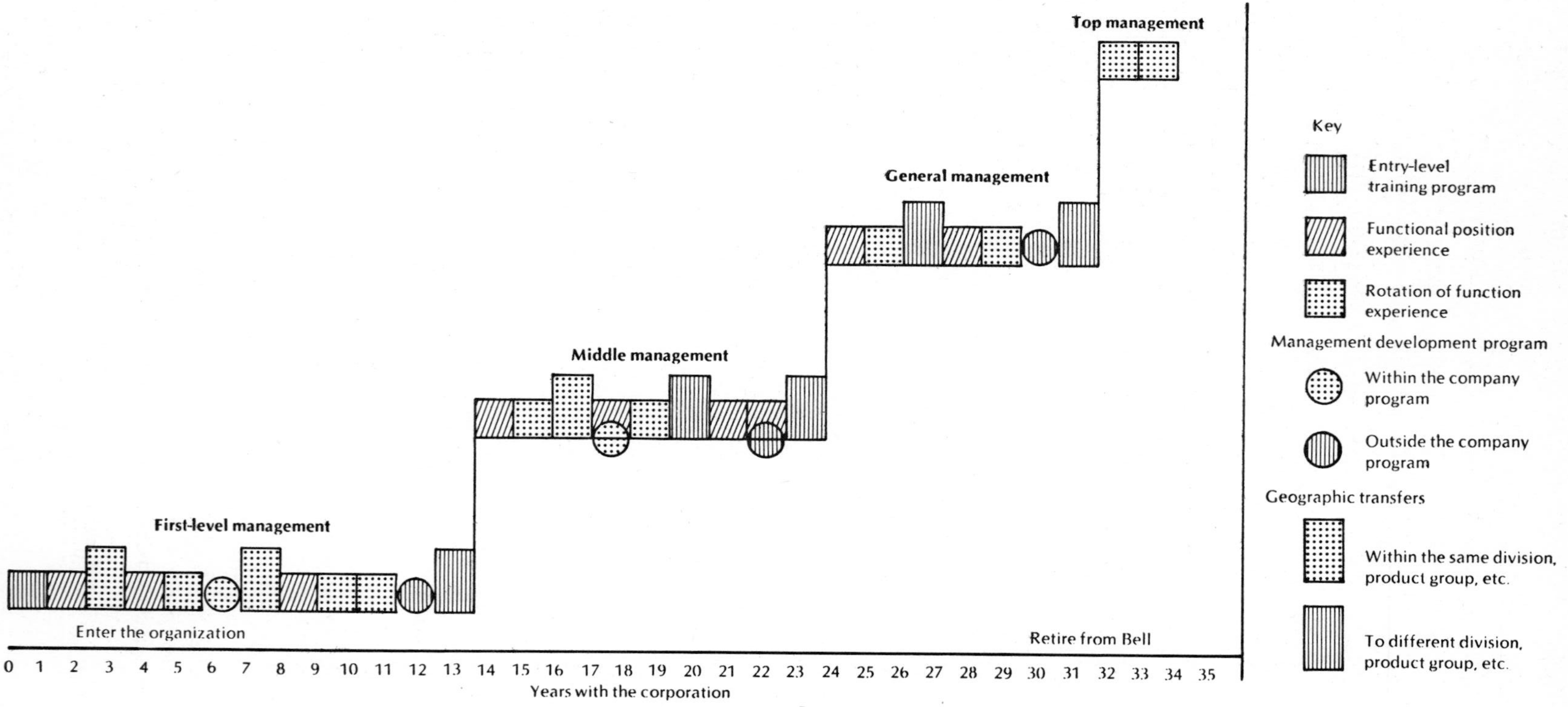

Key

	Entry-level training program
	Functional position experience
	Rotation of function experience
Management development program	
⊙	Within the company program
◐	Outside the company program
Geographic transfers	
	Within the same division, product group, etc.
	To different division, product group, etc.

Top management

General management

Middle management

First-level management

Enter the organization

Retire from Bell

Years with the corporation

0 1 2 3 4 5 6 7 8 9 10 11 12 13 14 15 16 17 18 19 20 21 22 23 24 25 26 27 28 29 30 31 32 33 34 35

them to military careers). So this system attempts to match Air Force needs with the assignment and training patterns desired by the officer.

Figure 2 is a schematic representation of a career profile. There are, however, specific career plans developed for each specialty, specifying the men of different kinds of position experience and education desirable for each. . . . Each career specialty has a career management officer whose function is to serve as an advisor on career development for that group of officers to help assure proper utilization of these men and serve as an advisor to them.

This system seems to be well thought out and a comprehensive program for career development. Whether it is operative and helpful to Air Force employees is an empirical question. Asking a number of Air Force officers on an informal basis if the system exists "except on paper" raised doubts in my mind that it does. Perhaps it is too new at this point in time.

One recent study of manpower planning provides some interesting data on the extent of career management in industry. David Robertson[20] surveyed 522 American manufacturing firms with at least $1 million in assets, 5,000 or more employees, and major employment in at least two geographically separate cities. He received 250 usable replies that represent the universe and with minimal nonrespondent bias. Some interesting findings relevant to our interest will be reported.[21] First, he found that the larger the company, the more likely it was to forecast manpower needs systematically for longer periods of time. With regard to training programs that involved rotation of positions for new employees, he found that about half of the smaller companies (under 25,000 employees) employed such programs

whereas some three-fourths of the larger firms used them. Robertson indirectly touched on an important aspect of career planning when he looked at "promotion from within" policies. He found that three-fourths of the companies vary somewhat from the strongly held value "promote from within," and the other fourth does so occasionally. There are substantial differences in cross-functional transfers between functions. Robertson says:

About 87 percent of the companies report that production executives ordinarily advance to their positions through the ranks. . . . Sixty percent of research positions . . . are filled from within . . . but departmental policy of 81–95 percent of the companies call for inclusion of managers outside the incumbent's immediate group or section as potential candidates.[22]

Robertson points out that 40 percent of accounting managers normally are promoted from within the local department as compared with only 12 percent of sales managers. The most-to-least geographically mobile executives Robertson found were sales, production, personnel, finance engineering, accounting, and research personnel.

Later[23] Robertson investigated companies which began an executive's career with rotational training programs and those which practiced cross-functional transfer policies in their promotion practices; there was a high correlation. However, he found differences along industry lines: "Managers in the textile and leather industry, for example, apparently maintain a greater degree of functional specialization than managers in the oil, rubber, and plastic industry."[24] Remember, however, that Robertson is looking at company practices. These are not necessarily planned that way. Robertson also found interesting patterns in cross-

---

[20] David E. Robertson, "Managerial Transfer Practices and Internal Mobility in Large Manufacturing Firms," unpublished Ph.D. thesis, University of Wisconsin, 1970.

[21] The findings reported in this section are found in Robertson, chapter 3, pp. 31–70.

[22] Ibid., p. 53.

[23] This section relies on pp. 93–105 of Robertson's thesis.

[24] Ibid., p. 96.

FIGURE 2
Career Profile for Any Air Force Specialty

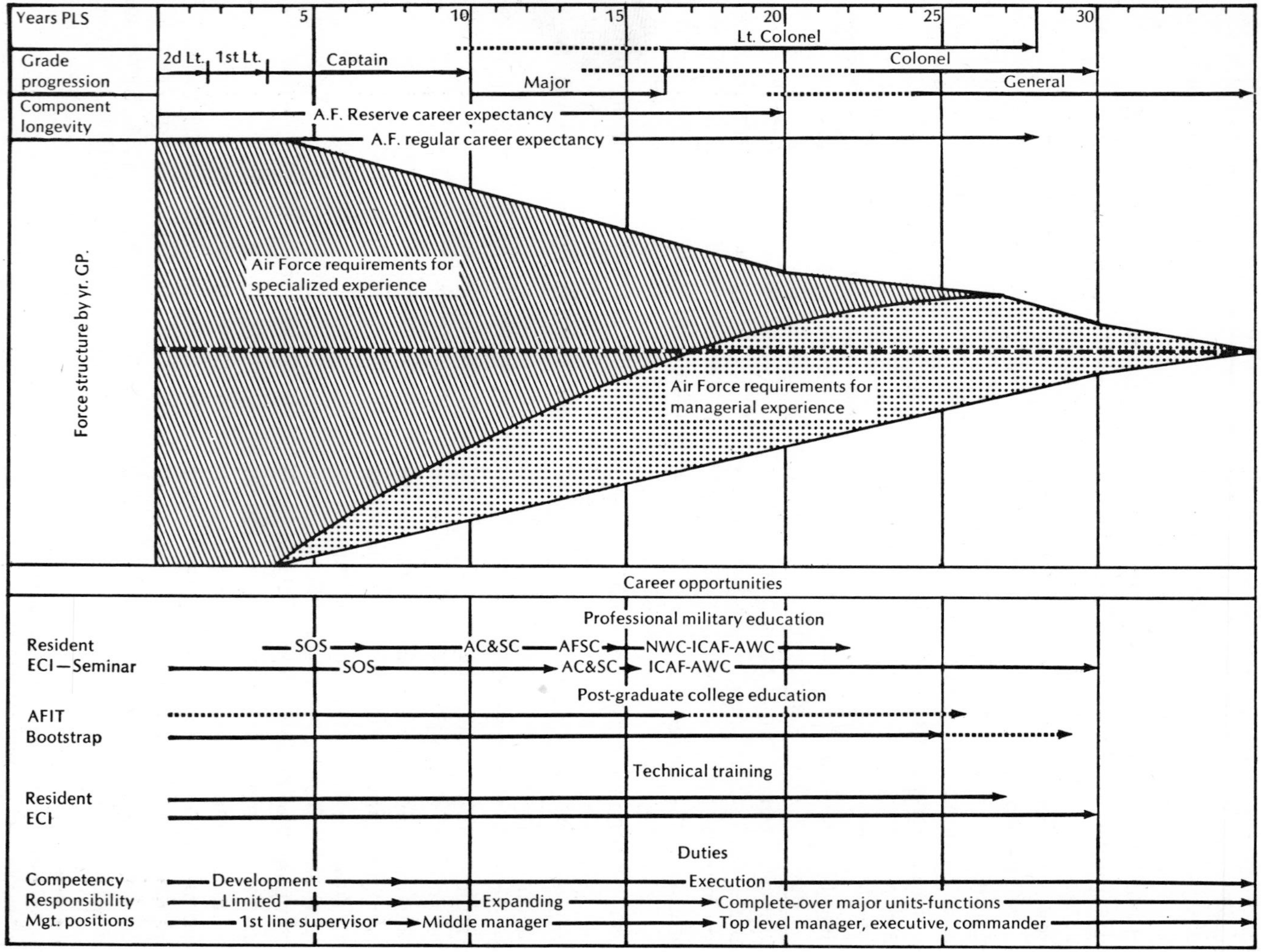

functional transfer, though these varied in intensity by industry. He found that:

Engineering is the most common originating department providing personnel for subsequent assignment to other functional areas. The four most frequently indicated routes of transfer between departments were: engineering to research; accounting to finance; engineering to sales; and engineering to production. Viewing the same data in terms of receiving functions, it was found that marketing accepts personnel from other areas more than any other function.

Production appears to be the second most heterogeneous receiving function in cross function transfers.[25]

Career management, then, involves planning the paths along which employees travel, including coaching, counseling, and evaluating the promotability of the employee, selection of the positions the individual passes through, the off-the-job training he or she receives, and the geographic transfers that he experiences. . . .

17. AN ASSESSMENT OF ASSESSMENT CENTERS*
ANN HOWARD†

As anyone familiar with the traditional psychometric literature can corroborate, the whole idea of assessment centers is preposterous. The basic principle requires that candidates, usually for management positions in organizations, go through a series of individual and group tests and exercises in one concentrated period while being evaluated by a group of assessors. The absurdity is that most of the procedures used to predict future job success are the very ones experience has demonstrated do not work. For example:

1. Clinical, not actuarial, predictions typically are relied upon, although most studies have shown the latter to be more accurate (37, 41).
2. Multiple predictors are used in spite of evidence that clinical prediction may be worse with the inclusion of more than a few variables (2).
3. Projective tests may be included, al-

though their reliability and validity are highly questionable (31).
4. An interview is usually an integral part of the process, in spite of its dubious validity (35).
5. Personality tests are often included, although it has been claimed that they have little or no value for personnel selection (27).
6. Situational tests are relied on most heavily, although they are still in an embryonic stage compared to classical psychometric tests and failed dismally at predicting the performance of clinical psychologists (30).
7. Managers are asked to integrate all this information and predict behavioral traits as well as potential success, even though psychologists are still struggling to demonstrate that even they can do it well (15, 37).

Where did such an extravagant idea as assessment centers come from? The credit is usually given to the Germans, from whom it was copied by the British and then by the Americans in World War II for use in selecting candidates for the Office of Strategic

*Source: *Academy of Management Journal* 17 (1974): 115–34.

†Ann Howard is currently with the American Telephone and Telegraph Company, Basking Ridge, New Jersey. This article was written when she was a doctoral candidate at the University of Maryland and Director of Research for L. F. McManus Co., Inc., Worchester, Massachusetts.

25 Ibid., pp. 109–10.

Services (40). And did it work for the OSS? The war ended and everyone went home, so no one really knows.

This would be an appropriate place to end this assessment except for one intriguing fact. Psychologists involved in these endeavors over the last few years have been thoughtfully and professionally demonstrating that assessment centers work. How is this possible? A combination of weak psychometric methods cannot be expected to lead to strong predictions any more than an accumulation of weak materials can be expected to produce a substantial building. The purpose of this review is to examine the structure of assessment centers, study the data concerning their uses and efficacy, and try to discover how such an apparent contradiction of psychometric experience can function successfully.

THE ARCHITECTURE OF ASSESSMENT CENTERS

Although the use of multiple assessment methods has been reported previously (15, 42), this review is confined to those operations which have been designated specifically as assessment centers. This means not merely multiple methods of assessment but the inclusion of situational tests and the use of multiple assessors. The "center" is really more a set of procedures than a physical location, and the "architecture" described here refers to the design of the components of those procedures.

The first industrial use of an assessment center is generally attributed to AT&T (6), and other centers have been more or less variations on AT&T's theme, as Finkle put it (21). A highlighting feature is that candidates are evaluated not on what they have done in present or past jobs but on how they are likely to cope with a new type of position. This involves using various situational tests as well as incorporating some of the more classic selection procedures, such as aptitude tests and interviews. Assess-ments are conducted at least partially in groups, which permits observing group interactions as well as obtaining peer ratings.

The organization of an assessment center typically follows a prescribed set of steps. The similarities and diversities in centers are explored below as these steps are described. Information on the various centers was compiled from a review of published articles and solicited unpublished material.

The Ojectives of the Program

The original industrial experimentation with assessment center techniques at AT&T was research oriented and designed to follow the development of managerial personnel. The first applied use of the assessment methods was in the selection from current employee populations of candidates for either first level or higher-level management. The selection function is being expanded gradually to include areas other than management, such as sales, engineering, and revenue agents and auditors (16). Expectations are that the application of these methods to rank-and-file employees will also be investigated in the future (7). As the centers have progressed, the possible advantages of the procedures for the training and development of both assessors and assessees have become more apparent, and some programs have changed their objectives to reflect this additional purpose.

The Dimensions to Be Assessed

Among programs to assess managerial candidates, the number of dimensions of effective performance in the companies studied here varied from about 10 to 52. Several companies have factor analyzed criteria to try to explicate the most important constructs. Generalizing from the managerial dimensions selected and factored, the following seem to be important: (a) leadership, (b) organizing and planning (c) decision-making, (d) oral and written communications skills, (e) initiative, (f) energy, (g) analytical ability, (h) resistance to stress, (i) use of delegation, (j) behavior flexibility, (k) human relations competence, (l) originality, (m) controlling, (n) self-direction, and (o) overall potential.

Tests and Exercises to Tap the Dimensions

A unique contribution of assessment centers is the inclusion of situational tests in the assessment battery. The rationale behind using such exercises is that they simulate the type of work to which the candidate will be exposed and allow his performance to be observed under somewhat realistic conditions. Contrary to the aptitude test approach, samples, not signs of behavior, are used for prediction (44).

Situational tests measure more complex or dynamic behavior rather than aptitudes or traits isolated by more traditional psychometric tests; for example, interpersonal skills, leadership, and judgment. Videotapes or films may be used to help capture these dynamics for evaluation purposes. The stated intention of the OSS staff (40) was to measure the Gestalt, or whole, integrated personality. The modern extension of this idea, in process-oriented terms, is that the whole personality is observed in interaction with simulations of the future job environment.

The In-Basket. This simulation is one of those most frequently used in assessment centers and is usually considered the most important (8). Although commercially prepared in-baskets are available, the most relevant simulations are developed from actual in-basket items in the appropriate offices of the participating company. Typically, the candidate is faced with an accumulation of memos, reports, notes of incoming telephone calls, letters, and other materials supposedly collected in the in-basket of the job he or she is to take over. The candidate is asked to dispose of these materials in the most appropriate manner by writing letters,

notes, self-reminders, agenda for meetings, etc.

In many companies completion of the in-basket exercise is followed by a questionnaire or an interview by one of the assessors, in which the candidate is asked to justify his decisions, actions, and nonactions. Ratings of performance may be subjective evaluations or highly standardized checklists.

The Leaderless Group Discussion. The participants in the leaderless group discussion are usually given a discussion question and instructed to arrive at a group decision. Topics may include such things as promotion decisions, disciplinary actions, or business expansion problems. Sometimes participants are given a particular point of view to defend, although they know the group must eventually come to a mutually agreeable decision. Dimensions that can be revealed in the leaderless group discussion include interpersonal skills, acceptance by the group, individual influence, and leadership (10).

Management Games. Management games usually require participants to solve problems, either cooperatively or competitively. Stock market tasks, manufacturing exercises, and merger negotiations are common. Selection of games, whether commercial or homemade, should be geared to the level of the job concerned. The games often bring out leadership, organizational abilities, and interpersonal skills (10). Some games also permit observations under stress, especially when conditions suddenly change or when competition stiffens.

Individual Presentations. Subjects are often given time to make an oral presentation on a particular topic or theme. Presentations are typically short, 5 to 10 minutes, but they allow the assessors to observe oral communications skills, persuasiveness, poise, and reaction to the stress of making a group presentation (10).

Objective Tests. All types of paper and pencil tests of mental ability, personality, interests and achievement (reading, arithmetic, general knowledge) are used. The tests are generally standardized, marketed instruments, although a few companies have developed their own. Usually two companies will not use the same combination of tests or even duplicate single tests.

Projective Tests. Although only a few companies use projective tests, sentence completion and TAT cards are the most popular. The projectives are used to get at some of the more obscure behavioral characteristics, such as need for achievement or originality (21).

Interview. Most centers have an interview between at least one assessor and the participant. Current interests and motivation, as well as general background and past performance, are sought (10). Interviews vary between companies in terms of structure, standardization of interpretation, and the general climate in which they are conducted (21).

Other Techniques. Written exercises, such as autobiographical essays or open-ended history questionnaires, may be required of participants before entering the center (10), or creative writing assignments may be made. Some companies have a mock interview between the participant and an applicant for employment or an employee in an appraisal situation. Since such interviews are often an important part of a manager's job, their inclusion in the assessment process has some face validity. The assessor can observe such things as interpersonal skills and empathy and attitude toward the job and the company (10).

One of J. C. Penney's exercises is the "Irate Customer Phone Call," in which the assessee must display tact and diplomacy to handle a customer's unreasonable demands. A company may also use informal meetings, such as lunches or cocktail parties, to gather information about participants.

The Assessors

A typical assessment center will have four to six assessors in anywhere from a 4:1 to 1:1 ratio to assessees (10). The assessors may be psychologists, members of management, or both. Management members usually are two or three levels above the position for which the candidates are being assessed and not in a supervisory capacity over them.

Most importantly, the assessors are trained for their job. They become familiar with the exercises by participating themselves, watching videotapes, or observing actual performances as nonvoting members of the assessment team. The behavioral dimensions to be assessed are defined, and assessors are given practice and instruction in how to recognize these behaviors. Assessor training varies widely in duration, from brief orientations to two or three weeks of intensive training. Companies highly interested in training managers in appraisal techniques will change assessors frequently, while those most interested in producing a stable selection program or in saving money on training will make changes less often.

The Assessees

Typically, assessees are in their first management position or are being considered for management. Candidates for other jobs are rapidly being included in assessment programs, however. Assessees are usually nominated by their supervisors to attend the center. There is some contradiction in this, since a basic purpose is to find a better way of rating potential than reliance on the supervisor's judgment.

Operating the Center

The time to run a center varies from a day to about a week, including time for assessor evaluations and report writing. The length of assessment ordinarily should increase with the responsibility level of those being assessed (9). Group exercises usually are run with a maximum of six candidates per group, and at least two assessors observe each group. Schedule rearrangements and alternating assignments of assessors can allow the processing of two six-candidate groups at one time.

The Evaluations

Peer and self-ratings and rankings may be part of the evaluation process. The official assessors typically write reports, skill by skill, exercise by exercise, and candidate by candidate according to their respective assignments. The reports are read aloud in a final evaluation meeting where each assessee is rated by every assessor on each predefined behavioral dimension. Meaningful differences of opinion are discussed and either resolved or noted. Final reports usually are written in a narrative style, relating remarks to specific behaviors and specifying the candidate's strengths, weaknesses, and developmental needs.

Feedback

Feedback of results to candidates is handled differently in various organizations according to the original objectives of the program. Those highly concerned with management development emphasize the directions in which the candidate should move in the future. Others concerned with training may stop in the middle of the assess-step in the architectural design of an assessment program and offer feedback and discussion of particular exercises. Oral feedback is much more frequent than written. Line management or assessment center personnel may provide it either automatically or on request only.

Research

Research on the effectiveness of the program is critical, since programs constantly need to be reviewed, critiqued, and improved if they are to be effective. This final step in the architectural design of an assessment center could be the one which deter-

mines the applicability of all of the other steps.

STRUCTURAL SUPPORT: WILL THE BUILDING STAND?

The basis of acceptance for any selection and classification procedure must be its reliability and validity. An examination of research on these two questions follows.

Reliability

In many assessment center exercises and in the final evaluations each participant is evaluated by more than one assessor. Accordingly, interrater reliability becomes a matter of some importance, in addition to the reliability of individual measures. A summary of reliability data is shown in Table 1.

It should be noted that the AT&T studies of the in-basket, projective tests and interviews probably had inflated reliability estimates, since the interrater reliability was determined for the written report of a procedure, not the procedure itself. Two raters in high agreement on what a report says is a far less potent finding than two raters in high agreement on how a candidate performs in a situational exercise. The reliability coefficients do indicate, however, that the reports presented clear evaluations from which consistent ratings could be made.

In summary, based on the data available, interrater reliabilities for assessment evaluations and for several assessment components seem sufficiently high to support their further use. There appear to be no advantages of ratings versus rankings or psychologists versus managers in terms of reliability.

Validity of Overall Assessment Ratings

What must be regarded as "The Study" in assessment center validity is AT&T's Management Progress Study (6), which was predictive and "uncontaminated"; i.e., results

TABLE 1
Summary of Interrater Reliability Studies of Assessment Procedures

Source	Company	Variables	Assessors	Interrater Reliability
Thompson (43) .... (N = 71)	SOHIO	13 dimensions	2 psychologists	Ratings, .73–.93, $\bar{r}$ = .85[a]
Thompson (43) .... (N = 71)	SOHIO	13 dimensions	3 managers	Ratings, .78–.95, $\bar{r}$ = .89[a]
Thompson (43) .... (N = 71)	SOHIO	Potential	2 psychologists	Ratings, .89[a]
Thompson (43) .... (N = 71)	SOHIO.	Potential	3 managers	Ratings, .93[a]
McConnell & Parker (36) ...... (N = 12)	AMA client	(a) 12 categories (b) Potential	5 managers 5 managers	Ratings, .64–.90[a] Ratings, .83[a]
McConnell & Parker (36) ...... (N = 12–48)	6 AMA clients	Overall management ability	5 managers	Ratings, .85–.98[a]
Greenwood & McNamara (26) .... (N = 288)	IBM	(a) Task force game (b) Leaderless group (c) Mfg. problem	All pairs of 3 alternating observers	(a) Ratings, .70; Rankings, .71 (b) Ratings, .66; Rankings, .64 (c) Ratings, .74; Rankings, .75
Bray & Grant (6) .... (N = 355)	AT&T	(a) Leaderless group (b) Mfg. problem (c) In-basket	2 psychologists 2 psychologists 2 psychologists	Ratings, .75; Rankings, .75 Ratings, .60; Rankings, .69 Ratings, .92
Grant, Katkovsky, & Bray (25) .... (N = 355)	AT&T	9 variables from projective tests	2 psychologists	Ratings, .85–.94[a]
Grant & Bray (24) .... (N = 355)	AT&T	18 variables from interview data	2 psychologists	Median = .82 college, .72 noncollege[a]

[a] Internal consistency estimates, correction for number of assessors.

were retained for research purposes only and not released to management to influence promotion decisions. The researchers administered the assessment procedure to 422 male employees of six Bell Telephone companies beginning in 1956, stored the results, and waited eight years before pursuing information on the assessees' progress in the company. While many may view eight years of waiting as an almost unbelievable display of forbearance, the authors admit that by their own standards they were impatient—they had intended to wait ten years. Comparisons made in 1965 of management level achieved by men assessed six to eight years previously are shown in Table 2. Validity for the assessment predictions was amply demonstrated.

Point biserial correlations were .44 for the college group and .71 for the noncollege group. Of the total number of men who reached middle management, 78 percent were correctly identified by the assessment staff. In contrast, among those in both groups who had not progressed further than first level management, the assessors predicted that 95 percent would not reach middle management within ten years. Note that these predictions still had two years to run; later communications from the company indicate that even greater accuracy was achieved.

Correlations between assessment ratings of general effectiveness and salary increments were also given for four samples of individuals who had at least six years of tenure in management since being assessed: (a) Company A, 54 college men, $r = .41$; (b) Company C, 27 college men, $r = .51$; (c) Company B, 83 noncollege men, $r = .45$; (d) Company C, 39 noncollege men, $r = .52$. All correlations were significant at $p < .01$. Combined with the data in Table 2, the usefulness of AT&T's overall assessment ratings for predicting management success seems well established.

Another AT&T study with newly hired candidates for sales positions also used an uncontaminated, predictive validity paradigm (5). The primary criterion of performance was a six-month field review by an experienced team from AT&T headquarters which regularly makes such inspections. Where the assessment judgment was "more than acceptable," 100 percent of the salesmen met the review standards. Comparable success figures for those judged "acceptable," "less than acceptable," and "unacceptable" were 60 percent, 44 percent, and 10 percent, respectively, producing a chi-square value of 24.19 ($p < .001$). Again the predictive validity of AT&T's overall assessments was evident, this time for the job of salesman and over a short time interval.

TABLE 2
Relationship between AT&T Assessment Staff Prediction and Management Level Achieved

Prediction if Make Middle Management within Ten Years	Status in July 1965		
	Percent 1st Level Management	Percent 2d Level Management	Percent Middle Management
		College[a]	
Yes .... (N = 62)	2	50	48
No or ? .... (N = 63)	11	78	11
		Noncollege[a]	
Yes .... (N = 41)	7	61	32
No or ? .... (N = 103)	60	35	5

Note: Adapted form Bray and Grant (6).
[a] χ^2 significant at $p < .001$.

Problems of criterion contamination have confounded predictive validity studies other than those described above, since assessment ratings were used in promotional decisions. Where assessment ratings were used primarily to make the first promotion, the effect on later promotions was not felt to be large, however. A summary of these contaminated criterion studies is shown in Table 3.

From the studies done to date, overall ratings of potential or performance from assessment center procedures generally have shown impressive predictive validity, especially for managerial jobs. Unfortunately, use of the ratings for decision making about assessees' careers somewhat restrains an overwhelming acceptance of the findings. Nevertheless, "clean" predictive validity has been demonstrated, but only in two studies with both at the same company. . . .

Contributions of Various Program Components

The contribution of the components of assessment programs has been evaluated in two different ways; first, how much each influenced assessors' overall ratings and, second, the degree to which each component related to measures of job success. The first method is of interest from a process viewpoint, but the latter is the more direct way of establishing the validity of the component. No matter how impressed an assessor may be with a particular assessment component, its validity should be established empirically before it is accepted as an integral part of a program. . . .

[The review suggests that] ratings of candidates based on the totality of assessment procedures . . . have validity superior to any of the specific components. Since the situation tests represented a unique contribution to the process and were relied upon heavily, it was usually assumed that these were what made the difference, although specific data often were not reported. The in-basket's contribution usually was considered critical, although it mainly tapped administrative skills and was thus more narrow in scope than some of the other exercises. Other situational tests were so varied and data were so seldom reported on them that conclusions are difficult to draw. The mental ability tests seemed to work for some companies but not for others; personality tests showed moderate to little success, but they continue to be used. The projectives and interviews were more successful than expected from their past reputations. More research evidently is needed on the various components of assessment centers and their integration. . . .

ARCHITECTURAL AESTHETICS AND BLEMISHES

Aesthetics

Many have claimed that there are additional benefits to be obtained from assessment centers beyond selection and placement of employees. These "architectural aesthetics" include the following benefits.

Help with the Criterion Problem. Installation of assessment procedures may force better job analyses and identification of the important criteria for success on a job. Such a rigorous process has been aptly described in connection with an analysis of the job of foreman (1). Another way assessment centers may help with the criterion problem is by training assessors to evaluate more accurately the performance, behavior, and potential of others. Assessors have been shown to have greater agreement in ratings of different assessee traits (43), but it has not yet been demonstrated that assessors will experience a transfer of training in rating subordinates under the unstandardized conditions of the normal work experience.

Training Assessors. Benefits of assessor training have been claimed not only in the form of a partial solution of the criterion problem but through (a) improvement in interviewing skills, (b) broadening of observation skills, (c) increased appreciation

TABLE 3
Summary of Validity Studies of Overall Assessment Ratings Where Ratings Were Used for Promotions

Source	Company	Criteria	Time	Validity
Wollowick & McNamara (45) .... [N = 94 men, lower and middle management]	IBM	Position code	3 yrs.	$r = .37^{***}$
Dodd (18) .... [11 groups, various jobs, N = 11–72]	IBM	Position level & salary	1–4 yrs.	Significant for 8 of 11 groups; r .29 to .63
Kraut & Scott (34) .... [N = (a) 67 Sales, (b) 141 Service, (c) Admin., 1st line mgt.]	IBM Office Products Division	Percent promoted to 3 higher levels of management	up to 5 yrs.	(a) $\chi^2 = 16.18^{**}$ (b) $\chi^2 = 10.60^{*}$ (c) $\chi^2 = 6.66$ ns
Thompson (43) .... [N = 71]	SOHIO	Ratings from supervisors' interviews	6–27 mos.	$r = .64^{***}$
Finley (22) .... [N = (a) 109, (b) 119]	SOHIO	Supervisors' ratings, potential	30–62 mos. 9–29 mos.	(a) $r = .65^{***}$ (b) $r = .63^{***}$
Carleton (14) .... [N = 122]	SOHIO	Supervisors' ratings, potential	2½–5 yrs.	$r = .65^{***}$
Moses (39) .... [N = 5,943]	AT&T	(a) 2 or more promotions (b) Management level	7 yrs.	(a) $\chi^2 = 12.39^{***}$ (b) $r = .44^{***}$
Campbell & Bray (13) .... [N = 471 1st-level supervisors, assessed vs. nonassessed]	AT&T	Last appraisal + ratings & rankings from interview (performance)	Several years	55 percent of those promoted before center installed rated "above average performers" vs. 68 percent of those assessed "acceptable."*
Campbell & Bray (13) .... [N = 471 1st-level supervisors, assessed vs. nonassessed]	AT&T	Last appraisal + ratings & rankings from interview (potential)	Several years	28 percent of those promoted before center installed rated "high potential" vs. 50 percent of those assessed "acceptable."*
Byham & Thornton (10) .... [N = 37 supervisors processed by assessment vs. 27 supervisors placed traditionally]	Caterpillar Tractor Co.	Job performance	—	ns (small N + restriction of range of criterion).

$* p < .05$
$** p < .01$
$*** p < .001$

of group dynamics and leadership styles, (d) new insights into behavior, (e) strengthening of management skills through working with simulations, and (f) broadening one's repertoire of responses to problems. No well-designed training studies have validated these promises, however; as has been pointed out previously, firms do considerably more management research on selection than on training and development (12).

Development of Assessees. Since many exercises, [such as] the in-basket and oral presentations, were used formerly as training exercises, many assume they serve such purposes in assessment centers, even without immediate feedback of results (10). Again, evidence supporting this training benefit has not been convincingly provided. Claims for increased self-insight (9) have not been evaluated with pretests or control groups, and statements by assessees that they felt the program was informative and useful for self-development (33) cannot be accepted as firm empirical demonstrations of the developmental value of assessment centers.

Minority Group Selection. Recent government interest in the fairness of selection tests for minorities has stressed that selection procedures must be job related, and the simulated aspects of assessment centers do have face validity in this respect. One study bearing on this problem at AT&T (39) demonstrated that there were highly significant correlations between performance in a one day approximation of the company's longer Personnel Assessment Program and performance in the latter, regardless of race or sex. The research design in this study more closely resembled alternate-form test reliability than predictive validity, however; thus the minority group fairness question for assessment centers is not yet sufficiently answered.

Face Validity. The simulation exercises in particular have high face validity, and the whole process has been claimed to be received favorably by managers, especially those who may be mistrustful of tests (21). Some assessee questionnaires have also indicated that the majority consider the procedures useful and objective (16, 33).

Attitude Changes. It has sometimes been claimed that assessees may change their attitudes in the direction of a clearer understanding of some of the problems facing the manager and the necessity for making some unpopular decisions (10), but so far the evidence is anecdotal.

In summary, the bonus benefits, or architectural aesthetics, of assessment centers sound promising but are largely without research support.

Blemishes

On the other side of the coin, there are those who cite "architectural blemishes" in the process, or possible negative outcomes for both individuals and organizations. These include:

The "Crown Prince or Princess." Those who do outstandingly well in assessment centers may find that they have become a crown prince or princess. Management may treat them so well that their future success becomes a self-fulfilling prophecy, the morale of those without royal status may decline, and the validity coefficients for the assessment center process may become inflated. No research has substantiated these potential coronation effects, however.

The "Kiss of Death." A candidate who does poorly at an assessment center may feel that he has been given the kiss of death as far as his future with the company is concerned. This could result in some undesirable attrition, since the candidate may be quite competent in the job he is now performing. Research on turnover of assessees so far has been inconclusive.

Stress. If a candidate gets the impression that his entire career is on the line based on a few days "on stage," the stress effects could be quite strong. It would seem important that the data from the procedure not be made of the pass-fail variety or kept too long in an employee's file. On the other hand, defenders of the procedures reply that since stress is a typical part of a manager's job, a candidate should be stressed to see how he copes with it. It would still seem important to keep stress in the exercises within limits.

The Nonnominee. The feeling that an individual may be part of the "out group" if he or she has not been selected to participate in the assessment process (which may become a status symbol) is another dimension of employee attitudes that needs to be empirically tested.

The "Organization Man." Some have raised the issue of whether or not assessment centers may not proliferate the model of the conforming organization man and serve to eliminate the unusual or imaginative managers that are believed to be needed in the future. A study at SOHIO showed that assessments correlated negatively with conformity for one small sample, however (14). An IBM study indicated that supervisors may nominate those higher on conformity and lower on independence, but that the assessment procedure itself does not select this type of individual (19). The organization man may be the other side of the nonnominee problem; the most able and not the least able may be denied access to the assessment center. The implication is that it is the nomination procedure and not the assessment procedure that creates the organization man syndrome. The supervisory nominations should perhaps be supplemented by self-nominations, peer nominations, personnel records, or assessment of everyone at a job level if numbers are not too large.

Costs. Estimates of costs have ranged from the price of a few meals to $5,000 per candidate, exclusive of staff salary (10). Installation costs are the highest, but to these must be added assessors', assessees', and psychologists' time, travel, accommodations, and meals, plus materials, from rating sheets to videotapes. Various cost-saving devices might include completing all possible procedures before arrival at the center, conducting exercises on company property over weekends, and combining small companies with similar jobs in a multiple company center, perhaps in a synthetic validity paradigm. In the end, these costs must be weighed in the context of current selection ratios against the possible gains in selection and training in some kind of a utility model.

In summary, the architectural blemishes, or possible negative outcomes of assessment centers, have much the same status as the architectural aesthetics; they appear reasonable, but for the most part they lack supporting data. . . .

BUILDING BETTER CENTERS

[If assessment centers do indeed violate much of the past psychometric literature, as indicated in the introduction to this review, does that mean the findings in the literature have been proven wrong? In this writer's opinion, not at all. The assessment center concept seems much more evolutionary than revolutionary. The critical lesson from assessment centers has been learning how to use all these techniques most appropriately for a given situation. Rather than throwing away old tools, psychologists have learned to reexamine them, use them better, and use them together.

The importance of situation-related validation research for those attempting to use assessment centers should be emphasized. Because their initial industrial development was grounded in research, it is often casually implied that, therefore, any assessment center will work. But each situation will probably require a little different architecture and constant monitoring with continuous research. Or one of these days, as so often happens with behavioral science techniques, a Big Bad Wolf may blow the house down.]

REFERENCES

1. Acker, S. R., and M. R. Perlson. *Can We Sharpen Our Management of Human Resources?* (Olin Corporation, June 1970).

2. Bartlett, C. J., and C. G. Green. "Clinical Prediction: Does One Sometimes Know Too much?" *Journal of Counseling Psychology* 13 (1966): 267–70.

3. Bentz, V. J. "The Sears Longitudinal Study of Management Behavior." Paper presented at the 79th Annual Convention, American Psychological Association, 1971.

4. Bentz, V. J. "Validity of Sears Assessment Center Procedures." Paper presented at the 79th Annual Convention, American Psychological Association, 1971.

5. Bray, D. W., and R. J. Campbell. "Selection of Salesmen by Means of an Assessment Center," *Journal of Applied Psychology* 52 (1968): 36–41.

6. Bray, D. W., and D. L. Grant. "The Assessment Center in the Measurement of Potential for Business Management," *Psychological Monographs* 80, 17 (1966), Whole No. 625.

7. Bray, D. W., and J. L. Moses. "Personnel Selection," in *Annual Review of Psychology* (Palo Alto, Calif.: Annual Reviews, 1972).

8. Byham, W. C. "Assessment Centers for Spotting Future Managers," *Harvard Business Review* 48, 4 (1970): 150 ff.

9. Byham, W. C. "The Assessment Center as an Aid in Management Development," *Training and Development Journal* (December 1971): 10–22.

10. Byham, W. C., and G. C. Thornton, III. "Assessment Centers: A New Aid in Management Selection," *Studies in Personnel Psychology* 2 (1970): 21–35.

11. Campbell, D. T., and D. W. Fiske. "Convergent and Discriminant Validation by the Multitrait-multimethod Matrix," *Psychological Bulletin* 56 (1959): 81–105.

12. Campbell, J. P., M. D. Dunnette, E. E. Lawler III, and K. E. Weick, Jr. *Managerial Behavior, Performance and Effectiveness* (New York: McGraw-Hill, 1970).

13. Campbell, R. J., and D. W. Bray. "Assessment Centers: An Aid in Management Selection," *Personnel Administration* 30, 2 (1967): 6–13.

14. Carleton, F. O. "Relationships Between Follow-up Evaluations and Information Developed in a Management Assessment Center." *Proceedings of the 78th Annual Convention, American Psychological Association,* 1970.

15. Cronbach, L. J. *Essentials of Psychological Testing,* 3d ed. (New York: Harper & Row, 1970).

16. DiCostanzo, F., and T. Andretta. "The Supervisory Assessment Center in the Internal Revenue Service." *Training and Development Journal* (September 1970): 12–15.

17. Dodd, W. E. "Will Management Assessment Centers Insure Selection of the Same Old Types?" *Proceedings of the 78th Annual Convention, American Psychological Association,* 1970, pp. 569–70.

18. Dodd, W. E. "Summary of Assessment Validities." Paper presented at the 79th Annual Convention, American Psychological Association, 1971.

19. Dodd, W. E., and A. I. Kraut. "The Prediction of Management Assessment Center Performance from Earlier Measures of Personality and Sales Training Performance. A Preliminary Report." (IBM Corporation, April 1970.)

20. Dunnette, M. D. "Multiple Assessment Procedures in Identifying and Developing Managerial Talent," in P. McReynolds, ed., *Advances in Psychological Assessment,* Vol. II (Palo Alto, Calif.: Science and Behavior Books, 1971).

21. Finkle, R. B. "Managerial Assessment Centers," in M. D. Dunnette, ed., *Handbook of Industrial and Organization Psychology* (Chicago: Rand McNally, 1976).

22. Finley, R. M., Jr. "Evaluation of Behavior Predictions from Projective Tests Given in a Management Assessment Center." *Proceedings of the 78th Annual Convention, American Psychological Association,* 1970.

23. Ghiselli, E. E. *The Validity of Occupational Aptitude Tests* (New York: Wiley, 1966).

24. Grant, D. L., and D. W. Bray. "Contributions of the Interview to Assessment of Management Potential," *Journal of Applied Psychology* 53 (1969): 24–34.

25. Grant, D. L., W. Katkovsky, and D. W. Bray. "Contributions of Projective Techniques to

Assessment of Management Potential," *Journal of Applied Psychology* 51 (1967): 226–32.

26. Greenwood, J. M., and W. J. McNamara. Interrater Reliability in Situational Tests," *Journal of Applied Psychology* 31 (1967): 101–6.

27. Guion, R. M., and R. F. Gottier. "Validity of Personality Measures in Personnel Selection," *Personnel Psychology* 18 (1965): 135–64.

28. Hinrichs, J. R. "Comparison of 'Real Life' Assessments of Management Potential with Situational Exercises, Paper-and-Pencil Ability Tests and Personality Inventories," *Journal of Applied Psychology* 53 (1969): 425–32.

29. Jeswald, T. A. "Research Needs in Assessment—A Brief Report of a Conference," *The Industrial Psychologist,* 9, 1 (November 1971): 12–14.

30. Kelly, E. L., and D. W. Fiske. *Prediction of Performance in Clinical Psychology* (Ann Arbor: University of Michigan Press, 1951).

31. Kinslinger, H. S. "Application of Projective Techniques in Personnel Psychology Since 1940," *Psychological Bulletin* 66 (1966): 134–49.

32. Korman, A. K. "The Prediction of Managerial Performance. A Review," *Personnel Psychology* 21 (1968): 295–322.

33. Kraut, A. I. "A Hard Look at Management Assessment Centers and Their Future," *Personnel Journal* 51 (1972): 317–26.

34. Kraut, A. I., and G. J. Scott. "The Validity of an Operational Management Assessment Program," *Journal of Applied Psychology* 56 (1972): 124–29.

35. Mayfield, E. C. "The Selection Interview —A Re-evaluation of Published Research," *Personnel Psychology* 17 (1964): 239–60.

36. McConnell, J. H., and T. C. Parker. "An Assessment Center Program for Multi-organizational Use," *Training and Development Journal* (March 1972): 6–14.

37. Meehl, P. E. *Clinical versus Statistical Prediction: A Theoretical Analysis and a Review of the Evidence* (Minneapolis: University of Minnesota Press, 1954).

38. Meyer, H. H. "The Validity of the In-Basket Test as a Measure of Managerial Performance," *Personnel Psychology* 23 (1970): 297–307.

39. Moses, J. L. "The Early Identification of Supervisory Potential," *Personnel Psychology,* in press.

40. Office of Strategic Services (OSS) Assessment Staff. *Assessment of Men* (New York: Rinehard, 1948).

41. Sawyer, J. "Measurement and Prediction, Clinical and Statistical," *Psychological Bulletin* 66 (1966): 178–200.

42. Taft, R. "Multiple Methods of Personality Assessment," *Psychological Bulletin* 56 (1959): 333–52.

43. Thomson, H. A. "Comparison of Predictor and Criterion Judgments of Managerial Performance Using the Multitrait-multimethod Approach," *Journal of Applied Psychology* 54 (1970): 496–502.

44. Wernimont, P. F., and J. P. Campbell. "Signs, Samples and Criteria," *Journal of Applied Psychology* 52 (1968): 372–76.

45. Wollowick, H. B., and W. J. McNamara "Relationship of the Components of an Assessment Center to Management Success," *Journal of Applied Psychology* 53 (1969): 348–52.

18. BASIC PATTERNS IN UNION CONTRACTS: (SENIORITY)

BUREAU OF NATIONAL AFFAIRS

Provisions on seniority, defined as employment service credit, are found in 92 percent of the contracts in the Basic Patterns sample. Seniority is used most often to determine an employee's ranking for purposes of layoff, promotion, and transfer.

In 80 percent of the contracts containing seniority provisions, seniority is based on the length of an employee's continuous service. An additional 5 percent compute seniority on the basis of time actually worked or on a combination of length of service and job qualifications, such as ability and fitness.

The order of layoff is determined to some extent by seniority in 85 percent of the contracts, seniority being the sole consideration in 42 percent. . . .

Accrual of seniority usually follows a probationary period on the job, which is provided for in 71 percent of the contracts. Under 60 percent of the provisions for probation, the employer retains full authority to discipline or discharge probationary employees. At the end of the probationary period, which usually lasts from one to three months, an employee's seniority goes back to the date of his hire.

Probationary periods are provided in at least half of the contracts in all industries with the exceptions of printing, construction, maritime, and services.

Loss of seniority occurs for a variety of reasons stated in 77 percent of the contracts. Under 88 percent of the contracts containing these provisions, seniority is lost after layoff; 65 percent specify a uniform length of time for all employees, and 23 percent key retention of seniority to length of service.

Seniority is revoked for failure to respond to recall in 82 percent of the contracts stating reasons for loss of seniority and for unauthorized absence in 47 percent. In addition, 37 percent of the provisions for loss of seniority cite failure to report after a leave of absence; 16 percent, the expiration of sickness or disability leave; and 11 percent, taking a job elsewhere while on leave.

Seniority lists are required by more than half of the contracts. Under 49 percent of the provisions for lists, the company must post the list in the plant or office; under 82 percent management must keep the list up to date or revise it at regular intervals. More than a fourth of the seniority list provisions permit the union to protest the list, most commonly within 30 days of posting.

PROMOTION

Seniority is assigned a role in determining promotions in almost 70 percent of the contracts.

TABLE 1
Probationary Periods (frequency expressed as percentage of contracts)

	Provided	30 Days	60 Days	90 Days	6 Months	Other
All industries	71	22	14	14	3	18
Manufacturing	80	25	16	15	3	21
Nonmanufacturing	50	14	9	12	5	5

Source: Bureau of National Affairs (Washington, D.C., 1975), pp. 75.1 to 75.5. Copyright © 1977 by The Bureau of National Affairs, Inc.

Seniority is the sole factor in promotion in 4 percent of the agreements.

Seniority is the determining factor in promoting employees in 34 percent of the contracts. Under these provisions, the most senior employee is promoted if he is qualified for the available job.

Seniority is given equal consideration with other factors in determining promotions under 4 percent of the contracts.

Seniority is a secondary factor considered only when other factors are equal in 25 percent of the agreements.

Industry pattern. Clauses providing that seniority shall be the sole or determining factor in promotion appear in at least half of the contracts in food, rubber, paper, petroleum, mining, furniture, fabricated metals, primary metals, and utilities.

TRANSFER

Seniority is considered in granting employees' requests for transfers in 48 percent of the sample contracts, compared to 38 percent in the 1970 study.

Seniority is the sole factor in granting employees' requests for transfers under 5 percent of the contracts.

Seniority is the determining factor in transfers in 26 percent of the contracts. Under these provisions the senior employee is permitted to transfer if he can do the job.

Seniority is a secondary factor in granting requests for transfers in 14 percent of the agreements. Under these provi-

TABLE 2
Consideration of Seniority in Promotion (frequency expressed as percentage of contracts)

	Applied in Some Degree	Sole Factor	Determining Factor	Secondary Factor	Equal with Other Factors
All industries	69	4	34	25	4
Manufacturing	76	5	39	26	3
Nonmanufacturing	54	2	21	22	5

POSTING OF VACANCIES

Job vacancies must be posted, usually for a specified period of time, under 52 percent of the sample contracts. Bidding procedures are included in 50 percent of the contracts, and 70 percent of the procedures specify a time limit within which bids must be submitted. Bidding in advance of job openings is permitted in 21 percent of agreements containing bidding procedures.

Trial periods on new jobs are called for in 29 percent of the sample.

sions seniority is considered when other factors are equal.

Seniority is given equal consideration with other factors in authorizing transfers in 2 percent of the contracts.

Industry pattern. Seniority is considered in granting requests for transfers in at least half of the contracts in chemical, electrical machinery, machinery, fabricated metals, paper, transportation equipment, communications, utilities, food, textiles, lumber, rubber, primary metals, and transportation.

TABLE 3
Consideration of Seniority in Transfer (frequency expressed as percentage of contracts)

	Applied in Some Degree	Sole Factor	Determining Factor	Secondary Factor	Equal with Other Factors
All industries	48	5	26	14	2
Manufacturing	53	5	30	15	2
Nonmanufacturing	37	4	17	12	2

TABLE 4
Seniority Provisions (frequency expressed as percentage of contracts)

	Probationary Periods	Lists Required	Vacancies Posted	Factor in Layoffs	Factor in Promotions	Factor in Transfers	Status upon Transfer to Other Department	Status upon Transfer to Non-bargaining Unit Job	Status upon Transfer to Supervisory Job
All Industries	71	58	52	85	69	48	30	43	36
Manufacturing	80	67	57	93	76	53	35	51	42
Foods	59	55	76	99	83	59	31	34	24
Textiles	77	83	50	94	78	56	56	33	44
Apparel	67	11	11	55	33	11	11	22	11
Lumber	71	100	71	99	100	57	—	43	43
Furniture	100	67	50	83	67	33	17	33	50
Paper	71	50	72	100	93	57	43	43	21
Printing	25	13	13	64	—	—	—	—	—
Chemical	88	56	75	88	63	50	38	38	44
Petroleum	86	86	29	100	86	43	29	29	57
Rubber	100	50	50	67	67	50	33	50	50
Leather	75	25	50	75	50	25	25	25	25
Stone, clay and glass	69	69	54	87	85	31	15	31	46
Primary metals	88	68	76	96	88	60	28	48	32
Fabricated metals	95	95	68	84	79	58	53	63	37
Machinery	91	88	64	100	79	61	36	67	61
Electrical machinery	81	54	58	97	81	54	31	73	42
Transportation equipment	91	82	37	97	74	71	51	83	69
Nonmanufacturing	50	39	41	69	54	37	18	25	22
Mining	58	67	75	91	92	42	17	42	58
Construction	4	13	—	4	—	—	—	—	—
Transportation	79	84	79	95	63	68	53	53	47
Maritime	25	36	13	50	25	13	13	13	—
Communications	67	33	56	100	89	56	33	33	33
Utilities	70	50	90	100	100	90	50	50	20
Retail trade	72	39	28	89	61	33	11	28	33
Insurance and finance	50	33	67	50	67	33	—	17	—
Services	42	11	16	79	53	26	—	5	—

Provisions for temporary transfers are included in 38 percent of the contracts. Under 72 percent of these clauses, temporary transfers are determined solely by management, and 69 percent limit the duration of the transfer, most often to less than two weeks.

Special transfer rights for disabled or aged employees, no longer able to perform their regular work, are found in 28 percent of the contracts. Under three-fourths of these provisions, employees are permitted to bump to jobs they are able to perform; under a quarter, employees are given preference for lighter work.

EFFECT OF TRANSFERS ON SENIORITY STATUS

Seniority upon transfer from one department to another is considered in 30 percent of the contracts. An employee who transfers immediately carries his seniority to the new department under 22 percent of these contracts. Under another 20 percent of the provisions, the employee retains his seniority in his old department for a specified period of time, while 16 percent of the clauses provide that an employee's seniority will be carried to the new department after a time.

Seniority upon transfer from the bargaining unit—other than to supervisory positions—is dealt with in 43 percent of the contracts. Under 21 percent of these provisions an employee retains his bargaining unit seniority, while under 17 percent he continues to accumulate it. Seniority is retained for a while and then lost under 27 percent and accumulated for a time and then retained under 13 percent. Under 5 percent seniority accumulates for a specified period and then is lost, and under another 5 percent seniority is lost immediately upon transfer from the unit.

SENIORITY AND SUPERVISORY JOBS

Seniority status of supervisors in the event of return to the bargaining unit is considered in 36 percent of the agreements. The most common practice, specified in 26 percent of the provisions, is continued accumulation of seniority while outside the unit. An additional 20 percent allow an employee to retain his seniority indefinitely, and 22 percent permit retention for a limited time only. Seniority is accumulated for a specified amount of time and then lost under 6 percent. Seniority is lost immediately upon promotion to a supervisory job under 2 percent of the provisions.

Industry pattern. Provisions dealing with supervisors' seniority are included in at least half of the contracts in the following industries: furniture, petroleum, rubber, machinery, transportation equipment, and mining.

7

LEARNING AND TRAINING

THE CONCEPT OF TRAINING

Training may be thought of as a *planned process* whose organizational purpose is to provide *learning experiences* that will enhance *employee contribution* to the goals of the organization. There are three important characteristics of this definition. First, the term *planned process* indicates that training should be a series of predetermined, interrelated steps rather than a haphazard activity undertaken for uncertain purposes. These steps include determining (1) training needs, (2) specifying training objectives, (3) designing training content and techniques, (4) evaluating the effectiveness of the training, and (5) modifying the training process if necessary for future applications. The likelihood that training will be effective, we feel, is directly related to how much of a planned process it actually is in the organization. The second part of the definition to note is its *reference to learning*. Successful training programs must be able to answer questions such as "What is to be learned (training objectives)?" "How can we maximize learning during training?" and "How can we help the learning to persist on the job?" Finally, our definition implies that *training needs evaluation* and that the ultimate criterion of effectiveness, though difficult to measure, would be employee contribution to organization goals.

TRAINING VERSUS DEVELOPMENT

A distinction is sometimes made between the terms *training* and *development*. In part, the distinction is based on who participates in the process (non-managers are trained; managers are developed). Also, the content of the learning experience may serve as the basis for the distinction (training is aimed at enhancing specific skills for a specified job; development is designed to provide new ideas and concepts that may be useful for present and/or future jobs). However, the distinction is somewhat artificial since it is based on characteristics of the process, rather than its purpose. The purpose of both training and development is to provide learning experiences. Because of this, and for simplicity's sake, only the term *training* will be used in this chapter to describe any such learning experience.

TRAINING DIFFERENCES AMONG ORGANIZATIONS

While almost all organizations engage in training, the nature and extent of training varies substantially. There are a number of reasons for this variability. First, training may be thought of as an alternative to recruitment and selection strategies. Rather than invest resources in recruitment and selection, organizations may attempt to accomplish the same objective (ensuring acceptable job effectiveness) by investing those resources in training. To some extent, forces outside the control of the organization may dictate the amount of reliance that must be placed on training. For example, if the labor market is *tight* (low unemployment rates and large numbers of vacancies), the organization will probably have to lower its hiring standards in order to fill its job vacancies. Invariably, this will create pressure to invest more heavily in initial training for new employees. In a related manner, the training investment will depend partly on the cost of hiring employees who turn out to be unacceptable performers. The greater the cost, the greater the need for training as a way of attempting to minimize the cost. Finally, as jobs change, so do the requirements for effective performance on them. To the extent that the new requirements must be met by the organization's current employees, training will be necessary. A variety of circumstances thus influence the nature and extent of training by the organization.

INTRODUCTION TO READINGS

A Training System Model

I. L. Goldstein presents a model of a training (instructional) system that illustrates how training can be viewed as a planned process. This process begins with an assessment of training needs, which is based on an analysis of the organization, the jobs, and the individuals on the jobs. Training objectives are then established on the basis of this assessment.

Once objectives are established, the training itself needs to be planned. This involves considering both how to effectively (a) *facilitate* learning during training itself and (b) *maintain* that learning back on the job. As Goldstein notes, this involves a careful blending of the type of training technique to be used and the numerous learning principles (for example, motivation of trainees, reinforcement, knowledge of results, whole versus part learning, and transfer). While any particular training technique implicitly uses certain principles of learning, the technique is only one of many factors influencing the amount of learning that occurs and is retained. It is thus necessary to view this phase of the training process as one of designing the total training environment, rather than simply choosing a particular technique.

In Goldstein's model, evaluation of training effectiveness is considered an integral part of the training process. The information derived from evaluation serves as a source of feedback for potential modifications of the program to be used in the future. This feedback loop indicates that training should be a continual process in the organization.

Management Training and its Evaluation

William Kearney elaborates on problems of program evaluation in the context of *management development* (his term) efforts. He first summarizes the two major reviews of the literature on the effectiveness of such programs. (One is by Miner; the other is by Campbell, Dunnette, Lawler, and Weick.) The latter review is particularly useful since it classifies studies according to the type of research design and the type of criterion measure used for program evaluation. Both of these considerations have major implications for what can reasonably be concluded about the true effectiveness of the various management development programs.

In the case of research designs, Kearney illustrates some of the types of designs that might be used to evaluate effectiveness and the acceptability of the designs (see Table 1). For example, design I is labeled unacceptable because there is no control group (no program group) that can be used as a basis of comparison with the experimental group (program group), and because the criterion measure was obtained only after the training program (period T_1 posttest). It is thus not possible to assess whether there was any change (due to no pretest measure), let alone whether any change that might have occurred was the result of the training program (due to no control group). Design II uses both a pretest and posttest, thus permitting assessment of change. Unfortunately, without a control group, it is impossible to say how much (if any) of the change was due to training. This design is thus also labeled unacceptable. Kearney also labels design III (experimental and control groups, with only a posttest for both groups) unacceptable. This is a debatable label. If people are *randomly* assigned to the two groups, they should be about the same on the pretest even though it actually is not obtained. Because of this, any posttest differences between the two groups is probably due to training, and not to a possible difference between the groups before training.

The first acceptable design (IV) is labeled as such because it has both experimental and control groups and pretest and posttest measures. The higher order designs (V, VI, and VII) are even more acceptable because of the greater degrees of experimental control they permit. Unfortunately, in most organizational situations use of these designs is not practical. Design IV is about the best that can reasonably be expected. The value of this design can be improved by adding more than one posttest to it, which is something that Kearney incorrectly implies is not possible.

Use of a second posttest becomes very relevant to the distinction between *internal* and *external* criterion measures. Internal measures get at change directly relevant to the training itself, and external measures assess changes that occur back on the job. For example, assume an organization conducts a training program whose objective is to change managers' knowledge about a new budgeting technique. A logical internal criterion measure might be a knowledge test that is given to trainees before, and immediately after, the training program. A likely external measure would be some assessment of the extent to which the managers actually use the technique effectively once they are back on their jobs. Due to any number of reasons, the managers may become knowledgeable about the technique in training, but fail to apply that knowledge by using the technique on their jobs. For example, the superiors of the managers may prefer to have the managers use existing budgeting procedures. Or, the managers might actually forget the new procedures. In any event, if only the internal measure (with an immediate posttest) had been used, it would not be legitimate to make inferences about the impact of the training program on the managers' job behavior. Only through the use of an external measure (second posttest) could such changes be gauged. Internal and external measures thus complement each other, and the use of both in training evaluation is desirable.

As should be obvious, however, internal measures have a number of advantages over external measures. Generally, they are easier and quicker to develop, they yield an immediate indication about change due to training, and they are not as subject to outside forces (such as the superiors of the managers cited in the previous example). But notice the price that is paid for too great a reliance on internal measures. Very simply, the price is that we learn little about the effectiveness of programs in producing changes in actual job behavior. This is aptly indicated in the Campbell et al. review summarized by Kearney, particularly in the case of general management and human relations training programs where primarily internal measures have been used.

Interaction Modeling: A Possible Breakthrough

Skepticism about the probable effectiveness of traditional supervisory training programs is voiced by William Byham and James Robinson. They describe a type of training for supervisors known as *interaction modeling*. It seeks to directly change specific job behaviors of supervisors, rather than such things as human relations attitudes. Trainees are shown models of a supervisor and subordinate interacting in a given problem situation (for example, handling a subordinate's complaint). Specific behavioral steps that the supervisor can use to successfully resolve the problem are also shown. Trainees can thus model their own behavior after the supervisor's behavior shown in the example. In addition to these models, Byham and Robinson indicate a number of other characteristics of interaction modeling that may facilitate learning. These include an emphasis on positive feedback, active practice in handling predetermined problems, practice in handling related problems trainees actually face in their jobs, and numerous review sessions of the previously learned behaviors.

Interaction modeling also explicitly recognizes the importance of taking steps to ensure that the learning that occurs during training will be maintained and used on the job. In part, this is accomplished by having the interaction situations in training closely parallel the kinds of interactions the trainees are actually confronted with on their jobs. Equally important, however, is the fact that the trainees' immediate superiors themselves receive an abbreviated form of interaction modeling. In this way, the superiors are able to recognize the value of the learning and reinforce the trainees' use of their newly acquired skills back on the job. Interaction modeling thus exemplifies the careful blending of technique and learning principles called for by Goldstein.

Byham and Robinson also review the studies that have been conducted on the effectiveness of interaction modeling. The evidence from these studies is generally quite favorable and the quality of the research is such that considerable confidence can be placed in the results. All of the studies used an experimental and control group. Some also used both pretest and posttest criterion measures. When only posttest measures were used, care was taken to ensure that the experimental and control groups were comparable before training. Finally, a wide variety of criterion measures, both internal and external, have been used in the studies. We thus are able to assess the effectiveness of interaction modeling in producing both immediate and sustained changes in behavior. These results may also be used to suggest possible modifications in existing programs that may further enhance the effectiveness of interaction modeling. Indeed, Byham and Robinson conclude by suggesting some other changes that might be made in terms of applications to other interaction situations.

19. A SYSTEMATIC APPROACH TO TRAINING
I. L. GOLDSTEIN

INSTRUCTIONAL TECHNOLOGY

While the term *technology* commonly refers to the development of hardware, *instructional technology* refers to the systematic development of programs in training and education. The systems approach to instruction emphasizes the specification of instructional objectives, precisely controlled learning experiences to achieve these objectives, criteria for performance, and evaluative information. Other characteristics of instructional technology would include the following.

1. The systems approach uses feedback to continually modify instructional processes. From this perspective, training programs are never finished products; they are continually adaptive to information that indicates whether the program is meeting its stated objectives.

2. The instructional-systems approach recognizes the complex interaction among the components of the system. For example, one particular medium, like television, might be effective in achieving one set of objectives, while another medium might be preferable for a second set of objectives. Similar interactions could involve learning variables and specific individual characteristics of the learner. The systems view stresses a concern with the total system rather than with the objectives of any single component.

3. Systematic analysis provides a frame of reference for planning and for remaining on target. In this framework, a research approach is necessary to determine which programs are meeting their objectives.

4. The instructional-systems view is just one of a whole set of interacting systems. Training programs interact with and are directly affected by a larger system involving corporate policies (for example, selection and management philosophy). Similarly, educational programs like the *Sesame Street*

Source: From *Training: Program Development and Evaluation*, by I. L. Goldstein. Copyright © 1974 by Wadsworth Publishing Company, Inc. Reprinted by permission of the publisher, Brooks/Cole Publishing Company, Monterey, California.

TV program are affected by the social values of society.

The various components of the instructional-systems approach are not new. Evaluation was a byword years before systems approaches were in vogue. Thus, the systems approach cannot be considered a magic wand for all the problems that were unsolved before its inception. If the training designer were convinced that his program worked, a systems approach would be unlikely to convince him that his program required examination. However, the systems approach does provide a model that emphasizes important components and their interactions, and there is good evidence that this model is an important impetus for the establishment of objectives and evaluation procedures. As such, it is a useful tool that enables designers of instructional programs (as well as authors of books like this one) to examine the total training process.

Figure 1 presents one model of an instructional system. Most of the components of this model (for example, derive objectives and develop criteria) are considered important to any instructional system, although the degree of emphasis changes for different programs. . . . This [selection] provides an overview of the complete system and the relationships among the components.

ASSESSMENT PHASE

Assessment of Instructional Need

This phase of the instructional process

FIGURE 1
An Instructional System

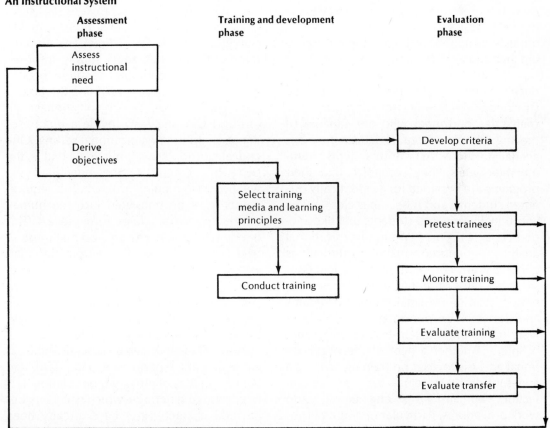

* There are many other instructional-system models for military, business, and educational systems. Some of the components of this model were suggested by these other systems.

provides the information necessary to design the entire program. An examination of the model indicates that the training and evaluation phases are dependent upon the input from the development phase. Unfortunately, many programs are doomed to failure because trainers are more interested in conducting the training program than in assessing the needs of their organizations. Educators have been seduced by programmed instruction and industrial trainers by sensitivity training before they have determined the needs of their organization and the way the techniques will meet those needs. The need-assessment phase consists of organization analysis, task analysis, and person analysis.

Organizational Analysis. Organizational analysis begins with an examination of the short- and long-term goals of the organization, as well as of the trends that are likely to affect these goals. Often, this analysis requires that upper-level management examine their own expectations concerning their training programs. Training designed to produce proficient sales personnel must be structured differently from programs to train sales personnel who are capable of moving up the corporate ladder to managerial positions. As school systems examine their goals, they recognize that their programs are designed for academically oriented students, and it becomes clearer why vocationally oriented students feel like second-class citizens. When organizational analysis is ignored, planning difficulties abound. Many corporations have spent considerable sums of money retraining personnel because the original training programs and decisions on performance capabilities were based on a system that soon became obsolete. Another aspect of the organizational analysis focuses on training programs and supporting systems—for example, selection, human-factors engineering, and work procedures. Particular operating problems might best be resolved by changes in selection standards or redesign of the work environment.

Task Analysis. The second part of the need-assessment program is a careful analysis of the job to be performed by the trainees upon completion of the training program. The task analysis is usually divided into two separate procedures. The first step is a *job description* in behavioral terms. It is not a description of the worker. The narrative specifies the individual's duties and the special conditions under which the job is performed. The second procedure, most commonly referred to as *task specification*, further denotes all the tasks required on the job so that eventually the particular skills, knowledge, and attitudes required to perform the job will become clear. Thus, a brief description of the job of a gas-station attendant might state that the employee supplies cars and trucks with oil, water, air, and gas, changes oil, and lubricates autos and trucks. The task specification provides a list of tasks that includes: collects money, makes change, and provides directions to customers. These statements supply information about the behaviors required regardless of the individual performing the task.

Person Analysis. The organizational analysis and task analysis provide a picture of the task and the organizational setting. One critical consideration is missing—that is, the behaviors required of the individual who will be in the training program. Job requirements must be translated into the human attributes necessary to perform the task. This is a difficult, but necessary, job that must be based on inferences drawn from the analysis of the organizational and task components. The determination of the learning environment and instructional media is directly dependent on the particular types of behavior necessary to perform the task.

Another facet of person analysis is the examination of the performance standards and the capabilities of the target population. It is important to determine which necessary behavioral characteristics have already been learned by the prospective trainees. Too many training programs are exercises in boredom, because they focus on skills already acquired. The determination of the target population is also necessary. Some training programs are designed for individuals who are already in the system, while others are for trainees who are not yet part of the organization. In any case, it is senseless to design the training environment without acknowledging the characteristics of the groups to be trained.

Behavioral Objectives

From information obtained in the assessment of instructional needs, a blueprint emerges that describes the behavioral objectives to be achieved by the trainee upon completion of the training program. These behavioral objectives provide the input for the design of the training program as well as for the measures of success (criteria) that will be used to judge the program's adequacy. The following is an example of one behavioral objective for our gas-station attendant.

By reading the gasoline pump, the employee can determine the cost of the product and provide correct change to the customer without resorting to paper and pencil for computations. Performance will be judged adequate if the employee:

1. Always provides correct change for single items (for example, gas) up to the total cost of $10;
2. Always provides correct change when the customer pays cash ranging up to $100;
3. Successfully completes 20 trials by providing the correct change.

Similar statements could be designed for instructional systems in a variety of settings. For example, the following behavioral objective is appropriate to the solution of a particular servicing aspect of a Xerox machine (Cicero 1973).

Given a tool kit and a service manual, the technical representative will be able to adjust the registration (black line along paper edges) on a Xerox 2400 duplicator within 20 minutes according to the specifications stated in the manual (p. 15).

Well-written behavioral objectives specify what the trainee will be able to accomplish when he successfully completes the instructional program. They also indicate the conditions under which the performance must be maintained and the standards by which the trainee will be evaluated (Mager 1962). Thus, objectives communicate the goals of the program to both the learner and the training designer. From these goals, the designers can determine the appropriate learning environment and the criteria for examining the achievement of the objectives. . . .

TRAINING-DEVELOPMENT PHASE

The Training Environment

Once the objectives have been specified, the next step is designing the environment to achieve the objectives. This is a delicate process that requires a blend of learning principles and media selection, based on the tasks that the trainee is eventually expected to perform. Gilbert (1960) described the temptations that often lead to a poor environment.

If you don't have a gadget called a teaching machine, don't get one. Don't buy one; don't borrow one; don't steal one. If you have such a gadget, get rid of it. Don't give it away, for someone else might use it. This is a most practical rule, based on empirical facts from considerable observation. If you begin with a device of any kind, you will try to develop the teaching program to fit that device (p. 478).

Gilbert's remarks are equally appropriate for any device or method, from airline simulators to educational television.

From the assessment of instructional need, the skills and knowledge necessary to perform the job becomes apparent. Now the performance required must be matched with the characteristics of the various media. "The best available basis for the needed matching of media with objectives . . . is a rationale by which the kind of learning involved in each educational objective is stated in terms of the learning conditions required" (Briggs, Campeau, Gagné, and May 1967, p. 3). This is the same process that gardeners use when they choose a certain tool for a certain job. In the same manner, trainers choose airline simulators that create the characteristics of flight in order to teach pilots; however, the simulator is not usually considered appropriate to teach an adult a foreign language. The analysis of job tasks and performance requirements, and the matching of these behaviors to those produced by the training environment, is, at this point, as much an art as a technology. Although the preceding examples of pilot training and language learning are misleading because they represent obvious differences between tasks, there could be significant improvements in the design of training environments if more emphasis were placed on this matching of training environments to required behaviors.

Learning Principles

In training environments, the instructional process involves the acquisition of skills, concepts, and attitudes that are transferred to a second setting (for example, on the job or in another classroom). The acquisition phase emphasizes learning a new task. Performance on the job and in the next environment focuses on transfer of learning to a second setting. Both theoretical and empirical sources of information are available to aid in the design of environments to improve worker performance. Unfortunately, a definitive list of principles from the learning environment that could be adapted to the training setting has not completely emerged. The learning literature is weak in describing the variables that affect man, especially those pertaining to various forms of skilled behavior. Basic research has centered on the more simple behaviors for which there are available laboratory tasks. However, learning theorists have progressed to a stage of development at which it is clear that the choice of the proper learning variable or level of that variable cannot be based on random option. Learning variables interact with the training environment. Thus, it is not appropriate to ignore the information from the learning literature or to accept a particular variable (for example, feedback or knowledge of results) as useful for all tasks. An illustration of these interactions is provided in a review by Gagné (1962), which suggests that feedback —one of the most sacred variables—is not effective in improving performance on some types of motor-skill training. This does not mean that feedback is not a potent variable for some tasks. It does, however, imply that there are complex interactions that will require consistent research before definitive answers can be found. . . .

EVALUATION PHASE

Since the development of a training program involves an assessment of needs and a careful design of the training environment, the trainee is expected to perform his job at acceptable criterion levels. Unfortunately, this statement of faith displays a sense of self-confidence that is far from justified. Careful examinations of the instructional process disclose numerous pitfalls resulting from mistakes or deficiencies in our present state of knowledge. The assessment of the instructional need might have omitted important job components, or the job itself might have changed since the program was designed. In other instances, there are uncertainties about the most appropriate training technique to establish the required behaviors.

Unfortunately, few programs are evaluated. Indeed, the word *evaluation* raises all sorts of emotional defense reactions. In many cases, the difficulties seem related to a failure to understand that instructional programs are research efforts that must be massaged and treated until the required results are produced. An experience of mine may illuminate this problem.

A community agency was offering a program for previously unemployed individuals to help them obtain jobs. A colleague and I were invited to visit and offer suggestions about improvements to the program. Our questions about the success of the program were answered by reference to the excellent curricula and the high attendance rate of the participants. A frank discussion ensued related to the objectives of the program, with particular emphasis on the criteria being utilized to measure the adequacy of the program—that is, how successful the participants were in obtaining and holding jobs. This discussion led to the revelation that the success level simply was not known, because such data had never been collected. Of course, it was possible that the program was working successfully, but the information to make such a judgment was unavailable. Thus, there was no way to judge the effectiveness of the program or to provide information that could lead to improvements.

The evaluation process centers around two procedures—establishing measures of success (criteria) and using experimental and nonexperimental designs to determine what changes have occurred during the training and transfer process. The criteria are based on the behavioral objectives, which were determined by the assessment of instructional need. As standards of performance, these criteria should describe the behavior required to demonstrate the trainee's skill, the conditions under which the trainee is to perform, and the lowest limit of acceptable performance (Mager 1962).

Criteria must be established for both the evaluation of trainees at the conclusion of the training program and the evaluation of on-the-job performance (referred to as transfer evaluation in the model). In educational settings, the criteria must pertain to performance in later courses, as well as to performance in the original environment where the instructional program was instituted. One classification (Kirkpatrick 1959, 1960) for this purpose suggests that several different measures are necessary, including reaction of participants, learning of participants in training, behavior changes on the job, and final results of the total program. Other serious issues pertain to the integration of the large number of criteria often needed to evaluate a program and to the difficulties (for example, biased estimates of performance) associated with the collection of criterion information. . . .

In addition to criterion development, the evaluation phase must also focus on the necessary design to assess the training program. Some designs use proficiency measures before and after training (pre- and post-tests), as well as continual monitoring to be certain that the program is being implemented as originally designed. Other designs include control groups to determine if any of the training effects could be caused by factors that are unrelated to the training program. For instance, some startled trainers have discovered that their control group performed as well as trainees enrolled in an elaborately designed training program. This often occurred because the control groups could not be permitted to do the job without training. Thus, they either had on-the-job training or were instructed through a program that existed before the implementation of the new instructional system. . . . There are situations in which it is not possible to use the most rigorous design because of cost or because of the particular setting. In these cases, it is important to use the best design available and to recognize those factors that affect the validity of the information.

A training program should be a closed-loop system in which the evaluation process provides for continual modification of the program. An open-loop system, in contrast, either does not have any feedback or is not responsive to such information. In order to develop training programs that achieve their purpose, it is necessary to obtain the evaluative information and to use this information for program modifications.

The information may become available at many different stages in the evaluation process. For example, an effective monitoring program might show that the training program has not been implemented as originally planned. In other instances, different conclusions might be supported by comparing data obtained from the training evaluation or transfer evaluation. If the participant performs well in training but poorly in the transfer setting, the adequacy of the entire program must be assessed. As indicated by the feedback loops in the model (refer again to Figure 1), the information derived from the evaluation process is utilized to reassess the instructional need, thus creating input for the next stage of development.

Even in those instances in which the training program achieves its stated objectives, there are continual developments that can affect the program, including the addition of new media techniques and changes in the characteristics of trainees. These changes often cause previous objectives to become obsolete. The development of training programs must be viewed as a continually evolving process....

REFERENCES

Briggs, L. J., Campeau, P. L., Gagné, R. M., and May, M. A. *Instructional Media: A procedure for the Design of Multi-Media Instruction, a Critical Review of Research, and Suggestions for Future Research.* Palo Alto, Calif.: American Institutes for Research, 1967.

Cicero, J. P. Behavioral Objectives for Technical Training Systems. *Training and Development Journal* 28 (1973): 14–17.

Gagné, R. M. Military Training and Principles of Learning. *American Psychologist* 17 (1962): 83–91.

Gilbert, T. F. On the Relevance of Laboratory Investigation of Learning to Self-Instructional Programming. In A. A. Lumsdaine and R. Glaser, eds., *Teaching Machines and Programmed Instruction.* Washington, D.C.: National Education Association, 1960.

Kirkpatrick, D. L. Techniques for Evaluating Training Programs. *Journal of the American Society of Training Directors* 13 (1959): 3–9, 21–26; 14 (1960): 13–18, 28–32.

Mager, R. F., and Beach, K. M., Jr. *Developing Vocational Instruction.* Belmont, Calif.: Fearon, 1967.

20. MANAGEMENT DEVELOPMENT PROGRAMS CAN PAY OFF

WILLIAM J. KEARNEY

In 1966 the *Wall Street Journal* reported that 500,000 American managers attended some form of management development program—about twice the number in 1961.

Very likely, over 1 million American managers are similarly involved today. The amount of money that American industry spends on management development is not known precisely, but one source estimates that it is more than several billion dollars.[1]

[1] Thomas Bray, "Obsolete Executives," *Wall Street Journal,* January 24, 1966, p. 1.

While there are more managers today, the reason for this increased activity is an implicit belief in the benefit of such programs. There may be occasional interruptions in this trend; yet, the upswing in expenditures is likely to continue.

John Miner's recent study for the Bureau of National Affairs brings home again an important point concerning management talent for the next 15 years: it will be in short supply. Managerial talent for middle- and upper-level positions normally includes persons in the 35–54 age range. Because of the low birthrate during the Great Depression, there will be fewer in this group. Miner suggests that more pressure to meet this shortage will fall on management development efforts. Women, blacks, and other minorities heretofore not in this group will be available and seeking development opportunities. Moreover, there may have to be a reduction in the lower age limit of persons to be considered for these positions. This shortage will further intensify the need for accurate identification and expeditious development of managerial talent.[2]

Because rising costs are likely in the foreseeable future and the shortage of managerial talent is growing, businesses are rightfully concerned about expenditures for management development efforts. More concern is surfacing these days on what employers really get for development dollars. Must such expenditures be considered simply a demonstration of interest in employees, a means of rewarding loyalty and building morale, a method of improving job satisfaction, a device to encourage employees to work hard for advancement? Or is managerial performance *improved?* The evidence that is marshaled is often weak. Sometimes the evidence ultimately leads to a simple declaration of faith in employee efficacy. To be convincing, judgments need to be based on more than the opinions of

the participants of such programs, the opinions of their superiors, or the opinions of organizational third parties. Even differences in participants' performance rankings may not be enough.

While it is true that we do not know a great deal about the effectiveness of management development programs, we do know more than some of our popular notions would suggest. Such evidence that we have, at least in some instances, is more convincing than that commonly cited (participant opinions, supervisory opinions, or expert judgement). That is, the picture is not as bleak as it is often thought to be. Yet, we do need to know and learn more about the impact of management development efforts. Business organizations can do something to provide the answers and, in so doing, help themselves.

RESEARCH REVIEWS

Two separate major reviews and critiques of research studies on management development effectiveness exist at the present time. In the first—by Miner—the reviewer's focus is on the rigor of the research design and classification of studies using experimental and control groups, with before-and-after measurement at one extreme of a continuum. Those using no control group with before-and-after measurement are at the other extreme. The change variables, however, do not always focus on managerial effectiveness. In some cases they are measured by standard tests or supervisory rankings.[3]

The second review was conducted by J. P. Campbell, M. D. Dunnette, E. E. Lawler, and K. E. Weick. The authors very carefully arrange the research studies on a continuum ranging from those utilizing a very rigorous research design (experimental and control groups with before-and-after measurements) to those using only an after-measure-

[2] John B. Miner, *The Human Constraint: The Coming Shortage of Managerial Talent* (Rockville, Md.: The Bureau of National Affairs, 1974), p. 4, and pp. 143–54.

[3] John B. Miner, *Studies in Managerial Education* (New York: Springer, 1965).

ment.[4] Similarly, indications of managerial effectiveness range from the more definitive results or job behavioral factors to imprecise items like supervisory opinions or rankings. Each of these reviews contains some reports of studies that meet the more stringent requirements of research design, although these studies are not in the majority.

Miner examined 38 research studies dating from 1948 to 1963. Over half of those cited were conducted in the five years prior to 1964. A variety of management development techniques were represented in these 38 studies. In presenting his findings Miner states:

Contrary to what a reading of much of the literature on management development seems to imply, there has not only been a considerable amount of research done in the field, but the results have almost without exception been positive. Practically every published report indicates that some change has occurred, although generally some of the pretest-posttest comparisons do not reveal a reliable difference. Even if we agree that studies producing negative results are less likely to be published, the evidence for the positive effects of management education is impressive. Many of the studies suffer from methodological differences, but these differ from investigation to investigation. And there are a number of well-designed evaluations. Inadequacies of method, therefore, can hardly be used to explain away the over-all trend of the findings. There can be little question as of 1964 that these techniques represent a major source of change.[5]

With respect to particular management development techniques, Miner feels that no one technique is most effective:

Lectures, discussion techniques, role-playing, case analyses and T-groups all have been shown to have an impact. However, comparative studies have indicated some superiority for certain procedures in specific instances.[6]

Miner summarizes his findings and conclusions with a very positive outlook on the impact of management development efforts on managerial effectiveness. Yet, he believes this impact also poses a problem:

Viewing the research as a whole it is difficult not to become optimistic, perhaps even enthusiastic, about the potential of management education. We are apparently only beginning to recognize what can be accomplished, especially in areas such as motivational and emotional development. . . . The possibilities for the misuse of social influences in this area are at least as great as those existing in the field of advertising, and probably greater, since the subject is less free to escape from the influence attempt. . . . We are now clearly beyond the point where we can brush the problem aside, contending that the techniques "really don't work, anyway." There is every reason to believe, at least in the case of management education, that they do work.[7]

The second and more recent major review of empirical studies was performed by Campbell, Dunnette, Lawler, and Weick. In addition to some reviewed by Miner, studies conducted between 1965 and 1970 were included. The authors used a format of discussion which distinguishes the studies on the basis of the research design. Two categories were used. Studies having "some control" were defined as those using experimental and control groups with pretesting and posttesting or a posttest only. Those identified as having "few controls" were defined as using pretests and posttests but no control groups.

An important addition to this format, which was not explicitly built into the Miner review, was the classification of the studies into two additional groups: those which attempt to demonstrate some change in behavior relevant to the training itself and those which are directly concerned with changes in job behavior. In the former category are such criteria as attitude measures, tests of decision making ability, and general opinions concerning whether the training was successful. These are internal criteria

4 J. P. Campbell, M. D. Dunnette, E. E. Lawler III, and K. E. Weick, Jr., *Managerial Behavior, Performance and Effectiveness* (New York: McGraw-Hill, 1970).

5 Miner, *Studies in Managerial Education*, p. 38.

6 Miner, *Studies in Managerial Education*, p. 40.

7 Miner, *Studies in Managerial Education*, p. 48.

that measure effect indirectly. External criteria constitute the latter category and include such objective measures of a manager's performance as turnover or grievances in the manager's unit and ratings of job performance by superiors, peers, or subordinates. In the latter case an attempt has been made to directly estimate the effects of training in actual job behavior. In regard to the former judgment, it remains to be demonstrated whether the behavior changes observed have anything to do with managerial effectiveness.

Campbell, Dunnette, Lawler, and Weick added a third classification scheme to the studies that they reviewed on the basis of program content: (1) general management programs; (2) general human relations programs; (3) problem solving and decision making; (4) T-group and laboratory programs; and (5) specialty programs. Overall, 73 studies in these categories using external or internal criteria were reviewed. Briefly, their findings are as follows:

First, about 80 percent of the general management and human relations programs showed results on most of the criteria used. The authors concluded that these types of programs do, in fact, lead to results in a variety of settings. Yet, 29 of the 35 studies in these categories used internal criterion measures. Over one-half of these were concerned with particular attitudinal content rather than job behavior. Thus, one cannot say for sure that an attitudinal change is accompanied by a change in job behavior.

Second, the authors found that T-group training and laboratory methods do produce behavioral change in the work environment but that it is difficult to identify the nature of the changes. Furthermore, these changes are not easily related to actual job effectiveness.

Third, generally negative results were indicated in the studies on programs to improve problem solving and decision making, but because there were so few of these studies the authors drew no conclusion.

Fourth, too few studies comparing two or more development methods or techniques were available to make any generalization as to the superiority of one technique over another (each having the same intent or change goal).

Campbell, Dunnette, Lawler, and Weick conclude their review of research studies by commenting that the empirical literature available to them does not demonstrate conclusively that what is learned in a training program makes an individual a better manager. These authors are clearly not as optimistic as Miner concerning the impact of management development training programs on managerial effectiveness. Yet, they are not pessimistic either.

Research on the effects of management development *has* demonstrated significant effects, and it *has* made a contribution to knowledge. It will undoubtedly continue to do so. However, what we have tried to make clear is that the problem is much more complex than the efforts to attack it to date would seem to imply. Trying to assess the effects of management training on an organization by administering a narrow range of criteria before and after a relatively short-term teaching effort made up of a number of techniques which are not differentially understood can convey only so much information. It is not that management development research has been of no value; rather there simply has not been enough of the varying kinds of efforts it will take to map out a significant number of the relationships in the system.[8]

Herein lies the crux of the question raised earlier and the contribution that business organizations can make in answering it. We have seen that some evidence exists concerning the effectiveness of management development programs. This evidence suggests that programs do have an impact but precisely to what extent we are not sure. The question now becomes What can academicians and businessmen do to clarify the picture? Most of the available empirical evidence is a product of academic research—that is, research performed by academicians using as subjects managers who are participating in management development programs that the researchers may be offering. It is probable that much of the research in the future will continue to be per-

----

[8] Campbell, Dunnette, Lawler, and Weick, *Managerial Behavior*, pp. 287–88, and p. 326.

formed in this manner because of academicians' interest in such matters and the opportunities for research presented by such situations. Yet, much more can be accomplished through the efforts of businessmen themselves.

First, businessmen can encourage research on the effectiveness of all management development programs offered to their managers.

Second, the study must be based on an adequate research design to insure confidence in the findings.

Third, the research must attempt to focus on and use clear-cut, direct indicators of managerial effectiveness rather than global measures or purely results measures.

Fourth, every effort should be made to publish the findings of all such research in appropriate business journals so that others may share in this information. We should keep in mind that positive and negative research findings are equally valuable.

Given the rough estimate of current spending for management development programs, research covering even a small percentage of these programs would result in a substantial gain of information. But this will only occur through the help of businessmen.

RESEARCH DESIGN

When evaluation research is to be conducted, two crucial matters are of central importance in determining the quality of the findings and ultimately the confidence that can be placed in them. The first is the research design. The second is the selection of criteria for measuring managerial effectiveness. If these issues are handled properly, the conclusions drawn from the research efforts will not be suspect.

A minimally acceptable research design is a must. The prime concern is to insure that any changes in managerial effectiveness can be traced conclusively to the program itself or to some other variable. Many previous studies of effectiveness do not meet this standard and, as a result, are not accepted with confidence.

Table 1 portrays several research designs that might be used. They range from those that are inadequate and are unacceptable to those that are more than adequate and are acceptable. Those labeled inadequate are so

TABLE 1
Research Designs

	Design	Pretest	Stimulus	Period T_1 Posttest	Period T_2 Posttest	Adequacy of Research Design
I.	Experimental group		Program	X		Inadequate design (unacceptable)
II.	Experimental group	X	Program	X		
III.	Experimental group		Program	X		
	Control group		No program	X		
IV.	Experimental group	X	Program	X		Adequate design (acceptable)
	Control group	X	No program	X		
V.	Experimental group	X	Program	X		More than adequate design (acceptable)
	Control group 1	X	No program	X		
	Control group 2	X	Placebo	X		
VI.	Experimental group	X	Program	X		
	Control group 1	X	No program	X		
	Control group 2	X	Placebo	X		
	Control group 3		No program	X		
VII.	Experimental group	X	Program	X	X	
	Control group 1	X	No program	X	X	
	Control group 2	X	Placebo	X	X	
	Control group 3		No program	X	X	

designated because it is not possible to attribute with any degree of certainty the results of the posttest to the impact of the development program.

Research design IV (see Table 1) is an acceptable design and the one most likely to be widely used. This design more clearly ascertains the impact of the program by examining the state of the experimental and control groups, which are alike in all important respects—before the program, as well as after the program. Any changes in the posttest can then be traced with more certainty.

Research designs V, VI, and VII provide for progressively greater control and correspondingly increase the confidence merited by the findings and conclusions. Design V provides a check for greater motivation that might be induced in the subjects by the research situation. In addition, design VI checks the possibility of the subjects learning through the pretest those areas of behavior or knowledge that are apparently important to the examiners and for which they might prepare themselves for the posttest. Finally, design VII adds a second posttest to determine the extent of knowledge retention or behavior change at a more distant time.

Research design IV, while it does not check for motivation effects and pretest learning, is acceptable. It combines the adequacy of design with the practicality of many business and development program situations. Thus, this design should constitute the minimum for any evaluation research.

A recent study of 141 organizations with 1,000 or more employees indicates that only 5 (3.5 percent) of the 141 firms that evaluate their management development programs use this design. Furthermore, none of these firms report using it as a primary evaluation tool. This would seem to indicate that much remains to be accomplished in doing an adequate job....

21. INTERACTION MODELING: A NEW CONCEPT IN SUPERVISORY TRAINING

WILLIAM BYHAM and JAMES ROBINSON

Can training measurably improve supervisory skills in such areas as increasing productivity, reducing employee absenteeism, handling discrimination complaints, and overcoming resistance to change? Although many managers would be skeptical, a number of leading companies such as American Telephone and Telegraph (AT&T), Boise Cascade Corporation, General Electric, Kaiser Corporation, RCA, IBM, Olin Corporation and B. F. Goodrich are attempting to change supervisory behavior in these critical areas, as well as others, and there is research to show the effectiveness of several of the training programs.

These training programs use a new training concept called *interaction modeling*, which is quite different from traditional supervisory training programs. No theory is taught; instead, for each situation, practical steps for handling are provided. Positive models of behavior are presented and on-the-job application is stressed.

Interaction modeling programs differ according to individual needs and objectives of using organizations, but most have the following elements in common:

1. The subject matter is targeted to *real*

Source: Reproduced by special permission from the February 1976 *Training and Development Journal.* Copyright © 1976 by the American Society for Training and Development, Inc.

needs of the group by identifying, prior to training, the difficult human interaction situations confronted by the supervisors to be trained, e.g., improving work habits, utilizing effective disciplinary action, delegating responsibilities, orienting new employees, etc.

2. Six supervisors are trained at one time.
3. The training is structured so that one difficult human interaction situation is learned at a time.
4. A step-by-step approach for handling each difficult interaction situation is provided.
5. A positive model using the step-by-step approach shows learners how each difficult situation can be handled successfully.
6. Practice in handling the difficult situations is provided each learner in the classroom.
7. Confidence is developed as supervisors discover they are developing skills to handle difficult situations which previously they had not been able to handle effectively.
8. A receptive and supportive on-the-job environment is built so that the trained supervisors do in fact use their skills on the job.

BUILDING SKILLS

. . . To illustrate how an interaction modeling training program works, we will use as an example the *Interaction Management* training system, which is the most widely used supervisory modeling program in business and industry. Although Interaction Management contains elements common to all interaction modeling programs, it has some unique elements not found in other programs.

The Interaction Management system consists of 20 skill modules, each dealing with a specific, difficult interaction situation faced by supervisors. An organization can choose any number of these modules to design a

training program to meet the specific needs of its supervisors. In addition to skill modules, a program is made up of:

1. An introductory module, providing an overview of the entire program and explaining the concepts that thread through all the modules.
2. Review modules in which participants discuss their on-the-job use of skills acquired in training. The opportunity for additional practice in handling difficult on-the-job situations is also afforded.
3. A diagnosis and review module is designed to help participants correctly diagnose critical situations and choose the most appropriate skill for each situation. It also provides participants with an opportunity to plan on-the-job applications.

A separate, but integrated, part of the system is a one and one-half day training workshop for the managers of the supervisors being trained.

FIGURE 1
Example of Interaction Modeling Critical Steps for Improving Work Habits

1. Describe in detail the poor work habit you have observed.
2. Indicate why it concerns you.
3. Ask for reasons and listen openly to the explanation.
4. Indicate that the situation must be changed and ask for ideas for solving the problem.
5. Discuss each idea and offer your help.
6. Agree on specific action to be taken and set a specific follow-up date.

Supervisory skills are successfully learned in an Interaction Management program because the supervisor sees immediate application of the skills being learned. The elements that make up the skill are clearly defined, a model is provided, and practice in using the elements is provided.

A key ingredient in any learning situation is a motivated learner. This is accomplished in an Interaction Management program by focusing on the actual needs of the supervisors and by providing them a sense of "ownership" in the program. Before the Interaction Management modules to be used in the program are determined, a needs-analysis questionnaire is utilized to gather information about what employee situations are causing difficulty for the supervisors to be trained. The needs-analysis information makes possible the construction of an effective training program aimed specifically at the supervisors' needs. The supervisors know it is a tailored program, developed to help them. They see it as relevant to their problem situations and their success on the job. They have a sense of ownership and enter the program with the expectation of benefiting.

The critical steps provide a sequence of events to be followed during an interaction between a supervisor and a subordinate. The steps provide an organized way of handling employee interactions while still appreciating the differences in the subordinates with which supervisors must deal. The critical steps are a fundamental part of each interaction modeling module and provide a structure for an effective human interaction.

Providing directions on how to accomplish a task is a central part of all learning theories, but it is absent from most supervisory and management training programs. Traditionally, trainers have said that there is no "one right way" to deal with people, and because of this, most training programs have provided no real direction. Interaction modeling programs recognize that while there may be many ways of handling a situation, a supervisor needs one way that works. The fact that there may be more ways is not important.

Following the steps in order is stressed so supervisors do not skip over steps such as "Ask the employee's help in solving the problem" in their haste to define action steps. But varying the amount of time devoted to each step is encouraged in recognition of differences in the individuals with

whom the supervisors interact. Thus, while Interaction Management provides an ordered, systematic approach, it still takes full cognizance of individual differences.

While the critical steps indicate the type of information to be covered during an interaction, a film or videotape model shows the supervisors how to handle the situation. In the film, a supervisor successfully deals with the type of interaction situation being studied in that specific module. . . .

Interaction Management programs stress confidence building. The positive model, which is an integral part of all interaction modeling programs, graphically shows the supervisors that specific, difficult employee situations can be handled satisfactorily from the supervisor's point of view *and* from the subordinate's point of view. The critical steps provide a road map and give the supervisor confidence that if the critical steps are followed, a successful conclusion will result. The emphasis in the skill practice exercises is that the discussion with the employee will be effective if the supervisors follow the critical steps.

The principle way that confidence is built is through positive reinforcement. Throughout an Interaction Management program, the accent is on the positive; that is, on what the trainee is doing well. A participant may start out very insecure and hesitant, even to the point of being afraid to enter into a skill-practice exercise. However, with each skill-practice being positively reinforced by the classroom administrator and his or her peers, and with the participant gaining insight from watching the successful peer behavior, the participant learns to handle difficult situations and solve problems. . . .

TRANSFER OF TRAINING

The importance of a receptive on-the-job environment in which a supervisor can try out skills learned in training has been well documented through the years. In the classic study done at the International Harvester Company,[1] it was found that training actually produced a negative effect on the performance of supervisors when they returned from the training to a real life situation where their bosses held values counter to the values taught in the training program. Thus, an important consideration in the Interaction Management system is creating a receptive and a positively reinforcing environment.

In the Interaction Management program, managers of the supervisors being trained attend a one and one-half day workshop (or three half-days) in which the following takes place:

1. They view a film which defines the purpose of the program, provides examples of the three basic human interaction concepts that underline all the programs, and shows how a typical skill module is conducted.
2. They take part in some of the same skill-building modules in which their subordinate supervisors are being trained.
3. They have the opportunity to handle in skill-practice exercises many of the same situations that the supervisors also handle.
4. They are trained in how to work with their subordinate supervisors in diagnosing supervisory problems, in determining the most appropriate interaction skills to use and in gaining agreement on the desired outcome of the problem situations. For example managers are taught how to help supervisors define the specific causes of a problem and outline specific interaction goals prior to deciding on the substance of the actual employee discussion. Difference in work-habit problems and job-performance problems are particularly stressed as confusion between the two

often results in ineffective discussions with employees.

5. Managers are taught how to effectively reinforce their subordinate supervisors' use of the Interaction Management skills on the job.
6. Managers also consider their impact as "managerial models" upon their subordinate supervisors and are taught to be "positive models" of effective supervisory behavior. . . .

VALIDITY STUDIES

For a new training concept, a surprising amount of effectiveness research has already been conducted. . . .

LEARNING OF NEW SKILLS

Two studies have found that supervisors trained in interaction modeling programs do gain the skills which they were taught. In an AT&T study,[2] a large group of first-level line supervisors were identified in two telephone companies. Special care was taken to insure that these supervisors were representative of typical first-level supervisors. In each company, 100 supervisors were randomly assigned to training or control groups after being matched by sex, age, department, length of service, and number of subordinates. One group received the interaction modeling training (called Supervisory Relationships Training in the Bell System) and the other group received no training. . . .

The results showed the performance of the trained supervisors to be dramatically superior to that of the untrained supervisors. Table 1 summarizes the overall judgment made by the evaluation team. Of the trained group 84 percent of the supervisors were

[1] Fleishman, Edwin A., "Leadership Climate, "Human Relations Training and Supervisory Behavior." *Personnel Psychology*, 6 (Summer 1953); 205–22; and Walker, Charles L., Jr., "Education and Training at International Harvester." *Harvard Business Review*, 27 (September 1949): 542–58.

[2] Moses, J., and Ritchie, D., "Assessment Center Used to Evaluate an Interaction Modeling Program." *Assessment and Development Newsletter*, Development Dimensions, Inc., January 1975; and American Telephone and Telegraph. Human Resources Development Department. *Analysis and Evaluation of Supervisory Relationships Training.* 1975.

TABLE 1
Percent Distribution of Overall Judgment Ratings

Overall Judgment	Percent Trained	Percent Untrained
Exceptionally good or above average	84	33
Average	10	34
Below average or poor	6	33
	100	100

seen to perform "exceptionally good" or "above average" in their handling of the problem discussions. On the other hand, of the untrained supervisors only 33 percent were rated this way.

A General Electric study similar in concept was used to evaluate their Managerial Skills Behavior Modeling course.[3] Sixty-two middle-level managers from six diverse company locations were randomly selected and trained. An additional 62 middle-level managers from the same six businesses were randomly selected to serve as an untrained control group.

Trained judges collected data within a month of the managers completing the course and also four months later. Like the AT&T study, the data consisted of evaluations of how well the trained and untrained managers handled simulated situations typical but not identical to the training situations. The judges did not know who had been trained and who had not been trained when they watched the three simulations. Analysis of the results revealed that the trained managers performed significantly better than the untrained managers (.05 level of significance).

APPLICATION OF SKILL

While the two studies reported above indicate that a skill was learned, they do not necessarily prove that trainees actually went back and changed their performance on the job. Such results are much more difficult to determine. Self-report data strongly show that supervisors feel they are making use of the skills acquired in training. An indication of actual on-the-job performance can come from the perceptions of subordinates of the supervisor. Two studies on subordinate reaction have been reported. A GE study, which surveyed subordinates of trained and untrained managers before training, immediately after training and four months after training, found no significant difference between the subordinates' perceptions of trained and untrained supervisors.[4]

A possible explanation for the lack of positive results may lie in their use of written questionnaires to collect the data. It is very difficult to get across subtle behavioral concepts to untrained people via a written document. Also, the GE questionnaire tended to focus on the employees' overall perception of the supervisor rather than skill in specific areas. The author of the study notes that the questionnaire evaluated whether the subordinates perceived their managers as being "good guys," i.e., being considerate, allowing them freedom, encouraging participation, being flexible, etc., not whether they improved in specific one-to-one situations.

A study conducted by Agway, Inc., which used trained interviewers to collect data on the specific behavior taught in the training program, did produce evidence of positive transfer of training.[5] The study involved asking employees in a data processing and office management operation questions regarding how their supervisors handle interpersonal situations similar to those taught in interaction modeling training. . . .

[3] Burnaska, R. F., "The Effects of Behavioral Modeling Training upon Managers Behaviors and Employees' Perceptions." Paper presented at the 83rd Annual Convention of the American Psychological Association, Chicago, August 1975.

[4] Burnaska, "Effects of Behavorial Modeling Training."

[5] Adams, D., and Engfer, R., *Validating Behavior Modification: A Pre and Post of the Effects of Interaction Training on Supervisory On-the-Job Behavior.* (In press)

TABLE 2
Differences in Average Percentage of Correct Responses

Area of Question	Pre (n=25)	Post (n=19)	Difference	Control (n=24)	Trained (n=19)	Difference
Orienting a new employee	29%	54%	+25	48%	54%	+ 6
Overcoming resistance to change	26%	50%	+24	24%	50%	+26
Reducing absenteeism	63%	87%	+24	69%	87%	+18
Handling emotional situations	51%	68%	+17	46%	68%	+22
Using effective follow-up action	30%	47%	+17	37%	47%	+10
Teaching an employee a new task	54%	66%	+12	52%	66%	+14
Reducing tardiness	58%	68%	+10	46%	68%	+22
Handling employee complaints	49%	58%	+ 9	60%	58%	− 2
Improving employee performance	82%	81%	− 1	63%	81%	+18

The experimental design involved getting the data from the subordinates of the 19 supervisors in a department before they were trained and seven months after training. Data was also obtained from the subordinates of supervisors in a roughly matched department to form a control group.

Table 2 shows some of the results of the study. For example, in the area of orienting a new employee, prior to their supervisors being trained, 29 percent of the subordinates said their supervisors used the "correct" method and 54 percent after their supervisors were trained. Thus, the net change was 25 percentage points.

The ultimate goal of many training programs is to affect the "bottom line" in terms of increasing productivity or decreasing costs. This kind of proof of the effectiveness of a training program is always the hardest to come by because measures are usually very contaminated by other factors. Nevertheless, three studies have already been reported that show the large potential profit impact that can come about from using an interaction modeling program.

A large manufacturer used [an] index that reflected effective utilization of employee and equipment resources as a criterion with which to evaluate the performance of four

trained and four untrained supervisors.[6]

Table 3 shows the differences in those work groups supervised by the trained and untrained supervisors. The data was collected during the ten weeks prior to training and during the ten weeks after training.

TABLE 3

Trained		Untrained	
Group	Net Change	Group	Net Change
T_1......	6	U_1..........	−20
T_2......	4	U_2..........	− 7
T_3......	0.1	U_3..........	−21
T_4......	−9	U_4..........	−21

PRODUCTIVITY DROPS

As can be seen, productivity of the untrained group dropped significantly. The researchers attributed this to a bad work climate caused by deteriorating general business conditions. Three out of four of the trained groups showed an improvement. The researchers concluded that the trained supervisors were more able to deal with the adverse effects of the poor business conditions (declining orders) than the untrained

---

[6] Goldstein, Arnold P., and Sorcher, Melvin. *Changing Supervisor Behavior.* New York: Pergamon Press, 1974.

supervisors. The great practical importance of the improvement is stressed in the study. It is noted that a 1 percent overall increase in the plant represented an annual savings of many thousands of dollars per year if it was sustained for that length of time.

Sales increases resulting from using an interaction modeling program have been reported by a large office equipment manufacturer.[7] Trained sales, service, and administrative teams showed a 7.89 percent increase in sales while each of three untrained teams registered an average of 2.18 percent decrease for the same time period.

Employee turnover reduction was the goal of an early GE study.[8] Both hard-core employees and their first-line supervisors were trained on how to take and give constructive criticism, how to ask for and give help, and how to establish mutual trust and respect. After six months, 70 percent of the 39 hard-core employees who, along with their supervisors, had been trained were still working. Only 30 percent of 25 untrained employees hired at the same time remained.

One of the principles on which Interaction Management is based is that participants in the program develop skills for handling interaction situations which generalize past the specific problems dealt with in a modeling program. An indication that this actually happens can also be obtained from the AT&T research described earlier. In addition to having the trained and untrained supervisors handle situations taught in the interaction modeling training program, the supervisors were also assessed on their ability to handle a unique problem not considered in the training program—namely, employee theft.

Differences between the trained and untrained groups of the same magnitude as those recorded in Table 1 were found. This indicates that not only were specific skills learned, but also that general skills of dealing effectively with employees were learned and could be generalized to novel situations.

MAINTENANCE OF SKILL

The last area of concern about a training program is how long the skills will be used on the job. In theory, interaction modeling programs are self-reinforcing. The successful handling of a situation, using the critical steps taught in an interaction modeling program, should produce a positive feeling of accomplishment immediately after the discussion with the employee and thus encourage further applications. In addition to this self-motivation aspect of the program, reinforcement by the managers of the supervisors is a powerful incentive for further applications.

Little evidence of skill maintenance is available, but a strong indication that skills are maintained or increased can be found in the GE study described earlier.[9] In the GE research, trained and untrained managers were evaluated before, immediately after, and four months after training using performance in behavioral simulations as rated by trained judges as the criterion. The four-month-after results were more positive than the immediately-after comparisons indicating that for at least four months, skill utilization increases instead of diminishes. . . .

"PROMISING" FUTURE

Many supervisory training programs have shown great promise, have gained wide public acceptance for a time, and then have been forgotten. Will interaction modeling programs follow the same route?

We think not, for two reasons. First, early research has shown that the program is

---

[7] Smith, P. E., *Management Training to Improve Morale and Customer Satisfaction.* (In Press).

[8] Burnaska, "Effects of Behavioral Modeling Training."

[9] Burnaska, "Effects of Behavioral Modeling Training."

effective. The "death toll" for many training programs was their inability to prove their contribution through research. From the research that has already been conducted and research that is underway, it appears organizations using interaction modeling programs will be able to show that their programs are making meaningful contributions that can pay off in better employee relations and cost savings. Second, interaction modeling is a learning process, not a theory being taught. This is an important distinction which makes interaction modeling more adaptable than specific theories which have come and gone in the training area.

Initial applications of the interaction modeling concept in industry have been to train first and second level supervisors, but there is no reason why the same concepts cannot be applied in many other training areas. The training of higher managers is an obvious next application. In fact, some organizations have already developed training programs for higher managers based upon interaction modeling concepts. IBM has developed a training program to teach managers how to handle attitude survey feedback data, and GE has a middle management program. Any situation that involves human interaction is a possible application. A major program using the method to train department store salespeople is now under development. A nurses training college has developed an interaction modeling program to train nurses how to deal with common nurse-patient interactions. Customer contact positions such as bank tellers, airline personnel and police officers are examples of obvious further possible applications. With ingenuity and foresight there is no limit to the kinds of applications that can be conceived by the training professional.

8

COMPENSATION

Organizations want their compensation policies to make a significant contribution to both participation and effectiveness objectives of the personnel/human resource function. Compensation is absolutely essential to insure participation in most organizations. Indeed, the enormous resources allocated to compensation or pay (we will use the terms interchangeably) is clearly aimed primarily at obtaining and retaining a workforce. Most organizations, however, also hope to facilitate their effectiveness objective with compensation as well.

TYPES OF COMPENSATION AND ACTIVITIES

Compensation Levels and Structures. It must be recognized that there are several dimensions of pay that organizations must develop policies on. A fundamental one is called the pay *level*. It refers to the average pay for a particular job. Note that level refers to pay for the job and not what individuals receive. Individual employees may be paid more or less than the level depending on their performance, seniority, and so on.

Another dimension is called the pay *structure*. Structure refers to the relationship of the pay associated with different jobs. These two dimensions of compensation are illustrated in Figure 1. The pay levels for the four jobs are shown by the intersection of the dotted lines with the dollar axis. The structure is shown by the slope of the line connecting the pay levels of the different jobs.

In establishing compensation levels and structures, the organization must consider a number of issues. Chief among them, of course, are economic issues. The organization must maintain control over its pay program so that it does not expend too much of its resources on this particular organizational expense. Ultimately, the organization's ability to pay will be an influential determinant of its pay levels and structure.

At the same time, however, the organization must have pay levels and a

FIGURE 1
Compensation Levels and Structure

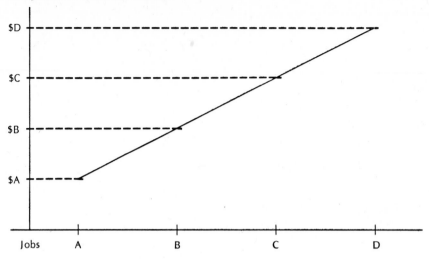

structure which will allow it to attract and retain a workforce. Its pay level must be competitive with other organizations employing individuals with similar job skills. Its structure must be seen as *equitable* (fair) so that employees find working for the organization acceptable.

Job Evaluation and Wage Surveys. Organizations typically engage in several activities to accomplish their pay level and structure objectives. One important activity is called job *evaluation*. There are a variety of job evaluation plans that differ on specific procedures. However, they all share three important steps.

1. Step one requires that jobs be analyzed. Recall that job *analysis* identifies the activities performed on the job and the skills necessary to perform the activities. The job *description* is simply a written summary of the job analysis. These job descriptions become the basic source of information for the remainder of the job evaluation.
2. A second step requires that the factors on which pay will be based be identified. The number and kind of factors varies by specific evaluation technique, but they usually involve the skill level necessary to perform the job and the responsibility associated with the job.
3. The third step involves the actual evaluation of the job descriptions on the factors previously identified. Again, different job evaluation plans vary somewhat in this regard.

Whatever the specific plan, the job evaluation procedure results in a hierarchy of jobs for pay purposes. This hierarchy indicates which job should receive the highest pay, which next highest, and so on. In most job evaluation plans, the dollar pay level for the job is *not* established. Before dollar pay levels are assigned, organizations will conduct or participate in a wage *survey*. These surveys are performed by having a number of organizations, often in a single labor market, indicate the current pay rates for their jobs. Wage surveys are admittedly rather crude indicators of market pay practices because jobs vary from organization to organization even though job titles may not. They are, however, the only way organizations have for identifying market pay conditions.

Pay System. Another dimension of compensation pertains to how employees on the same job may receive different rates of pay. We refer to this as the pay *system*. In some pay systems there will be only a single pay rate for each job and hence all employees on that job will receive the same pay. In other systems employees on the same job have different pay rates. Such differences could be due to a pay policy in which high-seniority employees receive a higher rate than do low-seniority employees. This type of policy obviously is aimed toward the participation objective. Pay differences on the same job could also be due to a policy in which higher pay rates are given to higher job performers than lower job performers. Systems of this sort are called *incentive* or *merit systems*. Achievement of the effectiveness objective underlies these systems. Finally, pay differences among people on the same job could be due to a combination of seniority and performance differences among the employees. Mixed systems like this attempt to achieve both participation and effectiveness.

Choice of a pay system depends substantially on the type of technology that is used and the type of product produced. It is generally agreed that incentive systems require a technology (a) that is employee-paced rather than machine-paced, (b) where the tasks to be performed are repetitive, and (c) that is fairly stable. The product or output must be easily measured and be of a type where quality is not particularly important or can be easily controlled. In such situations employees have an opportunity to regulate their own work pace so that the monetary incentive associated with high productivity can have the desired impact on behavior. Easily identified outputs and repetitious tasks are necessary so that measurement of productivity is not an insurmountable problem. Finally, technology must be stable so that productivity standards can be maintained over time.

Incentive systems have been shown to be effective in raising productivity over comparable nonincentive systems in many instances. Their use, however, is very demanding in terms of administrative costs and problems. Inadequate administration of incentive systems can easily result in lower efficiency than is typically obtained under other pay systems. These latter experiences of failure, sometimes well publicized, have probably been influential in the declining use of incentive systems among American organizations. At present, less than one third of manufacturing employees are working under such systems.

Pay Form. A final compensation dimension, pay *form*, refers to the composition of the pay that is received by the individual. The major portion of pay one receives is direct *take-home* pay. A rapidly growing proportion, however, is indirect in the form of *fringe benefits*. Approximately one third of an average employee's compensation is now paid in fringe benefits. Some of these benefits are required by the government, such as social security payments required of both employer and employee and workmen's compensation payments required of the employer. Privately sponsored benefits such as life and health insurance constitute another major category of fringe benefits. Also very important are employer payments for nonwork including vacation and retirement programs.

The rapid growth of fringe benefits is due to a number of factors. Laws such as social security have had an obvious and direct impact. Graduated federal and state tax laws have encouraged the development of fringe benefits that defer income such as retirement programs. Reduced insurance rates for groups versus individuals has allowed organizations to provide benefits to employees at a lower cost than the individuals could provide the same benefits to themselves. Employees and their unions have also undoubtedly encouraged employers to provide increasing amounts of fringe benefits. Employers, moreover, have often been quite willing to increase the relative amount of pay going to fringe benefits so long as the total compensation costs were increased no more than if a greater proportion went to direct pay.

One fairly recent trend worth special note is the greater individualization of organizational benefit programs. Research has shown that there are large differences among employees in their preferences for various types of benefits. For example, increased retirement benefits are relatively more attractive to older employees, and health insurance is relatively more attractive to employees with children. In response to these different preferences, some organizations have gone to so-called *cafeteria-style* benefit programs. These programs allow the employee to choose, within limits, the proportion of their pay that will be direct and indirect, and within indirect benefits, the relative mix of different types of fringes.

CONSTRAINTS ON PAY SETTING

The discussion so far has focused on market, organizational, and technological factors that influence the compensation-setting processes. Such a discussion would be seriously deficient if it did not explicitly consider the impact of two outside institutions on all aspects of the organization's pay program. The outside institutions that have the most significant impact are government and unions.

Government Regulation.   We have already indicated that certain federal and state regulations have had both a direct and an indirect impact on the form of pay. A substantial amount of legislation has also had a significant impact on other dimensions of pay, particularly level and structure.

The most direct impact in this vein has been the *minimum pay* laws established at the federal level and by many states as well. To make matters more complex, there is not one but several federal laws pertaining to minimum wages. The most comprehensive in terms of the number of people covered is the minimum wage established in the *Fair Labor Standards Act*. Most employers doing interstate business are required to pay a legislatively determined minimum wage to its employees. Higher minimums are established for employers doing business with the federal government in the *Davis-Bacon* and *Walsh-Healey Acts*.

The immediate impact of an increase in minimum wages appears to be primarily in the pay levels of those jobs that are below the new required rate. Usually only a minority of jobs must have their pay levels raised immediately to comply with the legal increase. Obviously, such changes serve to compress pay structures. Over time, however, it is typical for structures to be reestablished to the initial shapes by extending the amount of the increase in the minimum wage to all jobs in the structure. Thus, minimum pay increases have an apparent impact on pay structures as well as on pay levels.

At several times during the last four decades, we have also had *maximum wage* laws. These laws have been put into effect during war periods where there were very high-labor demands and the danger of inflation was great. At present, we have no maximum wage laws that are operative.

We also have federal and state laws regulating the *hours* of work that can be performed or performed without economic penalty to the employer. Again, the most significant law in terms of the number of people covered is the *Fair Labor Standards Act*. It requires that nonexempt employees (loosely defined as nonsupervisory personnel) be paid time and one half their regular pay rate for hours in excess of 40 during any week. The law was passed in 1938 and is aimed at encouraging organizations to employ additional people rather than having existing employees work overtime.

It is difficult to say exactly how large an impact laws regulating hours have had on organizational pay programs. One impact may be that pay levels are increased by overtime pay requirements. But total labor costs may be less by paying overtime than by hiring new employees. Costs of recruiting, selecting, and training new employees may exceed the costs of overtime pay to current employees. Another impact is on the pay structure if overtime pay is common for some jobs but not others. For example, first-level supervisors usually do not receive overtime pay, while their subordinates do receive such benefits. Under these circumstances it is possible for the subordinates' total pay to be the same, or even greater than, the supervisor's total pay, even though the supervisor receives a higher hourly wage.

Unions. Many organizations negotiate over compensation matters with one or more unions. Unions are typically interested in all aspects of the compensation process. A number of these interests often conflict with the policies the organization would prefer to implement.

One overriding concern of unions is that members be treated equitably in matters of pay. This leads them to be particularly concerned about the pay structure and pay system. Unions frequently oppose job evaluation procedures if they believe that the resulting structure puts some employees at an inappropriate pay level relative to others. Since organizations also want pay equity from their structure, there is frequently a basis for accomodation on this issue.

Another equity issue is unions' typical concern and frequent objection to incentive-pay systems or even merit-pay systems. Unions generally argue that they do not oppose pay for performance in principle. However, they charge that the administration of most pay for performance systems is inadequate so that the resulting pay differentials between people are unfair. This concern has frequently lead unions to argue that compensation rewards (and other rewards such as promotion) be based largely or exclusively on seniority.

Of course, the most likely source of union management conflict regarding pay has to do with the establishment of compensation levels. A major negotiating goal of unions is almost always to obtain an increase in the pay level above what the organization desires. Many of the work stoppages that occur have resulted because the two parties could not agree on a mutually acceptable pay level. There is a substantial amount of evidence that union members do receive higher, although usually not substantially higher, pay levels than comparable nonunion employees.

INTRODUCTION TO READINGS

Internal Wage Structure

We indicated that the pay-setting processes in organizations were complex and depended on a number of factors including economic, technological, and institutional ones. The first selection by E. Robert Livernash focuses on the process of *setting pay* (he uses the term wage) *levels and structures* in some detail. His analysis begins with a discussion suggesting the inadequacy of an economic model of pay level setting which depends on a labor demand and supply for each job. It is inadequate in part because most organizations have production processes that require simultaneous increases or decreases in demand for a variety of jobs. The pay rate for a single job is thus usually not critical to how many persons are employed on that job. Traditional economic analysis is also deficient on the supply side. Livernash argues that employees will not try to change jobs for minor differences in pay rates because they have built up security in their own organization through seniority.

He then proceeds to develop an alternative model to explain pay setting in organizations. There are four important concepts in this model. One is the *job cluster* which refers to a grouping of jobs within the organization. Jobs in a cluster are frequently similar in job content. Pay rates within narrow clusters are highly related. If one job receives a pay increase, all within the cluster are likely to receive a similar increase.

The second concept in the model is the notion of a *key job*. Key jobs are usually important to the organization because they involve critical skills and/or constitute an important portion of the organization's total compensation costs. Pay changes are introduced into the job cluster through key jobs. The key job is, therefore, more important to the pay-setting process than are other jobs in the cluster.

Concept three is concerned with the fact that pay rates between clusters are connected by the *wage structure*. Livernash views the wage structure as connecting pay rates among key jobs. Pay changes in one cluster thus have an impact on the pay changes in other clusters through key jobs.

However, *internal* pressure generated through the wage structure is only one component in the pay-setting process. *External* or market forces are still present to a greater or lesser degree. These forces are applicable to those key jobs that are used in a variety of organizations (so that a market can exist). External pay pressures occurring through the *wage contour* that links key jobs in an organization to similar key jobs in other organizations is the fourth concept.

A diagram of the major sources of influence is shown in Figure 2. It shows two clusters of four jobs each. Cluster 1 has key job 1 (K_1) and three nonkey jobs $A-C$; cluster 2 has key job 2 (K_2) and nonkey jobs ($D-F$). A change in pay for nonkey jobs is most heavily influenced by the key job in that cluster. Pay changes in the key jobs are influenced internally by other key jobs in the organization and externally through the wage contour. Actually, Figure 2 is an

FIGURE 2
Organizational Pay-Setting Process

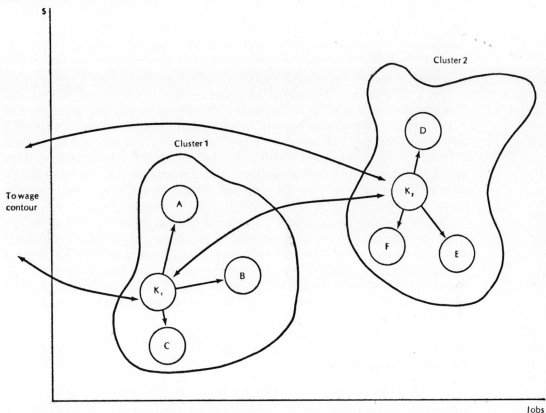

oversimplification of the model, but it should aid you in understanding the Livernash article.

Livernash points out that these various forces are generally worked out through the job evaluation process. He views successful job evaluation as accommodating both internal and external forces. Note also his discussion of union responses to job evaluation. He shows a good sensitivity to the concerns unions have regarding pay issues.

The Livernash model is descriptive rather than predictive. That is, you could not test it as you might some rigorous mathematical model. Nevertheless, if you read it carefully you will be rewarded with a good understanding of organizational pay-setting processes.

Supplemental Compensation

We indicated earlier that a rapidly growing form of compensation was in indirect benefits. The paper by A. N. Nash and S. J. Carroll, Jr., considers this form of compensation. They discuss the growth and the reasons for the growth of these benefits. The major portion of their paper describes the types of mandatory and voluntary benefits most frequently available to employees.

New Approaches to Pay

Both the Livernash and the Nash and Carroll papers describe pay issues as they relate to jobs or to most or all employees. We suggested at the outset, however, that the pay individuals receive often may vary around the pay level for the job. Edward Lawler's article examines several new approaches to pay that focus primarily on pay-setting issues as they apply to the individual.

One such step in individualizing the pay system that Lawler discusses, and that we discussed earlier, is *cafeteria-style* benefit programs. Another, *skill evaluation* pay plans, goes beyond traditional job evaluation in an important way. Recall that job evaluation generally pays for the skill required to perform the particular job in question. Skill evaluation pay plans additionally pay individuals for personal skills they acquire. This encourages employees to obtain additional job skills and hence provides greater flexibility in allocating employees to jobs.

One of the most novel issues discussed by Lawler is the possibility of individual participation in the development of pay programs. He briefly describes several situations where substantial employee participation in the development of pay programs seems to have resulted in improved work behaviors and attitudes. Participation in the development of pay plans is potentially the most significant individualizing effort of all since it brings employees directly into the managerial decision-making process.

Impacts of Pay on Employees

The last selection in this chapter by Lee Dyer, Donald Schwab, and John Fossum focuses on recent evidence about the influences pay has on employee attitudes and behaviors. It will help your understanding of this paper to recognize that Dyer et al. put pay into several dimensions, similarly to the way we did in the introductory remarks. Their use of the term pay *magnitude* is similar to our use of the term pay *level,* and their pay *contingency* relates to our pay *system.* They use pay *form* identically to the way we have.

The authors argue that pay magnitude is the major compensation dimension influencing job choice decisions for most individuals. They base this argument primarily on the evidence which indicates that except for the wage or salary, job seekers have relatively little information about the jobs they are applying for. On the other hand, Dyer et al. suggest that employee satisfaction and decisions of whether to stay or leave an organization are perhaps more complex. This complexity results because feelings about fairness or equity regarding pay enter into these attitudes and decisions as well as does the magnitude of pay. Equity feelings, in turn, depend on a number of factors.

The authors rely heavily on expectancy theory in their discussion of the impact of pay on job performance (see the reading by Donald Schwab in Chapter 2). They conclude that the pay system and how it is administered is critical to whether or not pay can encourage higher productivity. The essential elements they suggest are whether or not pay rewards are contingent on high performance and whether or not employees perceive that linkage to exist.

The obvious implication of their discussion is that the organization must be concerned with different dimensions of pay for different types of behaviors and attitudes. At a more fundamental level, Dyer et al. raise the intriguing possibility that a given dimension may have both positive and negative impacts on employees. For example, an incentive may motivate high performance, but due to problems of administering the system, it may also cause dissatisfaction with the system. This sort of possibility is one of the reasons that pay administration is so frustrating and yet so challenging.

22. THE INTERNAL WAGE STRUCTURE
E. ROBERT LIVERNASH

"Internal wage structure," as used in this paper, refers primarily to single plants or establishments. The term applies particularly to more complex structures, such as exist in many manufacturing plants, but also to simpler craft structures, with modifications in emphasis.

The concept of the internal wage structure is a significant approach to wage-rate analysis. As thinking shifts from the more or less exclusive role of impersonal market forces to encompass union and management policies, some adaptation of approach is necessary. Abstracting the internal wage structure for consideration has the advantage of staying within an organizational unit and dealing with a problem having realistic administrative scope. In such an approach the discussion of "market," "administrative," and "institutional" forces can be blended together.

This approach necessarily puts in question the thought of applying "demand and supply" independently to each wage rate in a plant. There simply is no compulsion of market forces adequate to explain the detailed determination of wage differentials. Internal standards of job comparison are a much more adequate explanation of many wage differentials than are market forces.

Source: "Abridged from Internal Wage Structure in *New Concepts in Wage Determination* by Taylor & Pierson. Copyright © 1957 by McGraw-Hill, Inc. Used with permission of McGraw-Hill Book Company."

From this point of view, the wage rate for one particular job in a plant cannot be divorced from the wage rates for other jobs within the same plant.

INSTITUTIONAL AND TECHNICAL BACKGROUND

Most areas of production and distribution are dominated by a highly integrated process and a narrowly specialized labor force. The "job" is a narrow base for wage analysis, apart from its immediate technical reference. Many "occupations" have disintegrated with technical advance; remaining occupations are often subdivided over a wide range of skill.

The Production Process and the Demand for and Supply of Labor

While some jobs still provide a reasonably distinct occupational category, the great proportion of factory jobs are specialized and constitute a narrowly subdivided task within each industry. They cannot typically be regarded as independent of related jobs.

The integrated production process creates a wide but variable area of joint demand for labor. An expansion or contraction of production is rooted in a technology which requires "balanced lines," with relative labor requirements on many jobs held to fixed ratios.

There are similar difficulties on the supply side in attempting to conceive of independent supply curves for each particular job. With relatively small differences in the amount and kind of training, workers can shift over a fairly wide range of related jobs.

Thus, modern technology has created a job structure which does not lend itself to a very satisfying explanation of internal wage differentials by a simple demand-and-supply approach. Fixed ratios of employment on so many jobs make it difficult to conceive of differentiated demand among these jobs. Joint demand blurs the demand concept for the purpose of the wage-differential problem. Discrimination between jobs from the point of view of supply is at least as difficult, except as a concept to maintain an incentive for promotion.

The Seniority System and the Labor Market

A further constraint on the relationship between wages and the market is that the vast proportion of job vacancies in any plant or company is filled today, not by hiring from the outside, but by promotion from within the organization. The policy avoids criticism of holding back those already employed in favor of outsiders and is a basic part of increasingly elaborate programs to build morale and security by encouraging a lifetime view of employment with a given organization.

Probably a worker would not decide to leave one employer simply on the basis of a higher wage rate in another plant. While seniority is a strong influence in promotion, its almost unqualified application to layoff brings greatly enhanced job security with continued years of employment. Each year also finds increasingly elaborate benefit plans related in amount to length of service. In this world of seniority, an employee would certainly be peculiar if he judged his economic position only in terms of his wage rate.

Most particular wage rates are thus not directly or closely related to a local labor market from an employment point of view. Employees enter and leave plants from the lower-paying "bottom" jobs. Expansion brings more rapid promotion. Recession brings layoff or demotion and downgrading for low-service employees. While seniority patterns differ, layoff schedules illustrate the indirect connection between many jobs and the labor market.

Wage Administration and Wage Inequities

Particular wage rates are set by administrative decision within the firm. Managements have increasingly worked toward a stable structure frequently based upon job evaluation in the local plant. Unions have increasingly accepted a stable structure but have worked to broaden the base of comparison and are more qualified in their acceptance of evaluation. Union skepticism toward job evaluation has many facets. Perhaps the greatest fear is of the use of evaluation to freeze unions out of the wage-differential area or to restrict wage-differential policy too narrowly. Related to this is fear of an overly scientific, as contrasted with a looser equity, approach.

Real differences in philosophy may create administrative conflict in adjusting wage rates with technological change. It is not easy for a union to allow a job rate to be reduced, particularly with increased output per hour on a machine, regardless of the logic of the job analysis. Craft rivalry, traditional wage relationships, and the numerical significance of particular groups within the union may give a shallow ring to "logical" job relationships so far as the union leader is concerned.

On the other hand, with a reasonable voice in policy and administration, a union may find evaluation constructive and desirable from its point of view. Even in unions with official positions opposing evaluation, acceptance in particular situations is commonplace. There at least would appear to be a growing accommodation of management and union attitudes in this area.

The development of job evaluation has been a real force in the creation of simplified rate structures. Moreover, the widespread use of particular job-evaluation plans, such as the National Metal Trades plan, has created more nearly identical wage structures in geographically separated labor markets. Within communities, the increasing prevalence of similar evaluation plans has had the same effect. Finally, the use of job evaluation in collective bargaining on an industry basis, most notable in basic steel, has created nearly identical detailed wage structures throughout an industry or segment of an industry.

Collective bargaining, with or without job evaluation, has been an influence in creating and extending simplified and more uniform wage structures. While this influence is, perhaps, less obvious in the absence of job evaluation, many bargained structures are closely analogous to evaluated structures; and the "removal of inequities" is a common part of the bargaining process, as is the diminishing of differentials for the same job within and between labor markets.

As collective bargaining first developed in the mass-production industries, wage inequities were an obvious avenue for union activity within wage structures that had not been subject to centralized managerial control and had more or less just grown. Nor were union representatives too concerned, during the organizational phase of union development, with just what constituted an inequity. As unions became going concerns, constant wage inequities were no more attractive to them than to management. Contracts began to restrict the area of wage grievances; wage-structure standards were developed.

In the light of our present knowledge, neither the general impact of collective bargaining upon the wage structure nor the impact of management and union policies viewed separately can be stated simply. But attitudes and actions "for and against" such policies as job evaluation, wage incentives, rate ranges, automatic progression, freezing wage rates by contract, revising rates with changing technology, arbitrating wage rates and production standards, and other policies are clearly continuously influencing wage structures. Also significant are factors such as craft rivalries, the degree of conflict or accommodation in union-management relations, and the character of leadership in union and management organizations.

The discussion thus far has attempted to make clear that an operational type of wage-differential theory relating each plant rate to a market rate through the employment process is highly unrealistic. This is not to say that there are not "labor-market forces," both in an employment and a wage-comparison sense. It is to say, however, that not every wage rate is of equal significance and that systems of rates must be explained and related to their economic and administrative context and environment.

SOME WAGE-STRUCTURE GENERALIZATIONS

The background considerations previously discussed tend to suggest that the wage structure requires special analysis. Each single wage rate is not simply a subcase of the general case of demand for and supply of labor for the firm. But how can the process of wage comparison be analyzed to place this process within a meaningful framework?

As a starting point, three propositions are advanced and then discussed. These propositions are related and can be of different significance for different firms. They are as follows:

1. In internal wage-rate comparisons of job content and job relationships, any given job is not related to all other jobs in an equally significant manner. Some jobs are closely related as to wage significance, others more remotely related. While such job relationships have no

simple, single basis, the larger relationships develop around key jobs.

2. In the external comparison of job rates in the firm to labor-market rates, each job within the plant structure is not related to a market rate in an equally significant manner. Not only are there obvious variations in the "mix" of different types of plants and jobs in different labor markets, but there is again no single, simple type of relationship. Joint integration to the market and to the internal structure, however, evolves around key jobs.

3. In relating the wage structure to labor cost, each job rate is not of the same significance as an element of labor cost. While most particular jobs are a small proportion of total labor cost, some are not, and employment at different wage rates varies widely in labor-cost significance—with the bulk of labor cost concentrated within a fairly narrow range of "production" rates.

The first two points are stated in terms of wage *comparison*. The significance of comparison is left open for development. Internal comparison is advanced predominately as an equity concept inherited in large part from valuation in the market place, but applied in its wage-administration and job-content context to create "fair" wage rates. External comparison is also meaningful in an equity sense relative to wage rates paid elsewhere.

Internal Job Comparisons and Job Clusters

Internal job-content comparison as a basis for wage-rate determination is stronger within certain groups of jobs than between them. It is difficult to give a single name to the job groups within which internal comparison is most significant, but they may be called job clusters. There are broad job clusters containing narrower clusters. Broad clusters may be illustrated within

manufacturing as (1) managerial—executive, administrative, professional, and supervisory; (2) clerical; and (3) factory. Within each broad group, narrower clusters are obvious. Within the factory group are maintenance, inspection, transportation, and production. Within production are certain smaller groups, varying with the nature of the industry.

Job-content comparison as a basis for wage-rate determination is felt to be strong within narrow clusters, somewhat weaker between narrow functional groups, and of least significance in relating broad clusters. An added notion must be introduced to this. Each cluster contains a key job or several key jobs. Wage relationships within a narrow group and among such groups revolve around key jobs. Within clusters, the primary determinant of nonkey job rates is the job-content comparison with the key job. Among clusters, the basic consideration is the relationship among the respective key jobs.

The Nature of Narrow Job Clusters

There is no single basis of classification for narrow job clusters. Geographical location within a plant, organizational pattern and common supervision, related and common job skills, common hiring jobs, and transfer and promotion sequences, as well as a common production function, tie jobs together. The notion of a common production function deserves some emphasis, however. Departments frequently signify separate job groupings as they relate to different phases of production, thus constituting a functional group of related jobs.

Look quickly at a few industry structures. A shoe factory is divided into departments of cutting, stitching, lasting, making, and packing. We can recreate the historical process from the cobbler to the crafts to the specialized jobs. Today departments take the place of earlier crafts, but each department is organized around a phase or function of production. In textiles there is a spinning room, a weaving room, a carding room. Steel integrates coke ovens, blast furnaces, open hearths, and mills. On a ship we find the engine room, the deck department, and the steward's department. Endless examples of the nature and organization of the production process reveal such job groupings, typically signified by "division" and "departmental" lines but based upon different production functions integrated into a larger whole.

There can be no rigid classification of narrow job clusters. Sometimes a department is so large and diverse that it does not constitute a meaningful wage group. A related work group or a skill family may cut across departmental lines. In other cases, departments, skill groups, and related jobs may reinforce a single relationship. There is reality, however, in the concept of degree of wage relationship and job-content comparison in terms of groups of jobs.

Job Clusters and Wage Relationships

Within a narrow job cluster, wage relationships are predominately based upon a job-content comparison. The skill required (including job knowledge) is the primary differentiating factor, but there are modifications in job placement relative to responsibility, working conditions, and physical effort (in the sense of heavy or light work). These relationships are influenced somewhat by custom and tradition and are mutually interdependent with promotion and transfer sequences. A wage differential of five cents per hour between two jobs within such a group is typically quite meaningless in terms of ability to hire or retain employees in a market sense and is also insignificant in terms of labor cost.

Close association of employees on cluster-type jobs creates an environment that forces close comparison of jobs and allows a type of direct comparison more meaningful than where jobs are less closely integrated. Within such a group, evaluation typically works out with reasonable preci-

sion and normally preserves a high proportion of existing wage relationships. Job content does not, however, create a completely rigid hierarchy. Minor differences in placement can and do exist among the same jobs in different companies.

[Normally, there can be either one or several] key jobs within a job-cluster group. A key job may simply be a "good" cross-comparison job because of similarity of job content, but usually a key job has significance because of its importance as to number of employees or key skill.

Primarily, key jobs are the more important jobs, the dominant jobs, within a group. Nonkey job relationships are built around key jobs. A nonkey wage range may be adjusted with minor or major social disturbance within the group, but with little or no impact outside the group. This is a significant limiting aspect of wage relationships. Adjust a key job, and it may well pull all or most of the nonkey jobs with it; and there will typically be repercussions outside the particular cluster—major or minor, depending on the strength of the ties with one or more other groups.

Internal comparison between key jobs in different clusters tends to be less precise and of a somewhat different character than comparisons within a group. As comparison is made among jobs that are very different in type and kind of job content, the area of judgment as to the "correct" relationship widens. Consciously and unconsciously, judgment leans more upon external market relationships or established internal relationships as the differences in job content and "social distance" increase.

Key Jobs and Market Comparison

While recognizing these differences among key-job relationships, the general point may be illustrated by the common procedure in applying job evaluation. The problem of rating the key jobs is quite different from rating the nonkey jobs. The first step, creating the "skeleton" by placing key jobs within the evaluation scale, is much more difficult than filling in jobs once the skeleton is created. Where, for example, should the key maintenance jobs or the key office jobs be placed relative to the key production jobs? In the case of office jobs this direct question is typically avoided, since a different evaluation plan is almost always used. With the maintenance jobs there is a considerable area of judgment.

Putting the question even more broadly, certain jobs are "key" jobs from a market comparison point of view. This list of key jobs is not necessarily identical with the list of internal key jobs. Some wage structures are keyed to the labor market at only a few points. Not all companies or plants are in an identical market position. In a high-paying industry, reference to the labor market may be almost exclusively to other companies and plants within the industry. In lower-paying plants and industries, market comparisons may be more directly related to local hiring conditions. But with all these relationships, the close association with job content becomes a weaker basis for wage determination.

Issues Arising from Technological Change

Before leaving the subject of internal wage comparisons, special mention must be made of the impact of technological change. Wage-rate grievances are most commonly associated with new or changed jobs; wage relationships are continuously forced to adapt to this dynamic factor.

Technological change may change the skill and responsibility required in performing the job. It may also alter working conditions and physical effort. On balance, one can only speculate as to the total effect. "De-skilling" creates obvious headaches and problems and consequently attracts attention; upgrading, however, can certainly not be neglected.

The most troublesome wage problem arises when the skill content of a job is reduced. Workers are conscious of the advantage to the company of greater production per hour and lowered unit product cost. They wish to share in the gains of technology, or at least not to suffer a job-rate reduction. Industrial relations effects vary, of course, with the size of the group, promotion opportunities, layoff or demotion necessities, protections to present incumbents, and other factors. But sharing gains with all workers is "pie in the sky," and it is far easier to gain acceptance of new methods if the rate can be sweetened a bit. The logic of rate relationships may be submerged in such situations.

Wage-Structure Adjustment to Market-Rate Influence

The influence of the labor market upon the wage structure can best be approached by a descriptive type of analysis. Individual firm and industry variations in the general level of wages are assumed to be a major source of rate dispersion. Consider in this setting the degree of dominance of particular market rates and the source of such dominance.

To start with some simple examples, in a small city one inquires of a high-paying firm what they pay an industrial nurse and why. The explanation is given that the job is evaluated and comes out as x dollars. Upon further discussion, we find that the personnel man feels that, in truth, the evaluation is definitely on the low side; but, after all, they're paying 25 percent more than the local hospitals. In a low-paying firm, we find that they pay the switchboard operator the identical rate paid by the telephone company. We ask whether that isn't high in terms of their other office jobs. The answer is yes, but they always hire a trained operator; the rate is really quite independent of other office rates; and it causes no "trouble." Consider an over-the-road trucking rate in a low-paying mill. Do they meet the trucking-firm rate? No, but they aren't organized, yet, and they do have the rate up so high that they would hate to have to argue it with some of their skilled production workers. In fact, they're not at all sure that they shouldn't sell their trucks and contract the work.

In all these examples, the wages in question constitute peripheral rates for the companies discussed. These rates tend to be paid for hiring-jobs and they do not constitute internal key-job rates for significant clusters within the company. They also have in each instance been pulled out of "consistent" internal alignment by market-rate influences.

In thinking of examples of market-rate influences, a series of considerations arises relating to how necessary it is to meet or at least come close to market rates and how difficult it is in terms of mutually interdependent wage relationships and cost effects within the firm. The pull of internal consistency through internal key jobs must be taken into account. This pull is around the central core of the general rate structure. There is also the pull of the market, which may be over a broad general group or quite specific as to a single job. The pull of the market may be essentially an equity comparison or quite directly related to hiring.

One cannot draw a hard and fast distinction between market influences and internal relationships. But there are differences in degree of influence. Internal relationships are strongest within narrow functional groups, though even here the amount of the wage differential is more a part of a broader picture than is the rank order of jobs. Among clusters, the internal ties are stronger: (1) in relating a narrow group to a larger group of which it is a distinct part; (2) within roughly comparable skill bands; and (3) where closely comparable or identical jobs are found in several functional groups. As concerns comparisons and ties between broader clusters, the inter-nal forces grow weaker and the market ties, including historically established relationships, become stronger.

THE MEANING AND SIGNIFICANCE OF JOB EVALUATION

In approaching job evaluation here, the primary question is the relation of the evaluation process to the internal and external wage forces under discussion.

Job evaluation is not a rigid, objective, analytical procedure. Neither is it a meaningless process of rationalization. If a group of people with reasonable knowledge of certain jobs rate them, for example, on the basis of minimum required training and experience, there will be a high degree of general agreement. The application of group judgment through the rating process normally produces an improved rate structure, but extreme attitudes as to the accuracy of rating are difficult to defend.

The results of job evaluation may be judged from two levels: wage relationships among key jobs or relationships within clusters. As to the first, job evaluation is tested by the degree of correlation achieved between points for key jobs and accepted wage relationships among the jobs. If this correlation does not work out in a reasonably satisfactory way, job evaluation weights and points have to be adjusted. If the correlation is satisfactory as a general relationship, some few jobs may still present a problem. Suppose a key job with an agreed-upon rate falls some distance away from the line of relationship between job evaluation points and wage rates. Which is to give way, the points for the job or the agreed rate? Neither can be regarded as the supreme standard, and judgment is likely to result in some jobs being dropped as key jobs, where points are accepted as controlling, and in other jobs being rescored where the evaluation is thought to be less satisfactory than the agreed rate. There is nothing wrong with this kind of trial-and-error testing; job evaluation does not automatically resolve debatable relationships among key jobs, particularly when there is a conflict between internal standards and external comparisons or when strongly held traditional relationships exist.

Within narrow groups, gross disturbance of existing relationships is not likely to be found. Creating a simplified system of labor grades, with one wage rate or rate range for each labor grade, gives rise to many small wage changes as part of the simplification process, but the rank order of job placement within narrow functional groups will not typically be changed significantly, except for some small proportion of out-of-line rates. These out-of-line rates are most frequently associated with past technological change of a "de-skilling" character. They may also result from overly successful grievance adjustments or from poor judgment in decentralized wage administration.

In reviewing the results of a typical job evaluation, one is likely to find some major changes in relations among key jobs and clusters: day workers may advance substantially relative to incentive workers; skilled groups, such as maintenance, may gain relative to the semiskilled; particular "low-wage" departments may increase in relative position. Within narrow groups, most past relationships will remain, with a minority of clear-cut out-of-line rates being meaningfully corrected. Also, with the many small simplification wage changes, jobs may go up or down slightly and, in process, achieve a somewhat more consistent placement, particularly with respect to the degree of wage recognition given to unfavorable working conditions.

What significant points for wage determination can one draw from the practice of job evaluation? The following may be singled out:

1. Job evaluation was created as an administrative response to a social environment allowing freer union and employee criticism. In this environment, authority and secrecy of rates no longer held criticism in check, and piecemeal adjustments of rates provided no lasting solution. Thus, standards and policies for the wage structure as a whole had to be developed to meet the changed social environment.

2. Job evaluation probably strengthened and broadened the influence of internal comparison. In part, this may have produced an over-emphasis on logical relationships. In part, it reflected the union representatives' enlarged scope of interest, as contrasted with employee feelings of injustice, and introduced the "over-all" point of view of the wage specialist. In particular cases, job evaluation has been part and parcel of the process of removing interplant differentials in multiplant firms and geographical differentials within an industry.

3. Job evaluation can and typically does accomplish a reasonable adaptation to internal and external forces at the time it is introduced. Can this adaptation remain appropriate over a period of time? There appears to be no general answer to this question, but it should be examined in terms of the relationships among and within clusters.

On the whole, job evaluation appears to reflect—in its introduction, in its problems and adaptations, and by its absence—the wage forces described in this [selection]. In its formal approach, evaluation does not recognize the substructure character of wage relationship; it hides it by the administrative grouping of jobs into labor grades. But under the surface, the jigsaw puzzle of relating job groups is involved. Internal relationships can be proclaimed as primary wage policy in certain wage environments, whereas by contrast such a policy in other areas results in rough sailing. Adjustments over a period of time require study to clarify the kind of adaptations which are developing.

23. SUPPLEMENTAL COMPENSATION

A. N. NASH and S. J. CARROLL, JR.

The number of different compensation methods has increased significantly over the years. The scientific-management approach after the turn of the century emphasized the use of economic rewards for motivating workers to perform at higher levels. This emphasis on economic rewards, together with the development of standard methods and standard times, gave impetus to the construction of a large number of incentive-wage systems. Most of the original incentive plans for individual workers are still used today. Group- and plant-wide incentive systems have evolved from these. World War II gave impetus to the development of numerous types of fringe-benefit plans, because fringes were the only form of compensation increases that was allowed.

Today over 30 percent of all compensation involves such *supplemental compensation;* the worker receives a supplement to the regular wage or salary without being required to spend additional time or energy. This [selection] will discuss the various types of supplemental compensation and worker attitudes toward them and will make some recommendations for using them.

GROWTH OF SUPPLEMENTAL COMPENSATION

Payments for supplemental compensation now average approximately 31 percent of payroll, or a little more than $2500 per employee (U.S. Chamber of Commerce 1972). The rate is approximately 35 percent for the larger companies. During the past 20 years, supplementary compensation payments have expanded more than twice as

Source: From *The Management of Compensation,* by A. N. Nash & S. J. Carroll, Jr. Copyright © 1975 by Wadsworth Publishing Company, Inc. Reprinted by permission of the publisher, Brooks/Cole Publishing Company, Monterey, California.

fast as wages and salaries in industry in the United States (Gordon and LeBlew 1970; Oswald and Smyth 1970). After adjustments for inflation, such compensation grew at the rate of 9.6 percent per year between 1929 and 1967, compared to a growth rate of 3.9 percent for wages and salaries. In addition, the growth rate for fringes has been increasing in the past few years (U.S. Chamber of Commerce 1972).

There are a number of reasons for the rapid growth of this type of compensation. A very important factor was the imposition of wage controls by the United States government during World War II. To avoid inflation during this period, the government encouraged employers to increase supplemental compensation and to maintain direct compensation at existing levels. Other important historical events in the growth of supplementary compensation were decisions—by the National Labor Relations Board and the United States courts—that the Taft-Hartley Act of 1947 requires employers to bargain collectively with unions on pensions and group insurance programs if the union wishes to negotiate on these subjects. The Wage Stabilization Board during the Korean War also exerted pressure for more supplemental compensation in place of direct compensation increases.

In addition to these pressures from outside the firm, management felt pressure from the union and from employees for supplementary compensation. Unions asked for increased benefits for their members as a means of increasing their status and of settling union-management disagreements dealing with direct compensation. In addition, employees had a rising standard of living that enabled them to live above a hand-to-mouth existence, and their interest in various employee benefits to supplement their basic wage increased. Other factors that have contributed to the growth in supplemental compensation include increased attention to economic security by the major political parties, changes in the tax laws that are favorable to supplemental compensation, and a growing acceptance by management of a more paternalistic management philosophy.

TYPES OF SUPPLEMENTAL COMPENSATION

Over 200 different types of supplemental payments have been listed (Heneman and Yoder 1965). There is often disagreement about whether a particular employer's expenditure is direct or supplementary compensation. For example, extra payments for suggestions, high attendance, and good safety records are classified as indirect or supplemental compensation by some, but probably are more appropriately classified as incentive payments. Premium pay for late shifts and for overtime is often considered supplemental compensation but should probably be considered part of direct compensation. Different supplements to direct compensation have been classified in various ways by different authorities. In this chapter the various types of supplementary payments will be classified as employee-security payments and nonwork payments.

Employee-Security Payments

Employee-security payments represent one of the largest proportions of expenditures on supplementary compensation, altogether about 14 percent of payroll (U.S. Chamber of Commerce 1972). These payments are used primarily to provide employees and their families with protection against loss of income due to insufficient work, sickness, disability, loss of life, or old age. Many, but not all of the programs, designed to protect the employee from

these events and thus provide him with more security, are social insurance programs that the employer is required to provide.

Mandatory Employee-Security Programs

OASDI. The Old-Age Survivors and Disability Insurance program was initiated by the Social Security Act of 1935. It is a federal program and is administered by the Social Security Board of the Department of Health, Education, and Welfare. Virtually the whole labor force is now eligible for OASDI benefits. The primary benefit under this program is a monthly payment to formerly employed individuals who retire after age 65 (62 if one takes reduced benefits). Dependents of such retired personnel also receive monthly benefits. Additional benefits under this program include monthly payments to permanently and totally disabled workers, monthly payments for surviving dependents of deceased employed people, burial allowances for deceased workers, and some medical benefits for those who have retired. Eligibility for benefits depends on the number of quarters covered and the type of benefit involved. Fully-insured status comes after 40 quarters of coverage for most individuals. Survivors' benefits can be received if the deceased was in covered employment for a sufficient number of years (which varies with age), and eligibility for disability benefits depends on age at time of disability. Under the program, retirement benefits are reduced if more than a certain amount of wages is earned after retirement. However, retired personnel are allowed to have income after retirement without limit if it does not consist of wages or salaries. Benefits are paid for by a tax on both the employer and the employee of 5.85 percent each of the first $13,200 in wages or salaries paid the employee. Taxes will be over 6 percent for the employee and employer in 1978. The present minimum monthly benefit is $135 for those with 25 years of coverage who retire at 65. The maximum family benefit is now $721.80.

Unemployment Compensation. All states require employers with at least four employees to contribute to the costs of providing unemployment benefits to workers laid off because of lack of work. The amount the employer must contribute for the provision of unemployment compensation (Brinker 1968; Heneman and Yoder 1965) by the state depends on his unemployment experience, or on how many individuals from his organization draw unemployment compensation in a given period of time. The taxes levied on an employer may range from 3 percent to .01 percent of payroll. This act makes it worthwhile for an employer to stabilize employment as much as possible or at least to find jobs for workers who are laid off permanently, because such activities reduce the tax contribution to be paid by the employer. The amount of unemployment compensation received by an unemployed person and the length of time he receives such benefits vary with his previous earnings and length of employment. However, typically the maximum amount of time that benefits can be received is 26 weeks. Benefits equal at least one-half of the average weekly compensation of the unemployed person in about half of the states (Hickey 1971). Individuals receiving benefits must be available for work in their normal occupational field. Causes for ineligibility for benefits include pregnancy, school attendance, and unemployment due to a strike. The laws in the various states vary considerably (Brinker 1968; Heneman and Yoder 1965).

Workmen's Compensation. All states have workmen's compensation laws (Brinker 1968; Heneman and Yoder 1965). Such laws were established separately by the various states, starting about 1908. By 1920 most states had passed such legislation. The purpose of these programs is to protect the worker against the effects of job-connected illness. These laws were passed primarily in response to public opinion. Before such legislation existed, it was very difficult for an injured worker to collect any benefits for a job-connected accident under existing common-law rules. This created great hardships for injured workers and also for the communities that had to support such workers on welfare (Carroll 1967). The benefits provided under workmen's compensation include medical expenses and compensation for the income lost because of employment-caused accidents or illnesses. Disabilities may be permanent or temporary. Individuals with permanent disabilities normally receive a lump-sum payment for their disability. The amount of the payment depends on the severity of the disability. An individual with a temporary disability, such as a broken leg, receives weekly payments until he or she returns to work. Such payments typically amount to between 40 percent and 60 percent of lost wages because of maximum benefits allowed in most states. Medical payments are limited to specific amounts in only a few states. Average workmen's compensation costs are about 1 percent of payroll but amount to as much at 30 percent of payroll for some industries in some states. As with unemployment compensation, experience rating is used and employers with higher accident rates have to pay higher premiums. In different states different institutions collect premiums and disburse benefits. Often private insurance companies handle this by selling to individual firms insurance policies that cover these losses for on-the-job accidents and illnesses. Sometimes the state provides the insurance coverage. It has been suggested that workmen's compensation programs should be put under the control of the federal government to provide more consistent benefits, that workers should contribute to the program so that benefits can be increased, and that the program should be extended to cover off-the-job accidents.

Private Employee Security Programs

Guaranteed Wages. Many firms have adopted guaranteed employment plans that assure a specific number of weeks of employment (Kaplan 1947; Heneman and Yoder 1965; Allen and Randle 1954). Such plans are designed to protect the employee against a sharp drop in his income because of lack of work. Procter and Gamble has had such a plan since 1923, the Hormel Company since 1931, and the Nunn-Bush Shoe Company since 1932. Organizations with such plans feel that the plans improve morale, help prevent economic depressions (if adopted on a wide scale), reduce turnover and illness, improve productivity, reduce resistance to technological change, and encourage management to plan carefully. These plans do have some disadvantages. They can result in excessive labor costs and can reduce operational flexibility. If such plans are taken for granted by the employees, the plans are of little or no value in motivating or satisfying employees. The guaranteed-annual-wage (GAW) plans differ in amount of employment guaranteed. For example, the Hormel plan guarantees 52 checks a year at least equal to regular full-time pay. Procter and Gamble guarantees 48 weeks of work a year; but by special vote the board of directors can cut the length of each work week by one-quarter. These plans seem to have diminished in popularity over the years. It seems likely that in the future the federal government will guarantee all families in the United States a certain income (Green and Lampan 1967). Currently six alternative plans are being discussed. Some of these would benefit all of the poor in the country and some only the working poor, but they would not benefit most employees in the nation because most workers are above the poverty level.

Supplementary Unemployment Benefits. SUB was first introduced in the automobile industry in 1955 (Becker 1968; Beier 1969; Slichter, Healey, and Livernash 1960). Employers agree to contribute to a fund that is used to supplement the unemployment compensation received by workers who are laid off. SUB plans are in effect in the steel, rubber, glass, and automobile industries. Over 2,500,000 workers are covered. Benefits to workers, under SUB in the automobile industry, now amount to 95 percent of usual take-home pay, less $7.50. The rubber industry pays 80 percent of gross pay. The advantages of being laid off now are so great that the principle of *juniority* has been established in the automobile industry. This requires the firm to lay off the most senior worker first when there is insufficient work. Benefits are paid out of a fund to which the employer contributes a specific amount for each man-hour worked. The employer usually is not liable for more than the amount of money in the fund.

Severance Pay. Severance pay, unlike SUB or GAW, is designed to assist the employee who has lost his job permanently (Heneman and Yoder 1965; Slichter, Healey, and Livernash 1960). Such payments provide compensation to a worker at a time when he is looking for and training for another job. The amount of compensation paid is often related to length of service plus level of earnings and varies considerably from one organization to another. A common practice is to provide one week's pay for each year of service. Approximately one fourth of all union contracts contain a severance-pay provision, and the number of firms with a severance-pay program has risen steadily but slowly over the years.

Private Pension Plans. Some 76 percent to 81 percent of all potentially eligible employees in private industry are covered by private pension plans (Holland 1966). Private pension plans are either contributory or noncontributory. A contributory plan is one in which the employee contributes to his retirement benefits; in a noncontributory plan, only the employer pays into the retirement fund. Most private pension plans today are noncontributory (Heneman and Yoder 1965). Virtually all government pension plans are contributory. Private and government pension plans may be vested or nonvested. Vesting allows the employee to claim the employer's contribution to the retirement fund when he retires, even if he changes his place of employment before retirement. In a nonvesting retirement program, the employee loses his claim to the employer's contributions if he does not retire from that organization. An employee always, of course, has a right to any of his own contributions to a retirement plan. Sometimes an employee gains vesting rights after a specified number of years of employment. Today most plans provide for vesting rights at some point before retirement (Levine 1965). However, because this is not necessarily early vesting, many workers will not receive retirement benefits if they have not been employed for long enough when they leave the labor force. One study of 87 pension plans found that, of 6.7 million workers who left their jobs between 1950 and 1970 and who were covered by a pension plan, 5.9 million lost all their pension benefits (*Washington Post* 1971). Because of this problem, the vesting provisions have increased in 75 percent of existing plans (Davis 1969). In addition, union demands have increased the number of portable plans where member employers contribute to a central fund and workers can change jobs among employer members of a fund without losing retirement benefits (Levine 1965). Congress has recently passed legislation to alleviate the problem of lost benefits under private pension plans. The amount of benefit received from a pension plan usually depends on length of service and earnings level. Retirement-benefit levels have been increasing rapidly in the last decade. For example, the normal retirement benefit increased by 40 percent from 1964 to 1968 (Livernash 1970). Retirement income for long-service employees who re-

ceive benefits from private pension plans and from OASDI will soon approach preretirement earnings after taxes (Davis 1969). Most retirement-benefit programs are funded (Heneman and Yoder 1965). That is, money is paid into a fund to insure that the employees concerned will be able to obtain benefits when they are eligible. The administration of such retirement funds involves difficult investment decisions and has created some economic problems. Federal legislation regulates the administration of such funds.

Health Insurance and Sick Leave. These benefits provide protection against hospitalization costs and loss of income arising from accidents or illness occurring from off-the-job causes (Heneman and Yoder 1965; Slichter, Healey, and Livernash 1960; *Monthly Labor Review* 1970). About 82 percent of all workers are covered by these benefits. In recent years there has been a significant increase in major medical benefits, which provide protection against very high medical expenses, and an increase in income protection or compensation for loss of salary due to the illness or accident. The income-protection plans take over when normal sick leave is used up and may continue to provide income to age 65 if there is long-term disability insurance coverage (Bjorhus 1966). The costs of such protection have increased very rapidly in the past few years. Hospital costs have risen rapidly, increasing 441 percent from 1946 to 1967 (Somers 1969). Because of this and other problems, there is increased interest in government programs in this area. Health-related fringe benefits provided by some organizations have been expanded to include such items as prepaid dental care, coverage for prescription drugs necessitated by a health problem, and such risks as organ transplants, abortions, and vasectomies. It would seem that fringe benefits in the health area have not reached their limit yet (Bellotto 1961; Foegen 1967, 1972; Perham 1971).

Life Insurance. In 1968 some 96 percent of all workers were covered by some form of life insurance (U.S. Chamber of Commerce 1970). This is typically term life insurance and is provided on a group-contract basis, because of the low cost of such an arrangement and because many occupations are uninsurable except on a group-contract basis. The primary purpose of life insurance is to assist the employee's family in adjusting to the loss of income resulting from the death of the wage earner. The average amount of insurance held by an employee is not known, but in 1965 the average amount of life insurance per family in the United States was a little less than $15,000, with great variability in amounts held by different families (Brinker 1968). This would, of course, account for only a very small proportion of the income losses arising from the deaths of wage earners. The amount of compensation needed to make up the total income loss to a family over a deceased wage earner's life expectancy is shown in Table 1. This informa-

TABLE 1
Economic Loss to Dependents of Deceased Railroad Worker

Summary of Calculations	
Lost earnings for next 27 years as adjusted for anticipated wage increases of 5 percent a year	$483,026
Lost value of certain fringe benefits as adjusted for anticipated wage increases of 5 percent a year over 27 years	24,152
Lost railroad retirement benefits for husband and wife for 7 years as adjusted for price increases at 2 percent a year ..	60,248
Lost widow benefits under railroad retirement for 6 years as adjusted for price increases at 2 percent a year	19,779
	587,205
Less personal consumption expenditures for working life	125,587
Less survivor benefits to family as adjusted for price increases of 2 percent a year ..	101,095
	227,095
Economic loss to dependents as adjusted for price and wage increases	360,110
Reduced to present value at 3 percent a year over 34 years	
Total	$223,268

tion is from a report made to a court (Carroll 1968) about the economic losses sustained by the family of a railroad worker when he died. The report took into consideration anticipated future changes in the wage level and the supplemental-compensation level.

Integrating Public and Private Security Programs

It is obvious that there are a large number of both private and government programs. Because the government programs are mandatory, the private plans are typically adjusted to them. The private plan is established to supplement compensation received from the social insurance program. Thus, many private pensions supplement OASDI retirement benefits, and SUB programs supplement unemployment-compensation programs. Much more could be done, however. In administering a supplemental-compensation program, each organization should examine the compensation that its employees or their dependents would receive if income was stopped or reduced because of various contingencies, and should then determine what the organization's supplemental-compensation program should provide. In such decisions, the probability of the contingency occurring and its effects on the family when it does occur should be carefully evaluated.

Nonwork Payments

A large number of nonwork payments are made by organizations. These include holidays that are paid but not worked, call-in pay, severance pay, vacation pay, pay for military or National Guard service, sick leave, family allowances, and pay for jury duty. Such payments amount to about 7 percent of payroll (U.S. Chamber of Commerce 1970). Vacation pay makes up the greatest proportion of this cost (five percent). Organizations vary in the extent to which they offer alternative nonwork payments. Virtually all firms offer paid holidays and vacations (98 percent); a much smaller proportion provide pay for jury duty and National Guard service (U.S. Chamber of Commerce 1972). There is a trend toward allowing more holidays and longer vacations than have been paid for in the past.

The number of paid holidays granted each year and the length of vacations have steadily increased (Bureau of National Affairs 1972). Currently more than 50 percent of union contracts provide for nine or more holidays a year. A typical union contract requires 1 week of vacation after 1 year of service, 2 weeks for 3 years of service, 3 weeks for 10 years of service and 4 weeks for 20 years of service. There has been a 50 percent increase in the number of vacation weeks taken by employees in 1970 as compared to 1960. Recent innovations include such hard-to-believe fringe benefits as a "to-hell-with-it clause" in a union contract, providing extra days off when employees don't feel like coming to work, and "off-track betting breaks," which permit employees a few minutes off to place or collect bets (Foegen 1967, 1972).

Hundreds of different types of services are offered to employees. Virtually all of these provide assistance, contribute to satisfaction or well being, or help employees save money or time. Such services include baby sitting, beauty parlors, burial plots, cafeterias, company stores, counseling, educational assistance, financial advice and assistance, income-tax service, legal aid, music at work, scholarships for children, and vacation facilities.

REFERENCES

Allen, J. L., and Randle, C. W. "Challenge of the Guaranteed Annual Wage." Harvard Business Review 32 (1954): 37–48.

Becker, J. M. Guaranteed Income for the Unemployed. Baltimore, Md.: Johns Hopkins University Press, 1968.

Beier, E. H. "Financing Supplemental Unemployment Benefit Plans." Monthly Labor Review 92 (1969): 31–35.

Bellotto, S. "New Fringe Benefits." Administrative Management 32 (1961): 24–26.

Bjorhus, R. E. "Group Insurance Protection." Personnel Journal 45 (1966): 668–73.

Brinker, P. A. Economic Insecurity and Social Security. New York: Appleton-Century-Crofts, 1968.

Bureau of National Affairs. Wage and Salary Administration. Personnel Policies Forum, Survey #92, Washington, D.C., 1972.

Carroll, S. J., Jr. "A Short History of Workmen's Compensation." In G. G. Morgis, L. P. Beauregard, and E. P. Shoub, eds., State Compensatory Provisions for Occupational Diseases. Bulletin 623, Bureau of Mines, Washington, D.C.: U.S. Department of the Interior, 1967.

Carroll, S. J., Jr. Unpublished report, 1968.

Davis, H. E. "Negotiated Retirement Plans—A Decade of Benefit Improvements." Monthly Labor Review 92 (1969): 11–15.

Foegen, J. H. "Far Out Fringe Benefits." Personnel 44 (1967): 65–71.

Foegen, J. H. "Is It Time to Clip the Fringes?" Personnel 49 (1972): 36–42.

Gordon, T. J., and LeBlew, R. E. "Employee Benefits, 1970–1985." Harvard Business Review 48 (1970): 94.

Green, C., and Lampan, R. J. "Schemes for Transferring Income to the Poor." Industrial Relations 6 (1967): 121–37.

Heneman, H. G., Jr., and Yoder, D. Labor Economics. Cincinnati: Southwestern, 1965.

Hickey, J. A. "Status Report on State Unemployment Insurance Laws." Monthly Labor Review 94 (1971): 22–30.

Holland, D. M. Private Pension Plans: Projected Growth. National Bureau of Economic Research. New York: Columbia University Press, 1966.

Kaplan, A. D. H. The Guarantee of Annual Wages. Washington D.C.: The Brookings Institution, 1947.

Levine, M. J. "The Influence of Vesting and Profitability on Pension Plan Liberalization." The Personnel Administrator 10 (1965): 14–16.

Livernash, E. R. "Wages and Benefits." A Review of Industrial Relations Research 1 (1970): 79–144.

Monthly Labor Review Changes in Health and Insurance Plans 93 (1970): 32–39.

Oswald, R., and Smyth, J. D. "Fringe Benefits on the Move." *American Federationist* 77 (1970): 18–24.

Perham, J. "Ferment in Fringes." *Dun's Review* 98 (1971): 34–36.

Slichter, S. H., Healey, J. J., and Livernash, E. R. *The Impact of Collective Bargaining on Management.* Washington, D.C.: The Brookings Institution, 1960.

Somers, H. M. Economic Issues in Health Services. In N. W. Chamberlain, ed., *Economic Issues.* Homewood, Ill.: Richard D. Irwin, 1969.

U.S. Chamber of Commerce. *Employee Benefits 1969.* Washington, D.C., U. S. Chamber of Commerce, 1970.

U.S. Chamber of Commerce. *Employee Benefits 1971.* Washington, D.C., U.S. Chamber of Commerce, 1972.

Washington Post. "Pension Plan Study Reveals Big Majority Gets No Benefits." April 1, 1971, A–3.

24. NEW APPROACHES TO PAY: INNOVATIONS THAT WORK

EDWARD E. LAWLER, III

The experiences of the few organizations that have been willing to innovate in the area of pay administration suggest that significant improvements can be made. Cafeteria-style fringe benefit programs, lump-sum salary increases, and employee participation in pay decisions are yielding improvements in both productivity and the quality of worklife. Although these and other innovative pay practices probably aren't right for all organizations, they apparently will benefit many.

Despite the potential advantage of these new pay practices, most organizations seem hesitant to abandon traditional approaches to wage and salary administration. Consequently, they are failing to get the maximum return possible on the money they spend on pay. The reasons are many and involve some basic misunderstandings about how pay can affect employee behavior. Two issues, especially, should be clarified:

Source: Reprinted by permission of the publisher from *Personnel*, September–October 1976, © 1976 by AMACOM, a division of American Management Association.

Pay is important. The writings of behavioral scientists such as Herzberg and Maslow seem to have convinced many executives that pay is not all that important to employees and that it can only be a source of dissatisfaction. Thus, when executives seek ways to increase motivation and productivity, they tend to forget about pay-system changes, concentrating instead on approaches such as job enrichment, team building, and management training. But research on the effects of pay does not support this view. Rather, just the opposite seems to be true. Pay seems to have a strong impact on satisfaction and consequently on absenteeism and turnover. Further, when pay is tied to performance, evidence has shown that it also contributes to motivation.

Pay is part of a total system. All too often executives fail to take a system viewpoint when they consider approaches to improving organizational effectiveness. Because of this, they think it is possible to install programs such as management by objectives and job enrichment in their organizations without changing the pay system.

Nothing could be further from the truth. Organizations are complex, interrelated systems; to operate effectively, all the subsystems must be in harmony. If changes are made in one important area (for example, job or organization design), changes are required in others to maintain the balance among all subsystems. Thus, because pay is important and pervasive in organizations, almost any important organizational change is likely to require a change in the pay system. The reverse of this is also true, that is, almost any pay-system change requires changes in other aspects of the organization if it is to be effective.

Cafeteria Fringe Benefits

The typical fringe benefit program provides equal amounts of benefits such as life insurance and health insurance to all members of the organization who are at similar levels. Typically, hourly employees have one fringe benefit package, salaried employees another, and top management still another. While this approach emphasizes the differences between levels of an organization, it fails to emphasize significant differences among people at the same organizational level. Research quite clearly shows that what is a valued benefit to one employee is not always a valued benefit to another. When studies ask employees to allocate a hypothetical raise among a number of benefits, factors such as age, marital status, and number of children influence which benefits a person prefers. For example, young unmarried men want more vacation time, while young married men are willing to give up vacation for higher pay. Older employees want greater retirement benefits; younger employees want more cash.

That many people do not receive the fringe benefits they want has some interesting implications for the degree to which fringe benefit programs contribute to the quality of worklife a person experiences and to organizational effectiveness. Essen-

tially, it means that most fringe benefit programs fail to contribute optimally to both. They end up costing the organization money for benefits that are not valued by employees and that do not contribute to their satisfaction and desire to work for the organization.

One way to improve employee satisfaction with fringe benefits, at virtually no cost to the organization, is to introduce a cafeteria-style fringe benefit compensation plan. Under this plan, employees receive the amount of money the organization allocates for their total pay package and spend it as they wish. The choice brings home to employees rather clearly just how much the organization is spending to compensate them and ensures that the money will be spent only on the fringe benefits they want. Thus it can increase employee perceptions of the value of their pay package and also increase their pay satisfaction, improving organizational effectiveness by decreasing absenteeism and turnover and generally allowing the organization to attract a more competent workforce.

While the cafeteria approach creates some practical problems, they are far from insurmountable. Obviously, the plan will complicate the bookkeeping aspects of wage and salary administration, but with computer assistance, this difficulty can be overcome. Probably the most serious practical problem with the cafeteria approach is the difficulty in pricing benefits and determining their availability in advance. The cost and availability of many fringe benefits (for example, life insurance) are based on the number of people who subscribe to them. In large companies, however, this is unlikely to be a serious problem since a minimum number of participants probably can be guaranteed in advance. Smaller companies may have to try to negotiate special agreements with insurance companies and others who underwrite the benefit package, or they may simply have to take some losses when the plan first goes into effect.

Despite the practical problems with cafeteria-style plans, two organizations, the Systems Division of the TRW Corporation and the Educational Testing Service (ETS), have put them into effect. The largest and first plan was implemented at TRW in the fall of 1974. Although far from a full cafeteria plan since it only offers a limited number of choices and requires everyone to take minimum levels of important benefits, it does, nevertheless, put all 12,000 employees in the organization on the plan, allow for new choices each year, and give employees choices among significantly different benefit plans. (For example, TRW employees now can choose among four hospital plans.) It should be noted that the plan is supported by an extensive computer software program, that its introduction was preceded by more than a year of development work, and that it was tried in an organization that has a good record of communicating effectively with its employees. (Over 80 percent of TRW's employees changed their benefit packages.) The ETS plan covers a smaller number of employees (less than 3,000), but provides more opportunities for choice than does the TRW plan.

Skill-Evaluation Pay Plans

The pay systems of most organizations are built upon job-evaluation programs that first describe the job and then assess the characteristics of it. Once a job has been evaluated, it is compared to a survey of what other organizations pay for jobs with similar characteristics in order to set the pay for the job at a level that is in line with the outside market. This approach has many weaknesses including its failure to reward individuals for all the skills they have and to encourage individuals to learn new job-related skills. Most of these problems occur because job-evaluation plans treat employees as job holders rather than as individuals.

In an attempt to improve traditional job-evaluation plans, some organizations in the United States and abroad have introduced skill-evaluation pay plans. Most of these plans pay people according to the number of jobs in the organization they can perform and do not take into account the job the person actually does at a given time. This has the effect of focusing on the individual more than on the job and of encouraging individuals to learn more skills.

Like most new approaches to management, it isn't clear when or where skill-evaluation pay plans were first used. They have been most frequently used in plants structured around work groups that practice a high level of job rotation. Skill-based evaluations seem to fit well here because effective job rotation requires individuals who have a variety of skills. At this point, this approach has enjoyed limited acceptance in the United States: Procter and Gamble has used it in four of its new plants, and General Foods has used it in its Topeka, Kansas plant.

The Topeka plant provides a good example of how this kind of plan works. All nonmanagement employees receive a standard starting rate when they first enter the plant. After they have mastered five different jobs, they move up to the next higher pay rate. After they have mastered all the production jobs in the plant, which usually takes a minimum of two years, they move to the top or plant rate. Employees are given encouragement and support to learn new skills. Members of the person's work team decide when a person has actually mastered a new set of skills. After people learn all the jobs, they continue to rotate among the same jobs; at this point their only opportunity for additional pay lies in acquiring a specialty rate, which is given to individuals who have gained expertise in a skilled trade (for example, plumbing or electricity).

Skill-based plans seem to contribute to organizational effectiveness in several ways. They increase the flexibility of the workforce and give employees a broader perspective of how the plant operates. This seems to lead to a more adaptive production system and to better decision making by all members of the workforce. An attitude survey that I recently conducted at Topeka showed that the plan there also contributes to a spirit of personal growth and development and is seen as a very fair way to administer pay.

Despite their high degree of promise, skill-based plans are not without problems. They require a large investment in training, which can take many costly forms including formal classroom education, as well as having inexperienced individuals on the job. It is interesting to note that most of the plants where skill-based plans have been successfully used are essentially process production plants (for example, chemical and bulk food), where having individuals know a number of jobs helps create a flexible workforce and one that understands the total plant as a system. The latter is particularly important in process plants where jobs are highly interrelated. This is in marked contrast to many service and unit production organizations where jobs are very independent. It is also important to note that these plans usually lead to high-wage levels. Because of the plan, employees become more valuable and they have to be paid accordingly. Finally there is the danger of the organization ending up with a highly trained workforce that wants to continue to develop but has nowhere to go. This problem can be overcome by such things as group incentive plans and inter-plant transfers, but it needs to be anticipated.

Lump-Sum Salary Increases

Although organizations speak in terms of annual salary increases, in fact, all but a few organizations actually give raises by adjusting the regular pay checks of employees. This approach allows employees no flexibility with respect to when they receive their raises. To get the full amount of their "annual increase," they have to wait a full year. It also often has the effect of perceptually "burying" a raise; after it is divided up among regular pay checks and tax deductions are made, very little change occurs in take-home pay.

Recognizing these problems, some organizations have instituted lump-sum salary-increase plans in order to make their salary increase more flexible and visible and to communicate to their employees that they are willing to innovate in the area of pay administration. Under these programs, individuals are given the opportunity to decide when they will receive their annual increase. Just about any option is available including receiving *all* of it in one lump sum at the beginning of the year. Employees can also choose to have it folded into their regular salary check, as has been done in the past. Each year, employees can make a new choice. They are not bound by any of their past choices, and each year they have the opportunity to allocate not only the current year's raise but the raises from all the years since the program began.

Money advanced to employees is treated as a loan; if they quit before the end of the year, they have to pay the company back for the proportion of their pay increase they have not yet earned. Also, since the money is advanced to individuals prior to their earning it, they are charged interest at a low rate to offset the cash-flow problems it causes companies. Although this somewhat reduces the attractiveness of lump-sum advances, practice indicates that most individuals still prefer to take the money early.

Unfortunately, there is little research on how effective the lump-sum program is. All that can be reported so far is that it appears to be a practice that helps both the organization and the individual employee. It costs individuals nothing, and they gain the opportunity to shape their income to fit their unique needs and desires. The costs involved to an organization are minimal. Like a cafeteria fringe benefit program, it requires extra bookkeeping and recordkeeping. Also, in some situations money undoubtedly will be lost because employees quit and don't pay back the advances they receive.

On the plus side, all other things being equal, organizations that give individuals the choice of when they will receive their increases should have a competitive advantage in attracting and retaining employees. Like other practices that make organizations more attractive, it can pay off in a number of ways—better selection ratios, lower turnover, and lower absenteeism. These, in turn, will result in lower personnel costs and a more talented group of employees.

Giving lump-sum increases also serves to increase the visibility and saliency of the amount of a salary increase. A large raise tends to come across clearly as a large amount of money; however, a small raise tends to come across as just what it is—a small increase. Thus, increasing the saliency of the amount of a raise may or may not be functional for an organization.

If pay is administered in an arbitrary and nonperformance-based manner, then it is hardly functional to increase the saliency of the size of an increase. On the other hand, if an organization does a "good" job of administering pay, and increases are based on performance, then the lump-sum approach has the potential of making pay a more effective motivator because it will be more clearly seen as tied to behavior.

Communication and Pay

Secrecy about management pay rates seems to be an accepted practice in most business organizations. When asked why they favor secrecy, most executives argue that most individuals prefer secret pay. However, they don't point out that secrecy also gives pay administrators more freedom in administering pay since they don't have to explain their actions. Yet, despite the apparent advantages of secrecy, some organizations are making pay information more public (Corning Glass and Bell Laboratories, for example). The reasons for this are significant and suggest that many organizations can profit from greater openness.

My research shows that secrecy tends to cause people to overestimate the pay of individuals at the same organization level and that the greater their overestimation, the greater their dissatisfaction. Thus pay secrecy may do more to cause pay dissatisfaction than to reduce it.

Secrecy may also reduce motivation. The motivating power of pay depends on the rather delicate perception that performance will lead to a pay increase. This perception requires belief in the honesty of the organization and trust in its future behavior. Secrecy does not contribute to trust; openness does. It allows people to test for themselves the validity of an organization's statements and communicates to individuals that the organization has nothing to hide.

But making pay information public will not in itself establish the belief that pay is based upon performance. All it can do is clarify those situations where pay actually is based upon performance but that fact is not obvious because salary information is not available. For example, in one organization with a merit-based pay plan and pay secrecy, a survey showed that employees believed there was only a moderate relationship between pay and performance. But another survey, conducted after the company became more open about pay, showed a significant increase in employees' perceptions of the degree to which pay and performance were related. The crucial factor in making this change to openness successful was that pay actually was tied to performance. Making pay rates public where pay is not tied to performance will only reduce the power of pay to motivate.

Openness about pay can have another important effect. It can motivate managers to make better pay decisions. Secrecy makes it difficult for individuals to obtain the kind of factual information that is needed to question the salary or the raise they have received and the validity of what supervisors tell them about the relative size of their raise. Thus secrecy, in a sense, protects supervisors from challenges to their pay decisions.

Making pay public, however, can be counterproductive in still another way. Supervisors may decide to pay everyone equally in order to avoid the uncomfortable situations of telling some individuals why they are receiving less than others.

How much information about pay should be made public? Should everyone's salary be made public, or only pay ranges for the various kinds of jobs? The answer depends on the situation. Consideration must be given to how well performance can be measured. If it is difficult to measure, as it often is in high-level jobs, then open pay needs to be approached carefully because it will be difficult to administer pay in a way that will clearly tie it to performance. If the organization has always had strict pay secrecy, then it would be foolish to try to move to complete pay openness overnight.

As a beginning, an organization might release some information on pay ranges and median salaries for various jobs. Most individuals want at least this amount of information to be made public. Next, the organization might give out information on the size of raises and who is receiving them. Finally, the organization could move to complete openness, but only when it has, as a whole, become more open and is characterized by a high level of trust among superiors, subordinates, and peers. Few organizations are ready now for complete openness; it simply goes too much against the political climates and power politics that exist.

Participation in Pay Decisions

The most important decisions that need to be made about pay include pay-system design and individual wage amounts. Al-though these decisions typically are made by top-management, some organizations are experimenting with having them made by the individuals who are affected by them.

The results of these efforts often have been quite positive. For example, a building maintenance company that was concerned about absenteeism asked several groups of employees to design an attendance bonus plan for themselves. The same plan was then installed in other areas in the company. The results showed the importance of participation in the design process. Attendance increased in all groups where it was applied, but it increased the most in the groups that developed it.

As part of another study, the employees of a small manufacturing plant were asked to design their own pay system. The result was a new pay program that called for an 8 percent increase in the organization's salary costs and a significant realignment of employee salaries. A survey of the company six months after the new system went into effect showed significant improvements in turnover, job satisfaction, and satisfaction with pay and its administration.

Why did this occur? The workers seemed to feel better about their pay because the additional information they received gave them a clearer, more accurate picture of how it compared with that of others. Further, participation led to feelings of ownership of the plan and produced a plan where actual pay decisions were made by their peers. These factors led to feelings that the pay system was fair and trustworthy.

It also seemed that the new pay rates themselves were more in line with the workers' perceptions of what was fair and that pay satisfaction would have increased somewhat even if the employees hadn't developed commitment to the plan. This is not surprising, of course, since what constitutes fair pay exists only in the mind of the person who perceives the situation, and in this situation the plan allowed the people with the relevant feelings to control pay rates directly. Thus, not only did employee participation lead to more understanding and commitment, it also seemed to lead to better decisions being made.

In yet another situation a company has asked its executives to redesign their own bonus system. It is too early to report on the long-term effectiveness of this move, but it is not too early to report that the executives worked hard to develop a new plan and that the new plan was seen as reasonable by top management.

The situation with respect to decisions about how individuals will be treated within an established pay structure is different from the one concerning pay-system design. In the Topeka plant of General Foods and others around the world, this decision is made by peers. The limited research done so far suggests that when peers are given the opportunity to make decisions, they behave responsibly and make decisions that result in high pay satisfaction and high commitment to the organization.

There typically are problems, however. Probably the most important of these is the difficulty peer groups have in saying no to a pay-raise request when there are no limits on how many individuals can receive raises or good performance ratings. This is a particular problem where there are no clear-cut objective standards for what constitutes doing a job well. Some organizations have tried to solve this problem by giving the group a lump sum of money to allocate among the group members. This prevents the group from deciding that everyone is doing well and deserves the maximum increase the organization can offer. It doesn't, however, prevent the group from deciding to give everyone the same raise. This often is not functional because it means that pay isn't related to performance in a motivating way; yet it seems to be a frequent outcome because individuals have trouble talking about each other's performance, particularly when there are no agreed-upon standards. Most groups that have handled this issue successfully not only have had agreed-upon standards but have also engaged in considerable group process work and have expert process consultation. Fi-

TABLE 1
Summary of New Practices

	Major Advantages	Major Disadvantages	Favorable Situational Factors
Cafeteria fringe benefits	Increased pay satisfaction	Cost of administration	Well-educated, heterogeneous workforce
Lump-sum salary increases	Increased pay satisfaction; greater visibility of pay increases	Cost of administration	Fair pay rates
Skill-based evaluation	More flexible skilled workforce; increased satisfaction	Cost of training; higher salaries	Employees who want to develop themselves; jobs that are interdependent
Open salary information	Increased pay satisfaction, trust, and motivation; better salary administration	Pressure to pay all the same; complaints about pay rates	Open climate; fair pay rates; pay based on performance
Participative pay decisions	Better pay decisions; increased satisfaction, motivation, and trust	Time consuming	Democratic management climate; workforce that wants to participate and that is concerned about organizational goals

nally it is important to note that participation in pay decisions takes up employee production time and this has a cost.

Deciding What Will Work for You

At this point, the reader is probably thinking, "All these new approaches are interesting, but will they work in my organization? How can I decide which ones to try?" The summary in Table 1 provides an overview of the different practices and lists the advantages and disadvantages of each. A major advantage of most of them is increased satisfaction and job attractiveness. Although this may not have an immediate direct impact on profit or organizational effectiveness, it nevertheless is a significant advantage since it can reduce absenteeism, turnover, and tardiness. These in turn have significant impacts on profits and organizational effectiveness.

Also shown in Table 1 are some of the situational factors that favor each of the new approaches. The importance of these situational factors cannot be emphasized too strongly; the potential advantages of these practices can be realized only if they are installed in a situation that is favorable to them.

Two situational factors in particular, the management style of the organization and the condition of the present pay system, must be considered at length. Executives who are interested in trying these pay practices in their organizations should first ask, "What management style do I want to see used in my organization?" If the answer to this is participative or democratic, a different set of pay practices are applicable than if the answer is authoritative or top down. The second question that should be asked is "Are the present pay rates in my organization basically fair and equitable?" If the answer to this is yes, then several new practices are applicable that are not applicable if the answer is no.

The chart in Figure 1 shows how the answers to the questions concerned with management style and pay fairness affect the applicability of pay practices. It assumes that an effort is being made to use pay as a motivator and that therefore a clear visible relationship between pay and performance is desired. Basically it suggests that most of the new practices are best applied in organizations having a participative management style. In most cases, these practices have been implemented after a participative management style has been

FIGURE 1
Guide to Choosing among New Approaches to Pay Administration

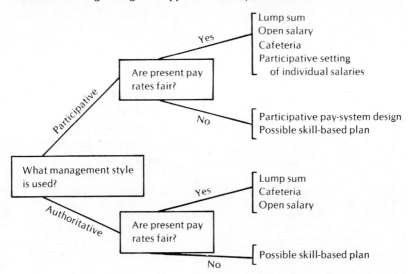

adopted, but a few organizations have experimented with using changes in pay administration practices as a way of moving the organization toward a more participative management style. In these situations pay-system changes have been used as an important change lever in a larger change program. It is also apparent that most of these practices are applicable only when a good basic pay structure is in place. Openness, salary information, and cafeteria benefit programs are not substitutes for a good basic salary system that sets fair salaries. They can, however, often lead to significant advantages when a good basic salary plan is in place.

25. IMPACTS OF PAY ON EMPLOYEE BEHAVIORS AND ATTITUDES: AN UPDATE[1]

LEE DYER, DONALD P. SCHWAB, and JOHN A. FOSSUM

Available evidence regarding the general impacts of pay on organizational behaviors and attitudes is reasonably clear on two points. First, Herzbergian pronouncements notwithstanding, pay is probably the single most important reward that an organization has to work with. Second, many, and perhaps most, organizational attempts to use pay for motivational purposes fail to produce the desired behaviors and often lead to high levels of pay dissatisfaction as well.

The present paper reviews literature on the impacts of pay in an effort to suggest mechanisms to help ameliorate the latter conclusion. In the past few years especially, this literature has become very large so that the present paper can deal with but a portion of it. Readers concerned with the issues raised here should also examine more comprehensive reviews by Heneman and Schwab; Lawler; Nash, and Carroll; and Opsahl and Dunnette.[2]

Organizations can potentially influence many types of behaviors and attitudes with pay. This review will consider several important ones although it is recognized that others might also be of interest in particular circumstances. Specifically, it will examine the potential impacts of pay on (a) decisions to join organizations; (b) behaviors within organizations such as performance and absenteeism levels; and (c) pay satisfaction and dissatisfaction and decisions to leave organizations.

There are several aspects or dimensions of pay that require consideration when investigating its impacts on these behaviors and attitudes. One such dimension is the *magnitude* of pay. Questions of pay levels for jobs, pay rates for individuals, and piece rates per unit of output all relate to pay magnitude. A second important dimension is the extent to which pay is *contingent* on a behavior of interest to the employer. For example, pay is almost completely contingent on employee performance under an individual piece-rate plan, somewhat less so under a group incentive or a merit pay plan, and not at all so when pay is based

[1] This article is based on a program presented by the authors at the Annual Meeting of the American Compensation Association, Boston, November 1976.

Source: *The Personnel Administrator*, in press.

[2] H. G. Heneman III, and D. P. Schwab, "Work and Rewards Theory," in D. Yoder and H. G. Heneman, Jr., eds., *Motivation and Commitment* (Washington, D.C.: Bureau of National Affairs, 1975), pp. 1–21; E. E. Lawler III, *Pay and Organizational Effectiveness: A Psychological View* (New York: McGraw-Hill, 1971); A. N. Nash and S. J. Carroll, Jr., *The Management of Compensation.* (Monterey, Calif.: Brooks/Cole, 1975); and R. L. Opsahl and M. D. Dunnette, "Role of Financial Compensation in Industrial Motivation," *Psychological Bulletin* 66 (1966): 94–118.

on time worked (beyond whatever minimal level of performance may be required to maintain one's job). The contingency between pay and performance is generally of greatest interest, although recently interest also has been shown in pay systems that attempt to make pay contingent on work attendance.

A third important dimension of pay is its *form*. This refers to the extent to which employees receive their pay in straight wages or salaries versus receiving them in fringe benefits such as insurance payments and pension plans. Underlying all of the previous issues is the way in which a particular pay plan is *administered* or *controlled*. While several facets of administration and control are of interest, particular attention is focused on the issue of pay secrecy in this paper.

It is important to bear in mind that the significance of pay depends on which of the foregoing facets of pay and which specific behavior or attitude is being considered.[3] Much of the confusion and controversy surrounding the impacts of pay undoubtedly results because of the failure to identify the specific aspects of pay that impact on particular behaviors or attitudes.

PAY AND JOB CHOICE

Economists have long been interested in the impacts of pay on the decision to join organizations. Indeed, pay levels for jobs and pay differentials between jobs were seen as the major if not exclusive mechanism for allocating the workforce to needed occupations in both classical and neoclassical economics. Labor economists began to challenge the efficacy of the market mechanism and the assumptions underlying it shortly after traditional economics came under Keynesian attack. These economists (much of their work is

reviewed in Parnes[4]) observed that there were very substantial wage level variations for similar jobs in local labor markets.

On the basis of these observations, it has sometimes been concluded that wage level is not an important determinant of job choice. If it were, according to this reasoning, wage levels for similar jobs would be much more homogeneous than observed, since employees would leave low paying organizations and seek work in high paying organizations. In the process, the former organizations would be required to raise pay levels to attract a labor force; the latter could maintain or perhaps reduce their pay levels.

It should be pointed out, however, that most of the investigators who actually studied these labor markets did not conclude that pay was unimportant. Rather, they concluded that market wage variability comes about as a result of the very limited knowledge job seekers (and employers) have about market conditions and the institutional and other constraints which serve to prevent equilibrium conditions.[5]

On the importance of wages there is general agreement. Indeed, because of the pervasive lack of market knowledge among job seekers, it is assumed that *job choice depends primarily on the type of work and wage level offered by the employer*. There has been a long standing debate on how job seekers establish this wage rate[6] but there is relatively little doubt that the ma-

3 Heneman and Schwab, "Work and Rewards Theory."

4 H. S. Parnes. *Research on Labor Mobility: An Appraisal of Research Findings in the U.S.* (New York: Social Science Research Council, 1954).

5 L. G. Reynolds, *The Structure of Labor Markets*. (New York: Harper, 1951); G. J. Stigler, "Information in the Labor Market," *Journal of Political Economy* 70 (1962): 94–105; and C. Kerr, "The Balkanization of Labor Markets" in E. W. Bakke, *et al.* eds., *Labor Mobility and Economic Opportunity* (New York: Wiley, 1954), pp. 93–109.

6 R. Gronau, "Information and Frictional Unemployment," *American Economic Review* 61 (1971): 290–301; Reynolds, *Structure of Labor Markets*; and D. P. Schwab, "Job Seekers Perceptions in the Choice of Minimum Acceptable Wage," Unpublished doctoral dissertation, University of Minnesota, 1968.

jority of job seekers establish minimum wage magnitude criteria which must be satisfied to make a job offer acceptable.[7]

We are not suggesting that type of job and pay magnitude are the only interests of job seekers. However, given the limited knowledge and job opportunities typically available, these are generally the only criteria job seekers can actually utilize. Where job seekers have greater knowledge and more opportunities, we can expect that additional criteria will be considered. Such opportunities and knowledge are probably most prevalent among skilled blue collar, professional, and managerial job seekers.

PAY AND INTRAORGANIZATIONAL BEHAVIOR

Several different psychological orientations have developed as to how pay may impact on job behavior. One orientation has been referred to as cognitive, in the sense that it relies heavily on an individual's ability to think for its explanation of behavior. An important cognitive formulation called *expectancy theory* has been formulated by Vroom to aid our understanding of organizational behavior.[8]

Insofar as a potential reward such as pay is concerned, the critical cognitive component of expectancy theory has to do with a person's belief about the linkage or contingency between a behavior (such as performance or attendance) and a reward (such as pay). The stronger the belief that the desired reward will follow the behavior, *ceteris paribus,* the stronger the motivation to engage in that behavior.

Note that it is the perception that the reward is contingent on the behavior that is essential. As expected, however, employee perceptions closely parallel organizational realities. Thus, both experimental

and field studies have found that perceptions regarding the link between performance and pay were highest when actual linkages were highest.[9] In a study by Schwab, for example, these perceptions were highest for workers on individual incentives, next highest among workers on group incentives, and lowest for hourly paid workers.

There is also substantial evidence that these perceptions manifest themselves in actual behavior. Numerous studies have found that the highest performing employees tend to have the strongest beliefs that high performance leads to increases in pay.[10]

There is another tradition in psychology associated most notably with B. F. Skinner that arrives at predictions which also are of interest when considering the impacts of pay. This tradition emphasizes the *reinforcement* history of an individual in explaining his behavior. In its most elementary form, the reinforcement model posits that a positive reinforcer (such as pay) linked contingently to a behavior increases the likelihood that the behavior will occur

---

[7] H. R. Sheppard and A. H. Belitsky, *The Job Hunt* (Baltimore: Johns Hopkins Press, 1966).

[8] V. H. Vroom, *Work and Motivation* (New York: Wiley, 1964).

[9] R. D. Pritchard, D. W. Leonard, C. W. Von Bergen, Jr., and R. J. Kirk, "The Effects of Varying Schedules of Reinforcement on Human Task Performance," *Organizational Behavior and Human Performance* 16 (1976): 205–30; and D. P. Schwab, "Impact of Alternative Compensation Systems on Pay Valence and Instrumentality Perceptions," *Journal of Applied Psychology* 58 (1973): 308–12.

[10] B. S. Georgopoulos, G. M. Mahoney, and N.W. Jones, "A Path-Goal Approach to Productivity," *Journal of Applied Psychology* 41 (1957): 345–53; G. Graen, "Instrumentality Theory of Work Motivation: Some Experimental Results and Suggested Modifications," *Journal of Applied Psychology Monograph* 53, 2 (1969): 1–25; E. E. Lawler III, "Ability as a Moderator of the Relationship Between Job Attitudes and Job Performance," *Personnel Psychology* 19 (1966): 153–64; L. W. Porter and E. E. Lawler III, *Managerial Attitudes and Performance* (Homewood, Ill.: Richard D. Irwin, 1968); J. R. Schuster, B. Clark, and M. Rogers, "Testing Portions of the Porter and Lawler Model Regarding the Motivational Role of Pay," *Journal of Applied Psychology* 55 (1971): 187–95; and D. P. Schwab and L. Dyer, "The Motivational Impact of a Compensation System on Employee Performance," *Organizational Behavior and Human Performance* 9 (1973): 215–25.

in the future. While at this general level reinforcement predictions about behavior are similar to expectancy predictions, the former does not resort to internal states of the individual for its explanation.

There have been a number of studies investigating behavioral consequences of pay in a reinforcement context. As with expectancy studies, these investigations have generally found performance to be higher when pay is contingently linked to performance.[11] Similarly, several studies have found that absenteeism can be reduced by making pay rewards contingent on attendance.[12]

There is a potential controversy between expectancy and reinforcement approaches regarding the *scheduling* of rewards. Expectancy theory would seem to predict that behavior-pay beliefs will be highest, and hence, the behavior of interest also highest, when a reward follows every desired behavior (a so-called continuous reinforcement schedule). A piece-rate individual incentive system where the performer is paid at the conclusion of each unit embodies such a schedule. Experimental psychologists studying nonhuman behavior, however, have often found that some sort of partial reward schedule (where the subject receives a reward after only a portion of correct behaviors) results in the highest levels of performance. Recently, a number of investigators have focused on the question of reward schedule as it pertains to monetary rewards of organizational behavior.[13] While it is premature to draw definite conclusions, there is reason to believe that partial reinforcement schedules result in performance levels as high or higher than continuous schedules.

The general point regarding the impact of pay on intraorganizational behavior, however, should not be lost in this discussion. *The critical dimension of pay in this context is whether or not it is contingent on the behavior to be influenced.* Magnitude of pay, except at extreme and probably unrealistic levels, has little if any impact on the intraorganizational behaviors discussed.[14] Form of pay can also be expected to have negligible impacts on performance and absenteeism unless differential contingencies are involved.

SATISFACTION AND TERMINATION

Satisfaction and termination are combined into a single section because it is reasonable to assume that if pay influences the latter, it is primarily through the former. Probably the best explanation of this process has been provided by March and Simon.[15]

[11] D. J. Cherrington, H. J. Reitz, and W. E. Scott Jr., "Effects of Contingent and Noncontingent Reward on the Relationship Between Satisfaction and Task Performance," *Journal of Applied Psychology* 55 (1971): 531–36; J. L. Farr, "Incentive Schedules, Productivity and Satisfaction in Work Groups," *Organizational Behavior and Human Performance* 17 (1976): 159–70; Pritchard, et al., "Effects of Varying Schedules"; J. T. Toppen, "Money Reinforcement and Human Operant (Work) Behavior: Piecework Payment and Time Payment Comparisons," *Perceptual and Motor Skills* 21 (1965): 907–13; and S. Wyatt, *Incentives in Repetitive Work: A Practical Experiment in a Factory*, Industrial Health Research Board, Report No. 69 (London: H. M. Stationery Office, 1934).

[12] E. E. Lawler III, and J. R. Hackman, "Impact of Employee Participation in the Development of Pay Incentive Plans: A Field Experiment," *Journal of Applied Psychology* 53 (1969): 467–71; and E. Pedalino and V. U. Gamboa, "Behavior Modification and Absenteeism: Intervention in One Industrial Setting," *Journal of Applied Psychology* 59 (1974): 694–98.

[13] C. J. Berger, L. L. Cummings, and H. G. Heneman III, "Expectancy Theory and Operant Conditioning Predictions of Performance Under Variable Ratio and Continuous Schedules of Reinforcement," *Organizational Behavior and Human Performance* 14 (1975): 227–43; Pritchard, et al., "Effects of Varying Schedules"; G. A. Yukl and G. P. Latham, "Consequences of Reinforcement Schedules and Incentive Magnitudes for Employee Performance: Problems Encountered in an Industrial Setting," *Journal of Applied Psychology* 60 (1975): 294–98; and G. A. Yukl, K. N. Wexley and J. D. Seymore, "Effectiveness of Pay Incentives Under Variable Ratio and Continuous Reinforcement Schedules," *Journal of Applied Psychology* 56 (1972): 19–23.

[14] Note, however, that absenteeism is probably also related to satisfaction in much the same way that voluntary turnover is. Thus, to the extent that satisfaction is dependent on the magnitude of pay, so also will absenteeism be affected.

[15] J. G. March and H. A. Simon, *Organizations* (New York: Wiley, 1958).

They hypothesized that voluntary (employee initiated) turnover is positively related to the perceived *ease* of leaving (which is a function of labor market alternatives) and the perceived *desirability* of leaving (a function of dissatisfaction).

While March and Simon's theory has not received much research attention in its entirety,[16] there is a substantial amount of evidence linking voluntary turnover to dissatisfaction.[17] A case in point has been provided by Hulin.[18] He investigated the satisfaction of clerical workers in an organization experiencing unusually high voluntary turnover relative to organizations employing similar types of workers in the same labor market. The employees studied experienced low satisfaction with their pay and promotion opportunities. Sometime after the organization modified its policies regarding pay and promotion, Hulin found that satisfaction with these two issues increased significantly and that voluntary turnover declined substantially to levels comparable with organizations in the labor market.

The question of how pay impacts on employee satisfaction is probably the most complex issue considered in this paper. One attempt to unravel the complexities involved has been presented by Dyer and Theriault.[19] In their model, pay satisfaction is viewed as being determined by (1) the perceived adequacy of pay system administration and (2) the perceived equity of amount of pay received. Equity of pay, in turn, is seen as reflecting the degree of discrepancy between the amount of pay a person feels he *actually* receives (largely a function of pay level) and the amount of pay he feels he *should* receive.

There is a lot of evidence showing that pay magnitude and pay satisfaction are positively related.[20] However, the relationship is typically not strong, suggesting that other factors are also involved. These other factors are probably the ones that determine an individual's perception of the amount of pay he should receive (pay referents in Goodman's terms[21]), and they are of several types. Most frequently suggested are social comparisons involving work outcomes and inputs. Pay, of course, is a major outcome, although others may also be considered. Inputs, alternatively, are of two kinds: (1) the nature of the duties and responsibilities inherent in the job and (2) the personal attributes (for example, training, experience, performance level, seniority, and the like) the individual brings to the job. The amount of pay a person feels he should receive is increased (and the perceived equity of a given pay level decreased) when he sees others earning more pay and/or when he feels others who are comparably paid are performing less demanding work or bringing fewer qualifications to their jobs.

Social comparisons are only one factor involved in determining a person's perception of the amount of pay he should receive. This perception is also influenced by a person's (1) sense of financial need (determined by his past earnings, his family and other financial obligations, and changes that occur in the cost of living); (2) perception of the financial condition of his employer (that is, its ability to pay); and (3) perception of the value of nonmonetary rewards received from his job, including

---

16 D. P. Schwab and L. Dyer, "Turnover as a Function of Perceived Ease and Desirability: A Largely Unsuccessful Test of the March and Simon Participation Model," *Proceedings of the 34th Annual Meeting of the Academy of Management* 34 (1974): 35–46.

17 L. W. Porter and R. M. Steers, "Organizational, Work, and Personal Factors in Employee Turnover and Absenteeism," *Psychological Bulletin* 80 (1973): 151–76; and Vroom, *Work and Motivation.*

18 C. L. Hulin, "Effect of Changes in Job Satisfaction Levels on Employee Turnover," *Journal of Applied Psychology* 52 (1968): 122–26.

19 L. Dyer and R. D. Theriault, "The Determinants of Pay Satisfaction," *Journal of Applied Psychology* 61 (1976): 596–604.

20 Heneman and Schwab, "Work and Rewards Theory."

21 P. S. Goodman, "An Examination of Referents Used in the Evaluation of Pay," *Organizational Behavior and Human Peformance* 12 (1974): 170–95.

fringe benefits and degree of psychological satisfaction experienced. Thus, for example, a given pay level will be seen as less equitable by a person experiencing financial pressures who works in a financially well-off company offering few benefits except the pay.

As complex as the discussion has been, it has thus far disclosed only some of the complexities of the pay satisfaction puzzle. As mentioned earlier, the equity issue is only one facet of the model. Also important in determining one's overall satisfaction with pay is an individual's perception of the way the organization administers its wage and salary plan. Over and above perceptions of pay equity or inequity, pay dissatisfaction is probably induced when individuals feel that: (1) the wrong criteria are used to determine their pay (a clear example here is the use of a merit criterion among employees who do not feel that performance should be a major consideration in determining their pay); (2) the criteria used to determine their pay are unclear; (3) the criteria used to determine their pay are not accurately assessed (e.g., inaccurate performance appraisals in merit-pay plans), and (4) the organization violates either explicit or implicit expectations with respect to pay. In other words, a sense of inequity is likely to be exacerbated if employees also perceive that the pay system is designed to reward the wrong personal inputs or job demands or that it is administered in a careless or capricious manner.

PAY SECRECY

The degree of openness or secrecy associated with a pay system is one of the more controversial issues in the literature and will be briefly considered here because of its implications for the issues already considered. Lawler has argued that pay systems shrouded in secrecy prevent recipients from accurately assessing the existence of any contingencies between pay and perform-

ance.[22] He also has argued that secrecy leads to fallacious pay comparisons with others that may result in a greater dissatisfaction with pay than would be the case if social comparisons were made based on knowledge of actual pay rates.

Other research, however, has shown that partially open pay systems (that is, communication of salary ranges) do not necessarily lead to more accurate pay comparisons.[23] The evidence is about evenly divided on whether open pay policies has a positive[24] or no impact[25] on pay satisfaction. In addition, Schuster and Coletti found professional employees to be about evenly divided on whether or not they even wanted pay levels to be published.[26]

Considering the small number of studies done and the conflicting results thus far, conclusions about the effects of pay secrecy would be premature. Nevertheless, contingency-based reward systems have the greatest potential for increasing employee motivation to perform when the pay-performance link is firmly established. This cannot be done without communications concerning the general relationship between differential performance levels and differential wage increments. The impact of openness on pay satisfaction, however, probably varies depending on the type of information communicated and the degree of care the

---

[22] E. E. Lawler III, "Managers' Perceptions of Their Subordinates' Pay and of Their Superiors' Pay," *Personnel Psychology* 18 (1965): 413–22; and Lawler, *Pay and Organizational Effectiveness*.

[23] G. T. Milkovich and P. H. Anderson, "Management Compensation and Secrecy Policies," *Personnel Psychology* 25 (1972): 293–302.

[24] Milkovich and Anderson, "Management Compensation"; and P. Thompson and J. Pronsky, "Secrecy or Disclosure in Management Compensation," *Business Horizons* 18, 3 (1975): 67–74.

[25] J. A. Fossum, "Publicity or Secrecy? Pay and Performance Feedback Effects on Satisfaction," *Proceedings of the 36th Annual Meeting of The Academy of Management* 36 (1976): 370–72; and Nash and Carroll, *Management and Compensation*.

[26] J. R. Schuster and J. A. Coletti, "Pay Secrecy: Who is For and Against It?," *Academy of Management Journal* 16 (1973): 35–40.

organization has used in pricing jobs and in determining individual rates of pay.

ADMINISTRATIVE IMPLICATIONS

While the evidence concerning the impacts of pay on employee behaviors and attitudes is somewhat inconclusive and ambiguous, one can extrapolate from available theory and research a number of implications that are applicable to the design and administration of compensation plans. These relate to all of the major elements of compensation systems previously discussed.

Pay Magnitude. If the employer is to attract new employees and keep them satisfied with their pay, the wages and salaries offered should approximate the wages and salaries paid to employees in other organizations with whom comparisons are made. Wage and salary surveys have obvious utility for this purpose. Their maximum value will be realized, however, *only* if: (a) the jobs surveyed are those which applicants and employees consider appropriate for comparison purposes and (b) the results and the uses made of the survey are unambiguously communicated to applicants and employees. The implementation of a competitive wage and salary policy has the greatest potential payoff in terms of attracting and satisfying employees when employees are aware of the policy. It should be remembered however, that there is little reason to believe that competitive wages and salaries per se will enhance employee performance or attendance levels.

Pricing Jobs. Pay satisfaction is enhanced when an organization's policy is perceived as embodying an equal pay for equal work philosophy and when differentials across jobs are seen as justified in terms of differences in the nature of work performed. Job evaluation can help create an equitable structure of pay rates. But job evaluation will perform this function adequately *only* when the system takes into consideration those factors employees feel they should be compensated for, weighted

in a manner they perceive as appropriate. The formulation of such a system may require employee inputs in the job evaluation process via actual participation in the establishment of the plan or through the use of employee opinion surveys.[27] Again, however, note that a pay structure perceived as fair by employees has implications primarily for employee satisfaction with pay; it will have little or no impact on the organization's ability to attract employees or to motivate them to perform.

Pricing Job Incumbents. It is through the system used to price job incumbents that the motivational potential of pay must be realized. The key issue here is the degree of contingency established between pay and the desired behavior. This, in turn, requires an accurate measure of the relevant behaviors (a particular problem with performance) and enough openness to clearly establish the linkages in the minds of employees.

Several caveats are in order concerning the impact of contingent pay on employee satisfaction or dissatisfaction with pay: First, not all employees look with favor on the principle of merit pay; some (many?) employees do not see performance as a personal input on which pay ought to be based. In such cases, merit pay systems can be expected to lead to dissatisfaction with pay. Second, a poorly administered plan can drain the reservoir of goodwill even when employees favor merit pay in principle. Third, even employees who favor the principle of merit pay and see their employers' systems as well run seldom feel that performance is the only personal input for which they should be paid. Thus, a satisfactory pay plan grounded in merit may also have to incorporate formal recognition of other employee inputs (for example, education, training, experience, or seniority) and such extraneous factors as the cost of living. Pay increments based on these other

[27] L. Dyer, D. P. Schwab, and R. D. Theriault, "Managerial Perceptions Regarding Salary Increase Criteria," *Personnel Psychology* 29 (1976): 233–42.

factors must be clearly differentiated from those based on performance. If they are not, the desired contingency between pay and performance will be diminished as will the positive effect of pay on motivation to perform.

Pay Form. The relative amounts of compensation allocated to indirect pay may have some implications for the organization's ability to attract new employees and to satisfy and retain current employees. To achieve these goals, the fringe benefits package must be clearly understood by applicants and employees and must be perceived by them as meeting their needs. The latter requirement has been approached in a small number of organizations through the use of cafeteria plans.[28] Communications concerning fringe benefits, however, remains a continuing problem in most organizations.

Cost-of-Living Adjustments. The satisfaction model earlier reviewed suggests that periodic pay adjustments should be made to reflect the effect of inflation on employees'

---

[28] E. E. Lawler III, *Improving the Quality of Work Life: Reward Systems.* A report prepared for The Office of The Assistant Secretary for Policy Evaluation, and Research of the U.S. Department of Labor, June 1975.

financial needs. If such increases are financially impossible or considered undesirable, this fact, along with the reasons for the situation should be communicated to employees. There is some reason to believe that such communications, if seen as legitimate, can partially mitigate the negative effects of declining real income. Of course, any cost-of-living adjustments (as any increments related to inputs other than performance) must be clearly distinguished from merit increases if the motivational impact of pay is to be maintained. Nothing is gained from either a motivational or attitudinal point of view by granting all increments under the general label of merit pay.

Good Faith. Pay policies and procedures, whether explicitly stated or simply implied by virtue of past practice, are an integral part of the "psychological contract" established with employees. Good faith requires that the pay system be changed only when absolutely justified. When modifications are necessary, the nature of the alterations and the reasons for them must be clearly explained. They should be made with every bit as much care as any other significant organizational change.

9

LABOR-MANAGEMENT RELATIONS

A major purpose of unions is to strengthen employee input to the determination of employment conditions affecting them. Thus, unions seek to improve the wages, employment security, and the general working conditions of their members.

To accomplish this purpose, unions attempt to represent groups of employees. This requires that individuals be induced to join the union. It also requires that the employer *recognize* the union as a legitimate employee representative. Recognition can be done voluntarily by the employer, but more typically it is established through a government-monitored election process where the organization's employees vote to decide if they want to be represented, and if so, by which union.

Once recognized, unions *negotiate* with employers about the employment conditions that will apply for some specified time period, typically one to three years. This negotiation has direct implications for all of the personnel/human resource functions. Compensation, internal staffing, hours, and safety policies, in particular, are likely to be covered in the negotiation process.

After a contract has been agreed to, usually the union indirectly participates in its *administration* through the *grievance process.* Such a process leaves the day-to-day contract administration to the employer. The union, however, can grieve if it feels that the organization is violating the contract through its administrative activities. The union and organization then attempt to resolve the grievance in a mutually agreeable manner. If they cannot, the last step in the grievance process ordinarily is *arbitration·* Arbitration involves bringing in an outsider (agreeable to both union and management) who decides how the grievance should be resolved. Both union and management agree that they will accept the arbitrator's decision as final and binding. Thus, unions not only participate in the establishment of personnel/human resource policy but also in the administration of those policies.

As you can see, the subject matter of labor-management relations is quite complex. Space limitations do not allow us to deal with all facets of it. However, we do want to highlight some of the major trends occurring in the private and public sectors and some of the recent problem areas in labor-management relations. This will facilitate a good general understanding of labor-management relations and increase your appreciation for the complexity of the process and the numerous impacts it has on both employers and unions.

PRIVATE SECTOR TRENDS

The *National Labor Relations Act* (Wagner Act) was passed by Congress in 1935 and thus constitutes a landmark year in the history of labor-management relations. The Wagner Act is important because it gave nonsupervisory employees in the private sector a legally protected right to organize unions and bargain collectively with management. Prior to that time, workers had struggled to organize and bargain, but without any legal protection to do so. At best these attempts met with limited success, and they involved relatively small numbers of workers.

Union membership climbed very rapidly, after the passage of the Wagner Act until the middle 1950s. It grew from somewhere around 3 million members to about 17 million members. This represents an increase in the percentage of the nonagricultural workforce that was organized from about 13 to around 35 percent. Since then, union membership has continued to increase but at such a slow rate that the percentage of the workforce that is organized has been declining. This *stagnation* is due in part to the fact that the easy-to-organize (particularly employees in manufacturing, mining, transportation, and construction) are already organized. In addition, the percentage of the workforce that such blue-collar workers represent has been declining. These declines have been partially offset, however, by increases in union membership among white-collar employers.

There has been an equally significant, though less readily apparent, trend in the private sector. That has been a continual expansion in the number of issues that labor and management negotiate over and reduce to writing in the labor contract. Federal law requires labor and management to bargain over wages, hours, and other terms and conditions of employment. Legal interpretation of this requirement has become increasingly broad, thus expanding the scope of bargaining. For example, the scope has expanded over the years to include such issues as Christmas bonuses, pensions, plant relocation, subcontracting, safety rules, work clothing, and performance appraisal.

PUBLIC SECTOR TRENDS

Relative to the private sector, the history of collective bargaining in the public sector is quite short. Significant public sector unionism only goes back to about 1960. Despite the short history, membership growth in the public sector has been quite spectacular. In large part, this was facilitated by an enabling legal environment, much as was the case in the private sector. Federal employees were given the right to organize and bargain collectively in two executive orders issued by President Kennedy in 1962. Many state and municipal governments have also passed legislation granting collective bargaining rights to employees. The provisions in this legislation are frequently patterned after federal legislation in the private sector. A major exception to this is that strikes are prohibited for all federal employees and most state and local employees.

Trends in the scope of bargaining for public employees are less discernible. In general, the scope of bargaining tends to be narrower than in the private sector. This is primarily due to a desire by both judicial and executive branches of government to maintain merit principles in public employment. These merit principles are specified in the law and usually administered as part of the civil service system. For example, federal employees cannot bargain over such issues as transfers and promotions, discipline and discharge, or grievance procedures. Prohibited bargaining issues at the state and local government level also occur, though the specific prohibitions will vary from jurisdiction to jurisdiction.

Expansion in the scope of bargaining at the federal level seems unlikely in the near future. At the state and local level, however, chances of expansion may be somewhat greater. For example, if the state law merely requires bargaining over terms and conditions of employment (as occurs very frequently), interpretation of such a clause may become broader and broader, just as has occurred in the private sector. On the other hand, legislative bodies may tighten up such loose clauses by specifying in detal the issues that are and are not subject to bargaining. The effect of this would probably be to reduce the scope of bargaining. On balance, therefore, it would seem that any expansions in bargaining scope will occur quite gradually.

BARGAINING IMPACTS ON LABOR AND MANAGEMENT

The most immediate impact of the bargaining relationship on management is that it must bargain with labor to jointly decide terms and conditions of employment. General economic conditions, as well as conditions peculiar to the organization, however, will greatly influence the specific terms of the agreement. The relative willingness of management and labor to agree with each other is also an important factor in avoiding a strike. In addition, bargaining invariably creates pressures for greater centralization of decision-making in the organization on all employment issues. Likewise, expansion in the number and complexity of bargaining issues creates a need for trained labor relations specialists. Such impacts, in turn, may very well lead to enhanced status and authority for the personnel/human resource function in the organization (see Chapter 1).

The bargaining relationship also has multiple impacts on the union and its leaders. Since the leaders are elected officials, they must be constantly attuned to members' needs and desires. Failure to do so may result in members failing to vote to ratify (accept) a new contract or attempting to vote the leadership out of office. Often compounding these representation problems that leaders face is the existence of competing interests among the rank-and-file membership which makes it difficult to please everyone (for example, skilled versus unskilled workers). Finally, the effectiveness of the union in achieving its goals is directly linked to the administrative qualities of the leadership. Increasingly, being an effective manager is a major requirement for being an effective union leader.

INTRODUCTION TO READINGS

Labor-Management Relations in 1976

In any given year, the patterns and issues of labor-management relations are broad and complex. This is aptly illustrated in the article by Leon Bornstein that deals with some highlights of labor-management relations in 1976. After describing the general economic setting and giving contract settlement and strike figures, Bornstein summarizes specific settlement provisions in a variety of industries all involving large numbers of workers—primarily in the private sector. This is followed by brief summaries of pay developments for federal employees and union affairs regarding problems of leadership and of organizing new groups of workers. While you will obtain the details in his paper, we would like to make some summary statements that take into account our previous comments on labor-management relations.

First, a glance over the provisions of the new settlements indicates how broad the scope of bargaining tends to be in the private sector. Actually, the scope is even broader than indicated, since Bornstein focuses primarily on economic issues and ignores the vast number of noneconomic issues also bargained over. One also sees some expansion in scope occurring. Some examples are the new personal holiday plan to reduce hours of work in the auto industry (see Chapter 11 for a further treatment of work hours) and new requirements regarding air-conditioned cabs in the trucking industry.

General economic conditions were of extreme importance in shaping bargaining demands and settlements. In general, inflation caused major attention to *escalator clauses* or cost of living provisions to protect workers against an erosion in purchasing power. High unemployment levels lead to such things as demands for reduced hours in order to "spread" the work, lowered wage demands over previous years to guard against layoffs, and increased financial benefits to workers if they were laid off.

Specific economic conditions also influenced labor-management relations. For one thing, they had a strong bearing on the occurrence and length of strikes in the auto and rubber industries. They also created some special bargaining problems. As examples, both the apparel and printing industries were confronted with major problems of efficiency and labor costs.

Conflicting interests between skilled and unskilled workers occurred within many unions. The major problem was the perception by skilled workers that the pay differential between themselves and unskilled workers was too narrow. The usual solution was to provide skilled workers an extra pay increase on top of the general increases granted to all workers. The United Auto Workers went even further and gave the skilled workers an absolute veto power over the acceptance of any contract, even though they are a minority of total membership.

Finally, there were some major problems regarding internal union leadership and management. There was considerable turmoil within several major unions, all of which involved demands for and/or changes in top leadership.

In addition, the Teamsters Union was faced with continual investigation by the U.S. Department of Labor, which alleged mismanagement of a $1.4 billion pension fund.

While subsequent years will never be quite like 1976, the Bornstein article illustrates well the problems unions create for the personnel/human resource function. The union, after all, must deal with the changing economic conditions and the impacts that these conditions have on union membership. Similar influences are having impacts on the organization. These influences and the problems they create must be resolved through contract negotiation and administration processes.

Unionization of Professional Employees

We previously noted that the overall decline in the percentage of the labor force that is unionized has been slowed by an increase in unionization among white-collar workers. An excellent example of this is the increase in union membership among professional employees in both the private and public sectors. The article by Dennis Chamot discusses the reasons for this increase, the bargaining issues of concern to professional employees, and the impacts of professional employee organizing on management.

Chamot advances a number of reasons for the growth of professional employee unions. One is simply the changing composition of the workforce, where the percentage of white-collar employees has been steadily increasing (see the data in his Exhibits 1, 2, and 3). Another factor is the increased legal protection we previously noted for public sector employees, many of whom are professionals. Finally, Chamot speculates that undesirable changes in the nature of the professional's job (for example, less autonomy) have caused professionals to view the union as a mechanism for regaining, or at least preventing further erosion of, their withering professional stature. Chamot apparently feels these forces are so strong that eventually all professionals will be unionized. ("Unionization of a particular group may be delayed, but the general outcome is inevitable.") Needless to say, this is a debatable conclusion.

Many of the bargaining issues discussed by Chamot are very traditional ones (for example, salaries, work schedules, job security). However, the scope of bargaining has increased to include many issues associated with the role of the professional and the ability to uphold professional standards. One example is educators bargaining over class size limits and over who will determine course content. Chamot sees a very uneven growth in the scope of professional bargaining issues, however, depending on each union's circumstances and bargaining priorities. He neglects to mention that for public employees, the growth will also depend on how tightly scope is defined by legislatures and the courts.

Chamot also reviews the impacts of unionization on management, and many of these are in keeping with our earlier discussion. One fairly unique impact in the case of professionals is that the actual structure of decision-making on a day-to-day basis may change. For example, nurses in a hospital may obtain representation on previously all-physician committees that deal with health care policies and procedures. Thus, as we suggested before, the scope of bargaining and bargaining impacts on management are interrelated issues.

Critical Problems in the Public Sector

The rapid growth of unions in the public sector invites comparisons with private sector unionism in order to discern major differences between the two and to see if there are some experiences in the private sector that could profitably be applied in the public sector. Charles Redenius begins his article by summarizing and projecting forward growth trends among public employee unions. He then proceeds to identify a number of differences between the private and public sectors that make collective bargaining in the public sector unique. These include the monopoly power of government units, the essential nature of some (but not all) government services, constant intrusion by the courts into illegal public employee strikes, and a maze of complex, everchanging law.

Not only is the law complex but, as Redenius points out, the forces influencing how it is written are very different from those in the private sector. This creates some difficulties unique to the public sector. Consequently, the private sector is not a totally appropriate model for the public sector.

There are two exceptions where the private sector experience can be helpful according to Redenius. First, the private sector teaches us that lack of bargaining ability and experience by both labor and management representatives creates many unnecessary problems. Since the skills of negotiators in the public sector are generally quite low, Redenius makes some specific recommendations on how these skills could be upgraded through training.

The second exception pertains to how public employee strikes might best be prevented, or ended if they occur. Redenius forcefully argues that experience in the private sector demonstrates how undesirable it is to use involuntary procedures for preventing and settling strikes. The two major procedures are *compulsory arbitration* (terms of the contract are required to be settled by a third party, if labor and management cannot agree themselves) and *judicial intervention* (a court issues an injunction declaring the strike illegal and ordering strikers back to work). While there involuntary procedures are often effective in preventing or ending disputes, Redenius offers a number of reasons for thinking that they actually tend to harm the collective bargaining process in the long run. He strongly favors a reliance on voluntary procedures under most circumstances.

26. INDUSTRIAL RELATIONS IN 1976: HIGHLIGHTS OF KEY SETTLEMENTS
LEON BORNSTEIN

During 1976, industrial relations transpired in an economic setting which was generally improved over 1975 but still of serious concern, particularly with respect to prices and unemployment. Collective bargaining during the year was heavy, as labor-management negotiations occurred in such key industries as trucking, automobile, electrical equipment, rubber, and meatpacking.

Source: *Monthly Labor Review* 100, 1 (1977): 27–36.

Unions continued to seek protection against inflation through cost-of-living wage escalator clauses. An escalator clause was established in the rubber industry following a four-month strike, and ceilings on the size of escalator adjustments were removed in the trucking and electrical equipment industries. Concern with the threat of unemployment led to some improvements in the size, duration, or employer financing of layoff benefits, notably in the automobile and electrical equipment industries.

Negotiators also tailored a number of settlements to alleviate special difficulties facing some industries. For example, the piecework system in the ladies apparel industry was revised to encourage and permit modernization and expansion of operations and thus stem a decline in the number of firms and employment. The can industry, beset by low profits, changing technology, and other problems, negotiated a contract extension with the Steelworkers.

Perhaps the most novel contract provision was the "Scheduled Paid Personal Holiday Plan" established in the automobile industry. The United Auto Workers, which negotiated the change, viewed the plan as a step toward its goal of a four-day workweek.

Union affairs were dominated by continuing clashes within the United Mine Workers Union and the beginning of what will apparently be a bitter contest for the presidency of the Steelworkers Union. In addition, the federal government was investigating direction of the Teamsters' pension fund by its union and management trustees.

The Economic Setting. A continued high rate of unemployment and a lower (though still historically high) rate of inflation combined to moderate bargaining settlements. Although employment reached record levels, the jobless rate in November 1976 was 8.1 percent, marking the first time in 1976 that it had reached the 8-percent level. The rate had dipped to a 1976 low of 7.3 percent in May, edged up to 7.5 percent in June, and held at the 7.8–7.9 percent level through October.

Total employment was a record 88.1 million in November, 4.0 million above the March 1975 recession low. This gain did not appreciably lower the unemployment rate because of growth in the labor force. The civilian labor force rose 2.8 million in the first 11 months of 1976, to 95.9 million.

The rate of inflation, as measured by the Consumer Price Index, was 5.3 percent for the 12-month period ended in October, an appreciable improvement over the 7-percent rise in 1975 and a large improvement over the record 12.2-percent rise during 1974. Although safely out of the double-digit range, the recent figures were still markedly above those in the 1952–65 period, when the annual rise in the Index was consistently under 3 percent. (The Index rose at an average annual rate of 4.8 percent in the 1966–73 period.)

Bargaining, Settlement, and Strike Statistics. About 4.4 million workers were covered by major (1,000 workers or more) contracts expiring or subject to wage reopening in 1976, compared to 2.5 million in 1975. (Although approximately one American worker in five in the total labor force is a union member, only one in nine is included in an agreement covering 1,000 workers or more in the private nonfarm sector.) Principal negotiations occurred in automobile and farm equipment manufacturing (800,000 workers), trucking (450,000), electrical equipment manufacturing (200,-000), rubber (70,000), and meatpacking (55,000).

Preliminary BLS [Bureau of Labor Statistics] figures showed that major collective bargaining settlements in the first nine months of 1976 generally provided lower wage increases than agreements reached throughout 1975. Wage gains averaged 8.9 percent in the first contract year (10.2 percent in 1975), and 7.0 percent a year over the life of the agreements, compared with 7.8 percent in 1975. Wage and benefit gains combined (in contracts covering 5,000 workers or more) averaged 9.4 percent for the first year (11.4 percent in 1975) and 7.2 percent a year over the life, compared to 8.1 percent the prior year. During the first nine months of 1976, negotiators added automatic cost-of-living escalator clauses in 41 settlements covering 233,000 workers, primarily in the rubber and apparel industries. This brought to 6.0 million workers—or 60 percent of all workers in major bargaining units—the total covered by such clauses. This was double the number covered by escalator clauses in 1971 and triple the number in the mid-1960s. (Escalation was eliminated in five agreements covering 77,000 workers.)

Idleness due to work stoppages increased in the first nine months of 1976. According to preliminary BLS figures, idleness caused by work stoppages amounted to 0.22 percent of the estimated working time through September, higher than the 0.17 percent for the first nine months of 1975, but lower than the 0.26 percent for the comparable 1974 period. A total of 33.6 million days of idleness were registered through September 1976, 8.3 million more than in the first nine months of 1975. The major strikes were in the automobile industry, in which 170,000 Ford Motor Co. employees were out for nearly a month, and in the rubber industry, in which 70,000 workers were out for four months. A three-month walkout that had an impact out of proportion to the number of workers involved began on September 15, when 17,000 members of the Teamsters Union struck United Parcel Service facilities along virtually the entire East Coast, slowing company deliveries throughout the country and diverting deliveries to the already over-burdened U.S. Postal Service.

Important Settlements

Autos. In terms of number of workers affected, the automobile industry topped the list of bargaining settlements. The Automobile Workers reached agreement with Ford Motor Company, Chrysler Corporation, and General Motors Corporation for almost 700,000 workers. (Bargaining at American Motors Corporation carried over into 1977.) Key terms at all three companies included additional employee time off under a new "Scheduled Paid Personal Holiday Plan" that the union hailed as a step toward its goal of a four-day work-week, increased employer funding of Supplemental Unemployment Benefits, and increased union participation in company decisions on subcontracting and use of outside facilities. Based on past practice, these accords were expected to set a pattern for about 100,000 workers the union represents at automotive parts manufacturers.

The automobile negotiations began after a severe downturn in the industry in 1974–75, which had resulted in substantial layoffs, reduced workweeks, and subsequent interruptions in Supplemental Unemployment Benefits payments to laid-off General Motors, American Motors, and Chrysler employees because funds ran out. Thus, the major demands formulated at the UAW's prebargaining convention centered on means for reducing the possibility of layoffs and increasing financial protection for employees who are laid off.

There were also several demands of special importance to skilled trades workers, including calls for special pay adjustments to widen the pay differential between these workers and production workers and for restriction of company rights to contract out work and shift work among its facilities. Gaining these demands was viewed as critical to the negotiations because the union had already promised the skilled workers at each company the right to veto any settlement, regardless of the acceptance vote by other employees. (The union had also promised the skilled workers veto power in the 1973 bargaining, but later accepted a settlement at Ford despite its being rejected by skilled workers.)

After some preliminary discussions with each of the "Big Three" companies, the union zeroed in on Ford, in keeping with its usual strategy of selecting a target and pressing for a settlement there. When the contract expired on September 14, the 170,000 Ford workers struck. Production continued at GM, Chrysler, and American Motors under contract extensions.

Ford and the UAW then began intensified negotiations until a settlement was reached on October 5 on companywide issues. Some production resumed immediately after worker approval of companywide terms, but the last of the workers did not return to work until November 1, when the last of the accords on local issues was reached.

The new holiday plan, which is in addition to the existing "regular" holiday plan, gives employees with a year's seniority 12 "personal" holidays during the contract term—5 during the second year and 7 during the third year. The time off is to be taken in single-day units throughout the workweek, and all eligible employees will have an equal opportunity to compete for particular days. To minimize production disruptions, the days off cannot be taken during the summer vacation season, and employees must work the day before and the day after a personal holiday in order to be paid for it.

The accord also added a regular holiday, July 3, 1978, bringing the total to 37 during the 1976–79 contract term, compared with 40 during the 1973–76 agreement. The lower total resulted from year-to-year fluctuations in the number of paid holidays required to comply with an existing provision that employees receive unbroken paid time off from Christmas through New Year's Day. There were no changes in the vacation schedule, which calls for a maximum of five weeks after 20 years' service.

Although laid-off Ford workers did not suffer any interruptions in Supplemental Unemployment Benefits payments during the 1974–75 downturn, Ford agreed to increase its contribution to the fund, to reduce the possibility of such interruptions in the future.

Over the term, general wage increases ranged from 66 cents an hour for employees in the lowest rated jobs to $1.06 for those at the top, compared to increases ranging from 45.5 to 81 cents under the prior agreement. Skilled workers also received an additional 20 or 25 cents under the new agreement to widen the differential between them and production workers, one of the key demands formulated at the prebargaining convention. There were no changes in the escalator formula, which provides for a one-cent-an-hour adjustment for each 0.3-point rise in a composite price index (1967 = 100) derived from the official indexes issued by the U.S. and Canadian governments. Escalator gains had totaled $1.09 during the 1973–76 contract.

The existing six-year pension agreement, which does not expire until 1979, was not subject to bargaining, but Ford did agree to a union proposal for a onetime bonus to retirees, financed solely by a temporary diversion of money from the active employees' cost-of-living allowance. The graduated bonus, payable on January 1, 1978, to those who retired prior to September 15, 1976, ranged up to $600 for retirees with 30 years' service or more.

Skilled workers won several of their key aims. In addition to the special pay adjustment for skilled workers, the company pledged to retain all "new die machining, fabrication, repair and tryout work" in present plants to the extent the company's requirements "can reasonably be met" and agreed to discuss proposed moves of such work with the union prior to making a decision.

After the Ford settlement, the union turned to Chrysler, where a similar settlement was reached on November 5, averting a strike scheduled for that day. Next came General Motors. After a 12-hour "mini-strike" by 69,000 of GM's 390,000 hourly workers, an accord was reached November 19. Production workers at all three companies approved the contracts by wide margins, but the approvals by skilled workers were close at Ford and Chrysler. The agreements expire September 14, 1979.

A major issue at General Motors had been the union's contention that the company had adopted a so-called "southern strategy," that is, actively resisting union attempts to organize employees at new company plants in the southern states. The company denied this, contending that union defeats in several representation elections resulted from the attitudes of the plants' employees, rather than from corporate policy. This issue was resolved when the company agreed to "neither discourage nor encourage" union organizing efforts.

Farm and Construction Equipment. During the automobile negotiations in August and September, the Automobile Workers union was also negotiating with the "Big Three" argicultural and construction equipment companies—Deere and Company, Caterpillar Tractor Company, and International Harvester Company—on renewal of agreements expiring on September 30. About 100,000 workers were involved.

Using the same "divide and conquer" strategy as in automobiles, the UAW first concentrated on Deere. Employees struck on October 1 and remained out until an agreement was reached on November 8. The focus was then shifted to International Harvester, where a November 19 accord ended a one-day strike. Bargaining was still in process at Caterpillar when this article was completed. The contracts at Deere and International Harvester, both for three-year terms, differed in some respects.

The Deere contract specified an initial wage increase of 33 to 43 cents for hourly paid employees and an equivalent 27 to 36 cents in base rates for incentive-paid employees and for all employees to receive 3-percent increases in the second and third years. The International Harvester accord provided for an initial increase of 34 to 43 cents and for 3-percent increases in the sec-

ond and third years and skilled workers received 20 or 25 cents more during the first two years. The escalator clause at Deere will provide for quarterly adjustments of 0.14 percent for each 0.3-point movement in the CPI (1967 = 100), instead of 0.17 for each 0.3-point movement. The formula at International Harvester continued to provide for quarterly adjustments of one cent an hour for each 0.3-point movement in the CPI.

Other terms at Deere included an increase to six and one-half days a year, from two and one-half, in the maximum paid time off employees are permitted to take under the "bonus hours" program established in 1973 for rewarding perfect weekly attendance. This program was a precursor of the "Scheduled Paid Personal Holiday Plan" adopted in the 1976 automobile negotiations, although the plans differ in approach and in the resulting amount of paid time off.

At International Harvester, the similar "attendance bonus plan" was terminated in favor of improvements in the regular paid vacation plan. The change consisted of an additional week of paid time off for all eligible employees except those with 3 but less than 5 and 10 but less than 15 years' service, who received an additional week and a half. The result was a schedule ranging from 2 weeks for employees with 6 months but less than 3 years' service to a maximum of 5 for those with 20 years' service. The unchanged vacation schedule at Deere ranged from 1 week for employees with 6 months but less than 3 years' service to 4 weeks for those with 20 years' service.

Unlike the situation in the automobile industry, pension plans were up for renegotiation at these companies. The parties raised the normal rate to $16 a month for each year of credited service and agreed to give foundry employees with 25 years of service 1.2 years of credited service for each year actually worked. Thus employees with 25 years of service could retire immediately under the existing "30-and-out" eligibility requirement. The accelerated retirement provision was similar to one prevailing in the automobile industry after the 1976 settlements.

A new provision of importance to skilled workers specified that the companies must give the union advance written notice prior to subcontracting out tool and die work that would result in layoffs within the company. This will give the union time to pressure the companies to revise their plans.

Rubber. What had promised to be one of the bellwether industrywide negotiations of 1976 led instead to the most protracted test of strength of the year. By the time the four-month walkout by 70,000 Rubber Workers against the industry's Big Four producers ended in early September, settlements had already been reached in meatpacking and electrical equipment manufacturing, both of which had originally been slated to follow rubber, and perhaps be influenced by any settlement in rubber.

The URW's decision to strike Firestone Tire and Rubber Company, Uniroyal, Inc., Goodyear Tire and Rubber Company, and B. F. Goodrich Company simultaneously was a departure from its usual practice of striking only one company and then attempting to extend the terms to the other firms. In making the change, the union believed that the federal government and the automobile manufacturers would pressure the tire companies for an early settlement, but this did not happen, because the automobile companies had stockpiled large quantities of tires in anticipation of a walkout, and the government kept hands off. In addition, the companies maintained limited tire production during the strike, as some supervisory and office employees were shifted to production jobs. The impact was also reduced because production continued at some other firms in which employees are represented by other unions or are not represented by any union and because URW-represented employees at a few smaller companies defied the union leadership and signed interim agreements assuring them the same terms as those eventually won at the Big Four companies.

At the outset of negotiations, URW President Peter Bommarito emphasized that the union's chief bargaining aim was a "catch-up" wage increase, a general wage boost on top of that, and the introduction of an "uncapped" cost-of-living escalator clause. Both Bommarito and union members were smarting from the 1973 bargaining round, when wage increases were limited by stabilization policies, and the tire producers were able to conclude agreements that did not provide cost-of-living clauses. As a result of the inflation since 1973, the union fell further behind workers in the automobile industry, who have been protected by a cost-of-living clause since 1950. In presenting the case for the union's wage and cost-of-living demands, Bommarito pointed out that wages of the Rubber Workers had fallen 32 cents behind those of the Auto Workers in 1967, 50 cents behind by 1970 negotiations, and $1.35 by the start of 1976 negotiations.

The new escalator clause provided for a one-cent adjustment for each 0.4-point change in the CPI (1967 = 100) in the first two years, with the formula liberalized to one cent for each 0.3-point change in the third year, with no limits on adjustments.

In describing the settlement, Bommarito said:

This COLA [cost-of-living adjustment] clause is really worth more for the URW membership than the general wage increase earned in this contract. It means, for all practical purposes, that Rubber Workers will have COLA from now on and we will have true inflation protection in the worst of times.

The contracts also provided for an immediate 80-cent-an-hour general wage rise, with additional increases for Firestone, Goodrich, and Uniroyal workers to equalize pay differences resulting from the 1973 settlements. Wages were raised 30 cents an hour in the second year and 25 in the third year for all Big Four employees, and those in skilled trades receive an additional 25 cents the first year and 15 cents in the second.

The settlement also liberalized a number

of benefits, including pensions and Supplemental Unemployment Benefits, and provided for strengthening the industry's Joint Occupational Health and Safety Program.

Trucking. Removal of a ceiling on cost-of-living adjustments was a key feature in the settlement between the Teamsters and several employer associations. The accord, reached in April, covers 450,000 truckdrivers and related employees. Under the new escalator clause, employees will receive a pay adjustment in April 1977 calculated at one cent an hour for each 0.4-point rise in the CPI (1957–59 = 100) during the preceding 12 months and an adjustment in April 1978 calculated at one cent for each 0.3-point rise in the 1967 = 100 Index during the preceding 12 months. The clause in the previous contract had provided for adjustments in July 1974 and 1975 not to exceed 11 cents on each date. The employees received a total of 22 cents in "cost-of-living" payments as a result, but they would have received 77 cents more had there been no maximum.

Other wage terms were an immediate 65-cents-an-hour increase for the 350,000 local cartage drivers, followed by increases of 50 cents on April 1 of 1977 and 1978. Over-the-road drivers, who number 100,000, will receive increases of 1-, 1.25-, and 1.25-cents per mile on the same dates.

The three-year accord also established three days annual sick leave and required employers to provide over-the-road drivers with single sleeping quarters in hotels and motels and air-conditioned truck cabs. The employer contribution for pension and health and welfare benefits was increased by a total of $17 a week, but virtually all of the money was expected to be used to meet the increased cost of existing benefits and to meet the requirements of the Employee Retirement Income Security Act of 1974, rather than for major improvements.

Electrical Equipment. Settlements in electrical equipment manufacturing followed the trucking accord. General Electric Company and Westinghouse Electric Corporation, in three-year agreements signed in midyear with three electrical workers' unions (the International Union of Electrical Workers, the United Electrical, Radio, and Machine Workers, and the International Brotherhood of Electrical Workers) and other unions, also agreed to elimination of caps on escalator clauses. The new pacts provided for annual escalator adjustments calculated at one cent an hour for each 0.3-percent rise in the CPI up to 7 percent and above 9 percent during the preceding 12 months, with no credit toward the adjustment for that portion of any CPI rise between 7 and 9 percent. The 200,000 workers had received 41 cents an hour in adjustments—the maximum permitted—under the previous clause. Without the limit, they would have received an additional 48 cents an hour.

Other wage terms at both companies included an immediate wage increase of 60 cents an hour and second- and third-year increases of 4 percent or 25 cents an hour, whichever is greater. Certain skilled workers also received an additional immediate pay adjustment ranging from 5 to 50 cents an hour.

There were a number of other benefit improvements at both companies. These included a sixth week of paid vacation after 30 years' service and larger cash payments to laid-off workers who are covered by each company's income extension aid plan.

Apparel. A new method of setting piece rates was adopted in the January settlement between the Ladies' Garment Worker's Union and dressmaking firms for 55,000 workers in eight eastern states. Within a few months, similar terms were agreed to for 125,000 workers in the children's wear, sportswear, and coat and suit industries.

The new pay system, already in effect in the union's contracts in some other parts of the nation, permits piece rates to be lowered if the introduction of new machines or more efficient methods enables the employees to maintain or increase their income. The intention was to encourage employers to modernize operations by enabling them to lower their labor cost per unit of output.

Sol C. Chaikin, president of the union since 1975, said the change was necessary to revitalize the industry, particularly in New York City, where it has been affected by higher costs of doing business, and by competition from nonunion and foreign firms. The New York City garment industry now employs 200,000 people, down from 325,000 in 1947.

The 40-month contracts also set guaranteed minimum hourly rates for pieceworkers and specified that piece rates be set to yield the average worker 25 percent above the hourly guarantee. Other terms included general wage increases totaling 23 percent for pieceworkers and 25 percent for hourly workers, an additional paid holiday, and increased employer financing of pension and welfare benefits. The agreement will expire on May 31, 1979, matching the expiration dates the union had won in some earlier agreements. Common expiration dates were part of the union's goal.

In men's apparel, 90,000 workers in a number of states were covered by contracts negotiated by the Amalgamated Clothing and Textile Workers and firms in the shirt, pants, and outerwear industries. The three-year shirt and pants contracts provided for wage increases totaling 75 and 80 cents an hour, respectively, and the 38-month outerwear contract provided for increases totaling 95 cents. All of the agreements established wage escalator clauses, but the annual adjustment in September 1977 will be payable only to the extent the increase computed under the formula exceeds the 30 cents deferred wage increase scheduled for the same month, and the September 1978 adjustment will be payable only to the extent the computed amount exceeds the scheduled 35 cents deferred increase. In any case, each escalator increase cannot exceed ten cents.

Cans. In August, the Steelworkers and four major container companies—American Can Company, National Can Corporation, the Continental Group, and Crown Cork and Seal Company—negotiated an eight-month extension of their existing contracts to October 31, 1977. The extended contracts provided for hourly wage increases ranging from 17 to 23.3 cents an hour on March 1, 1977 and specified that any additional amounts provided in the first year of a subsequent contract be made retroactive to March 1, 1977. As a result, 1977 negotiations in the can industry will follow rather than precede the union's talks with companies in the steel and aluminum industries. The can companies and the union said that the extension would give them additional time to study the impact of a number of problems—such as the introduction of new types of cans and increased competition from bottlemakers—on the "job security of employees and the growth of the companies."

Meatpacking. Settlements in the meatpacking industry, which covered about 70,000 workers, did not include any major innovations. The Meat Cutters settled first with Wilson and Company and afterwards reached similar accords with John Morrell and Company, Swift and Company, and Armour and Company, and a number of smaller companies.

However, the Wilson contract provided for somewhat liberalized semiannual cost-of-living adjustments, computed at one cent an hour for each 0.3-point rise in the Consumer Price Index (1967 = 100), instead of for each 0.4-point rise in the 1957–59 = 100 Index. General wage increases totaled 60 cents, and the company and union were to jointly allocate 1,500 pay adjustments of five cents an hour to individual jobs requiring certain skills. Benefit improvements included a rise in the pension rate to $13 a month, from $8.50 a month, for each year of service.

Printing. Four major settlements centered on union and management responses to changing conditions in the printing and publishing industry. Among the conditions are changes in technology, with resulting shrinkage or even virtual elimination of some printing trades; intensified competition from television and radio; and an increase in suburban newspapers and job shops, often at the expense of city firms with higher labor costs and less efficient facilities.

Two contrasting approaches to dealing with these changes were evidenced in labor management negotiations at the two daily newspapers in the nation's capital. The *Washington Post* won some crew-size reductions and strengthened its control over work scheduling and the introduction of new technology and methods. At the *Washington Star*, which, unlike the *Post*, was operating at a loss, a number of unions agreed to concessions intended to restore profitability. In two settlements in New York City and Chicago, lithographers deviated from the usual provisions of past agreements in an effort to improve the position of their employers.

The struggle at the *Washington Post* began on October 1, 1975, when the pressmen's contract expired and they walked out, after allegedly damaging the presses. Members of some unions refused to cross the picket lines, and members of other unions struck because their agreements also expired. But the newspaper continued to publish, with the aid of supervisory employees and most members of the Newspaper Guild, who refused to back the pressmen because of the alleged acts of sabotage.

In February, the newspaper reached three-year agreements with some trades that called for a $60 wage and benefit package and, in some agreements, for reductions in crew sizes and eased rules on contracting out work. At the end of 1976, the *Post* was operating the presses with a crew of 150 newly hired employees, while the members of the Printing Pressmen's union were still technically on strike and insisting that all 204 members must be rehired, or none would return.

The *Washington Star* accord with ten unions provided for the elimination of 200 of 1,700 jobs within 18 months as part of a cost-reduction effort expected to save $6 million. To induce 100 of the 270 printers to leave, the newspaper offered them termination bonuses up to $18,000, depending on when they departed, or, as an alternative if they were between age 57 and 62, early retirement at 40 to 50 percent of final-year earnings.

The New York City agreement between the Metropolitan Lithographers Association and Local 1 of the Amalgamated Lithographers (an affiliate of the International Typographical Union) provided for total wage increases of up to $40 a week over the 26-month term, plus benefit improvements. However, the association announced that it expected the cost increases to be offset by provisions that gave the 100 firms "significant relief from contractual and traditional restrictions on the assignment and scheduling of work." About 8,000 workers were involved.

In Chicago, 13 percent of the 3,500 lithographers covered by the new agreement with the Chicago Lithographers Association were reportedly unemployed as a result of plant shutdowns, plant relocations, and reduced operations. The local of the Graphic Arts International Union cited this as the reason it agreed to no annual pay increases in its two-year contract. The pact did, however, provide for continuation of the wage escalator clause and for increased employer financing of health and welfare benefits.

Canning. Some 60,000 cannery workers in California, represented by the Teamsters, approved a three-year settlement on July 31, ending an 11-day strike in which growers and processors lost millions of dollars in unprocessed fruits and vegetables. The new contract provided for a total of $1.35 to $1.57 in hourly wage increases. Under the prior agreement, the wage increase was $1.07 to $1.49, including gains of 54 cents an hour under a cost-of-living escalator clause. There is no escalator clause in the new contract, but the union did win some improvements in supplementary benefits.

San Francisco Strike. About 1,800 craft employees of the city of San Francisco suffered pay cuts of up to $5,300 a year after the Board of Supervisors, in June, reaffirmed an earlier decision on the matter. The March 30 decision had precipitated a 39-day walkout by the trades workers, but the impact was minimal because 16,000 other city workers had accepted contracts calling for small wage increases and remained on the job.

The supervisors' position was that the voters had mandated the pay cuts when they repealed a section of the city charter requiring the city to pay its craft-workers wages comparable to similar jobs in private enterprise. The unions had contended that pay cuts were not authorized and that all the voters did was repeal the parity concept. Among the trades affected were carpenters, whose $21,800 a year pay was reduced to a $17,240–$20,800 range, electricians ($21,620) reduced to $16,430–$19,850, machinists ($22,250) to $17,040–$21,300, plumbers ($24,100) to $16,750–$20,220, and streetsweepers, whose $17,300 pay was cut to $12,000–$14,460.

Rails. The United Transportation Union terminated its ten-year strike against the Florida East Coast Railway. The walkout, the longest in U.S. railroad history, began when the company eliminated some train-operating jobs it considered unnecessary and asserted greater control over work schedules. The railroad continued to operate during the strike, using nonunion replacements. A company spokesman said the only way the strikers could resume working for the road was "to bid for jobs, take a physical, and re-read the rules on how to operate a railroad." Existing three-year contracts in the railroad industry do not expire until December 31, 1977.

Federal Pay, Pensions

Unions representing federal employees reacted bitterly to the size of the scheduled October pay increase set by President Gerald R. Ford. The increase for the 1.4 million white-collar employees covered by the General Schedule pay system ranged from 4.19 to 8.98 percent, and the 2.5 million members of the Armed Forces, Foreign Service workers, and Veteran's Administration medical personnel received a comparable increase because their salary levels are linked by law to those of the GS employees.

The minimum 4.19-percent increase applied to GS employees in certain pay steps of grade 5 of the 18-grade system, and the maximum 8.98-percent increase applied to those in the lowest step of grade 16. Other employees in grade 5 and those in the lowest four grades received increases slightly larger than 4.19 percent. Employees in the upper steps of grade 15, most employees in grades 16, and all employees in grades 17 and 18 received a 4.76-percent increase; their pay rates were increased by larger amounts (ranging up to 11.83 percent for grade 18), but a statutory ceiling prevented them from receiving the full amount.

Members of Congress, federal judges, and certain political appointees would have received an October increase of 4.83 percent under a 1975 law granting them annual increases linked to those for GS employees, but a bill signed into law on October 1 specifically excluded them from receiving the 1976 increase.

President Ford also signed legislation that eliminated the permanent 1-percentage point bonus federal retirees had received on top of each of their periodic cost-of-living adjustments. The bonus had been introduced in 1967 to compensate retirees for the two-month delay between the increase in the Consumer Price Index needed to trigger a pension increase and the actual payment of the higher amount. It had been criticized because the resulting cumulative rise in pensions had exceeded the percentage rise in the CPI.

Union Affairs

Mine Union. The year was marked by a series of controversies within the United

Mine Workers union as President Arnold Miller engaged in a running dispute with the executive board and other dissident leadership factions while attempting to deal with strike-prone members in the pits.

At the beginning of the year, UMW vice president Mike Trbovich informed the Department of Labor of alleged mismanagement of union funds by Miller. The Department investigated and ruled that there were some instances of lax controls and documentation, but there was no "willful intent" to violate the law and no basis for legal action. After the finding was announced in May, the executive board reinstated Trbovich, who said he had been suspended in April by Miller for filing the charges of mismanagement. Miller said he imposed the suspension because Trbovich refused to accept an organizing assignment.

This was followed by a wildcat strike that started in West Virginia in June over a job-posting dispute which eventually involved 90,000 miners in seven states. As the walkout spread, the strikers defied Miller, who repeatedly ordered them to return to work, and the executive board, which threatened to expel them. The stoppage ended after a month, when Miller was able to persuade 300 local union officers to endorse a back-to-work order, leading to its acceptance by the strikers.

At a ten-day convention that began September 23, dissident forces won approval of a resolution advancing the union's scheduled November 1977 presidential election to June 1977 and specifying that the winner serve as the union's chief negotiator for the fall 1977 bargaining to replace the soft coal agreement expiring December 6, 1977. (If Miller loses, he will be permitted to finish his term, which expires December 22, 1977.) Other results of the convention were mixed, with Miller winning on some disputed issues and the opposition winning on others.

Teamsters. An investigation of the Teamsters pension fund continued throughout the year, as the federal government sought to determine if the trustees had made loans to persons associated with organized crime and had engaged in other questionable practices. The investigation is being conducted by the Department of Labor, the Department of Justice, and the Internal Revenue Service.

At the behest of the Labor Department, in October, 11 of the 16 trustees resigned, joining one who had resigned earlier. The board was revamped to comprise ten members—five from the unions and five selected from the various employer associations. Teamsters' President Frank E. Fitzsimmons and Roy L. Williams, head of the Central Conference of Teamsters, remained on the board, as did two management officials. Three Teamsters officials and three management officials became new trustees.

The Department of Labor had requested changes in the makeup of the board because it doubted that the old board had the competence and willingness to make imminent decisions on some of the fund's major loans. It said the investigation would proceed despite the resignations and restructuring.

The $1.4 billion fund, established in 1955, and officially titled the Central States, Southeast and Southwest Areas Pension fund, covers 380,000 active members of the union and 71,000 retired persons from 300 locals in 33 states. In October 1976, employer contributions to the fund reportedly averaged about $25 a week for each active employee.

Textile Merger and Boycott. The 160,-000-member Textile Workers Union and the 350,000-member Clothing Workers merged and formed the Amalgamated Clothing and Textile Workers Union, with Clothing Workers' chief Murray H. Finley as president. Sol Stetin, who headed the Textile Workers, was selected as senior executive vice president. Delegates to the union's founding convention approved a national boycott of J. P. Stevens and Company products designed to aid in a continuing drive to organize 40,000 of the textile firm's unorganized employees. The company labeled the boycott "an improper use of the combined power of many unions."

Other Union Developments. Stating the current leadership has "grown soft," Edward Sadlowski, 38, announced he would seek the presidency of the 1.4-million Steelworkers in the union's scheduled February 1977 election. Sadlowski, director of the Steelworkers' Chicago area district, said he would seek tougher contract provisions on job security and on occupational health and safety issues. He also attacked the Experimental Negotiating Agreement between the union and the steel industry, claiming that it deprived workers of some bargaining strength by limiting their right to strike. Opposing him will be Lloyd McBride, the union's current director for the St. Louis district, who is backed by President I. W. Abel. Abel was not eligible to run again because he had reached the union's mandatory retirement age.

International Union of Electrical Workers president, Paul Jennings, 58, retired for health reasons on June 1, and the executive board selected David J. Fitzmaurice, to complete the term of office ending in December. Fitzmaurice, 61, who had been secretary-treasurer of the 250,000-member union since 1968, won a four-year term, according to unofficial election results.

Letter Carriers' president, James Rademacher, 54, stepped down from the post he held since 1968. He reportedly had become "worn down" over dissension within the 200,000-member union. In November balloting, J. Joseph Vacca was elected as Rademacher's successor.

C. L. Dennis, 68, president of the 238,000-member Brotherhood of Railway and Airline Clerks, retired on November 1 and the union's executive council chose Fred Kroll to complete the remaining two and one-half years of Dennis' term. He reportedly stepped down because of the lingering effects of a recent injury and because of an intraunion dispute involving his son, L. F. Dennis, who had just resigned as the union's director of organization.

California Farm Organizing. Union representation elections resumed among California farmworkers in November, after the Agricultural Labor Relations Board, which conducts the balloting, was restored to full strength by the appointment of members to replace three who had resigned. The Board had run out of operating funds in February and was unable to gain additional funds from the legislature until July. The Board may run into difficulties in future fiscal years, because California voters rejected a constitutional amendment that would have required the Legislature to grant the board the money necessary to carry out the Agricultural Relations Act of 1975.

The voters also turned down a proposition that would have written into the law a board ruling permitting union organizers to campaign on growers' property for three hours a day. Cesar Chávez, head of the United Farm Workers, had argued that such access was necessary because many workers live on the farms and seldom leave the property. Growers opposed the provision, claiming that it violated their property rights. The proposition was vital to the unions because it would have prevented the board from ever reversing its decision.

As the elections resumed in November, the tally stood at 192 victories for the Farm Workers, 119 for the Teamsters, 19 for other unions, and 25 for "no union," with the results of 59 other elections in dispute.

During the slowdown of organizing efforts in California, the Farm Workers gained 6,000 members on the East Coast, as an independent union, the Association of Agricultural Workers, merged into the United Farm Workers. The association, headquartered in Hartford, Conn., operates in New York, Connecticut, New Jersey, Massachusetts, Delaware, and Pennsylvania. Growers recruit the workers from Puerto Rico, and they enter the mainland under the Farm Labor Contracts Registration Act of 1963.

27. PROFESSIONAL EMPLOYEES TURN TO UNIONS

DENNIS CHAMOT

In March 1975, the nation witnessed a relatively minor, but rather dramatic event. More than 2,000 doctors in New York City went on strike for four days. In the best tradition of more conventional trade unionists, they walked picket lines and demanded improvements in pay, hours, and working conditions. It should be noted that this was an honest-to-goodness labor dispute and not the increasingly common but, in union terms, less significant protest of malpractice insurance problems by established doctors.

This action (and similar, more recent ones in Washington, D.C., Chicago, and Los Angeles) caught many people by surprise. After all, who needs a union less than a doctor? When put in proper perspective, however, these developments are neither strange nor unexpected, and they have important implications far beyond the medical community.

In fact, the men and women who participated in these strikes, and the many more doctors who are currently in unions, are not the highly paid, independent practitioners one usually thinks of. They are, instead, hospital interns and residents, *employees* of large bureaucratic organizations. Thus the similarities between them and other employed professionals are far greater than the more obvious differences.

There are currently almost 3 million members of unions and employee associations who are classified as professional and technical.[1] They include public schoolteachers, college professors, musicians, actors, journalists, engineers, nurses, and doctors, among others.

The American work force as a whole is changing. "White collar" now describes one half of all working people, and this figure has been increasing steadily (see Exhibit 1). The fastest-growing segment, professional and technical employees, currently accounts for one seventh of the total work force, and is expected to increase to one sixth within ten years (see Exhibit 2). Paralleling these changes has been the upsurge in white-collar union membership, which, in the past decade and a half, increased by over 1 million (to 3.8 million), and now accounts for 17.4 percent of all union membership; another 2 million employees are in state and professional associations that engage in collective bargaining (see Exhibit 3).

WHITE-COLLAR UNION GROWTH

Several white-collar unions have experienced spectacular growth over the past few years, with much of the increase occurring in the public sector. For example, by mid-1975, the American Federation of Teachers (AFT) claimed 450,000 members, four and one half times its 1963 membership. Furthermore, one in ten AFT members is on a college faculty. If the professors belonging to other unions are added, it appears that 20 percent of the American professoriat, on over 420 campuses, have been organized— virtually all within the past decade.

Similarly, the American Federation of State, County, and Municipal Employees (AFSCME) and the American Federation of Government Employees (AFGE) each tripled its membership between 1963 and 1975. It should be noted that many unions represent for collective bargaining purposes more people than are indicated by membership

[1] U.S. Bureau of Labor Statistics, *Directory of National Unions and Employee Associations 1973* (Washington, D.C.: U.S. Government Printing Office, 1974).

EXHIBIT 1
The Changing U.S. Work Force

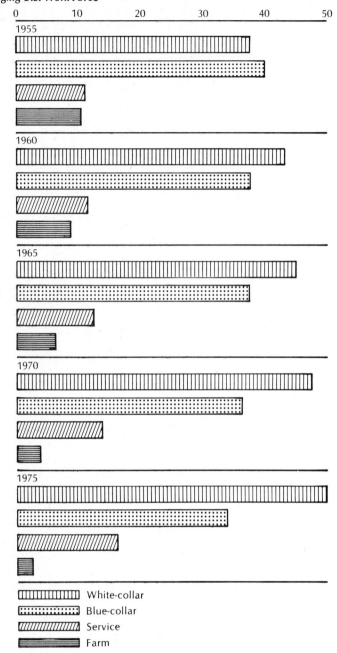

Sources: U.S. Department of Labor, *Handbook of Labor Statistics, 1974*, Bureau of Labor Statistics, 1974, and Press Release, Bureau of Labor Statistics, March 1975.

figures, e.g., AFGE has about 325,000 members but represents over 600,000 federal employees.

By contrast, the United Brotherhood of Carpenters and Joiners' membership expanded by only 11 percent in the decade 1963–73. Both the Auto Workers (UAW) and Teamsters, mostly blue-collar unions that

EXHIBIT 2
White-Collar Workers in U.S. Work Force

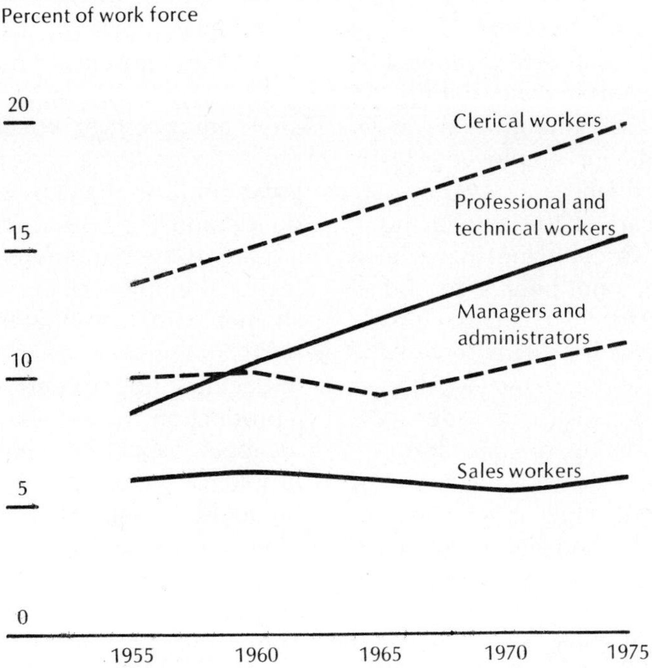

Percent of work force

Source: U.S. Department of Labor, *Handbook of Labor Statistics, 1974,* Bureau of Labor Statistics, 1974.

EXHIBIT 3
Union Membership Growth by Thousands (relative to 1963)

Year	AFT	AFSCME	AFGE	CWA	SEIU	UAW	Teamsters	Carpenters
1963	1.00	1.00	1.00	1.00	1.00	1.00	1.00	1.00
1965	1.41	1.07	1.31	1.05	1.09	1.09	1.03	1.03
1967	1.76	1.28	1.88	1.15	1.18	1.31	1.13	1.08
1969	2.33	1.66	2.78	1.28	1.32	1.37	1.20	1.07
1971	2.90	2.02	3.07	1.51	1.48	1.38	1.26	1.11
1973	3.51	2.40	2.76	1.59	1.64	1.30	1.27	1.11
1973 (thousands..	249	529	293	443	484	1,394	1,855	820

AFT: American Federation of Teachers
AFSCME: American Federation of State, County and Municipal Employees
AFGE: American Federation of Government Employees
CWA: Communications Workers of America
SEIU: Service Employees' International Union
UAW: United Automobile, Aerospace, and Agricultural Implement Workers of America
Teamsters: International Brotherhood of Teamsters, Chauffeurs, Warehousemen, and Helpers of America
Carpenters: United Brotherhood of Carpenters and Joiners of America
Source: U.S. Department of Labor, *Directory of National Unions and Employee Associations,* Bureau of Labor Statistics, 1963–73.

are trying to increase white-collar membership, did only slightly better (about 30 percent, although from a larger base).

Growth is not the only measure of success when one is dealing with a finite system. Organization is proceeding slowly in some areas because most eligible workers in these fields are already in unions. This is true, for example, in the performing arts, where union membership is the accepted norm among professional and supporting personnel.

Historically, unions have been most successful among blue-collar workers. Why the rapid and sustained increase in white-collar interest? In the public sector, at least, the situation was helped by changes in the appropriate laws. The Wagner Act, passed in 1935, applied only to workers in the private sector. However, under President Kennedy's Executive Order 10988 in 1962, followed by new laws in state after state during the 1960s, collective bargaining rights were granted to government employees. Many were quick to use them.

This is only a part of the answer, however, since the laws could not have been changed if there had not been a good deal of pressure already for the changes. Furthermore, union interest has increased in the private sector, too, and here the legal framework has been available for decades, permitting, if not mandating, organization.

At the heart of the matter is the nature of modern employment, which is likely to consist of very routine, nonchallenging jobs. Here the problem for nonprofessional white-collar employees is in many ways identical to that of their blue-collar colleagues. It is only natural, then, that they should choose similar means to solve those problems. As the white-collar work force rapidly expands, union successes continue apace.

SPECIAL PROBLEMS OF PROFESSIONALS

The large number of professional employees presents a more complex situation. Although it is beyond the scope of this article to examine in detail individual professions or industries (which differ from group to group even within the same profession), several important generalizations may be drawn.

It might be useful at this point to note that the word *professional* has two rather different connotations. The first emphasizes the external, economic aspect of the job. A person is a professional because he or she is paid for services rendered. This is one of the differences between Arnold Palmer and a weekend golfer. It is this definition I use

in discussing problems with salaries, termination policies, and the like.

The complementary definition involves an internal, psychological view. The professional sees himself as a member of a special group to which admission is gained only after advanced or specialized study. He seeks recognition among his peers and takes great pride in the knowledge he has acquired and the opportunity to use it.

One of the big differences between professional employees and all other nonmanagement workers is that the professional expects that he will have a major role to play in deciding how to perform his job. Unlike a production worker or a secretary, the professional expects to help determine the problems he will work on and the approaches toward their solution. All too often, his expectations fall far short of reality. Dissatisfaction may result from inadequate technical support, insufficient opportunity to pursue interesting ideas, excessive interference by superiors, lack of sufficient input to project assignment decisions, and so on. Whether or not there are overriding economic considerations behind these decisions, the professional employee frequently feels he is not treated with the respect he deserves.

Back in the "good old days," the individual professional enjoyed a one-to-one relationship with his client. He experienced a great deal of autonomy both in making decisions and in determining work assignments and conditions. Further, he had sufficient control to effectively determine adequate compensation.

The professional-client relationship today has been radically altered. Today's professionals are no longer self-employed, independent practitioners, but are instead employees of ever-larger organizations. No matter what the nature of the employing institution—corporation, university, or government agency—few individuals within it feel they have sufficient personal bargaining power to effectively control their careers or their jobs.

The problem is that we are dealing with two very different viewpoints. As Archie Kleingartner of the University of California at Los Angeles put it some years ago in a discussion of industrial engineers:

Management equates professionalism with loyalty to management and perceives unions as threatening the loyalty of engineers. Any engineer who joins a union is perceived as disloyal, and by extension as behaving unprofessionally. [However,] management opposition to engineer unionism reflects purely managerial interests more than a concern for high professional standards. I would guess that management opposition would be just as strong if professional societies attempted to bargain.[2]

Authority and Decision Making

Discussion with representatives of several unions that are active in organizing professionals confirms that dissatisfaction with policies relating to authority and decision making is a major issue. For example, at most campuses where faculties have unionized in recent years, the primary concerns were job security and the somewhat related but much broader subject of university governance. Colleges and universities are moving away from the old system of collegiality and are increasingly employing full-time administrators who exercise considerable authority. Attempts to impose business practices (e.g., measurement of faculty "productivity") by people who are perceived, at least, as having insufficient teaching experience, threaten established notions of professional responsibilities, duties, and prerogatives. Unionization is looked on as a way for a faculty to improve its bargaining position with an administration that has grown too powerful in areas that have been traditionally the domain of the educators.

Current union contracts have provisions safeguarding these areas:

---

[2] Archie Kleingartner, "Professionalism and Engineering Unionism," *Industrial Relations*, May 1969, p. 235.

- The contract between the Southeastern Massachusetts University Faculty Federation (AFT Local 1895) and the university trustees states: "The faculty shall have the responsibility to determine course content and texts."
- A recent contract between the faculty union (AFT Local 1600) and trustees of Cook County Community College, District No. 508, has sections limiting class size and teaching loads.
- The Rhode Island College Chapter of the AFT apparently felt that more basic problems existed, because the contract it negotiated in 1972 with the Rhode Island Board of Regents declared: "Each fulltime faculty member shall be assigned office space."

In these, and in many other cases, the faculty felt it needed a union to secure rights in areas that are at the heart of its ability to perform its professional duties.

Salary and Work Schedules

Where unions have been active in organizing employees of hospitals and other health care facilities, it has been found that issues involving quality of patient care (e.g., the number of doctors in clinics or emergency rooms, the improvement of nursing and technician staffs, the improvement of X-ray services, the availability of physical therapists, and so on) are of great concern at all professional levels. Salary is the other major issue, although this is far less important at the higher pay levels. Nurses, for example, are much more interested in salary improvement than the better paid pharmacists, but both groups seek greater impact on institutional decision making.

In many cases, concerns overlap: interns demanding shorter schedules will work fewer hours, but they will also provide better care if they get proper sleep; professors fighting enlargment of classes (or elimina- of some) are protecting their jobs, but they are also vitally concerned with the effects of proposed changes on the quality of education.

In the federal sector, salary cannot be an issue because the unions are forbidden by law to bargain over congressionally set pay levels. In 1973, NASA engineers at Huntsville, Alabama joined the International Federation of Professional and Technical Engineers (AFL-CIO). A key issue in the campaign was employee disgruntlement over an extremely complex and rigid organizational structure, which they felt would be changed by a union. One might note that, even before they organized, these engineers were earning an average salary of about $20,000 a year. Engineers in federal, state, and municipal agencies have turned to unions in large part because of a strong desire to have greater impact on managerial decisions.[3]

Although the general concerns noted here seem to be fairly universal, the details of every organizing campaign or bargaining session are different. We are, after all, dealing with groups of *employees,* and, professional or not, they worry about wages, hours, and working conditions.

Furthermore, since professional employees are only human, they do not like to be taken advantage of. For example, they are exempt from the maximum hours provisions of the Fair Labor Standards Act. In other words, they are entitled to work overtime for free. As Robert Stedfeld, editor of the magazine *Machine Design,* wrote a few years ago:

Some companies have discovered a new cost-cutting gimmick—force engineers to work overtime without pay. The company saves money. Engineers can be laid off, and the regular work load is imposed on the remaining engineers. The engineers being unfairly exploited are afraid they will lose their jobs if they protest, so they take it.[4]

This situation is still fairly widespread, especially in R&D. Hours are set for the non-exempt clerical and support staff, but the professional employees—scienstists, engineers, computer people, and the like—are expected to begin work at least as early as the secretaries and feel a great deal of indirect pressure to stay quite a bit later each day than the official quitting time. The worst offenders are those employers who offer services to others. Here, the pressures can be quite intense as contract proposal or termination deadlines approach.

It should be noted that these pressures are applied to all members of the professional staff, not just to those who are eager to get ahead. Some companies formalize the system by offering compensatory time off, but this is not the norm. Even where this option does exist, it is often abused. For example, one plant has some restrictions on how the compensatory time is taken, limiting it to days approved by the supervisor, and to no more than one day at a time. The rules may be bent a bit, but, in fact, a large part of the overtime put in by those engineers is never paid for in any way.

A recent study of overtime trends by the U.S. Bureau of Labor Statistics shows that nearly a quarter of all professional and technical employees regularly work more than 40 hours a week, but only 18 percent are paid for overtime.[5] Furthermore, one half of all workers on extended work weeks are white collar, and this number has continually increased, even though overtime for blue-collar workers has fluctuated with changes in general economic conditions.

The reader, especially one in a managerial or executive position, may see nothing wrong with this. The point, though, is that affected employees do. They do not like being required to work overtime routinely. This is particularly true when non-

---

[3] For a more general look at scientists and engineers, see Dennis Chamot, "Scientists and Engineers: The New Reality," *American Federationist,* September 1974, p. 8.

[4] Robert Stedfeld, editorial in *Machine Design,* April 15, 1971, p. 65.

[5] Diane M. Westcott, "Trends in Overtime Hours and Pay, 1969–74," *Monthly Labor Review,* February 1975, p. 45.

exempt assistants draw premium pay while their professional colleagues get only titles.

Grievance Procedures

Another serious problem for the employed nonunion professional is the lack of a realistic grievance procedure. If problems arise, as they invariably do, he is encouraged to complain to his immediate supervisor or perhaps to the personnel department.

Both the supervisor and the personnel people are representatives of the employer; further, their future careers and rewards are in the hands of that same employer. Should the disagreement between the professional and the employer be a serious one that cannot be easily resolved without cost to the company (either in dollars or in "managerial prerogative"), then the employee probably will not get satisfaction through the only channels open to him. His choice is to accept the unilateral decision of the employer or resign. In neither case is the employee able to demonstrate sufficient professional status to influence the outcome. This can be very discouraging.

It should be emphasized that lists of specific grievances are not as important as are the deficiencies of the system for dealing with them. To be sure, the complaint may be very serious to the individual involved (e.g., dismissal, involuntary transfer, insufficient salary increase, improper job assignment). But, whatever the nature of the specific dispute, a modern organization is not set up to deal directly with individuals. Authority for settling disputes is usually much higher up in the hierarchy than the immediate supervisor or personnel person with whom the complainant tries to bargain.

Frequently, policies are too inflexible in any case, as the following examples show:

A few years ago a physicist at a major corporation was offered a 10 percent salary increase. He asked if he could have instead an additional week of vacation (which was worth much less in dollar terms). He was refused.

Sometimes a clash may occur over issues of quality of work rather than individual benefits, as in the case of three professional employees of the Bay Area Rapid Transit (BART) in San Francisco. The three, a systems engineer, a programmer analyst, and an electrical engineer, became increasingly concerned with defects in the automated train control system being developed by a contractor and with the manner in which the installation and testing of this system was being carried out. When their supervisors continued to disregard their warnings, they complained to the BART board of directors. After a public hearing, the board voted to support management. Shortly thereafter, the three engineers were fired.[6]

Several months later, a BART train overran the station at Fremont, injuring several passengers. Other failures of the automatic system occurred frequently. These three engineers were never rehired by BART and have instituted a court suit.

Whatever the nature of the grievance, if refusal defies common sense, the professional employee in particular feels slighted, impotent, and unsatisfied. Moreover, as the BART engineers found, he may discover that bucking the system invites catastrophe.

Job Security

The fear of layoffs among white-collar and professional employees has increased greatly in recent years. There are many contributing factors, but the most important are probably the widespread layoffs of engineers and other white-collar workers that occurred in the early 1970s and the

---

6 See John T. Edsall, *Scientific Freedom and Responsibility* (Washington, D.C.: American Association for the Advancement of Science, 1975), p. 37.

continually poor job market for (and, hence, oversupply of) recent college graduates.

Employees at professional levels used to be encouraged to believe they were a valuable talent pool and a part of the management team. It has come as a shock to them to realize that they are no longer as sheltered from the effects of general economic declines as they once were. They can be fired for any reason (except, ironically, for union activities—these are protected by law). Notice, severance pay, continuation of company-paid health and life insurance after separation, company assistance in locating new employment—all of these benefits are conferred solely at the discretion of the company. Frequently, policies in these areas are inadequate. And unlike laid-off blue-collar workers, professional employees have virtually no chance of being recalled.

This situation is unfortunate even if the person who is fired is professionally incompetent. But when incompetence is the excuse given for terminations in cases of personality clashes, square pegs in round holes, and economic exigency, then a reasonably sophisticated labor pool can determine for themselves that a colleague is being shafted. It takes only a few clear-cut examples to do a great deal of psychological damage. A union, while it could not prevent a layoff, would eliminate much of the arbitrariness otherwise possible.

A case in point is provided by the American Federation of Musicians, which represents symphony orchestra members, among others. For example, the union at the Detroit Symphony recently won a demand that dismissal proposals be submitted to a committee consisting of 15 musicians elected by the orchestra members. At least 10 must give their approval before management can dismiss a player. Furthermore, a union can negotiate the right of recall, a right that is virtually nonexistent for nonunion professionals.

REASONS FOR RELUCTANCE

There certainly seem to be a lot of reasons for professionals to join unions, and many have. How, then, can we explain the reluctance of some segments (e.g., scientists and engineers) to do so?

A major reason is that unorganized professionals frequently have rather limited knowledge of what unions are and what they can do. They tend to think of unions in terms of not too accurate blue-collar stereotypes: complex and rigid work rules, excessive reliance on seniority, narrow jurisdictional lines, dictatorial power in the hands of union leaders, and so on. They are unaware of the flexibility of collective bargaining and the legal safeguards that exist for protecting their right to influence internal union policies. In short, they need realistic models for professional unions.

No one group's problems are unique, even among professional employees. The questions that are being asked today were asked and answered years ago by other professionals; it is an ongoing, evolutionary process. The renowned educator John Dewey held membership card No. 1 in the American Federation of Teachers, and the highly respected journalist Heywood Broun helped found the Newspaper Guild.

More recently, such professionals as Theodore Bikel, Charlton Heston, Walter Cronkite, and Ed Sullivan have been very active in the affairs of their unions. In the technical world, Albert Einstein spoke in favor of unions for "intellectual workers" 30 years ago. Nobel laureates Linus Pauling and Harold Urey recently wrote in support of unionization among scientists.

Unionization of a particular group may be delayed, but the general outcome is inevitable. There are, after all, inherent differences of interest between employers and those they employ. While they have a common general goal—the success of the business—they often have very different views on specific issues. A prime example should suffice: a major source of income for the employee, his salary, is an expense for the employer. The latter will want to minimize the same flow of dollars that the employee seeks to increase. No matter how enlightened the compensation policy, one is ultimately faced with the basic decision of how to divide limited available dollars between employees and stockholders.

There are only two ways to reconcile the differences, economic and otherwise: either unilateral management decision making or some kind of bilateral, employer-employee system for reaching compromises. (Individual bargaining, philosophically most acceptable to professionals, is totally unrealistic for most employees of large organizations.) It is inevitable that management decisions will not always parallel the personal interests of affected employees. Since employees lack strength as individuals, the logical approach is to join together to support each other.

RESULTS OF UNIONIZATION

Let's take the bad news first. At the very least, and perhaps most important, management flexibility will be reduced. The union will quickly seek to negotiate a contract, and the company is bound by law to bargain with it in good faith. In the course of such negotiations, many areas that were formerly in the exclusive domain of management will become negotiable.

It is probably worthwhile to stress my major caveat—one must not overgeneralize, especially when dealing with unions of professionals. It is fair to say that such unions will be concerned with salaries and fringe benefits. However, in some cases, these may already be at satisfactory levels, so that the main emphasis will be on other areas. In still other instances, the general level of benefits may be satisfactory, but the distribution may be at issue (e.g., a desire for more vacation with very little pressure for major salary increases). In any

event, the union's priorities will vary tremendously from place to place, depending almost entirely on local conditions.

The biggest noneconomic change would probably be the establishment of a bilateral grievance system. Quite obviously, this would significantly affect management flexibility. It might require a major overhaul of personnel practices. The union becomes the official representative of that group of employees, and as such, the union, not the individual employee, must be dealt with. Indeed, it could be illegal to make a deal with a particular employee without the knowledge and acquiescence of the union.

Where abuses were rampant in the past, the union might be interested in having the contract contain sections dealing with overtime (number of hours, as well as extra pay), type of allowable work, relocation policies, and the like.

Uniquely professional concerns will be of interest to the union, too, reflecting the desires of the members. These will vary from one group to another but might include requests for additional technical or supporting staff, tuition refund plans (or improvements thereto), formal peer input to promotion or termination decisions, and the like.

Besides less flexibility in dealing with professional staff, management will probably also face higher costs. In addition, time will have to be spent on contract negotiation and administration. Still, all of the changes can be (and have been) adjusted to.

Unionization need not be all bad for management. A few years ago, the Conference Board surveyed several companies that had recently been involved in successful organizing drives.[7] About forty percent saw some advantage to the company as a result of the unionization of their white-

7 Edward R. Curtin, *White-Collar Unionization*, Personnel Policy Study No. 220 (New York: The National Industrial Conference Board, Inc., 1970).

collar employees. Some of their comments are indicative:

> The presence of the union has made the company much more sensitive in the handling of employee relations matters.
>
> [It] forced us to formalize and administer properly a merit review program.
>
> We gained insight into a group of dissatisfied employees. . . .[8]

Improved worker morale may be the biggest benefit. The union helps employees regain the professional stature and pride that in recent decades were submerged beneath the corporate monolith. The individual union member does not have the freedom enjoyed by members of the learned professions in years past, but, by joining with his peers, he can once again participate meaningfully in decisions that affect his professional life. The result should be more productive, less dissatisfied employees.

CONCLUSIONS

We are dealing here with several rather fundamental assumptions:

1. The fraction of professionals who are employed by others will continue to grow.
2. In spite of similarities in educational backgrounds and mores, professional employees and those who employ them have inherently different viewpoints about many aspects of the job situation.
3. White-collar and professional employees will continue to be attracted to unions in ever-growing numbers.

There should be little disagreement with the first two points. As to the third, all trends point to the increasing organization of professionals. The most important factor is the growing size and impersonality of employing organizations. This will make the professional ever more remote from the center of decision making and will inevitably increase his frustrations. It is this professional malaise, rather than strictly monetary considerations, that in the long run will result in a union.

A progressive management will recognize that a unionization attempt at the very least indicates widespread employee discontent with existing conditions and that professional employees in particular desire a stronger voice in solving their problems. The union provides the employees with such a voice.

Should management be less than enlightened, then the union will at least fight to obtain for its members a greater measure of dignity and a larger share of the economic rewards.

---

[8] Curtin, *White-Collar Unionization*, p. 66.

28. PUBLIC EMPLOYEES: A SURVEY OF SOME CRITICAL PROBLEMS ON THE FRONTIER OF COLLECTIVE BARGAINING

CHARLES REDENIUS

The decade of the 60s saw the beginning of the shift in the thrust of the organization of labor from the private sector of the economy to the public sector. The 70s have seen an acceleration of that trend. The growth of public employee organization is even more dramatic when we contrast that growth with trends in union membership in the total labor force. Since 1960, membership in public employee organizations has more than doubled to almost 5 million. As of 1975, about one third of the public employee work force was organized.[1] By contrast, union membership as a proportion of the labor force has undergone a decline since 1953, falling from a little more than one fourth to a little over one fifth.[2]

Given the prospect of the continued growth of public employee collective bargaining, the public sector will soon provide more than enough newly organized workers to offset and even reverse the decline in union membership. Unless the organization of service workers in the private sector accelerates rapidly, and there is little evidence indicating the likelihood of such a development, this trend of rapid public employee organization will continue to be the frontier of collective bargaining.

Public employee bargaining has become so pervasive that hardly a week passes that we do not hear of, or read of, public employees engaging in collective bargaining or resorting to strike action when negotiations fail to produce a contract. Public employee unions range across the entire spectrum of governmental activities.[3] Whether we speak of the national government, state governments, local government, or special districts, especially school districts, the impact of public employee unionism is apparent even to the most casual observer. We can safely state that the continued growth of the public sector will be more than matched by the continued growth of public employee unions.

KEY DIFFERENCES

This continued growth will bring into sharper focus some of the key differences between collective bargaining patterns in the public sector as opposed to those in the private sector.[4] Let us briefly review a few of these differences. First, public employee bargaining differs from the private

Source: Reproduced from the September 1976 issue of the *Labor Law Journal*, published and copyrighted 1976 by Commerce Clearing House, Inc., 4025 W. Peterson Avenue, Chicago, Illinois, 60646.

[1] U.S. Department of Labor, Labor-Management Services Administration, *Summary of State Policy Regulations for Public Sector Labor Relations*, (Washington, D.C.: U.S. Government Printing Office, 1975), p. i. Hereafter cited as *Summary of State Policy*.

[2] U.S. Department of Labor, Bureau of Labor Statistics. *Handbook of Labor Statistics 1975—Reference Edition* (Washington, D.C.: U.S. Government Printing Office, 1975), p. 389, Table 158. The one fifth figure is for 1972, the last year reported.

[3] For federal employee unions see, U.S. Department of Labor, Labor-Management Services Administration, *Register of Federal Employee Unions* (Washington, D.C.: U.S. Government Printing Office, 1975). For state employee unions see, U.S. Department of Labor, Labor-Management Services Administration, *A Directory of Public Employee Organizations* (Washington, D.C.: U.S. Government Printing Office, 1974).

[4] The following sources provide some different perspectives on this subject: W. H. Holley, Jr., "Unique Complexities of Public Sector Labor Relations." *Personnel Journal* 55 (February 1976): 72–75; Louis V. Imundo, Jr., "Some Comparisons Between Public Sector and Private Sector Collective Bargaining," *Labor Law Journal* 24 (December 1973): 810–17; and Lee C. Shaw and R. Theodore Clark, Jr., "The Practical Differences Between Public and Private Sector Collective Bargaining," *UCLA Law Review* 19 (August 1972): 867–86.

sector in that public employees work for governmental units that almost always have a monopoly or near monopoly of the services in a community. The importance of this difference can readily be seen when we examine the effects of work stoppages by public employees on a community.

Let us cite some examples: governmental units provide, usually on an exclusive basis or nearly so, postal service, water and sewage disposal, elementary and secondary education, sanitation services, and police and fire protection. The disruption of these services is felt by every part of the service area. A coordinated work stoppage, although never attempted and highly unlikely, given the lack of public employee union integration, could quickly bring a community to its knees. Thus, the impact of a public employee strike is immeasurably heightened by the fact that there are usually no readily available and adequate alternatives to governmental services.

Second, certain governmental services are deemed "essential" to the well-being of the community. Fire and police protection, garbage collection, health care, and perhaps education are services that cannot be disrupted without severe consequences for the community as a whole. The more extreme opponents of public employee collective bargaining, and the strike action taken when such bargaining is unsuccessful, see a society on the brink of anarchy. Although it is dated, Calvin Coolidge's statement about the 1919 Boston police strike (while he was governor) "There is no right to strike against the public safety by anybody, anywhere, anytime," still commands wide support among legislators and judges. Indeed, 37 states prohibit public employee strikes by statute and/or case law.[5] It is difficult to argue that a strike in the private sector would have such disruptive consequences or provoke such a strong reaction by legislators and judges.

Third, most bargaining conflicts in the private sector are resolved without recourse to litigation and judicial intervention. This is often not the case with work stoppages by public employees. Most states, as noted above, have laws expressly denying public employees the right to strike. Such laws, of course, do not prevent strikes. When such strikes do occur, governmental officials in these states are tempted to resort to litigation rather than tackle the difficult process of negotiating a contract.

It is interesting to note that in certain respects the seeking of judicial intervention by public officials is a repetition of the early experiences of collective bargaining in the private sector. The end results is a dragging out of the collective bargaining process because judicial intervention can not come to grips with the issues in dispute nor can it produce a contract.[6] The most that can be hoped for by litigation is that public employees will be forced back to work. It will come as no surprise that public employees bitterly resent the issuance of an injunction just as an earlier generation of employees in the private sector resented such action.

There are still other characteristics shaping the environment of public employee collective bargaining that should be mentioned at this point. An important characteristic that is almost always ignored, or commented upon casually, is that public employees can best be characterized as service workers. In terms of labor force participation rates, public employees make up a negligible fraction of workers engaged in agriculture, commerce, and manufacturing.

The importance of this characteristic lies in the fact that the organization of public employees has been vastly more successful than the organization of service workers in

---

[5] *Summary of State Policy,* cited at note 1. See the heading "Strike Policy" under each state for particulars.

[6] The Wisconsin experience with judicial intervention is instructive. See my "Participant Attitudes Toward a Judicial Role in Public Employee Collective Bargaining," *Labor Law Journal* 25 (February 1974): 94–113.

the private sector. This fact has dual implications: Public employees are, as noted earlier, at the frontier of collective bargaining, and consequently the private sector will be emulating, in certain respects, the experience of public employees in their collective bargaining experiences, strategies, and outcomes rather than the other way around as it has been up till now. This seems especially important when we note another characteristic of bargaining in the public sector.

Both service sectors, the public and the private, are highly heterogeneous. Public employees, concentrating only on those already organized, have made their presence felt in virtually every area of governmental activity. This means there exist organizations at the federal level and the state and local levels covering virtually every type of public employee. Organizers of service workers in the private sector should be able to profit from examining the successes of these groups. The surface heterogeneity of the service sectors may be underlaid by some commonalities that would be revealed after a careful scrutiny of the experiences of successful organizations in both sectors.

A final characteristic of the public employee collective bargaining setting is the complexity of the legal environment. Employees and employers in the private sector, whether in agriculture, commerce, manufacturing, or service, and whether competing in a local, regional, or national market, come within the jurisdiction of either the National Labor Relations Act (Wagner Act) or the Railway Labor Act. Their legal environment, although it may be tedious in some respects and complex in still others, is a model of clarity and simplicity when we compare it with the multiplicity of laws confronting public officials and their employees who want to organize and bargain collectively.

Nor is this legal environment a fixed and unchanging one. In 1975, 17 of 20 state laws on labor relations dealt with the collective bargaining rights of public employees.[7] Thus, whereas the bargaining setting in the private sector is characterized by its relative simplicity, clarity, and stability, the bargaining environment of the public sector is characterized by complexity, lack of clarity, and change.

But even this does not fully state the case. In 23 of the states, public employee organizations operate either wholly or partially in the absence of protective legislation.[8] Without the benefit of such legislation or case law, public labor unions are at a severe disadvantage when compared with public employee organizations in states with public labor relations laws. Public officials cannot be legally compelled to bargain in good faith; a union cannot legally be designated as the exclusive representative of the employees for bargaining purposes; and the legal status of a collective bargaining **agreement** is even questionable. These are only some of the most important disadvantages. Yet, bargain they must, and the absence of a fixed legal environment coupled with their inexperience with collective bargaining are two of the most difficult obstacles that must be overcome.

THE CONSEQUENCES OF INEXPERIENCE

The rapid growth of collective bargaining in the public sector has brought to light the inexperience of both public officials and public employees in grappling with the problems of negotiating a contract, establishing a grievance procedure, and defining the new employer-employee relationship. Many public officials now expected to act as "management" have had little or no training in dealing with labor

7 Deborah T. Bond, "State Labor Legislation Enacted in 1975," *Monthly Labor Review* 99 (January 1976): 18.

8 *Summary of State Policy*, cited at note 1. See the headings, "Coverage," and "Authority and Date," under each state for particulars.

organizations. In the past they have been able to rely on civil service commissions,[9] personnel offices, or school administrators to handle most employer-employee matters. That is no longer the case in many instances.

The same is true for public employees. Until the last decade and a half, public employees were likely to be passive and docile employees. Exerting their influence through labor organizations is new to them, and they have not yet learned to identify those situations when it would better serve their interests to temper their emerging militance. Instead of dealing with their immediate supervisor, they are expected to bargain directly with public officials who are now seen as merely their employers.

Thus, collective bargaining has introduced some of the features of an adversarial relationship into a setting which heretofore had been, or could be, characterized as paternalistic or collegial. Indeed, in the field of higher education, one of the major objections to collective bargaining, pointed out by faculty and administration alike, is that it will destroy the collegial relationship and replace it with an adversarial one. There is no doubt collective bargaining is seen as an almost wholly negative development by advocates of this position. Despite this widely held view, 60 institutions of higher education opted for collective bargaining in the last year alone, bringing the total to 461.[10] The implication seems to be that one can champion the adversarial system in the courtroom but be quick to decry its supposedly corrosive effects elsewhere.

However, if we examine the collective bargaining situation more carefully, we might find that the higher level of tension between public officials and public employees could be traced to the inexperience of both parties, and the difficulties in adjusting to new relationships with one another. Such a dramatic change as the adoption of collective bargaining is certain to have an impact on behavior patterns and that impact may initially be an adverse one. But as the parties gain experience in negotiating contracts and resolving grievances, and in adjusting to their new relationships, most of the deleterious side effects initially attributed to the adversarial nature of collective bargaining may be considerably alleviated or disappear altogether.

That has certainly been the experience of collective bargaining in the private sector. The level of violence and abrasiveness which occurred during the early days of the organization of the automobile industry, for example, is not apparent today. Since that level has not been and is unlikely to be matched by public employee bargaining, the long-term diminution of the initial adverse experiences will be less dramatic but nonetheless markedly perceptible.

As the parties gain confidence in their abilities to negotiate contracts and resolve grievances, we are also quite likely to see a reduction in the number of disputes brought into the courts. Judicial intervention in public employee bargaining disputes can be viewed as an indicator of inexperience with collective bargaining and/ or a lack of confidence in one's abilities to resolve disputes without outside assistance. Those who have had experience with judicial intervention quickly learn that such intervention will not resolve the dispute, produce a contract, or even, in some instances, avert a work stoppage. Again the experience of the private sector is instructive. Most bargaining disputes are resolved without judicial intervention, or outside mediation of any kind. Indeed, the parties to such disputes resist outside assistance, preferring to resolve their disputes in their own way.

---

[9] The relationship between civil service and public employee bargaining is explored in Charles Feigenbaum, "Civil Service and Collective Bargaining: Conflict or Compatibility," *Public Personnel Management* 3 (May 1974): 244–52.

[10] Philip W. Semas, "Faculty Unions Add 60 Campuses in 1975–76 Academic Year," *Chronicle of Higher Education* 12 (May 31, 1976): 5.

Perhaps we ought not to recapitulate in the public sector the experiences of the private sector. Instead of gaining experience in a trial-by-error fashion, public employers and public employees could be taught the skills necessary to negotiate contracts and establish grievance procedures. The mere fact that we have such a broad range of disciplines dealing with labor relations in our schools and colleges indicates we believe such skills can be taught. The learning which would occur could only be put to the test in a real bargaining situation. If successful, the teaching of these skills would produce a healthier bargaining climate. The division of interest between employer and employee would be just as real and just as formidable, but the skills necessary to reconcile differences would reduce the amount of wasted energy and concentrate it on the issues in dispute.

An alternative to the academic teaching of these skills would be to institute training programs in collective bargaining.[11] At the state level, these programs could be coordinated by a public labor relations agency and should be open to state and local officials and public labor organization representatives. This type of program would have a dual benefit. It would equip both public officials and employee representatives with the skills necessary for collective bargaining. It would also, as a result of "management" and "labor" participation, create a greater awareness of the perspectives and problems each brings to the bargaining table. To restrict a training program to only public officials would seriously impair, if not defeat, the effectiveness of such an effort. Indeed, there do not seem to be sound reasons for excluding labor representatives from a training program of this nature.

---

[11] Such a program has been advocated for state and local public managers. See William D. Torrence, "Collective Bargaining and Labor Relations Training of State-Level Management," *Public Personnel Management* 2 (July 1973): 256–60. The national government operates a Labor Relations Training Center to meet this need at the federal level.

THE INEFFICACY OF THIRD PARTY INTERVENTION

However, before programs of this type can be implemented successfully, the state legislatures must be educated to write public employee bargaining laws that place strong incentives on voluntarism in collective bargaining and strong disincentives on reliance on involuntary third party intervention. The process of negotiating a labor contract is a difficult and complex one. If state legislatures enact statutes that obviate facing this difficult task directly, then we can expect employers and employees alike to seek an easy way out. Ultimately, however, a labor contract satisfactory to both parties can come about only through the willingness of those parties to engage in the give and take that is an inherent characteristic of the collective bargaining process. Intervention by a third party that thwarts, or even by its presence diminishes, this willingness can only prolong the process.

None of this is meant to imply that mediation, fact finding, and nonbinding recommendations are to be ruled out. Quite the contrary is the case. All these "tools" are useful in facilitating the collective bargaining process. Note: they facilitate. They cannot be substituted for that process.

Mediation can perform an invaluable service in certain instances where rancor between the parties or a breakdown in communication has either emotionally overheated or stalemated the bargaining process. In instances like these, mediation can bring *willing* parties together by *facilitating* the give and take which must occur. Fact finding can insure that both parties share a basic understanding of the issues in dispute. It can create channels of communication by establishing a common framework. As a result, fact finding can, in those instances, expedite the bargaining process.

Nonbinding recommendations can also play an invaluable role in bringing the parties in dispute together. The recommendations reveal how a third party would reconcile the differences. This gives the parties an opportunity to reassess their bargaining positions. Involuntary third party intervention, however, which attempts to *control* the bargaining process, by endeavoring to define the issues and then resolve them, can only result in an involuntary agreement which is unlikely to gain the support of either party if indeed the third party can force acceptance upon the disputants.

The involuntary impasse procedures which must be eschewed are binding abritration and judicial intervention.[12] Let us examine each of them in turn. Compulsory arbitration is often advocated as the "solution" to bargaining impasses. However even in states where compulsory arbitration is mandatory when bargaining breaks down, it is difficult to evaluate the results of arbitration.[13] Most statutory provisions are concerned more with preventing or ending work stoppages than they are with encouraging voluntarism in the bargaining process by the threat of an involuntary technique.

Thus, these procedures are likely to have an adverse effect rather than a positive one on the willingness of public officials to bargain in good faith. They realize, as well as the unions, that the strike weapon's effectiveness is considerably diminished when mandatory arbitration procedures can be invoked. On the other hand, a weak union can increase its bargaining leverage significantly if it can invoke arbitration.

The weakness, then, of binding arbitration is twofold. One, it is difficult to write a statutory procedure that does not affect the bargaining leverage which can be exerted by one or the other of the parties. The result is that such a procedure benefits one party and penalizes the other. Second, it often inhibits the bargaining process by diminishing incentives for voluntary negotiation in favor of reliance on a third party to issue a formal award. If access to arbitration is not strictly limited, voluntary agreements will undergo a marked decline.

Judicial intervention has been tried and found wanting in both private sector and public sector collective bargaining. The history of the private sector, with judicial intervention especially in the early days of collective bargaining, provides experiential evidence in support of this statement. Although certain segments of management might deny it, most would agree that the efficacy and efficiency of collective bargaining has gained as the result of the passage of the Norris-LaGuardia Act and the Wagner Act. The fact that labor and management in the private sector negotiate most of their collective bargaining contracts without the use of involuntary impasse resolution techniques indicates in a very important way their understanding of the best method of reaching agreement.

Even the federal executive branch recognizes the inefficacy of judicial intervention. The injunctive relief available under Taft-Hartley in private sector "national emergency" disputes is sought only when all else fails, including the threat to invoke its provisions. Binding arbitration and other involuntary impasse resolution techniques are used only as a last resort. Thus, when involuntary techniques are utilized, it means failure in some respect.

---

12 For other views on impasse procedures see Thomas P. Gilroy and Anthony V. Sinicropi, "Impasse Resolution in Public Employment. A Current Assessment," *Industrial and Labor Relations Review* 25 (July 1972): 496–511; Joseph R. Grodin, "Arbitration of Public Sector Labor Disputes: The Nevada Experiment," *Industrial and Labor Relations Review* 28 (October 1974): 89–102; and Richard P. McLaughlin, "Collective Bargaining Suggestions for the Public Sector," *Labor Law Journal* 20 (March 1969): 131–37; Paul D. Staudohar, "Some Implications of Mediation for Resolution of Bargaining Impasses in Public Employment" *Public Personnel Management* 2 (July 1973): 299–304; and William R. Word, "Toward More Negotiations in the Public Sector," *Public Personnel Management* 2 (September 1973): 345–50.

13 Grodin, "Arbitration of Public Sector Labor Disputes," pp. 92–94.

MEAGER SUCCESS

Likewise, the limited history of bargaining in the public sector also supports the nonutility of judicial intervention. It can force public employees back to work in most instances, but judicial intervention has had meager success in producing any other positive results. This can be traced, not only to its inappropriateness in the bargaining situation, but also to the character of the instruments which the judiciary can wield. The injunction can stop a strike, but it does so at the expense of fostering bitterness on the part of employees who are forced to work without a contract. Nor does the injunction compel the public employer to bargain in good faith. With the employees back on the job, the pressure to negotiate is considerably diminished if not altogether absent.

If public employees resist a back to work order, the judge can punish such resistance summarily by use of the contempt power. Normally this takes the form of heavy fines for the union, and possible imprisonment of union leaders. Since union leaders and their attorneys rarely seek injunctions, nor do statutes usually provide for such a step by public employees, judicial intervention is weighted in favor of public employers. Seldom, if ever, is an injunction issued against a public employer. Consequently, they are not often, if ever, faced with the threat of fines and/or imprisonment.

The widespread disaffection among labor and management in both the public and private sectors with involuntary techniques for resolving collective bargaining disputes indicates that such techniques do not enjoy a preferred position in their hierarchy of values. Thus, a general rule against involuntary third party intervention either in the form of binding arbitration or judicial intervention can be persuasively argued. It cannot force unwilling parties to bargain. It cannot remove either the difficulty or complexity inherent in the bargaining process. It cannot resolve the issues in dispute. It cannot effectively forge an agreement which will receive the support of the parties to the dispute.

The use of involuntary procedures, then, appeals not to the parties to bargaining disputes but rather to legislators, judges, and labor relations scholars.[14] State legislators in particular seem to be attracted to involuntary impasse resolution techniques when writing public labor relations laws. These techniques are often coupled with a ban on strikes by public employees.[15] When we contrast such laws with laws governing collective bargaining in the private sector, the difference is glaring.

The theoretical grounds for the differences between labor laws governing the public sector versus labor laws governing the private sector are usually attributed to the character of public employment.[16] However, the actual differences between bargaining in the private sector versus bargaining in the public sector are very often more differences in degree than differences in kind.

The differences are great enough to justify separate labor laws, but both should be characterized by voluntarism and any departure from that norm should be subjected to careful analysis. With the exception of "essential" services, there do not

---

14 The literature on involuntary impasse procedures far outweighs that of articles concerned with voluntary collective bargaining models. The materials cited in footnote 12 could easily be doubled or tripled. There is a surprising paucity of research exploring collective bargaining models given the norm of voluntarism that characterizes labor relations in both the public and private sectors.

15 The Connecticut public labor relations law is a good example.

16 One of the theoretical grounds for differentiating public employment from private employment is the concept of state sovereignty. For an elucidation of the ramifications of this concept see Abraham L. Gitlow, "Public Employee Unionism in the United States: Growth and Outlook," *Labor Law Journal* 21 (December 1970): 766–78; and Anne M. Ross, "Public Employee Unions and the Right to Strike," *Monthly Labor Review* 92 (March 1969): 14–18.

seem to be adequate grounds for discriminating against public employees by insisting on involuntary procedures not imposed on private sector collective bargaining.

Thus, a necessary element in the improvement of the environment for public employee bargaining must be laws that rule out involuntary third party intervention in bargaining disputes except when "essential" services have been disrupted by a work stoppage. The definition of "essential" services and what would constitute an acceptable minimum level of such services should be carefully spelled out to insure the integrity of such laws. To insure their evenhandedness, these laws should attempt to create a comprehensive framework for public employee bargaining, one that matches, insofar as possible, the voluntarism of the bargaining framework established for the private sector.

IMPACT OF POLITICAL CONSIDERATIONS

Public labor laws are written in an environment quite different from that for labor law governing the private sector. State legislators are responding to a different set of pressures and the "clients" of such laws are employees of the state. This means decision making in regard to public labor laws is more likely to be dominated by political considerations than economic considerations or questions concerning the nature of collective bargaining.[17] Since legislators always have one eye on the next election, they will be slow to write laws which they think might jeopardize their chances of reelection. Permitting public employees to strike, or more accurately not placing a prohibition on work stoppages, would seem

to imply that legislators were condoning the disruption of governmental services.

Let us cite just one example. Education is a core value to most middleclass Americans. If legislators do not ban teacher strikes, they might be perceived as allowing teachers to do great damage to the education of our children by disrupting the learning process. It is not surprising to learn that many states ban teacher strikes. As noted earlier, the trouble with such bans is they do not prevent strikes and they usually encourage school boards to seek judicial intervention which cannot resolve bargaining disputes. However, the real damage done in these instances is that such bans encourage disrespect for the law. The other impasse resolution route, requiring arbitration in teacher disputes, has nearly as many pitfalls for school boards and teachers alike. Indeed, school boards are as likely to reject arbitration as unions.

The appeal of judicial intervention or binding arbitration, in public employee disputes, then, is more clearly due to political considerations than it is to economic factors, or to the insufficiencies and/or inadequacies of collective bargaining. Until such time as public employee unions are able to effectively counter such political considerations with pressure of their own, state legislators will continue to respond to what they perceive as most threatening to their continuance in office.

Public officials must bargain, not only in the context of this politicized legal environment, but also within the constraints of allowable budgets and tax revenues.[18] These constraints are much more severe at the state and local level given the nature of the property tax, sales tax, and the narrow limits of the income tax. By contrast, the federal sector has access to revenues which are much more elastic. In fact,

[17] For two different perspectives on the impact of political considerations see Thomas M. Love, and George T. Sulzer, "Political Implications of Public Employee Bargaining" *Industrial Relations* 11 (February 1972): 18–33; and Clyde W. Summers, "Public Employee Bargaining: A Poiltical Perspective," *Yale Law Journal* 83 (May 1974): 1156–2000.

[18] For a case study see Milton Derber, Ken Jennings, Ian McAndrew, and Martin Wagner, "Bargaining and Budget Making in Illinois Public Institutions," *Industrial and Labor Relations Review* 27 (October 1973): 49–62.

if the federal government did not return a large fraction of the revenue it collects to to the states, state governments would be unable to function without some drastic modifications in their access to resources.[19]

The impact on state programs of these constraints is also immediate. Given limited resources, what is allocated to wage increases, cannot be allocated for implementing or expanding programs. This is particularly the case in education. In an era of scarce resources, increases in teacher salaries will have an impact on the curriculum. That impact, unfortunately, will largely be a negative one. Special services such as counseling, individual tutoring, and secretarial assistance will be cut back. Special enrichment programs including music appreciation, the arts, and extracurricular activities are also likely to suffer. It is easy to appreciate the manifold problems faced by school boards in their collective bargaining efforts. Perhaps the most disturbing fact about these problems is that they lie outside the decision-making capacity of the public officials most directly affected.

The collective bargaining setting for public employees is thus hedged with difficulties from a number of directions. Public labor relations laws which are the result of political considerations, economic constraints which are largely outside the control of public officials, and increasing taxpayer resistance are just some of the more important problems. The private sector is not confronted by these types of difficulties. They may argue that their problems are just as formidable, but surely the problems they face are different in kind. In coming to grips with these difficulties, the experiences of the private sector will be of little utility. Once again we see the meaning of being on the frontier of collective bargaining.

_____

[19] The fraction for 1973–74 was 17.5 percent. See U.S. Department of Commerce, Bureau of the Census, "Governmental Finances and Employment at a Glance," (Washington, D.C.: Subscriber Services Section (Publications), January 1976), p. 1.

Without the experience of the private sector to rely on, the short-range future is unlikely to be an unclouded one. Public employee collective bargaining will be breaking new ground and that experience will shape the bargaining process and its outcomes as surely as the industrial union experience was different from the craft union experience. Each type of union shaped the bargaining process in its own way, and each process led to different outcomes.

To improve the bargaining process for public employees will require further modifications in the legal environment, perhaps greater local control over economic constraints, and tax revenues derived from greater reliance on income rather than property or sales. This last will distribute the tax more equitably.

CONCLUSION

The continuing growth of the public sector and the accompanying surge of public employee organization increases the need for a comprehensive effort to reconcile the rights of public employees to bargain collectively with the safeguarding of the public well-being. Since the American political system at both the federal and state levels responds to problems with incremental adjustments, we can expect this task to occupy legislators for some time to come. Most state public labor laws now on the books have nearly all of the features—secret elections, provisions for exclusive representation, enumeration of unfair labor practices, impasse resolution techniques quite often coupled with a ban on strikes, and labor relations agencies—which have been touted as necessary to the collective bargaining environment.

Despite these laws, public employee bargaining still suffers from some major deficiencies. The absence of public labor relations laws in other states represents an opportunity to write laws that would correct these deficiencies. However, what is needed is a comprehensive national framework for public employee collective bargaining to parallel the Wagner Act and the Railway Labor Act. Such a federal law would insure some minimal level of uniformity rather than the existing patchwork of state laws.

This development, unfortunately, is unlikely given the recent Supreme Court decision in *National League of Cities* v. *Usery*,[20] which invalidated federal wage-and-hour regulations for state employees. This decision would seem to virtually rule out a federal law granting collective bargaining rights to all public employees at the state and local levels regardless of whether there was pertinent state law or not. Thus the effort to overcome the deficiencies of the public employee collective bargaining environment must be concentrated on the state level, especially in those states without public labor relations laws.

These laws must more carefully take into account the key differences between bargaining in the public sector versus bargaining in the private sector. The accommodation of these differences is essential to the definition of the collective bargaining rights of public employees. In this way these rights can be reconciled with the safeguarding of the community's well-being.

Second, state laws should include provisions for instituting training programs in collective bargaining practices which would be open to both public "managers" and public labor representatives. These workshop programs would temper the inexperience of both managers and union officials while at the same time acquainting them with each other's perspective.

Next, public labor relations laws should foster voluntarism in collective bargaining insofar as possible. Public employees must be able to perceive themselves as being on an equal footing with their counterparts in the private sector. This means that utilization of involuntary impasse resolution techniques must be ruled out except under carefully prescribed conditions such as the failure to maintain a clearly defined minimum level of an "essential" service.

Finally, legislators and the public alike have to begin to recognize the legitimate claims of public employees. This would seem to be the only way legislators will be able to write public labor relations laws which are not largely the result of political considerations. Legislators may be unwilling to take such political risks and the public is certainly averse to higher taxes. But unless these steps are taken public employees will continue to be treated inequitably.

If the states can avail themselves of this opportunity to take a comprehensive look at public employee collective bargaining, they will demonstrate the vitality of the federal system as a laboratory for the resolution of social problems of the first order.

---

[20] 44 *U.S. Law Week* 4974 (June 22, 1976); (S Ct 1976) 12 EPD ¶ 10,996.

10

SAFETY AND HEALTH

ACCIDENTS AND THEIR CAUSES

An accident is typically defined as the occurrence of physical damage. This broad definition implies that accidents involve damage to both human and nonhuman objects, both at and away from work. Our concern here is with the causes and reduction of those accidents that are *work related* and involve human illness or injury.

In general, we know relatively little about accident causes. There are, however, three major possibilities—*bad luck or chance, characteristics of employees,* and *characteristics of the work environment.* Many people feel that bad luck or chance is the primary cause of accidents. Thus, it is chance that determines whether or not an accident will occur and which individuals will suffer the illness or injury. Undoubtedly, chance plays a role in the *occurrence* of accidents. But, to say that chance *causes* accidents does not seem warranted. Rather, accidents are better thought of as being caused by characteristics of employees and/or the work environment. Then if the specific employee and environment characteristics can be identified, steps can be taken to control or reduce accidents.

Employees may cause accidents if they engage in accident behavior. *Accident behavior* is defined as unsafe behavior that *might result* in an accident. It can occur without an accident happening; for example, an employee who drops a heavy object may not be injured or injure anyone else. On the other hand, it seems likely that most accidents involve some degree of accident behavior. An example of an exception to this would be accidents due purely to mechanical or equipment failure.

There are many studies that have looked at the relationship between specific employee characteristics and accident behavior or accidents. The variables include such things as age, length of service, vision, eye-hand coordination, and willingness to take risk. Unfortunately, a solid consistent pattern of evidence does not seem to emerge from these studies.

Part of the reason for this lack of consistency results from problems of measuring accident behavior and accidents. If accident behavior is to be predictable, it must be stable. That is, each employee's accident behavior must remain consistent over time, whether it is at a high, medium, or low level. To the extent it is not consistent, it is difficult to predict. In addition, many studies use such measures as "number of accidents involved in" as a substitute for measures of accident behavior because the latter are difficult to obtain. Number of accidents may be a poor substitute because, as we pointed out, the number of accidents employees experience may not be that strongly related to the number of accident behaviors they engage in.

An organization will usually find interdepartmental differences and sometimes very large differences in accident rates. Such differences suggest that characteristics of the work environment are causing accidents (assuming that employee accident behavior does not systematically differ among jobs or departments). It would obviously be desirable to be able to identify the characteristics of the work environment that are responsible for the differences in accident rates. Again, our limited knowledge requires that we be somewhat speculative about the probable causal variables. Included in this list would be such things as machine and work tool design, temperature and noise levels, exposure to toxic materials, and chemical agents, work methods and flows, and housekeeping practices. Complicating things even more is the possibility that combinations of these variables have an impact on accidents in specific situations.

REDUCING ACCIDENTS

How we attempt to reduce accidents obviously depends first of all on what we know (or assume) to be their causes. It also depends on what we know (or assume) to be the relative importance of the causes. If the greatest percentage of accidents is due to employee characteristics, then other things equal, this is where to focus our efforts in reducing accidents.

Approaching accident reduction through employee characteristics may involve both selection and training programs. In selection, the concern is with identifying those applicants most (and least) likely to experience accidents or engage in accident behavior. This would require that the organization conduct validation studies to determine which predictors (for example, age, vision) are related to accidents and accident behaviors (see Chapter 5). Here, the previously mentioned problems of measuring accidents and accident behaviors would surface.

The training approach would involve attempting to change employee characteristics that cause accidents and accident behaviors (for example, failure to follow standard work procedures). As with any training program, the major concerns would be designing a program that will facilitate learning of how to reduce accidents during training and taking steps to ensure that the learning will be maintained back on the job (see Chapter 7).

The work environment approach to accident reduction frequently involves efforts to reduce or eliminate specific hazards and unsafe environmental characteristics, build safer tools and machines, and provide protective equipment to employees. These are the types of activities that one would observe in a typical organizational safety program.

Further impetus for accident reduction through the creation of safer work environments is provided by the *Occupational Safety and Health Act* (OSHA) of 1970, which applies to all private employers whose business affects interstate commerce. OSHA is aimed at (a) the establishment of mandatory safety standards, and (b) enforcing compliance through a system of inspections and penalties (fines and jail sentences) for failure to meet standards. OSHA is administered by the Occupational Safety and Health Administration within the U.S. Department of Labor, which has the responsibility for both establishing and enforcing the standards.

It is important to recognize that OSHA requires the *employer* to be knowledgeable about, and to comply with, the safety standards. That is, OSHA generally does not attempt to reduce the accident behaviors of *employees* or to make them responsible for these behaviors. The ultimate effectiveness of OSHA in reducing accidents thus will be limited by two things. First, it will be limited by our ability to identify the true work environment causes of accidents and establish appropriate standards. Second, to the extent that accidents are caused by characteristics of employees, OSHA will have little, if any, impact on accident reduction.

OSHA is by no means the only piece of legislation concerned with job safety and health. There is considerably more legislation at both the federal and state level that is similar in principle to OSHA in that it seeks to prevent accidents through the establishment and enforcement of safety standards.

Also, special mention should be made of another important type of legislation—*workmen's compensation* (WC) laws found in all 50 states. WC is basically an insurance system whose purpose is to provide financial benefits to employees if they should suffer a work-related illness or injury. WC laws are primarily designed to protect employees from the economic hardships of accidents, rather than to prevent accidents.

Accident prevention is considered in the *experience rating* feature of WC laws. WC benefits are financed by employers through the purchase of insurance premiums. In states with experience rating, the size of the premium depends on a rating of the employer's accident experience. The more favorable the experience, the lower the premium. Experience rating is designed to provide employers with an economic incentive to undertake accident reduction programs. The effectiveness of experience rating in achieving this objective, however, has long been a matter of controversy.

INTRODUCTION TO READINGS

OSHA: Problems and Prospects

A review of the major provisions of OSHA, some of its general impacts on organizations, and examples of specific impacts on retail organizations are provided in the article by Joseph Barry Mason. He begins by citing numerous accident statistics regarding frequency and cost on a national basis. These statistics indicate that the toll from accidents is a staggering one, and they go a long way in explaining why federal legislation in the form of OSHA was felt necessary.

Mason then proceeds to present the major provisions of OSHA, which are too numerous to summarize here. They pertain to employer coverage and responsibility, federal agencies created, recordkeeping requirements, types of safety standards, inspection for compliance with standards, and penalties for noncompliance.

The extensiveness of OSHA would suggest that OSHA's impacts on organizations are considerable, and Mason's discussion aptly illustrates that this is indeed the case. Mason suggests some general impacts on corporate strategy in the areas of purchasing, small businesses, labor-management relations, and public relations. In regard to purchasing, for example, these impacts include such things as contract provisions with suppliers and subcontractors, employer responsibilities when suppliers and contractors are on the employer's premises, and the leasing of equipment.

Perhaps a more graphic illustration of OSHA's impact is contained in Mason's discussion of what OSHA means to retail organizations. He provides long, detailed checklists of the specific things a retail organization would have to do in order to be in compliance with the relevant safety standards. Estimates of the costs of compliance are also given.

Numerous times in his article, Mason touches upon an issue discussed earlier. Namely, to what extent are accidents caused by characteristics of employees as opposed to characteristics of the work environment? He notes, as we did, that under OSHA, employers have responsibility for providing a safe and healthy work environment, but employees have no corresponding responsibility to reduce accident behavior. Mason also cites some sources who claim that employee characteristics play a much larger role in accidents than work environment characteristics. Given our lack of knowledge about accident causes, it would seem wise not to take such claims too seriously. They do point out, however, a major controversy that is likely to continue for years to come. Moreover, we should recognize that OSHA alone, even if skillfully administered, will not eliminate accidents.

OSHA: The Problem of Penalties and Compliance

The mere fact that there are specific standards and penalties for noncompliance with the standards under OSHA does not necessarily guarantee employer compliance with those standards. This point is cogently made and illustrated in the article by Darold Barnum and John Gleason.

They argue that the employer's decision to comply or not to comply with a safety standard can be treated as an investment decision. In particular the compliance decision depends on an estimate of the expected cost (fine) of a violation relative to the opportunity cost of compliance (the money that could be invested in something else, rather than being used to correct a violation). If the expected fine is less than the opportunity cost of compliance, then the employer has little economic incentive to correct the violation.

Barnum and Gleason then go on to use actual compliance data from OSHA records to determine the expected cost of a violation. Their computations indicate that the expected cost is so low ($1.82) that there is, in fact, little economic incentive for employers to correct violations of standards. Using this same approach, they conclude by suggesting ways of increasing the expected cost of a violation in order to increase employer compliance with standards.

Safety, Health, and the Older Worker

Older workers often face tremendous problems in obtaining jobs. Much of this is due to the assumption by employers that the performance of older workers will be less than that of younger workers because of declining health. It is also frequently believed that problems of safety will be greater for older workers, resulting in such things as higher accident rates and higher insurance premiums for medical insurance and Workmen's Compensation.

The article by Mary Youry describes a pilot program (called GULHEMP) that has been designed to assist older workers and employers in overcoming these traditional barriers. The program is based on the assumption that chronological age itself is not a good indicator of ability to perform effectively and safely on the job. Instead, the abilities of people and the abilities required by the job should be directly assessed. In turn, individuals can be matched to jobs for which their abilities are suitable.

There are two basic features of the GULHEMP program. The first is a very thorough physical examination of the individual to determine physical abilities and what the individual can do. The second is a very thorough job analysis to determine the physical ability requirements and environmental factors of the jobs. During job analysis, possible changes in the job itself to make it more compatible with older workers' abilities are also noted. The ability profiles of the individual and the job(s) are then compared to determine the best match. All in all, the program seems to be quite effective and perhaps we will see more like it in the future.

29. OSHA: PROBLEMS AND PROSPECTS
JOSEPH BARRY MASON

The Williams and Steiger Occupational Safety and Health Act (OSHA) became law in 1970. The act now covers some 60 million workers and 5 million work places.[1] As such, it probably has more impact on the American worker than any legislation since the Wagner Act of 1935.

The need for such legislation was clear.

Between 1969 and 1973 more persons were killed at work than in the Vietnam war. Further, 2.2 million persons are disabled on the job each year, with a resulting loss of 240 million man-days of work, a loss much greater than that caused by strike.[2] The National Safety Council has estimated that the cost of wage losses, insurance costs, medical expenses, and related costs such as time spent investigating and reporting accidents

Source: © by the Regents of the University of California. Reprinted from *California Management Review* vol. 19, no. 1, pp. 21–28, by permission of the Regents.

[1] Lawrence P. Ettkin and J. Brad Chapman, "Is OSHA Effective in Reducing Industrial Injuries?" *Labor Law Journal*, April 1975, p. 236.

[2] House Committee on Education and Labor, Occupational Safety and Health Act, RH #91–1291, 91st Congress, Second Session, 1970.

exceed $3.9 billion annually.[3] Cost to employers for workmen's compensation coverage as a part of the insurance cost is more than $4.8 billion.[4]

Even ignoring human pain and suffering, the economic costs of job-related accidents are astounding. Equally disturbing is the fact that from 1958 to 1970 the accident frequency rate increased more than 33 percent.[5] It was against this background of tragedy and economic loss that the Occupational Safety and Health Act was passed.

Currently, inspections are increasing in all types of businesses. For example, it was recently stated that "Retail inspections, like OSHA inspections in general, are on the upswing . . . there were 2,228 July-November last year [1974] versus 1,209 in the same 1973 period."[6] January 1975 inspection data for retailing showed that 875 inspections were made in establishments employing over 42,000 persons. Only 12 percent of the firms inspected were found in compliance with safety regulations; more than 3,400 violations were found.[7]

This article reviews the key provisions of the Occupational Safety and Health Act, presents an overview of the emerging problems and controversies since the passage of OSHA, and offers guidelines in addressing the problem of job-related safety.

AN OVERVIEW OF THE OCCUPATIONAL SAFETY AND HEALTH ACT[8]

Employee Coverage. OSHA covers all employers whose business affects interstate commerce.[9] The only employees exempted are those employed by federal, state, and local governments, and special provisions also have been made for them. The size of the business is irrelevant. For example, OSHA officials have said of the small business proprietor, "We appreciate it is more difficult for him to comply, but if we find violations, he will be cited. Ignorance, as in common law, is no defense with OSHA."[10] Employers who are already subject to the standards established by another federal agency are not covered by the act if the other agency continues its duty of enforcement.

OSHA Standards. The act provides for four kinds of standards. These are (1) interim standards, put into effect as soon as it is practical and based on already existing federal guidelines; (2) consensus standards, which are developed after obtaining the views of interested parties and which are typically those established by various trade associations;[11] (3) permanent standards that would replace or supplement interim standards if the interim standards are determined not to be in the best interest of employees' safety; and (4) temporary emergency standards, which can be issued quickly when a finding suggests that employees are exposed to a serious hazard.

In response to its congressional mandate, OSHA has established five priority areas for inspection.[12] The first priority is situations that pose an immediate danger to the health or safety of workers. The second priority is where a fatality has occurred. The third

[3] U.S. Department of Labor, *Job Safety and Health*, Number 1 (Washington, D.C.: U.S. Government Printing Office, November–December 1972), p. 32.

[4] U.S. Department of Labor, *The President's Report on Occupational Safety and Health* (Washington, D.C.: U.S. Government Printing Office, May 1972), p. 1.

[5] Don Cordtz, "Safety on the Job Becomes a Major Job for Management," *Fortune*, November 1972, p. 113.

[6] "OSHA Chief Doesn't See It the Way Chains Do," *Chain Store Age Executive*, April 1975, p. 17.

[7] Ibid.

[8] For more detailed information, see Marjorie

Gross, "The Occupational Safety and Health Act: Much Ado about Something," *Loyola of Chicago Law Journal*, 1972, p. 247; and Horneberger, "Occupational Safety and Health Act," *Cleveland State Law Journal*, 1972.

[9] Stephen R. Kirklin, "OSHA: Employer Beware," *Houston Law Review*, November 1973, p. 429

[10] "The Book on OSHA Rules: Do It Anyway," *Iron Age*, October 19, 1972, p. 17.

[11] "OSHA: A Worthwhile Law with Several Uncorrected Faults," *Industry Week*, October 14, 1974, p. 21.

[12] William A. Steiger, "OSHA: Four Years Later," *Labor Law Journal*, December 1974, p. 726.

priority is an inspection based upon a valid employee complaint. The fourth priority consists of target industry and target health hazards. The last category is a general inspection of all industries.

New Agencies Created. OSHA was responsible for the creation of three new federal agencies: the Occupational Safety and Health Administration within the U.S. Department of Labor; the National Institute of Occupational Safety and Health in the Department of Health, Education and Welfare; and the Occupational Safety and Health Review Commission, an independent agency of the Executive Branch.[13]

The Occupational Safety and Health Administration is given the authority to develop standards, conduct inspections, determine compliance with the standards, and initiate enforcement actions against employers who they believe are not in compliance. The National Institute of Occupational Safety and Health (NIOSH) performs research, training, and educational programs in occupational safety and health. Its most important contribution is the recommendation of new standards. The Occupational Safety and Health Review Commission adjudicates enforcement actions of the Department of Labor when they are contested by employers, employees, or unions. The Occupational Safety and Health Administration only proposes penalties. The Review Commission has the sole authority for assessing penalties.

Employer Penalties. The responsibility of the OSHA inspector is to determine that an establishment is in compliance with the appropriate standards. If a violation is noted, it is reported to the OSHA area director, who then proposes a violation and informs the employer of the proposed penalty. If the employer disagrees with the citation or the proposed penalty he may contest it by advising the Labor Department within 15 working days of the citation.

When notification is received that an action is being contested, the Review Commission is notified and the adjudicatory process begins. The commission assigns the hearing to an administrative law judge. The hearing typically occurs in the community where the alleged violation took place or as close to the community as possible. It is the responsibility of OSHA to prove that the violation has occurred. Following the hearing, the judge may issue an order to affirm, modify, or vacate the citation or proposed penalty. The order is final after 30 days unless the commission reviews the decision. If an employer decides not to contest the citation, he must correct the situation that is in violation of the standards. If he cannot do so within the proposed abatement period, he can seek an extension.

Penalties provided by the act include fines up to:

- $10,000 for each violation by any employer who willfully or repeatedly violates the obligations of the act, or regulations, standard, rule, or order issued in connection with it.

- $1,000 upon employers receiving a citation for a violation, serious or otherwise.

- $1,000 a day upon an employer who fails to correct, within the time permitted for correction (or after review proceedings for a contested order), a violation for which a citation has been issued.

- $10,000, or imprisonment for not more than six months ($20,000 and one year for a second offense), upon an employer who willfully violates any standard, rule, or order, or regulations prescribed, if such violation causes death to any employee.

- $1,000 or up to six months imprisonment for any person giving advance notice of any inspection.

- $10,000 or up to six months imprisonment, or both, for knowingly making a

---

13 Robert D. Moran, "How to Obtain Job Safety Justice," *Labor Law Journal*, July 1973, pp. 387–88.

false statement, representation, or certification.

$1,000 for each violation upon an employer who violates any of the posting requirements.[14]

Types of Regulations. There are two basic types of OSHA regulations: horizontal regulations, which apply to all industries and relate to such features as fire extinguishers, electrical groundings, and machine guards; and vertical provisions, which apply to particular industry groups such as construction.[15]

The various OSHA regulations typically call for minimum safety and health precautions. Ordinarily these are consensus standards that have been derived from previous legislation developed by such organizations as the National Fire Protection Association or the American National Standards Institute. Consensus standards traditionally have been benchmarks against which an employer could measure his company's performance. None of the consensus standards was initially designed with the idea that they would become legislative minimums to which an employer must conform. One writer said:

Business took the position that we already live by consensus standards so let's write them into the act. But the fact is that they have never read them nor has anyone else who was involved in this legislative process.[16]

Employer Responsibility. Responsibilities for OSHA violations reside almost entirely with the employer. As has been stated:

Congress has required the employer to be responsible for every unsafe working condition. For example, the employee can perform an un-

safe act, against the direct order of the employer, and the employer will be liable under workmen's compensation laws in some states, as well as under OSHA. . . . An employee deliberately could create an unsafe or hazardous condition, report it, and the employer specifically is barred from discriminating against the employee under the act.[17]

Thus, no incentive exists for employees to follow OSHA's standards except for their innate concern for their own safety. Significantly, the National Safety Council estimates that 75 to 85 percent of industrial accidents are caused by persons who lack "safety consciousness."[18]

Requirements for Recordkeeping. Three forms of records are required: a log of occupational injuries and illnesses, a supplemental record, and a summary record. These records remain at the place of business and must be made available for examination by federal or state safety inspectors. An occupational injury or illness must be logged within six working days after the notification, and any lost workdays should be recorded. With appropriate summaries, the logs will indicate what occupations or departments are incurring injuries or illnesses and show the areas to be checked during safety inspections.

The act also requires that the records be located at the lowest possible organizational level. This is necessary to provide records for safety inspectors as close as possible to the point of operations. This also prevents pooling of information so that high-frequency injuries are not averaged with statistics from other areas where safety problems are minimal.[19] The only instances in which records are not needed are minor injuries requiring only first aid treatment. OSHA defines first aid as "One-time treat-

---

14 Edward J. Kehoe, "The Federal Occupational Safety and Health Act: Its Impact on Management, Safety, and Public Relations," *Public Relations Journal,* August, 1972, p. 25.

15 Fred K. Foulkes, "Learning to Live with OSHA," *Harvard Business Review,* November–December 1973, p. 60.

16 "OSHA: A Worthwhile Law with Several Uncorrected Faults," *Industry Week,* October 14, 1974, p. 21.

17 Ronald L. Tatham and James H. Coogan, "OSHA: Anticipating Problems Between Purchasing Manager and Supplier," *Journal of Purchasing,* November 1973, p. 63.

18 Foulkes, op. cit., p. 62.

19 "How the Safety Act Affects Banks," *Banking* May 1972, p. 61.

ment and subsequent observation of minor scratches, cuts, burns, splinters, and so forth which do not normally require medical care."

For firms with branches, it is a sound idea to keep separate records for each of the various branches. This enables inspection to occur at the lowest possible level and as near as possible to the site of the occurrence.

IMPACTS ON OVERALL CORPORATE STRATEGY

Impact on Purchasing. One writer has stated that "The purchasing triangle of quality, delivery and price may well be enlarged to a rectangle of quality, delivery, price and safety."[20] The purchasing agent as the company's primary interface with suppliers must be familiar with the provisions of the act and with its still-evolving standards so that he can insure that products purchased meet the requirements of OSHA.

The act clearly makes each employer responsible for the safety and welfare of his employees. However, less clarity exists as to how the actions of suppliers, customers, and independent contractors affect his duty as an employer. Emerging areas of concern include: A buyer's responsibility to insure supplier compliance with the act, legal exposure to a buyer in the event a supplier fails to comply, a buyer's legal recourse against a supplier who fails to comply, and a buyer's responsibility when suppliers, customers and independent contractors come on the buyer's premises.[21] A buyer is not prohibited from dealing with a supplier who violates the act, nor is he required to obtain assurances from a supplier that he is complying with all appropriate provisions of the act. Thus, as a buyer he is not legally required to refer to or incorporate the act as part of his purchase order.

For a variety of reasons, however, it is desirable for a buyer to refer to the act in contracts with suppliers.[22] For example, a buyer may wish to protect himself against a situation where a supplier is temporarily prohibited by a court order from continuing production of an item until the safety hazard is corrected. Thus, the purchasing agent would find it desirable to structure a contract so that the supplier assumes the risk for a work stoppage and delay in delivery which results from his violation of OSHA regulations.

Buyers also find it to their advantage to insist that goods purchased comply with OSHA standards and regulations. Many suppliers, however, are reluctant to guarantee in broad terms that their products meet OSHA standards. Consequently, some buyers are solving this problem by knowing the OSHA requirements and including these requirements as part of the specifications for purchase. A failure to meet the requirements would be a breach of contract.

Another area of concern is the responsibility of a subcontractor or subsupplier when on the premises of the buyer. An employer may incur liability under OSHA if he allows employees to be exposed to any hazardous conditions which may be created by a subcontractor. A buyer thus would want to have a written statement that whenever a subcontractor is on the premises all activities conducted by him are in accordance with OSHA.

The final area in which a buyer may have additional responsibility is in the leasing of equipment. Appropriate language probably should be included in a lease agreement to insure that equipment and machinery are properly "guarded," as specified in OSHA standards. Overall, buyers increasingly are seeking the broadest possible contractual coverage regarding possible OSHA requirements when dealing with suppliers.

---

[20] "Purchasing—OSHA's Man in the Middle," *Purchasing*, February 6, 1973, p. 37.

[21] John D. Jackson, "Let the Standards Do the Talking," *Purchasing*, February 6, 1973, p. 47.

[22] Ibid.

It appears that the risks involved will be passed on by most firms in the form of negotiated express warranties or insurance against the risk of OSHA enforcement. As has been stated, "In both situations the cost eventually will be borne by the consumer, who ultimately must pay for the safe environment of production as an added cost of consumer goods."[23]

Financial Impact on Small Businesses. Various legislative amendments have been offered to exempt small businesses from OSHA requirements. This probably is not in the public interest, however. Approximately 30 percent of the nation's work force is in businesses with fewer than 25 employees, and these small businesses have the highest injury rates.[24] Also, if small businesses such as subcontractors were exempted from the act, unsafe practices by their employees could cause unnecessary risks for workers on larger jobs. Finally, it is possible that if the small business proprietor were excluded from the act, large businesses might be placed at a competitive disadvantage because compliance with OSHA is expensive.[25]

Small businesses have a particularly difficult time complying with the standards because the cost for improvements in working conditions is often prohibitive, and the owner of a small business may have difficulty understanding the standards and how they relate to him. A special feature of the legislation amended the Small Business Act to provide loans to businesses for meeting health and safety requirements. Any small business is eligible for such a loan "if it is likely to suffer substantial economic injury" without such assistance. Businesses must, however, meet normal SBA standards as to employment and size in terms of sales volume.

The major areas likely to require corrective expenditures by virtually all businesses have been stated as follows:

Companies will have to take a stronger position on enforcing existing internal rules and regulations concerning maintenance and house keeping. This could mean that additional maintenance personnel must be hired.

Internal Safety programs may have to be beefed up, primarily to insure that employees are informed of their responsibilities under the act and are complying with requirements.

Purchases of personal protective equipment will continue to increase for such items as safety shoes and glasses.

General in-plant utility equipment might have to be purchased or installed, including such items as ladders, scaffolding, railings, fire extinguishers, and first aid kits.

The area that may require the greatest single expenditure is in major machinery and equipment purchases and plant modifications to meet OSHA standards; this includes ventilating equipment, noise- and vibration-control equipment, roll bars and backup alarms on materials-handling equipment, machine guards, fire doors, new walls and flooring, and so on.[26]

OSHA generally is not welcomed by small businesses. As was recently stated:

OSHA will probably destroy more businesses than lack of financing will. . . . When OSHA regulations slipped through Congress, there was not a coherent body that scrutinized what the effects would be. OSHA is the glaring example of how uncoordinated our government activity can be and how punitive they can be on small business in a very unintentional manner.[27]

Labor-Management Relations. The act may have a major impact on contract negotiation and administration as employees become familiar with their rights under the act. Unions are likely to become increasingly concerned with upgrading working conditions in addition to establishing special benefits for affected workers. Thus, employers are going to have to engage in more

---

[23] Tatham and Coogan, op. cit., p. 67.

[24] Foulkes, op. cit., p. 63.

[25] See Jack R. Nicholas, Jr., "OSHA, Big Government and Small Business," *MSU Business Topics*, Winter 1973, pp. 57–64.

[26] J. Daniel Coogan, Jr., "Financing Compliance with OSHA," *Industrial Development*, May–June 1973, p. 11.

[27] "Small Business: The Maddening Struggle to Survive," *Business Week*, June 30, 1975, p. 98.

safety training for their supervisors and employees. They must also become more diligent in disciplining employees for not complying with safety work rules. This action may lead to more grievance procedures by the union. Therefore, OSHA may have major negative impacts on management-labor relations.

Public Relations Programs. When a firm is issued a citation, the notice must be posted until the violation is corrected or for three working days, whichever is longer. Thus, even if a violation can be corrected in ten minutes, the citation must remain visible for three days. Serious violations can bring major adverse publicity. Also, as has been stated:

The citation, particularly if it is upheld, may provide a third-party accident victim or his family with an excellent basis to sue directly the corporation, its officers, plant manager, etc., while at the same time collecting workmen's compensation from his own employer.[28]

Increasing attention must be given to the public relations function in explaining management's side to the community, to employees, to stockholders, and to the news media when violations are noted. Proper coordination of the public relations function can minimize problems with employees. OSHA can have a negative impact on management-labor relations if the situation is not handled properly and may seriously damage the employer's reputation with his various publics.

The specific impacts of OSHA vary by type of business, and it is not possible to highlight all of them. However, a brief focus on retailing as one type of business may serve as an example of the type of general problems that may be encountered by virtually all businesses.

OSHA AND RETAILING

John H. Stender, assistant secretary of labor for occupational safety and health,

points out that OSHA standards are records of historical problems in that "Most violations are the obvious, such as improper wiring, electrical equipment not grounded, unsafe stairs or ladders, obstructions, inadequate or unmarked egress, or no fire extinguishers."[29] Apparently OSHA inspection data are reflective of this view. In fiscal 1974 for supermarkets, variety stores, and department stores, the standards violated most often "pertained to the electrical code, portable fire extinguishers, means of egress, guarding floor and wall openings and holes, power transmission apparatus, handling materials, and personal protective equipment."[30]

George Groves, safety director for Food Fair, points out that "80 percent of wholesale and retail-related accidents are due to unsafe *acts* by employees versus only about 20 percent due to unsafe *physical* conditions." He goes on to state that "many OSHA inspections have little or nothing to do with job safety or health."[31]

The costs of necessitated changes in retail structures are likely to be quite high because of necessary changes in old buildings and providing for the new requirements in new buildings. Old buildings, for example, may not meet such standards as the electrical code and are likely to require ripping out of old wiring and installation of new equipment. One supermarket executive who asked not to be identified recently indicated that changes in one ten-year-old, 12,000-square-foot store would approximate $3,000. He went on to say that if all of these changes had to be made immediately, it would come close to bankrupting the company because of the hundreds of the stores it operates.[32]

---

28 Kehoe, op. cit., p. 26.

29 "OSHA Chief Does Not See It the Way Chains Do," p. 17.

30 Ibid.

31 "The OSHA Tangle," *Chain Store Age Executive*, April 1975, p. 15.

32 "Chain's Plan Takes the Sting out of OSHA," *Chain Store Age*, August 1973, p. E–27.

Mack Wilhite, head of the 1,900-store Flemming Company, indicates that:

OSHA regulations combined with more stringent Department of Agriculture and state laws will make sanitation considerations extremely important and add to costs. It is not unreasonable to expect that they will add $1.00 to $1.50 per square foot to the cost of constructing new stores.[33]

The consensus among various design experts and manufacturers reveals that the following changes probably will be necessary in new and remodeled stores:

More use of expensive flooring—quarry tile with nonslip sealed grout for preparation areas.

Sealed walls and overhead tiles capable of being washed down with germicidal cleaning agents.

Shielding on slim lines and other lights over preparation areas.

Grounded three-pronged outlets throughout the store. Waterproof outlets in areas to be sanitized.

All preparation equipment designed for easy cleaning and sanitizing. This means waterproofing of electrical components and more expensive finishing on machines.

Separate work areas, saws, sinks, and coolers will be needed for red meats, poultry, and fresh fish.

Sinks and other fixtures should meet national sanitation standards. Woods and other natural products will have to be replaced by more expensive materials in most cases. Stainless steel of higher quality will have to be used.

Separate sinks will have to be provided in each perishable prep area; they must be equipped with dispensers of germicidal solutions.

Sprinkler systems will be required almost without exception.[34]

Many people are beginning to believe that a meaningful program of self-inspection is the key to being in compliance with OSHA. Self-inspection and training programs, as well as assignment of more enforcement activities to the states, seem to be the direction OSHA is heading. For example, 26 states now have OSHA-approved programs.[35]

Organizational responsiveness is necessary for a meaningful self-inspection program. Top management should also give consideration to safety and health records in supervisory evaluations. Likewise, increased employee and supervisory training programs are desirable.

Compliance can be obtained from OSHA by calling an OSHA regional office and asking questions. Another possibility for assistance is the workmen's compensation insurance carrier for a firm. Insurance companies have a major incentive in offering advice and counsel because it gives them a differential advantage over competition. Insurance companies may, however, carry out inspections using their own standards. Thus, an insurer's requirements may not cover all areas specified by OSHA.

George Matwes, safety director for Bamburger, has prepared the list shown in Table 1 as an OSHA Self-Inspection Checklist for stores in the Bamburger chain. The 42 items provide a viable check list for all groups that may be interested in self-inspection. The list can be modified to fit the needs of a particular firm.

DISCUSSION

An enlarged sense of social responsibility and increasing numbers of accidents led to

---

[33] "The OSHA Man Is Coming and He's Changing Your Buying Habits," *Progressive Grocer*, December 1972, p. 35. For further information on sanitation requirements, see Joseph Barry Mason and Morris L. Mayer, "Regulation of Sanitary Practices in the Food Industry: New and Emerging Guidelines," *MSU Business Topics*, Summer 1975.

[34] "The OSHA Man Is Coming," p. 15.

[35] "OSHA Chief Does Not See It the Way Chains Do," p. 17.

TABLE 1
Suggested OSHA Checklist for Retailers

1. OSHA poster is posted in appropriate location.
2. OSHA Form 100 (Record of Occupational Injury and Illness) maintained.
3. Regular employee and customer accident reports, with any follow-up reports kept in orderly fashion.
4. All new employees are being indoctrinated in safety by films, pamphlets, and so forth.
5. Parking lot meets requirements (striping, speed limit signs, lighting, snow and ice removal, maintenance).
6. Stairways clear of debris or obstructions.
7. Exits marked and lighted properly, not blocked.
8. All floor mats must not slide or curl up, must be butted.
9. Glass panels marked by decals.
10. All stairways more than 88 inches wide have center handrail.
11. Main aisles at least 36 inches wide; clear of boxes, etc.
12. Fixtures should not have extensions that could trip people, or sharp corners.
13. All display counters should be free of nails, broken glass, or easily knocked over counter displays.
14. Stock drawers must be closed when not in use.
15. Check for open carpet seams, tears or folds in carpet.
16 Check for holes in floor, missing tiles, or slippery spots.
17. No obstructions in or near elevators; escalators properly maintained.
18. Doors that are not exits must be marked ("office," etc.).
19. Any door that is an exit must be unlocked when employees are in the building.
20. All aisles must be properly striped; clear of debris.

21. Material or stock not stacked within 18 inches of sprinkler.
22. Hazardous and flammable material stored properly.
23. Employees trained in equipment use.
24. All rolling ladders have wheel locks and rubber "crutch" tips.
25. All pulleys and saw blades have guards
26. All grinders have hood guards; table not more than 1/8 inch away from grinder.
27. All equipment designed with interlocks should not have interlocks made inoperable.
28. All electrical equipment, wall sockets, and plugs should have three-prong plugs and be grounded.
29. Extension cords not strung across walk areas without being properly covered.
30. All electrical hand tools should be grounded.
31. "Temporary wiring installations" are not acceptable.
32. Fan blades less than 7 feet off the floor must be "mesh guarded."
33. Fire extinguishers must be readily accessible, charged in the past year, and hung properly.
34. Fire doors must work properly and not be blocked.
35. No smoking signs posted where necessary; rules enforced.
36. Monthly fire drills conducted.
37. Emergency lighting system working properly.
38. Floors clean and free of grease or spills.
39. Flues, ducts, and hoods clean, relatively free of grease.
40. Meat-cutting and all other machines have guards on blades, pulleys, and cutting edges and are grounded.
41. Refrigerators and other food and storage areas kept clean and at proper temperatures.
42. No excessive noise levels (over 90 decibels).

Source: "The OSHA Triangle," *Chain Store Executive*, April 1975, p. 16.

passage of the Occupational Health and Safety Act. The federal government now has adopted as national domestic policy that the cost of safety can no longer be balanced against the cost of accidents. Similarly, John J. Sheehan, legislative director of the United Steel Workers of America, has stated:

The safety of workers should not be traded off in terms of wage costs. Safety is an *issue of public policy* and the cost of doing business, and *not the cost of dealing with the unions*. While collective bargaining can and does supplement public sector regulation, it cannot substitute for it.[36]

Preventive safety and health can be made to work for retailers and other businesses. Such an approach may help to reduce workmen's compensation costs, hospitalization costs, and perhaps lost time from accidents. One corporate officer of a large corporation has stated, for example, "We have cut out lost-time per million man-hours by almost 50 percent," while the manager of another smaller company has pointed out that it has "Reduced its workmen's compensation costs by 25 percent in a one-year period."[37]

OSHA is not without its problems, how-

[36] John J. Sheehan, "OSHA and Job Safety Plans," *Monthly Labor Review*, April 1974, p. 44.

[37] Foulkes, op. cit., p. 88.

ever. Employers talk about vagueness in the standards and complain that different OSHA inspectors are likely to provide different answers to the same question.

Another area of uncertainty relates to the assessment of penalties for violations. It has been pointed out that many people believe that the fining process is criminal in nature, which assures an accused firm of all of the constitutional guarantees of a criminal proceeding.[38] However, the federal government apparently feels that fines and penalties are regulatory and that traditional constitutional safeguards, which abound in criminal cases, are not applicable in administrative matters.

In a similar vein, it has been stated that the:

Act presumes that the employer is responsible for every injury even if an employee caused the harm when acting against a direct order of the employer. . . . There is no incentive for employees to follow OSHA standards other than innate concern for their own safety, a reality that predated OSHA.[39]

He further states that:

Congress has placed in the hands of the Secretary of Labor a grant of power unprecedented in the history of the United States. Although the problem must have a high priority in America, it can never be so compelling as to require an approach that subverts the Constitution.[40]

Regardless of the various controversies surrounding the implementation of OSHA, it is a reality that will continue to become even more of a factor in business. As was recently stated, "So to that list carrying the inevitable entries, death and taxes . . . now add OSHA compliance."[41] Much pressure for legislative relief is being exerted, however. Thus, it behooves management to stay alert to possible changes in the legislation that could affect their business. For example, a U.S. District Court has held that OSHA inspectors cannot enter a business for an inspection without a search warrant. The decision is being appealed to the U.S. Supreme Court because a judge will not issue a warrant without justification. Such justification is often difficult to show prior to inspection. If the decision of the District Court is upheld, effective enforcement of the law would be very difficult.[42]

30. A PENALTY SYSTEM TO DISCOURAGE OSHA VIOLATIONS*

DAROLD T. BARNUM and JOHN M. GLEASON

In passing the Occupational Safety and Health Act of 1970, Congress recognized that if the law were to be obeyed there had to be effective enforcement mechanisms, including meaningful penalties for violations. If OSHA is to achieve its objectives, OSHA sanctions must encourage employers to obey the law. This paper examines,

from a decision-theory point of view, the effect on employer behavior of federal penalties for first-instance violations. OSHA penalty provisions and administration are discussed, their expected consequences are analyzed, and recommendations for more effective public policy are suggested.

* Source: Monthly Labor Review 98, 10 (1975): 40–42.
[38] Tatham and Coogan, op. cit., p. 64.
[39] Kirklin, op. cit., p. 446.

[40] Ibid., p. 449.
[41] "OSHA and the Metal Working Industry," Iron Age, June 21, 1973, p. 38.
[42] "A Hobbled OSHA Seeks Relief," Business Week, April 12, 1976, p. 95.

Categories of Violations

Penalties are assessed under the act for several types of violations, including non-serious, serious, and willful categories. Conditions classified as "nonserious violations" have a direct and immediate relationship to employee health or safety, but will not generally result in death or serious physical harm. Although penalties can range from "$0" to $1,000, the mean fine for the period July 1972 through December 1974 was only $14.99. Of the 591,160 violations cited during this period, 98.53 percent were classified as nonserious.[1]

"Serious violations" are conditions that would likely result in death or serious physical harm if an employee were injured. Penalties of $1,000 for each violation are assessed, although the amount can be reduced by up to 50 percent at the inspector's discretion. In fact, the mean fine for the July 1972–December 1974 period was $618.66 for the 1.22 percent of the cited violations that were classified as serious.[2]

Finally, an employer commits a "willful violation" by deliberately and knowingly violating the law or regulations, or by being aware of a hazardous condition and making no reasonable effort to eliminate it. Penalties of up to $10,000 can be imposed for each willful violation, although the mean penalty for the July 1972–December 1974 period was only $866.44. Furthermore, less than 0.25 percent of the cited violations during this period were classified as willful.[3]

Whether or not a given condition will result in a penalty is often uncertain, because of administrative shortcomings and nonuni-form enforcement. Regulations are often inaccessible, vague, and constantly changing, making it difficult for an employer to know if a situation is or is not a violation (or will remain a violation) of safety standards. There is additional randomness in the enforcement process: discovered violations are sometimes not cited, and, even when cited, their classification as to seriousness is not uniform.

The Compliance Decision

Assume the rational economic employer feels that it is in violation of OSHA. The conditions that could lead to citation can be corrected by installing safety equipment and devices. However, suppose an alternative opportunity is available in which the employer can invest the funds, if it chooses not to correct the conditions. The employer is faced with a decision problem: Should it correct the conditions, or should it invest the funds in the alternative project?

The purpose of OSHA sanctions is to encourage employers to correct unsafe and unhealthy conditions.[4] Such encouragement will not be provided by the sanctions as long as the opportunity cost of corrections greatly exceeds the expected cost of penalties.

Although cost-of-compliance data are not now available, it is clear that the opportunity cost of correcting almost any violation will be far greater than the most likely expected fine, taking into account the low probability of being inspected in a given year, the uncertainty of penalties and classification as to seriousness, and the relatively low level of penalties. A decision-theory approach based on historic inspection and citation data yields an expected fine of $1.82 for a violation. In effect, expected fines of this size almost invite the employer to violate the law, because the discrepancy between compliance costs and fine levels is so great. In fact, low fines give the impres-

---

[1] *Field Operations Manual* (Washington, D.C.: Occupational Safety and Health Administration, U.S. Department of Labor); and "Current Report," *Occupational Safety and Health Reporter* (Washington, D.C.: Bureau of National Affairs, 1974–75), pp. 342 and 1311.

[2] *Field Operations Manual;* and *Occupational Safety and Health Reporter,* pp. 342 and 1311.

[3] *Field Operations Manual;* and *Occupational Safety and Health Reporter,* pp. 342 and 1311. This category includes willful, repeat, and imminent danger citations.

[4] 29 U.S.C. sec. 651.

sion that the government is not taking violations too seriously, making it even more likely that the employer will make its decisions on purely economic grounds.

The obvious implication is to substantially increase the cost of sanctions by increasing the fine levels, the probability of being fined, or both. For example, recall that the mean fine for nonserious violations (which constitute 98 percent of all violations) is $14.99, although fines of up to $1,000 are possible under the current law. There is little doubt that this average should be substantially increased.

Likewise, the probability of being cited could well be increased. Most employers have less than a 10-percent chance of being inspected in any given year. Because many true violations discovered by inspectors go uncited, the probability of being cited for a given violation is certainly far less. The probability of citation can be increased by many means, such as increasing the number of inspections, increasing the proportion of discovered violations that are cited, and increasing the skill of the inspectors in discovering violations.

But whether the expected cost of sanctions is increased by larger fines or by higher probabilities of being fined, it is crucial to set the expected cost of sanctions at a level higher than the opportunity cost of compliance. Currently, fine levels are based on the gravity of the violation rather than on the cost of compliance. Because the objective of the act is to reduce unhealthy and unsafe conditions, fines should be set at levels that would encourage employers to comply. These levels are those at which the expected fines are greater than the opportunity costs of compliance, regardless of the gravity of violations.

31. GULHEMP: WHAT WORKERS CAN DO

MARY YOURY

"I was GULHEMPed," the older man said to his friend. "Now I have a job." GULHEMPed? The friend looked blank. And no wonder. Except for a small, but efficient, operation in Portland, Maine, an aircraft factory in Canada, a physician who specializes in industrial health, and The National Council on the Aging, Inc., few people have ever heard of GULHEMP.

But for those few, GULHEMP has great significance. It is the key to opening the door to a closed job market; it can mean life renewed for the discouraged and emotionally moribund; it is a giant step toward changing American industry's attitude toward the aging process.

Here is what the odd-sounding acronym

stands for:[1] G–General physique; U–Upper extremities; L–Lower extremities; H–Hearing; E–Eyesight; M–Mentality; and P–Personality. The combination forms the name of a unique system for testing an employee's physical condition and providing a parallel analysis of a particular job. GULHEMP aims to match workers to specific jobs, to underscore an individual worker's physical capacities for job performance, and to make it clear to all concerned that capacity and ability—not chronological age—are the determining factors in job performance.

The GULHEMP technique was developed by Dr. Leon Koyl. It has been implemented and tested in an industrial setting and, for

_____
[1] M and P factors are no longer utilized as measures in the system due to possible conflict with Equal Employment Opportunity Commission requirements.

Source: *Manpower* 7, 6 (1975): 4–10.

more than 14 years, has been applied successfully at deHavilland Aircraft, Ltd., in Toronto, Canada.

ACCENTUATES THE POSITIVE

Unlike most employee health evaluations, GULHEMP does not stress the negative aspects of a worker's physical condition. Typical health reports note "heart condition" or "arrested pulmonary tuberculosis" and include functional limitation statements such as "cannot lift heavy loads" or "continuous pressure ill-advised." Managers and supervisors learn only what the worker should not or cannot do. GULHEMP is the reverse; it emphasizes what individuals, regardless of age or disability, *can* do in a specific job role.

In June 1970, the GULHEMP system became the focal point of operations for the Industrial Health Counseling Service (IHCS) in Portland, Maine. The Maine Employment Security Commission (MESC), through a grant from the Manpower Administration of the U.S. Department of Labor, had contracted . . . to set up IHCS as an experimental project. . . .

EXAMS ARE THOROUGH

Local firms that use IHCS services pay $25 for the physical examination of an employee or prospective employee, plus $75 for a job analysis. The dual process begins as soon as an individual walks through the IHCS door. First there is the physical examination. . . . The . . . examination lasts about an hour and includes extensive testing by modern equipment that checks hearing and visual capacity, heart and pulmonary function, ability to lift and push, and the range of the individual's mobility. . . .

JOB PROFILE IS DEVELOPED

A job analysis is performed to obtain information about the job and its fitness requirements. An assessment is then made to insure that a particular worker (whose physical abilities have been determined by the IHCS medical examination) can meet these requirements.

An illustration of how the system can work involves a post office employee whose job had for two decades required that he stand at a machine for long hours at a time. With no warning, the man's perfect attendance record was suddenly marred by frequent absences. An analysis of his job and a medical examination which showed that he was afflicted with high blood pressure, varicose veins, and diabetes led to the conclusion that the job was no longer appropriate for him. He sits at a desk now, doing different work but still employed by the post office.

Gary E. Whitney, for the past three years manager of the Maine Employment Security Commission office in Portland, enthusiastically praised IHCS and the service it performs. "IHCS is a very important part of the total employment picture here," declared Whitney, "and the spinoffs are electrifying." . . .

Last August, 137 middle-aged and older workers—30 percent of them between 40 and 45—applied for jobs at the employment security office. Whitney pointed out that prospective employers who consider such persons "too old" for certain types of jobs tend to change their minds when confronted with GULHEMP and physical examination results. Evidence of the physical capacity to do a job involving physical activity is a plus for the jobseeker; the IHCS material is an added tool employment security counselors can use to persuade employers to hire older clients. In the past year, jobs in the metal and machine trades of three separate industries have been filled by older workers whom employers had considered ineligible before GULHEMP results indicated that they could perform the work.

Whitney said IHCS has helped to change the employment security office image. Once the accent was "unemployment, negative" he explained. Now it is positive, particularly for people in the "older age" bracket, because the chance of job placement is enhanced by GULHEMP and the IHCS screening process. Before the IHCS breakthrough, older workers seemed to resent counselors and acted as if they were hindering rather than helping. Many, after halfheartedly agreeing to talk with counselors, failed to show up for appointments. Pessimistic attitudes and outlook altered radically when word got around that people were landing jobs after exposure to the IHCS program.

"What a difference!" stated Whitney. "The entire IHCS program is a fantastic success. I think it should be incorporated physically as part of the employment security operation. Today our agent booking there is solid." . . .

Efforts are underway to export the program to other states and, at the same time, to keep Portland's facility going. Potential sources for the broad base of financial support needed to maintain the facility are the fees charged for service; the Comprehensive Employment and Training Act; the Administration on Aging of the Department of Health, Education, and Welfare; the Community Chest; and contracts with additional organizations for specific industrial health and manpower services. By supporting the project now, the Maine Employment Security Commission is helping to insure the place of IHCS as a permanent industrial health facility. The commission would continue to gain special services and benefits at diminishing cost as other agencies pick up a share of the IHCS budget.

Data collected from participating companies leave no question of the project's multiple benefits. The overall goal is to convince others in industry of the inherent truth: Age is never a barrier to working, only physical limitations are. And these can be measured and fully compensated for by using a yardstick called GULHEMP.

part IV

INNOVATIONS IN WORK

11

HOURS OF WORK

The hours that employees work have always been a source of concern to personnel/human resources. For example, extended work hours often have compensation implications because they involve overtime payments. As another example, part-time work opportunities can alter recruiting practices. Students and homemakers may become potential employees if an organization is willing to employ persons less than 40 hours per week.

Periodically, hours of work can become especially important to personnel/human resources and to organizations because of substantial changes in hours of work that effect all or nearly all of the workforce. Such changes are ocurring in some organizations at present. The purpose of this chapter is to describe these changes and to discuss their implications for employee attitudes and work behaviors.

Historical Trends in Hours

The vast majority of full-time, nonfarm employees work five days per week, and most of those work 40 or more hours during that time. This five day, 40-hour workweek (we will refer to it as the 5/40), however, is a fairly recent phenomenon, occurring only within the last 30 to 40 years. In the early 1800s the typical workweek was six days, sunrise to sunset. From about 1850 until the 1930s there was a quite steady reduction in average weekly hours from around 70 to 40. This came about both by a decrease in workdays per week (from six to five) and hours per day (from 12 to 8). Average weekly hours increased during World War II, but after the war average weekly hours returned to about their prewar level. Since that time, there has been hardly any decline in average weekly hours, and the 5/40 has become firmly entrenched as the standard workweek.

Reinforcing the 5/40 as a standard is the operation of premium or overtime pay for hours worked in excess of 8 per day and/or 40 per week. Such requirements are frequently contained in labor contracts. Federal legislation also plays an important role here. The *Fair Labor Standards Act* requires time and one-half pay for hours worked in excess of 40 per week. The *Walsh-Healey Public Contracts Act,* which applies to federal contractors, requires time and one-half pay beyond eight hours per day. Executive, administrative, and professional employees are exempt from overtime provisions of both acts, even though these employees often work in excess of 40 hours per week.

While average weekly hours have leveled off since World War II, this has not been the case for average *yearly* hours. Here there has been a continuous, but gradual, decrease due to an increase in paid time-off from work. The two major contributing factors have been (1) an increase in the number of paid holidays and (2) more liberal (lengthy) paid vacations. In effect, such increases have helped to reduce average weekly hours *per year* to below 40.

Future Trends in Hours

What will happen to average yearly hours in the future? It is probably safe to conclude that average yearly hours will continue to decline, but at a slow rate. The costs of paid time-off have increased rapidly, and this may cause organizations to resist the rate of liberalization that has occurred in the past.

Conclusions about average weekly hours are more hazardous. These will be influenced by a host of factors such as changes in the composition of the labor force, unemployment rates, changes in real earnings, and the birthrate. If recent history is any indicator of the future, however, no drastic reduction in average weekly hours appears likely in the foreseeable future.

While changes in average weekly hours are thus likely to be quite modest, there is a distinct possibility of a more rapid change in the way hours are scheduled. The basic trend here will be a shift away from the typical schedule in which all employees start and stop work at the same time for five days (that is, the standard 5/40).

One alternative currently being tried by many organizations is the 4/40, in which employees work four ten-hour days per week. This schedule shortens the workweek, but with no reduction in average weekly or yearly hours. Employees receive a lump sum block of leisure in the form of one extra day per week, usually making possible a three-day weekend. An even more extreme example is the 7/70 work schedule that some hospitals are experimenting with. Here employees work seven consecutive ten-hour days, and then are off for seven days. Compared to the 4/40, this creates much larger blocks of leisure and also slightly reduces average yearly hours since employees work 70, instead of 80, hours in each two-week period.

Another alternative to the typical 5/40 is flexible working hours or *flexitime.* While employees still work a five-day week, they can vary their starting and stopping times. The major constraint is that all employees must be present during a core time each day (for example, 10:00 A.M. to 2:00 P.M.). In some plans, employees are required to work eight hours everyday, so the only flexibility is when to start work. In more liberal plans, the month is considered the basic work period and *carryforward* hours are permitted. Carryforward hours means that employees may work more than 40 hours one week, and then work a reduced (by the number of hours over 40) number of hours in the next week. For example, if an employee worked 50 hours in one week, the same employee could carry forward 10 hours and thus work only 30 hours the next week. Thus, flexitime permits a choice of small leisure time blocks each work day, whereas the 4/40 creates a one day block of leisure.

INTRODUCTION TO READINGS

The Four-Day, 40-Hour Week

Advantages of, and problems with, the 4/40 are pursued in the article by Ben Buisman. He begins by briefly tracing the evolution leading to the 5/40. Buisman then describes the basic 4/40 and some slight variants of it. For example, some organizations allow employees to forego coffeebreaks, and thus they work something less than a ten-hour day. Even then, however, employees still work above the eight-hour day standard. This is of great concern to organized labor, Buisman notes, since labor fought long and hard to win the eight-hour day. It also creates overtime pay problems, and Buisman describes a couple of ways that organizations have dealt with them.

The advantages and (occasionally) disadvantages of the 4/40, both to employees and the organization, are then reviewed. From the employees' perspective, the advantages cited are numerous. Surprisingly, however, Buisman says little about two potentially major problems: (1) What impact does the 4/40 have on employee stress, fatigue, and safety? (2) How well are employees able to cope with, or adjust to, their increased leisure time? The latter question, it might be pointed out, has been raised historically everytime a reduction in hours has been considered.

For the organization, a long list of claimed advantages is presented. It includes such things as better recruitment, reduced absenteeism, and increased productivity. You should note, however, that most of these cited advantages are simply based on surveys of managers' opinions about the 4/40 in their own organizations. There is considerably less hard, empirical evidence to support these contentions.

Buisman also describes a number of possible disadvantages of the 4/40 and claims that failure rates among organizations that have implemented the 4/40 are estimated to range from 8 to 15 percent. The major cause of failure appears to be inadequate planning and implementation by management. To counter this, a number of suggestions are made regarding the assessment of 4/40s likely success during the planning process.

Flexitime

Descriptions of flexitime, problems associated with it, and possible solutions to these problems are dealt with by John D. Owens. To do this, he draws heavily on the experiences of European organizations where flexitime originated in 1967. After describing basic flexitime systems, Owens briefly summarizes the evidence on the advantages of flexitime to employees and organizations. As with the 4/40 workweek, the list of advantages is long and mostly based on testimonial types of evidence.

Flexitime is not equally applicable in all organizations, and Owens describes some of the major factors influencing its probable applicability. He also indicates that certain work schedule modifications, and work reorganization (for example, job rotation), could be undertaken to broaden flexitime's applicability.

A number of controversies between labor and management surround flexitime and are discussed by Owen. For example, labor charges that flexitime may be just another management attempt to increase productivity without increasing employees' earnings. Overtime problems also come into play. Owens describes ways in which management could greatly (and coercively) reduce overtime with flexitime. If employees are used to overtime pay, this may not sit too well with them. Alternatively, use of carryforwards could increase overtime, which obviously clashes with labor's stance on the eight-hour day. In addition, the federal statutes would have to be revised to permit carryforwards, which would in turn make them more difficult to enforce.

In short there are a variety of potential problems with flexitime. Owens concludes his article by looking at European experiences with these problems and how most of them have been overcome. It is this successful resolution of problems in Europe which leads Owens to optimistically predict flexitime's "extension to a much larger proportion of the American workforce."

32. FOUR-DAY, 40-HOUR WORKWEEK: ITS EFFECT ON MANAGEMENT AND LABOR

BEN A. BUISMAN

The currently accepted "normal" five-day and 40-hour week is only a few decades old. Eighteenth-century workers, especially those engaged in agriculture, toiled dawn to dusk, six days a week. In the 1830s, American labor unions began pressing for shorter workdays. Management opposed this position, citing moral and economic factors. Labor felt that if the workers had more time with their families and more time to read, they would become better citizens and better educated. Management

stated fears of a collapse of American society because increased leisure would lead to more mischievousness. They also felt they would face increases in costs of production, leading to business failures and widespread unemployment.[1]

The ten-hour, six-day week began in skilled trade groups and government employees in the mid-1800s. Semiskilled and unskilled workers did not see these benefits until after the Civil War.

Again the craft unions led the way to

Source: *Personnel Journal* 54 (November 1975): 565–67.

[1] Don Hellriegel, "The Four-Day Workweek: A Review and Assessment," *MSU Business Topics*, Spring 1972, p. 39.

the eight-hour day (but still six days a week). This trend began in the 1890s, and by 1920 many industrial union members were working an eight-hour day.[2]

The next major change occurred in the 1920s with the unions pressuring for a five-day week. The depression years of the late 1920s and early 1930s aided the union's argument, spreading available work to more union members. Governmental pressure in the form of the Walsh-Healey Public Contracts Act and the Fair Labor Standards Act added impetus. The idea spread, led by large industry and large unions until, by the early 1950s, the five-day, 40-hour week was the most common job structure in the United States.[3]

WHAT IS THE FOUR-DAY WEEK?

The most commonly heard answer to the above question is "four ten-hour days per week." But the work periods discussed here take many forms. By far the largest group of employees working a shortened workweek *are* working four days and 40 hours, but many others are trading their coffee breaks and cleanup time for shortened hours. For these, the workday may mean nine or less hours. Some employers feel they get as much work done in four nine-hour periods as they did in five regular days due to savings in start-up, and that scheduled downtime for maintenance can now be done in the fifth day.

Another form of the four-day week is the four-on, four-off scheme in firms that require continuous operation. The Cromwell Corporation, a machining company in South Bend, Indiana, has four crews, each working four ten-hour days with four days off. This scheme gives the company 20 hours of operation per day, seven days a

week. The additional four daily hours are used for routine maintenance and cleanup.[4]

The kinds of firms trying the four-day week cover a wide range. Most are engaged in manufacturing, are small, and nonunion. A few are retail outlets, either working two overlapping shifts to accommodate peak customer loads, or only open four days a week. But one of the earliest examples of the four-day week can be seen in the large fuel oil and gasoline delivery industry.[5]

Firms are approaching the requirement to pay overtime rates for any hours worked over eight per day by either reducing the base pay so that the weekly base plus overtime remains the same as before or paying the overtime rate, stating that the increased productivity of the four-day week justifies the pay increase. Most are paying for 40 hours, even though the workweek may be somewhat less.[6]

Another obstacle is that many state laws prevent women from working more than eight hours per day. Some states will grant waivers if the workweek does not exceed 40 hours.

LABOR'S VIEW

Organized labor has taken two separate stands on the issue. One group takes the position that the ten-hour day is an erosion of the long and hard-fought battle for the eight-hour workday. Joseph Cointin, a regional official of the Machinists Union, states:

This business of working ten-hour days strikes at the heart of what our unions have accomplished for us over the years, and the shift to four ten-hour days in a work-week that is taking place

[2] Clyde E. Dankert, F. C. Mann, and Herbert R. Northrup, *Hours of Work* (New York: Harper and Row, 1965), pp. 19–44.

[3] Hellriegel, "The Four-Day Workweek," p. 40.

[4] John L. Schohl, "4 Days On, 4 Days Off," *4 Days, 40 Hours*, ed. Riva Poor (Cambridge: Bursk and Poor Publishing, 1970), pp. 169–70.

[5] Riva Poor, *4 Days, 40 Hours* (Cambridget: Bursk and Poor Publishing, 1970), pp. 19–29.

[6] Poor, *4 Days, 40 Hours*, p. 30.

in many sections of the country can only wreak havoc in the universal eight-hour day that unions so long fought for.[7]

An opposing view comes from Howard Coughlin, six-times president of the Office and Professional Employees International Union, who sees the four-day, 40-hour week as a wedge toward the four-day, 32-hour week that has been for some time a goal of organized labor. He cites the fact that many companies converting to the four-day week require less than 10 hours per day.[8]

The general view is that most organized labor will not make a stand for the four-day week. Rank-and-file support is usually lacking. The four-day, 40-hour week threatens the eight-hour workday.

In the majority of companies working the four-day week, the movement was initiated by management. They usually polled their workers beforehand and of course had to negotiate the change with the union. The unions generally acquiesced, usually holding only for overtime pay after eight hours and/or pay for 40 hours.[9]

The reaction of individual workers involved in the four-day week has been for the most part favorable. A few people left their jobs because of conflicting schedules with their spouses or children or found the long day too tiring. But the majority favored the three-day weekend, especially because one of the days, Friday, for example, let them take care of banking, dentist appointments, and other transactions previously requiring time off from work. The three-day weekend allows more time for recreation and travel. Another consideration is that the four-day week means only four trips to and from jobs, and different traveling hours

than the eight-hour schedule, reducing commuting time and traffic congestion.[10]

MANAGEMENT'S VIEW

As stated, most of the impetus for the four-day week has come from management. Reasons given are many and varied; the most often heard: to increase employees' morale[11] and as a corollary, to improve employee recruitment. For Lowell Manufacturing Company, a textile firm in a labor-tight New England town, the only reason for initiation of the four-day week was to attract more and better-qualified employees. By being a pioneer, with the subsequent publicity, they received a sharp increase in the number of job applicants.[12]

But administrators can see some negative aspects. The long weekend may lead to employee moonlighting. Scheduling can be a headache, especially for those employees who deal with the "five-day" world, such as salesmen, and shipping and receiving personnel. Most companies elect to retain their sales force and all or part of their office staff and shipping and receiving people on a five-day schedule. This, then, can lead to communication problems with the four-day production workers. And supervisory employees find themselves working extra long hours trying to reduce this confusion.[13]

A study[14] by the American Management

[7] "Two Views of the 4-Day Workweek," *U.S. News & World Report,* May 3, 1971, p. 57.

[8] "A 4–Day Work Week Is Inevitable," *Administrative Management,* May 1970, pp. 22–23.

[9] D. Quinn Mills, "Does Organized Labor Want the 4-Day Week?", *4 Days, 40 Hours,* ed. Riva Poor (Cambridge: Bursk and Poor Publishing, 1970), pp. 61–69.

[10] James L. Steele and Riva Poor, "Work and Leisure: The Reactions of People at 4-Day Firms," *4 Days, 40 Hours,* ed. Riva Poor (Cambridge: Bursk and Poor Publishing, 1970), pp. 105–22.

[11] "Shorter Work Week Results in Higher Employee Morale," *Administrative Management,* February 1972, p. 90.

[12] L. Erick Kanter, "An Industrial Pioneer Rescued by the 4-Day Week," *4 Days, 40 Hours,* ed. Riva Poor (Cambridge: Bursk and Poor Publishing, 1970), pp. 39–46.

[13] William B. Werther, Jr. and John W. Newstrom, "Administrative Implications of the Four-Day Week," *Administrative Management,* December 1972, pp. 18–19.

[14] Kenneth E. Wheeler et al, *The Four-Day Week, An AMA Research Report* (New York: American Management Association, Inc., 1972), p. 19.

Association of 143 involved companies found that production had increased in 62 percent of the companies and declined in 3 percent. Profits were up in 51 percent of the firms and had decreased in only 4 percent. A study of 71 companies by the Bureau of National Affairs reports that 79 percent of the managements approve of their change to the four-day week and 73 percent consider the change permanent.[15]

Levy[16] presents three case histories:

At Thomas Lipton & Sons, a work week of three 12-hour days for some 1,300 employees in three plants was initiated last January. According to Dominick Belsante, director of industrial relations, management's primary motivation was "a great need for increased productivity." By optimizing the use of equipment each day, Belsante reports, "productive hours have increased by 16 percent while quality control has been maintained at a high level."

At Scoville Manufacturing's General Hose & Coupling subsidiary, where some 400 employees have been working four nine-and-a-half-hour days for about a year, manager Thomas Nagle measures the productivity factor in "absolute pieces" of auto air-conditioning components produced; this has increased 8 to 10 percent since the institution of the four-day week. "But the most remarkable gain," says Nagle, "is that our absenteeism rate has been cut almost in half." Nagle figures that better attendance is also a quality improvement. "If you have to get Janie to do Joanie's job while she is off getting a tooth filled at the dentist," he explains, "product quality can suffer."

Still another concern citing productivity gains is Kraftco's Sealtest Foods division. Now in the second year of a 4-40 experiment at its ice-cream plant in Omaha, where about 30 employees work four ten-hour days at straight time, the company has reduced overtime to "practically zero." But more important, advises personnel director David Campbell, in a production process that requires strictly sanitary conditions, Sealtest has been able to cut one day's start-up operation each week, and subsequently one clean-up operation, thus reducing what he calls "quality risks."

THE FUTURE

The four-day week has not been a 100 percent success. Some firms have tried it and have returned to their previous work schedule. Failure rates are estimated to be from 8 to 15 percent. The AMA study cited inadequate planning and poor management techniques as the most common reasons. Early "successes" have been declared failures after the novelty wore off, a symptom of the Hawthorne effect.

Hellriegel[17] suggests a three-step evaluation approach applicable to a firm considering the four-day week. A "won't work" response to any step is suggested as precluding an effective implementation of the plan and avoids the pitfalls of trial and error.

The first step involves looking at the organization and evaluating the four-day workweek on how it will affect the nature of the organization's processes (unit, batch, or continuous), the utilization of capital and resources (can downtime and maintenance be scheduled to "off" hours for greater productivity?), customer response, competitive response, legal implications, and the union position.

If results of the first step are favorable, then the second step involves evaluating conditions relating to the employees. Here Hillriegal insists on open communications between management and workers about the pros and cons of the proposed plan to reveal early potential dissatisfaction. To be

15 Robert Levy, "How's the Four-Day Week Working?" *Dun's*, July 1972, pp. 52–54.

16 Levy, "How's the Four-Day Week Working?" p. 53.

17 Hellriegel, "The Four-Day Workweek," pp. 43–47.

considered are the workers' reactions to the change in the hours of work, remuneration, tiredness and boredom. Exogenous to the organization, but affecting worker attitudes, are transportation, family life and off-job time utilization.

With open communications, Hellriegel suggests that the third step, measuring and evaluating worker attitudes about the proposed plan, can at least be tested before implementation. Employees can be tested on how they now perceive the organization and how they would perceive it with the new plan, their attitudes about the plan and their feelings about job satisfaction and morale with or without the effects of the plan.

If all three steps show positive results, implementation of the plan should lead to increases in organizational effectiveness: more and better output because of positive human factors—less absenteeism, turnover, tardiness, and lower training and recruitment costs.

But after implementation, all stages need continuous re-evaluation and checks to see if the expected results occur. Pre-implementation assumptions may have been incorrect and the workers' perceptions may change when faced with working with it. By breaking the problem into stages, however, trouble areas can be pinpointed and perhaps corrected. For example, worker attitudes can be examined by further testing and the plan changed to correct problems. If negative results occur because of a factor inherent in the plan that can't be corrected, the plan can be abandoned.

33. FLEXITIME: SOME PROBLEMS AND SOLUTIONS

JOHN D. OWEN

The new systems of flexible hours scheduling, which allow the employee some degree of individual choice as to when he works, have usually been well received by employees in Europe and the United States. Yet, only a few labor spokesmen have praised the idea, and almost none have actually urged its adoption. As a striking example of the hostility of some segments of organized labor, during the recent hearings on a bill to permit widespread experimentation with flexible hours systems for federal employees, the principal opposing witness was the president of the American Federation of Government Employees, the largest union of federal employees.[1]

A major purpose of this paper is to try to explain this apparent paradox by exploring the problems as well as the advantages flexible hours systems bring to management and labor. The paper will focus on the "flexitime" system and will discuss

[1] Testimony of Clyde M. Webber, U.S. Congress, House Committee on Post Office and Civil Service, 1975, "Alternative Work Schedules and Part-Time Career Opportunities in the Federal Government," Hearing No. H621–11 (October 7) before the Subcommittee on Manpower and Civil Service, Congress of the United States, Ninety-Fourth Congress, Second Session, pp. 117–29, on Bills H.R. 9043 and H.R. 6350, which would authorize employees and agencies of the government to experiment with flexible and compressed work schedules as alternatives to present work schedules.

some methods that have been developed for dealing with the problems that commonly arise.

Although flexible hours scheduling is very new in the United States, many European workers have had some form of it for several years. In both areas the initiative for the flexitime system has come mainly from employers, with organized labor often initially cautious or even hostile. In a number of instances, however, European labor representatives have come to take a positive view of flexible hours schedules as experience with them has accumulated, partly because the fears raised by early reports turned out to be groundless and partly because methods of alleviating the problems that the systems did in fact create for labor were developed.[2]

THE FLEXITIME SYSTEM

Flexible hours schedules can take a number of forms, but all variants offer the individual some control over his work schedule. The popular "flexitime" form provides the most choice to the employee, and will be given primary attention in this paper.[3] In a typical flexitime system, the employer sets a "core" time during which all employees must be present—as, for example, from ten to twelve in the morning and two to four in the afternoon. He also sets a "bandwidth" within which all hours must be worked—say, 6:00 A.M. to 6:30 P.M. In

addition, certain restraints are imposed in the interest of the worker's health—for example, he may be required to take at least 45 minutes for lunch and be limited to no more than ten hours of work a day. Also, the employee is still required to put in the same total working time—such as an average of 40 hours a week—as he would under a conventional work schedule.

In the most limited variant, schedule flexibility is confined to daily starting and ending times, and the worker must continue to put in eight hours each day. In less limited plans, he may vary his total daily hours. In still more generous plans (more common in Europe than in the United States), he may even carry hours forward from week to week and month to month, although an upper limit, such as no more than 10 hours per week and 20 hours per month, is usually placed on these carryforwards.

The flexitime system was first introduced in 1967 at the Messerschmidt Research and Development Center, outside Munich, Germany. It has spread very rapidly since then. Although accurate data on its coverage are not available, it has been estimated that about a third of the Swiss labor force has a flexible scheduling system. Estimates for Germany run as high as 5 or 10 percent of the white-collar labor force. In addition, a million or more workers in England, France, Scandinavia, and elsewhere in Europe have the flexitime system. Although heavily concentrated in white-collar occupations, flexible hours scheduling has been extended to some European blue-collar factory and service workers as well.[4]

The introduction of flexitime into the United States is a much more recent phenomenon. Apart from a few early pioneers,

---

[2] Stephen Baum and W. McEwan Young, *A Practical Guide to Flexible Working Hours* (London: Kogan Page, 1973), for a review of English and German experience. See also the union position papers in *L'horaire variable ou libre: rapport du groupe d'études réuni à la demande du Premier ministre* (Paris: La Documentation Française, 1972); and *L'horaire libre en 1974: synthese des travaux du groupe d'études réuni à la demande de M. Gorse, ministre du Travail et de l'emploi, et présidé par M. de Chalendar* (Paris: La Documentation Française, 1974).

[3] In some forms of flexible hours scheduling, the employer offers the employee a choice among several alternative schedules. Once chosen, the schedule is then fixed for a stated period of time. It is arguable whether this degree of flexibility should qualify the system as flexitime.

[4] See Alvar O. Elbing, Herman Gadon, and John R. M. Gordon, "Time for a Human Time Table," *European Business*, no. 39 (Autumn 1973), pp. 46–54. See the discussion by CATRAL (Comité pour l'étude et l'aménagement des temps de travail et des temps de loisirs dans la région parisienne), in *L'horaire libre en 1974* for additional estimates.

most installations of the system have occurred since 1973. Yet, it has been estimated that several hundred thousand employees in this country already have some
form of flexible hours system.[5]

Government officials have been generally favorable to the flexitime system because it helps to ease the congestion of
commuter and other social-overhead facilities, and because it can allow industry
to bring more full-time workers—especially women into the labor force.[6]

Most employees, both here and abroad,
also react favorably to flexitime. In a typical survey, a large majority are in favor of
the system, a minority are more or less
indifferent, and only a very small percentage are actively opposed. Those who prefer
the system report that they seem to have
more time for leisure activities and discharging family responsibilities, even
though their worktimes are not reduced.
They frequently report less aggravation
and less time spent in commuting; easier
access to retail and service outlets; and
greater ease in handling children's schedules and other family matters. The last set
of factors is at least partly responsible for
the great popularity the system has enjoyed
among working women. Those who prefer
to work standard hours, however, can retain their old schedules under flexitime,
and many exercise this right. Those few

who actively dislike the system are often
those who find themselves inconvenienced
by the nonstandard hours of their fellow
employees, which may make it harder for
them to do their own work or may break
up their car pool when other members decide to commute outside the rush hour.[7]

Managements that have experimented
successfully with the system report a number of advantages. Employee morale is generally improved, sometimes to the point of
lowering quit rates, a direct benefit to
management. Tardiness is eliminated as a
problem and part-day absences reduced;
many managers also report that full-day
absences are reduced. Some employers believe that when employees can pick their
starting times, they are more likely to
arrive at the job ready to work, reducing
startup costs. Other employers report that
some employees will voluntarily work late
when the work demands it, taking off compensatory time in slack periods, thus further increasing productivity. Reductions in
overtime and other productivity gains have
also been reported.[8]

On the other hand, many employers who
have considered the system have not installed it, and a few who have tried it have
abandoned it as unworkable. To many of

[5] On the basis of her survey, Virginia Martin,
Hours of Work When Workers Can Choose (Washington, D.C.: Washington's Business and Professional
Women's Foundation, 1975), estimated that in 1975
as many as 1 million American employees already
had some form of flexible hours schedules.

[6] A number of studies of individual firms report
that employees use flexitime to avoid the commuter
rush. More direct evidence is available from Winter-
thur, Switzerland, where a majority of the workforce
has some form of flexible work schedules: a significant reduction in rush hour congestion has been
measured there, with a consequent saving by the
local mass transit system. See Alvar O. Elbing and
John R. M. Gordon, "Self-Management in the Emerging Flexible Organization," *Futures* (August 1974).
On the effects on female labor-force participation,
see Heinz Allenspach, "Flexible Working Time: Its
Development and Application in Switzerland," *Occupational Psychology* 46, 4 (1972): 209–15.

[7] For discussion of American experience, see "New
Flexible Hours Increase Productivity at First National
Bank of Boston," mimeo (First National Bank of Bos-
ton, 1974); United States Social Security Administra-
tion, "Report on BDP Flexitime Study Midpoint Sur-
vey," mimeo (Washington, D.C.: 1974); and Robert T.
Golembiewski, Rick Hilles, and Munro J. Kagno, "A
Longitudinal Study of Flexitime Effects: Some Conse-
quences of an OD Structural Intervention," *Journal of
Applied Behavioral Science* 10, 4 (1974): 503–32.

For a survey of European experience, see George
Moller Racke, "The Effects of Flexible Working Hours"
(Ph.D. dissertation, University of Lausanne, Switzer-
land, 1975); Michael Wade, *Flexible Working Hours
in Practice* (Essex: Gower, 1973); Baum and Young,
A Practical Guide to Flexible Working Hours; and J.
Harvey Bolton, *Flexible Working Hours* (Wembley:
Anbar, 1971).

[8] See Alvar O. Elbing and John R. M. Gordon,
Flexible Working Hours (Geneva: International Labor
Office, 1975) and "Self-Management in the Emerging
Flexible Organization"; Allenspach, "Flexible Work-
ing Time"; and Martin, *Hours of Work When Workers
Can Choose.*

these employers, it seems that a system that permits workers to come and go as they see fit would necessarily lead to anarchy in production, and that its costs would far exceed any benefits to management from improved employee morale or other gains in personnel relations.[9] A closer look at the successful application of flexitime by some managements, however, will explain how it has been made to harmonize with efficient production under a variety of circumstances.

APPLICABILITY OF THE SYSTEM

Either a white-collar or a blue-collar setting can accommodate a flexible hours scheduling system. It is the technical requirements of the work and the way in which workflows are organized that determine whether the system will work.

Flexible schedules can be introduced with relative ease in situations in which employees work in isolation from each other. The 300 employees in the highly publicized flexitime experiment of the Social Security Administration in Baltimore, who compare material displayed on an individually controlled viewing machine with typed material on their desks, provide a perfect example. Their interaction with other workers is minimal.[10] Even in other, more complex jobs, if only a part of the day must be spent in contact with others, the remaining worktime can be spent in isolation on a flexible schedule. As long as confining the necessary interactions to the core periods when all are present does not impose a cost, flexitime can be imposed without reducing efficiency.

In yet other situations, workers can be isolated from each other at a relatively small cost. In batch production layouts, for example, buffer stocks can be built up between each work station so as to permit schedule flexibility, such as in the Swiss watch industry where employees now maintain an inventory of three hours or more between work stations.[11] It is difficult to introduce flexitime in an assembly line, however, because of the close interactions among workers. Special problems are also posed by the service-on-demand jobs—such as the switchboard operator, the supplier of emergency services, and the employee in retail trade and service industries—because employees in these jobs must be in personal contact with the users of their services.

In addition to the independence of each worker, the number of people doing, or able to do, the same job plays a role in determining the applicability of the flexitime system. Large numbers can operate to reduce the effects of random variations in the schedule preferences of employees. In a batch-type production layout, for example, if there are 50 operators at each step in the production process, a buffer stock need only be kept between each group of 50 workers. When flexitime is introduced, this buffer stock will have to be increased, but the increase will be relatively minor because the variations in starting and quitting times among employees within each group will offset each other.

The positive effects of many employees doing, or capable of doing, the same job are also found in the service-on-demand type of job: the more workers, the more likely that schedule preferences will offset one another, thus minimizing the efficiency loss in providing service. There are also special cases, of course, in which flexitime may work precisely because service demands are

[9] See Karen Legge, "Flexible Working Hours—Panacea or Placebo?" *Management Decision: The European Review of Management Technology* 12, 5 (1974): 264–80.

[10] U.S. Civil Service Commission, *Legal Limitations on Flexible and Compressed Work Schedules for Federal Employees* (Washington, D. C.: U.S. Government Printing Office, 1974). This volume presents information from interviews with representatives of the U.S. Civil Service Commission who are monitoring the experiment.

[11] At the Omega watch factory in Switzerland, inventories permit a margin of three to eight hours beteen employees. See the statement by the Federation of Swiss Employers Association, "L'horaire variable en Suisse," in *L'horaire libre en 1974.*

not uniformly spread out over the standard 40-hour week. In retail trade, for example, customers may prefer to shop in the early morning, or in the evening, or on certain days of the week; under these circumstances, the standard workweek is itself suboptimal from the viewpoint of the employer and management may have to pay overtime, use part-time workers, or adopt other expensive expedients to supplement the regular work schedule. In that kind of situation, it is possible that the choices under a flexitime system will yield a pattern that is superior to, or at least not much worse than, that obtained by the standard workweek.

The applicability of flexitime can be greatly broadened by modifying the freedom given to employees under the system or by changing the organization of the work. The simplest modification is to permit employees to choose a nonstandard schedule, but then to insist that each adheres to his new schedule for some specified period. (The purist would argue that this system should then no longer be called "flexitime.") Another modification—much more highly regarded by the advocates of flexitime—is for central management to insist that whatever schedule arrangements are chosen, and however often these are changed, productivity must not suffer. Under that modification, each work group and its supervisors must arrange hours and workflows in such a way that the individual employee is allowed the flexibility he values most, while still maintaining the productivity of the group.[12]

The applicability of flexitime has been further broadened in some establishments by a reorganization of work responsibilities. Since the number of people doing, or capable of doing, the same job contributes to the success of flexitime, job enlargement or job rotation has often proved to be

the most straightforward and successful method.[13] More complicated changes in job structures are also possible: to take a popular example, if secretarial services are pooled, then secretaries can arrange to have at least one of their number on duty and available to take dictation throughout the entire bandwidth period, while typing and other tasks that do not require interaction with others can be scheduled to permit maximum freedom to the employee group. In practice, a combination of work reorganization and small group autonomy can succeed; indeed, some optimistic advocates of flexitime believe that as techniques for introducing the system are gradually improved, it will eventually be extended to a majority of the workforce.

UNION ATTITUDES

Union attitudes toward flexitime are conditioned by the treatment of the union organization in any new scheduling scheme, as well as by the bread-and-butter issues raised for the membership by flexible hours. Negative reactions by some unions in this country may be ascribed, in part, to the fact that such schemes have typically been sponsored by employers. In any event, there is evidence from European experience that if the employer introduces the system without involving the union in its design and implementation, a negative

___

12 See Elbing and Gordon, "Self-Management in the Emerging Flexible Organization," for a discussion of the positive uses of small work-group autonomy under a flexitime system.

___

13 One large English insurance company, which introduced flexitime after a considerable investment in preparatory planning, found it profitable under the new system to apply job rotation or enlargement not only to clerks but also to such very specialized and technical occupations as that of insurance underwriter. The company first reorganized all work units into sections of at least 12 people, then had workers within each section learn the jobs of some or all of the others in the group, and then gave the section chief autonomy in allocating work assignments and worktime schedules with the group. (Interviews with D. Jubb, General Manager, London and Manchester Insurance Company, and Maurice Reynolds, National Secretary, Insurance Section, Association of Scientific, Technical and Managerial Staffs, representing the London and Manchester employees).

union attitude is more likely to develop.[14] Close labor-management cooperation can help head off union suspicion that flexitime is a purely management-oriented policy and can assure prompt resolution of specific union problems under the new system. If a union local customarily holds meetings at lunchtime or just after work, for example, the introduction of flexible schedules could have a negative effect on attendance. A labor-management compromise frequently adopted in Europe is to revert to a common lunch or quitting time on the days when union meetings are held.[15] Labor representatives can also point out, and help to resolve, specific problems of hours, earnings, and work intensity that might otherwise lead to conflict.

Labor union spokesmen have argued that under some circumstances flexitime will increase the amount of time given by the employee for the same weekly wage; reduce the employee's monthly earnings while increasing the intensity of his work; and encourage longer hours of work. They have also claimed that flexitime increases management profits without raising wage rates, although the increase derives from a more effective, and often a more intensive use of labor.

Each of these points requires serious consideration. An obvious corollary of the claim that management gains from reductions in tardiness or part-day absences (because workers are more likely to make up lost time) is that more labor will actually be supplied for the same wages.[16] If the lost time is the result of oversleeping, taking time out for a haircut or hairset, or

some other frivolous cause, most employees will agree that management is within its rights to expect makeup time, but they will not extend this principle to occasions such as a visit to a doctor. Moreover, some labor spokesmen have argued that when increased employee time is put in under a flexitime system—even as a makeup for frivolous absences—the earnings of the workers should increase or there should be some other form of compensatory reward.

OVERTIME EFFECTS

Employees working under a flexitime system may spontaneously decide to stay late in order to finish a job, voluntarily offset these hours by taking time off in a slack period on another day, and so reduce overtime costs (at least if overtime premiums are calculated on the basis of weekly or monthly, rather than daily, hours). Or they may simply work more effectively while on the job (presumably because they are at work at times when they are psychologically prepared rather than at times determined by a time clock), and hence need less overtime to complete their tasks. In either case, union reaction may be unfavorable: if the employer's overtime payments are reduced, this means there has been a reduction in the gross earnings of employees,[17] and if management is also obtaining the same amount of work from employees as before, this usually means there has been an increase in the intensity of work.

There is much greater scope for reducing overtime under a flexitime system when the workers' hours choices are further limited by management. The gains to management in this area are likely to be greatest where the demand for employee ser-

---

[14] See the position paper by the Confederation General du Travail in *L'horaire libre en 1974,* and Testimony of Webber.

[15] See discussions in *L'horaire libre en 1974.* See also Henri Bernard and Michael Ghanadian, "Alternative Work Schedules," mimeo (Paris: Trade Union Advisory Council of the Organization for Economic Cooperation and Development, 1974).

[16] See Bernard and Ghanadian, "Alternative Work Schedules."

[17] See the discussion of the overtime problem in Bernard and Ghanadian, "Alternative Work Schedules," *L'horaire libre en 1974,* and Testimony of Webber.

vices varies over the week or month. A very crude method management can use to ensure that the distribution of hours under a flexitime system will match company requirements—thus reducing overtime payments—is for the employer to tell the employee the schedule he should "volunteer" to work, threatening him with sanctions, either directly or by implication, if he should "choose" otherwise. It is difficult to find examples of such gross violations of both the spirit and the letter of the flexitime agreement, and in unionized firms, of course, grievance procedures are available to eliminate such coercion. Nevertheless, well-informed European trade unionists and government officials continue to fear that such practices will become common, especially in small- or medium-size businesses in the trade and service sectors, if flexitime becomes widely accepted.[18]

It is easier to find examples of a more subtle form of management pressure, which, without violating the flexitime agreement, does induce workers to change the distribution of their working hours so as to minimize overtime payments. Consider the following hypothetical case, developed from an actual British example.[19] Employees in an office customarily work late Wednesday nights to accommodate a weekly rush of payroll work, but Mondays and Fridays are slack times. Before the introduction of flexitime, each worker put in 44 hours a week and was paid time-and-a-half for the four hours of overtime on Wednesday. Workers like long weekends, however, and so when flexitime was installed, most asked to have a portion of Monday or Friday off. Management agreed on the condition that the time be made up when the worker was needed—on Wednesdays.

This was an entirely legitimate management policy, but it can be shown that most workers may have been worse off as a result.

Assuming that each worker in this office made five dollars hourly, three alternatives need to be appraised. (a) In the original situation, with 44 hours of work, everyone's weekly pay was $230 and all worked Wednesday nights but had a relatively easy time Mondays and Fridays. With flexitime the employer in effect offered the worker the following choice. (b) In 40 hours of work per week for $200, the employee could work Wednesday nights and take either Monday morning or Friday afternoon off. Because overmanning is eliminated on those days, however, the employee must exert himself more than before on the Mondays or Fridays he does work. (c) Or, in 40 hours of work per week for $200 an employee could work a standard 8:00–4:30, five-day workweek, but again, because overmanning is eliminated, each worker must exert himself more than before on Monday and Friday.

Under flexitime, alternative a was no longer available to the worker, because the employer could meet his Wednesday night needs without offering overtime. Some workers, however, may well rank the three alternatives: $a>b>c$. These workers could be worse off under the flexitime system because their most preferred option is no longer available. In fact, where most employees have become dependent on overtime earnings to maintain their living standards, those made worse off by the system could constitute a majority of the workforce.[20]

On the other hand, some unionists fear that flexitime could lead to longer working hours, an objection with particular force in the United States where it is feared that the flexitime system would undermine legal limitations on working times. The Fair Labor Standards Act (FLSA) requirement of

---

[18] *L'horaire libre en 1974*, p. 26.

[19] Many of the objective conditions were as described in the text. However, management recognized the possibility that a sharp reduction in overtime would alienate the staff, and so did not in fact take full advantage of the opportunity to cut overtime costs.

[20] See Bernard and Ghanadian, "Alternative Work Schedules," for a discussion of this problem among low-paid British workers.

an overtime premium after 40 hours a week and the Walsh-Healy and Public Contract Acts requirements (for those employed in government or in companies working on government contracts) of overtime payments after eight hours a day now protect the working schedules of millions of employees; they are especially important for those workers whose schedules are not already regulated by a union contract. The advocates of flexitime argue, however, that workers should be allowed to carry hours forward from day to day, or even from week to week, in order to gain the full benefits of the system. (Were this not done, flexible scheduling would necessarily be confined to variations in daily starting and quitting times.) To facilitate these "carry-forwards," American labor laws could be modified to continue to require the payment of overtime premiums only in those situations in which extra worktime in a day or week was ordered by management, not when an employee chose a long workday or workweek in order to have compensatory time off at another date. This revision of the federal statutes, however, would clearly make it more difficult to enforce the hours laws.

Moreover, union spokesmen have argued that even if the law is not revised to permit carryforwards of time from one day to the next, the introduction of a flexitime system can make enforcement more difficult. Under the flexitime system, normal business hours are extended and each employee has a different starting and stopping time, thus complicating the job of the government inspector.[21] Because of the various problems flexitime raises in the enforcement of hours legislation, some union opponents actually regard the spread of the system as a step backward in the historic struggle for a shorter workday and workweek.

Another possible source of controversy between labor and management is over the distribution of benefits. Even if make-up time, overtime loss, and similar problems are resolved in a satisfactory manner (at least in the sense that most workers feel that the gains far outweigh the losses in being able to modify their own working hours), unionists question the rationale for permitting management to retain all residual benefits from the introduction of the system. In their view, insofar as higher productivity results from a more intensive use of labor under flexitime, at least a portion of the resulting gain should be distributed to labor in the form of higher earnings.[22]

RESOLUTION OF PROBLEMS

Examples of the successful resolution of all these problems through either collective bargaining or preventative management action designed to head off a potential union objection are available. European experience shows that the makeup time issue can be settled, in part, by breaking down incidents of lost time into those from justifiable and those from unjustifiable causes; the overtime problem can be alleviated if management avoids pursuing an aggressive policy of overtime reduction in situations where there is such a tradition of large overtime payments that workers regard them as a permanent prerequisite. These and similar problems are further alleviated when productivity gains—including those resulting from makeup time or from a reduction in overtime payments—are divided between higher hourly wages and higher profits, so that workers actually obtain a financial benefit, as well as greater freedom, in rearranging their schedules.[23]

[21] See the position paper by the Confederation General du Travail in *L'horaire libre en 1974.*

[22] See the discussion in Racke, "The Effects of Flexible Working Hours."

[23] Of course, the replacement of standard hours schedules by the new flexitime system will require an additional union effort to negotiate the continued protection of employee rights under the new system. Where union resources are already strained, this additional cost may itself constitute a reason for union resistance to a proposed change in schedule provisions.

The nonunion or weakly organized sectors present a different problem: concern for those groups that are economically weak but that currently enjoy legal protection from competitive market pressures on their wages and hours. There is no doubt that the extensive development of flexitime systems could make enforcement of the wage and hours provisions of the FLSA and Walsh-Healy and Public Contract Acts more difficult, especially if the laws are amended to permit voluntary carryforwards of worktime. If the use of flexible scheduling continues to spread, one can predict that the wage and hours division of the U.S. Department of Labor will have to allocate more resources to the effective enforcement of hours and overtime payment regulations. In Europe, a special commission of the French government established to study the management of work and leisure time—CATRAL—examined this issue and proposed that a random sampling procedure be used by French labor inspectors. In this way, CATRAL believes, sufficient resources can be expended in intensive investigations at selected sites to assure that the rights of the employees are being fully protected under flexible hours systems. It is hoped that the threat of inspection will act as a sufficient deterrent to all employers, so that the expense of a full census of employers need not be incurred.[24]

But while there is an obvious need to assure that bogus flexitime schemes are not used to victimize workers, there does not appear to be a very strong case for going further and using labor legislation to restrict or eliminate *genuine* flexitime schemes. The experience with flexitime in this country to date suggests that the effects of flexitime on employees tends, on balance, to be positive or neutral. Drawbacks such as the need to make up time missed or a possible loss in overtime income are offset (or even more than offset) for most

workers by the positive advantages of the system.[25]

That is not an accidental result. If an employer is to obtain a profit advantage from a genuine flexitime system, he will usually have to obtain an improvement in employee morale with its related personnel benefits. Otherwise, introducing this rather complicated new system with its unpredictable effects on efficiency is simply not worthwhile. A further constraint on the employer results from the need for a high degree of employee cooperation in order to make a genuine system of flexitime work. There are many ways in which an unpopular flexitime system can be sabotaged ranging from a simple refusal to choose schedules that conform to job needs (in the more sophisticated variants where management has delegated autonomy to the small work group) to actual physical interference with the individual time-recording devices. Hence, it has not been in management's interest to take such advantage of the system's full potential for reducing overtime income and increasing work effort that employees become disenchanted with flexible scheduling.

SUMMARY AND CONCLUSIONS

The new systems of flexible hours scheduling have not been in operation long enough and are not sufficiently widespread to provide definitive measures of their social potential. Experience to date suggests, however, that the flexitime system can make a contribution to ameliorating commuting congestion and other broad social problems of interest to government.

Where the system has been introduced and successfully maintained, it has been popular with employees and profitable to management. One reason for this outcome is the importance of employee cooperation and satisfaction in achieving the gains ex-

---

[24] See *L'horaire variable en 1974,* pp. 18–19

[25] See footnote 7.

pected. But there remain specific problems that must be worked out by business, labor, and government if such positive resolutions are to be obtained in a wide variety of job situations. Labor productivity must be maintained in each case without undermining the earnings, hours, and working conditions of the workforce. Where flexible scheduling is introduced in the union sector, a fair division of the productivity gains of the system, if any, must be negotiated. The organizational interests of the labor union must also be accommodated in the design and implementation of the new system. In the nonunion sector, it is important that legal enforcement mechanisms prevent bogus coercive flexitime systems from being unilaterally introduced at the expense of labor.

Many European examples of the successful resolution of all these problems are on record. If the problems can be as readily solved under American conditions, one might expect a diminution of union, as well as management, resistance to flexitime and its extension to a much larger proportion of the American workforce.

12

JOB REDESIGN

The jobs that employees perform periodically change because technologies change and organizational products and services change. Changes in jobs necessarily influence the persons who perform those jobs. Such changes have implications for the pleasantness of the work, opportunities to interact with other persons, amount of variety in what one does, and so on. These job changes, however, usually receive relatively little attention because they are not planned, but rather they are a consequence of other changes in the organization.

There have also been systematic attempts to change the character of jobs directly. These sorts of efforts and the resulting job changes have received much more attention. When *scientific management* was popular in the early 1900s, jobs were often *simplified*. It was assumed that such changes would allow employees to learn their tasks more rapidly and become more proficient at them, because they could repeat the same simple operation over and over.

JOB ENRICHMENT

The emphasis on efficiency through job simplification has been questioned by an increasing number of persons concerned with work. Indeed, within the last 15 years or so, a few organizations have begun to systematically change jobs away from simplification. Typically these changes have increased the number of job activities and have been deliberately designed to make the job more challenging. This approach to job redesign is frequently called *job enrichment*.

Job enrichment advocates believe that most employees seek personal growth in their work. Making work more demanding and challenging is thus seen as a way to increase employee motivation to perform well on the job. Implicitly, at least, it is assumed that the increase in motivation resulting from job enrichment will more than offset any decrement in the abilities the employee will have for performing the more complex job.

It is not the purpose of this chapter to debate the merits of job enrichment. Some job enrichment programs have apparently succeeded; others have clearly failed. One reason for the failures may have been the misguided assumption that all individuals are motivated by the same types of *intrinsic* (work related) rewards that job enrichment is designed to provide. (In this regard see Reading 3 in Chapter 2. Schwab points out that there are substantial individual differences in the types of rewards people seek in work so that not all people are likely to find job enrichment motivating.) Another reason for failure may have been inadequate attention given to the personnel/human resource implications of changes in job content.

IMPLICATIONS FOR PERSONNEL HUMAN RESOURCES

In Chapter 1 we suggested that personnel/human resource activities were aimed at facilitating a correspondence between individuals and the jobs they performed. This correspondence pertained to (a) the skills and abilities possessed by individuals and those required by the job and (b) individual expectations regarding what the job should provide by way of rewards and what rewards the job actually provides.

A change in the job will alter the correspondence along both dimensions. Note that the specific reason for the job change is not important in this regard. The correspondence will be altered whether the job change stems directly from a planned job enrichment program or indirectly from a change in the organization's technology.

Whatever the reason, the change creates immediate problems for the personnel/human resource function. Perhaps most obvious is the importance of the job change for training. If job enrichment is successful in increasing the challenge associated with performing work then it must almost certainly increase the skills required to perform the job. Thus job enrichment will probably require added training of existing employees.

Job change will also likely require changes in staffing practices. If employee abilities necessary to perform the job are altered, existing external staffing predictors are likely to require change. The job change will also result in the need to change the way performance is measured on the job. Either of those changes will affect the existing predictor-criterion validity relationships. Change in performance measurement obviously requires alteration of the performance appraisal system.

Job enrichment is also likely to require changes in internal staffing. Frequently job enrichment involves the elimination of some jobs as tasks are combined into a smaller set of more challenging work assignments. Job consolidation of this sort will change the composition of transfer and promotion routes throughout the organization.

Changes in jobs have some of the most important implications for compensation. Employees will expect that an upgrading in job content will result in an upgrading in pay levels. Unions frequently object to job enrichment programs because they fear that such programs increase the work productivity of employees without providing additional compensation. Pay structures will also undoubtedly be altered since the enrichment activities will not affect all jobs similarly.

In short, job enrichment will necessarily have a profound impact on virtually every personnel/human resource activity. If an organization decides to engage in a job enrichment program it must carefully coordinate the job changes with the personnel/human resource activities performed. Failure to do so will almost certainly doom the job enrichment efforts to failure.

INTRODUCTION TO THE READINGS

Work Design

The first paper (actually a book chapter excerpt) by J. Richard Hackman is included to familiarize you with the job enrichment concept and to illustrate how it is utilized in organizations. Hackman provides several brief examples of enrichment efforts. Some of these have been viewed as successful in terms of improved work performance and/or attitudes and others have been unsuccessful.

Hackman argues that job redesign is more consequential than many behavioral science attempts to improve employee performance and attitudes. He suggests that this greater importance results because redesign (a) changes the relationship between the employee and the job, (b) changes employee behavior, (c) provides opportunities for other organizational change, and (d) can rehumanize rather than dehumanize individual employees. While the latter point is obviously a value judgment, there can be little argument about the other observations he makes.

Hackman discusses the impact of job redesign primarily in terms of its implications for employee attitudes and behaviors. Job changes also have substantial implications for the way the organization is administered. The change in the relationship between the employee and the job is especially important for the operation of personnel/human resources as we have previously noted.

Redesign in a Coal Mine

The article by Ted Mills on job redesign in a coal mine is an excellent illustration of the difficulties and promise of a job enrichment program. This particular program grew out of a specific set of problems experienced by the coal industry, namely declining productivity and high accident levels. An underground mining company was found by the National Quality of Work Center that was willing to undertake a work redesign experiment. In addition participation was sought and obtained from the United Mine Workers.

The degree of union involvement in this program is worthy of special emphasis. Mills indicates that the union's main interest was the potential of the program for reducing mine accidents. That concern and the company's agreement that no one would lose employment because of the program was sufficient to gain active union support during the early stages of the project.

Jobs were redesigned primarily by having employees rotated through different jobs. Miners were given extensive training to acquire the needed new skills. Their responsibility for performance, safety, and discipline were increased, as was their pay. The total program thus involved substantially more than a simple job rotation system.

The program was introduced in one of the mine's three underground sections. It appears, moreover, to have been an initial success. Production in the experimental section was substantially higher than in the other sections, and there were fewer accidents. It was generally agreed that the program was successful after a year. You will see, however, that problems began to emerge thereafter. The company unilaterally decided to implement the change program in another section of the mine. This angered the union and many of the members. Some employees in other sections of the mine, as well as those working on the surface, wanted to be included in the program while others did not. The early union-management cooperation gave way to a more traditional adversary form of relationship. The program continues, however, after four years. Not all parts of the mine have been redesigned, but the experiment has spread beyond the original section. Mills believes that the program has been at least partly successful in achieving both productivity and safety goals.

In reading this account you should get a feel for some of the complexities involved when so fundamental a change as job design is considered. Such changes and the potential for positive results that they hold is one of the more exciting possibilities in the personnel/human resources field.

34. WORK DESIGN
J. RICHARD HACKMAN

Every five years or so, a new behavioral science "solution" to organizational problems emerges. Typically such a solution is first tried out—with great success—in a few forward-looking organizations. Then it is picked up by the management journals and and the popular press and spreads across the country. And finally, after a few years, it fades away as disillusioned managers, union leaders, and employees come to agree that the solution really does not solve much of anything.

Source: From *Improving Life at Work: Behavioral Science Approaches to Organizational Change*, by J. Richard Hackman and J. Lloyd Suttle (pp. 96–104). Copyright © 1977 by Goodyear Publishing Company. Reprinted by permission. Portions of this chapter are adapted from Hackman (1975b), Hackman and Oldham (1975; in press), and Hackman, Oldham, Janson, and Purdy (1975). Bibliographic assistance was provided by Kenneth Brousseau, Daniel Feldman, Linda Frank, Andrea Miller, and Irmtraud Streker.

It looks as if the redesign of work is to be the solution of the mid-1970s. The seeds of this strategy for change were planted more than two decades ago, with the pioneering of Charles Walker and Robert Guest (1952), Frederick Herzberg and his associates (Herzberg, Mausner, and Snyderman 1959; Herzberg 1966), Louis Davis (1957, 1966), and a few others. Successful tests of work redesign were conducted in a few organizations and were widely reported. Now, change programs involving work redesign are flooding the nation, stories on "how we profited from job enrichment" are appearing in management journals, and the labor community is struggling to determine how it should respond to the tidal wave that seems to be forming (Gooding 1972).

The question of the moment is whether the redesign of work will evolve into a robust and powerful strategy for organizational change—or whether, like so many of its behavioral science predecessors, it will fade into disuse as practitioners experience failure and disillusionment in its applications. The answer is by no means clear.

Present evidence regarding the merits of work redesign can be viewed as optimistic or pessimistic, depending on the biases of the reader. On the one hand, numerous published case studies of successful work redesign projects show that work redesign can be an effective tool for improving both the quality of the work experience of employees and their on-the-job productivity. Yet, it also is true that numerous failures in implementing work redesign have been experienced by organizations around the country—and the rate of failure shows no sign of diminishing. Reif and Luthans (1972), for example, summarize a survey, conducted in the mid-1960s, in which only 4 firms implementing job enrichment described their experiences with the technique as "very successful." Increasingly, other commentators are expressing serious doubts about whether job enrichment is really as effective as it has been cracked up to be (Fein 1974; Gomberg 1973; Hulin and Blood 1968).

Unfortunately, existing research findings and case reports are not very helpful in assessing the validity of the claims made by either the advocates or the skeptics of work redesign. In particular, an examination of the literature cited in Hackman (1975a) leads to the following conclusions.[1]

1. Reports of work redesign successes tend to be more evangelical than thoughtful; for example, little conceptualizing is done that would be useful either as a guide to implementation of work redesign in other settings or as a theoretical basis for research on its effects.

2. The methodologies used in evaluating the effects of changes in work design often are weak or incomplete. Therefore, findings reported may be ambiguous and open to alternative explanations.

3. Although informal sources and surveys suggest that the failure rate for work redesign projects is moderate to high, few documented analyses are available of projects that failed. This is particularly unfortunate because careful analyses of failures often are among the most effective tools for exploring the applicability and the consequences of this or any other organizational change strategy.

4. Most published reports focus almost exclusively on assessing the positive and negative effects of specific changes in work content. Conclusions are then drawn about the general worth of work redesign as a change strategy. Yet, there is an *interaction* between the content of the changes and the organizational context in which they are installed; identical job changes may have quite different effects in different organizational settings (or when installed using different processes). Existing literature has little to say about the nature or dynamics of such interactions.

5. Rarely are economic data (that is, direct and indirect dollar costs and benefits) analyzed and discussed when conclusions are drawn about the effects of work redesign projects, even though many such projects are undertaken in direct anticipation of economic gains.

In sum, it appears that despite the abundance of writing on the topic, there is little definite information about why work redesign is effective when it is, what goes wrong when it is not, and how the strategy can be altered to improve its general usefulness as an approach to personal and organizational change.

This [selection] attempts to advance cur-

---

[1] Similar conclusions are reached by Katzell and Yankelovich (1975), after a very thorough review and analysis of selected prototype studies of the effects of work redesign.

rent understanding about such questions. It reviews what is known about how the redesign of work can help improve life in organizations and attempts to identify the circumstances under which the approach is most likely to succeed. It reviews current practice for planning and installing work redesign and emphasizes both the pitfalls that may be encountered and the change strategies that have been shown to be especially effective. And, at the most general level, it asks whether this approach to organizational change is indeed worth saving, or whether it should be allowed to die.

WHAT IS WORK REDESIGN?

Whenever a job is changed—whether because of a new technology, an internal reorganization, or a whim of a manager—it can be said that work redesign has taken place. The present use of the term is somewhat more specialized. Throughout this [selection], work redesign is used to refer to any activities that involve the alteration of specific jobs (or interdependent systems of jobs) with the intent of increasing both the quality of the employees' work experience and their on-the-job productivity. This definition of the term is deliberately broad to include the great diversity of changes that can be tried to achieve these goals. It subsumes such terms as *job rotation, job enrichment,* and *sociotechnical systems design,* each of which refers to a specific approach to or technique for redesigning work.[2]

There are no simple or generally accepted criteria for a well-designed job, nor is there any single strategy that is acknowledged as the proper way to go about improving a

job. Instead, what will be an effective design for one specific job in a particular organization may be quite different from the way the job should be designed or changed in another setting. There are, nonetheless, some commonalities in most work redesign experiments that have been carried out to date. Typically changes are made that provide employees with additional responsibilities for planning, setting up, and checking their own work; for making decisions about methods and procedures; for establishing their own work pace within broad limits; and sometimes for relating directly with the client who receives the results of the work. Often the net effect is that jobs which previously had been simplified and segmented into many small parts (in the interest of efficiency from an engineering perspective) are put back together again and made the responsibility of individual workers (Herzberg 1974).

An early case of work redesign (reported by Kilbridge 1960) is illustrative. The basic job involved the assembly of small centrifugal pumps used in washing machines. Prior to redesign, the pumps were assembled by six operators on a conveyor line, with each operator performing a particular part of the assembly. The job was changed so that each worker assembled an entire pump, inspected it, and placed his own identifying mark on it. In addition, the assembly operations were converted to a batch system in which workers had more freedom to control their work pace than they had had under the conveyor system. Kilbridge reports that after the job had been enlarged, total assembly time decreased, quality improved, and important cost savings were realized.

In another case, the responsibilities of clerks who assembled information for telephone directories at Indiana Bell Telephone Company were significantly expanded (Ford 1973). Prior to the change, a production line model was used to assemble directory information. Information was passed from clerk to clerk as it was processed, and each

---

2 Because the aim of the present chapter is a *general* examination of what kinds of changes in jobs lead to what kinds of outcomes under what circumstances, there is no need to join in the occasional haggles that develop over the specific meaning of the various terms used to refer to such changes. Readers who wish to sort out the specific connotations of the various terms used in the literature are referred to expositions by Rush (1971, pp. 12–17) and by Strauss (1974, pp. 38–43).

clerk performed only a very small part of the entire job. There were a total of 21 different steps in the workflow. Jobs were changed so that each qualified clerk was given responsibility for all the clerical operations required to assemble an entire directory—including receiving, processing, and verifying all information. (For large directories, clerks were given responsibility for a specific alphabetical section of the book.) Not only did the new work arrangement improve the quality of the work experience of the employees, but the efficiency of the operation increased as well—in part because clerks made fewer errors, and so it was no longer necessary to have employees who merely checked and verified the work of others.

In recent years, work redesign increasingly has been used as part of a larger change package aimed at improving the overall quality of life and productivity of people at work. A good example is the new General Foods pet food manufacturing plant in Topeka, Kansas (Walton 1972, 1975). When plans were developed for the facility in the late 1960s, corporate management decided to design and manage the plant in full accord with state-of-the-art behavioral science knowledge. Nontraditional features were built into the plant from the beginning—including the physical design of the facilities, the management style, information and feedback systems, compensation arrangements . . . and career paths for individual employees. A key part of the plan was the organization of the workforce into teams. Each team (consisting of from 7 to 14 members) was given nearly autonomous responsibility for a significant organizational task. In addition to actually carrying out the work required to complete that task, team members performed many activities that traditionally had been reserved for management. These included coping with manufacturing problems, distributing individual tasks among team members, screening and selecting new team members, and participating in organizational decision-

making (Walton 1972). The basic jobs performed by team members were designed to be as challenging as possible, and employees were encouraged to further broaden their skills in order to be able to handle even more challenging work. Although not without problems, the Topeka plant appears to be prospering, and many employees experience life in the organization as a pleasant and nearly revolutionary change from their traditional ideas about what happens at work.

THE UNIQUENESS OF WORK REDESIGN AS A STRATEGY FOR CHANGE

The redesign of work differs from most other behavioral science approaches to changing life in organizations in at least four ways (Hackman 1975b). Together, these four points of uniqueness make a rather compelling case for work redesign as a strategy for initiating organizational change.

1. Work Redesign Alters the Basic Relationship between a Person and What He or She Does on the Job. When all the outer layers are stripped away, many organizational problems come to rest at the interface between *people* and the *tasks* they do. Frederick Taylor realized this when he set out to design and manage organizations "scientifically" at the beginning of this century (Taylor 1911). The design of work was central to the scientific management approach and special pains were taken to ensure that the tasks done by workers did not exceed their performance capabilities. As the approach gained credence in the management community, new and more sophisticated procedures for analyzing work methods emerged, and industrial engineers forged numerous principles of work design. In general, these principles were intended to maximize overall production efficiency by minimizing human error on the job (often accomplished by partitioning the work into small, simple segments), and by minimizing time and motion wasted in doing work tasks.

It turned out, however, that many workers did not like jobs designed according to the dictates of scientific management. In effect, the person-job relationship had been arranged so that achieving the goals of the organization (high productivity) often meant sacrificing important personal goals (the opportunity for interesting, personally rewarding work). Taylor and his associates attempted to deal with this difficulty by installing financial incentive programs intended to make workers *want* to work hard toward organizational goals and by placing such an elaborate set of supervisory controls on workers that they scarcely could behave otherwise. But the basic incongruence between the person and the work remained, and people-problems (such as high absenteeism and turnover, poor quality work, and high-worker dissatisfaction) became increasingly evident in work organizations.

In the past several decades, industrial psychologists have carried out a large number of studies intended to overcome some of the problems that accompanied the spread of scientific management. Sophisticated strategies for identifying those individuals most qualified to perform specific jobs have been developed and validated. New training and attitude change programs have been tried. And numerous motivational techniques have been proposed to increase the energy and commitment with which workers do their tasks. These include development of human relations programs, alteration of supervisory styles, and installation of complex piece-rate and profit-sharing incentive plans. None of these strategies have proven successful. Indeed, some observers report that the quality of the work experience of employees today is more problematic than it was in the heyday of scientific management (cf., *Work in America* 1973).

Why have behavioral scientists not been more successful in their attempts to remedy motivational problems in organizations and improve the quality of work life of employees? One reason is that psychologists

(like managers and labor leaders) have traditionally assumed that *the work itself was inviolate*—that the role of psychologists is simply to help select, train, and motivate people within the confines of jobs as they have been designed by others. Clearly, it is time to reject this assumption and to seek ways to change both people and jobs in order to improve the fit between them.

The redesign of work as a change strategy offers the opportunity to break out of the "givens" that have limited previous attempts to improve life at work. It is based on the assumption that the work itself may be a very powerful influence on employee motivation, satisfaction, and productivity. It acknowledges (and attempts to build on) the inability of people to set aside their social and emotional needs while at work. And it provides a strategy for moving away from extrinsic props to worker motivation and to move instead toward *internal* work motivation that causes the individual to do the work because it interests him, challenges him, and rewards him for a job well done.

2. Work Redesign Directly Changes Behavior—and It Tends to Stay Changed. People do the tasks they are given. How well they do them depends on many factors, including how the tasks are designed. But no matter how the tasks are designed, people do them.

On the other hand, people do *not* always behave in ways that are consistent with their attitudes, their levels of satisfaction, or what they cognitively know they should do. Indeed, it is now well established that one's attitudes often are *determined* by the behaviors one engages in—rather than vice versa, as traditionally has been thought (Bem, 1970; Kiesler, Collins, and Miller 1969). This is especially true when individuals perceive that they have substantial personal freedom or autonomy in choosing how they will behave (Steiner 1970).

Enriching jobs, then, may have twin virtues. First, behavior is changed; and second, because enriched jobs usually bring about increased feelings of autonomy and personal discretion, the individual is likely to develop attitudes that are supportive of his new on-the-job behaviors (cf. Taylor 1971). Work redesign does not, therefore, rely on changing attitudes first (for example, inducing the worker to care more about the work outcomes, as in zero defects programs) and hoping that the attitude change will generalize to work behavior. Instead, the strategy is to change the *behavior,* and to change it in a way that gradually leads to a more positive set of attitudes about the work, the organization, and the self.

Moreover, after jobs are changed, it usually is difficult for workers to slip back into old ways. The old ways simply are inappropriate for the new tasks, and the structure of those tasks reinforces the changes that have taken place. Thus, one need not worry much about the kind of backsliding that occurs so often after training or attitude modification activities, especially those that occur off-site. The task-based stimuli that influence the worker's behavior are very much on-site, every hour of every day. And once those stimuli are changed, behavior is likely to stay changed—at least until the job is again redesigned.

3. Work Redesign Offers—and Sometimes Forces into One's Hands—Numerous Opportunities for Initiating Other Organizational Changes. When work is redesigned in an organization so that many people are doing things differently than they used to, new problems inevitably surface and demand attention. These can be construed solely as *problems,* or they can be treated as *opportunities* for further organizational change activities. For example, technical problems are likely to develop when jobs are changed—offering opportunities to smooth and refine the work system as a system. Interpersonal issues also are likely to arise, almost inevitably between supervisors and subordinates and sometimes between peers who now have to relate to one another in new ways. These issues offer opportunities for developmental work aimed at improving the social and supervisory aspects of the work system.

Because such problems are literally forced to the surface by the job changes, all parties may feel a need to do something about them. Responses can range from using the existence of a problem to justify that "job enrichment doesn't work," to simply trying to solve the problem quickly so the work redesign project can proceed, to using the problem as a point of entry for attacking other organizational issues. If the last stance is taken, behavioral science professionals may find themselves pleasantly removed from the old difficulty of selling their wares to skeptical managers and employees who are not really sure there is anything wrong. Eventually a program of organizational change and development may evolve that addresses organizational systems and practices that, superficially at least, seem unrelated to how the work itself is designed (Beer and Huse 1972).

4. Work Redesign, in the Long Term, Can Result in Organizations That Rehumanize Rather Than Dehumanize the People Who Work in Them. Despite the popular inflation of the work ethic issue in recent years ... there is convincing evidence that organizations can and do sometimes stamp out part of the humanness of their members—especially people's motivations toward growth and personal development (cf. Kornhauser 1965).

Work redesign can help individuals regain the chance to experience the kick that comes from doing a job well, and it can encourage them to once again *care* about their work and about developing the competence to do it even better. These payoffs from work redesign go well beyond simple job satisfaction. Cows grazing in the field may be satisfied, and employees in organizations can be made just as satisfied by paying them well, by keeping bosses off their backs, by putting them in pleasant work rooms with pleasant people, and by arranging things so that the days pass without undue stress or strain.

The kind of satisfaction at issue here is different. It is a satisfaction that develops only when individuals are stretching and growing as human beings, increasing their sense of competence and self-worth. Whether the creation of opportunities for personal growth is a legitimate goal for work redesign activities is a value question deserving long discussion; the case for the value of work redesign strictly in terms of *organizational* health easily can rest on the first three points discussed above. But personal growth is without question a central component of the overall quality of work life in organizations, and the impact of work redesign on the people who do the work, as human beings, should be neither overlooked nor underemphasized. . . .

REFERENCES

Beer, M., and Huse, E. F. "A Systems Approach to Organization Development." *Journal of Applied Behavioral Science* 8 (1972): 79–101.

Bem, D. J. *Beliefs, Attitudes, and Human Affairs.* Monterey, Calif.: Brooks/Cole, 1970.

Davis, L. E. "Toward a Theory of Job Design." *Journal of Industrial Engineering* 8 (1957): 19–23.

Davis, L. E. "The Design of Jobs." *Industrial Relations* 6 (1966): 21–45.

Fein, M. "Job Enrichment: A Reevaluation." *Sloan Management Review* 15 (1974): 69–88.

Ford, R. N. "Job Enrichment Lessons from AT&T." *Harvard Business Review*, January–February 1973, pp. 96–106.

Gomberg, W. "Job Satisfaction: Sorting Out the Nonsense." *AFL-CIO American Federationist,* June 1973.

Gooding, J. *The Job Revolution.* New York: Walker, 1972.

Hackman, J. R. *Improving the Quality of Work Life: Work Design.* Washington, D.C.: Office of Research, ASPER, U.S. Dept. of Labor, 1975 (a).

Hackman, J. R. "On the Coming Demise of Job Enrichment." In *Man and Work in Society,* edited by E. L. Cass and F. G. Zimmer. New York: Van Nostrand-Reinhold, 1975 (b).

Hackman, J. R., and Oldham, G. R. "Development of the Job Diagnostic Survey." *Journal of Applied Psychology* 60 (1975): 159–70.

Hackman, J. R., and Oldham, G. R. "Motivation Through the Design of Work: Test of a Theory." *Organizational Behavior and Human Performance,* in press.

Hackman, J. R., Oldham, G. R., Janson, R., and Purdy, K. "A New Strategy for Job Enrichment." *California Management Review,* Summer 1975, pp. 57–71.

Herzberg, F. *Work and the Nature of Man.* Cleveland: World, 1966.

Herzberg, F. "The Wise Old Turk." *Harvard Business Review*, September–October 1974, pp. 70–80.

Herzberg, F., Mausner, B., and Snyderman, B. *The Motivation to Work.* New York: Wiley, 1959.

Hulin, C. L., and Blood, M. R. "Job Enlargement, Individual Differences, and Worker Responses." *Psychological Bulletin* 69 (1968): 41–55.

Katzell, R. A., and Yankelovich, D. *Work, Productivity and Job Satisfaction.* New York: The Psychological Corporation, 1975.

Kiesler, C. A., Collins, B. E., and Miller, N. *Attitude Change.* New York: Wiley, 1969.

Kilbridge, M. D. "Reduced Costs Through Job Enrichment: A Case." *The Journal of Business* 33 (1960): 357–62.

Kornhauser, A. *Mental Health of the Industrial Worker.* New York: Wiley, 1965.

Reif, W. E., and Luthans, F. "Does Job Enrichment Really Pay Off?" *California Management Review,* Fall 1972, pp. 30–37.

Rush, H. M. F. *Job Design for Motivation.* New York: The Conference Board, 1971.

Steiner, I. D. "Perceived Freedom." In *Advances in Experimental Social Psychology,* edited by L. Berkowitz. Vol. 5. New York: Academic Press, 1970.

Strauss, G. "Job Satisfaction, Motivation, and Job Redesign." In *Organizational Behavior: Research and Issues,* edited by G. Strauss,

R. E. Miles, C. C. Snow, and A. S. Tannenbaum. Madison, Wisc.: Industrial Relations Research Association, 1974.

Taylor, F. W. *The Principles of Scientific Management.* New York: Harper, 1911.

Taylor, J. C. "Some Effects of Technology in Organizational Change." *Human Relations* 24 (1971): 105–23.

Walker, C. R., and Guest, R. H. *The Man on the Assembly Line.* Cambridge, Mass., Harvard University Press, 1952.

Walton, R. E. "How to Counter Alienation in the Plant." *Harvard Business Review*, November-December 1972, pp. 70–81.

Walton, R. E. "From Hawthorne to Topeka and Kalmar." In *Man and Work in Society*, edited by E. L. Cass and F. G. Zimmer. New York: Van Nostrand-Reinhold, 1975.

Woodward, J. *Management and Technology.* London: H. M. Stationary Office, 1958. *Work in America.* Cambridge, Mass.: MIT Press, 1973.

35. ALTERING THE SOCIAL STRUCTURE IN COAL MINING: A CASE STUDY

TED MILLS

In the past five years, all over the Western world, there has been a substantial growth of interest—reflected in increased experimentation and activity—in the human contribution to work performance. With major organizations such as the United Automobile Workers and General Motors in the vanguard, American labor and management in both the public and private sectors are beginning to pay significantly more attention to the growing body of expertise in a field increasingly called "the quality of working life," which focuses on the overall development of the human resource in enterprise.

COAL MINING PRODUCTIVITY

In order to develop and explore the quality of working life concept, the National Quality of Work Center has conducted a number of diverse experiments in various industries. None of these industries is more fascinating for such exploration than underground coal mining, the subject of this case study. For one thing, coal mining is hard, hazardous, health-jeopardizing work, as everyone—particularly miners and their

union—is aware. More significantly, available data, though very crude, indicate that the industry's productivity has declined precipitously during the past decade. Unofficial productivity figures for the entire industry, including the highly productive strip mining operations, are bad enough; the figures for underground mining alone are far worse. For example, Consolidation Coal's big underground Ireland mine in the Ohio River area showed a decrease in daily production per miner from 25 tons in 1966 to 10.6 in 1974, with the rate continuing to fall in 1975 despite investments of millions of dollars in ultramodern technology to try to stem the decline.

Whenever productivity declines, of course, the overriding question for management and unions alike is, why?

In the coal mining case, some managers suggest that when stringent new state mining safety laws and the Federal Coal Mine Health and Safety Act of 1969 took effect, with inspectors crawling around the mines to enforce them, productivity plummeted. But, curiously, the productivity decrease after the new laws were passed was not significantly greater than the years before the federal act took effect; productivity just continued its downward march.

Source: *Monthly Labor Review* 99, 10 (1976): 3–10.

Another possible explanation for the productivity decrease is that miners, like other Americans, had become increasingly better educated, with higher expectations from their work, with consequently increasing resistance to the dismal conditions and work organization of most underground mines.

For these reasons, underground coal mining seemed, in 1973, an intriguing place to implement some of the emerging quality of working life notions. These notions postulate, among other things, that joint union and management efforts to involve employees in the decisions that affect their lives on the job can and will have measurable impacts on their attitudes toward work, employer, union, and even themselves as human beings. According to the quality of working life approach, when you change the quality of the individual's experience at work, you will find employees in turn changing both the quantity and quality of the work they are asked to do. When the quality of working life is high, in other words, improved productivity may be one of the important consequences. This notion is sometimes stated as "change the work, change the worker."

Most mining managements have traditionally assumed that there are essentially only two ways to remedy falling productivity underground: Sweetening the paycheck, or increasing capital investment in mining machinery. Until the experiment launched by the National Quality of Work Center, few mine managers or union leaders had considered that restructuring work systems underground, providing miners with new insights about their (and their machines') performance of work, might have a measurable positive impact on productivity in mining.

THE AGREEMENT

In 1973, I was able to persuade the National Commission of Productivity to support a quality-of-working-life experiment in a coal mine (the experiment later shifted, along with the rest of our Quality of Work Program, to the National Quality of Work Center when that organization was founded in 1974). We found a mine president (Warren Hinks of the Rushton Mining Company) who was intrigued by the notion of working with his people as well as his machines. And we found that the newly elected president of the United Mine Workers of America (Arnold R. Miller, himself a victim of black-lung disease) was intrigued by the potential of the quality-of-working-life effort to improve the health and safety of underground mine workers. We found that Professor Eric Trist, a social scientist from the Wharton School of the University of Pennsylvania who had done classic work on socio-technical work restructure in British mines more than two decades before, would be available and interested in participating in the project. Dr. Gerald Sussman, a research psychologist from the Pennsylvania State University, and Grant Brown, a Penn State mining engineer, formed the rest of the Trist team.

In mid-1973, the mine president, the United Mine Workers president, and the consultant team met for the first time, in the UMW building in Washington. Hinks and Miller signed an experiment-launching agreement which stipulated, among other things, that either party could end the experiment by just a phone call, that no miner would lose a job because of the experiment, and, most important of all, that the experiment would be "jointly owned" by the management and the union during its 18-month lifetime.

In all of the National Quality of Work Center's many, diverse projects across the country, all of them in unionized workplaces, this "joint ownership" is of major significance to the potential success of each project. To the participants it means that neither management nor union is running the project, but rather both at once, co-operatively. To the consultants, it means their "client" is both the management and the union members who make up the labor-management committees formed in every project.

In all Center projects, there are two or more such labor-management committees, situated at various levels from the top of the organization to the bottom. The top tier committee usually comprises two or three senior executive officers of the entire organization (often including the chief executive officer) and two or three senior officers of the international union (often including the president). The focus of this committee is organizationwide; the joint objective at this level is eventually to spread the first experimental efforts (if they prove beneficial) throughout the organization.

This top committee—which may be called a "core committee" or a "steering committee" or whatever—identifies a divisional, second-tier area of the organization where the union and management feel the first active shopfloor experiment should be inaugurated. In large operations (two Center projects involve organizations with more than 50,000 employees and unions of more than 500,000 members), such second-tier areas are usually operating divisions or regions. The Center encourages these divisions or regions to form second-tier divisional or regional labor-management committees of 6 to 10 management and union officers from that level. They in turn identify one or more plants or work organizations for experimental activity, where plant-level committees (usually with 12 to 14 members, evenly divided between managers and union members) are established.

As this case history shows, there are good reasons for urging such a multi-tier approach to quality-of-working-life projects in organizations of any size. One reason is *sanction:* participants at the plant level where the first experimental efforts occur are reassured that both their union and their management, all the way up to the top, jointly approve of, and are even part of, the experiment. (More than once, Rushton coal miners were heard to justify their commit-ment to the experiment by saying, "Arnold Miller's for it.") Another reason is *visibility:* What happens in a plant far from organizational or divisional headquarters is known, monitored, and evaluated at each level; the danger of "encapsulation"—achieving something impressive that no one beyond the local workplace knows or cares about—is significantly lessened. But perhaps the most important reason for the multi-tier structure is the built-in impetus and potential it provides for eventually spreading or *diffusing* a successful experiment from the first workplace to others, first within the division by the division-level committee and then from one division to another by the top-level committee. Sanction from the top adds prestige, encouragement, and a sense of importance to work-change activities at the workplace level; organizationwide visibility creates higher level awareness of what is achieved; the potential for diffusion makes experimental efforts far more significant, justifiable, and cost-effective, for if they provide the hoped-for benefits to the management and union sponsors, the built-in structure can spread those benefits throughout the organization.

IMPLEMENTATION

The Rushton mine was a small, independently owned 235-worker mine in central Pennsylvania, not part of a larger organization as are most other Center projects. (It subsequently became an owned subsidiary of Pittsburgh Power and Light Co.) Nevertheless, it had two tiers of committees. The 12-member top-tier steering committee, which included the mine president and superintendent and the president of the UMW local, would eventually authorize the formation, in each affected underground section of the mine, of section committees, comprising one supervisor and one union member in each of the section's three shifts, for a total of six members per section.

It took the mine's steering committee a while to realize that its joint diagnosis of mine work structures and work performance was quite different from the traditional adversary and money matters usually discussed in labor-management meetings. But slowly, under the guidance of the Trist team, committee members began to learn how to examine all work-related aspects of underground mining, one by one, and to devise notions for improving them.

After four months of weekly steering committee meetings, a carefully prepared 15-page report which they called "the document" was finally drawn and jointly approved. It covered many points and recommended many major changes, most of them organizational. But unfortunately, it concerned itself almost exclusively with the establishment of a new experimental underground section operating under brand new principles (for the United States) of human organization in mining. The major points of "the document" were:

1. An experimental section would be established in the mine, comprising 27 volunteers, 9 to a shift.

2. Every worker in the experimental section would be on top pay. This meant the experimental section would cost at most $324 more each week than other sections, not a prohibitive cost factor to the mine's management.

3. All members of each crew would be, or would be trained by the company to be, capable of performing any job in the section, from continuous miner operation to roof bolting. The entire crew would also be given special training in state and federal mine safety laws, so each miner would know what constitutes a violation. Each crew of the experimental section, therefore, would be an autonomous workteam.

4. Each of the three crew foremen in the section would henceforth have responsibility and authority primarily for the safety of the crew. The responsibility to management for the day-to-day production of coal by the crew was transferred to the entire workteam of nine men now without a boss.

5. Grievances by any member of the section would be dealt with primarily by the crew involved, in what is sometimes called "peer discipline." If the crew couldn't cope with a grievance itself, it would then be processed through the local union's formal grievance machinery.

A meeting of the full membership of the union was called to approve "the document." The vote of those attending was strongly in favor. By that membership approval, production at the mine had legally become—although experimentally only—a joint worker-management responsibility.

An important factor in the deliberations of the steering committee, in the final membership vote ratifying the document experimentally, and in the entire mine's initial acceptance of the experiment was an explicit search for ways to improve the safety of the miners. This emphasis on safety underlay Miller's initial interest and official UMW endorsement of the project. It underlay the decision to entrust foremen with primary concern for crew safety, instead of production. Safety improvement, in many ways, was the motivation for the entire initial effort.

Once the document was ratified, the next step was to call for volunteers for the new experimental section, called "2 South." The list was quickly subscribed. Then came training for the three crews of the all-volunteer section. The miners worked at the jobs they had originally bid for, but they were encouraged to begin learning every job in the crew and to familiarize themselves with state and federal safety laws. On February 24, 1974, each of the three new crews of 2 South elected one miner to be a member of the section committee, management appointed five members, and the "official" implementation of the experiment underground was underway.

THE FIRST YEAR'S RESULTS

Some ten months later, in January 1975, at a labor-management conference in Buffalo sponsored by the National Commission on Productivity and Work Quality, miners, foremen, and managers from Rushton told of their experiences to date. From what they said to the large audience, it was obvious that they felt that the new social system of the experimental section and the new role of foremen in that section were working. The change was evident, they said, not only in what they did, but also in how they felt.

A 25-year-old miner, since promoted to foreman, put his feelings this way:

Suddenly, we felt we mattered to somebody. Somebody trusted us. . . . The funny thing is, in the new system, the crew, we don't really get tired any more. We probably work twice as hard as we did before, but we don't get tired. . . . It's like you feel you're somebody, like you feel you're a professional, like you got a profession you're proud of . . . all 27 guys in all three shifts.

A section foreman, also since promoted and now assistant director of training, spoke candidly about the radically changed foreman function. He told the audience that it took a lot of personal adjustment not to be (or act like) a "boss" any more, but that once he learned the new system, he found that he had more time to study safety problems coming up, time that the old system had never allowed him. His relations with his crew were first-rate, he said, but he pointed out that now they respected him because of what he knows, and not just because he was boss. He liked that.

Warren Hinks, the mine president, spoke last. He said that the impact of the experiment underground was reaching upward into his management and the management style of the mine as a whole; it was changing much of his own and his subordinates' notions about mine management, above ground as well as under.

In February 1975, a few weeks after the conference, the three full crews of the 2 South experimental section gathered, as scheduled, for one of the all-day critique and training sessions that occurred about every six weeks. But this session turned out to be special. For the first time since they

had joined together, the 27 miner members and 3 foremen of 2 South were shown actual management figures for their performance. The figures were for only one month, January 1975, but it was the first feedback to the crews of their effectiveness as a section compared with the nonexperimental sections of the mine.

The miners were astonished. As a section, they had mined 25 percent more coal than the poorest section of the mine. This achievement was even more impressive because a roof cave-in had rendered their mine inoperative for 5 of the 21 working days that month, or almost 25 percent of the working days. And their section's operating cost (covering materials, timbers, bolts, maintenance, and so forth) was almost 40 percent under that of the poorest section. As a result, the cost of clean coal produced by the experimental section in January 1975 was $1.16 a ton, $0.71 under the mine average of $1.87 and $1.58 under the poorest section, whose clean coal that month cost $2.74 a ton.

To members of the local and international unions, however, the experimental section's safety record for the first year of operation was even more impressive. In 1974, one of the mine's nonexperimental sections had amassed 37 federal safety violations, and the other had 17; the experimental section had incurred only 7. The other two sections reported 25 accidents in 1974, 5 of them involving lost time. The experimental 2 South section reported only 7 and just 1 lost-time accident (which the crews insisted was an unavoidable fluke).

The 2 South section that racked up these impressive performance and safety records for about its first year of operation differed from the other two sections only in its social or organizational structure. The technology used by all three sections was the same most of the time. Mine services were the same. What was different was 2 South's autonomy as a work unit. (The performance data cited are management's figures for one month only, however, and during that particular month, conditions in 2 South's section of the mine were generally better than those encountered by the poorest section, though that advantage may have been roughly canceled out by 2 South's five down days from the roof cave-in.)

Both the miners in the experimental section and management were delighted by these figures. It seemed clear that in every way—in the changed self-estimate of the crews, in their productivity, and in their safety record—the experimental section was working more impressively than anyone had hoped. On that snowy day in 1975, with the experiment a year old, it would have been understandable to describe the new system as enormously successful, with major ramifications for improved safety and productivity in the mining industry. But any euphoria that may have been experienced that day was soon to be dispelled.

THE RISING STORM

In late 1974, with the new push on for coal as an energy source, the management unilaterally decided to start a fourth section in the mine. A decision was made—unfortunately without consulting the union—that the fourth section (to be called 5 Butt) would operate under the new system, which everyone, miners and management and consultants, now referred to as "autonomous." The joint steering committee was presented this decision as a fait accompli, which rankled many union members, particularly the representative of the UMW International.

This new section was also to be composed only of volunteers. But this time, the volunteers for 5 Butt were mostly "yellow hats," or apprentice new miners. Older miners, most of whom seemed to prefer to stay with the crews they'd worked with for years, did not rush to this section as the committee had anticipated. So an appreciable number of the members of the new 27-man section were greenhorns, brand new to mining, who were to earn top mine pay

from the start, a factor that helped set off the coming storm.

Another factor was ignorance, or inadequate communications throughout the mine, or both. Beginning in late 1974 and mounting in the spring, the rumor-mill began to operate full blast among the mine's rank and file. One highly persistent—and untrue—rumor was that the "autonomous" sections, and they alone, had made a deal with management by which any productivity increases would be shared; the other sections, the rumor went, were to have no such sharing. Additionally, dissident union members not in the two experimental sections, and particularly those in above ground work, began to say that they too wanted top mine pay. Why should "yellow hats" get it when workers with years and decades of seniority did not?

At a local union meeting in March 1975, one of the dissident miners proposed that the top-pay provisions of the experimental sections be extended to the entire union membership, or the union would exercise its right to terminate the project. The proposal was accepted by the members present.

Now faced with a legal union mandate to devise a formula for diffusing the experiment to the full mine population if it was to be continued at all, the embattled steering committee sought to find some formula which would be acceptable to the mine's management, to the local union leadership, to the rank and file, and to the United Mine Workers International. Moreover, the formula would have to be acceptable to all concerned as a permanent solution which could continue beyond the soon-to-expire 18-month experimental period. For the union, the formula had to apply equitably throughout the entire mine operation and not violate national agreements between the UMW and the Bituminous Coal Operators of America (BCOA). And for management, it had to be a formula that would not price the mine's labor force out of competitive range.

Nevertheless, by June 1975, a formula ("document no. 2") had been devised which was acceptable to the steering committee, the United Mine Workers contract officials in Washington, the mine management, and all officers of the local. Throughout July, members of the research team and the steering committee endeavored to explain the details of the complex new "document" to the entire workforce, meeting in groups of eight to ten miners at a time. In essence, the new document offered each underground miner in all sections of the mine the option of accepting or refusing the "experimental" autonomous principles of job-rotation at top pay. It offered every worker 90 workdays at top pay while training for the new type of work system. At the end of 90 days, workers would take a proficiency test. If they passed, they would be permanently assigned to an autonomous section at the new rate of pay.

It didn't work. Perhaps the formula was just too complex. Perhaps its provisions were wrongly conceived or inadequately explained. Perhaps the miners in the more productive experimental sections had developed—as some others charged—a holier-than-thou smugness about their way of life that angered their peers. Perhaps it was political factionalism within the local. Perhaps too many of the older miners were too tradition-bound or too close to retirement to welcome major changes in their ways of working. Perhaps the persistent false rumor of a local-union sellout to management had sunk in.

Whatever the reasons, the local union rejected the new document in mid-August 1975, by a razor-thin margin of 79 against, 75 for, with 16 absent.

The vote rocked the consultants, the local union leadership, and the mine management, who had jointly devised the formula and had been convinced it would easily pass. It rocked the United Mine Workers officials in Washington and in the UMW's regional district, who had given it their endorsement.

Legally, the vote was merely a rejection of the new formula. But the stunned local union leadership interpreted it as more—as rank-and-file rejection of the whole experiment, ending the cooperative joint union-management decision-making phase. The union leaders, aware that almost half the membership of the local (and perhaps more than half, had the absent members been present) wanted to continue and expand the experimental conditions, asked management to continue the new work systems in the autonomous sections, so cherished by the miners in them, exactly as they were, but as a unilateral management decision. Also at the union's request, the name of the steering committee was changed to the training and development committee (under a clause in the national BCOA-UMW contract permitting union-management cooperation in those areas). But unlike the steering committee, the new training and development committee was no longer—officially—a decision-making body. It was to recommend to management, which would make all decisions unilaterally.

In the fall of 1975, several things happened. Almost immediately after the vote against the new formula, there was a perceptible fall-off in productivity and an accompanying rise in safety violations throughout the mine, particularly in the formerly "yellow-hat" second autonomous "5 Butt" section. The former steering committee continued to meet regularly under its new name, with exactly the same faces around the table as for the previous two years, with continuing counsel from the research team. In October, it began deliberating a new formula. Warren Hinks, the mine president, noted with a smile that by the time that formula was set into place in the mine in October 1975, the newly named training and development committee had reassumed all of the steering committee's old labor-management decision-making functions, as if the August vote had never happened.

The mine still contained a large percentage of workers unconvinced that the autonomous mode of the experimental volunteer sections was a good way to mine coal. The committee's new formula gave such miners an option. Management announced that for a period of one year, all workers except new "yellow-hat" entrants in the entire mine—above ground and below—would be paid the top rate for their area of the mine, and all would be given training in all the jobs performed in their areas. Those who showed no interest or willingness to learn jobs other than their own would revert to the contract rate for their job, which usually would be less pay. Because this was a management decision recommended by the committee, there was no formal debate among the miners.

In August 1976, the Rushton project entered its fourth year. The initial experimental phase was dead; the research team felt it expired long before the August 1975 brouhaha, when the focus at the mine began—through peer pressures, primarily—to turn its focus from two sections underground to the new focus on the entire mine. Even the terms used around the mine have changed: "autonomous" has largely dropped out of currency; no one now refers to "the program" or "the experiment" as they used to. According to President Hinks, today miners and managers, in referring to the new participative social system, simply talk about "our way of working."

Since October 1975, the focus of "our way of working" has been increasingly on managers and foremen, on the sound assumption that mine personnel at those levels often require more understanding and reassurance about participative management than do the underground miners on whom the initial phase focused exclusively. In July 1976, a leadership effectiveness course for managers was inaugurated. The old section conferences of the experimental period are still full-day meetings to examine social and interpersonal work problems, but they now occur half as often as in the old days of 1974. Miner training has been shifted underground, where workers train with the mine's machines, and a new machine-maintenance consultant has been retained.

In late 1975, the third of the mine's four sections—1 East—voluntarily adopted "our way of working" as an autonomous unbossed workteam, with no formal fanfare and no new "document" to set it up. Its safety record has changed dramatically since then, from five lost-time accidents with one fatality under the traditional system in 1974 to one lost-time accident in 1975 under the new system, and one thus far through 1976. (The first experimental section, 2 South, improved its splendid one lost-time 1974 record to none in 1975 and none thus far in 1976). Nor is it coincidence, perhaps, that of five promotions in the mine since mid-1975, all have come from the 2 South section: four miners promoted to foreman and managerial positions, and one foreman promoted to assistant training director. Further, perceiving the value of the extra training the experimental crews had received, the mine management brought in a new training consultant to expand such training throughout the mine. And the renamed steering committee, now operating as before but under its new alias, has been wrestling with a soon-to-be-proposed gain-sharing plan (requested in the original "document no. 1"), reportedly to resemble a modified "Scanlon plan" for profit sharing. Clearly, there were spinoffs from the original experiment, not specifically bottom-line productivity improvements, which had significantly increased the effectiveness of the entire mine and the utilization of its human resources.

"Our way of working" is still very much in place at Rushton, operating under different names, and with its new, minewide focus. Yet, it has not entirely won. Pockets of hard-nose resistance in management and among the workers remain unbudged, although Hinks says many of those are slowly and suspiciously "coming around." The fourth section, 2 North, will as yet have none of "our way of working" (and has had four lost-time accidents thus far in 1976). There have been several wildcat strikes, at Eastertime a big one (about bidding for a single temporary job). Problems, lots of them, remain.

LESSONS AND QUESTIONS

When questioned in August 1976 about his prognosis for the future of "the way we work" at Rushton, the mine president—still as committed to its principles as in 1973—identified his feelings as "positive." He paused, then added, "but not euphoric." He said, looking backward, that a lot of good things have happened, and, although there's no way to know for sure, a lot of bad things have probably been avoided. Generally, most officers of the local union share Hinks' cautious optimism for the future; they agree that labor-management dialogue and joint consultation are probably permanently imbedded in the organization. An unpublished 1976 report by UMW officials, however, is critical of what Rushton has actually achieved in terms of major safety advances. The report does not treat the three-year lost-time and accident performance of 2 South, and more recently 1 East, as significant.

With the benefit of hindsight, however, almost all who have been involved with the project concur that what is most significant about the still unfinished Rushton story is not whether the new participative social system works in underground face mining in the United States. Its feasibility as a more human, more effective, measurably safer way of mining coal has been proved beyond a reasonable doubt, as every Rushton miner who has worked in it will vouchsafe. What remains to be seen, however, with implications for every underground mine operation in the United States, is if the new work-restructuring approaches can be successfully applied to a *total mining organization,* at every level of that organization, above ground as well as under ground, and particularly with mine managements.

The dissidence, suspicion, and hard-core resistance that developed at Rushton and culminated in the negative vote of August 1975 suggest an important lesson: although initiating socio-technical change activities through a single "shopfloor" workplace unit may be a useful or even mandatory "entry" device into an organization and the best or only way to get an organizational change program going, it must quickly be expanded throughout the workplace, or peer-pressure troubles are certain to arise. A study of the negative August 1975 vote reveals that all those who had personally experienced the new social system in action voted for continuance and expansion; almost uniformly, those who voted against had not been touched by the experimental activity. And because those untouched miners had no personal, experiential understanding of the new social system in action, they perceived, quite understandably, the key issues involved to be traditional issues such as equity in pay, which they did understand.

Another hindsight judgment worth noting is that once 5 Butt, the second experimental section, got underway, the steering committee, perhaps considering its experimental task accomplished, ceased to meet regularly. Many involved suggest that had it continued to meet regularly, it might have been able to both perceive and take remedial action against the rising suspicions, dissidence, and minewide thrust. The permanent function of labor-management bodies at every level may be as much to observe, diagnose, and take regularly scheduled soundings as it is to make implementive decisions.

Perhaps the most useful lesson to be learned by the Rushton story to date is a lesson in scale. At the inception of the effort, it was a small, one-section "shop-floor" experiment in the effectiveness of autonomous workteams in mining coal underground. That was the totality of the original "experiment" inaugurated by Miller and Hinks, a small, joint search for innovative mining techniques which might bring greater safety and perhaps productivity to coal production. But it could not stay small. By early 1975, it was evident (looking backward) that peer pressures were already transforming that first experiment into a totally different effort: the mandatory diffusion of the same participative notions to the entire organization. The latter had, and still has, a scale of hugely different proportion and complexity. For what might be called the second, evolutionary stage focusing on the whole mine, involved not just one kind of work, workers, and technology (digging coal underground) but many. It involved electricians, maintenance workers, bulldozer operators, clerks, supervisors, managers, and trainers. It involved an entire organization to be introduced slowly and effectively to "our way of work."

The basic lesson is that tactical "entry at the bottom," however initially effective, always has in it the larvae of the obligatory second stage which, if not accommodated by carefully preplanned strategies for growth, will grow hungrily and finally burst out of their chrysalis.

The Trist research team had conceived the total organization as the experimental locus from the outset. The two experimental sections—2 South and 5 Butt—had been conceived and structured as but initial efforts within a broader, minewide plan of project growth. But the tactics of entry had obscured from the mine population this larger multi-tier vision: the visible focus to the participants remained too long underground and too long on just two sections. Had management, local and international union, miners, and the consultant team worked from the outset to eventually bring work restructure and new participative systems to all, the Rushton story might have

been quite a different story, avoiding the traumas of 1975 and 1976. True, full sanction from top to bottom was present from the start. To most of the mine organization, however, strong, organizationwide visibility and preconceived commitment to diffusion were missing.

Many still-unanswered questions remain for time, the mine's union and management, and present and future consultants to answer. The key question, of course, is whether, in the ad hoc, ex-post-facto manner in which the minewide focus arrived, two years after the experiment began, "our way of working" can and will spread effectively to the rest of the mine, as President Hinks hopes. Another significant question is whether the crews working under the new system will sustain their performance permanently, both in safety and productivity, or whether in a delayed "Hawthorne effect," it will subside down to status quo ante or worse. Still another question is the impact that the labor-management cooperation and joint decision-making will have on collective bargaining, both locally at Rushton and perhaps nationally on BCOA-UMW national agreements.

What could happen at Rushton if Arnold Miller is replaced as UMW president and a new Mine Workers regime appears, or if Warren Hinks retires as mine president? Is enough built into the system to survive such change? What will happen as one by one the original leaders of the experimental effort are replaced by younger, newer figures? How deeply fixed, in other words, are the notions of cooperation and autonomy? How much are they merely the temporary objectives of a currently convinced group that will disappear in time?

Underlying these questions are deeper ones. Assuming that the new system will effectively spread minewide, what will be the long-run effect on productivity in mining? On mine safety? On new technology? On the union and the management? Some union pessimists still claim that in the long run, success of the new system will undermine the union's strength and weaken the union irreparably through gradual disappearance of the adversary attitudes. Some managers still claim, in almost equal pessimism, that success of the new system will permanently undermine "management's right to manage" and hand the power of mine management over to the approval of the men and their union.

Each of these questions reaches beyond events in a small coal mine in central Pennsylvania. Each opens up other long-range questions about mine safety and human productivity in American underground mining in the energy-hungry future. A year from now, in mid-1977, a Ford Foundation-funded study of Rushton from 1973 to 1976, prepared by Dr. Paul Goodman for the Institute of Social Research at the University of Michigan, will reveal not-yet-available documented details and data of the impact of the initial experiment and its minewide evolution on miner attitudes, mine effectiveness in dollar terms, union relations, and the like. But like this article, that report will not have an end. The end will be written, as a continuing learning process, by a handful of coal miners and their bosses struggling to learn whether they can work better together, and how to do it.

13

EQUAL EMPLOYMENT OPPORTUNITY

We noted in Chapter 1 that government regulations are an important source of influence on the personnel/human resource function. *The Wagner Act*, for example, gave employees the right to form unions and bargain with employers over the terms and conditions of employment (see Chapter 9). Certain personnel/human resource activities were affected by the *Wagner Act*, particularly compensation and internal staffing. However, the fairly recent laws and executive orders pertaining to *equal employment opportunity* (EEO) have had an even more profound impact on the total personnel/human resource function. The present chapter examines EEO regulations and their widely felt effects on virtually all personnel/human resource activities.

THE LEGAL FRAMEWORK

Title VII of the *Civil Rights Act* (as amended) and *Executive Order 11246* (as amended) form the basic legal framework of EEO requirements for organizations. These and other relevant legislation are described below.

Title VII. In 1964 Congress passed *Title VII*, which prohibits discrimination on the basis of race, color, religion, national origin, and sex in all employment practices. This includes recruitment, external and internal staffing, training, performance appraisal, and compensation. These provisions apply equally to employers, unions, and employment agencies. A federal agency—the *Equal Employment Opportunity Commission* (EEOC)—was created to administer and enforce *Title VII*. The EEOC was given the responsibility to investigate discrimination charges and to attempt their resolution through voluntary means, such as persuasion, negotiation, and conciliation. The EEOC did not, however, have the power to take cases directly to court.

This limited enforcement power was the primary reason that *Title VII* was amended by the *Equal Employment Opportunity Act* of 1972. Under these amendments, alleged violators can be taken to court if voluntary efforts to resolve a complaint are not successful. This key provision greatly expanded the powers of the EEOC. Another major change was to expand coverage to include most *public* employees and employees of *educational* institutions. With this change, most of the nation's workforce is protected by *Title VII*.

When the EEOC investigates a discrimination charge, it first seeks facts to determine if there is probable or reasonable cause to conclude that discrimination has occurred. For example, in the area of selection, the EEOC might examine the rejection rates for males and females to determine if the selection process is having an *adverse impact* on females. Or, the percentage of females in each job may be compared with the percentage of qualified females available in the labor market for each job to determine if females are being *underutilized*. Once the EEOC interprets such facts as indicating probable cause, the burden of proof then shifts to the employer to demonstrate that discrimination has not occurred.

What happens if the employer is taken to court and the court upholds the discrimination charge? *Title VII* permits the court to order remedies for the discriminatory practice(s). Often these remedies will apply to all members of an *affected class* (for example, females), even though only one member of the class may have filed the original charge. The reason for this is the belief that employment discrimination is *systemic*, meaning that the total employment system is discriminatory and thus has an adverse impact on all members of an affected class. In other words, courts have tended to view individual charges as being simply symptoms of broad patterns of discrimination within the organization.

One common remedy is for the court to award a back-pay settlement. This can be extremely expensive since it will likely apply to all members of the affected class, and since *Title VII* permits the award to go back to two years prior to the time that charge was originally filed. Another common remedy is for the court to order that the organization undertake an *affirmative-action* plan. This will usually include a requirement that the organization establish goals and timetables for the hiring, promotion, and training of minorities and/or women. In fact, the court itself may write the affirmative-action plan including the actual goals and then continue to monitor the organization in order to ensure compliance with the plan. Obviously, affirmative action can often involve substantial changes in virtually all of the organization's personnel/human resource policies and programs.

Executive Orders. *Executive Order (EO) 11246* was issued by President Johnson in 1965 and amended shortly thereafter by *EO 11375* to extend coverage to women. It prohibits employment discrimination on the basis of race, color, religion, national origin, and sex and applies to most organizations that have contracts or subcontracts with the federal government. Unlike *Title VII*, however, it *requires* that most covered organizations must develop and implement affirmative-action programs. The specific requirements for these programs are spelled out in what is known as *Revised Order No. 4*.

Basically, the employer must do a *utilization analysis* on a job-by-job basis for minorities and women. This involves determining the number and percentage of minorities and females on each job. Their representation or utilization is then to be compared with their availability in the labor market, according to a number of specific criteria. When the comparisons indicate that there is underutilization, the employer must establish goals and time-tables for the selection, promotion, and training of members of the under-utilized groups. Moreover, the employer must make a *good faith effort* to achieve these goals. Employers not in compliance with the order face the possibility of such penalties as cancellation of contracts and prohibition from bidding on future contracts.

Other Regulations.   Two other important pieces of federal legislation are the *Equal Pay Act* of 1963 and the *Age Discrimination in Employment Act* of 1967. The *Equal Pay Act* requires equal compensation for males and females on jobs requiring equal skill, effort, and responsibility and performed under similar working conditions. The *Age Discrimination in Employment Act* pro-hibits discrimination against individuals from 40 to 65 years of age. Both laws are administered by units within the Department of Labor.

It should also be noted that there is considerable EEO legislation that has been passed by state and local governments. In many respects, these laws are patterned after the federal legislation and executive orders.

As can be seen, the legal framework of EEO is massive and complex, de-spite its short history. Moreover, you should recognize that the framework is in a constant state of flux. Periodic changes occur in the interpretations of the laws by the courts and in the guidelines and regulations being issued by the enforcement agencies. These types of changes place an even greater burden on the organization's EEO efforts.

An extremely important example of this involves the legal status of affirma-tive-action programs. Despite the requirements for them, the legality of affirmative-action programs has never been ruled on by the U.S. Supreme Court. As of this writing, however, there is an affirmative-action case before the U.S. Supreme Court—*Bakke* v. *University of California-Davis*. The medi-cal school at the University has an affirmative-action plan for recruiting and admitting minority students. Bakke is a white applicant who was denied ad-mission to the school, despite the fact that he allegedly was more qualified than some minority applicants who were admitted. Regardless of the specific ruling by the Supreme Court in this case, you can see what a major new impact it may have on the personnel/human resource function.

INFLUENCES ON PERSONNEL HUMAN RESOURCE MANAGEMENT

Our discussion of EEO's legal framework indicates that the law can and does have a substantial influence on personnel/human resource management. The precise nature and extent of the influence will vary among organizations, making it difficult to present too many generalizations. There are some general points, however, that illustrate the typical influences likely to occur or that already have occurred.

The most pervasive influence of EEO law is that the organization must examine *all* of its personnel/human resource policies and programs to determine if they are having adverse impacts. When adverse impacts occur, the reason(s) for this must be determined. This requires deciding whether the adverse impact is justifiable on grounds of job-relatedness or business necessity. If the impact cannot be so justified, the courts will likely rule that the practices are discriminatory.

The importance of such assessments was underscored in 1971 by the Supreme Court in the case of *Griggs* v. *Duke Power Company*. The case involved the company's use of specific test score and educational requirements for transfers and promotions. Since, on the average, blacks scored lower than whites on the tests and had lower educational levels, use of the requirements had an adverse impact on blacks. The company did not have any empirical validity evidence that the test and educational requirements were related to success on the jobs to which employees would transfer or be promoted. For this and other reasons, the Supreme Court unanimously ruled against the company. In the Court's words:

. . . Congress has placed on the employer the burden of showing that any given requirement must have a manifest relationship to the employment in question.

If an employment practice which operates to exclude Negroes cannot be shown to be related to job performance, the practice is prohibited.

Thus, when a practice is having adverse impact for reasons that are not job related, the practice must be changed. This will require extensive planning of what changes are necessary and how they will be implemented. While occasionally the planning will involve only a limited aspect of personnel/human resources (for example, validating selection devices), the far more usual occurrence is that many, if not all, aspects of personnel/human resources will be involved.

For example, suppose an organization concludes that females are underrepresented in most jobs at all levels of the organization. It then decides to increase representation. To do so requires answering a series of interrelated qestions. For example, the organization must ask how many additional women will it be able to accommodate, and when, in each job? Are there sufficient numbers of qualified women available? What recruitment sources will it use? What effects will the increased recruitment have on starting salaries and on overall pay levels for jobs? How will increased representation influence the kinds of benefits the organization offers and the costs of the benefits? Does the organization have valid selection devices? How will it assess the women's job performance and how important will the assessments be in promotion decisions? For that matter, will enough vacancies be occurring to even have a meaningful promotion program? What training programs will be necessary, both for initial jobs and to enhance promotability to future jobs? For those women who will be in jobs where employees are represented by a labor union, what changes in the labor contract will have to be negotiated with the union? Could the organization end up with two EEO programs—one for union and one for nonunion women? These merely illustrate the questions that must be considered if the sex composition of the workforce is to be appreciably altered.

The essential point is that most EEO efforts are extremely complex and they require extensive planning. Usually it will be the personnel/human resource department of the organization that will be responsible for these efforts. Often such efforts require an increase in authority of, and support for, the personnel/human resource department (see Chapter 1 for an elaboration).

Successfully conducted EEO programs are likely to require that the personnel/human resource department exert an increased amount of control over line management. Increased control is necessary to ensure consistent planning and implementation of EEO policies and programs. Moreover, the potential costs of noncompliance are so great that unusually strong control must be exerted. Part of the control will involve a constant monitoring of line management's performance in administering the EEO policies and programs. Another more stringent form of control will require that line managers obtain approval *in advance* for certain actions. For example, the personnel/human resource department may require that it have final approval of all selection and promotion decisions. The overall effect of these controls will be to place tight constraints on line managers and the amount of authority they have to make personnel/human resource decisions by themselves.

INTRODUCTION TO READINGS

An Overview of Legal Trends

As we noted, the various EEO statutes are having considerable influence on all aspects of personnel/human resource management. In their article, William Holley and Hubert S. Feild discuss court cases illustrating both current interpretations of the law and impacts of these interpretations. Their discussion includes issues regarding recruitment and selection, promotion, training, performance appraisal, discipline and discharge, grievance administration, compensation and benefits, maternity benefits, and layoffs.

A common theme underlying these cases is the previously mentioned concept of adverse impact. Almost every case reviewed by Holley and Feild involved the occurrence of adverse impact. The burden of proof was, therefore, invariably on the employer. Only a very small number of employers were able to successfully defend themselves. To date, employers generally have been unable to justify practices that have an adverse impact in terms of their job-relatedness and/or the costs of changing the practices. Part of the reason for these judicial decisions has been that employers provided insufficient documentation to buttress their claims (for example, use of performance rating scales that were not developed on the basis of a careful job analysis). In some instances, courts disagreed with employers about the meaning of the documentation that was provided. These decisions reinforce a point we made earlier—the organization must examine and justify all of its employment practices in great detail.

In many of the cases, the court imposed certain remedies on the organization in addition to their requiring that the employer stop a particular practice. While we indicated that two of the most common remedies involve back pay and affirmative action, the latter includes a large number of specific remedies that are tailor-made to each situation. You will see this most clearly in the cases involving recruitment, selection, promotion, and training.

The Testing Issue

Title VII permits the use of professionally developed ability tests, provided they are not designed, intended, or used to discriminate. This particular provision has been the subject of considerable controversy and litigation. To help interpret this provision, the EEOC issued a set of testing *guidelines* in 1970. The article by Bonnie Sandman and Faith Urban summarizes the specific content of the guidelines and how the courts have interpreted the testing provision of *Title VII,* particularly in light of the guidelines. (You will find this article more understandable if you first read, or review, Chapter 5 on external staffing.)

The thrust of the guidelines is that when adverse impact (for example, different rejection rates for males and females) occurs through the use of a test, the employer must present evidence that the test is valid. Three types of validity evidence are suggested: empirical or criterion-related, content, and construct. The guidelines indicate in some detail how to conduct the validation studies and establish certain standards for what makes an acceptable validity study.

A very controversial requirement of the guidelines is that of *differential validity*. Differential validation requires that a criterion-related validity study must be done separately by race/sex group if it is *technically feasible* to do so. The requirements are based on the possibility that a test might be valid for one group but not for another group. If so, the test should obviously only be used on the group for which it is valid. Sandman and Urban note that many people feel there is no convincing evidence that differential validity actually occurs. At this point, it is best to recognize that differential validity will remain a very controversial issue for some time to come.

Sandman and Urban indicate that the guidelines have been taking on great importance due to two Supreme Court decisions—*Griggs* v. *Duke Power Company* and *Moody* v. *Albemarle Paper Company*. They suggest that the effect of these two decisions has been to make the guidelines become "etched in stone tablets," rather than serve as merely guidelines to acceptable testing practice. Since their article, however, there has been another Supreme Court case involving testing. In *Washington* v. *Davis*, the Supreme Court specifically rejected the notion that the guidelines are a set of standards that must be slavishly adhered to in all respects.

The current status of the guidelines is uncertain for another reason. After reviewing what they feel are other unresolved issues dealing with testing and the guidelines, Sandman and Urban conclude by suggesting that help may be forthcoming in the form of a new set of guidelines. After publication of this article, these new testing guidelines (*Federal Executive Agency Guidelines on Employee Selection Procedures*) were put into force by the Department of Labor, Department of Justice, and the Civil Service Commission. The EEOC has refused to agree to these guidelines, however, and retains the ones it previously issued. The result is that now there are two, sometimes contradictory, sets of testing standards that apply to many employers. Because of this, it seems safe to predict substantial confusion and litigation in the years ahead.

Sex-Role Stereotypes

As we have indicated, EEO laws and regulations touch virtually all aspects of personnel/human resource management and often require substantial changes in policy and practice. While this may reduce broad patterns of systemic discrimination, it may not have much effect on the occurrence of more subtle forms of discrimination. An example of this is the concept and influence of sex-role stereotypes, described in the article by Benson Rosen and Thomas Jerdee.

They begin by showing how males may have deep-rooted concepts of a female's role in an organization, and how these sex-role stereotypes can have subtle, and often unintentional, impacts on female employees. These impacts occur primarily in the context of personnel decisions regarding such things as job assignments, training opportunities, performance appraisal, and compensation. In addition, Rosen and Jerdee suggest that females may fail to win the support and confidence of their supervisor. This may trigger a chain of events in which females may end up performing in a manner that reinforces the supervisor's sex-role stereotype.

To overcome such problems, Rosen and Jerdee argue that males need some form of awareness training and describe a program they have developed. The program is aimed at providing managers with a first hand opportunity to examine their own sex-role stereotypes. This is accomplished by having the managers participate in exercises structured in such a way that they are required to deal with situations in which their own sex-role stereotypes may influence their decisions and behaviors. These influences are then shown to the managers and discussed in order to increase the managers' awareness.

The authors conclude by stating that this approach ". . . has a lasting impact when participants return to their jobs." This is almost certainly too strong a conclusion. No evidence is provided to support it (see Chapter 7 on learning and training for how one would evaluate the effectiveness of such a program). Moreover, there is the assumption that making managers more aware will actually change managers' job behavior. As we noted in Chapter 7, this largely depends on whether the new behaviors are constantly rewarded back on the job. Unless the organization already has a total EEO effort underway, it seems rather unlikely that awareness training itself will have any lasting impact on the reduction of discrimination. It is probably best to conclude that awareness training and total EEO programs must work hand in hand for both to be of maximum effectiveness.

EEO and the Union

Title VII applies to labor unions, as well as employers and employment agencies. This often overlooked fact, and its implications for the union, are explored in the article by Herbert Hammerman and Marvin Rogoff. They note that, under current interpretations of Title VII, the union may be financially liable for discriminatory practices even though it was the employer who was directly responsible for the practices. Being party to a labor contract that specifies or creates discriminatory terms and conditions of employment amounts to at least implicit support for them. Thus, the question becomes —How can the union guard against discrimination charges and the possibility of financial liability? Two methods are suggested by Hammerman and Rogoff: grievance-arbitration procedures and affirmative-action programs.

In the first method, discrimination charges would be processed through the grievance procedure. The last step in the procedure would be arbitration where an arbitrator would make the final decision on the charge. Such a process has considerable appeal in terms of simplicity, convenience, and speed. Unfortunately, due to a Supreme Court decision (Gardner v. Denver), the decisions would not be final and binding. The authors explain the reason for this and some modifications that could be made in a typical grievance procedure to partially overcome this problem.

The union itself would initiate and sponsor an affirmative-action program in the second method. Such a program could be initiated with or without management cooperation. The "ideal" features of such a program, and the numerous obstacles in getting it implemented, are detailed. The authors conclude by giving examples of actual affirmative-action programs that have been undertaken by three national unions.

36. EQUAL EMPLOYMENT OPPORTUNITY AND ITS IMPLICATIONS FOR PERSONNEL PRACTICES
WILLIAM H. HOLLEY and HUBERT S. FEILD

Court cases and administrative decisions are helping to clarify the meaning of personnel practices for equal employment opportunity. Several studies[1] concerning the impact of civil rights legislation on selected personnel practices have been conducted, but case law and administrative decisions in this area have been so dynamic that much has occurred since these studies. This article presents a review of the current legal status of some of the more pertinent personnel practices of organizations, both private and public. Since the well-publicized consent decrees in the steel industry and American Telephone & Telegraph Co. with the accompanying expense of attorney fees, back pay, court costs, loss in executive time, much attention has been devoted to equal employment opportunity at all levels of management. The cases cited herein were selected primarily on the basis of their significance in depicting the current interpretation of the laws and secondly as examples of typical cases affecting

Source: Labor Law Journal 27, 5 (1976): 278–86.

[1] Fred Luthans, "The Impact of the Civil Rights Act on Employment Policies and Practices," Labor Law Journal 19, 6 (1968): 323–28, George Cooper and Richard B. Sobol, "Seniority and Testing Under Fair Employment Laws: A General Approach to Objective Criteria of Hiring and Promotion," Harvard Law Review 82 (1969): 1598–1636; and Floyd L. Ruch, "The Impact on Employment Procedures of the Supreme Court Decision in Duke Power Company," Personnel Journal 50, 4 (1971): 777–83.

personnel practices. The personnel practices addressed include (a) recruitment and selection,[2] (b) promotion and training, (c) performance appraisal, (d) discipline and discharge, (e) grievance administration, (f) compensation and benefits, (g) maternity benefits, and (h) layoffs and recalls.

Court decisions and administrative interpretations of existing legislation have made and will continue to make significant alterations in many of the more traditional personnel practices. These decisions and interpretations affecting personnel practices are based on several key statutes which have been in effect for just over a decade. The most predominant, the Civil Rights Act of 1964 as amended in 1972,[3] prohibits discrimination in employment on account of race, color, religion, sex, or national origin except in certain instances where religion, sex, or national origin is a bona fide occupational qualification reasonably necessary for the normal operation of a particular organization.

Executive Orders 11246[4] and 11375,[5] which cover organizations with federal government contracts in excess of $10,000, prohibit discrimination in employment. In addition, the accompanying Revised Order No. 4[6] requires contractors with 50 or more employees to develop an affirmative action program which must include (a) a set of specific and results-oriented procedures to which a contractor must make a commitment to apply in good faith, and (b) an analysis of areas within which the government contractor is deficient in utilization of minority groups and goals and timetables to which the contractor must direct good faith efforts in correcting these deficiencies.

Another statute, the Equal Pay Act of 1963,[7] prohibits discrimination in compensation on account of sex, where skill, effort, responsibility, and working conditions are equal. These specific statutes do not include all laws which address various types of discrimination, but they cover the important personnel practices regarding discrimination based on race, sex, religion, and national origin.

RECRUITMENT AND SELECTION

In the recruitment and selection of personnel, organizations attempt to recruit and select the "most qualified" persons for the positions at wage rates commensurate with the duties and responsibilities of the specific jobs. Although organizations seek this objective, the activities surrounding these processes cannot be conducted without giving attention to court orders and administrative decisions regarding equal employment opportunity. For example, when the court found a gross disparity between the percentage of nonwhite persons in Minneapolis and the percentage of nonwhite persons employed by the Minneapolis Fire Department, the city of Minneapolis was required to hire one minority for every two nonminority applicants until the percentage of minorities in the work force of the fire department approximated its proportion in the general population.[8]

In a similar situation, the state of Mississippi in Morrow v. Crisler[9] was required to conduct recruitment visits in such a manner as to achieve maximum nondiscriminatory

---

[2] Testing, an important part of the selection procedure, will not be covered because adequate explanation would require considerable space and the subject has been covered previously. For excellent references, see Bonnie Sandman and Faith Urban, "Employment Testing and the Law," Labor Law Journal 27, 1 (January 1976): 38–54; and W. C. Byham and M. E. Spitzer, The Law and Personnel Testing (New York: American Management Association, Inc., 1971).

[3] Equal Employment Opportunity Act, March 1972, Public Law No. 92–261.

[4] Executive Order 11246, September 24, 1965, 3 CFR 169 (1974).

[5] Executive Order 11375, October 13, 1967, 41 CFR 60–2.10 (1975).

[6] 41 CFR 60–2.10 (1975).

[7] 29 CFR 800 (1975).

[8] Carter v. Gallagher, 452 F. 2d 315 (CA-8, 1971), 3 EPD ¶ 8335; cert. denied, 406 U.S. 950 (S. Ct., 1972), 4 EPD ¶ 7818.

[9] Morrow v. Crisler, (DC Miss, 1971), 4 EDP ¶7541; (CA-5 1973), 5 EPD ¶ 8563.

coverage and maintain appropriate records covering job applicants and employees. The Georgia Power Company was required to recruit at predominantly black colleges,[10] and Central Motor Lines was ordered to undertake a recruiting program aimed at black communities, to contact civil rights and local job training organizations for minority applicants, to advertise, either by radio or newspaper, to the black community, and to report its progress to the court every six months.[11]

Regarding the selection of personnel, employers must expend considerable efforts in assuring that the job specifications are appropriate for the job, and the legal interpretations require that organizations today do not establish job specifications that have discriminatory effects. For example, the refusal to employ male applicants with long hair may be illegal unless the employer's grooming code can be rationally justified, e.g., the community's negative reaction to long hair of males.[12] Further, refusal to hire a minority member who has an arrest record may be a violation of the law if employment statistics demonstrate that use of arrest records in selecting employees operate to bar minorities in a far greater proportion than nonminority applicants. An exception would be where the employer can show a proper justification that there is a reasonable business purpose for inquiring about the prospective employee's arrest record.[13]

Many other examples can be cited to demonstrate the impact of civil rights legislation on recruitment and selection. These include nepotism policies which unfairly preclude nonwhites from employment opportunities,[14] as well as other artificial requirements, e.g., poor credit ratings,[15] records of gambling,[16] word-of-mouth recruiting,[17] background investigations,[18] preference to former employees and close friends and relatives in the existing work force,[19] exclusion of males for flight attendant positions,[20] refusal to employ females with preschool age children,[21] and adverse personnel reports without an opportunity of rebuttal.[22] Cases involving such issues have been found to serve as grounds for employment discrimination.

PROMOTION AND TRAINING

For years, organizations required or have provided training to those individuals who are qualified or who can qualify for supervisory positions. Many times promotion opportunities have been coupled with training. Now both promotion practices and training have come under fire from the EEOC and the courts.

In one case, an employer was found to have violated Title VII by relying upon its foremen to recommend hourly employees for presupervisory training programs and promotion to salaried positions when (a) foremen based their recommendations upon subjective and vague standards with no written instructions involving qualifications for promotion, (b) a disproportion-

[10] U.S. v. Georgia Power Company, 474 F. 2d. 906 (CA–5, 1973), 5 EPD ¶ 8460.

[11] U.S. v. Central Motor Lines (DC NC 1971), 4 EPD ¶ 7624.

[12] Willingham v. Macon Telegraph Publishing Company, 482 F. 2d 535 (CA–5, 1973), 6 EPD ¶ 8701.

[13] Gregory v. Litton Systems, Inc., 472 F. 2d. 631 (CA–9, 1972), 5 EPD ¶ 8089.

[14] U.S. v. Iron Workers, Local 1, 438 F. 2d. 679 (CA–7, 1971), 3 EPD ¶ 8098.

[15] EEOC Decision No. 72–0427, August 31, 1971, CCH EEOC ¶ 6312.

[16] EEOC Decision No. 71–2682, June 28, 1971, CCH EEOC ¶ 6288.

[17] Cited at footnote 10.

[18] Pennsylvania v. O'Neil, 473 F. 2d. 1029 (CA–3, 1973), 5 EPD ¶ 8448.

[19] Lea v. Cone Mills (DC NC 1969), 2 EPD ¶ 10,087; (CA–4, 1971), 3 EPD ¶ 8102.

[20] Diaz v. Pan American Airways (DC Fla, 1972), 5 EPD ¶ 8473.

[21] Phillips v. Martin Marietta Corporation, 400 U.S. 542 (US Ct, 1971), 3 EPD ¶ 8088.

[22] EEOC Decision No. 72–2103, June 27, 1972, CCH EEOC ¶ 6368.

ately small percentage of black hourly employees were transferred or promoted to salaried positions, and (c) hourly employees were not notified of the qualifications necessary for salaried positions. As the remedy, the employer was required to post notices of the qualifications for every salaried position, to post announcements of pre-forman training classes, and to assert that no hourly employee was denied consideration for a salaried position.[23]

In a similar case, the employer's promotion procedure was held to be in violation of Title VII when the employer used supervisory recommendations as the predominant factor in making promotion decisions in that (a) supervisors had not been furnished written instructions specifying the qualifications necessary for promotion, (b) promotion standards, e.g., work experience, desire for improvements, and leadership potential, were considered vague and subjective, and (c) employees had not been notified of opportunities or qualifications necessary for promotion.

As the remedy, the judge ordered the company to (a) furnish supervisory personnel with written instructions delineating objective criteria and specific qualifications necessary for promotion or transfers, (b) post detailed notices of all job vacancies and training programs on bulletin boards, (c) establish a management committee to insure that no employee is denied consideration for promotion solely for the reason that the employee is not supported by the supervisor's recommendation, and (d) continue giving qualifications paramount consideration in promoting employees and providing training opportunities.[24]

Organizations have used seniority as a basis for personnel decision-making regarding promotions and have designed lines of progression for employees to move up in the organization, but these practices likewise have been shown to have discriminatory effects. In Local 189 and Crown Zellerbach v. U.S.,[25] the courts found that segregated seniority lists and lines of progression had a discriminatory impact against black employees who were primarily employed in low-paying jobs without the opportunity to move into a line of progression to high-paying jobs. To remedy these discriminatory effects, the court converted the seniority system into a plantwide system providing advancement opportunities to those black employees who had accumulated sufficient plantwide seniority.

In Jones v. Lee Way Motor Freight, Inc.,[26] the employer's refusal to grant requests for transfers from black city drivers to over-the-road positions was decided in favor of the plaintiffs when the company could not justify a transfer policy requiring employees to surrender their accumulated seniority as a city driver. The judge concluded that this policy tended to bar black employees from applying for over-the-road jobs having a better line of progression. In another case, Bing v. Roadway Express, Inc.,[27] the court ruled that black workers transferring from city driver positions to better paying over-the-road driver positions were to be permitted to carry some of their departmental seniority accumulated in a city driver position to the over-the-road driver position.

"Promotion-from-within," an organizational practice designed to improve morale, to provide rewards for past performance, and to take advantage of an individual's training and experience with the company, is another personnel practice which has been seriously questioned by the courts and the EEOC. Even though "promotion-from-

23 Rowe v. General Motors Corporation, 457 F. 2d. 348 (CA–5, 1972), 4 EPD ¶ 7689; (CA–5, 1972), 4 EPD ¶ 7689.

24 Baxter v. Savannah Refining Corporation (CA–5, 1974), 7 EPD ¶ 9426.

25 Local 189 v. U.S., 416 F. 2d. 980 (1969) 60 LC ¶ 9289; cert. denied. 397 U.S. 919 (1970).

26 Jones v. Lee Way Motor Freight, Inc., 431 F. 2d. 245 (CA–10, 1970), 63 LC ¶ 9504, 2 EPD ¶ 10,283.

27 Bing v. Roadway Express, Inc., 485 F. 2d. 441 (CA–5, 1973), 6 EPD ¶ 8878.

within" is considered an accepted employment practice, it has been shown to have discriminatory effects under certain circumstances. In one case, for instance, an employer filled three of four vacancies by promoting from within, but failed to show legitimate reasons for not hiring a qualified black female who had applied for any one of the four vacant positions. Although the court recognized the potential importance and validity of the "promotion-from-within" practice, the judge concluded that such a practice could not serve as a valid defense to a charge of unlawful hiring practices when the vacancies had been filled by persons whose backgrounds were "conspicuously unimpressive" when compared with that of the better-qualified female applicant.[28]

PERFORMANCE APPRAISAL

Performance ratings have frequently been used as a basis for making decisions regarding wages, promotions, training, test validation, transfers, and layoffs.[29] However, they, too, have come under serious attack from the EEOC and the courts. Industrial relations directors have become very cognizant of the possible discriminatory effects of performance ratings when used in personnel decision-making. The EEOC and the courts have discovered discriminatory factors in performance evaluation systems in several cases.

The Zia Company was found to have discriminated against Spanish workers when it used invalid performance ratings in making layoff decisions.[30] Albemarle Paper Company improperly validated its selection tests when it compared the tests results with sub-

jective ratings of supervisors who had been given only vague standards by which to judge employee performance.[31] Further, a municipal government was found in violation of the law in that it used performance ratings which had not been developed from careful job analyses as a basis for making promotion decisions.[32] Lastly, another municipal government was found violating the law when the average scores given to black employees were lower than those given to white employees, and when performance ratings which had not been validated were used as one of the criteria for making promotion decisions.[33]

DISCIPLINE AND DISCHARGE

Employers reserve the right to discipline and discharge employees for "just cause" in order to preserve order and to assure an acceptable level of productivity, but now employers must be careful in disciplining and discharging minority employees. One employer was found in violation of Title VII when it dismissed a minority employee whose wages were garnisheed even though the employer had justified the discharge on the grounds of additional expense and time involved in answering letters and telephone calls from the employee's creditors. The court ruled that the employer had not correlated the wage garnishments with work efficiency, and thus the effect of such a dismissal policy was deemed racially discriminatory.[34]

Another employer was required to reinstate a black employee who wore his hair in an Afro-style after the court decided that the employer's grooming rules had not

[28] Gates v. Georgia Pacific Corporation, 492 F. 2d. 292 (CA–9, 1974), 7 EPD ¶ 9185.

[29] Hubert S. Feild and William H. Holley, "Performance Appraisal—An Analysis of State-Wide Practices," Public Personnel Management 4, 3 (May–June, 1975):145–50.

[30] Brifo et al. v. Zia Company, 478 F. 2d. 1200 (CA–10, 1973), 5 EPD ¶ 8626.

[31] Moody v. Albemarle Paper Company, 474 F. 2d. 134 (CA–4, 1973), 5 EPD ¶ 8470, 422 U.S. 405 (1975).

[32] Allen v. City of Mobile, 331 F. Supp. 1134 (DC Ala. 1971), 4 EPD ¶ 7582; cert. denied 412 U.S. 909, (US 1973) SCt, 5 EPD ¶ 8656.

[33] Harper v. Mayor and City Council of Baltimore, 359 F. Supp. 1187 (DC Md, 1973), 5 EPD ¶ 2650.

[34] Johnson v. Pike Corporation of America, 332 F. Supp. 490 (DC Cal, 1971), 4 EPD ¶ 7517.

taken into consideration racial differences and cultural symbols of various groups.[35] Another court required reinstatement of a white female employee who had been discharged under the guise of suspicion of criminal activities after the court discovered that the "real" reason for the discharge was that she had been dating a black person.[36] Sex discrimination was found when a female employee was discharged for living with and having an affair with a fellow male employee, while in the same case the male employee was not discharged.[37]

The guiding principle which has been used in these cases is the degree to which the employment standards have been found to be bona fide occupational qualifications; thus, an employer will not be guilty of discrimination automatically. For example, in *Boyce* v. *Safeway Stores, Inc.*,[38] the court upheld a discharge of a male food clerk whose head and facial hair did not conform to written grooming standards that had been previously established for all employees who had regular contact with the public. The judge believed that the grooming code was not arbitrary but was reasonable as a bona fide occupational qualification.

In another case, the discharge of a bellman from a sensitive security job at a hotel was upheld in *Richardson* v. *Holter Corporation of America*[39] after the employer learned that the employee had been convicted of a serious crime even though the plaintiff had established a prima facie case by presenting statistics revealing that black persons were convicted of these crimes in considerably higher proportion than whites in the same population.

GRIEVANCE ADMINISTRATION

In dealing with employees in the work environment, employers are often faced with employee grievances regarding various types of discrimination. Prior to 1974 under the deferral to arbitration policy,[40] employees were expected to use the internal grievance machinery to resolve disputes. In 1974, in *Alexander* v. *Gardner-Denver Company*,[41] the Supreme Court refused to adopt the rule of deferral to arbitration decisions and relegated the arbitration process to an ancillary role.

The Court explained that there should be no deferral to arbitrator awards in Title VII cases and concluded: (a) the function of the arbitrator is to effectuate the intent of the parties rather than the requirements of enacted legislation, (b) the specialized competence of arbitrators pertains primarily to the law of the shop, not the law of the land, and (c) the process in arbitration is usually not equivalent to judicial fact-finding. It then added that the arbitral decisions may be admitted as evidence but accorded only such weight as deemed appropriate.

With this case as the landmark, employers now seem to have two choices regarding grievance administration of discrimination cases. They can continue to resolve discrimination grievances in arbitration if the employee chooses this route, and then, if the grievant petitions the EEOC, enter the arbitrator's decision as evidence. Or, they can prevent dual coverage of discrimination cases by exempting certain discrimination cases from the grievance-arbitration machinery.

COMPENSATION AND BENEFITS

Employers put forth substantial efforts to design wage and salary systems which aid in recruiting, retaining, and motivating pro-

---

35 EEOC Decision No. 71–2444, June 10, 1971, CCH EEOC ¶ 6240.

36 EEOC Decision No. 71–1902, April 28, 1971, CCH EEOC ¶ 6281.

37 EEOC Decision No. 71–2678, June 28, 1971, CCH EEOC ¶ 6287.

38 *Boyce* v. *Safeway Stores, Inc.*, 351 F. Supp. 402 (DC D of C, 1972), 5 EPD ¶ 8077.

39 *Richardson* v. *Hotel Corporation of America*, 332 F. Supp. 519 (DC La, 1971), 4 EPD ¶ 7666.

40 *Collyer Insulated Wire*, 192 NLRB 837 (1971), CCH NLRB ¶ 23,385.

41 *Alexander* v. *Gardner-Denver Company*, 415 U.S. 36 (US 1974) S. Ct., 7 EPD ¶ 9148.

ductive employees, but these efforts must be made within the parameters of legislation regarding discrimination. Any differentials in compensation will be ruled legal only when they are based on factors other than sex, e.g., seniority, merit, or quantity and quality of production.

In *Shultz v. Wheaton Glass Company*,[42] the company which compensated female employees at 10 percent less than their male counterparts was required to pay back wages to all female employees who performed equal work. *Corning Glass Works*[43] violated the law by paying a higher base wage to male night shift inspectors than it paid female inspectors on the day shift. The company contended that day shift work was not performed under similar working conditions as the night shift, but the Secretary of Labor and the courts disagreed. Because the higher wage was paid in addition to a separate night differential paid to all employees on the night shift, the court concluded that wage differentials between sexes cannot be justified under the guise of "working conditions."

For a company to pay wage differentials based on sex, it must prove justification for such differentials. Robert Hall Clothes, Inc. was able to justify its wage differentials, but only after it showed that men's clothes were higher priced and better quality, thus causing a higher profit margin and sales volume per employee in the men's department.[44]

MATERNITY BENEFITS

The question of providing maternity benefits to female employees during absences from work due to pregnancy remains unresolved. In *Geduldig v. Aliello*,[45] the Supreme Court ruled that a provision in the California Unemployment Insurance Code, which excludes disability caused by normal pregnancy and childbirth from coverage under the state disability insurance program, was not unconstitutional and did not violate the Equal Protection Clause of the 14th Amendment.

This decision, at first glance, seemed to lay to rest this most controversial personnel issue; but, its finality was short-lived. A Court of Appeals (3rd Circuit) ruled that the *Geduldig* decision did not necessarily apply in the *Wetzel v. Liberty Mutual Insurance Company*[46] case. The appeals court concluded that the exclusion of pregnancy-related disabilities from the employer's income protection plan was a violation of Title VII if the same plan covers other disabilities caused by voluntary activities such as drinking, smoking, and engaging in athletic activities.

In a similar case now before the Supreme Court, *Gilbert v. General Electric*,[47] a Title VII violation was found when the employer failed to pay sickness and accident benefits to female employees for periods of absence due to childbirth or other pregnancy-related disabilities despite the employer's claim that pregnancy inclusion would increase insurance costs and that pregnancy was voluntary. With this issue now before the Supreme Court, a final decision should soon be forthcoming.

LAYOFFS AND RECALL

Periods of recurring economic recessions and insufficient demand force organizations to face the issue of layoff and recall. In many instances, these practices are regulated by provisions negotiated in collective bargaining agreements giving high priority to seniority. In a Louisiana case, District Court Judge Cassiby ruled that the "last hired, first

[42] *Shultz v. Wheaton Glass Company*, 421 F. 2d. 259 (DC NJ, 1970) 64 LC ¶ 32,413.

[43] *Corning Glass Works*, 474 F. 2d. (1973), cert. granted, 414 U.S. 1110 (1973).

[44] *Hodgson v. Robert Hall Clothes, Inc.*, 473 F. 2d. 589 (CA-3, 1973), 5 EPD ¶ 8434.

[45] *Geduldig v. Aliello*, 94 U.S. 2485 (1974).

[46] *Wetzel v. Liberty Mutual Insurance Co.*, 511 F. 2d. 199 (CA-3 1975), 9 EPD ¶ 9942.

[47] *Gilbert v. General Electric*, 375 F. Supp. 367 (DC Va, 1974), 7 EPD ¶ 9282.

fired" layoff and recall practices violated the Civil Rights Act because the employer's hiring policy of hiring only white employees for many years had prevented blacks from accumulating any relevant seniority.[48] The Court of Appeals over-turned this decision and allowed the use of the long-established seniority system for determining who would be laid off and rehired even though use of the seniority system resulted in the discharge of more blacks than whites, even to the point of eliminating blacks from the company's workforce.

This decision was justified on three grounds. The company's hiring policy had not been discriminatory for over ten years. The seniority system which was determined to be racially neutral was adopted without the intent to discriminate. And individual employees who were laid off under the seniority system were not themselves subject to prior employment discrimination.[49]

Prior to this Fifth Circuit decision, a district court in Illinois had ruled that affirmative action programs would be "utterly frustrated if the layoffs were to be effectuated solely in accordance with the seniority clause."[50] Thus, the court ruled that layoffs should be allocated among minority workers and nonminorities in such a way that minority workers would have the same percentage representatives after the reduction in force as they had prior to the layoffs,[51] but this decision likewise was overturned on appeal.[52] The court reasoned that:

Title VII mandates that workers of every race be treated equally according to their seniority. . . . Title VII speaks only to the future. Its back-

ward gaze is found only on a present practice which may perpetuate past discrimination. An employment seniority system embodying the 'last hired, first fired' principle does not of itself perpetuate past discrimination. To hold otherwise would be tantamount to shackling white employees with a burden of a past discrimination created, not by them, but by their employer. Title VII was not designed to nurture such reverse discriminatory preferences.[53]

Even though these Circuit Court decisions may have laid to rest at present the question of whether or not the "last hired, first fired" practice is discriminatory, they have not resolved other serious questions. For example, what effect would continuing discriminatory hiring practices after 1964 have? Even though the "last hired, first fired" practice is racially neutral, could not certain individuals who have been treated discriminatorily also be adversely affected by such practices? If so, what remedy would restore them to an equitable position? These are only a few of the questions that will still have to be resolved in the near future.

CONCLUSION

Because the expenses of not complying with the legal requirements of equal employment are exorbitant, management at all levels must be cognizant of the current legal status of the more pertinent personnel practices. This importance becomes even more apparent in organizations when the percentage of minorities in the work force is disproportionately low when compared to that of the population. Thus, when this disparity occurs, the burden of proof shifts to the employer to show justification and validity of their personnel practices and to show that these personnel practices are bona fide occupational qualifications. In the event that the organization cannot show justification and validity, they often bear enormous costs.

48 *Watkins* v. *Steelworkers, Local 2369,* 369 F. Supp. 1221 (DC La, 1974), 8 EPD ¶ 9766.

49 *Watkins* v. *Steelworkers, Local 2369,* 516 F. 2d. 41 (CA–5, 1975), 10 EPD ¶ 10,319.

50 *Waters* v. *Wisconsin Steel Works,* 502 F. 2d. 1309 (CA–7 1974).

51 *Ibid.*

52 *Waters* v. *Wisconsin Steel Works,* cited at footnote 50. Also, see *Jersey Central Power and Light Company* v. *IBEW Local Unions,* (DC NJ, 1974), 8 EPD ¶ 9759; (CA–3, 1975), 9 EPD ¶ 9923.

53 *Waters* v. *Wisconsin Steel Works,* cited at footnote 50.

37. EMPLOYMENT TESTING AND THE LAW

BONNIE SANDMAN and FAITH URBAN

Title VII of the Civil Rights Act of 1964 states:

. . . It shall be an unlawful employment practice for an employer to give and to act upon the results of any professionally developed ability test provided that such test, its administration, or action upon the results is designed, intended, or used to discriminate because of race, color, religion, sex, or national origin (Section 703A).

The act authorized the establishment of a Federal Equal Employment Opportunity Commission (EEOC) to which it delegated the responsibility of preventing and eliminating unlawful employment practices as defined in the title.

This article[1] will focus on the judiciary decisions regarding the use of professionally developed tests in the employment situation. Basic EEOC guidelines will be reviewed and the courts' interpretation of the guidelines will be noted. Landmark cases in this area will be briefly summarized. Judicial decisions regarding the use of unvalidated tests, deficient validity studies, and adequate validity studies as well as court pronouncements regarding test usage will be noted. Some "prophecies" regarding the use of tests in the employment area and potential conflict situations between the judicial and psychological points of view will also be explained.

As a result of Title VII, which prohibited the use of any discriminatory employment test, numerous employees have accused their respective employers of violating this particular law. In *McDonnell-Douglas Corporation* v. *Green*,[2] the Supreme Court ruled on the exact role of the plaintiff and defendant in a Title VII case. The complainant carries the initial "burden of proof" in establishing a prima facie case of discrimination. To do so he must demonstrate that (1) he is a minority group member, (2) he has applied and qualified for a particular job opening, (3) he has, despite his qualifications, been rejected, and (4) after he was rejected, the employer continued to seek applications from persons similarly qualified to the complainant. After this prima facie case has been made, the "burden of proof" shifts to the employer. The employer must "come forth with proof on non-discriminatory reasons for his actions . . ." (p. 969).

The employer's required "proof" may fall under the guise of "business necessity" or "job relatedness." In *Jones* v. *Lee Way Motor Freight, Inc.*,[3] it was stated that:

Where a policy (or a practice or procedure) is demonstrated to have discriminating effects, it can be justified only by a showing that it is necessary to the safe and efficient operation of the business . . . that is, a business necessity (p. 899).

In *Arrington* v. *Massachusetts Bay Transportation Authority*,[4] it is noted that:

The difficult issue . . . is the determination of the level of business relevance necessary to justify the utilization of a test. It is one thing to demand that a test be designed to measure abilities relevant to job performance and be an accurate determinant of those abilities, but quite another to decide what showing is adequate to indicate that a particular test is performing that function successfully. (p. 373)

The EEOC has issued the *Guidelines on Employee Selection Procedures*. These guidelines:

Serve as a workable set of standards for employers, unions, and employment agencies in deter-

Source: *Labor Law Journal*, 27, 1 (1976): 38–54.

[1] The authors are grateful to Dr. Robert Guion for his assistance in this article.

[2] (S. Ct., 1973) 5 EPD ¶ 8607.

[3] 431 F. 2d 245 (CA–10, 1970) 63 LC ¶ 9504.

[4] (DC Mass 1969) 61 LC ¶ 9375.

mining whether their selection procedures conform with the obligations contained in Title VII of the Civil Rights Act of 1964.[5]

The standards focus primarily on the development and use of properly validated procedures as a means to eliminate discrimination in employment testing.

According to the EEOC guidelines, the "test" category includes:

. . . Measures of general intelligence, mental ability, and learning ability; specific intellectual abilities, mechanical, clerical, and other aptitudes; dexterity and coordination; knowledge and proficiency of occupational and other interests; and attitudes, personality, or temperament.[6]

In addition to the above, this category also includes . . .

Personal history or background requirements, specific educational or work history requirements, scored interviews, biographical information blanks, interviewers' rating scales, scored application forms, etc.

TERMS

It is also necessary to define several terms which frequently appear in the literature on employment testing. A working knowledge of these terms is mandatory in understanding the implication and meaning of fair employment cases. For further detailed definitions the reader is referred to the EEOC guidelines themselves or to the *Principles for the Validation and Use of Personnel Selection Procedures* published by Division 14 of the American Psychological Association in 1975. Knowledge of the following terminology, taken from the latter publication, constitutes a fundamental understanding of important principles in the testing area.

Sometimes tests and other measurable characteristics are called predictors, because they are used to predict certain cri-

teria such as job performance or academic achievement. The validity of a test or measure is the degree to which inferences may be made from the measure. In other words, a test purported to predict job performance, through a research study, has been shown to be correlated with a certain measure of job performance (criterion). This correlation is the test's validity when used to predict job performance. The greater the correlation, the stronger the relationship, thus the greater the validity of the measure in that context.

Three main types of validity are frequently recognized: construct, content, and criterion-related validity. Construct validity is the degree to which scores, obtained through a specified test or other assessment procedure, may be interpreted as measuring or reflecting a specified trait.

Content validity is the degree to which scores on a test may be accepted as representative of performance within a specifically defined content domain of which the test is a sample. For example, a test of achievement in algebra would be a sample of problems representative of the class of problems encountered in the study of algebra.

Criterion-related validity, sometimes called empirical validity, is a statistical statement of the existence of a relationship (correlation) between scores on a predictor and scores on a criterion measure.

A fourth type of validity mentioned in the original EEOC guidelines, differential validity, refers to the notion that a particular test which is valid for a specific group of individuals may not be equally valid for another group of people. The term job analysis refers to any method which is used to determine the elements of a particular job which the incumbent must know in order to successfully perform the job.

The EEOC guidelines outline how to go about showing a test's relationship to the job. While not law, these guidelines have been given the force of law in the practical sense:

---

[5] Fed. Reg. Title 29, Chap. XIV.
[6] Fed. Reg. Title 29, Chap. XIV.

Nevertheless these guidelines undeniably provide a valid framework for determining whether a validation study manifests that a particular test predicts reasonable job suitability. Their guidance value is such that we hold they should be followed absent a showing that some cogent reason exists for noncompliance.[7]

LANDMARK DECISIONS

There have been many court decisions regarding fair testing in employment. Certain decisions, because of their frequent citation by the courts and their level of judicial review, have set the trend for much of the legal thinking on the testing issues. Looking at these cases in chronological order reveals the courts' increasing demand on employers to follow EEOC guidelines *specifically*. The most recent decision, *Moody* v. *Albemarle Paper Company*,[8] for example, requires employers, not only to validate their tests in the traditional sense, but also to do a differential validity study. This is a significant and controversial holding. Several psychologists who have studied the validity of ability and achievement tests have found little evidence of "differential validity."

In *Griggs* v. *Duke Power Company*,[9] Duke Power could not require a high school education or the passing of standardized general intelligence tests as a condition to employment since neither were significantly related to successful job performance. Duke Power used the Wonderlic Personnel Test and the Bennett Mechanical Aptitude Test to qualify employees for transfer to "inside" jobs even though these tests operated to disqualify Negroes. The court said that arbitrary and unnecessary barriers to employment, such as the tests used by Duke Power, are to be removed when the barriers operate to discriminate.

The touchstone is business necessity. If an employment practice which operates to exclude Negroes cannot be shown to be related to job performance, the practice is prohibited. Diplomas and tests are useful servants, but Congress has mandated the common sense proposition that they are not to become masters of reality.

The court further concluded that the EEOC's construction of 703 (h), which requires that employment tests be job-related, comports with congressional intent.

In *U.S.* v. *Jacksonville Terminal Company*,[10] a test devised by the personnel supervisor had been a factor in both initial job assignment and transfer decisions since 1967. The court found that the Terminal had not adequately borne the burden of showing that the examination had a "manifest relationship" to the employment in question. The court relied on the Griggs case, which demanded a substantial proof of a relationship between test scores and job performance: " . . . certainly the safest validation method is that which conforms with EEOC guidelines" (p. 893).

Test scores of blacks had been compared with the predicted, not the actual, job performance of blacks. The "predicted criterion" was supervisory estimation of employee job potential for a higher job, The court concluded:

. . . Finding no job-related objective criteria for a specific group of jobs in the department, . . . the Terminal must ascertain and publicize such qualifications which shall be applicable to all employees, group 1 incumbents, as well as candidates.

In *Bridgeport Guardians, Inc.* v. *Commission*,[11] it was demonstrated that the passing rate for whites on a police test was three and one-half times that for Negroes and Puerto Ricans. The use of the test was criticized because the city was us-

---

[7] (CA–5, 1973) 5 EPD ¶ 8460.

[8] (S. Ct., 1975) 9 EPD ¶ 10,230.

[9] 91 S. Ct. 849, 401 US 424, 3 EPD ¶ 8137.

[10] 451 F. 2d 418 (CA–5, 1971) 3 EPD ¶ 8324.

[11] (CA–2, 1973) 6 EPD ¶ 8755.

ing an old examination which tested non-job-related skills.

Many of the vocabulary and arithmetic questions on the exam were only superficially or peripherally related to police activity. The stress on vocabulary and verbal skills often produces cultural bias (p. 1344).

No job analysis, construct validity, content, or predictive validity of the test was demonstrated. The cut-off score was arbitrary. The remedy: the court enjoined the use of the test and required a validation study.

REVERENCE

In *United States* v. *Georgia Power*[12] several important issues were addressed by the court and a demonstrable reverence for EEOC guidelines was evident in this landmark case. The court ruled that (1) the test evaluator made no attempt to show that the test did not screen out Negroes as Negroes; (2) a differential validity study was not performed despite its feasibility; (3) the employer made no indication that he even attempted to satisfy the provisions of the EEOC guidelines; (4) the test evaluator's "self-described" guess at validation was not adequate; (5) the testing of current employees was not uniform; and (6) "even without regard to guidelines, the evaluator's study was improper since he used theoretical testing schemes as his premise instead of employer's actual testing procedures" (p. 587).

This case is particularly valuable because it demonstrated an extensive application of the EEOC guidelines as the basis for the ultimate judicial decision. Additionally, the court noted that a differential validity study was required where technically feasible. . . .

SUMMARY AND CONCLUSIONS

After a complainant has presented a prima facie case of discrimination in a

12 (CA–5, 1973) 5 EPD ¶ 8460.

Title VII case, the employer bears the "burden of proof." It is the employer who must demonstrate that the tests used as the basis of his employment decisions are related to adequate performance on the job. This "job relatedness" can be shown through a validity study. The contents of such a study have been outlined in the EEOC guidelines. The courts have interpreted these guidelines (*Griggs*) as comporting with Congress' intent in Title VII of the 1964 Civil Rights Act.

In the landmark decisions discussed, one sees the court's increasing reliance on the validity evidence of tests as per the EEOC guidelines. Have these guidelines been etched on "stone tablets"? In the recent Supreme Court decision, *Moody* v. *Albemarle*, this pre-occupation with specific suggestions in the guidelines is quite evident. Due to the poorness of the *Albemarle* validity study, the Court demanded an overwhelmingly thorough validation study to demonstrate the job relatedness of the test in question. Such specific interpretation of the guidelines may cause severe pressures on the employer. While a "differential validity" study (where technically feasible) and an "adequate job analysis" are but two of the Court's demands in *Albemarle*, the "state of the art" in the testing area will certainly hamper the demonstration of such judicial requirements.

The stringent application of the guidelines may dissuade employers from the continued use of formal employment tests.

Employers may turn to such selection devices as the interview, personal history blank, and training programs in order to escape the Court's demand to validate formal tests. As defined in the guidelines, however, "tests" is an extensive category, covering such instruments as interviews, personal history blanks, and training programs when such devices are used to predict success on the job. To date, the court has made few rulings on the use of such "informal" tests. The legal safety that these devices presently provide an employer may be short lived. At some time in the future, the court may demand the same validity evidence of these informal tests as is now required of formal tests.

It is expected that evidence of the reliability and validity of the criterion used in a validation study will also be required. For the most part, the courts have addressed themselves only to the "lack of objectivity" in a given criterion. With the court's continued emphasis on validity studies in general, it is expected that the court will demand some specific evidence of the validity of the criterion itself.

One also notes a continued preference for predictive validation studies rather than content or construct validation studies. It must be noted, however, that the guidelines themselves call for an empirical validation study (predictive or concurrent) only where technically feasible. These reviewers ask, "What is the use of an empirical validity study for the sake of an empirical validity study when it is not warranted?"

The *Griggs* decision demanded a "meaningful" validation study. It is conceivable that given a certain set of circumstances, a certain type of validation study may be more appropriate than another type. It is also possible that under a different set of circumstances no validity study may be possible or even reasonable. For example, must a typing work sample test be shown to have "predictive" validity? The issue of feasibility is one which the court must consider in demanding validity evidence of a test. Additionally, it appears that concurrent validity studies have usually been overlooked (by "expert witnesses" and the courts alike) as a means of empirical validation.

ISSUES

The judicial pronouncements also reveal the courts' increasing sophistication as to psychological terminology and methodology. While the courts are certainly cognizant of some important testing issues, these reviewers feel the judiciary, as a whole, is deficient in some important areas of psychological thinking. In many cases, the courts' definitions of basic psychological terms is clearly at odds with the definitions employed by psychologists. Without clear agreement by psychologists and the judiciary on the terms they are using, it is inconceivable that they will ever come to grips with some of the more important conceptual issues.

One such issue . . . which confronts these two groups is that of practical versus statistical significance. Early court decisions were seemingly content with a statistically significant relationship of a test with the job. It now appears, however, that statistical significance is not enough. "Practical significance" of the test must also be evident.

Psychologists determine the statistical significance of the test; the court determines the "practical significance." This trade-off may have repercussions in the legal testing area because it will be up to the courts, in effect, to decide "how good is good enough?" Now, if "practical significance" is related to the business necessity concept, the pronouncement of "practical significance" is surely in the court's jurisdiction. To demand a correlation coefficient equal to or greater than .30 as evidence of "practical significance" is certainly a step in that direction.[13]

One must question if this is actually the court's decision to make. Strict proscriptions of "practical significance" are somewhat unrealistic. Sample size and sensitivity of the measuring instrument are but two of the many situational factors which must be considered in establishing the "practical significance" of a correlation coefficient. Decisions of this nature appear to be better suited to the industrial psychologist than to the judiciary.

Another legal issue which must be re-

---

[13] For example, *Boston Chapter NAACP v. Beecher* (DC Mass, 1974) 7 EPD ¶ 9162.

solved is the burden of "proving the alternative." A validated test, with a disparate impact, can continue to be used if no other equal alternative, with less disparate impact, is available. Who is to prove the infeasibility of other alternatives? The *Moody* v. *Albemarle* decision decreed it was the burden of the plaintiff; *Chance* v. *Board of Education* gave the burden to the defendants. The EEOC guidelines state the defendant is to prove the infeasibility of other alternatives. Who, exactly, has the "burden of proof" in this area? How does one "prove the negative"?

Before leaving the legal reader totally dismayed at some of the important questions requiring answers, the reviewers feel

obligated to acknowledge that some help may be on the way. This "help" is in the form of newly drafted testing guidelines proposed by the Equal Employment Opportunity Coordinating Council (EEOCC). There is one small drawback, however. Two previous drafts have been shelved. It appears that the third draft may have a similar fate. According to a recent article[14] on the new guidelines, "even the staff members didn't think they were workable, or presented a coherent, uniform government position on testing issues."

It appears that, rather than holding our breaths and waiting for these new "stone tablets," it would be beneficial to resolve some of the questions raised here.

38. ON-THE-JOB SEX BIAS: INCREASING MANAGERIAL AWARENESS*

BENSON ROSEN and THOMAS H. JERDEE

In recent years, many organizations have extensively revised personnel policies and procedures pertaining to women. Recruitment and selection procedures have been changed to comply with Affirmative Action and Equal Employment Opportunity guidelines and job titles and job descriptions have been rewritten, breaking long-standing traditions that certain jobs are exclusively the male domain. Some organizations have initiated new programs to help women with career planning. All of these changes have provided women with better access to employment opportunities and raised their aspirations toward higher level managerial positions.

Although more and more women are moving up to executive levels, many others still face obstacles stemming from deep-

rooted attitudes about women's roles in organizational and family life. Even the most enlightened managers have difficulty in shedding deeply ingrained expectations regarding women's managerial and professional abilities and commitments. These negative stereotypes may cause subtle, unintentional sex discrimination in a variety of decisions, involving job changes, specific task assignments, development activities, and job-related social activities. Although these decisions often cannot be covered by specific formal policies, they can nevertheless be harmful to the self-image and career progress of females. Before we examine solutions to the problem of sex bias, it is important to have a clear understanding of its nature and its harmful effects.

* Source: *The Personnel Administrator,* 22 (January 1977), pp. 15–18.

14 89 LLR 158, p. 158.

CONSEQUENCES OF SEX BIAS

Women are vulnerable to various kinds of differential treatment when it comes to *job assignments*. In some instances it has been alleged that women have been assigned to organizational housekeeping roles, including keeping things neat, attending to details, making coffee, serving drinks, and taking minutes at meetings.

Women often have great difficulty gaining *experience* by developing close working relationships with older male executives. Executives who would not hesitate to accept a male protégé may fear that, regardless of how innocent, their motives would be questioned if they worked closely with a young woman.

Subtle sex bias can also create inequities in organizational *reward systems*. A recent labor department report indicated that some 96 percent of all jobs paying $15,000 or more in the United States are held by white males. One explanation for this staggering imbalance is that men are rewarded for excellent work in terms of money and promotion, while women are rewarded with honorary dinners, badges, and certificates of merit.

Two particularly destructive patterns of sex bias are *condescending treatment and withholding of supervisory support and encouragement* for career women. One female public relations director, for example, was forced to deal with the secretaries of her fellow executives rather than the executives themselves.

Finally, many women claim that they are judged more on how they behave than on what they accomplish. Male colleagues are evaluated on the quality and quantity of output, but females are judged on their manners, style of dress, and good humor, not on what they achieve.

Failure to win the support and confidence of their supervisors can have an adverse effect on women's abilities to succeed in managerial positions. The problems of Ruth Norris dramatically illustrate the destructive consequences of executive suspicion and lack of confidence. After five years as an administrative assistant, Norris was promoted to a managerial position. The general manager in Norris' division felt that women lacked decisiveness and interpersonal skills necessary in supervisory roles. He was concerned that if Norris performed poorly, it would reflect on him personally. Accordingly, the general manager assigned her to routine tasks and specified in detail the procedure and strategy for handling each departmental problem. Moreover, he monitored her behavior and was quick to criticize when she made mistakes. In these and other subtle ways the general manager conveyed his expectations that Norris was not likely to succeed in her managerial role.

Now let us consider the problem from Norris' perspective. She probably entered her new managerial role with some apprehension. Once in that role, she became sensitive to the fact that her job assignments involved low autonomy and routine work. She read this as a sign that she was expected to be less capable than her male counterparts. At first this motivated her to try harder. When she realized that her work was carefully scrutinized, her anxiety increased and she found herself making more mistakes and behaving in a rigid manner, often unable to cope with the day-to-day problems associated with her position. Her ineffective behavior confirmed her boss's expectations and reinforced his stereotype of female managers.

Figure 1 illustrates how Norris was a victim of an unfortunate cycle of expectations and self-fulfilling prophecies. The general manager's expectations regarding her probable failure caused a withholding of support and encouragement and ended in confirmation of his own expectations. Clearly, managerial skepticism and lack of support can be a powerful barrier to success for career-oriented women.

These examples illustrate that organizational efforts to promote equal employ-

FIGURE 1
The Self-Fulfilling Prophecy of Male Managerial Expectations

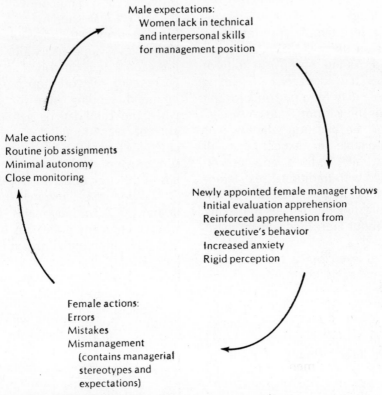

Male expectations:
Women lack in technical
and interpersonal skills
for management position

Male actions:
Routine job assignments
Minimal autonomy
Close monitoring

Newly appointed female manager shows
Initial evaluation apprehension
Reinforced apprehension from
executive's behavior
Increased anxiety
Rigid perception

Female actions:
Errors
Mistakes
Mismanagement
(contains managerial
stereotypes and
expectations)

Source: Reprinted from Rosen, B., and Jerdee, T. H. *Becoming Aware* (Chicago: Science Research Associates, 1976).

ment opportunities for women must go beyond mere legal compliance. Innovative training programs must be developed in order to establish a climate conducive to the achievement of affirmative action objectives. A primary emphasis of such programs must be to heighten managerial awareness of subtle forms of sex discrimination and to help managers deal with the problem. This entails helping managerial personnel to become aware of their own subconscious sex stereotypes and illustrating how sex stereotypes lead to unintentional sex discrimination in managerial decisions.

EXPERIENTIAL APPROACH

Unfreezing stereotypes that have been learned in childhood and reinforced by a lifetime of experience is obviously a difficult task, requiring much more than a simple memorandum or policy statement from top management. Recognizing this difficulty, many organizations have undertaken "management awareness" workshops. A promising approach for use in these workshops is experiential learning in which participants learn first-hand how sex bias influences managerial actions. Participants work through specially designed exercises, cases, and role plays in which they are motivated to examine feelings, define problems, and suggest positive actions for eliminating sex bias. The experiential learning materials help focus discussion on participants' own assumptions, expectations, and stereotypes.

As a way of demonstrating stereotypes, a workshop facilitator can ask participants to consider the problem of making predictions about an individual's behavior based on the knowledge of a particular stereotype. Consider, for example, the stereotype of a Texan as an oil millionaire, driving a luxury car and passing big tips. In spite of this stereotype, few managers are willing to countersign a loan for a person knowing only that he or she is from Texas. A discussion facilitator can question whether it is similarly reasonable to expect that all women share traits, abilities, and motivations associated with traditional sex stereotypes. Subsequent discussions can be directed at highlighting the dangers of making assumptions about individuals on the basis of stereotypes.

An in-basket exercise is another good way to help managers learn about the influence of sex stereotypes on everyday decisions. The in-basket consists of brief incidents depicting a variety of organizational problems. Participants are now aware that there are two versions of each in-basket incident which differ only in the sex of the key employee. Half of the workshop participants respond to a version involving a woman in the first incident, a man in the second incident, and so forth. The other half of the participants respond to a version with a man in the first incident, a woman in the second and so forth. By comparing recommendations made for the female and male version of each incident, the workshop facilitator can vividly demonstrate how sex bias influences decisions.

Responses to the incidents typically reflect two general patterns of sex bias: (1) there is greater organizational concern for the careers of men than for women and (2) there is a degree of skepticism about women's abilities to balance work and family demands.

ORGANIZATIONAL CONCERN

In one incident, for example, participants are asked to recommend an employee to attend a highly regarded supervisory training conference. Background information is provided for a candidate who is a business school graduate and who is described as "having demonstrated good potential for higher level supervisory positions." When this candidate is described as a male, about 60 percent of workshop participants recommend sending him for training, but when the candidate is a female, only 35 percent recommended the training. This case illustrates the tendency to be more supportive of the interests of male employees in the area of career development.

Another case illustrates the differential treatment accorded males and females when a company policy has been violated. Similarly, differential treatment of males and females in incidents involving job assignments and selection and promotion decisions illustrates to participants how their own decisions are influenced by unconscious sex stereotypes about women's motivation and ability for holding managerial roles.

JOB VERSUS FAMILY

Other incidents in the in-basket exercise focus directly on managerial expectations when career demands and family obligations conflict. For example, participants might respond to a case involving a family conflict. One spouse is depicted as a junior executive while the other is described as a freelance writer. The conflict centers on whether the junior executive could expect the freelance writer to attend a cocktail party where business associates are present, although the freelance writer finds the party boring. When the junior executive is male, typically about 70 percent of the workshop participants recommended that the spouse go to the party and not complain about it. When the junior executive is female, only 45 percent feel that her spouse should accompany her. The conclusion from this is that managers expect women to participate in the social activities associated with their husbands' careers; much less in the way of career support is expected from husbands of working women. The difference in expectations could make it easier for men to combine professional and social lives and thus give the appearance of complete dedication to work. Career women, on the other hand, might find it more difficult to combine their work and social lives and therefore might be seen as less dedicated to their work even though they spend as much time and energy on the job.

The in-basket exercise, if properly administered, minimizes defensiveness, yet clearly demonstrates the influence of sex bias on a range of managerial decisions. Because the workshop facilitator deals only with group results, no one participant is singled out for criticism.

The use of role-play exercises has also proven effective in management awareness seminars. When asked to assume the role of a female who has been victimized by discriminatory managerial decisions, men experience first-hand the kinds of organizational injustices women have been working to eliminate. One role-play situation, for example, might involve a man who is passed over for promotion because it is assumed that he will not relocate his family because of his wife's career. The goal here is to increase recognition of discriminatory practices and to create empathy for the victims of discriminatory behavior.

Case discussions are also a good way to illustrate questionable organizational practices. Cases can be created to focus attention on recent interpretations of equal rights laws. Other cases might reflect actual problems in the participants' own work situation. In the discussion of these cases participants are encouraged to suggest how organizational policies and practices can be revised to comply with the law. The use of cases in awareness workshops is a good way to increase familiarity with the legal issues surrounding employment of women. In addition, case discussions provide workshop participants with an opportunity to become actively involved in the process of revising discriminatory organizational practices.

It is often useful to include a case of reverse discrimination depicting a situation where males are victimized by sex stereotypes. Often the discussion of this case will lead to consideration of the psychological and ethical implications of sex stereotypes for both sexes.

In summary, there are many useful organizational strategies for promoting equal employment opportunities for women. A review of formal personnel practices to ensure their compliance with legislation regulating the employment of women is a critical first step. Creation of an affirmative action program to ensure continued compliance and to rectify past inequities represents a further commitment to the principles behind equal employment opportunity. Perhaps an even more important step is to create the kind of climate that is supportive of principles of equality for all employees.

We have described some ways to develop an organizational climate helpful in achieving affirmative action goals. Providing managers with the opportunity to examine their own biases and the effects of these biases on administrative decisions is a good place to start. Use of an experiential learning approach in which participants learn from data generated in exercises, cases and role-plays has a lasting impact when participants return to their jobs. These programs have the added value of demonstrating organizational concern and support for affirmative action goals. Genuine organizational support for equal employment opportunity will enable employees of both sexes to maximize their contribution to organizational goals.

39. UNIONS AND TITLE VII OF THE CIVIL RIGHTS ACT OF 1964

HERBERT HAMMERMAN and MARVIN ROGOFF

Labor organizations are in an anomalous and somewhat perilous position with respect to federal law on equal employment opportunity. The anomaly is that labor was in the forefront of the civil rights fight that led to the enactment of Title VII of the Civil Rights of 1964 and yet finds itself often indifferent and sometimes hostile to current trends in the interpretation and enforcement of that law. The peril is that developing theories of liability may sometimes result in legal fee and back-pay judgments against labor unions, in amounts that can be staggering.

Most unions, particularly industrial unions, feel they should not be held responsible for employment discrimination, because they are not responsible for hiring, nor for management policies and decisions that have historically restricted the upward mobility of minority groups and women in their industries. However, some courts have held that a union that has acquiesced in the perpetuation of the effects of such discrimination is itself guilty of discrimination and therefore is liable for its results.[1]

In the words of the Supreme Court, "Employment practices, though neutral on their face, cannot be maintained if they operate to freeze the status quo of prior discriminatory employment practices."[2]

Consequently, as explained by James E. Youngdahl, legal counsel of the International Woodworkers of America, AFL–CIO, all that is needed to impose liability is the coincidence of two conditions: A history of discriminatory hiring with segregated assignments into race- or sex-designated occupations, lines of progression, or departments, even if the discrimination occurred before the 1964 act took effect; and a seniority system that inhibits movement out of the historically assigned jobs, lines, or departments. The same reasoning has been applied to several other long-established and often socially sanctioned employment practices, especially institutionalized sex differentials, including sex-segregated jobs and wage schedules, different retirement ages, different benefits in health and welfare plans, the treatment of maternity leave, and state protective legislation limiting job or work availability for women.

For both employers and unions, there is no necessary concord between culpability (that is, the extent of discrimination) and financial liability. Often, there is an inverse relationship. For example, where company A has hired no members of minority groups and company B has hired minority-group members in proportion to their representation in the labor force but only into the lowest paying jobs, the liability of company B may be larger than that of company A, because of the larger number of back-pay recipients who may be identified at company B.[3]

How can a union protect itself against discrimination charges and avoid or minimize the danger of heavy financial liability? Two methods may be used concurrently: (1) A grievance-arbitration proce-

Source: *Monthly Labor Review* 9, 4 (1976), pp. 34–37.

[1] See *Albemarle Paper Company* v. *Moody*, 422 U.S. 405 (1975) (discussed in *Monthly Labor Review*, October 1975, pp. 56–57); *Myers* v. *Gilman Paper Corporation*, 392 F. Supp. 413 (D.C.–S.D. Ga., 1975); *Macklin* v. *Spector Freight Systems, Inc.*, 478 F. 2d. 979 (C.A.–D.C., 1973); *Johnson* v. *Goodyear Tire & Rubber Company*, 101 F. 2d 1364 (C.A 5, 1974).

[2] *Griggs* v. *Duke Power Company*, 401 U.S. 424 (1971); see *Monthly Labor Review* (June 1971):79–81.

[3] In some cases, however, courts have ordered employers with few or no minority employees to compensate rejected applicants, or workers who might have applied but for the existence of the discrimination.

dure adapted to Title VII that effectively handles discrimination complaints before they become charges that government must handle; and (2) a wide-ranging affirmative action program that can be initiated with or without employer cooperation, including bringing Title VII issues to the bargaining table and if necessary to the courts.

The principal difficulty of absorbing Title VII into the grievance procedure is that the result is not final and binding. In *Alexander v. Gardner-Denver Company,* a unanimous Supreme Court ruled in 1974 that Title VII provides individual rights independent of those contained in a collective bargaining agreement.[4] These rights may not be preempted, deferred, or otherwise replaced or waived by an arbitrator's decision.

However, the Court also ruled that an arbitrator's decision may be admitted as evidence and given whatever weight it deserves under the facts and circumstances of each case. The Court stated:

Where an arbitral determination gives full consideration to an employee's Title VII rights, a court may properly accord it great weight. This is especially true where the issue is solely one of fact, specifically addressed by the parties and decided by the arbitrator on the basis of an adequate record. . . .

To the extent that a grievance procedure is credible and effective in handling complaints of discrimination, it would absorb "the law of the land" into "the law of the shop"[5] and should achieve the following results:

1. Institutionalize in union contracts the principles and methods of equal employment opportunity, and thereby re-

duce resort to government procedures in handling of grievances.
2. Reduce the number of charges filed with the Equal Employment Opportunity Commission and its state and local deferral agencies.
3. Minimize government interference in labor-management operations.
4. Minimize financial liability in attorneys' fees and accruing back-pay.
5. Minimize resort to the federal courts.
6. Provide unions with stronger defenses for those cases that do reach the courts.

Experience has demonstrated that, in most instances, government is not a practical forum for convenient, inexpensive, and expeditious resolution of charges of discrimination. The time lag is too great, the procedural steps too many, and successful resolutions without resort to the courts too few.

A combination of affirmative action, in which unions take initiative to discover and change discriminatory patterns, and a revised grievance arbitration procedure adapted to the requirements of Title VII would seem to be the optimum means of eliminating discrimination and minimizing adverse consequences.

The following summarizes three provisions developed by the office of general counsel of the International Union of Electrical, Radio, and Machine Workers, AFL–CIO, and suggested by that office for inclusion in agreements:

1. A broad antidiscrimination clause covering employees and applicants for employment and including any term or condition of employment.

2. A requirement that the arbitrator apply Title VII, all other federal, state, and local antidiscrimination laws, and all applicable rules and regulations and judicial interpretations. The arbitrator's award must grant appropriate relief under the law and as granted by the courts. The arbitrator shall have the authority to direct the rewriting of contract provisions if required

---

4 415 U.S. 36 (1974); see *Monthly Labor Review,* (April 1975):69–70.

5 See the "Steelworkers Trilogy,"; *United Steelworkers* v. *American Manufacturing Company,* 363 U.S. 564 (1960); *United Steelworkers* v. *Warrior & Gulf Navigation Company,* 363 U.S. 574 (1960); and *United Steelworkers* v. *Enterprise Wheel & Car Corporation,* 363 U.S. 593 (1960).

by the award, or to specify necessary contract changes, which would then be binding upon the parties.

3. A provision that the grievant may appear as a party at arbitration, present evidence, and be represented by counsel, without limiting the right of the union to participate as it sees fit.

The key, then, is for unions to develop programs for the protection of Title VII rights. But there are major obstacles. First, of course, the leadership must commit itself to the effort. Next, it must resolve major problems of implementation with respect to politics, priorities, and resources. Politically, the program must be sold to the locals. Clearly, there are difficulties in convincing locals to push for better opportunities for minorities, when often they will be at the expense of the white male workers who are a majority of those voting for union officials. Priorities are a problem in that, to the extent the union wins bargaining concessions for minorities, the benefits may well come out of what could have been won for other workers. Finally, the resources needed for staff will not be inconsiderable.

We have set out what we believe to be the elements of an ideal equal employment opportunity program for industrial unions, with examples of unions that are meeting part or all of these objectives:

First, adopt and publish a firm policy statement, by national convention, spelling out how the union intends to help rid its industry of discrimination, including vestiges of past discrimination, and placing full responsibility on the international for providing leadership, resources, and guidance in its implementation.

Second, establish machinery for gathering and evaluating information on employment practices in all companies and bargaining units, on a continuing basis.

Third, require all locals, districts, and conference boards to negotiate contract provisions barring discrimination in em-

ployment and making equal employment opportunity complaints grievable up through arbitration.

Fourth, require all locals to establish special committees to undertake immediate and continuous equal employment opportunity review of collective bargaining agreements and employer work practices.

Fifth, assign to national full-time staff the responsibility for fair practices activities.

Sixth, include a report of equal employment opportunity progress and plans on the agenda of every policymaking body and assembly, including international, district, and state conventions, international executive boards, joint boards, conference boards, and local unions.

Seventh, include instruction on Title VII and its implementation in all training programs, courses, seminars, and institutes for officers, members, and staff at all levels.

Eighth, insure that all employee selection procedures and tests conform to Title VII, including those unilaterally applied by employers as well as those within collective bargaining agreements and joint apprenticeship standards.

Finally, as an employer in its own right, apply these eight initiatives to its own operations just as forcefully as it does in the industry with which it bargains.

One union that is moving on most of these points is the International Union of Electrical, Radio, and Machine Workers, AFL–CIO. The IUE has repeatedly adopted updated convention resolutions, keeping the issue alive and dynamic, following up with implementation programs by the international executive board. The union has also retained full-time social action and women's activities directors and involved substantial resources of their legal department.

The IUE program calls for local unions, with assistance of field staff and districts, to conduct midcontract reviews of collective bargaining agreements and employer work practices to ascertain discriminatory provisions or purposes; a checklist helps dig out the more obvious forms of racial and sexual discrimination. The international adds clout to the information retrieval effort by formally requesting of major companies data on sexual, racial, and national origin characteristics of new hires, incumbents, and applicants for posted jobs.

If Title VII violations are detected, the local is to write the employer to "request a meeting to bargain over the elimination of contractual provisions and noncontractual practices which are discriminatory, as well as substitution of nondiscriminatory provisions and practices."[6] As an example, the international provides suggested contract language applying EEOC guidelines to retention of seniority, payment of sickness and accident benefits, and taking of leave in connection with pregnancy disability, together with the legal backup for their position.

Employers who do not provide the requested data may be charged with violating the good faith bargaining requirement under section 8(a)(5) of the National Labor Relations Act, or IUE may file Title VII charges and follow up with suits in federal court.

IUE's suit against General Electric challenging discriminatory denial of sickness and accident benefits during absence because of pregnancy is the pivotal case on this issue for all private employers in the nation. That case is now being considered by the U.S. Supreme Court.

The Newspaper Guild, AFL–CIO, has likewise introduced equal employment opportunity into the mainstream of everyday bargaining. The Guild, which generally represents editorial, advertising, business, and other nonmechanical departments of newspapers, magazines, and wire services, has adopted a basically decentralized equal employment opportunity approach. Certain equal employment opportunity require-

ments (such as equal pay for equal work among reporters, proper recognition of pregnancy disability, and hiring goals for minorities and women) must be met for locally negotiated agreements to receive Guild approval.

Local unions are committed to uncovering violations, but the Guild does provide training and conferences to equip officers and committees to do their work. The Guild has, in fact, sent local negotiators back to the bargaining table to achieve wage parity for women's page and society reporters (all of whom are usually women) with general assignment reporters (mostly men). Local committees are likewise to review hiring standards for conformance to the formula set forth in *Griggs* v. *Duke Power Company*.[7]

Finally, after several successive convention rejections, the Guild has created its first national-level position to coordinate activities in human rights.

The International Woodworkers, AFL–CIO, has embarked on a modest program of seeking out cases of discrimination and then negotiating settlements with employers.

Perhaps the most important development in the Woodworkers' program is the special equal employment opportunity grievance process negotiated with Weyerhaeuser Company in its Oklahoma and Arkansas facilities. The process, embraced in an overall settlement agreement covering seniority and other issues, permits a grievant a choice of routes. He or she can choose the regular contractual process, or the special procedure, which allows the union only a bystander's role.

In the special process, the grievant deals directly with two strata of corporate management; then the issue goes right to an arbitrator. The grievant can select any representative, including outside attorneys or organizations. The arbitrator, one of a spe-

---

[6] Memorandum to all IUE locals from Paul Jennings, president, March 16, 1973.

[7] *Duke Power Company.*

cially prepared panel of equal employment opportunity experts, determines responsibility for the discriminatory act and assesses financial costs, including representation fees.

Thus, the union itself has proposed and negotiated a procedure that may take from it the responsibility and opportunity to handle employment problems, and give it instead to a rival apparatus.

This innovative process bears close watching for the quality of its operations and decisions and for its ultimate acceptability under the *Alexander* v. *Gardner-Denver* formula.

In a somewhat similar vein, the United Auto Workers recently negotiated for special local union fair practices committees to factfind equal employment opportunity grievances before they resume normal processing. Because the UAW-trained committees will reflect the ethnic, racial, and sexual makeup of the plant, it is assumed such grievances will benefit from extra care and savvy. Here, too, it is too early to assess the impact of the new system.